'Love'
in
A Course in Miracles

AN INQUIRY INTO ITS VIEWS ON
THE THEORY AND PRACTICE OF LOVE

by Theodore L. Kneupper, Ph.D.

2014

Mind Unlimited Press
135 Pink Road
Slippery Rock PA 16057

No part of this book may be reproduced, stored in a retrieval system, or transmitted in any form or by any means (electronic, mechanical, photocopying, recording or otherwise) without the written permission of Mind Unlimited Press.

'Love in 'A Course in Miracles'
An Inquiry into its Views on the Theory and Practice of Love
All rights reserved.
Copyright 2015 Theodore L. Kneupper, Ph.D.
v4.0 r1.2

Cover image © 2015 Theodore L. Kneupper, Ph.D. All rights reserved – used with permission.

Interior designs © 2015 Theodore L. Kneupper, Ph.D. All rights reserved – used with permission.

Author photo © 2015 Diane bowser. All rights reserved – used with permission.

Permissions and Disclaimers
Portions from *A Course in Miracles*, ed. 3, 2008, are reprinted with permission from The Foundation for Inner Peace, PO Box 598, Mill Valley, CA USA 94942 A Course in Miracles ® and ACIM® are registered service marks and trademarks of the Foundation for Inner Peace. www.acim.org

Portions from *A Course In Miracles Urtext Manuscripts*, ed. 1, 2008, by Douglas Thompson and Miracles in Action Press, LLC, used by permission from the editor.

A limited number of citations are from *The New Oxford Annotated Bible with Apocrypha*, Expanded Edition, Oxford University Press, 1973. Similarly, a number of dictionary definitions of important words are from *Webster's Third New International Dictionary*, Unabridged, Merriam-Webster, Inc., 2002. A few quotations are taken from St. Augustine's *Confessions*, translated by R.S. Pine-Coffin, Penguin, 1961.

The ideas presented here are the personal interpretations of the author and are not necessarily endorsed by the Foundation for Inner Peace or Miracles in Action Press. The book is the result of independent scholarly research and is in no way sanctioned by these or any other Course-related organization.

Paperback ISBN: 978-0-9862773-0-6
Hardback ISBN: 978-0-9862773-1-3

Library of Congress Control Number: 2014922186

PRINTED IN UNITED STATES OF AMERICA

FOR NANCY, ALEXANDER, ZACHARY
AND
ALL MY RELATIONS
MITAKUYE OYASIN

Table of Contents

Preface and Acknowledgments   vi

Ch. I   Introduction   1

Ch. II   'Love' (or 'absolute love')   24
     A. Love in God, the uncreated perfect Mind   24
         1. Love in God originally   25
         2. Love in God in response to separation   53
         3. Love in God 'after' Atonement is completed   65
     B. Love in created minds   66
         1. Love in created minds not in separation   68
         2. Love in created minds 'during' separation   74
         3. Love in created minds 'after' full completion of Atonement   81
     C. Love in the Universe of Love   82

Ch. III   'illusory love'   85
     A. Illusory love as based on ego-involvement   86
         1. Origin and characteristic of the ego   87
         2. Guilt as due to acceptance of the ego   89
         3. The inconsistency of the ego-idea   92
         4. The 'world' as result of the ego-error   93
     B. Core of the idea of 'illusory love'   95
     C. The characteristics of illusory love   100
         1. Cognitive characteristics of illusory love: its beliefs   100
         2. Affective characteristics of illusory love   117
         3. Behavioral characteristics of illusory love   132

Ch. IV 'imperfect love'   150
     A. Charity as imperfect love   151
     B. The nature of miracles   153
         1. Two different meanings of 'miracle'   153
         2. What miracles are not   154
         3. What miracles are   157
         4. The process of giving a miracle   164
         5. Effects of the miracle   181
         6. The Source of miracles   200
         7. Conditions hindering and helping miracles   201
         8. General contexts in which miracles occur   217
         9. Summary, and definition of 'miracle'   220
     C. The two primary concerns of imperfect love   220
     D. 'False charity'   222
     E. Sexuality as viewed by the Course   229

Ch. V 'perfect love'	231
A. Two meanings of 'perfect love'	231
B. Access to the realization of perfect love	233
1. The general problem for the separated mind	233
2. The holy instant as key	235
3. Content of the holy instant	245
C. The occurrence of experience of the holy instant	303
1. Two main types of experience of the holy instant	304
2. Conditions and practices promoting the experience of the holy instant	310
D. The process of returning to Love: Atonement	322
Epilogue	325
Appendix 1 The Separated Mind's Idea of 'God'	328
Appendix 2 'Light' in *A Course in Miracles*	341
I. The contrast of light with darkness	342
II. Two basic levels of light	349
III. Spirit as source/center of light	367
IV. Releasing of the Light	369
Selected Bibliography	380
Index	386

Preface and Acknowledgments

This book is the result of many years of philosophical and spiritual seeking that ranged widely. This began with an early interest in the teachings I was exposed to: first, my indoctrination into Roman Catholic beliefs and practices as a child; then, in early adulthood in my earnest search into the teachings of the less often discussed mysticism of that tradition, particularly in the form of the *Spiritual Exercises of St. Ignatius* as well as the theological elaborations of St. Thomas Aquinas. This was followed by a period of great skepticism and even agnosticism that came through the study of philosophy (most especially the philosophy of science.) Later in my 30's there resurged a more thoughtful inquiry into these matters focusing on the teachings of the East, particularly through the influence of my meetings with several highly realized mystics, as well as through the study and teaching of courses on oriental religions, mysticism, and psychical research. In that continuing search I was eventually led back to a re-examination of the teachings of Christianity under a very new and profoundly revolutionary expression as found in *A Course in Miracles*. The latter did not always meet with my assent, particularly in that my philosophical training made me greatly sensitive to its many apparent inconsistencies. However, a deeper intuition cautioned me not to dismiss it and that those 'contradictions' might actually be resolvable. But after years of resisting its practices, I eventually decided to test them by way of going through the 365 daily lessons of the Workbook, which I have completed three times, each time finding an even deeper understanding and practical application of what it means by 'giving miracles.' By no means do I assume that my present grasp of those teachings is complete, but in sharing my thoughts with other students of the Course, I've found that their responses indicate that it may be of help to others to express them in writing.

In the course of my development, there have been many important teachers. These began with my own parents' piety and devotion, which served as a starting orientation to the overall prospect of spiritual development. Then there were several mentors, the earliest being Fr. Alois Goertz, who guided me into the subtleties of the *Spiritual Exercises of St. Ignatius* and *The Spiritual Life: A Treatise on Ascetical and Mystical Theology* by Tanqueray, and then Brother John Totten, SM, who combined both the rigor of the philosopher and the vision of the mystic in his remarkable and inspiring manner as both instructor and personal counselor. Similarly, Prof. Jean Ladriere of the University of Louvain, where I did graduate studies focusing on the philosophy of science, served also as a guide to helping me mature to intellectual freedom from much of my earlier dogmatism while at the same time maintaining openness to what had not yet been dreamed of in our philosophies. Further, there were many colleagues in my career of teaching who supported this sense of open intellectual freedom, one of the most important being Prof. John Pauson. It was also my great good fortune to have befriended my first teacher on things oriental, Prof. Mohan Sharma, himself a master of the literatures of East and West and more importantly a man of deep mystical realization. Somewhat later, in a year of traveling through the East, I was again quite fortunate to meet and converse with some of the great masters, including the Hindu mystic Gopi Krishna, the Sufi masters Suleyman Dede and Hazrat Arah, Master Charan Singh of the Sikh tradition, the Dalai Lama and Dudjom Rinpoche of the Tibetan Buddhist tradition, the Buddhist Mindfulness master Munindra, Roshi Kobori of the Zen tradition, Master Hsuan Hua of the Ch'an tradition, and J. Krishnamurti who abandoned all traditions. Also in the 70's there were my conversations with the first person to introduce me to *A Course in Miracles*, Zelda Supplee, who in turn introduced me to the psychiatrist Gerry Jampolsky, one of the earliest professionals to write about the Course.

But brief encounters with any master, while they may have a strong effect of opening doors to new insights, have in my own view far less significance than long-term exchanges of serious inquiry. Most important in that respect have been my wife Nancy and my two sons Alexander and Zachary, who have taught me much in terms of very concrete family relationships. As well, there have been a number of seeker friends who have for many years shared their insights and questions by way of regular dialogues. Most especially I want to express my great thanks to Sam Giannetti and Skip Kline, whose philosophical acuity and penetrating insights have contributed much to the substance and the form of this present book. They have also been of great assistance in proofreading and offering important suggestions and help in readying it for printing. Additionally, I thank my friend Dr. Thomas Bodie for his help in proofreading the manuscript and offering his suggestions for improving it. As well, Doug Monkton of Miracles In Action Press and Robert Perry of Circle of Atonement have made several suggestions. Also, the patient and careful help of Sharon Isacco was extremely valuable in preparing the book for publication. Finally, I want to thank Dr. Diane Bowser for taking and preparing the author photo.

Years ago I had the opportunity to ask an artist how long it took him to complete his marvelous painting. "My whole lifetime till now," was his answer. At first I thought he was dodging my question, but later came to realize that he could not have honestly answered in any other way. For that reason, although the actual writing of this book has been carried out over a period of about two years, in reflecting on its origin the more accurate description is that it has taken a whole lifetime – and possibly many – till now.

My hope is that it will be of some use to students of the Course, to scholars of religion and spirituality, and to those who simply want to get a clear and coherent grasp of its teachings on love. While its organization may seem perhaps to be highly logical, something that comes to a mind through years of practicing academic philosophy, more important are the central insights. Although articulated in terminology drawing primarily from the Judeo-Christian tradition, I have sought to point out how its teachings are greatly like those found in other spiritual traditions.

I should also note that this book is only one phase of a larger undertaking, the next step of which is alluded to in several places here. The second book will be entitled *The Holy Spirit and Jesus in A Course in Miracles*, which attempts to clarify and disentangle some of the difficulties involved in the Course's assertions regarding those two entities. Eventually I hope to complete the original project that led to all of this, *An Inquiry into the Apparent Inconsistencies in A Course in Miracles and their Resolution*. However, the present inquiry on the meaning of 'love' as understood in the Course stands on its own as an attempt at a comprehensive clarification of what it means by that term and its connection with other important teachings central to the Course.

Chapter I. Introduction

The purpose of this inquiry. What has come to be known as A *Course in Miracles* is a remarkable writing, both in its origin, its teachings, and its philosophical insights, especially about the nature of love. Many popular books have been written with a focus on illuminating its teachings on love, including G. Jampolsky's *Love Is Letting Go of Fear*, Marianne Williamson's *A Return to Love: Reflections on the Principles of "A Course in Miracles,"* Kevin Rice's *The Game of Love: Changing the Rules Changes Everything*, and the Master Teacher's (Charles Buell Anderson) *Love: The Sum and Substance of Our Eternal Reality*. All of these contain some useful clarifications. Most recent is Mari Perron's *A Course on Love*, which she claims was, like the Course, dictated to her by Jesus, but offering new material that on certain points appears to be different from the original Course and quite unlike it in that its 'scribe' has chosen to step out of anonymity. More penetrating are Kenneth Wapnick's *Love Does Not Condemn: The World, the Flesh, and the Devil According to Platonism, Christianity, Gnosticism, and a Course in Miracles*, Joe Jesseph's *A Primer of Psychology According to A Course in Miracles*, and Robert Perry's *Special Relationships: Illusions of Love*. However, while these have offered valuable insights and clarifications, there has not yet appeared a thorough study of the Course's views that attempts to clarify with any precision the various meanings of the word 'love' as used within its lengthy teachings. The present book is the result of my attempt to comprehend the Course's central ideas on love and proposes to initiate dialogue toward greater comprehensive clarity and understanding regarding its teachings related to one of its most important ideas.

The Course has come to be widely studied not only in the United States, but throughout the world (it has been translated into 23 languages) and continues to grow in its readership. Thus, it has in recent years become an important alternative among the many spiritual paths that seekers have available. Although it is sometimes classified as 'New Age' spirituality by the establishment, which is perhaps a matter of wishful thinking in that it might be the hope that it is only a fad that will soon pass away, a closer appraisal is that the Course offers a profound teaching that could make it a major influence on humankind. While it is historically relatively 'new,' it contains a radically different interpretation of the teachings found in the Christian Bible and, even more importantly, a practical guide for spiritual realization of the very highest sort. Because the term 'love' is so pivotal to its teaching, what I am presenting here may prove to be useful to its students, its critics, and those simply interested in finding out what it teaches. As others have pointed out, its teachings are much closer to the views of Christian Gnosticism, but in important ways they differ from what is found in the ancient Gnostic writings.

The present book came to be written as the result of my larger concern that arose over many years of examining the Course along with other spiritual teachings and paths. Particularly in my experiences of seriously 'trying to practice' its teachings and closely and critically studying them, I found numerous passages that seemed to contradict one another. However, in light of the remarkable insights that came despite these apparent inconsistencies and the claim that its author was no one less than Jesus himself (a claim that I scoffed at when it was first told to me in 1973 or '74, when I saw a photocopy of the Course in its earliest typed version while visiting a friend in New York City), I launched into a project of carefully examining those apparent inconsistencies to see if they could be resolved. At present, that project has shown that all of the 60 'contradictions' that I have examined can actually be shown to be due to ambiguities in the language the Course was written in and can be logically resolved. Moreover, in 'locking heads' with them, they have disclosed an even deeper level of the teachings than I suspected was within them, much as the pondering of Zen koans unlock the serious student to the much deeper insights of the Buddhist teachings. Several of those apparent inconsistencies led me to recognize that it was vital to have a thorough discussion of what the Course means by 'love.'

Related to 'love,' two of the apparent inconsistencies I have found are:

"The opposite to love is fear"(Intro. to Text,1,3)[1], i.e., there is an opposite to love; vs.

"what is all-encompassing [love] can have no opposite" (Intro. to Text,1,3), i.e., there is no opposite to love.

and:

"The ego is totally unable to understand this, because it does not understand what it makes, does not appreciate it and does not love it."(Text,7,V,9,6), i.e., the ego does not love what it makes; vs.

"This sickly picture of yourself is carefully preserved by the ego, whose image it is and which it loves, and placed outside you in the world."(Text,20,III,5,6), i.e., the ego does love what it makes, that is, the image it makes of you.

These will be considered later.

The need for clarification of 'love' in the Course. *A Course in Miracles*, or more briefly the Course, makes 1,589 mentions of the term 'love' in its most widely studied version, and 1,717 mentions in the original version. It is clearly

---

[1] The referencing system will be explained shortly.

one of its most important notions. However, upon examining closely how the word is used, one finds that there are several very different meanings.

It is also important to note that right from its earliest pages there are some very puzzling statements about love, one of which is:

> "6 The course does not aim at teaching the meaning of love, for that is beyond what can be taught."(Intro. to Text,1,6)

This might be taken as saying that it is impossible to teach the meaning of the term 'love.' But that would be neither accurate, since even a dictionary can do that, nor useful to the student, whose task is to obtain a deeper understanding of what love is, since, without any way of clarifying what the term means, one would be engaging in a very confusing search. Rather, this statement is better understood as saying simply that the *full* meaning of the reality of love cannot be taught. The Course later makes clear that this meaning is found only through the complete realization of oneself, which is the same as the return to the complete knowledge of Reality that was integral to one's original state as a creation of God.

This is further clarified in:

> "5 You know not what love means because you have sought to purchase it with little gifts, thus valuing it too little to understand its magnitude. 6 Love is not little and love dwells in you, for you are host to Him. 7 Before the greatness that lives in you, your poor appreciation of your and all the little offerings you give slip into nothingness."(15,III,8,5-7)

That is, the current conditions of our minds obscure their full comprehension of love's meaning. It only has an inkling of what it is.

This primary meaning of love, which is more than a linguistic definition, is something that arises from the Source, God. As is stated:

> "3 The meaning of love is the meaning God gave to it. 4 Give to it any meaning apart from His, and it is impossible to understand it."(Text,15,V,10,3-4)

Thus, to truly understand the meaning of love would amount to having the same awareness that God has of it, which in the Course's view cannot occur as long as one is in the current state that it calls 'separation.' Hence, it is necessary to undo that condition, which occurs by removing the obstacles that obscure it. As it states:

> "7 It [the Course] does aim, however, at removing the blocks to the awareness of love's presence, which is your natural inheritance."(Intro. to Text,1,7)

This process of removing these blocks is the Course's central task.

Although love's full meaning cannot be taught, since the term 'love' has several meanings as used within the Course, it is very useful to understand what those various meanings are, particularly where their use in particular passages may lead to inconsistencies and other confusions. To that end, this inquiry is undertaken into how that term is used.

The origin, parts, and versions of *A Course in Miracles*. Before we go into our inquiry, however, it will be helpful to consider some important facts regarding the origin of the Course and its several published versions. According to our best information, it was written out in its first form now called "'Shorthand Notes" by Columbia University Medical School research professor of clinical psychology, Dr. Helen Schucman.[2] What is called the 'scribing' process began in 1965 and continued over a period of almost 13 years. She claimed only to have written, both in ordinary words and her own shorthand symbols, what she heard from a 'Voice.' Because of numerous statements in the dictated material, she eventually concluded that the actual 'Author' was Jesus of Nazareth, also known as the Christ, communicating to her from a higher plane. This was despite the atheistic position she held at the start. Her beliefs eventually shifted to a deep theism based on what was said to her. Thus, the earliest form of the Course is these "Shorthand Notes."

Intimately associated with the writing of the Course was Dr. William Thetford, Schucman's close friend and research colleague at Columbia. He produced the first typed version by regularly typing out the most recent new material she had added to the "Notes." This was done primarily by Schuman's reading the material aloud, which he then typed. His typed version has been called the "Thetford version," and both he and Schucman are usually referred to as the Course's 'Scribes.' There were apparently some modifications made by Schucman and quite possibly inaccuracies in the typing, since some discrepancies have been found between the "Notes" and the earliest available typed version, known as the "Urtext." Unfortunately, the Thetford version itself has not been made available for comparison with the "Notes." This has held back more complete determination of the nature of any changes that arose.

The material alleged to have been heard by Schucman includes, in its published form, several different volumes. These are:

1) "Text" (which will be referred to more briefly as T)
2) "Workbook for Students" (W)
3) "Manual for Teachers" (M)
4) "Use of Terms"(U), also titled "Clarification of Terms" (C)
5) "Psychotherapy" (P)
6) "Song of Prayer"(S)
7) "Gifts of God" (G)

The 4th, "Clarification of Terms," is disputed by some serious students as to

---

[2] The most extensive biography of Schucman, including many relevant details about her personal background and the process of the Course's being originally written, then prepared for publication, is Wapnick's *Absence from Felicity: The Story of Helen Schucman and her Scribing of A Course in Miracles*. Another biography, *A Course in Miracles: The Lives of Helen Schucman & William Thetford*, by Neal Vahle, was published in 2009. Also, her own *Helen Schucman Autobiography* gives important insights.

whether it was actually dictated by the Voice or only authored by Schucman and Thetford, although they both claimed these were communicated by the Voice. However, since the wider opinion is that it was 'scribed' from the Voice, I will treat it as that. It should also be noted that the 7th refers to a rather short disquisition that was published in 1982 as the last section of a larger book by that title (most of that book contains Schucman's 'inspired' poetry, which she did not claim had been dictated by the Voice). Finally, an eighth collection, called "Special Messages," is an assortment of generally brief material that does not seem to add substantially to or differ from the teachings in the rest of the material.

The Thetford version of the "Shorthand Notes" is also referred to as the "Thetford Transcript." Although it has not been published, it served as the basis for an editing process that produced several somewhat different versions, which were photocopied and circulated within a small group of early students of the Course. Eventually, sections of that material, usually extensively edited, were published as various printed versions.

The earliest printed version, which most students of the Course are familiar with, was published by the Foundation for Inner Peace in 1975. However, although it is claimed to be the 'complete Course,' some have concluded that this is not the case, since it deleted some 50,000 words from the "Shorthand Notes" (mostly from the 'Text') and also made a number of significant changes to the original words, as well as changes in punctuation and location of original material. Now known as the "FIP version," it has had three major editions, which will be referred to as FIP1, FIP2, and FIP3. The first edition made the material available as three separate volumes, known as "Text," "Workbook," and "Manual for Teachers," the last of which included the "Clarification of Terms." Later, two other volumes, "Psychotherapy" and "Song of Prayer," were also published separately. The most recent edition ('FIP3'), published in 2007, includes edited versions of all of these volumes, as well as a "Preface," the last part of which, 'What It Says,' is claimed also to have been dictated to Schucman by the Voice.

Other, more complete, versions of the Course have also emerged. The first of these is what is known as the "Hugh Lynn Cayce version," or HLC, which had been sent to the then head of the Association for Research and Enlightenment, Hugh Lynn Cayce. It included about 10,000 additional words omitted from FIP; that is, it omitted about 40,000 words from the "Notes." It was posted online in 1999, then made available in print in 2000 under the title *Jesus' Course In Miracles*. An annotated edition of HLC was published by Miracles In Action Press in 2009.

An even more complete version, known as the "Urtext," which contains the material deleted in the FIP and HLC versions and is much closer to the "Notes," was published online at miraclesinactionpress.org in 2000. This can be found in the site's section 'The Students and Teacher's Toolbox,' along with many other useful tools, including a searchable 'Concordance' of the "Urtext." In 2008, after a more thorough editing and the inclusion of numerous scholarly notes and several very informative 'Appendices' by the editor Doug Thompson, it was published in printed form under the title *A Course In Miracles Urtext Manuscripts*, by Miracles in Action Press. A second edition of that version is currently being prepared.

The last important publication of Course material is most of the "Shorthand Notes," also posted online at miraclesinactionpress.org in 2008. This is a collection of photocopies of most of the actual notebooks in which Schucman wrote down what she was allegedly hearing. A typed transcription of these "Notes" was published online in 2009 and is available at miraclesinactionpress.com/dthomp74/2008/TOOLBOX/Menus/Notesmenu.htm. Thus, the serious student or scholar can examine directly Schucman's immediate record of what she claimed to have heard from the 'Voice.'

An excellent discussion of all the versions, based on his careful and painstaking work, can be found in Doug Thompson's appendices of his *A Course in Miracles Urtext Manuscripts.* That same publication contains the most complete printed version of the Course now available. I should note that Thompson's tireless dedication to making the Course's various versions available has been a major contribution to our more complete understanding of its evolution.

The writings that we will examine and the referencing system. In the opinion of many, the Course's teachings stand as a major work in the literature on religious and spiritual life. Its primary purpose is to offer both theory and practice for aiding the student to come to the full realization of the Truth of what the student and all reality truly are. Its theoretical insights are found primarily in its first volume, "Text," and amplified in the smaller volumes "Manual for Teachers," "Clarification of Terms," and "Gifts of God." However, because the last contains no additional insights that seem relevant to the present book's inquiry, it will not be cited. The realization or actualization of the truth of those insights in living is the primary focus of the more practical second volume, "Workbook for Students," which gives 365 meditative lessons to be practiced each day for a year. The Workbook also contains important further discussions of central ideas. Other practical instructions as well as some further theoretical clarifications are found in "Psychotherapy" and "Song of Prayer."

Since the Course has been most widely read in one of the FIP editions, our study will focus on FIP3. Most of the passages cited are from that edition. For referencing those citations, I will employ its system. This gives the chapter number in standard numerals, the section number usually in Roman numerals (occasionally, where the chapter has an Introduction it uses 'In.'), then a paragraph number, and a line number or numbers. This information will be put in parentheses following the passage. For volumes other than the Text, there will also be a capital letter to indicate the volume. Thus, (6,II,3,4-7) refers to Text, Chapter 6, Section II, paragraph 3, lines 4-7; (S,2,II,6) refers to Song of Prayer, Chapter 2, Section II, line 6. Also, there are some passages in FIP that make use of special abbreviations, such as 'r' or 'fl.' These will be clarified in footnotes when they occur.

Further, for some passages cited where an important pronoun, like 'it' or 'he,' is used, what it refers to will be placed in brackets immediately after the pronoun. For example:

> "7 It [the Course] does aim, however, at removing the blocks to the awareness of love's presence, which is your natural inheritance "(Intr.,1,7)

This will allow the passages cited to be briefer.

Further, on occasion I will give citations from Thompson's *A Course In Miracles Urtext Manuscripts* (which will be abbreviated as UM). When doing so, I will make use of his reference system, which is somewhat different from that of FIP. For example, a passage not found in FIP is:

> "I want to finish the instructions about sex, because this is an area the miracle worker MUST understand."(UM, T 1 B 40b)

Here, UM refers to Thompson's *Urtext Manuscripts*, T to Text, 1 to Ch. 1, B to Section B, 40b to paragraph 40b of that section.

A brief summary of the four fundamental ideas of 'love' in English and in the Course. We first consider the meanings of 'love' in ordinary English, then outline the four basic meanings found in the Course. The remaining chapters offer more detailed discussions of those four meanings.

The English dictionary[3] defines 'love' both as a noun and as a verb. As a noun it means:

1a: attraction, desire, or affection felt for a person who arouses delight or admiration or elicits tenderness, sympathetic, interest, or benevolence
  b: an assurance of affection; e.g., 'give her my love'
2a: warm attachment, enthusiasm, or devotion, e.g., 'love of the sea'
  b: the object of such attachment
3a: the benevolence attributed to God as resembling a father's affection for his children
  b: men's adoration of God in gratitude or devotion
4a: the attraction based on sexual desire
  b: a god or personification of love (as Cupid)
  c: an amorous episode
  d: the sexual embrace, copulation
5: beloved person
6: a score of zero in tennis
7: *cap.* Christian Science: God
8: a delightful or superb example, instance, or occurrence

---

[3] I make use of *Webster's Third New International Dictionary of the English Language Unabridged*, 2002, for all English dictionary references.

Def. 6 can, of course, be excluded (derived from the French word 'l'oef' or 'the egg,' meaning 'zero'), which has nothing to do with the other meanings. Within those 13 meanings, there may be seen **four fundamental meanings** of the English noun 'love:'
1) a feeling of *attraction* to something (1a,b,8)
2) the more specific of the strongest sort of such feelings, *sexual* attraction and engagement in sexual relations (4a,b,c,d)
3) feeling of *attachment* to someone or something (2a,b, 5)
4) benevolent attitude and activity of *concern or caring for* (3a,b,7)

These correspond closely to what in some languages are given different names, as in Greek, 'epithumia', 'eros', 'philos', 'agape.'

The noun 'love' is probably a more abstract linguistic expression. More basic is the verb idea, which refers to the more concrete activity that one engages in. Thus, there are the following definitions of 'love' as a transitive verb:

1: to feel affection for, hold dear: cherish
2a: to feel a lover's passion, devotion, or tenderness for
 b: to engage in sex play
 c: to copulate with
3a: to cherish or foster with divine love and mercy
 b: to feel reverent adoration for
4a: to like or desire actively, be strongly attracted to
 b: to take pleasure or satisfaction in
5: to fondle, caress
6: to thrive in
7: to choose, prefer, like

As with the noun form, the verb's meanings correlate to the four indicated fundamental ones.

In the Course, the word 'love' is used as both a noun and a verb, and the meanings intended reflect three of the fundamental meanings in English. In the FIP version, the words 'sex,' 'sexual,' and 'sexuality' do not occur at all, nor does there seem to be even any indirect reference to sexual or erotic love. Also, although UM contains a long discussion about sexuality, it does not use the term 'love' to refer to sexual attraction or behavior. In fact, although sexuality is not considered intrinsically opposed to what it considers to be love, there are only three passages where 'love' is actually mentioned in relation to sexuality. One of these is:

> "Sex is often associated with the lack of love, but Revelation is purely a love experience."(UM, T 1 B 24i)

This is not to say that sexuality cannot be an expression of genuine love, even perfect love, but only that it is quite often lacking in that regard. In a second passage it is pointed out that love can be brought into situations involving sex:

> "Turn immediately to me by denying the power of the fear, and ask me to help you replace it with love."(UM, T 1 B 41u)

A third passage (UM, T 1 B41au) speaks of how love is excluded from sex in a specific context. Related to the Course's views on sexuality, there is the previously cited passage that was excluded from the FIP versions:

"I want to finish the instructions about sex, because this is an area the miracle worker MUST understand."(UM, T 1 B 40h)

It is at first perplexing that all material mentioning sexuality was edited out in FIP, especially in light of this strong assertion that it *must* be understood by the miracle worker. However, when one carefully examines what is contained in FIP regarding the 'body,' this deletion does not appear to be as serious a problem as it may at first seem. Indeed, what FIP does say about the body, when applied to sexuality, makes quite clear, if not explicitly so, the place of sexuality in the Course's teaching. Although sexuality is an important area of human existence that needs to be understood in relation to the Course's views on love, this will be left to another occasion, so that we can remain focused here on the primary concern of understanding its fundamental meanings of 'love.' However, to reiterate, throughout the material there is no place where the term 'love' is used in the sense of 'erotic love.' I will discuss this important topic at the end of Ch. IV.

For the Course, 'love' denotes either the most fundamental reality present in all 'perfect minds' (a term that will be clarified shortly), such as God and all created minds, or more limited notions of love found in 'separated minds' (also clarified shortly). It turns out that, for the Course, there are also four significantly different meanings for the term 'love.' As an overview, they can be characterized:

1. **absolute love**. This will be capitalized as 'Love.' This is the Course's most fundamental idea of love. It refers to the basic principle or 'energy' in any perfect mind that impels it to give, share or extend to any other mind. It is closest to meaning 4) of the four fundamental English meanings. As found in FIP, the word is often, but not always, capitalized as in:

    "7 Never forget the Love of God, Who has remembered you."(14,III,15,7)

    However, it should be recalled that if the Course was given to the Scribe by a 'Voice,' the capitalization was a choice made by her. Wherever this is the case, there is clearly a meaning in the sense of this foundational type of love, or love in the highest sense. Also, there are passages where the word is not capitalized, but the context makes it clear that the intended meaning is this foundational type of love.

2. **illusory love**. In great contrast to Love, there is within the Course an idea of love that it sometimes calls 'the illusion of love.' For brevity, this will be referred to as 'illusory love.' The following is an instance that refers to this notion.

    "5 If you seek love outside yourself you can be certain that you perceive hatred within, and are afraid of it. 6 Yet peace will never come from the illusion of love, but only from its reality."(16,VI,6,5-6)

Illusory love is one of the most problematic ideas and feelings for the separated mind. This is due to the fact that it involves a seriously misleading mode of awareness. As we will see, it is foundational to most of the experiences we think of as 'love,' and because it involves a major distortion of Love, it is an important focus of the Course's aim of healing.

    3. **imperfect love**. This is also a type of love that can manifest in separated minds, as in:

> "2 The Apostles often misunderstood it [the crucifixion], and for the same reason that anyone misunderstands it. 3 Their own imperfect love made them vulnerable to projection, and out of their own fear they spoke of the 'wrath of God' as His retaliatory weapon."(6,I,14,2,2-3)

As we shall later see, imperfect love is considered to be the result of the placing of limits on love, and has both positive and negative effects on the separated mind.

    4. **perfect love in the world.** This refers to love in its highest possible manifestation within the realm that the Course calls the 'world of perception' (also discussed later). For example:

> "4 Perfect love casts out fear."(1,VI,5,4)"

The Course uses the expression 'perfect love' in two different ways. One refers to Love, both as present and operating in God or in created minds. The other refers to the highest type of love realizable while within the world we experience. Indeed, it is this type of love that the Course seems to be intent on helping the separated mind to realize.

These four types of love may be thought of as characteristic of different 'phases' or 'modes' that it can be present within minds (also called 'spirits') that the Course holds to be the various sorts of entity that have existence of any sort. The first and original phase is that of Love in perfect minds, including the uncreated Mind of God and all those that are created. The second is illusory love, which dominates the plethora of imperfect minds in the state it calls 'separation.' The third, imperfect love, is the mode that arises in separated minds as they begin to move out of separation. The fourth, perfect love in the world, is the most developed mode that can be realized by minds remaining within the realm of separation.

    The basic types of mind. It will also be helpful here to understand the Course's view on the two main types of mind: **perfect minds** and **imperfect minds**. There are two sub-types of perfect minds: the one uncreated Mind of God and multiple created ones. What is characteristic of *perfect minds* is that they are fully aware of their own fundamental reality, which is Love, and from this Love they extend so as to create another perfect mind and have complete awareness of all that really exists, that is, of all perfect minds. Also, perfect minds exist in a mode that is entirely beyond time and space, which is called 'timelessness' or 'eternity.' The network of the collection of all perfect minds in their interrelationship is what the Course views as the truest reality called 'Heaven,' sometimes referred as the 'Universe of Love,' or what will also be called 'Reality.' This will be discussed at greater length in Ch. II.

Imperfect or separated minds have only a kind of 'provisional' existence as the result of the choice of a created perfect mind to focus its awareness on only a limited portion of what really exists and to become attached to that focused awareness. This is the core of the mode of awareness called 'perception.' In so doing, it generates within that created perfect mind a plethora of fragmentary imperfect minds. As part of upholding their continued limited awareness, each such mind further generates for itself first the idea of an 'ego,' with which it identifies. It then further attaches itself to a particular group of perceptions, which it thinks of as its 'body.' Central to this contracted perceptual awareness is the field of many other regions of space, as well as the shifting contents of its own perceptions, which is the foundation of time. Within that field, which is what it thinks of as the 'world,' it perceives other portions that it thinks of as other bodies, onto some of which it projects the idea of ego. Along with this there is the experience of suffering. The process of entering into this mode of awareness and the resulting state or condition are referred to as 'the separation.' The main consequence of all of this is that the separated mind not only experiences the contracted type of awareness with the suffering intrinsic to that, but it more seriously loses the awareness of Reality and of the Love that is at its core, which is indeed a major loss. However, there is a way to undo the separation. The Course's primary concern is to carry out that undoing through the process that it calls 'Atonement.'

Since any separated mind, including that of the present writer, the reader, any student of the Course and most other conscious beings in the world, has this seriously contracted awareness, what it thinks of and lives out as 'love' can be one of the three modes of love: illusory love, imperfect love, or perfect love. That is, it can experience varying degrees of love. The aim of the Course can be described as a matter of learning to realize the highest type of love, which ultimately involves returning to the state that the Course calls 'Heaven.'

General overview of the rest of this inquiry. In the following chapters, I will discuss the Course's views on 'love' in considerable detail, so as to present its teachings in a way that makes its various insights logically connected. A major concern is to make clear that its teachings on love can be understood as completely consistent or involving no contradictions.

Ch. II deals with the idea of 'Love,' which is both the most profound and possibly the most demanding for the reader due to the sometimes abstract concepts that the Course uses to explain it. However, with some patience and focused reflection, particularly if one tries to grasp the points of the cited passages, there may emerge a much richer or even more surprising insight than the view one held prior to considering what is explained. Such has been my own experience in grappling with these passages. A further reason for focusing first on 'Love' is that each of the other three meanings of 'love' are ideas of love that in some way fall short of the full meaning of 'Love.'

Ch. III focuses on 'illusory love.' This is the greatest deviation from Love, but also the notion of love that is in many ways closest to what is usually thought of when that word is used. In that chapter, many of the reader's ideas will probably be greatly challenged. But with openness, there may come a very important shift in what one thinks about love.

Similarly, when we come to 'imperfect love' (Ch. IV), the reader may find many beliefs about what is usually thought of as the 'noblest' or 'holiest' type of love, such as 'charity,' seriously challenged. It will also try to clarify the Course's understanding of what it calls 'miracles.'

And, in considering the discussion of 'perfect love' (Ch. V), the reader may come to much greater clarity and depth of insight about the form of love that the Course holds is possible for the human mind/heart to realize – even more importantly, about how it can be realized. Particularly important are clarifications of what it means by 'real world,' 'holy instant,' and 'holy relationship.'

Thus, the reader is urged to be patient throughout the more difficult sections, open to both what may be new and to what may be questionable in the old, and particularly to exercise one's own inner inquiry as one encounters these ideas. If one's belief system allows this, one may regularly call upon her/his deepest inner 'Light' of intelligence to illuminate what is presented. And if the reader finds it difficult to accept these views, there may at least come a better understanding of the Course's teachings regarding its views on the meanings of 'love.'

Considerations for the reader on how to approach the Course and this book. Before we enter our careful inquiry, it would be useful to consider how this can be approached most profitably. Anyone who decides to spend the time and energy it takes to study the Course or read the present book has a set of dispositions or orientations, based on his or her background, that will greatly color the task. Also, there is an overarching orientation of the author, both of the Course and of the present book, that illuminates what fills the pages of the writing. This is especially important to reflect on here, since the Course's authorship is alleged to have been none other than Jesus. Of course, whether this is true is greatly debated, and at first was even doubted by the Scribes. Its correctness or incorrectness seems to be entirely a matter of subjective evaluation, since there seems to be no way to 'objectively prove' whether it is true or false. The Scribes, as well as many students of the Course, eventually concluded that it is very probably the case, based entirely on the internal coherence of its teachings and the profundity of their insights, as well as the illumination they give to many of the things reported to have been said by Jesus in the New Testament, in spite of disagreements with some of the statements attributed to him there. In any case, such a claim has been rarely made for any other writing in the world's history, at least none that have come to have such an extensive and serious readership as the Course, although since the Course's appearance there have been a plethora of writings claimed to have been dictated by Jesus to other 'scribes.'[4]

A. Orientations the reader may have. In any case, there are several possible perspectives that anyone reading the Course or the present book may have. One is that of the **curious inquirer**, or a person who would simply like to get a better idea of what the Course is about, especially its views on love. Most likely such a person has either heard about the Course from someone enthusiastic about it or is only seeking an understanding of the nature of miracles or love, and drawn by the title. Some may have begun to read the Course itself from this perspective, but quickly found it very demanding. It is not a work that can be read casually, but calls for full attention. Many that I personally know have begun out of such curiosity, but after a few pages set the Course aside.

There is a much wider concern for the average person to get a better understanding of the nature of love. Our ordinary experience is that some of the greatest joys, but also the greatest sorrows, turn about what is called 'love.' When someone offers a thoughtful clarification of it, our interest is likely to be drawn to what is said. In my own case, this was one of the things that led me to persist in the study of the Course. Its insights on love are some of the most profound and comprehensive that I have come across. Thus, the person with the orientation of simply 'wanting to know' will hopefully find the present book helpful.

A second perspective is what might be called that of the **dissatisfied believer**. Some people sincerely dedicated to a set of religious or spiritual teachings, such as those of Christianity, Islam, Judaism, Hinduism, or Islam, have found that the scriptures and the interpretations they have followed contain great difficulties, in their being incomplete or inconsistent or deficient in the practices they prescribe. This moves them to look 'outside the box,' particularly among

---

[4] There have been several publications claimed to have been 'channeled' from Jesus, particularly since the Course was published. However, quite unlike the Course, these have almost invariably identified the 'channeler' and made that person the holder of the copyright. The names of these 'channelers' include Mari Perron, Kim Michael, Brent Haskell, Paul Tuttle, John Marc Hammer, and Tom Carpenter as well as others. A rather long list of publications of this sort can be found at otherjesussources.com/. A careful examination of these allegedly channeled documents would make it clearer as to the cogency of their claim regarding authorship. Robert Perry has written an insightful essay on this, which can be found at circleofa.org/library/articles/an-editorial-on-jesus-channeling. In light of the seriousness of these claims, it would seem to be an appropriate task of qualified scholars to evaluate those writings, particularly to compare them with the teachings in the Course so as to ascertain whether they agree or disagree with it, as well as to examine them for their own internal coherence and consistency.

teachings that seem to have surmounted those difficulties. For example, within traditional Christianity there is the extremely perplexing problem of how a God who is all-loving, all-knowing, and all-powerful could have created a world in which such enormous suffering occurs, or how He could send anyone to an everlasting hell. The disclaimer that 'it is a mystery' does not suffice for many thoughtful believers, who then extend their search for a view that is more coherent.

Those readers will approach the Course with many long-accepted ideas still intact and operating powerfully within their minds. This is also likely to occur for such persons reading the present book. However, if one attempts to provisionally set aside those past beliefs and simply try to understand the views offered, it may be possible to grasp just what they are. For example, one does not have to become an atheist in order to understand an atheist's views. In fact, by doing so one is led to a more mature and clearer understanding of one's own theism, and even possibly to see how to help the atheist come to a theistic position.

Related to this second perspective is that of the **protective believer**. That is, some readers may be so deeply committed to their own particular view that they feel compelled to enter into a struggle with any view that differs from their own. Recently there have been a number of such minds who have felt it their duty to condemn the Course as a 'work of the devil' and warn the rest of the world about it.[5] However, besides its placing them in a fear-filled and conflict-ready attitude toward their fellow humans, this perspective would make it almost impossible to understand the Course or its teachings as interpreted here. Nevertheless, it is also possible for such readers to adopt a sincere intention of trying to understand just what the Course's teachings are. Even if the Course is in error, by accurately understanding it, such readers will be able to discern more clearly the nature of those errors and offer what they think is a correction of them so as to help the brothers they consider errant. Indeed, the present author hopes that this book will serve to stimulate sincere dialogue between them and the Course community.

Yet another perspective is that of what can be called the **skeptical inquirer**. Such a reader is of a mind-set that holds all religious teachings as open to serious question, since the only valid approach to life is one that strives to be very much like that found in science. This view holds that the primary basis for finding true beliefs and reliable opinions is what is disclosed through sense-perception and carefully reflected on by logical scrutiny. In that view, religious and most spiritual teachings are based primarily on either imagination or emotion or a combination of the two, and cannot be verified by the scientific method. This would be particularly the case for something like the Course, which that view would

---

[5] For example, see the section 'Websites primarily critical of the Course' in our Selected Bibliography.

consider to have been generated by the Scribe's own emotional needs and their play upon her imagination.

It is quite possible that such actually occurred. Indeed, both Schucman and Thetford at first thought that to be the likely origin. However, as they began to grasp the profound coherence of the teachings, they realized that such an explanation could not adequately explain its contents: they were far too insightful and formed a remarkably coherent whole whose practical consequences in their lives and those of others who studied them served as a kind of empirical confirmation of what they taught.

Be that as it may, the skeptical inquirer, although disposed to dismissing the Course, for the sake of challenging its teachings may wish to understand just what it says. In this respect, such a person is much like the protective believer, and might also be called the 'protective disbeliever.' Hopefully, this present book will facilitate such a reader's coming more directly and quickly to a grasp of its views on love. Again, if one's primary intention is to find the truth and set aside error, it is hoped that this would also serve to promote a serious dialogue among both skeptics, believers, and other seekers.

Yet another orientation of the reader could be that of the **academic scholar**. The areas of professional scholarship that the Course is likely to be of interest to are Religious Studies, Biblical Studies, Theology, Philosophy, Psychology, and Sociology of Religion, even possibly Political Science. There have already been several persons in some of these fields who have expressed interest, either formally or informally, in its teachings: Kenneth Wapnick, Gerald Jampolsky, Norris Clark, Anton van Harskamp, and Douglas Thompson, to name a few. Since the Course has grown in interest around the world, it is clearly a phenomenon that calls for inquiry. The present volume should be especially useful for serious scholarly investigation, in that it focuses on its primary teachings and attempts to clarify them in a systematic and logically coherent manner.

The last sort of reader is one who is might be called a **serious seeker**. This could include those already personally involved in the study of the Course, as well as those following other religious or spiritual teachings, including sincere believers within the Christian tradition. Such a person's primary concern is simply to realize the truth, however it may be articulated in words. As pointed out, the Course is both voluminous and often unclear, sometimes even appearing to be inconsistent. This has led to its being variously interpreted by some of its most perceptive and astute students after many years of study. Ultimately, there is no better way to understanding its teachings than arduous thinking through and practicing of what it proposes. However, in this present work I offer a reflection that systematically considers some of its most important teachings and sets them forth in a way that may help in their own study. To my knowledge, no one else has attempted to do this regarding the term 'love.' Further, in the process of working through its teachings, particularly in attempting to resolve some of its most puzzling apparent contradictions, there have emerged a number of insights that seem to be contained within those teachings by implication, some of these quite remarkable when stated clearly as I have tried to do. By no means do I claim they are the final or only interpretations. But, by considering them, the serious seeker will very likely be prompted toward making even further discoveries. Indeed, I look forward to learning from others how the teachings might be alternatively understood, and, if my own views are in error, how they may be corrected. That is, this present volume should be thought of as one attempt at thinking through these profound teachings, so that the danger of slipping into the stance of the dogmatic and closed-minded 'true believer' is avoided. Thereby, there may occur the unfolding of the mind to a more vibrant and living presence of what may be called 'Truth.'

Thus, you, the person who may actually be engaged in reading this, are likely to find yourself as having one or the other of these different orientations, or perhaps even a combination of several of them. In any case, it would be good for you to reflect before continuing just what your own perspective may be so as to use what is said here most profitably. While this book is likely not as demanding as the Course itself, it does call for the effort entailed in careful thinking.

B. The perspective of the Course and its author. That said, let us turn to the overall orientation of the mind that authored the Course. It may be useful to recall the allegory formulated by Plato,[6] which likens the human condition to people who have spent all their lives chained inside a cave, so that all that they can see is what is projected on the wall before them. There they see objects moving past. They learn to be quite skillful in recognizing those objects and predicting what will happen in the processes they observe. Indeed, they think of those forms as what is 'real.' But then, one of the prisoners is released by a person who is not in chains and turned around to see what is actually happening. At first he resists, thinking that he is going insane, but gradually comes to discover that there is a fire behind the prisoners whose light sends out shadow-images formed by various objects, like puppets, that are being moved about and whose shadows are what he and they have been seeing. His releaser pulls him close to the fire, which blinds him until he becomes accustomed to its light, and slowly he recognizes that the fire and the puppets are actually what is 'real,' and that what he had called 'real' was only a faint imitation of that. But then, he is pulled even further upward toward the cave's entrance and finally out into the sunlight and the even more real realm of the objects of the outer world. Thus, he comes to the conclusion that the Sun is actually somehow what is most fundamentally 'real,' at least in terms of what he sees. Afterwards, he is told that he needs to go back down into the cave and release other prisoners still there. At first he hesitates, preferring to remain outside in the much more beautiful realm, but eventually is moved by compassion to carry out his orders.

---

[6] In his *Republic*, 514a–520a.

This allegory could be easily modernized to depict people chained inside a movie theater with 3-D images and stereo-sound, or even made more complete as depicted in the film 'The Matrix,' where the whole variety of sensory perceptions is generated by a computer and fed into the nervous systems of those imprisoned. The point, however, remains the same. That is, there is depicted the condition of our minds, which are generally convinced that the contents of their perceptions show them what is real and true. Then, there comes someone who has stepped beyond that condition so as to be aware of what is actually going on. His awareness is not dependent on the more limited mode of awareness, but is rather a complete encounter with what is truly real. That person then sees how minds dependent on limited perception move through a field of pleasure and pain, eventually coming to the ending of their perceptual experience which collapses with the death of their bodies and always dominated by anxiety in anticipation of their death, and greatly deprived of the tremendous beauty and freedom from suffering that is central to that higher mode of awareness.

Indeed, when one looks closely at most of the world's great spiritual teachings, they all seem to have originated when one or another person somehow managed to 'get outside the cave.' Buddha, Lao Tze, and Jesus are generally thought of as having reached that fully illuminated state, then taught others for the purpose of helping them realize that same state, variously called 'nirvana,' 'oneness with the Way,' or 'Heaven.'

While we cannot be certain whether the fully illuminated Jesus was the actual author of the Course, if we provisionally or hypothetically accept that, then its teachings would have to be a verbal articulation of insights that were present to his fully illumined or completely knowing mind. For us, who have not come to such a state, they will seem to be 'out of this world,' which is where they would have to originate if the world is the realm of what we perceive. In that sense, the teachings would have to be called 'revelation,' in the sense that their meanings are not accessible through the ordinary perceptual mode. Although the words are forms within the perceptual realm, their meaning is far beyond that.

Why such an illumined mind would be concerned with helping those still chained within the prison of perception, is indicated in both Plato's allegory and in the Course itself: compassion for those not yet free demands that the free help the imprisoned to freedom. Indeed, when one considers what the Course itself has to say about the whole process of finding true and complete freedom (variously called 'salvation,' 'redemption,' 'Atonement,' or 'Heaven'), its author seems to be convinced of two major things: one, that he has fully realized the Truth or known Reality; the other, that he is profoundly concerned with helping every mind come to that same realization.

Related to this, one finds within the Course itself the following passage:

"4 Let us raise our hearts from dust to life, as we remember this is promised us, and that this course was sent to open up the path of light to us, and teach us, step by step, how to return to the eternal Self we thought we lost."(W,rV,in,6,4)[7]

Here it is clearly stated that the primary purpose of the Course is to teach its students how to rediscover or be restored to the true Self they always are. In that sense, also in agreement with Plato, this is not so much a matter of learning something new, but of remembering what has been forgotten.

Further, the author shifts to the first person immediately after the previous passage:

> "1 I take the journey with you. 2 For I share your doubts and fears a little while, that you may come to me who recognize the road by which all fears and doubts are overcome. 3 We walk together. 4 I must understand uncertainty and pain, although I know they have no meaning. 5 Yet a savior must remain with those he teaches, seeing what they see, but still retaining in his mind the way that led him out, and now will lead you out with him." (W,V,in,6,1-5)

That is, the author identifies himself as a 'savior' of human beings, not by way of some sort of magical self-sacrifice as traditional Christianity tends to view Jesus, but as a teacher who is aware of their mode of awareness but who is also not limited to that mode and has a much fuller understanding of what is actually real. Again, this is quite like the 'releaser' of Plato's allegory.

Indeed, in yet another passage the Course's purpose is explicitly described as a one of releasing:

> "5 Can you to whom God says, 'Release My Son!,' be tempted not to listen, when you learn that it is you for whom He asks release? 6 And what but this is what this course would teach? 7 And what but this is there for you to learn?" (31,VIII,15,5-7)

Thus, not only is the Course's purpose to free the mind from the chains of ignorance of what it truly is, but to enable that released mind also to be the releaser of others – again, the same point made by Plato.

One last passage that elucidates the author's intention is as follows:

> "4 If the purpose of this course is to help you remember what you are, and if you believe that what you are is fearful, then it must follow that you will not learn this course. 5 Yet the reason for the course is that you do not know what you are." (9,I,2,4-5)

Here is made clear that the core of the release consists in a very simple realization: to remember what one is. This is not just a conceptual remembering, but rather a full and thorough realization that involves a radical transformation. As we will see later, this consists not in merely believing intellectually or emotionally, but returning to the full and unblocked mode of living and being that the Course calls 'Christ.' What is also indicated here is that the primary factor that blocks

---

[7] 'r' in 'rV' means 'Review' and 'V' refers to the fifth of these reviews.

one's mind from that is fear, particularly the fear of remembering what one is. But this will be discussed at greater length in the later chapters.

The reader may question all of this, but if one keeps it in mind while reading the Course, what one reads will likely take on a very interesting quality.

C. The Course's challenges. As will become much clearer in the chapters to follow, the Course is likely to challenge some of the views that the reader is likely to hold. This is not merely for the sake of challenging them, but to help the mind in chains break away from those chains. We may briefly consider two kinds of challenge: the first, to several traditional Christian beliefs; the second, to the dominant assumptions accepted by most in academia, particularly those accepting the dominant scientific or philosophical perspective.

Among those who think of themselves as Christians, there are significant beliefs that the Course calls into serious question, offering very powerful reasons to support that. Here is a brief list of some of the most important ones:

1. That God created the physical universe that we think of as existing in space and time.
2. That He created human beings as individual, separate beings in bodies, placing within them an ego similar, though limited, to the Ego that is His own.
3. That Adam sinned, which brought punishment to his descendants, and that sin is something very real that God abhors.
4. That the most severe punishment for sin is the everlasting condition of suffering in hell.
5. That God required that His only Son, incarnated as Jesus, suffer death by crucifixion so that humans could be redeemed and avoid hell.
6. That only Jesus is the Son of God.
7. That the only way to avoid hell and be assured everlasting happiness after death is through accepting Jesus as the Son of God and one's lord and savior.

All of these beliefs are squarely opposed by the Course. What is most interesting is that the basic reason for its rejecting them is that they are incompatible with the nature of God's being Love. Part of the intent of the present book is to clarify why the Course holds them to be contradictory to His being Love.

But the Course also challenges some of the fundamental assumptions or beliefs generally accepted within the academic world. These are summarized:

1. That the primary reality is what we think of as matter, or limited form that exists in and undergoes changes in space and time.
2. That the primary way of finding reliable beliefs or truth is through information given by sense-perception or its extension through instruments that can be perceived through the senses, and then reflecting logically on what that information discloses. Indeed, what is thought of as 'matter' is what is discoverable as present through this approach.

3. That the most important thing in human experience is the ego, the protection and preservation of which should be sought to extend as long as possible, along with its enjoyment of various sorts of pleasure (sensual, emotional, or intellectual) and the minimization of pain, and that the function of society is to facilitate the improvement of the ego-mode to the maximum.

Once again, while the Course recognizes that these beliefs, particularly the last, do indeed dominate the minds of most human beings, it views them as fundamentally false. Again, it does not merely propose a dogmatic dismissal of them, but rather offers some rather impressive reasons for their incorrectness and an explanation of why they are so widely accepted. The most dominant belief, which runs through both the traditional Christian (indeed also through most other religions, possibly with the exception of Hinduism and Buddhism) and the scientific view, is the primacy of the ego. The course actually makes explicit that this is the most problematic belief, as it states:

"1 The whole purpose of this course is to teach you that the ego is unbelievable and will forever be unbelievable."
(7,VIII,7,1)

Thus, it directs most of its teachings to helping the student see this as the major problem and how to correct this fundamental error, which is the foundation of the chain that imprisons one's mind and life.

Accordingly, many readers will very likely find the Course to be very demanding. This is not so much because its ideas are so difficult to grasp. Rather, it is due to the fact that they challenge one's own basic beliefs at the deepest level. The same is likely to hold for the present book, which is the result of my attempt to express the teachings in a logical order. What I have done here is a philosophical reflection on what can be thought of as a revelation or communication from a mind that is 'outside the cave;' that is, a mind directly aware of Truth in its fullness without any limitations. In that sense, this book can be thought of as a 'theological' treatise. But, as the Course points out:

"4 Theological considerations as such are necessarily controversial, since they depend on belief and can therefore be accepted or rejected. 5 A universal theology is impossible, but a universal experience is not only possible but necessary. 6 It is this experience toward which the course is directed. 7 Here alone consistency becomes possible because here alone uncertainty ends."(C,In.,2,4-7)

That is, while a philosophical or theological inquiry may be useful for clarifying and offering reasons to support or criticize various statements and insights, it can at best serve as only a useful means for opening to the direct intuitive experience of the insights that the Course proposes. It further claims that those insights are available to anyone who seriously seeks to listen, not merely to its words, but to the Teacher that is present within every mind that thinks it is limited. That Teacher it calls the 'Holy Spirit' or the 'Voice for God.'

D. The present author's perspective and intention. It will also be good for the reader to have some idea of my own orientation. As I briefly stated in the Preface, I have since my teenage years been a serious seeker of truth. That seeking has had two important perspectives, the one that might be called 'spiritual,' the other 'scientific.' The first began with an early interest in the mystical teachings of Christianity. The second expressed as a great interest in the natural sciences, especially physics and cosmology. This second interest became the dominating concern of my years of study in higher education, so that I eventually was drawn to the philosophy of science. Eventually, my dominant interests came back to what I see is the higher type of truth found in the spiritual teachings of the East and West, and in the field of inquiry called 'psychical research.' The latter attempts to some extent to apply the methods of science to 'higher' modes of cognition, particularly that of mystical experience. It was in this context that I was eventually led to the Course. Accordingly, I have applied my scholarly skills, particularly those developed in the study and practice of philosophical methods, to this present book.

My intention in this inquiry should also be clarified to you, the reader. I should note first that it is not to attack or destroy any beliefs you find useful or true. Nor is it to persuade you to accept the ideas taught by the Course. Of course, since it is my fundamental belief that truth is far better to believe than illusion, both for any individual and for society as a whole, it may turn out that some beliefs you have accepted will, through this inquiry, become clear to you that they involve illusions and thus need to be given up. That is precisely what has happened in my own mind. In following that step, which is a matter of one's choice, you may come to a view more intellectually and practically satisfying as a closer approximation to the truth.

Thus, my primary intention is to share the results of my own attempt to come to greater clarity about the Course's teachings. In doing that, there are two primary intellectual activities. The first might be called 'disambiguation.' That is, there are many places in the Course's words that involve some or even great ambiguity as to what the teaching actually is. This ambiguity lies to a great extent in the fact that English words sometimes have many different meanings. Thus, if one is to come to a clear understanding of the teaching, it is necessary to determine which of those meanings is intended by the author in any particular context. There is also, at times, an ambiguity in the grammatical expressions in which statements are articulated. Students of the Course have long noted this, asking what does 'it' or 'that' or some other pronoun refer to, and seeing that the statement's meaning is radically shifted depending on whether one or another referent is taken. Along with the concern of disambiguating the Course, there is also the even more challenging task of resolving what seem to be its inconsistencies, passages that appear to contradict one another logically. This was mentioned earlier. One of the great benefits of developing philosophical skills is that it sharpens the mind's sensitivity to inconsistency. Even more important, when matured, those skills facilitate one's coming to see how a contradiction is only apparent and how it may be resolved and lead to an even deeper or broader understanding of something only hinted at prior to resolving the apparent inconsistency.

A third important concern here, also a skill that comes in earnestly studying philosophy, is to offer a more systematically organized presentation of the Course's teachings. As originally formulated, the Course is arranged along a sequence of presentation that seems concerned with leading the student stepwise into a greater understanding of Truth. This pedagogical sequence moves back and forth between the student's strongly held ideas, which in the Course's view are often deeply illusory, and contrasting them with formulations much closer to what it considers to be the truth. In the sequence that I have chosen, there is first the attempt to give a clear formulation of the Course's most profound insights (Ch. II). That is followed by a discussion of how it views the illusory beliefs that dominate most minds (Ch. III); then, the insights that come into such a mind as it begins to move out from a state dominated by illusion (Ch. IV); and finally, the insights the developing mind comes to upon realizing the highest state possible within the realm of human form (Ch. V). Thus, this sequence, although more systematically organized than the Course, is intended primarily to lead to intellectual clarity. For anyone desiring to go beyond that and come to the more thoroughgoing existential realization of its teachings, I cannot see any better way than studying the Course itself.

E. The most profitable perspective for the reader. As a last reflection in this introductory chapter, I'd like to offer several suggestions for you to consider.

You are likely to have some or even serious reservations about the Course. These can range from its being authored by a perhaps mentally ill woman, or by a very clever team of psychologists trying to 'brainwash' people to accept a dangerous teaching (some have claimed it came about as a part of a CIA plot), or by the arch-deceiver Satan (also claimed by some critics), or that it is just an interesting philosophical writing by a very insightful woman. And some will regard it as a revelation by Jesus himself, whose intention was to correct many of the errors that have crept into interpretations of his original teachings as found in the New Testament and to offer a much more thorough and accurate elaboration of what is found there.

Whatever your orientation, I suggest that if you want to understand what it says beyond a superficial level, it will be very important to *listen* carefully to what is said here. One of my teachers observed: "Before you judge a thinker's ideas critically, it is important first to 'sit in his own armchair,' so to speak, and try to grasp just what he is saying from his own perspective. Then, after you have gotten a clear understanding of his view, you are ready to consider the next question: is it true?" That is precisely what I've sought to do regarding the Course. This entails what is sometimes called the 'provisional suspension of one's own beliefs.' For, as long as one insists on holding on to what one already thinks, one is unable to listen to what another is saying or understand what he is thinking, and quite likely excluding the possibility of enlarging one's own comprehension of the truth.

While this 'provisional suspension of one's own beliefs' may at first be difficult, it is quite possible for anyone sincerely dedicated to discovering the truth. Nor does that involve the giving up of one's beliefs. Indeed, if, on the one hand, those beliefs are true, further reflection on what another is saying will make clearer how one's beliefs are true and another's in error. But, on the other, if one is honest, it will also make clear in what sense those that one has accepted may be false, and how another's are true. In any case, you are urged to think through what is presented here (or in any book, including the Course) so as to decide for yourself whether it is true or not. This also includes whether what I present is an accurate interpretation of the Course.

Throughout such reflection, I would also suggest that you consider an insight found in both the teachings of many thinkers and the Course itself. That is, there is within each person's mind a level of awareness that is the final criterion of deciding whether to accept or reject ideas or information as reliable. This is sometimes called the 'inner voice,' the 'voice of Reason,' or 'inner intuition.' Plato tells of how his own teacher Socrates always turned to his inner guide, which he called his 'daimon,'[8] when deciding what to believe or do. The Course refers to that guide as the 'Holy Spirit.' But, it is also careful to point out that our minds can listen to *two* basic voices. The one is that of the ego, which often speaks quite loudly, but has a major problem in that its awareness is fundamentally confined to a very limited amount of information and insight. The other is that of the Holy Spirit, which generally speaks quietly and gently, but is the only reliable criterion in that it is aware of the whole of reality.

While you need to decide which voice you choose to listen to, it is hoped that you will find what is presented here to be illuminating and useful, in relation to the concern of understanding the Course, the nature of love, and particularly the quest of understanding yourself.

A final suggestion is that the reader may find Ch. II more comprehensible if it is read a second time after reading the other chapters. Although the teachings on 'absolute love' are the most abstract and thus most challenging, they are considered first because it is in light of them that the other three ideas of love make sense. Indeed, in my own study of the Course, it was only through coming to a better understanding of its view on 'love' in this most fundamental sense that the rest of its teachings could be seen as coherent, illuminated by this most profound idea.

---

[8] In Socrates' case, 'daimon' is best translated as 'guardian spirit.' It should not be confused with its other possible meaning, 'demon' or 'evil spirit.'

Chapter II. 'Love' (or 'absolute love')

We will focus first on Love, in the absolute or most fundamental sense, as present in God, then on Its presence in created perfect minds (both those that do not slip into separation and those that do), and on how it is present within the 'Universe of Love.'

A. Love in God, the uncreated perfect Mind. We begin by considering two important passages:

"7 God is Love and you do want Him."(9,IX,9,6-7)

and:

"God, being Love, is also happiness."(W,103)

That God *is* Love is a profound claim. It does not say that Love is an attribute of God, one of His characteristics. Rather, what is affirmed here is that the essential nature of God is simply what is referred to as 'Love.' In one sense, because we do not have, in our present condition, an awareness of His essential Nature, this word can only be an outer label of something about which we may have only an inkling as to what it means. However, by asserting that Love is the primary internal quality, activity, or mode of being of God, we are put on notice of two things. One is that until we completely realize or enter into full awareness of God, we can only dimly grasp what Love is. The other is that all meanings that we think of when we use the term 'love' are at best only outer, partial glimpses of what that term means in its fullness. In a sense, in this recognition we are drawn to It (Love/God), as is the point of the first passage. And, as the second passage indicates, only in the full awareness of It can there be complete satisfaction or happiness. Yet, as long as we remain outside that awareness, we can have no adequate concept or idea of what is actually involved within It. In that sense, God and Love, for separated minds are a kind of 'mystery.' In seriously considering It, the response can be one of great awe. If It begins to resonate within one's mind, this response can be one of great longing. But, as we shall later see, for the mind still strongly attached to the separated condition, that response can also be one of fear and a variety of impulses to remove oneself from Its Presence.

But the Course offers many further indications of what Love in God involves. Here we should distinguish two somewhat different modes or conditions: what God/Love is originally in Its primary state, and what It is in relation to the created mind's entering into separation.

1. Love in God originally. Love, in its most fundamental mode, is identified with the Entity the Course refers to as 'God.' Our concern will be to clarify what the Course means by 'Love' as present within that Entity.

a. Love's essential characteristics. It is especially important first to understand what for the Course seems to be Love's primary function. Then we will examine the most general features that belong to It in relation to that function.

i. The function of uniting. In one passage we find:

> "10 What God did not give you has no power over you, and the attraction of love for love remains irresistible. 11 For it is the function of love to unite all things unto itself, and to hold all things together by extending its wholeness."(12,VIII,7,10-11)

Here we need to focus on statement 11. In this, the Course is quite clear that the function of Love is *to unite all things*. This is based on what seems to be Its most interior or central characteristic: wholeness. That is perhaps best understood as the foundation of what makes Love, and anything It touches on, completely one. This may be difficult for our minds to grasp, accustomed as they are to thinking in terms of pluralities that involve many sorts of division, which are by their very meaning lacking in complete wholeness. Something we think of as a whole, for example, what we call a 'human being,' is not understood in its relationships with all other beings, but as a whole constituted of many parts. That being is only a 'partial whole.' However, despite that tendency, we do recognize wholes that are the unities of various parts: one's body is a whole of many limbs and organs; the collection of things we see belong to a whole that is the current field of visual perception; even the many moments of our experience we can think of as a whole that we might name 'our life till now' and recognize that this whole continues to enlarge itself as we continue to live. Thus, the notion of 'wholeness' is not altogether unfamiliar to us. While it may be difficult to understand what is the wholeness that is central to Love, which, as has been pointed out, is thought of as having its primary or original form in the Love that is God, we can perhaps come to a somewhat fuller grasp of what that may involve.

Ordinarily, we think of 'uniting' as what acts on what is in some way not united, composed of differing or separate parts or aspects, so as to bring all those parts or aspects together into a single whole. Thus, although we might have many different visual perspectives in seeing an apple, along with many touch, taste, and smell impressions of it, we think of it as a single thing: the apple that is sitting in a bowl. That synthesis or uniting of all those different perceptions is primarily by way of forming an idea, a concept, of this particular apple. In this, we do not necessarily conclude that all those different perceptions are somehow pulled together, but rather that the apple is the one entity or being from which all those differing perceptions are expressed. Of course, we do not perceive through our senses this single whole apple, but only *think* of it or hold it as an idea in our mind. While it may be the case that the formation of that idea was preceded by a sequence of many different perceptions, once it is present in the mind we hold it there in thought as a single whole about which we tie together any further perceptions we may have regarding it.

However, it is not intrinsic to a whole that it involves many different, separated parts. Its wholeness may express in parts or aspects, but in so far as it is a whole, the presence of parts is not necessary. This is perhaps most easily exhibited in the idea of a point. A point, by definition, has no parts, yet it is a single whole. We may think of parts or aspects related to it by considering its relationship with other points (or by visualizing it from different perspectives), but the point, as a point, is a simple single whole that has no parts or aspects in itself. Thus, we can form an idea of a whole that is in no way divided or divisible. If we now apply this to our thinking about God's Love, we can begin to recognize that Its wholeness can be, in itself, completely without parts or separate aspects. Whatever aspects or parts we may think of, such as Its relationship to things created, which may lead us to speak of differing relationships, these do not in any way undo the single wholeness that belongs to It. Nor should saying "Love is whole" be taken as implying that there are two different things because we use two different words or ideas. Similarly, to say "Love unites all things" should not be taken as implying that there is one thing, Love, and many other things that It unites. There is only one fundamental 'thing,' Love, which is present in all that we might want to refer to as 'things' – perhaps better thought of as 'processes.' Although that seems to involve asserting that the one single Whole is different from those other things, this does not follow; it only seems to be implied as a result of the way we interpret our use of the words.

The uniqueness of the wholeness of Love, which may be referred to as Wholeness, is indicated even further where the Course states that the function of Love is 'to hold all things together by extending its wholeness.' This can be understood as saying that the very nature of Love as Wholeness is to extend Itself. This is not to be taken in a spatial sense of going out to other things. Rather, it is better thought of as a logical extension, like the extension of an idea or concept to what it implies. In that, what arises is simply the same Wholeness of Love as present in a fuller realization of what it already is. What is 'produced' thereby is exactly the same Wholeness. But, because it is present in another, the quality of that Wholeness is rendered more intense. Again, this is not something that takes place by way of a temporal sequence, since, as we will see, there is only one Instant or Now in which this occurs. This also holds for any further extensions of that Wholeness/Love.

The result of this uniting or extending of Wholeness is itself a wholeness that in a sense is even greater or more intense than the original Wholeness. It also involves the intimate unity of all that follows from that extension. That is, that to which Love is extended is both completely one within itself and with that from which and to which It is extended. If we can appreciate the significance of this, we may begin to glimpse what seems to be the most fundamental characteristic of Love, of God, and whatever arises from It.

The centrality of oneness or unity as the function of Love is further clarified in the following:

> "4 God will come to you only as you will give Him to your brothers. 5 Learn first of them and you will be ready to hear God. 6 That is because the function of love is one."(4,VI,8,4-5)

Although this begins in reference to love present in or expressed by a separated mind ('you'), the point in statement 6 seems to be general for all forms or occurrences of love, including Love in God. We will focus on what this passage says about love in its fullest mode, that is, as Love in God. The assertion that 'the function of Love is one' may be taken in two ways. The first is that Its function is a matter of uniting (the point previously made). The second is that there are not several functions, but only a single function. If this is the sense, then it follows that, whatever else might be said to proceed from Love, all of that is to be understood as but an aspect of that single function. Given the primacy of oneness or unity as the essential characteristic of Love (and any variation of It, as in the love present in and expressed by creatures), this singularity of Its function seems to be central. One might use an analogy to light. That is, a white ray of light, when passed through a prism, is seen to exit in the many different colors of the spectrum. This might lead one to think that white light is actually a composite of many different colors or wavelengths. But, in this analogy, it would be more accurate to say that the many colors are only manifestations or expressions of the single, simple unitary white ray, or the white ray appearing to be modified into many different rays. Of course, this analogy has its limitations, since the disposition of physical theory is to insist on the primacy of the fragmented colors as being what is most real and the whiteness as only an appearance.

It is interesting, even illuminating, to consider that the term 'whole' is closely related to 'holy,' both etymologically and in the Course's view. These two words have the same root in the Greek word 'holos,' which means 'whole.' This connection is recognized in:

> "5 The creation is whole, and the mark of wholeness is holiness."(1,IV,4,5)

The point is that, since Love is that which unites or is the foundation of the Wholeness in God and all Reality, and God is considered to be what is most holy, the essential nature of holiness lies in the uniting function, or Wholeness, of Love. Thus, we can think of Love, which is God, as the primal 'energy' whose function is to unite all entities in Reality into a whole through its extension to include all of them. These entities the Course calls 'spirits' whose primary feature is their perfect minds. Further, this energy has two modes of uniting/extending: awareness and creating. The awareness of perfect minds is what is called 'knowing,' which makes all real beings present to or united with the spirit/perfect mind in which Love is present. In a sense, it is the 'receptive' mode of uniting, by which the mind 'holds' or 'contains' what it is aware of. The second is 'creating,' an 'active' or productive mode of uniting, which brings created spirits/perfect minds into being as extensions of Love, which makes Love present in them. These two modes of uniting/extending are discussed further as the next two characteristics of Love.

ii. Knowing awareness. For the Course, the most fundamental and perfect type of awareness is **knowing** or **knowledge**. This makes present all real beings. The mind in which Love is fully operative is totally or completely united with all those beings. This is the central insight in the following:

> "4 This Self alone knows Love. 5 This Self alone is perfectly consistent in Its Thoughts; knows Its Creator, understands Itself, is perfect in Its knowledge and Its Love, and never changes from Its constant state of union with Its Father and Itself."(W,rV,In,4,4-5)

Although this passage focuses on knowing in the Self, which is the fundamental reality of Love in the created entity that is the foundation of any separated mind, and only speaks of its knowing of 'Its Creator' (God), what is clear here is that knowing is primarily a matter of union. This awareness has nothing to do with perception, which in the Course's view is always partial and involves some separation between the one that is aware and what it is aware of. That is, knowing should not be thought of as involving any concepts, images, or any other sort of limited perception, since all of these involve some sort of selection and exclusion of what does not fall within them. It is better thought of as a direct intuition in which what is known is immediately present to or united with the knowing mind.

iii. Creating/extending. Although 'creation' and 'creating' have been referred to as central to Love, it is important to have some clarity on what the Course means by those terms. It was pointed out that creating is one of the two primary modes of unlimited extending/uniting. In fact, the Course, when originally written by Schucman, used the terms 'projecting'/'projection' as equivalent to 'creating'/'creation' and 'extending'/'extension.' However, because the word 'projection' was also used in the original material to refer to a second sort of activity of the mind, which is the mental activity of imposing a limited perceptual form onto what is found in awareness, the editors decided to reserve it for this more limited activity (very much in line with the way that word is used in psychology). Thus, the FIP versions were altered so that the words 'creating'/'creation' are used for the unlimited productive activity or extension of any perfect mind.[9] That

---

[9] The following are examples of this change:
"In the Creation, God *projected* his Creative Ability out of Himself toward the Souls which He created, and also imbued them with the same loving wish (or will) to create."(UM, T 2 A 4)
is changed in FIP to:
"In the creation, God *extended* Himself to His creations and imbued them with the same loving Will to create."(2,I,1,2)
Also:

is, although it is the nature of Love to extend to *all* other real entities/spirits/perfect minds, it does not extend in the same way to all of them. One mode of Love's extension, as was pointed out, is that of the *receptive mode* of awareness, which does unite with all of them so as to hold them present and affirm their existence. But the other mode, the *active mode* is that of creating, which brings an entity into existence and maintains that existence. However, we will see in what follows that the Course holds that each perfect mind creates, at least directly, only *one* other perfect mind. And, since the creating capacity is also given to any created mind by its being given Love, the created mind also must create yet another perfect mind. Accordingly, there is an infinity of perfect created minds in Reality. Although each is in union with all other perfect minds through Love's awareness (knowing), each directly creates only one other perfect mind, its single creature. This means that we must distinguish between the kind of extension that is knowing and the kind of extension that is creating. Without that, one is led to serious contradictions. Hopefully, this will become much clearer to the reader as we consider more fully the nature of creating as a primary characteristic of Love.

One passage reads:

> "3 To create is to love. 4 Love extends outward simply because it cannot be contained."(7,I,13,3-4)

From this we may see that the primary foundation of the creative act is Love. Because It cannot be contained, creating is not something optional for God. Since He is Love, He necessarily creates. He cannot *not* create.

This idea of creation as extension is profoundly different from what is found in most Western religious traditions, although it is perhaps closer to the views found in some forms of Hinduism and the mystical philosophy of Plotinus. The prevailing view in Christian thought is that God creates by producing separately

---

> "Whenever *projection* in its inappropriate sense is utilized, it ALWAYS implies that some emptiness (or lack of everything) must exist, and that it is within man's ability to put his own ideas there INSTEAD of the truth."(UM, T 2 A 5)

is changed in FIP to:

> "The *inappropriate use of extension*, or *projection*, occurs when you believe that some emptiness or lack exists in you, and that you can fill it with your own ideas instead of truth."(2,I,1,7)

This change is based on the fact that the word 'projection' in English has two very distinct meanings. The one is more general, which can be understood as close to 'extension' ('a moving outward'), which, in a sense, the act of creation as understood in the Course can be thought of. The other is a more restricted, psychological meaning, such as the way our minds project particular meanings onto things we perceive. The change made in FIP does appear to me to be a helpful one so as to avoid confusion, so that it reserves 'projection' for 'inappropriate use of extension.' So defined, creation is a type of extension, but not a type of projection.

existing things out of nothingness, and thus introduces into existence multiple entities that are limited and significantly different from the Creator. Another view is that creation involves an imposition of form upon some already existing thing, much as a potter is said to create a pot from clay, or more generally the idea analogous to what we call artistic creation. There are still other ideas of creation, such as those found in Hinduism's view of the origin of the universe as a dream arising in the mind of the Creator, or in modern scientific cosmology's different theories such as that of a single 'Big Bang' or an infinite series of 'big bangs,' which originate from what is thought of as a 'mathematical singularity.'[10]

The Course's view is perhaps best understood if we further consider its idea about the fundamental nature of the Creator or God. God is thought of as an entity that does not exist in space or time. Thus, He cannot be attributed any qualities related to physicality, such as change, occupying space, or enduring over any period of time. One might be tempted to think of God simply as a point, but another attribute the Course applies to Him is 'infinity' or 'unlimitedness.' (The non-temporality and infinity of God/Love are discussed below.) Again, this cannot be a boundless spatiality or temporality, since those two notions are not applicable. The key notion is that God is a 'spirit,' but of course, since that word is fraught with ambiguity, one must specify what this means. This is indicated in:

"3 *Spirit* is the Thought of God which He created like Himself."(C,1,1,3)

While this does not directly say that God is a spirit, it can be understood as implying it, since it states that what it means by 'spirit' is a Thought that is like Himself; that is, spirit is fundamentally an 'idea' or 'thought'. This turns about the primary characteristics of God, which are those of Love, which as we have seen includes awareness of all that really exists and the productive extension of creating. The awareness aspect of God is described by the Course in terms of what in our own experience most closely approximates the divine: what we call 'thought.' Indeed, God is at various places referred to as both being an idea or thought and having a thought or thoughts, as in:

> "4 That is because you recognize, however dimly, that God is an idea, and so your faith in Him is strengthened by sharing. 5 What you find difficult to accept is the fact that, like your Father, *you* are an idea."(15,VI,4,4-5)

and:

> "1 God created His Sons by extending His Thought, and retaining the extensions of His Thought in His Mind."(6,II,8,1)

and:

---

[10] Modern cosmology posits a single, undivided whole, which it calls a 'singularity,' as the foundational or initial reference point in the formation of the physical universe. This may indicate a profound convergence of the views of the Course and those of contemporary physics regarding the origin of the universe of perceptual experience.

"7 Only the Thoughts of God are true."(17,III,9,7)

A first and more general point that should be noted is that the use of the masculine nouns 'Son' and 'Father,' as well as 'brother' and 'man,' and the pronouns 'he' and 'him' should not be understood as implying any superiority of males over females, since sexual gender is completely inapplicable to the only truly real beings, spirits or minds, in what the Course considers to be the higher level of Reality. Also, within what it thinks of as this lower level of existence, the Course displays no preference whatsoever of males over females. While such a preference was prevalent in early Christianity and continues in much of what is found today in Christian thought and institutions, a careful reading shows that this is not the case for the Course. It could have been expressed without any difference in its teaching if it had used the words 'Daughter,' 'Mother, 'sister,' 'she,' and 'her' instead (although that would probably have generated a block to many students, particularly men, steeped in the biases of tradition). That masculine words were used seems to be entirely a matter of the Course's remaining in accord with the terminology of the prevailing Judeo-Christian and Muslim traditions, and even the traditions of the East, most of which imagine and conceptualize the 'higher' level as masculine. It has also been the dominant custom of English speakers to use the masculine form when referring to persons of either sex or the more generic meaning of any member of the human species. In the remainder of this inquiry, for consistency with the Course's way of speaking, we will also generally use the masculine forms of words when discussing its teachings. Hopefully, female readers will not take offense to that.

In the first passage cited above, it is made quite clear that both God and what He produces ('you') are in the most fundamental sense 'ideas' or 'thoughts.' This is what might be called the fundamental mode of existence.[11] In the second passage, it is made clear that the process of creating is one of extending or forming a further idea/thought. What is especially important here is that the thought produced by God, who is Himself a Thought, is quite different from our thoughts. Since He is a spirit, the thought that He thinks is also a spirit. That means this created thought has the properties of awareness and extending that is in God as the Original Thought. The second passage also states that His created thoughts, like our own thoughts, remains in His own Mind. That is, they are not separate from Him but rather exist by virtue of the very thinking process within God's Mind. Since this thinking process is rooted in and is an aspect of Love, it follows that the spirit that God thinks or creates is an expression of Love.

The second passage also makes use of the word 'Sons,' and at first reading seems to state that He created a plurality of entities or Thoughts that would have

---

[11] Such a view is quite close to the insight of one of the earliest Greek philosophers, Parmenides, who observed: "For to be aware and to be are the same." (*The Poem of Parmenides*, III, in the section called "The Way of Truth.") Here I have translated his word 'noein' as 'to be aware.'

to be understood as 'spirits' having their own awareness and creativity. Indeed, the third passage refers to a plurality of 'Thoughts of God,' and 59 other passages in the Course material[12] speak of the 'Sons of God,' or the equivalent 'God's Sons,' 'His Sons,' or 'Your Sons,' in the plural. However, we also find the following passages:

> "1 It should especially be noted that God has only *one* Son." (2,VII,6,1)

and:

> "Father, You have one Son. ... He is Your one creation." (W,262,1,1&3)

That God has 'one Son' ('only one Son') is repeated 16 other times in the Course,[13] so it is clearly not a slip-up in the note-taking and is something that is very central to the Course's view. At first, this seems to involve a serious inconsistency. However, some reflection makes clear that the phrase 'Sons of God' can be understood in a way that is fully consistent with the assertion that God has only one Son.

To see this requires that we have a fuller understanding of the nature of the extending process that is central to creating. An important feature of that is described:

> "1 Love is extension. 2 To withhold the smallest gift is not to know love's purpose. 3 Love offers everything forever. 4 Hold back but one belief, one offering, and love is gone, because you asked a substitute to take its place."(24,I,1,1-3)

That is, if Love held back anything in God's extending that creates His one Thought or Son, it would fail to be complete giving or extending. That is, it would not be Love. Hence, in His producing the Son He gives to the Son all of what He is, which is Love, and which includes both the complete awareness of knowing and the extending power of creating. This is radically different from the traditional Christian notion of creation, which holds that God only gives partially to what He creates. But, for the Course, such a limited idea of extending is completely contradictory to the very nature of Love, since it involves some degree of non-giving or non-loving. It follows from this view that the Son is completely like the Father (God) regarding his knowing and creating. But the Son differs from the Father in an important way: that the Son does not create the Father, although the Father creates the Son. This is indicated in:

> "1 God is more than you only because He created you, but not

---

[12] In the FIP version, the Text uses the expression 'Sons of God' or an equivalent 62 times, 12 in the Workbook, 1 in Manual for Teachers, 2 in Clarification of Terms, and 2 in Song of Prayer.

[13] At 9,VI,3,5; 10,III,2,5; 10,III,10,1; 26,III,1,3; W,20,3,5; W,99,9,3-4; W,137,14,4; W,187,10,2; W,200,7,1; C,1,1,4; P,2,VII,1,13. There are also at least 768 passages that speak of the Son in the singular ('the Son,' 'God's Son,' 'His Son.')

even this would He keep from you."(9,VI,4,1)

That is, God's act of creating does not produce a creature that has properties in any way inferior to God's. Their difference in so far as they are perfect minds is that their creative relationship goes from God, also called 'Father,' to the Son, but not from the Son to God. Thus, the Son, as a perfect mind with all the qualities of the Father's Mind, is a complete likeness of God. And when one connects this with passage (2,VII,6,1) cited above, the Course is asserting that every human (and even every nonhuman mind), *as it is created*, is this very sort of being. This gives a profoundly different meaning to the passage in Genesis, "Then God said, 'Let us make man in our image, after our likeness...'"[14]

To help make this somewhat clearer, we can use a diagram, as in Fig. 1, to represent it. From the 'God' circle flows an arrow ('creates') to the 'Son' circle. The 'Son' circle has the same content as the 'God' circle: Love, which both knows and creates. Thus, the Son perfectly reflects the perfect mind of God, and is hence itself a perfect mind.

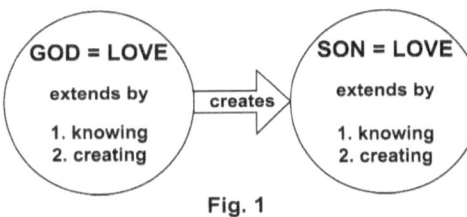

Fig. 1

Since God creates only one Son, Fig. 1 represents the creative action of God. Of course, as happens with any representation, Fig. 1 could lead to a misunderstanding, in that the 'Son' circle is outside and separated from the 'God' circle. Accordingly, we need to avoid reading into any representation more than is intended.

An alternative representation is in Fig. 2. There the 'Son' circle is concentric within the 'God' circle, and an arrow points inward to indicate the creative act. This more accurately represents the insight that the Son is a thought within God's Mind. But even here the image can be misleading, in that the 'Son' circle is smaller than the 'God' circle, and one might think that there is more within God than in the Son. However, representations such as Fig. 1 and 2 can be useful for helping us think of these insights as long as we are careful. Later, other diagrams will be given, using either the 'separate circle' form or the 'concentric circle' form, with the caution: be careful in interpreting them.

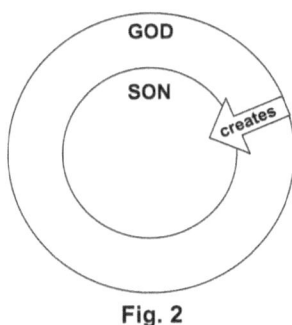

Fig. 2

Returning now to our main point, because the created Son has the full presence of Love within his being, and Love must also create, the Son likewise creates, or produces yet another perfect Thought, which is a spirit that is given Love in Its fullness. This is the Son's creature, as indicated in:

---

[14] Genesis 1: 26.

"5 It is *because* he is God's Son that he must also be a father, who creates as God created him."(28,II,1,5)

That is, the Son creates in the same way 'as God created him.' Since God created only one Son, if the Son's creative act is like God's, he also creates one creature. While the Course does not develop this to any great extent, we could name this creature of the Son 'Son$_2$.' This could also be represented, as in Fig. 3, which has a third circle for Son$_2$. In this way there is produced a plurality of

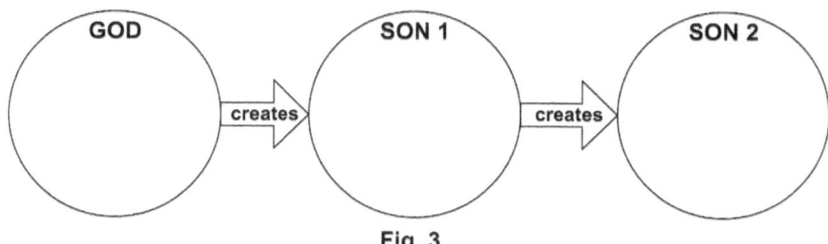

Fig. 3

three entities/spirits, but only one that is directly created by God. However, God indirectly is the Source of the Son's creature, so that Son$_2$ can more loosely be called another 'Son of God' (in human terms, he would be called a 'grandson' of God.) Thus, by enlarging the meaning of the phrase 'Son of God,' there are two Sons of God, one directly and the other indirectly created by God.

But further reflection makes clear that the creature of the Son, being also a perfect mind having Love as his essential nature, likewise has the same complete awareness and creative capacity as God's. Accordingly, Son$_2$ also extends to create his creature, which we may call 'Son$_3$.' Further, since Son$_3$ has the full perfection found in his own creator, he also creates to produce Son$_4$. Only a little further thinking makes it clear that there must also be Son$_5$ followed by Son$_6$, Son$_7$, etc., without end, so that there must be an infinity of creatures, each perfect, and each appropriately called a 'Son of God' in the extended sense. Thus, although God creates only one Son directly, there are indirectly countless Sons of God. Fig. 4 represents this, using ... to refer to a long series of steps not de-

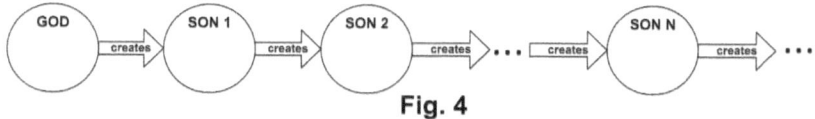

Fig. 4

picted, both within the sequence prior to Son$_n$ and extending without limit beyond Son$_n$. We could also use a diagram of concentric circles, but that has the limitation of running out of space for the infinity of interior circles. (This will be given later in Fig. 11.)

It also follows that each of these Sons of God, as perfect minds by virtue of their being constituted of Love, has complete awareness of all other perfect minds. This seems to be the deeper meaning of the Course's expression 'uni-

verse of love,' the ramifications of which are immense, as pointed out in:
> "10 The universe of love does not stop because you do not see it, nor have your closed eyes lost the ability to see. 11 Look upon the glory of His creation, and you will learn what God has kept for you."(11,I,5,10-11)

Thus, spirits or absolutely existing beings are most fundamentally something more like what we call 'ideas' or 'thoughts' than 'things,' which we almost invariably think of as being in space and time. In the passage cited earlier (17,III,9,7 on p. 30) that speaks of 'the Thoughts of God,' this seems best understood as similar to the point of the second passage (6,II,8,1 on p. 30) that seems to say that God has multiple 'Sons.'[15]

One other expression needs clarification here. The ordinary word 'extend' has a primary meaning that connotes spatiality. That is, we may extend a line segment beyond a given limit, or extend the area of our land-property to include more land. It also has a temporal meaning, as when we say we extended our visit from one to two hours, or the hot season extended beyond its usual date. However, there is also a more abstract meaning, which is called 'logical extension.' This is exemplified in mathematics where one can speak of the theorems of geometry as extensions of its axioms, or in law where one speaks of concrete applications of general legal rules or principles as their extensions.

Although some of our thoughts, particularly visual images, have spatial and temporal characteristics in their content, thoughts themselves are neither spatial nor temporal. Even the fact that they occur in minds whose bodies are located in space and at particular times does not mean that these minds are themselves spatial or temporal entities. While some thinkers may contend that they are (their reasons are highly problematic),[16] it is clear that the Course takes the opposite

---

[15] Robert Perry holds that the Course should be understood as saying that God directly created many individual Sons. (See his essay at www.circleofa.org/library/articles/are-there-many-sons-or-just-one-son/). One reason for his view is that the Course uses the expression 'Sons of God' so many times that it should be taken as its primary teaching. However, it does not seem that his view adequately explains the following: 1) how is this consistent with its clear assertions that God has only one Son? 2) what would differentiate the countless Sons created directly by God from one another? 3) why would all or many of those Sons make the decision to go into separation together? While Perry's essay is valuable, particularly in the questions that he raises related to the practical implications of the view that God created many Sons, without addressing these three questions, his view itself appears to involve serious problems. In the view offered here, while there is a plurality of Sons of God, that plurality arises from the creative power given to the one Son created by God. The plurality of minds within the world of perception consists of aspects or fragments of the Son's one perfect Mind.

[16] This is the predominant view among most neuro-scientists and many psychologists, as well as many contemporary philosophers who hold a materialist view of mind, although Nobel laureate neuro-scientist John Eccles held that mind does not exist in space.

view. From that perspective, the term 'extension' must be understood in a non-spatial and non-temporal way, that is, as logical extension.

Similarly, the assertion that 'Love extends outward' (7,I,13,4), which uses the spatial term 'outward,' should not mislead us to think of extension as involving spatiality. The central kernel of this notion of 'extending outward' is rather to be thought of as giving rise to something that is not itself identical to the source of the extending act. What is said to be 'outward' is simply another mind.

From this, we see that the Course's idea of 'extension' as 'creation' involves two primary features. One is that it is productive of another perfect being, a spirit with a mind that is also capable of knowing-awareness. The second is that it endows that being with specific qualities or characteristics. Earlier it was pointed out that what God communicates to what He creates, or what Love communicates to what It creates, is the fullness of all that is present within Him/It. This is what the Course considers to be the maximal giving that is central to Love.

One final point is the relation of Love to what the Course sometimes speaks of as the 'Will of God,' as in:

> "1 What is the Will of God? 2 He wills His Son have everything. 3 And this He guaranteed when He created him *as* everything. 4 It is impossible that anything be lost, if what you *have* is what you *are*."(26,VII,11,2-4)

From this, it may be seen that Love is not only what God wills, but is the very core of His Will or power of willing. In that sense, it is the 'energy' of Love that is present in this Will. It follows that Love is essentially the Will to unite all Reality, a 'Will to Wholeness.' Since this uniting is not a matter of choice, but necessarily follows from the very nature of Love, there is no choice in God's Will: He wills completely by the necessity of what He/Love is.

iv. Limitless/infinite. Intimately connected with the extending nature of Love is that It has no limits. Following the statement that was cited in our discussion of its creative character we find:

> "5 Being limitless it [Love] does not stop."(7,I,13,5)

This means that there is no boundary or end to that act. This negation of any limit should not be taken spatially or temporally, although that is the first way our spatio-temporal ways of thinking may be inclined to think of it.

Although it has been pointed out that the act of creating by its very nature extends to an infinity of creatures or 'Sons,' this limitless or infinite character of Love can be further developed. Since there is no limit surrounding the Love within the Mind of God, the act of creating involves the production of that same condition of having no limit in the mind that He creates. And, since to have no limit would involve no boundary on Its own creative act of communicating Its essential unity, there can be no existence where It is not, since that would involve a boundary or limit beyond which Love does not go.

Of course, when we think of something as limitless, our habits incline us to imagine something very large that extends without an end in a vast region of space. But such an image is misleading, since any notion of space involves spatial subregions as parts of it, and each such part by its very definition must have a limit. Similarly, we are inclined to imagine whatever we think of as existing in time as having limits, since time by its own definition is composed of sub-portions of time having limits. The complete negation of any limit thus makes such images radically inaccurate. Thus, if we want to have an idea that will not introduce distortions and lead to contradictions, we will have to let these images go. Indeed, the reflections of Immanuel Kant where he demonstrates how such conceptions necessarily lead to contradictory conclusions (his antinomy related to the notion of 'universe') make clear that any attempt to use such images is unreliable. At best, they can only serve as very weak aids for minds addicted to ideas like 'space' and 'time.'

The infinity of Love is also clearly stated in the following:

> "1 Creation is the sum of all God's Thoughts, in number infinite, and everywhere without all limit. 2 Only love creates, and only like itself."(W,pII,11,1)

As we saw in the previous section, the effect of Love's/God's creating the one Son by giving that creature that same Love requires that there be an infinite sequence of 'Thoughts' or spirits produced, which are within the whole of the created Universe of Love. This process of further extending can have no limit, since each mind produced by the extension in its essence is Love, which necessarily extends onward ad infinitum. If this is so, then the point made in the passage above, that 'God's Thoughts, in number infinite' can be understood as His distinct acts of awareness ('Thoughts') of each of those Son_n. Indeed, this seems to be the only way in which way we can make any sense of the full ramifications of statement 2 in this last passage and the earlier assertion that there are no limits whatsoever on Love.

v. Eternal or timeless, and beyond change. Closely connected with the unlimitedness of Love is its eternal character. As is stated:

> "6 It [Love] creates forever, but not in time."(7,I,13,6)

Although the term 'forever' has a temporal connotation, the primary point here is that Its primary mode of being is outside time. This reaffirms that creating should not be understood as involving a past, present, or future. Rather, although the word 'process' also connotes something temporal, it can be understood as the unfolding of all the logical consequences of the primary principle, Love, which unfolding occurs in a single instant. That instant is unlike the instants that we think of as composing the long series that are considered as the 'whole of time.' This Instant, when considered by a mind within time, must be thought of as occurring at all temporal instants, that is, 'forever,' but it is entirely outside that series. Thus, it is best called the 'Eternal Instant' or 'Eternal Now.'

This also means that this Instant has no boundary, either a 'beginning' prior to which it did not exist or an 'ending' after which it will not exist. The ideas 'was' and 'will be' simply do not apply to it. The only sense of a 'beginning' is that of the first or originating principle, which is better thought of as a logical 'first principle.' Similarly, the complete unfolding of that principle occurs 'all at once' in the single Instant, but there is no 'last' step in the infinite series that follows in this unfolding. That is, there is no cessation of that Instant. It also follows that there can be no change within the realm of Love, which includes God and all creatures that arise from Love's creative extension.

This last point is made even clearer in:

> "1 Love's meaning is obscure to anyone who thinks that love can change. 2 He does not see that changing love must be impossible. 3 And thus he thinks that he can love at times, and hate at other times. 4 He also thinks that love can be bestowed on one, and yet remain itself although it is withheld from others. 5 To believe these things of love is not to understand it."(W,127,2,1-5)

Thus, Love is essentially beyond all change. Not only is it impossible for It to cease, but It cannot alter its essential characteristics or change in any way. Since what we mean by time is meaningful only within a context of change (one may recall Aristotle's definition of time as 'the measure/number of change according to the before and after'),[17] Love is completely changeless. This changelessness/timelessness is the most fundamental meaning of 'eternity.' Thus, Love is eternal.

This is quite different for those emotions we often designate by the name 'love.' But for the Course, they are not love at all. They are, at most, as we shall see later, dim reflections or diluted expressions within the realm of time that may have some similarity to Love, possibly serving as occasions to opening to Its true presence. In that sense Love is not like what we call an emotion in the usual sense, which is related to our bodily states. That is, It does not exist as a temporal quality. However, that does not mean It cannot manifest within the realm of time. While that manifestation may be experienced as sometimes clear and at other times obscure or even absent, Love itself does not undergo any change. Rather, it is the changing receptivity of the separated mind that makes It appear to come and go. One might think of this as analogous to the Sun's light, which in itself is constant throughout the 24-hour period of a day, but is experienced in differing ways as clouds pass across a clear bright sky or as the earth moves so that we enter into the dark shadow we call 'night.' When we discuss 'illusory love,' it will be made even clearer how its changingness is opposed to Love, and how that idea of 'love' leads to much confusion in separated minds.

vi. All-inclusive. There is also another aspect of Love related to Its lack of limits. This is indicated indirectly in:

> "6 Love does not limit, and what it creates is not limited. 7 To give without limit is God's Will for you, because only this can

---

[17] *Physics*, Book IV, Ch. 11 (220a1,25)

bring you the joy that is His and that He wills to share with you. 8 Your love is as boundless as His because it *is* His." (11,I,6,6-8)

Here we are told that Love is directed toward 'you.' But we must remember that the Course's teachings are offered as an expression of Love, not only to a few particular individuals who might happen to read this version of it, but to *every* separated mind. (The Course itself speaks of the 'universal course,' of which the particular set of teachings called *A Course in Miracles* is only one articulation – see M,1,4,1-2). This means that Love is directed to everyone within the world of perception, that it excludes no one. Further, since it is the very nature of Love to be given without limits to whomever It is given, it follows that It is directed to every mind. Within the Course's view of Reality, this includes all perfect minds, such as God, the Son, the Holy Spirit, and the infinite series of created minds, as well as all imperfect, separated minds, since they are only aspects of a perfect mind from which they think they separated. Thus, within the realm called 'this world,' Love is given not only to all minds that have taken human form, or even some other sort of intelligent similar form, but every entity that displays any mentality. This is quite similar to the Mahayana Buddhist view of the Bodhisattva, whose compassion/love embraces *all sentient beings*, which are much the same as what the Course calls 'separated minds.' It also implies that, since there is within each separated mind the perfect mind that is its foundation, genuine love in each such mind must also be nonexclusive, directed to all other minds equally.

Related to this, what we usually think of as love is focused on one or very few other beings, excluding all the rest. But in so as far as this holds, in the Course's view it is a deficiency of Love, as is indicated:

"4 He [a separated mind] also thinks that love can be bestowed on one, and yet remain itself although it is withheld from others. 5 To believe these things of love is not to understand it."(W,127,2,4-5)

That is, because Love is what unites *all* that exists and thereby gives the all its existence, were something totally excluded from Love, it would not exist.

vii. Sustaining. A further essential aspect of Love is indicated in:

"I am sustained by the Love of God."(W,50)

The sustaining aspect refers to the idea that It supports or causes the continued existence of whatever It is directed to. For separated minds, it is that which ultimately makes possible their enduring existence over the many moments of time. This would involve the impossibility of the cessation of any of those minds, as long as they remain within time. Of course, at the ending of time they cease to exist as separate as they are fully restored to the awareness of their complete state of perfection as the perfect mind out of which they began their separation. For perfect minds, Love is the foundation of their remaining in the Eternal Instant.

viii. The Law of Love. There is also an expression used by the Course that is reminiscent of the teaching recorded in the Bible as given by Jesus. This centers on the idea of 'law,' which was a central notion in the Hebrew tradition. The older idea focused on the imposition of restrictions on behavior, such as the Ten Commandments (in fact, for the Hebrews there were many more laws than these ten; one listing gives 613 laws). Jesus on several occasions offered a much greater simplification, saying that the core of these laws is to love God and one's fellow human beings.[18] The Course puts it even more simply, calling it the 'Law of Love:'

> "3 You see what you believe is there, and you believe it there because you want it there. 4 Perception has no other law than this. 5 The rest but stems from this, to hold it up and offer it support. 6 This is perception's form, adapted to this world, of God's more basic law; that love creates itself, and nothing but itself."(25,III,1,1-6)

We need not go into the passage's point about perception here. What is important is the formulation of the 'Law of Love:' ***Love creates Itself, and nothing but Itself***. When we take into account all that has been already pointed out about Love, particularly in Its primary aspect of extending the wholeness or unity that is Its essential core, it is clear that this law has little to do with any sort of 'commandment,' which is something that one might choose to obey or disobey. It is a law more in the sense in which we think of the 'law of gravitation' or the 'law of causality,' in that it describes what necessarily follows in its presence. That we observe within the realm of perception situations where love seems not to operate, means only that Love is absent from that realm in so far as It fails to be in awareness. In the Course's view, this means that such a realm involves a great distortion or illusion, which appears to be present because one is not fully aware of what is really present, since there is nothing that actually exists that is not an expression of Love. Such perceptions lead a mind to think, "That's all there is," in which case it takes on a mode that is removed from the experience of Love's presence. In the Course's view, this is the same as experiencing suffering. But one can also respond to those perceptions as occasions for opening up to Love. Learning to do this is a primary concern of the Course.

Regarding the assertion, "Love creates itself," one might object that the very notion 'creating itself' involves a contradiction. Strictly speaking, that is correct, if the expression is understood as 'bringing into existence its own self.' This is due to the fact that in order for something to create (or do anything), it must exist. That is, it must exist prior (either temporally or logically) to the act of creating. But

---

[18] "... and you shall love the Lord your God with all your heart, and with all your soul, and with all your mind, and with all your strength.' The second is this, 'You shall love your neighbor as yourself.' There is no other commandment greater than these."(Mark 12: 30-31)

if Love were thought to produce Its own existence, it would mean that Love does not exist prior to Its existing. That is, if It did not exist prior to existing and It is said to bring Love into existence, that would imply that Love must exist if it is to create. Thus, Love would both exist and not exist prior to creating, which is a contradiction. However, if we recall that creating is an extending of Love which thereby produces something (the Son), and that what is produced is also Love in Its fullness, then there is no contradiction. That is, the expression "Love creates itself" should be understood as "Love creates another spirit/mind which is another instance or occurrence of Love."

Further, although the Course speaks in a way that seems to involve several different meanings for the word 'love,' this should not lead us to think it holds that in Reality there are several sorts or kinds of love. In fact, it clearly states there is only one love:

> "1 Beyond the poor attraction of the special love relationship, and always obscured by it, is the powerful attraction of the Father for His Son. 2 There is no other love that can satisfy you, because there *is* no other love. 3 This is the only love that is fully given and fully returned."(15,VII,1,1-3)

This refers to what has been called 'Love,' the primary and most essential idea of love, which is identical to God. This does not say that Love is not present in other beings or minds. On the contrary, it is Love that is given to and made present in them by the very act of their being created. Thus, because It is present in all absolutely real things (and even in all unreal things, which are only aspects of those real things), and because God is Love, it follows that God is present in all things. Or taken another way, because God creates all real things either directly or indirectly by His Thought, and that Thought exists within his Mind, it follows that all things are present in God. However we formulate it, the Course is quite clear that in an absolute sense there is actually no other love than Love.

b. Effects of Love. There are other points that the Course makes about Love, which we may think of as Its *effects*, or if one prefers, Its *secondary characteristics* or *aspects*. These effects are named by words familiar to us, no doubt because there is some similarity in those words' ordinary meanings to what the Course understands. However, we may find a much deeper illumination of what they refer to by thinking of their meaning in relation to what has already been said about Love.

i. Peace. The first that we consider is peace. One passage indicates that peace cannot be adequately understood except from the perspective of the Love that brings it:

> "4 Rest in His Love and protect your rest by loving. 5 But love everything He created, of which you are a part, or you cannot learn of His peace and accept His gift for yourself and as yourself."(7,VII,6,4-5)

Here it is made clear that without loving everything, which is intrinsic to Love, one cannot come to a true understanding of peace. Statement 4 seems to give a reason for that: when one realizes the presence of Love within oneself, extending It to all others, the mind is in a state of absolute or complete protection. Being in complete union with all, there is no possibility of opposition or conflict, either within oneself or with anything beyond oneself. Indeed, strictly speaking there is no 'beyond' oneself, since Love as realized is fully within oneself, and its presence there makes all other minds present to it also. One can liken it to the idea of a 'wormhole' in modern cosmology, which is an immediate connection with another object or location in the universe. However, this connection is not with only one or a few other objects or locations, but with all of them. In that relationship, all other minds are seen as completely one with (although not identical to) one's own mind. Thus, there is no ground or basis for opposition or conflict.

This is also the point made in the following:

> "5 Peace is the state where love abides, and seeks to share itself. 6 Conflict and peace are opposites."(23,I,12,5-6)

That is, in Love there cannot be the slightest trace of conflict. Conflict can only arise for a mind that is within a state where Love is in some way placed in unawareness by that mind. For the infinity of perfect minds that constitute Reality, since each is filled with Love, there is no conflict whatsoever. Indeed, what is there called 'peace' is but another name for the complete union that is Love itself. For minds in separation, which places Love's presence beyond their awareness, to the degree that there is unawareness of Love there is the presence of conflict. Yet, since those minds can also have some partial awareness of Love, to the degree they have that awareness there is peace.

ii. Joy/happiness. While peace is to some extent a negative idea (absence of conflict), it also has a positive meaning (the presence of the awareness of Love's unity or wholeness). But even more positive is the effect of Love the Course calls 'joy' or 'happiness.' The following passage makes an important point about that joy:

> "3 There is no difference between love and joy. 4 Therefore, the only possible whole state is the wholly joyous."(5,in.,2,3-4)

In this it can be seen that 'joy' is simply another name for love. If one focuses on the primary Love in God, it follows that Love might be called '**primary Joy**.' Statement 4 relates this Joy to the wholeness or unity that we have already seen is the essential trait of Love.

Here we may pause and ask, how is this Joy connected with the more limited feeling we are occasionally familiar with that goes by that name? The primary definition of 'joy' is 'the emotion excited by the acquisition or expectation of good: pleasurable feelings or emotions caused by well-being, success, or good.' Most people have such experiences, but these are generally quite limited and temporary. The problem that the separated mind encounters is as follows. When what it considers to be a desired good is either attained or about to be attained, some sort of joy is experienced. This 'good' can be either sensual gratification or a more subtle sort, such as the completion of a project or the affirmation that one is valued or loved by another person. But once that has happened there can be a turning of the mind toward another object of desire or toward the receding of that good from one's experience. Thus, such joy is only partial, brief, and followed by its opposite. However, what the Course proposes is that beyond these limited joys there is the Joy of Love, which involves the complete attainment of the unlimited Good, which is union with all of what is possible to have union with in a way that admits of no change or loss. Thus, Love by Its very nature is Joy.

Similarly, there is a close association between love and happiness, as is indicated:

> "1 Happiness is an attribute of love. 2 It cannot be apart from it. 3 Nor can it be experienced where love is not. 4 Love has no limits, being everywhere. 5 And therefore joy is everywhere as well. 6 Yet can the mind deny that this is so, believing there are gaps in love where sin can enter, bringing pain instead of joy. 7 This strange belief would limit happiness by redefining love as limited, and introducing opposition in what has no limit and no opposite."(W,103,1,1-7)

Although the term 'happiness' as understood in ordinary English involves more than the emotion of joy, it is clear that joy is an important part of it. Thinkers have offered various theories about what happiness consists in, but the dictionary gives a simple description that most of those theories would accept: 'a state of well-being characterized by relative permanence, by dominantly agreeable emotion ranging in value from mere contentment to deep and intense joy in living, and by a natural desire for its continuation.' If we compare this definition to the state described by the mind that has full awareness of Love, it becomes quite clear that happiness cannot but be present in such a mind. It is content, has intense joy, and being in a timeless condition has no possibility of being lost. However, the Course further points out (in statement 4) that there can be no real happiness in the absence of Love. This means that the conditions that separated minds sometimes call 'happiness' are, at most, pale imitations that fall immensely short of what true happiness is. That is due to the absence of the awareness of Love. Only if such a mind is fully awakened to that awareness can it be truly and completely happy. The Course proposes that this can only occur when such a mind completely moves out of the state of separation.

This view of happiness is summed up quite simply:

> "4 God, being Love, is also happiness."(W,103,2,1-4)

That is, since God has within Him the fullness of Love, He is completely satisfied and in a state of infinite Joy. Similarly, any other mind, if it is fully aware of Love's presence within it, recognizes that the presence of that Love constitutes its complete happiness. This echoes the point made by St. Augustine: "Our hearts are made for Thee, o God, and will not rest until they rest in Thee."[19]

---

[19] *Confessions*, I,1.

An even deeper teaching regarding Love's Joy is given in:
> "8 Joy is unlimited, because each shining thought of love extends its being and creates more of itself."(22,VI,14,8)

The point here is that Joy is not merely a celebratory feeling arising from perfect union with another mind. Undoubtedly that would bring with it an intense joy, in that the awareness of complete connectedness with that other mind would involve both the joy of giving Love to another and the joy of finding that Love returned. Perhaps the highest joy that we experience in our ordinary relationships is in the awareness that our gift is given to another, received by that other, and returned to us by that other, even if this experience lasts only briefly. But there is yet another aspect of Love that multiplies even more this joy of giving-receiving-returning unlimited Love. That is, the act of creating involves both the formation of another mind and the giving-receiving-returning of Love between the creating mind and the one created. But, as was pointed out, that created mind not only returns love to its creator; it also creates yet another mind with which it shares the Love that is its essence. Further, not only is there a loving connection between a creator and its creature, or between a creature and its further creature, but also between the earlier creator and its creature's creature. That is, Love in any one perfect mind extends to ALL other perfect minds, is received by all other perfect minds, and is returned to all other perfect minds. Thus, the intensity of Love, in any mind and in all of them, is multiplied by the total number of minds that arise by the creative process. Since there is an infinity of such minds, the resulting situation must be one of an infinity of unlimited Love, and with it an infinity of unlimited Peace and an infinity of unlimited Joy. Another passage, so concise and simple that one might miss its profound significance, seems to make this point:

> "2 Love would *always* give increase."(15,IX,4,2)

This can be applied to the situation that separated minds find themselves in, but its deeper and fuller meaning is seen in the relationship that is said to hold for perfect minds. Since Love's primary mode is not in space or time, this increase cannot occur in time, but all at once. In contemplating this as a possibility, our minds can only be in awe. And if one recognizes that this must actually be the case, he must ask: why tarry in this condition of separation?

iii. Gratitude. Although it is implicit, there is yet another effect or aspect of Love that is indicated by the Course:

> "2 Gratitude goes hand in hand with love, and where one is the other must be found. 3 For gratitude is but an aspect of the Love which is the Source of all creation. 4 God gives thanks to you, His Son, for being what you are; His Own completion and the Source of love, along with Him. 5 Your gratitude to Him is one with His to you."(W,195,10,2-5)

That Love involves gratitude was already indirectly pointed out in that it has three facets or 'moments:' *giving* from one mind to another, *receiving* by that other mind, and then a *returning* of Love by that other mind to the mind that originally gave. It is in this third aspect/moment that gratitude seems to consist. Ordinary human gratitude, as defined by the dictionary, is 'a state of being grateful: warm and friendly feeling toward a benefactor prompting one to repay a favor.' This involves an acknowledgment of the favor given and an inclination and willingness to return that benevolence. Of course, in a perfect mind, which is the only sort of mind that is capable of fully recognizing the gift given by another who gives it Love, there is both acknowledgment of the Love that has been given it and an immediate response of returning that Love to the one who gave it. Thus, there is perfect gratitude in a perfect mind in response to its being given Love. But even further, because this mind returns Love to the one who gave It, that original giver responds to this act of being given Love with gratitude to that mind returning It. When one thinks this through, this means that there is gratitude not only on the part of the creature, but also in its creator, and gratitude for the creature's gratitude. This holds not only for the original Creator, God, as is asserted in statement 4, but in the Son in relation to his creature, Son_2. One might think of this as a kind of 'feedback loop' in which Love is further intensified between the creator and the created. Even further, that 'loop' is not restricted to only those two minds that happen to be in the immediate creating-created relationship, but also holds among all perfect minds, since all minds give Love to all other minds. This again leads to an even deeper amazement, as we consider a Universe of minds related in the infinitely intensifying relationship of gratitude. This would seem to be another aspect of the infinite Joy that is present, both in God, in all other created minds, and in that 'Universe of Love' as a whole. One might liken this situation to an exponentially increasing fire, so that this Universe is in majestic resonance of growing Love, Joy, and Gratitude. However, this analogy should not be taken as involving any intensification over time, but rather as occurring all at once and lasting without diminishing and without ceasing. That we can have a dim glimpse of this, even within the state of separation, seems to be the gist of the practice that the Course proposes:

"Love is the way I walk in gratitude."(W,195)

Indeed, many of the later practices in the Workbook seem to focus on opening the separated mind to the mode that it will eventually experience, the one said to be fully enjoyed by all perfect minds.

iv. Freedom. A final effect or aspect of Love is indicated in the following:

"1 Love is freedom. 2 To look for it by placing yourself in bondage is to separate yourself from it."(16,VI,2,1-2)

This equation of Love with freedom should not be thought of in terms of the limited ideas of freedom that we as separated minds envision. Those ideas range widely. One of the most basic definitions of 'freedom' is 'the quality or state of not being coerced or constrained by fate, necessity or circumstances in one's choices or actions.' This is more an absence of limitations related to physical, emotional, or intellectual needs and activity. A further distinction that is sometimes made is one between this 'freedom from' and a 'freedom to.'

'*Freedom from*' is perhaps the more basic meaning. This is generally thought of in relation to things that are in some way 'outside' oneself, such as freedom from hunger, from poverty, from illness, from slavery and domination, from abuse by others, from injustices originating in individuals or society as a whole, or from suffering. '*Freedom to*' focuses on what originates from within, such as the freedom to act as one is inclined, to achieve one's goals, to create as one is inspired. Of course, both of these sorts of freedom are in relation to something limited, such as our body, our feelings, our thoughts. If one were to propose a notion of '*complete freedom,*' or freedom to be without any limitations, that would entail having no constraints whatsoever, either originating from outside or from within. Even further, one can think of a notion of freedom that involves being without any limitation on what one fundamentally is, what might be called '*absolute freedom.*'

When we consider the freedom that the Course asserts belongs to Love, we see that it must be absolute freedom. The freedom that is in Love involves the complete, willing embrace by a mind of all that can possibly bring it the full satisfaction that it is capable of. However, we must be careful to observe that this does not involve the absence of any necessity. The 'Law of Love' operates without exception in every mind, just as the 'law of gravity' operates on every mass. Yet, whereas gravity imposes constraints from outside, Love's requirements are entirely from within the mind. But the necessity here does not involve any limitations placed on the mind in which Love is the primary characteristic. God extends His Love by absolute necessity, just as does every created mind. Since It imposes no limitation, It involves no constraint, either from outside or from within. It is more a total 'letting be' of the mind so that it can be all that it can possibly be, as well as a letting be of all other minds in a similar manner.

Even when we take into consideration the presence of Love and the possibility of a mind's entering into the state of separation, we see how that freedom is quite remarkable. On the one hand, the original creating Mind (God) has only one possibility: to love without limit. It does not have the possibility of entering into separation, since that would entail that the ultimate Ground of Love would cease to have awareness of Love. And, since that awareness is essential to Love's existence, Love would cease to exist. Further, if Love were to cease to exist, the whole of Its effects would cease. That is, if God's Mind went into separation, all existence would cease, including all other perfect minds, as well as any separated minds that might arise from them. It would also entail that there would be a change in God, meaning that the Eternal Instant could not occur. And, if it could not occur, it would entail that there would be no original Mind of God. Thus, to hold that God's Mind could enter into separation involves a contradiction, and accordingly cannot be true.

Yet, the situation is different for a created mind. Since it has within it the full presence of all aspects of Reality, in its freedom it can direct awareness to either all those aspects or to any one or several of them. The possibility of doing this I call the **'Illusion Capacity'** or IC, which will be further explained later. That focused awareness on only some aspect does not lead to the cessation of Love within the universe, but only to Its suspension in so far as It is in focused awareness. As has already been discussed, the moment of focused awareness can further slip into the whole separation process, which produces countless separated minds and the world we are familiar with. However, God's Love remains flowing to the created mind, holding it on its deepest level in its perfect or complete awareness of the whole. This last is the basis of restoration of the created mind from its separated condition back to its wholeness. Although in separation it may experience the fragmentation of many moments (time) and many different places (space) and things (the perceptual universe), all of this occurs within the fraction of a moment in which it briefly turns away from awareness of the whole. Or, since the idea of a 'fraction' of an instant involves a serious problem logically, a less problematic way of putting this is that the focused awareness occurs on one level of the Son's Mind, while on another level His Mind remains in awareness of the Whole. Understood in this way, we see that there is no imposition by God or any other mind upon a created mind of any constraint preventing it from entering into separation. Since God's Love produced the created mind with this potential, and that potential is part of the created mind's essential nature, the exercising of that potential is entirely a matter of the separated mind's free inclination. While the Course does not address the question of whether that created mind could choose not to enter separation, it would seem that separation or the experience of illusion, that is, the activation of the IC, must occur in every created mind, since that would be part of its fulfilling its own potential. However, the degree to which separation occurs for any of those minds may not be the same for all of them. Here, we might think of the notion of 'angels' as being minds, some of whom are said not to have entered into separation, some of whom are said to have done so. Of course, this last point is only a speculative aside. In any case, this discussion perhaps offers a very different way to think of freedom with respect to Love.

    c. What Love does not involve. It has already been pointed out that Love does not involve any limits, space, time, or exclusivity. Those only seem to arise due to the separation. To complete our discussion of Love, we need also to consider the Course's view on several other things that It is not or does not involve.

    i. No fear. One of the earliest observations made in the Course's Introduction is:

> "8 The opposite of love is fear, but what is all-encompassing can have no opposite."(In.,1,8)

Fear is an emotional response to some type of pain or anticipation of pain, involving the tendency either to remove oneself from it, prevent it, or change it into something other than it is, that is, to negate in some way what is feared. But Love is understood to involve complete affirming, embracing, or willing of all that of which It is aware. That seems to be the point of saying it is all-encompassing.

Thus, in Love there can be no fear response whatsoever.

This is further clarified in:

> "3 Fear is really nothing and love is everything."(2,VII,5,3)

Fear can be seen to be nothing, in two ways. One is that from the perspective of Reality, anything that a separated mind might regard with fear is something that does not absolutely exist, or is nothing. The other is that the feeling of fear, being a response to nothing truly real, based on the fragmenting awareness of only an aspect of Reality, is not itself an aspect of Reality and thus does not truly exist. This is not to say that the separated mind does not generate something it feels as fear of something it perceives as fearful. However, this is only an unreal state without absolutely real existence. This is likened to the feeling one may have in a nightmarish dream, since the image that one feels fear of is only a formation of the mind while sleeping. On the contrary, since Love is present in all absolutely or truly real beings and is the foundation of their existence, It exists in a most fundamental way. However, fear only has a relative existence. Thus, the 'inconsistency' is only apparent.

In reference to the response to Love in created minds, particularly those in separation, the Course observes:

> "2 If fear and love cannot coexist, and if it is impossible to be wholly fearful and remain alive, the only possible whole state is that of love."(5,In.,2,2)

Thus, the complete opposition between Love and fear necessitates that fear can be experienced only to the degree that Love is not experienced. Minds that experience only Love, i.e., God and all other created minds in their perfect state, are in the state of complete union with all of Reality, a state of complete wholeness. That is, only in the full awareness of Love can a mind be truly whole and completely without fear.

Thus, it follows that any experience of fear involves the perception of something that does not actually exist:

> "11 His Love remains the only thing there is. 12 Fear is illusion, for you are like Him."(M,18,3,11)

What we call an illusion is a form, image, or idea that is held or contained in a mind but is without any reality that it corresponds to. An illusion is even more illusory, so to speak, if it includes the belief that it corresponds to some reality. This is the situation of most separated minds when they respond with fear to any form in their awareness. However, since a mind fully aware of Love cannot be involved in any illusion, it is impossible for it to have or feel any fear.

ii. No illusion. As the previous section pointed out, Love and illusion are completely incompatible. Indeed, that incompatibility is said to be the more fundamental basis of the incompatibility between Love and fear:

> "8 He [God] loves you, wholly without illusion, as you must love. 9 For love *is* wholly without illusion, and therefore wholly without fear."(16,IV,11,6-9)

This may seem to be a subtle point. For us, fear is a more salient experience than illusion. Indeed, in the Course's terms we are immersed in illusions even at times when we don't feel any particular fear, although as Heidegger points out, a fundamental characteristic of our mode of existence is a constant 'Angst' or anxiety that never leaves us even in our lighter moments; it always remains present in some way due to our 'Sein zum Tod,' 'being toward death.' But, although fear may be more manifest in our awareness as separated minds, its presence can only arise in absence of the fuller awareness of Love, which involves the complete awareness of Reality. That complete awareness is without any illusion; or, stated more positively, it is the same as the mind's possession of Truth.

This holds not only for God's Mind, but also for any other mind that is fully aware of Love:

> "6 Illusions have no place where love abides, protecting you from everything that is not true."(23,I,10,6)

Of course, the problem in separated minds is that they find it difficult to have full and complete access to the awareness of Love. To the extent that they do not have that complete awareness, they experience illusion and all the other consequences of Love's absence.

iii. No judgment. Besides the absence of these traits that belong to what is ordinarily called 'love' in our experience, there are several other traits incompatible with Love. Judging is one of them, as is clear in:

> "1 Love cannot judge. 2 As it is one itself, it looks on all as one. 3 Its meaning lies in oneness. 4 And it must elude the mind that thinks of it as partial or in part. 5 There is no love but God's, and all of love is His. 6 There is no other principle that rules where love is not. 7 Love is a law without an opposite."(W,127,3,1-7)

Intrinsic to judging is the formation of concepts, which divide what one is aware of between what is within the concept's meaning over against what is outside that meaning. Judgments are of two major sorts: factual and evaluative. *Factual judgments* basically assert that a thing or class of things belongs or does not belong within another class. For example, 'Barack Obama is a man," "All men are mammals," "No men are dogs." *Evaluative judgments* assert that a thing or class of things has or does not have a positive or negative value, as in "Gandhi was a morally good person," "All murderers are bad," "No Van Gogh paintings are ugly."

While this dividing seems to have importance for minds within separation, in the Course's view it also has the effect of further entrenching a judging mind in the separative mode. This is especially the case with evaluative judgments, which generally lead to feelings of desire and fear. However, a mind aware in the mode of Love can only have an awareness, as described in statement 2, of 'all as one.' Even the Course's assertions that seem to be judgments, such as "Love is one," "Love is creative," "Love is inclusive," "Love is unlimited," "Love is Joy," etc., are only modes of speaking to accommodate minds that are steeped in separation. Because we distinguish oneness, creativeness, inclusiveness, unlimitedness, joy, etc., from one another, it might seem that this implies that each of these characteristics is different from one another. However, the more accurate way of thinking is that they are all one and the same as Love.

What makes Love so different from other notions is that all other notions are essentially conceptual, and all concepts involve the positing of an opposite. For example, when one thinks of something as 'white,' he thereby generates at least implicitly the concept 'non-white.' If we take 'Love' as a concept, it similarly posits its opposite, 'non-Love.' (The same is true of the term 'God,' which in the view of the Course is identical to 'Love,' although each term may connote for us different characteristics.) But statement 7 above could be rephrased, "Love is without an opposite," the point also made in Introd.,1,8. That is, since 'Love' refers to a unique, all-embracing notion, anything that might be thought to fall outside Its range is simply nonexistent. In other words, the expression 'non-Love' is completely devoid of any real characteristic or of any real thing it might refer to. In this respect, 'Love' is completely unlike any other notion that our minds might think of, since those other notions all involve one or several concepts, connoting specific characteristics and referring to various entities. This peculiar nature of the idea 'Love,' making it completely unlike concepts, should make us very cautious about applying the usual laws of logic, which are the basic laws of conceptual relationships, to it. This does not mean that we cannot use those laws in thinking about Love, but that we need to exercise great care about not being led to conclusions that simply cannot apply to something so completely simple.

iv. No comparison. Related to the absence of judgment is Love's incompatibility with making comparisons. As indicated:

"1 Comparison must be an ego device, for love makes none." (24,II,1,1)

Although this statement refers to love within the context of the mode of separation, it is quite consistent with what was said above regarding Love, and thus can be taken to say: "In Love there is no comparison." This becomes obvious when we reflect that all comparison is a type of judgment. That is, when one makes a comparison, he holds an idea that can be expressed in the general form, "A is more than B" (e.g., "A is more valuable than B") or the reverse, "B is less than A." This involves taking the concept understood under 'A' and judging it in relationship to the concept understood under 'B.' Since judging is not possible with regard to Love, and comparing is a type of judging, comparing is not possible with regard to Love.

One exception might be thought of as holding within the realm of Love. It was pointed out that the Course holds that God differs from the Son in two ways. One is that He creates the Son, but the Son does not create Him. The other is that the Son has the capacity to choose the focused awareness of perception. In this sense, God can be said to be 'more than' the Son. However, in terms of what God and the Son are as perfect minds (in their awareness, creativity, and joy), they are completely alike or the same. If one objected that the Son would not exist without the Father's creating Him, and thus this makes Him greater than the Son, one would have to rejoin that the Father would not create or be a Father if the Son did not exist. As the Course points out:

> "1 Without a cause there can be no effects, and yet without effects there is no cause. 2 The cause a cause is *made* by its effects; the Father *is* a Father by His Son. 3 Effects do not create their cause, but they establish its causation. 4 Thus, the Son gives Fatherhood to his Creator, and receives the gift that he has given."(28,II,1,1-4)

In this passage are two important insights. The first is that God can be called 'Cause' or 'Father' only by virtue of His effect's (the Son's) giving Him that causal characteristic. Statement 2 could be restated: "Any cause is made a cause, or endowed with causality, by virtue of its having effects." The second insight is that God is not superior to His creature, the Son. It is only our greatly contracted awareness due to separation that makes us tend to think of God as superior in value and us as inferior. From the perspective of our separated mode of awareness, that judgment of comparison is correct. However, since separation is only an illusion, that judgment is in an absolute sense untrue. When one considers the Son's awareness of the Father, since both of them have the precisely same mode of awareness of Love, neither judges the other as inferior nor superior. The same is true of the relationship between the Son and his creature, or between any other creature and its creature in the 'Universe of Love.' All are completely equal in their likeness of one to another. And even what might be called a 'comparison of equality' has no place within their minds, since it would involve a kind of distraction from the far more salient feature of Love itself as what they both are and through which they are both related. Philosophically, this might be thought of as saying: "Within the realm of the perfect mind, there is not and cannot be any mathematics, which is a system of judging and comparing." Although mathematics might be useful for the separated mind in helping it move out of separation, once so used, it is completely abandoned.

v. No triumph. Another characteristic often attributed to what separated minds call 'Love,' particularly among traditional Christians, is that it is involved in some sort of battle that culminates in a victory of God and His followers over all the rest. This is especially the theme that is the usual interpretation of the last book of the New Testament, the so-called 'Book of Revelations.' From the Course's perspective, such an idea involves a misunderstanding of Love. As it states:

> "1 There are no triumphs of love. 2 Only hate is at all concerned with the 'triumph of love.' 3 The illusion of love can triumph over the illusion of hate, but always at the price of making both illusions. 4 As long as the illusion of hatred lasts, so long will love be an illusion to you."(16,V,5,1-4)

What is especially significant here is the point that a mind that associates triumph with Love (or real love in its human manifestation) intrinsically connects it with hate, so that such a notion of 'love' is not Love at all, but only an illusion of It. The ramification for the traditional interpretation, which associates love with any sort of battle or conflict, is that it has completely misunderstood It. This should give cause for serious reflection on the history of Judaism, Christianity, and Islam, as well as much that is found in their current thought and practice.

vi. No symbol. The last idea that the Course negates about Love, both within perfect minds and whatever way it might manifest in separated minds as genuine love, is that it cannot be symbolized, as indicated in the following:

> "1 The symbols of hate against the symbols of love play out a conflict that does not exist. 2 For symbols stand for something else, and the symbol of love is without meaning if love is everything."(16,IV,2,1-2)

Statement 2, if taken as expressed, seems to say that any symbol that is intended to symbolize love (and all the more, Love) is completely without meaning. The reason: a symbol is a sign (e.g., the written form 'love'), which is a restricted portion of the whole of what is Real that is intended to have a meaning other than the sign itself. However, Love includes both the portion that is the symbol/sign and everything else as well. Thus, what is intended to serve as a symbol for Love is actually a portion of Love whose meaning would be different from that portion ('something else'). But this would entail that the symbol is not itself a portion of Love, which it actually is. That is, the alleged symbol of Love involves a meaning which is self-contradictory, and therefore without meaning, in the sense that any self-contradictory form cannot refer to anything actually existing. The point here is that all symbols for love, such as 'love' and 'Love,' cannot refer to anything in Reality.

Of course, this means that every statement made either in the Course or in this discussion about Love or love, making use of the symbols 'Love' or 'love' to speak about what is in Reality, involve something that is strictly speaking without meaning. This would seem to require that all such statements have no value whatsoever. Indeed, if they are taken as having meaning when they actually don't, they involve an illusion in a mind so taking them. This would seem to make the whole Course itself an illusion that one must set aside if he is to come to Truth.

This is indeed a very puzzling problem for anyone who is attached to the Course's words. But it offers a very important correction to minds addicted to words and symbols. This does not mean that words/symbols cannot be useful tools to aid the separated mind to move out of its separated condition. Indeed, that is precisely what the Course proposes itself to be. But, the illusoriness of those words must be seen through. This point that Love or love cannot be symbolized is thus a correction that indicates that the mind must go beyond those symbols to the Reality itself. That is, one needs to keep in mind that the Course, whether having the formulation found in a book entitled 'A Course in Miracles,' or expressed in other concepts and symbols with other titles, must be completely gone beyond.[20] That occurs only in the state of awareness referred to as 'knowledge,' where one is completely aware of the totality of Love. The words/symbols have value in that they can be of help in bringing one, or better, restoring one to that awareness. Other traditions make use of the image of a boat or a ladder that one uses to cross to the other shore or climb up out of a cave. Once one has crossed or climbed out, the boat, the ladder ceases to have any value, except as a means for helping those not yet returned to knowledge. Perhaps their forms are seen as simply variations of the land of the other shore or the world outside the cave, as sparkling grains of the shore's sands or jewels forming part of the outer world. In the terms used by the Course, the symbols are 'seen' for what they actually are: aspects of the luminous realm of Love.

2. Love in God in response to separation. By this point, the question has probably occurred to the reader: if Reality is such as has been described, why do our minds perceive and think of what we call 'reality' as something very different from Reality as viewed by the Course? To answer this, we need to discuss the core of what it calls the 'separation' as a process and as the resulting condition that arises from that process. This can be explained by recognizing that the Son's mind (or any other created perfect mind) differs from God in the important way that has been referred to as its having the Illusion Capacity, IC, although the Course does not use that term. That is, while it is given the full awareness of all Reality, it also has the capacity to focus on only a part or aspect of Reality. Also, unlike God, it has the capacity to direct its will to maintain that focused awareness. In the case of the Son's mind, it has exercised a choice to enter into this focused state of awareness. This may also be represented as in Fig. 5A and Fig. 5B. In 5A, which depicts conditions in the Son 'prior' to separation, there is only a *potential* in His mind for activating the IC, so that it is completely whole as originally created. In Fig. 5B, the IC is activated and there is formed within the Son's mind a multiplicity of limited centers of awareness, or separated minds. Here only three small circles depict three such minds, sm_1, sm_2, and sm_3. That is, the separation is the result of a simple choice made within the Son's mind, which is indirectly described:

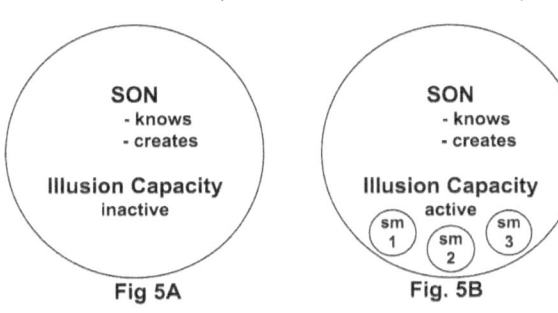

Fig 5A   Fig. 5B

> "3 To substitute is to choose between, renouncing one aspect of the Sonship in favor of the other."(18,I,1,3)

---

[20] One is reminded here of the the Buddhist *Heart Sutra of Perfect Wisdom*, which ends with the words "Gone, gone, gone beyond, gone beyond the beyond."

That is, within the Eternal Instant, the Son is on one level fully aware of all of Reality in the state of awareness called 'knowing,' but on another level his mind has chosen a condition of focused awareness. Because this focused awareness by its nature excludes, at least in that region of the Son's mind where it occurs, awareness of some aspects/parts of Reality, this is a very different mode of awareness. The Course refers to that mode as '**perception**.' As it states:

> "5 Only perception involves partial awareness."(3,V,8,5)

By choosing to fasten onto this focused awareness, the Son's mind enters into a twofold fragmentation of its awareness. The first is that on the level of the mind that chooses focused awareness there is a separation of itself from the level that is aware of God and the whole of Reality. As is pointed out:

> "1 A sense of separation from God is the only lack you really need correct. 2 This sense of separation would never have arisen if you had not distorted your perception of truth, and had thus perceived yourself as lacking."(1,VI,2,1-2)

But, since there are multiple different aspects that can be focused on, there also arises a similar focused awareness on them. That is, in other parts of the focusing level of the Son's mind there is a second fragmentation within the Son's mind into countless other partially aware minds. Each of these fragmented minds is occupied with a focused awareness and thus separates itself from the awareness of the whole mind of the Son and also separates itself from all those other separated minds.

The separation process further leads to the formation within each separated mind of two important ideas or mental forms that support the choice of being separated. The first is that of the 'ego.' This is an idea that basically sets one's own mind off from other minds, and further involves other ideas and feelings that support the separated state (these will be discussed further when we consider 'illusory love'). A second important means of consolidating the separated state is the separated mind's identification with a small region of what it perceives, which it thinks of as its 'body.'

> "2 Each body seems to house a separate mind, a disconnected thought, living alone and in no way joined to the Thought by which it was created. 3 Each tiny fragment seems to be self-contained, needing another for some things, but by no means totally dependent on its one Creator for everything; needing the whole to give it any meaning, for by itself it does mean nothing."(18,VIII,5,2-3)

That is, by virtue of its attachment to a body, it perceives other bodies and thinks of them as the centers for other separated minds. This is represented by Fig. 6 for only one separated mind, where the separated mind circle is enlarged within the Son circle. Within the separated mind circle is another circle for the ego-idea, and inside that is an even smaller circle for the body. Again, this is only a schematic representation and should be referred to with care.

Along with this consolidation of the separated condition, the mind divides up

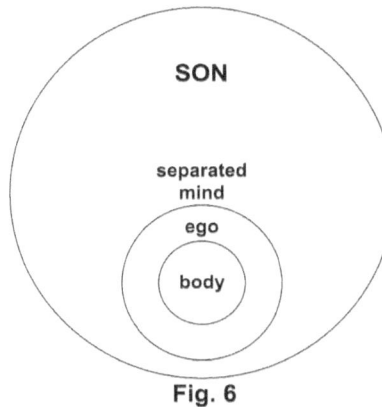

Fig. 6

those aspects that it perceives into what it thinks of as 'space.' And, because the contents within it undergo a shift in particular focus, it enters into the shifting perceptual structure of 'time.' As a result, separated minds experience and think of themselves as being in a spatio-temporal world of perception. Owing to their forgetting of the original condition and the process of separation from their own perfect mind with its awareness of all of Reality, their focused perceptual awareness leads them to form an idea of 'reality' whose primary characteristic is that it is the collection of what it and other separated minds agree on in their perceptions. That is:

"13 To them the separation is quite real."(M,5,III,1,13)

With that it enters into a mode of existing in a space-time order that includes uncertainty, change, competition with other ego-dominated and embodied minds, suffering, and eventually its own bodily death. However, all of this originates simply in the choice of actualizing the IC. Thus, we need to distinguish between **absolute reality**, or Reality, which consists of what truly exists (God and all perfect minds and their relationships resulting from the creativity of Love, which is essentially the same as what is called 'Heaven'); and **relative reality**, or what arises as the collection of things in the world of perception from the formation of the ego-idea. Although the latter seems to continue for a very long time, such as the billions of years recognized by modern science as the age of this universe, in the Course's view it is fundamentally only a complicated illusion, which is referred to as the 'dream of separation.' As it states:

"4 You dream of a separated ego and believe in a world that rests upon it."(4,I,4,4)

The careful thinker at this point may also ask: "If there is only one Eternal Instant of the Son's (or any perfect mind's) existence, how can it be possible for there to be the two moments as indicated here? First, that perfect mind has a potential for separation; then, it activated that potential. This seems to require two different moments and contradicts the view that there is only one. Indeed, the very notion of a 'process' of separation seems to indicate that it involves some sort of time, which necessarily entails more than one single moment or instant."

To be sure, the Course in describing the separation does make use of terms that usually involve time: 'process,' 'first,' 'then,' 'before,' 'after.' However, here we need to be careful, as in our use of spatial diagrams to represent things that are not spatial. That is, the use of those terms does not necessarily mean that what is being described is itself something in time. Rather, it can simply be a non-temporal mind's way of describing something not in time to a mind steeped in time.

We may approach this puzzlement by seeing it in the broader perspective of what is called 'sequence.'[21] A sequence involves a series of several components, in which those components have an order; that is, one 'follows' another. Indeed, the root of the word 'sequence' is 'sequi,' which in Latin means 'to follow.' One type of sequence we experience is that of time. Time's fundamental components are what we call 'moments,' and their order is such that one moment is earlier or later than others in that sequence. This is central to Aristotle's definition of time as 'the measure of change according to the before and after.'[22]

A second type of sequence is what we call 'spatial,' exhibited in the points of a line. Here there is an ordering of points in a kind of before and after (e.g., more to the right, more above, more in front of other points in the line). However, in this case, all components exist in the same moment. Thus, we actually experience a non-temporal sequence.

A third type of sequence, which we may call a 'logical sequence,' is more abstract. As an example, consider the general structure of Euclid's geometry. Here, there are several statements or insights that are accepted as fundamentally true (the axioms and postulates). From that set of fundamental insights there are numerous other insights or statements that are necessarily implied (the theorems and corollaries). Although it may take time for us to work them out and become aware of all those implications, they all follow at once immediately from the axioms and postulates. This sequence is entirely independent of time and space, although they may be applicable to things we experience in time and space.

The unfolding of all logically implicit insights can also be called a 'process.' Although for us that requires a series of moments in time, in itself that process is entirely outside of time. Here we also see a kind of 'before' of the axioms and postulates and an 'after' of the theorems. But there is no time involved at all within the 'logical process.'

This notion of 'logical process,' when applied to the Course's teaching on the separation, allows us to understand not only the two 'moments' or 'states,' first the potential of activating the IC, then the actual activation, as being both 'in the same moment of the one Eternal Instant.' The same is true of all the other consequences of the choice to activate the IC: the formation of the ego-idea, the body, and the space-time structure of the world with all of its events. Although for minds in separation it seems to take a very long sequence of moments in time, the whole process unfolds in a single instant, which is best thought of as a 'sub-

---

[21] This discussion is similar to, but more general than, the discussion earlier (pp. 35-6) of the idea of 'extension.'

[22] *Physics*, 220a25

set' or 'sub-level' of the one Eternal Instant. Thus, the separation is essentially a matter of experiences arising within a different region or level of the Son's mind due to its choice to activate the IC.

Accordingly, the question, how can the eons-long world of separation occur within a perfect mind that does not exist in time, is answered: it happens as only a tiny 'fraction' or on a 'sub-level' of the Eternal Instant that is so small it could be called an infinitesimal portion of it, although it seems temporally very long. As it states:

> "6 The instant the idea of separation entered the mind of God's Son, in that same instant was God's Answer given. 7 In time this happened very long ago. 8 In reality it never happened at all."(M,2,2,6-8)

Indeed, the Course's whole concern is to help the separated mind return to the full awareness of knowing, which is also described as 'awakening from a dream' to what has always been. Interestingly, it comments that when this is fully realized, the mind discovers that the separation *'never really happened.'* In a sense, the whole of the separation and its resulting world (what we call our universe) and all of time is no more than an infinitesimal minor 'blip' in the one Eternal Instant. When undone completely, the mind returns to its full awareness of Love and its creative extension. As it states somewhat more generally:

> "5 The tiny tick of time in which the first mistake was made, and all of them within that one mistake, held also the Correction for that one, and all of them that came within the first. 6 And in that tiny instant time was gone, for that was all it ever was."(26,V,3, 5-6)

But we postpone a fuller discussion of this till later.

Related to this question about the process of separation is another one: How can the sequence of creative acts in which the infinite number of created perfect minds is produced occur in the single Eternal Instant? From what we saw earlier, the answer should be clear. It is a logical sequence or process that unfolds completely in the single moment of the Eternal Instant.

Although God and all Reality, including the Son, do not exist in time, it has been pointed out that the Course indicates that the Son is able to take on two differing modes of awareness: the complete awareness of Love in all its aspects that is called 'knowledge' and the partial awareness, called 'perception,' that gives rise to the condition of separation. Within the one Eternal Instant, both of these modes arise. Each mode has different consequences. The perfect mode of knowledge includes the Son's act of creating something that is exactly like himself, what has been called Son$_2$. The further consequence is the infinite sequence of further created perfect minds.

However, the entry into separation due to taking on the imperfect mode of focused awareness also occurs within that same Instant. But, unlike the perfect mode, within the mind experiencing separation there arises the structure of time and space. That is, to the mind in separation it seems that there are many different moments (time) and different coexistent separated minds and things (space), which constitute 'the world.' Yet, on the more fundamental level all those moments and minds are simply expressions of the single mind of the Son occurring in the single Instant. As already noted, that these two modes occur within that single Instant requires that we think of there being *two levels* within the Son's mind, one that operates with perfect awareness, the other with separated or fragmented awareness. Further, since the Course also points out that the separation ceases upon completion of the Atonement, and what was experienced as a long duration of many moments by the separated mind is recognized as having occurred in the 'tiny tick of time' or even as 'having never happened,' we may think of the duration of the separation as only a 'blip' or a tiny fraction of the single Eternal Instant. This last point is the way that any perfect mind regards the separation.

   a. God's awareness of separation. However, God's awareness of the Son's mind includes His awareness of both levels, the perfect awareness and the imperfect awareness. While His awareness of that perfect awareness involves a recognition of the increase that brings infinite Joy and all the other aspects related to Love discussed above, His awareness of the Son's taking on the separative awareness has consequences in God's Mind. Yet, God's awareness, being solely the mode of knowing, does not involve any perception, as made clear in:

> "4 God does not perceive at all."(W,193,2,4)

Thus, His awareness of the Son's level of separation contains no details of what separated minds experience. Although God does not have direct awareness of the details that arise within that imperfect mode, He is aware that something is not operating for a 'fraction,' or more accurately, since a single instant cannot be subdivided, *on a 'level'* of the Eternal Instant within the Son's mind in a manner that reflects upon the Son's full awareness of Love. The situation is described:

> "7 The constant going out of His Love is blocked when His channels are closed, and He is lonely when the minds He created do not communicate fully with Him."(4,VII,6,7)

A similar point is made in:

> "1 God is lonely without His Sons..."(2,III,5,11)

This may at first seem quite perplexing and even inconsistent with the earlier assertion that Love in God involves the awareness of unlimited Joy. However, this is only due to our association of 'being lonely' with being unhappy. If we look at the meanings of 'lonely' in English, we find the following definitions:

- 1a: being without company: lacking companions or associates
-   b: cut off from company or neighbors
- 2: not frequented by human beings
- 3: affected by loneliness: dejected and unhappy as a result of being alone

Clearly, only the third definition involves the presumed negative emotional state.

The other three meanings cited here do not necessarily involve any sort of unhappiness. So we must ask which of those other meanings would be the better meaning to be applied here, since God is elsewhere in the Course said to be perfectly happy or joyful.

It seems that both 1a and 1b point to the most appropriate interpretation of the word. For 1a, if we consider what the situation of God would be in encountering the Son within that level or fraction of the eternal moment in which the Son is experiencing the state of separation, it would involve God's awareness of the Son's diminished awareness of and return of Love to God. In that sense, there would be to some degree a 'cutting off' from company or being without the fullness of the Son's company. That is, there would be a lesser degree of intensity of communication between God and the Son. Since God is elsewhere said to respond to the Son's experience of separation by giving the Son the correction to that experience by way of offering Him the Holy Spirit, it is clear that the Course recognizes that God has some sort of awareness of this diminished degree of communication. It is within that awareness that God 'feels lonely.' But that does not involve any diminishing of God's own joy or happiness. Indeed, since for God the whole of time (as experienced by separated minds) is within this 'fraction' of an instant, that lonely state would actually be analogous to the jostling of an atom in our own familiar experience of time, something that is unregisterable in our own time-consciousness. Thus, to say that God is lonely cannot involve any pain or sorrow, since God as Love is infinite Joy, and pain and sorrow are matters of perception. It is simply an awareness that within the Son's mind Love is blocked in some way on some level, primarily in the incomplete returning of Love from the Son to God.

This can be visualized with the help of Fig. 7. It focuses on the relation be-

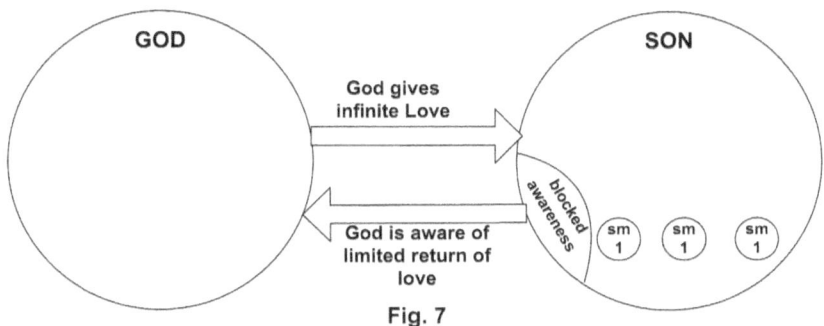

Fig. 7

tween God and the Son in so far as the Son has made the focused state of separation. This is the first 'phase' of the initial content of God's awareness of the Son. In the lower arrow, we need to think of this as representing His awareness of the level of the Son's mind that is not fully returning Love to Him, indicated by the 'blocked' area in the lower region of the Son circle. Since God has no perception, He cannot even be aware of the multiple separated minds.

This awareness that something is operating within the Son's mind bringing about its blockage to Love is immediately responded to by God with what is described as giving a 'plan:'

> "2 Atonement corrects illusions, not truth. 3 Therefore, it corrects what never was. 4 Further, the plan for this correction was established and completed simultaneously, for the Will of God is entirely apart from time. 5 So is all reality, being of Him. 6 The instant the idea of separation entered the mind of God's Son, in that same instant was God's Answer given. 7 In time this happened very long ago. 8 In reality it never happened at all."(M,2,2,2-8)

Here, we should be careful not to think of this 'plan' in terms of what we usually think of by that term. That would include the articulation of a goal the plan tries to achieve, steps to be taken to achieve that goal, and usually a time-line for executing it. When we recall that Love is a mode of awareness that does not involve any concepts or judgments and that it is outside time, and even further that it involves only knowledge and no perception, the most that we can reasonably attribute to what Love/God plans is the fundamental intention of establishing or communicating unity or wholeness, which is the essential feature of Love. The term the Course uses for the plan is 'Atonement.' From the perspective of God's awareness, this is simply the impulse of Love to fully establish the separated level of the Son's mind to its perfect awareness, or what is the same, the abandoning of the imperfect mode of separation.

c. God's formation of the Christ Mind/Holy Spirit. Central to this plan or impulse is God's holding the perfect level of the Son's mind within that level so that the whole of that mind does not slip into separative awareness. This is described:

> "1 The Holy Spirit is the Christ Mind which is aware of the knowledge that lies beyond perception. 2 He came into being with the separation as a protection, inspiring the Atonement principle at the same time."(5,I,5,1-2)

Although the passage makes clear that the two names 'Holy Spirit' and 'Christ' or 'Christ Mind' refer to the same entity, the Course sometimes refers to the one or the other in a way that, if we are not careful, might lead to the thought that they are two different minds. Those two different names are thus better understood as referring to the same entity, but thought of in somewhat different ways. It is also important to note that the Holy Spirit/Christ Mind comes into being as a response to the choice made in the Son to enter into separation. This seems best thought of as a creative response by God to the Son's choice.[23] Thus, the Holy Spirit is in a sense a further thought or 'creature' that exists within the Son's mind. Although the Course does speak of the Holy Spirit as a creature, His primary reality is as an aspect within the Son's mind, not as a different entity or 'spirit.' Perhaps the best way that this may be understood is seen in the expression 'as a protection.'[24] In this we see that 'Thought of God' has two meanings: 1) as a fully complete entity or 'spirit', as is the Son, also sometimes called 'Word,' much like the 'Logos' in traditional theology; 2) as an aspect of an entity, as are the Christ Mind and the Holy Spirit.

This may be further explained as follows. As God becomes aware that the Son has made the choice of separation, He recognizes that if this were to proceed fully throughout the Son's mind it would place the Son in a condition that could be incurably separated. Also in His awareness of the Son's making this choice is the blocking of the return of the intense Love and the lesser Joy that this entails. Thus, since Love in God wills only complete happiness and Joy for the Son, God responds by sending a 'pulse' of Love to the Son. This 'pulse' acts as a kind of illumination in the Son's mind that makes it fully aware of what that choice is leading to. One 'part' or 'level' of the Son's mind responds in a manner so as to pull back from the move toward separation, not because God forces it to do so, but because it sees the folly that this involves. This part/level of the Son's mind that desists from slipping into separation is the Christ Mind. It has accepted the pulse of protective Love. Indeed, if that did not occur, the Son would have entered totally into separation, and apparently would never be able to come to the awareness of what He had done and be unable to reverse that foolish

---

[23] Wapnick (and apparently others) regards 'Christ' as synonymous with 'the Son.' For example, without giving any reference for it, he states that Christ is "defined in *A Course in Miracles* as God's one Son" *(Love Does Not Condemn*, p. 448) and uses the word 'Christ' as having the same meaning as 'the Son.' Indeed, the Course does state that Christ is

"the Son of God as He created Him."(C,6,1,1).

However, it does not follow that 'Christ' and 'Son of God' have exactly the same meaning. A serious difference is that while the Son can enter into the separation, this is not possible for the Christ or Christ Mind, as in

"7 Christ knows of no separation from His Father..."(15,VIII,4,7)

Thus, although the Son is originally created perfect, his choice leads to the separation as occurring on one level of his mind. The notion of the Christ arises only as a result of God's preventing the complete collapse of the Son's mind into separation, along with the Holy Spirit, such as is explained above.

[24] The interpretation offered here avoids what would be a contradiction in the teaching, and will be briefly discussed later. For a much more thorough discussion of this and the overall nature of the Holy Spirit as viewed by the Course, see my next study *The Holy Spirit and Jesus in A Course in Miracles*.

choice. This is depicted in Fig. 8. That is, in response to God's awareness of the incomplete return of Love, He creates the 'protection' which establishes the Christ Mind in the Son as a level remaining fully aware (knowing) and the Holy Spirit as an aspect of the Christ Mind that can interact with separated minds (only three such minds are indicated for simplicity). The Holy Spirit is represented as a region within the dotted line surrounding all separated minds. Again, we need to be careful in thinking of this, since these two aspects of the 'blip'/level, along with the whole of time, occur in the 'infinitesimal sub-instant' of the one Eternal Instant. The Christ Mind/Holy Spirit and the whole of time would more accurately be thought of as two major levels of the Son's mind rather than as occurring at two different times.

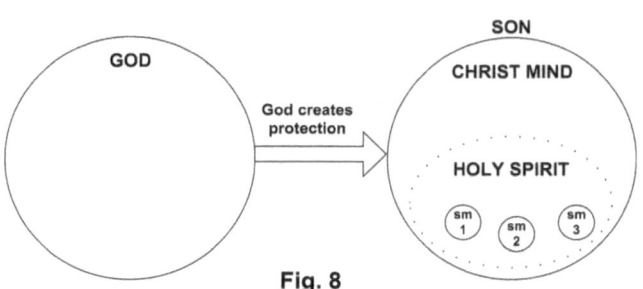

Fig. 8

Thus, 'Christ' refers to this level of the Son's mind that avoids making the choice of separation. This is described most succinctly in the following:

> "1 Christ is God's Son as He created Him. 2 He is the Self we share, uniting us with one another, and with God as well. 3 He is the Thought which still abides within the Mind that is His Source. 4 He has not left His holy home, nor lost the innocence in which He was created. 5 He abides unchanged forever in the Mind of God."(W,pII,6,1,1-5)[25]

That is, 'Christ' refers to the Son's mind in so far as it remains in its perfect state. We may think of it as the higher level of the Son's mind that does not slip into separation, but remains aware of Reality, i.e., only knows. Thus, Christ is the deepest Self of every separated mind.

But, although the Christ Mind does not slip into the dream of separation, there are other 'parts' or aspects of the Son's Mind that do so on this lower level. Since God has given complete freedom for making that choice, He cannot immediately void that choice, but is obliged by the very nature of Love within Him to respect it. Nevertheless, in so far as this level of the Son's mind has fragmented into numerous separated minds, God is aware of that 'loneliness' or lowered intensity of Joy, which they are also depriving themselves of, and that same impulse of Love generates a way to return them to the fullness of Joy and awareness of Love. The vehicle or means for that return is that aspect of the Christ

---

[25] The expression 'pII' refers to 'Part II' of the Workbook. Part II is divided into 15 sections, each of which begins with an introductory question followed by a response to it. The number following 'pII' is the number of the section/question.

Mind which the Course calls the 'Holy Spirit.' He may be thought of as the Christ Mind functioning as a link or 'bridging awareness' that enables the correcting process of the Atonement to connect to the various separated minds. This is described:

> "5 The Holy Spirit is God's Answer to the separation; the means by which the Atonement heals until the whole mind returns to creating."(5,II,2,5)

That is, the Holy Spirit is the Christ Mind in so far as it is given the function of helping all separated minds, those aspects of the Son's mind that by their choice slipped into the severely limited focusing or perceiving mode of awareness, be restored to their unity with the Christ Mind. A further description is given:

> "1 The Holy Spirit is described as the remaining Communication Link between God and His separated Sons. 2 In order to fulfill this special function the Holy Spirit has assumed a dual function. 3 He knows because He is part of God; He perceives because He was sent to save humanity. 4 He is the great correction principle; the bringer of true perception, the inherent power of the vision of Christ. 5 He is the light in which the forgiven world is perceived; in which the face of Christ alone is seen. 6 He never forgets the Creator or His creation. 7 He never forgets the Son of God. 8 He never forgets you. 9 And He brings the love of your Father to you in an eternal shining that will never be obliterated because God has put it there." (C,6,3,1-9)

Thus, the Holy Spirit is in charge of working out the details of the Atonement plan. For this reason, He has both knowledge (awareness of the full Reality) and perception. The nature of His perceptual awareness will be discussed later. This can be represented as in Fig. 9. Here, two separated minds are small circles, both surrounded by a larger dotted envelope to represent the Holy Spirit. The Holy Spirit can thus be thought of as the aspect of the Christ Mind that 'interfaces' with separated minds, acting as the deeper or higher 'communication link' between each of them and also between them and the Christ Mind.

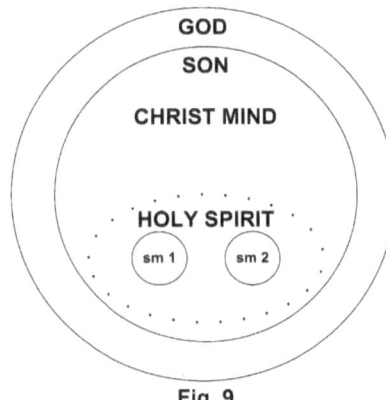

Fig. 9

A further important point about how the Holy Spirit connects with each separated mind is made in:

> "1 The Holy Spirit abides in the part of your mind that is part of the Christ Mind."(C,6,4,1)

From this we see that both the Christ Mind and the Holy Spirit should be thought of as 'located' or present *within* every separated mind. This might be better represented by a 'concentric circle' diagram as in Fig. 10. There, the outer circle is the 'grosser' form of the body and as we move progressively inward we come to the deeper or 'more interior' levels. In this way of diagraming, the Holy Spirit is more interior than the separated mind, and the Christ Mind is more interior than the Holy Spirit, while God is most interior. This means that the condition of separation is simply a matter of the separated mind's awareness being blocked from the full awareness of the Holy Spirit/Christ Mind by its focus on the ego, and the Atonement consists in removing or undoing any obstacles to that awareness. In the Course's view, when that occurs in a particular separated mind, it sees that it *is* the Christ. This is what happened with the historical person known as Jesus (and probably with others such as the person Siddhartha Gautama who became the Buddha).

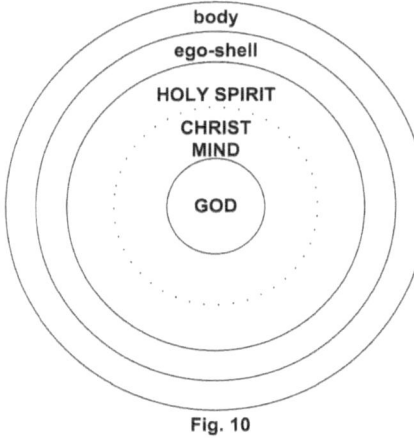

Fig. 10

A final point concerning the Holy Spirit relates to a statement that seems to say that He is a distinct creature produced by God:

> "2 The Holy Spirit, being a creation of the one Creator, creating with Him and in His likeness or spirit, is eternal and has never changed."(C,6,1,2)

This might lead one to think of the Holy Spirit as another entity, spirit, or mind that is different from the Son. But since the Course holds that God creates *only one Son*, if we are to avoid reading a contradiction into the Course's teaching, the Holy Spirit must be the same as the Son's mind as it remains in its perfection, that is, the 'Christ' or 'Christ Mind,' the point just discussed. In saying that the Holy Spirit is 'a creation of the one Creator,' this should be understood as asserting that He is an expression of Love that is integral to the very being of the Son, or better, that He is an *aspect* of that spirit, rather than a distinct creature. Thus, there is no difference between the Holy Spirit and the Christ Mind, except in the way one thinks of each. Accordingly, the Holy Spirit is the Mind that at once has an 'upward' awareness, or the awareness of knowledge of Reality, and a 'downward' awareness, or the perceptual awareness of what is occurring in the focused state of separated minds, and is given complete charge of working out the details of the plan for Atonement.

d. God's forgiveness. One further point is made by the Course regarding God's/Love's response to the Son's entering into separative awareness:

> "4 The sleep of forgetfulness is only the unwillingness to remember Your forgiveness and Your Love. 5 Let us not wander into temptation, for the temptation of the Son of God is not Your Will. 6 And let us receive only what You have given, and accept but this into the minds which You created and which You love."(16,VII,12,4-6)

This seems to say that in God there is forgiveness. This could be interpreted as saying that God somehow sees some sort of offensive behavior or thought within the separated mind and then forgives it. The rest of the passage would also seem to imply that God can see the various 'temptations' that we might fall into and steer us clear of them. But that cannot be the case if God has no perceptual awareness of any details within the experience of separated minds. As we saw, the Course clearly denies that He has any perception. Thus, the expression 'Your forgiveness' must be understood in a different way.

This is given further clarification in the following:

> "1 Yet although God does not forgive, His Love is nevertheless the basis of forgiveness. 2 Fear condemns and love forgives." (W,46,2,1-2)

At first, this might be taken as contradictory to the previous passage, which spoke of 'Your (i.e., God's) forgiveness.' But forgiveness can be understood as either an *act* of forgiving or a *state* which would result from such an act. That state, which in this case is the complete letting go or absence of fragmented awareness, can occur either from the act of forgiving (which is first aware of something amiss) or from an act which produces unfragmented awareness. We have seen that the latter is the original state that arises from Love. In that sense, Love may be said to involve forgiveness. In the last cited passage, statement 1 makes quite clear that there is no act of forgiving on God's part. However, Love is the foundation of forgiveness. Indeed, it is the very nature of all genuine types of love to forgive. In this we may find a deeper understanding of forgiveness as originating in Love. That is, since Love is the foundation of the undoing of the separation, which it brings about simply by allowing the focused awareness that is the separation's basis to be set aside or let go by any portion or aspect (what is called a 'separated mind') of that focused and separative mode of awareness, it is correct to say that in Love there is forgiveness. This is not forgiveness of any specific 'sinful' or 'negative' detail, but the undoing of the fragmenting mode that makes those details appear to be present within that awareness. From that perspective, God does not concern Himself about any details, since by undoing what makes possible all details (fragmented, piecemeal perceptions), those details, as experiences in separated minds, are thereby undone. In that sense alone does it make any sense to speak of 'God's forgiveness.'

3. Love in God beyond or 'after' Atonement is completed for all separated minds. Atonement is essentially the fulfilling of the plan for undoing or dissolving of the state of focused awareness whose consequence is separation and all its perceptions and suffering. It is completed within the same single Instant in which all creation is actualized and even separation arises.[26] Thus, in the Atonement's completion there remains only the state of perfect awareness that the Son's mind was given in its creation. In relation to the perfect mode, it is as if the 'blip' or level of separation does not exist or that it ever occurred. What specific consequence the Atonement might have upon the Son's mind, or on all the perfect minds within Reality, is not indicated within the Course. All that is indicated is that it is the state called 'Heaven,' which is the full awareness of Love's presence. As was pointed out earlier, the primary consequence is that its completion acts as a kind of intensifier of the Joy within all minds.

Here we might speculate that, since among the infinity of other created minds within the creation-sequence there is also the capacity to enter into separation, there may be a countless number of other separation-atonement 'blips,' each producing its own perceptual universe through the separation process and acting as another intensifier of that Joy through the completion of its atonement. In that case, the nature of the Joy that runs through the whole of creation would be vastly greater than anything our little minds have even considered. And if this is what the Course is pointing to, it would make any further delay in accepting the full Atonement all the more foolish, considering that any joy we might experience here is quite insignificant by comparison.

B. Love in created minds. Now we turn our attention to how the Course views love within what is the result of the creative act. The word 'creation,' as used in the Course, has several distinct meanings. Sometimes it refers to an *individual created entity or an aspect of a created entity*, at other times to *all of created entities* taken together, and at still others as the *act of creating*. While this is in accord with the ordinary English use of the term, to avoid confusion, I have reserved the term 'creation' only for the *process* of creating and the term 'creature' only for a *created entity*, and 'creatures' as *several or even all created entities*. As already pointed out, in the Course's view the only type of created entity is a spirit having a perfect mind, since creation can only produce what has all the properties of the creator. Thus, all creatures are spirits with perfect minds. While the Course sometimes speaks of 'thoughts' and other aspects of those spirits/minds as being created, all such thoughts/aspects exist as aspects or parts of some perfect mind, either God's or a created one's. Thus, it speaks of thoughts, love, and joy as being created, as in:

"2 God created love, not idolatry."(10,III,4,2)

and:

"1 Blessed Son of a wholly blessing Father, joy was created for you."(14,V,3,1)

---

[26] For clarity, we should distinguish between two sorts of completion of the Atonement: 1) as occurring in one particular separated mind, which might be called '**individual completion of Atonement**,' and 2) as occurring in all separated minds, which would be the '**full completion of Atonement**.'

These are not to be thought of as 'creatures' in their own right, but as aspects of creatures. In this sense, the Christ Mind and the Holy Spirit are most accurately thought of as aspects of the Son, rather than as different entities. Similarly, in a sense all separated minds, although not produced by God, are aspects of the Son. Those aspects can be called 'creatures' in a secondary sense.

As was made clear in our discussion of Love in God, creation is the process that necessarily follows from Love, and this process results in the extension of that Love to creatures. That is, Love is fully shared with and made present in whatever God creates. An important point is made in the following:

> "There is no love but God's. 1 Perhaps you think that different kinds of love are possible. 2 Perhaps you think there is a kind of love for this, a kind for that; a way of loving one, another way of loving still another. 3 Love is one. 4 It has no separate parts and no degrees; no kinds nor levels, no divergencies and no distinctions. 5 It is like itself, unchanged throughout. 6 It never alters with a person or a circumstance. 7 It is the Heart of God, and also of His Son."(W,127,1,1-7)

From this it is clear that the Course says that there are not two or many different 'loves,' one in God and the other or others in creatures, including His Son. Love not only unifies or unites, but there is only one love, what was earlier called 'Love,' that is present in any mind, whether it is God's Mind, the Son's mind, the Holy Spirit's Mind, or the minds of any other creatures. There are obviously different 'receptacles' of that single Love, and in that sense we may speak of 'God's Love,' 'the Son's love,' etc. But Love is not divided into many 'pieces' or 'portions' with those portions having different characteristics. Even within the multitude of separated minds, it is the exact same Love in each and every one of them. As is further said:

> "2 As it is one itself, it looks on all as one. 3 Its meaning lies in oneness. 4 And it must elude the mind that thinks of it as partial or in part. 5 There is no love but God's, and all of love is His. 6 There is no other principle that rules where love is not. 7 Love is a law without an opposite."(W,127,3,2-7)

This passage not only re-emphasizes the primary unitive function of Love, but also adds that this function is exactly the same in any mind in which it is present. Further, any thing or any mind where one might think of Love as being absent has no basis or principle. What this means is that, if a thing were completely deprived of Love, it would not exist or have being. That is, anything existing that seems to be without Love only has Love hidden to the mind to whom it so seems. That is, Love is the necessary basis for anything's existence. Earlier, it was pointed out that any thing or state one might think as 'existing' in the contracted and limited condition of separated minds is not absolutely existent in that condition. It may seem so to exist, but, in Reality, Love is present in it. Thus, the foundation of what is included in Reality is the presence of Love that gives it existence. Indeed, there may seem to be principles and laws that govern a 'realm' where Love is absent, but those principles/laws are themselves all illusory, in so far as they contain anything that is in opposition to the one Law of Love. Or, put more simply, only that absolutely exists or is absolutely real which is either Love or Its expression.

However, although Love is the same in every mind, that does not mean that, as present in the various minds, It does not manifest or express in different ways. We have already seen that within God's Mind It expresses as the primary originative creative act. Since God is not created and the Son is, Its expression is somewhat different in the Son. Similarly, Its expression is different in the Holy Spirit, in all others in the sequence of created minds, and even in the minds that arise in the state of separation. Here we will consider each of those other sorts of mind.

1. Love in created minds not in separation. Within the types of created mind, the Course gives the greatest number of indications regarding the Son.

a. Love in the Son. We have seen that the Son, although His Mind was created as perfect, has the capacity to enter the imperfect mode of separation. Indeed, one level or part of His Mind, the Christ/Holy Spirit remains in the perfect mode, while another level or part enters the imperfect mode. Furthermore, even the level that has come into the imperfect mode of separation will, from the separated mind's perspective, eventually return to the perfect mode. In this section, we will focus on what Love is in the Son in so far as His Mind is in the perfect mode.

Several passages make important points regarding what might be called the internal nature of the Son. The primary point is seen in the following:

> "6 The Love of God is in everything He created, for His Son is everywhere."(10,V,7,6)

The insight here, though at first quite simple on the surface, entails something quite profound. What seems almost obvious is that, if God creates by extending Love within Him to what He creates, that Love must be within the Son, His creature. But the reason given for this, that "His Son is everywhere," at first is puzzling. For one thing, since 'everywhere' is a spatial term, and space is not something applicable to the Son or any perfect mind, what could it mean to say "the Son is everywhere?" Further, how could His being everywhere be a reason for Love's being in everything?

Since 'everywhere' cannot be taken here in a spatial sense, it must be understood in a different way, one that is analogous to the spatial meaning. The Course's view is that the fundamental mode of existence for all things in Reality is mental, or as an idea. This means that if we think of God as a 'thing' in visual terms, having a location within the field of vision, such a thought necessarily entails that this 'thing' is either a part of the whole visual field, or perhaps even all of it. But, in so thinking, God is spatialized or imputed some sort of spatial mode of existence. Such an idea would be a distortion or illusion, leading one to think that other characteristics involved in spatiality are applicable to God. The

Course, addressing minds deeply steeped in spatial and temporal modes of thinking, whose language is also drenched with those modes, must make use of words having these connotations if it is to communicate with them. Accordingly, when it uses a term like 'everywhere,' if we are not to misconstrue it, we need to take care to remove the spatial content and come to its deeper meaning. The concept 'everywhere' involves several aspects or elements of meaning. One is the notion of 'all-inclusion' as in 'every.' In relation to Reality, that would include every entity that is within the realm of the Real, that is, every perfect spirit-mind. Although the word 'where' has a spatial meaning, which we generally think of as a point in space, that is not the only possible meaning it can have. Analogously, it can refer to any element or component of the whole collection of spirit-minds. Thus, the heart of the puzzlement lies in what is meant by a 'spirit-mind?'

Our habits of thinking usually associate with the word 'spirit' or 'mind' an image of some being, either a human or an animal or something like them, either existing in our familiar world or on some 'higher' plane within which awareness occurs and out of which come effects of that awareness, expressed in an action or behavior affecting other beings, particularly other spirits/minds. That image generally involves some sort of body, which has spatial location. Thus, throughout the history of human thought, we find ideas of 'spirits' or 'minds' associated with bodies, whether they are other human beings, animals, discarnate spirits like angels, demons, gods, or even what is called 'God.' Our habits of thinking, being based on body-experiences of minds, both our own and others', impel us to associate all minds with a kind of body, i.e., a form that occupies a definite region of space. This is well-documented in myths and legends found in almost all religions, as well as in more careful studies of people's experiences regarding 'higher' sorts of minds, as in near-death experiences, mediumship, 'ghost' experiences, hauntings, and many religious experiences.

However, the Course makes it quite clear that what it means by 'spirit' and 'mind' does not necessarily involve anything related to a body. As it states:

> "1 The term *mind* is used to represent the activating agent of spirit, supplying its creative energy. 2 When the term is capitalized it refers to God or Christ (i.e., the Mind of God or the Mind of Christ). 3 *Spirit* is the Thought of God which He created like Himself. 4 The unified spirit is God's one Son, or Christ."(C,1,1,1-4)

That is, 'spirit' is best thought of as a center of Love's extension, whose primary characteristics are being aware and creating. 'Mind' refers to such a center's capacity to extend. In perfect minds, that activity has no limits; in separated minds, there are limitations, imposed by the mind itself on that activity. Rather than thinking of mind as a 'thing,' it should be thought of as a 'thought' or 'idea.' Of course, even here many items we call 'thoughts' or 'ideas' involve spatial and temporal aspects, which are better called 'images.' By 'thought' or 'idea' the Course understands something that in awareness has no spatiality or temporality intrinsic to its meaning. (There can be thoughts/ideas about spatial and temporal aspects, but they are aspects of their content, not of their fundamental being as thoughts.)

Now perhaps we can better understand the statement, 'His Son is everywhere,' as saying that the Son, which is a spirit-mind and thus a thought or idea, is present to all other perfect spirits-minds. Those other spirits-minds, themselves thoughts, are both contained in the Son's mind as aspects of its content, and contain the Son's mind as aspects of their content. But the basis for that mutual presence of each within each is the Love that unites and gives being to all of them. This means that the Love that originates in God and extends to the Son, the only spirit-mind created directly by God, is also extended to the Son's creature, who, although primarily or immediately created by the Son, is thereby also secondarily or indirectly created by God. This holds for all minds that are created in the infinite sequence of creation, who are included in the 'everywhere' that has no space or time.

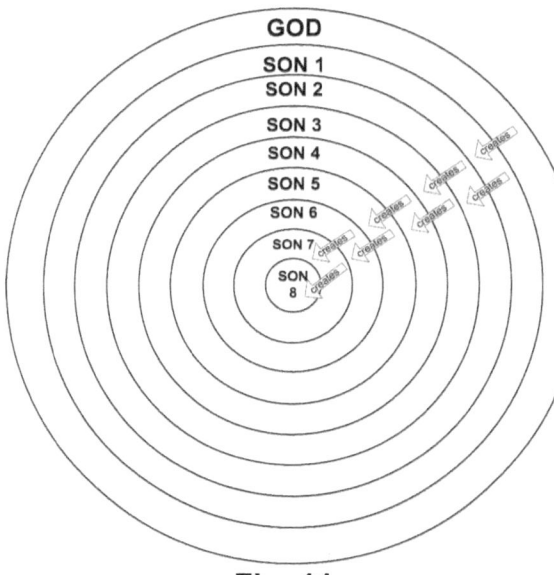

Fig. 11

To make this somewhat clearer, see Fig. 11 which represents what the Course thinks of as 'Reality' or 'the Universe of Love' by way of a set of concentric circles. The outer circle is God, the next within is the Son created directly by God, within that is Son_2 created by the Son, etc. (the diagram indicates only 8 such 'Sons of God,' but there should be an infinity of them.) This seems to better emphasize the notion that each creature is a *thought* within the perfect mind of its creator. Although there are further interior circles, the diagram has a problem in that we run out of space to draw the rest of the infinity of creatures ($Sons_n$). Fig. 12 compensates for this (with some loss of detail) by drawing a heavy circle to repre-

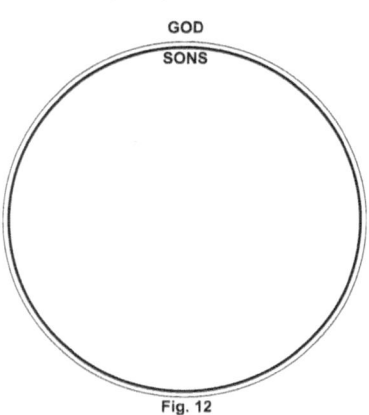

Fig. 12

sent the superimposition of all of the infinity of circles on one another within the God-circle. Although this makes each Son-circle indistinguishable from others in terms of their contents, it brings out the insight that each of them is where any of them is and also that each contains what any other one contains. That is, each of those perfect minds is where any of them is, i.e., that each is 'everywhere' or present to all that exists in Reality. Again, this should not be thought of as a 'where' in space or time, but in the non-spatial and non-temporal realm of absolute Reality.

Although what we have just said may be challenging to comprehend, since it stretches our thinking beyond its usual habits, we may next turn to points made about Love in the Son that are perhaps more easily grasped. Since the Love in the Son is the same as the Love in God, all of the attributes of God's Love belong also to that Love in the Son. The only attribute that is given specific further elaboration as found in the Son is that of creating/extending. It will be helpful to consider those passages. One is as follows:

> "3 Sharing the perfect Love of the Father the Son must share what belongs to Him, for otherwise he will not know the Father or the Son."(11,IV,8,3)

This emphasizes the importance of the Son's love going beyond itself. The primary 'going-beyond' is the movement back to the Creator that gave it Love. The significance of this moving beyond itself is that without it the Son cannot be aware of either the Creator (Father) or Himself. What this brings out is that the sharing of Love is what enables awareness to occur. The returning of Love to the Creator is what unites the Son's mind with the Father, and thus enables his awareness of the Father to arise. However, that sharing is also what enables the Son's Mind to have awareness (as knowledge) of itself. One might think that the Son would be aware of Himself by the fact that His mind is given both existence and awareness by the very presence of Love within His mind. What this brings out is that self-awareness cannot operate simply within a mind in its solitude or considered simply within itself. This seems to echo the observation made by some philosophers such as Martin Buber, that the 'I' (this is not the ego, but awareness of oneself) is constituted only in a relationship with a 'Thou' (awareness of another), which he calls the 'I-Thou' relationship. Of course, Buber's observation may only be based on reflections on human experience, which from the Course's perspective is within separated minds. The Course takes this even further by saying that a perfect mind, such as the Son's, cannot be aware of itself without having a relationship of love with another mind, its Creator's. If this is a principle for all perfect minds, it points to an interesting implication. That is, it would follow that God cannot be aware of Himself without sharing His Love with the Son. This would make Love the primary foundation of all awareness. That is, it would place Love as that out of which all awareness, even God's awareness of Himself, is generated. In a sense, this means that Love, or God, comes to Its/His awareness only by the act of creating.

But the creative extension of Love in the Son is not confined to its being returned to the Father. It also moves outward toward another entity or mind:

> "1 It is your Father's holy Will that you complete Himself, and that your Self shall be His sacred Son, forever pure as He, of love created and in love preserved, extending love, creating in its name, forever one with God and with your Self."(W,192,1,1)

This passage makes clear two important points related to the Son's creative act. One is that God's act of creating the Son involves an act of completing God. That is, without creating, God would be incomplete, so that His act of creating is completely necessary. The other is that the presence of Love in the Son not only involves a returning of that Love to God (what might be called an 'upward or inward movement'), but its doing precisely the same thing that God does with regard to the Son: producing the existence of another mind exactly like itself by extending Love within it to that other mind (a 'downward or outward movement'). And, just as by Love God is one with His Son, so is the Son by Love in him one with the Son's creature. This is articulated in a slightly different way in:

> "1 To think like God is to share His certainty of what you are, and to create like Him is to share the perfect Love He shares with you."(7,I,6,1)

The important point here is that the Son's creative act is like God's creative act. The only difference is that the Son is both created and creating, while God is creating but not created.

We saw regarding the creation that comes from Love in God, one of the effects that result from it is the intensification of the Joy already intrinsic to Love. This is further noted in the following:

> "9 Through our creations we extend our love, and thus increase the joy of the Holy Trinity."(8,VI,8,9)

Two points need comment. One is that, by the Son's creating a perfect creature filled with Love, the Joy that was intensified in God by His act of creating the Son further increases that Joy, both in the Son and in God. The second is the reference to 'our creations.' Since the Course affirms that there is only one Son of God, strictly speaking there is no 'we' or plurality in the Son. What we think of as 'we' or many minds is, in fact, the single mind of the Son that seems to be divided into many. Further, if the Son creates in a manner like God's act of creating, he can create only one creature, what was earlier called Son_2. So, what could this passage be referring to by using the plural 'creations?' If it is taken to mean that the Son creates many minds, then His creating is not like God's. However, this can also be taken as referring to the whole *sequence* of created minds, which originate in the act of creation by the Son who is earlier in the sequence. That is, because it is his creative act that leads to the rest of the sequence, it would not be incorrect to say that all subsequent members of that infinite sequence are the Son's creations. (Of course, by the same token, they are even more fundamentally God's creations.) If we take the passage in this way, it is clear that the Joy in the Father, the Son, and the Holy Spirit (the 'Holy Trinity') is augmented by its awareness of the joy in each mind within the infinite sequence.[27]

b. Love in the further created perfect minds. The Course says little about the creatures that proceed from the Son's creative extension. However, one passage offers a glimpse:

> "7 Your creations love you as you love your Father for the gift of creation."(8,VI,5,7)

Created by Love's sequential extension from the Son, each further Son_n has Love as its inner life. Accordingly, that Love extends from each of them back to its creator. Son_2 loves the Son as the Son loves the Father. Of course, since all in the sequence have their ultimate origination in the Father, they also love the Father. Indeed, there must be a flowing of Love to each and every mind produced in the creation, which if our notion of an unlimited sequence is correct, proceeds from each, first *back* to its creator and *on* to its creature, but then to all those preceding and proceeding in the sequence.

This may give a clearer meaning to the term that the Course mentions only once, the 'Universe of Love.'[28] It states:

> "10 The universe of love does not stop because you do not see it, nor have your closed eyes lost the ability to see. 11 Look upon the glory of His creation, and you will learn what God has kept for you."(11,I,5,10-11)

Three things are important here. The first is that the deluded state of separated minds does not in any way hinder the process of creation, either within the Son

---

[27] The Course's meaning of the term 'Holy Trinity' is quite different from that of traditional Christian theology. Briefly, although the Trinity is in a sense 'divine' as unlimited, perfect beings, only the Father is God in the proper sense as 'uncreated Creator.' The Son is His primary creature, produced by Him and like Him in all ways, except for the further possibility of forming limited minds as the 'maker of the world.' The Holy Spirit is also created by God in response to the Son's making the world (thus siding with Eastern Christianity on the 'filioque' controversy), but a part of the Son's perfect mind. In this view there is no problem of the 'mystery' of three persons as one God, which logically places the traditional view into what frankly seems to be a tri-theistic position and generates other serious problems concerning the functions of Father, Son and Holy Spirit. For the Course, those functions are quite definite, distinct, and clear. Retrospectively, the Course's view dissolves much of the controversy that generated much acrimony and even violence among those who thought themselves 'orthodox' and those who were labelled 'heretics.' A more complete discussion will be given in *The Holy Spirit and Jesus in A Course in Miracles.*

[28] The term 'universe' is used 106 times in FIP and 108 times in UM. Sometimes it refers to this whole network of perfect minds as 'universe of love,' 'universe of truth,' 'Universe of universes,' 'universe of all creatures,' 'universe that God created,' or simply 'universe.' In other places it refers to what is also called the 'world,' i.e., the whole that is included within the space-time field in which separated minds think they exist.

or in any other perfect mind. It only closes the separated mind off to the awareness of that process, while beyond it what is truly Real is untouched and unhampered by this infinite extension and exchange of Love. Second, although the separated mind has placed limits on its awareness ('closed your eyes'), its capacity for full awareness remains. Third, the expression 'universe of love' refers to this totality of numberless spirits-minds, each filled with Love, each creating through Love, and each related to all others in the unity that is the essence of Love. In the deepest sense, it is a 'universe,' a united diversity, whose internal unifying principle is Love.

2. Love in created minds 'during' separation. It has already been pointed out that separation is said to arise as the actualization of the potential in the created mind of the Son for focusing and identifying with aspects of Reality. However, God responds to this so as to bring about its correction or the undoing of its effects. We can think of the separation as involving three primary consequences. The first is the formation of the Christ Mind, the second is the formation of the Holy Spirit, and the third is the formation of numberless separated minds. Here we will consider Love as present in each of these three:

a. Love in the Christ Mind. In several passages we find two different ways the Christ Mind is referred to: most directly as 'Christ,' but indirectly as the 'Self.' Let us consider each:

i. Christ. Related to the first is:

> "5 Christ is the extension of the Love and the loveliness of God, as perfect as His Creator and at peace with Him."
> (11,V,7,5)

and:

> "1 Christ is God's Son as He created Him. 2 He is the Self we share, uniting us with one another, and with God as well. 3 He is the Thought which still abides within the Mind that is His Source."(W,pII,6,1,1-2)

Here, the Course offers its own particular meaning for the term that has long been a source of confusion, misunderstanding, and speculation within the Christian tradition. In this passage, we see that it is simply another name for the Son (who is the extension of the Love of God) in so far as His mind remains in the state of perfection. That is, 'Christ' refers to that mind in so far as Love is fully operative in the Son as the uniting (knowing and creating) 'energy' that is present in Him as a spirit. That is, strictly speaking, the Christ only knows.[29]

Since in the Christ Mind there is no obstacle to the awareness of Love's presence, and it is possible for individual minds in the world of perception to be

---

[29] This seems to be inconsistent with some passages that say the Christ perceives. However, this is resolved when we recall that the perception is present in the Holy Spirit and the Holy Spirit is the same entity as the Christ Mind. This will be clarified more fully in *The Holy Spirit and Jesus in A Course in Miracles*.

fully united with that Mind, this union is the basis of perfect love in the world. The Course holds that such union was realized by Jesus. Hence, he is currently called 'the Christ.' But such union is also possible for every separated mind. Indeed, the whole point of the Atonement is to bring that about, and the Course assures us that it is completely certain to occur. At that point, all separated minds that in time have no or only blocked awareness of the Christ realize they are actually that one perfect mind. This will be discussed further in Ch. V. From the Christ Mind's perspective, this has already occurred.

ii. The Self. Although we tend to think of the Son as something or someone different from ourselves, for the Course that is simply an illusion due to the separative mode of awareness our minds are enmeshed in. Echoing an insight found in the Hindu tradition, the Son is intimately present, though hidden, as the deepest Self of ourselves:

> "4 This Self alone knows Love. 5 This Self alone is perfectly consistent in Its Thoughts; knows Its Creator, understands Itself, is perfect in Its knowledge and Its Love, and never changes from Its constant state of union with Its Father and Itself."(W,rV,ln.,4,4-5)

That is, there remains within us the perfect mind in complete awareness, although we seem to have an awareness that is quite disconnected with that Self. Put simply, the Course holds that the Son/Christ is the true reality or Self of you and all other separated minds, despite what any of them may think or believe they are.

b. Love in the Holy Spirit. As we saw, the response of Love in God to the separation involves the 'creation' or, more accurately, the formation of the Holy Spirit, who has the function of carrying out the Atonement. It was also pointed out that the Holy Spirit has two modes of awareness, knowledge and perception. The presence of these two modes is what enables Him to relate to separated minds so as to guide them within the concrete conditions of the limited perceptions that they have generated for themselves back to the complete state of awareness of the Wholeness of Reality that is Love's knowledge. Since the Holy Spirit is the Christ Mind in so far as the Christ Mind has the function of carrying out the Atonement, it should be clear that this is also the basis of the Christ Mind's capacity to perceive (often referred to as the 'vision of Christ'). This Mind is presumably present or realized in Jesus, who claims to be the Author of the Course, and thus communicates by way of limited forms, such as the words heard by Schucman or other perceptual communications to separated minds. The use of the terms 'Christ Mind' or 'Holy Spirit' seems primarily to be a matter of emphasizing the difference between the function of being fully aware of Reality and creating without limits and the function of facilitating Atonement.

The facilitation of Atonement is the Holy Spirit's primary expression of Love within the world. In order for Him to be able to carry out that healing function, He must have awareness that allows Him to link with any separated mind. In the

Course's view, His awareness involves some sort of perception. Indeed, it was pointed out that His awareness involves both knowing and perceiving.

i. The Holy Spirit's perception. If we wish to have some understanding of how the Holy Spirit helps or guides all separated minds, we need to have a better idea of the nature of His perception. Here is offered an overview of the main features of this. A more complete discussion will be given in *The Holy Spirit and Jesus in A Course in Miracles*.

1) The Holy Spirit's perception involves only true perceptions. This is indicated in:

> "1 The Holy Spirit will teach you to perceive beyond your belief, because truth is beyond belief and His perception is true." (7,VIII,6,1)

Although briefly stated in the last clause, if taken for what is stated, it means that the only type of perception possible for the Holy Spirit is true perception. This means that, as perception, its content must be on some aspect or aspects of Reality. However, it differs from perception in the separated mind in that it does not make the second step of imposing a limit on that content or superimposing the content of one perception on that of another, which is false perception.

2) His perception is of all true perceptions in all separated minds. This is the point in the following:

> "9 He [the Holy Spirit] perceives only what is true in your mind, and extends outward only to what is true in other minds."(6,II,11,9)

That is, His perception includes what any individual separated mind ('your mind') truly perceives and what is true in all other separated minds. That is, He perceives all the true perceptions in all separated minds. This seems to be meant quite literally, which means that His perception is not only of those true perceptions at a particular moment in time, but at all times including both past and future.

3) His perception is the perception of the Real World. This is the point in:

> "9 The real world is all that the Holy Spirit has saved for you out of what you have made, and to perceive only this is salvation, because it is the recognition that reality is only what is true."(11,VII,4,9)

Briefly, what the Course means by the term 'Real World'[30] is in essence the totality of all true perceptions as an integrated whole. It is this perception, which involves awareness of how each true perception fits into the whole, that is the basis of His being able to help any separated mind move toward healing. This

---

[30] The expression 'real world' is not capitalized in the various versions of the Course. However, because it is such an important term and has a very special meaning, I've decided to capitalize it in this inquiry, although all citations referring to it will keep the Course's preferred form.

will be discussed at much greater length in Ch. V.

4) His perception is holistic. This seems to be the most important point concerning the Holy Spirit's perception, expressed in the following:

> "4 The Holy Spirit sees the situation as a whole."(17,VI,6,4)

Although brief and simply expressed, this contains a wealth of insight. The most important one is that although it is an awareness of particular aspects or details of what is real, that awareness of any detail involves how it fits within the context of the whole set of all true perceptions. What this means is that His perception of any one aspect includes or 'reflects' all the other aspects. That is, His Mind is aware of the totality or the whole of all aspects of Reality through its awareness of only one of them. This is very similar to the principle of what are called 'holograms.' It could be called a 'holographic perception.' In this sense, He has a kind of 'omniscience' that is extremely simple in its foundation.

5) His perception involves no illusions, including conflict. Two passages make this clear. The first is:

> "1 The Holy Spirit undoes illusions without attacking them because He does not see them at all. 2 They therefore do not exist for him. 3 He resolves the apparent conflict they engender by perceiving them as meaningless. 4 I have said before that the Holy Spirit perceives the conflict exactly as it is, and it *is* meaningless."(7,VI,6,1-4)

That is, since the Holy Spirit is only aware of true perceptions, He does not, indeed, cannot perceive illusions and the conflicts they involve in any way at all. While He perceives the true perceptions that the separated mind distorts into illusions and conflicts, He has no awareness of them as illusions or conflicts. (Statement 3 should not be understood as asserting that He perceives the actual conflicts, but rather only the true perceptions out of which they are composed.)

The reason for this is that this perception is grounded in His awareness of God, as indicated in:

> "7 There is no conflict anywhere in this perception, because it means that all perception is guided by the Holy Spirit, Whose Mind is fixed on God. 8 Only the Holy Spirit can resolve conflict, because only the Holy Spirit is conflict-free."(6,II,11,7-8)

Here we should recall that God's awareness, and thus the Holy Spirit's awareness of God, is one of total unity or union, which we saw can only involve complete peace or absence of conflict (conflict can arise only by way of opposition or disunity). The practical consequence for the separated mind is that the Holy Spirit's perception, if accessible to that mind, must be the basis for the complete resolution of all conflict.

This absence of any perception of conflict in the Holy Spirit's perception is the foundation of His ability to help separated minds be healed, which is the point of statement 8. That is, the absence of conflict in His perception of things as 'they really are' is what enables the separated mind, by 'tuning in' on that holistic perception, to correct the false perceptions that are the basis of its separated state. What this does is to shift that contracted mind's awareness to a condition of being connected with all else. That enables the separated mind both to be healed and to give healing to others.

6) His perception of things in time is from beyond or outside time. This last major point regarding the Holy Spirit's perception is found in the following:

> "5 The Holy Spirit stands at the end of time, where you must be because He is with you. 5 He has already undone everything unworthy of the Son of God, for such was His mission, given Him by God. 6 And what God gives has always been." (13,I,14,5-6)

That is, He perceives the whole of time, including every separated mind's condition, in one single mental act. From the perspective of the Holy Spirit, this is at the end of all temporal change. Of course, this is difficult for our time-bound minds to conceive, but not totally beyond our understanding. Indeed, as the passage points out, there is an aspect of our minds that is already there ('where you must be'), although we may not be aware of this. But to fully understand it one has to awaken to that awareness. Thus, although the Holy Spirit (and, of course, the Christ Mind) is outside of space and time, He can operate or communicate with minds immersed in the spatio-temporal framework and carry out His function of completing the Atonement.

ii. Special characteristics of Love in the Holy Spirit. Although Love in the Holy Spirit has the same characteristics that belong to God's Love, His special function involves Love's presence in Him as having several special characteristics.

1) The patient teacher. This is indicated in:

> "2 One Teacher is in all minds and He teaches the same lesson to all. 3 He always teaches you the inestimable worth of every Son of God, teaching it with infinite patience born of the infinite Love for which He speaks."(7,VI,7,2-3)

That is, Love moving through the Holy Spirit is what gives rise to His activity of teaching every separated mind, including the unlimited patience to respect the choice in each of those minds to accept or reject that teaching. This involves awareness and acceptance of the pace at which each mind makes the sequence of choices that are in line with its willingness to accept Atonement to whatever degree it is able. Of course, this patience is quite unlike human patience in that there is for the Holy Spirit no time of waiting, since His Mind is outside the time-framework and experiences the whole of time in a single instant, or more accurately as a sub-instant, aspect, or level of the Eternal Instant. He waits till that mind makes the choice to retrieve its original Christ Mind awareness and to listen to His guidance concerning how to do that. For this reason, the Holy Spirit may be thought of as literally 'having all the time in the world' to accomplish His assignment without any sense of being pressed, as we often experience, to meet some 'deadline.' Instead, from His perspective the Atonement is already accomplished.

2) Gentleness. A second special characteristic of the Holy Spirit's expression of Love is described:

> "8 The Holy Spirit sees only guiltlessness, and in His gentleness He would release from fear and re-establish the reign of love. 9 The power of love is in His gentleness, which is of God and therefore cannot crucify nor suffer crucifixion."
> (14,V,10,8-9)

This seems to be another aspect of His patience as a teacher, in that there is no forcing of His guidance in any way upon any separated mind. That is not to say that the receiving mind may not perceive that guidance with resistance, even feeling it is being 'oppressed' by it, but the experience of such is entirely that mind's construction.

3) The only judgment. A third unique property of Love in the Holy Spirit is in relation to the judging aspect of perception:

> "1 The only judgment involved is the Holy Spirit's one division into two categories; one of love, and the other the call for love. 2 You cannot safely make this division, for you are much too confused either to recognize love, or to believe that everything else is nothing but a call for love."(14,X,7,1-2)

This refers to how Love, operating in the Holy Spirit, responds to what He perceives. His perception of what is occurring in the totality of separated minds involves only a single evaluation or judgment of what is presented there. This places any particular aspect within one of the two basic categories, as either an expression of Love or a call for It. Thus, nothing in His perception discloses to His Mind anything as 'evil' or 'bad.' These are categories formed only by separated minds, the errors that the Holy Spirit looks past to see only in terms of their being either loving or a calling for Love. It is this perception that enables Him to offer counsel that is most appropriate to any particular separated mind. Of course, that counsel is itself an expression of Love in Him. Since the Holy Spirit's judgment is ultimately the only true one, the Course refers to this as the essence of the Last or Final Judgment.[31]

c. Love in separated minds. In the working out of the formation of multiple separated minds, there arises the experience of what we are familiar with as the 'world' composed of various bodies, including our own, within space and time, and the unfolding of the correction that is the Atonement. The Course often refers to those separated minds as the 'sons of God' and indicates a great concern for human minds. However, it does not seem necessarily restricted to human beings, but includes every separated mind. The Course is clear that each separated mind, although it has lost the full awareness of Love's presence within it and throughout the world it perceives, Love is still operating at its foundation.

---

[31] This will be clarified in *The Holy Spirit and Jesus in A Course in Miracles.*

That is because nothing, not even an illusion (which in absolute terms the world is), can exist without its being given existence by Love. Contemporary physics envisions all things as modifications of a fundamental 'energy,' which expresses either in a 'spread out' mode of what it calls 'fields' and waves within those fields, or in a 'consolidated' mode of particles or conglomerations of particles such as atoms, rocks, plants, animals, human beings, planets, stars and galaxies. Borrowing from physics, the Course's view might be expressed: the energy of all things in the physical universe is, at base, Love, although those things may be only dimly aware, or even completely unaware, of this. The Holy Spirit's awareness is more like the all-embracing 'field-mode,' and the separated mind's awareness is more like the 'particle-mode.'

However, the teaching is not concerned with developing a comprehensive theory of the physical world, and only offers so much theory as is helpful for its students. For them, it is important to have some glimmering of the far greater depths of their essential nature. The following points to that:

> "1 The Holy Spirit's Love is your strength, for yours is divided and therefore not real. 2 You cannot trust your own love when you attack it. 3 You cannot learn of perfect love with a split mind, because a split mind has made itself a poor learner."
> (12,V,4,1-3)

Were it not for the Holy Spirit's function of teaching the separated mind what it truly is, the separated mind would be at a loss and only spin about within the confines of the very limited perceptions and thoughts that it has become enmeshed in. This is very much like the Buddhist idea of 'Samsara' or the 'Wheel of Becoming,' in which the particular mind is imprisoned until it fully awakens. The Holy Spirit provides the 'thrust,' so to speak, for pulling that mind out of the bondage it has made for itself. That mind is so split or fragmented that it is unable to see what is really so. Although Love is the fundamental reality of the separated mind, it cannot recognize It without the illumination from the perfect mind itself to remind it of what it is.

In saying this, the Course does not deny that there have been individuals who have opened to their essential Love-nature prior to the writing of the Course or even the coming of Jesus. It states:

> "2 Are other teachers possible, to lead the way to those who speak in different tongues and appeal to different symbols? 3 Certainly there are. 4 Would God leave anyone without a very present help in time of trouble; a savior who can symbolize Himself? 5 Yet do we need a many-faceted curriculum, not because of content differences, but because symbols must shift and change to suit the need."(M,23,7,2-5)

Many teachers and their students have obviously heard the Holy Spirit's Voice and come to the full realization of their Love-nature. If one looks closely at the teachings of the major religions, although they have used other idioms and symbols 'to suit the need,' the greatest teachers have been clearly aware of a Voice, which guided them to great and even full realization of their true essence. Indeed, where we have information on their biographies we find among many of them indications of their being moved by a higher 'light' or 'voice' that led them to that realization. However, our primary concern here is to understand what the Course tells us about that process

3. Love in created minds 'after' full completion of the Atonement. The Atonement is fully completed when all separated minds have been restored to the full awareness of Love. One may ask what is the status of Love in all the minds that arose as a consequence of the separation, i.e., in all the particular separated minds, in the Christ Mind, and in the Holy Spirit.

a. In minds 'once' separated. Since all the countless separated minds have then come to the full realization of their being the one Christ Mind, or the perfect mind of the Son, those particular minds cease to have any existence whatsoever. Since they are only illusions and thus are not creations of God, the full awakening that occurs in every one of them simply dispels those illusions. Since both the separation and the whole process of the Atonement occur within but a 'fraction' of the one Eternal Instant outside time, it is recognized that they never really happened. Or, expressed in a more 'simultaneous' way congruent to the idea of there being a single Eternal Instant, the separation occurs in one very tiny region or level of the Son's perfect mind, so tiny that it is infinitesimal relative to the infinity of the Son's whole Mind. Thus, what appeared to be those countless fragments of the Son's Mind are fully reintegrated as the perfect mind of the Son, which has the fullness of Love that includes the awareness of the Universe of Love and the creative extension that produces the Son's creature.

b. In the Christ Mind. Since this is the Son's mind in so far as it is fully present to Love, that one mind drops all concern for accomplishing the Atonement, for which there is no need. Thus, it has no concern for healing any fragment of the Son's mind. While the Course does not offer any information about its status, since the Christ Mind is ontologically identical with the Son's mind, it exists in that more primordial unfragmented state, which is called 'Heaven.'

c. In the Holy Spirit. Since the Holy Spirit is also identical with the Christ Mind, but so named in so far as that mind has the function of bringing about the Atonement, it would seem that, since the Holy Spirit no longer has that function, He would simply be reabsorbed, as it were, into the Son's Mind. However, the Course states the following:

> "5 When the Atonement is complete and the whole Sonship is healed there will be no Call to return. 6 But what God creates is eternal. 7 The Holy Spirit will remain with the Sons of God, to bless their creations and keep them in the light of joy."
> (5,I,5,5-7)

Here we find the assertion that, because the Holy Spirit arose as a created aspect in the Son's mind, and what is created cannot be 'uncreated' or cease to exist, He continues to 'remain' in the presence of the 'Sons of God,' or what is also called the Universe of Love.³² This seems to be saying that this expression generated by the 'impulse' of Love from God to protect the Son's Mind from completely falling into separation, unlike the illusory separated minds, does not cease to operate. However, His operation is one of 'blessing' all the Sons of God (all created perfect minds). But ontologically, this seems to be much the same as the loving activity of the fully restored Son's mind, which is also the Christ Mind. The problem that we encounter here is that our ways of thinking lead us to view both the Christ Mind, the Holy Spirit, and the Son as different 'things' or entities that we think of as different 'substances' or self-existing forms. But the more appropriate way of thinking of them is as 'thoughts' that have an altogether 'non-thing-like' mode of being. Thus, they are better thought of as 'aspects' of the Mind of God, just as the Son is such an aspect, and as are all the other created perfect minds. Also, we should keep in mind that the formation or creation of all those created perfect minds occurs in the single Eternal Instant, so that there can be no possibility of the cessation or change of any of them. Again, as the Course, asserts from the perspective of that Eternal Instant, the separation never *really* happened.

C. Love in the Universe of Love, including minds in separation. To represent most fully how the Course views the combined structure of the Universe of Love and minds in separation, Fig. 13 is offered as a way of visualizing that. (I've chosen this image for the book cover.) The outer circle represents God,

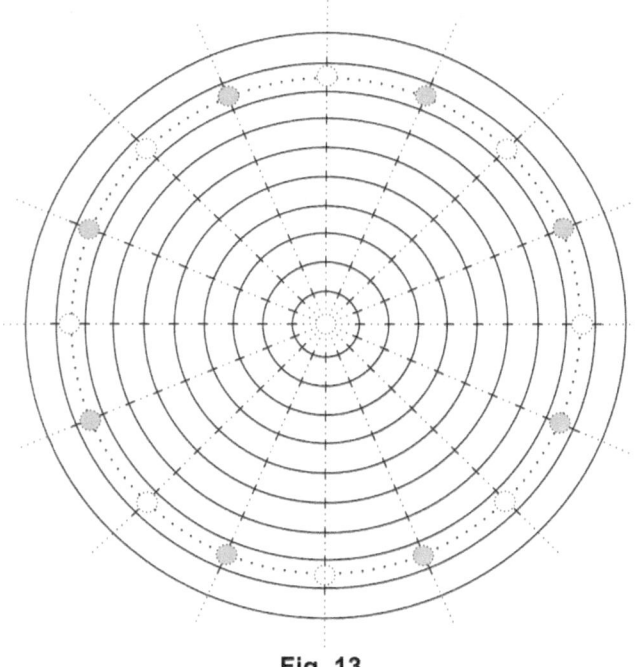

Fig. 13

---

³² For clarity, it should be noted that God did not create any separated mind; separated minds arise by their being *made* by the mind of the Son when it activates the IC. Thus, separated minds do not exist in an absolute sense, but only *seem* to exist or have relative existence.

and the interior concentric circles represent the first few of the sequence of creatures or Sons of God in the proper sense. That all of these are within the circle of a mind that creates them denotes the fact that their existence is as perfect Thoughts within the perfect mind that is either directly or indirectly their creator. Of course, the number of concentric circles is in fact infinite, which is not representable. Also, the flow of love could be depicted by dashes on the radial lines that connect each adjacent circle. (The dots on those radial lines can be thought of as indicating the presence of Love within the perfect mind.)

The smaller dotted circles within the circle just inside the God-circle represent a small selection of the numberless separated minds within the Son's mind. Some of these are shaded, to indicate they are in the condition of separation; the others without shading indicate those once-separated minds that have come to the maturity of the Atonement. Although while in separation and seeming to exist as separated minds, they are perceived by those minds to have had a very long temporal experience of dissociation from the full flow of Love from God and from all other created perfect minds. From the perspective of any perfect mind, Love remains without disturbance in its flow to every 'part' or 'aspect' of the Universe of Love. Also, we should recall that the undoing of the separated condition in any of those imperfect minds serves to give increase to the Joy of Love present in the Universe of Love. That the radial lines flow through each of the smaller dotted 'separated mind circles' indicates that Love in Reality always flows through them (or what might be thought of as regions of the Son's perfect mind). Similarly, within the Son-circle there is a dotted lined that runs through all of the smaller circles; this represents the presence of Love flowing from each to all the rest. For those no longer in separation, we would have to place a connecting dotted line from each to every other, but that would make the diagram too cluttered.

The central smallest circle filled with dots represents the infinity of created perfect minds that arise due to the unlimited creative process that each of those minds participates in. Also, that each of the perfect mind circles is smaller than the circle of the mind of its immediate creator needs to be corrected, since what is in the created mind is as complete as what is in its creating mind. That is, a more accurate representation would have the circles of all the created perfect minds exactly the same size, which would of course obscure the point that each of them is a distinct entity/mind/spirit. Finally, because the Course gives no details as to whether any of the created perfect minds subsequent to the Son (Sons,) make the choice of separation, I have entered 'separated mind' circles only into the circle representing the Son. However, it is quite possible that in some, or even all, of them there occurs the activation of the IC, in which case some (or all) would also have to contain smaller separated mind circles, both shaded ones for those in separation and unshaded ones for those having realized Atonement.

Finally, the radial dotted lines extending outward beyond the God circle represent the infinite or unlimited extension of Love that emanates from Him as the Source. Strictly speaking, there is no 'outside' region. Thus, the diagram should be considered only an aid to helping one grasp the insight, not a literal representation.

Chapter III. 'illusory love'

In a way, illusory love is one of the most important ideas for a student of the Course to understand. This is due to the fact that it is what most separated minds think of as 'love' and, being a major distortion of it, is the basis of many of the problems that prevent learning what love actually is. Because belief in it acts as such a block in understanding, we will examine it at length.

In Ch. 16 of the Course entitled, "The Illusion and the Reality of Love," there are several passages that refer to the 'illusion of love:'

1) "6 For the illusion of love will never satisfy, but its reality, which awaits you on the other side, will give you everything." (16,IV,2,6)
2) "5 The special love partner is acceptable only as long as he serves this purpose. 6 Hatred can enter, and indeed is welcome in some aspects of the relationship, but it is still held together by the illusion of love."(16,IV,3,5-6)
3) "3 The illusion of love can triumph over the illusion of hate, but always at the price of making both illusions."(16,IV,5,3)
4) "7 Find hope and comfort, rather than despair, in this: You could not long find even the illusion of love in any special relationship here."(16,VI,8,7)

From passage 1), illusory love is regarded as incapable of giving satisfaction. In Buddhist terms, it involves a fundamental dissatisfactoriness ('dukkha') or suffering. Of course, this is contrary to genuine love. From passage 2), it is found in what the Course calls 'special love,' which will be discussed at length below. From passage 3), it exists only in the context of its contrary illusion of hate. This perhaps is the kernel of insight sometimes expressed in the view that love cannot exist without hate. Such was the view of Heraclitus that the universe operates by two basic principles, love and hate. From passage 4), illusory love is the foundation of what the Course refers to as the 'special relationship,' which we will also discuss below.

Although the idea of an 'illusion of love' is referred to in these passages, a close reading of other passages makes it clear that sometimes when the term 'love' is used without the qualifier 'illusion of,' they actually refer to illusory love. This can be gathered from the context. In what follows next I will try to clarify the nature of illusory love and the way it is present in special relationships, particularly in special love relationships.

First we will discuss how the Course views illusory love as stemming from the separated mind's formation of and involvement with the ego and the consequences that arise from that involvement.

A. Illusory love as based on ego-involvement. Here we consider how illusory love arises due to the separated mind's attachment to the ego-idea and then the overall nature of illusory love. The basis of illusory love lies in its close association with the ego. It is important to be clear about what the Course means by this term. While it would merit its own full discussion, I will briefly describe its central characteristics.

Two essential features of the ego are described in:

> "1 The ego is the part of the mind that believes in division. 2 How could part of God detach itself without believing it is attacking Him? 3 We spoke before of the authority problem based on the concept of usurping God's power. 4 The ego believes that this is what you did because it believes that it *is* you."(5,V,3,1-4)

That is, the ego is the fundamental idea in the separated mind that supports its belief in or *acceptance of division* or separation. As applied to one's own mind, this involves the mind's accepting the belief that this part of the mind is what one actually is. This originates in the mind's choice to think that it is something different from what it truly is. That is, although the mind is both unlimited and the creature produced by God, it chooses to think that it is limited and that it is its own creator or 'author.' The latter is the essence of what is here called the 'authority problem.' This is further described in:

> "2 If you made the ego, how can the ego have made you? 3 The authority problem is still the only source of conflict, because the ego was made out of the wish of God's Son to father Him. 4 The ego, then, is nothing more than a delusional system in which you made your own father. 5 Make no mistake about this. 6 It sounds insane when it is stated with perfect honesty, but the ego never looks on what it does with perfect honesty. 7 Yet that is its insane premise, which is carefully hidden in the dark cornerstone of its thought system. 8 And either the ego, which you made, *is* your father, or its whole thought system will not stand."(11,In.,2,2-7)

That is, following its forming the ego-idea, the mind then looks back upon itself through that 'ego-lens' and thinks of itself as being the product of the ego. That is, it thinks that the ego made the mind that made it. This is essentially based on the intention to 'author' or form everything that arises in its awareness, or to be God, the primary Creator or true Author of Reality. This occurs simply out of its choice to maintain the focus of awareness on the limited aspect or aspects that it chooses to be aware of. From this arises a very complex 'system' of ideas, beliefs and other perceptions, which it thinks of as fundamental to 'the world.' However, when seen clearly, that system is basically a delusion that it has fabricated.

Within that system, the mind is thought of as something generated by the ego, rather than the reverse which is in fact true: that the ego is generated by the mind by its own choice.

If this is compared to the Genesis story of 'Adam's fall,' it gives a very different meaning to what is there thought of as Adam's 'sin.' Many have been puzzled why God would have made so much ado over Adam's eating a fruit. The fruit, in the Course's terms, would symbolize an aspect of reality, which the separated mind focuses on and attaches to. That is only symbolic of the choice in the creature's mind to cease recognizing the whole truth of what it actually is and to attempt to think something that is not true. This can be understood as trying to 'usurp' the role of God by thinking what is false, i.e., its own chosen limited thoughts.

The primary falsehood is the 'lie' of the ego.[33] This is the original error, which the confused mind thinks of as the 'original sin.' (See the discussion below on the belief in sin.) Because on a deep level the separated mind recognizes it has made this choice, it experiences both the unfolding of that choice's consequences and the deeper recognition that it has taken on a false belief or slipped into an illusion.

1. Origin and primary characteristics of the ego. Put simply, in order to maintain or uphold the belief that it is limited and separate, the mind generates the idea of an 'ego' to which it attaches itself. A further passage brings out four other primary characteristics:

> "1 Everyone makes an ego or a self for himself, which is subject to enormous variation because of its instability. 2 He also makes an ego for everyone else he perceives, which is equally variable. 3 Their interaction is a process that alters both, because they were not made by or with the Unalterable. 4 It is important to realize that this alteration can and does occur as readily when the interaction takes place in the mind as when it involves physical proximity. 5 Thinking about another ego is as effective in changing relative perception as is physical interaction. 6 There could be no better example that the ego is only an idea and not a fact."(4,II,2,1-6)

Here is made clear that the ego's *origination* lies in the very mind that accepts it. It is something constructed by that mind, not by God or any other power outside the mind. In agreement with the philosopher David Hume, it is highly *variable and shifting* in its content. And because its content is one of dividing one portion

---

[33] From the perspective of the course, the 'Fall' story's placing the origin of the lie in the 'serpent' is a major example of projection. Called 'the father of lies,' what the serpent symbolizes is actually the ego itself. That is, the 'temptation' does not come from outside the mind, but from within it. Thus, what is theologically thought of as 'Satan,' 'the devil,' etc., is essentially the ego-idea itself.

of what is present in Reality from other portions, in its own formation it simultaneously forms similar ideas for certain other portions of the realm it perceives, constructing a world of *multiple egos*. Of course, the mind's own ego is primary among these, both in that mind's awareness and in importance among the 'world of egos' that it sees itself a part of. However, we see here what the Course considers the ego most truly to be: simply an *idea* that only exists in the mind (or minds) that accept it. In that sense, it is only a fabricated form in the mind, although it is attributed by that mind the greatest reality.

One might think that this idea-nature of ego makes it a concept. However, the following passage indicates that it would not be correct to call it that:

> "4 Every symptom the ego makes involves a contradiction in terms, because the mind is split between the ego and the Holy Spirit, so that whatever the ego makes is incomplete and contradictory."(3,VI,7,4)

That is, the very meaning of the ego involves contradictory implications. This means that this idea, although seeming to be a concept, is actually a contradictory form itself. Since any genuine concept must be consistent, the word 'ego' cannot refer to a concept, but is rather very much like 'square-circular plane figure,' only a symbol or image. We will discuss the core inconsistency of the ego-idea below, but this passage points to the consequence that whatever is produced out of its presence in the mind ('whatever the ego makes') involves inconsistency – an application of the principle expressed in: 'Garbage in, garbage out.' Of course, that means that there are major effects on any mind that accepts it. Indeed, the beliefs, emotions and behavior that will be discussed below describe the principal effects.

It should also be pointed out that where the Course makes assertions that 'the ego does this or that,' as in the above passage that talks about 'what the ego makes,' this should be understood with care. Strictly speaking, the ego, being only a self-contradictory form, can do nothing. However, a mind that attaches itself to the ego, which we could call an 'ego-dominated mind,' does things that are peculiar to its having taken on the ego idea. Thus, the first clause of statement 4 above should be understood as saying: "Every symptom that the ego-dominated mind makes involves a contradiction in terms..." Throughout what follows in this discussion, wherever it is asserted that 'the ego does x' this should be understood as a shorter way of saying 'the ego-dominated mind does x.' This clarification will help us to avoid needless confusions or problems that would otherwise arise if we attributed some sort of independence of activity to the ego. It is only the mind that adopts it that is the source of any activity attributed to ego.

The symbolic or sign nature of ego is indicated in statement 1 and its contradictoriness in statement 3 of the following:

> "1 The ego is idolatry; the sign of limited and separated self, born in a body, doomed to suffer and to end its life in death. 2 It is the 'will' that sees the Will of God as enemy, and takes a form in which it is denied. 3 The ego is the 'proof' that

strength is weak and love is fearful, life is really death, and what opposes God alone is true."(W, pll,12,1,1-3)[34]

The point that it is 'idolatry' refers to the idea that 'ego' is only an image ('eidola' is the Greek word for 'image,' from which we get the term 'idol'), but one set up as having supreme importance and functioning much as a god. Because it encloses the volitional activity that is central to any mind, it makes the mind engrossed in it think of that volition as opposed to the volition of minds it thinks are outside it, particularly to the volition of God. Indeed, because it is only a self-fabricated illusion and God's Will is Truth, which entails undoing all illusions, the mind accepting the ego must regard God as its 'enemy.' Out of this it moves that mind to negate or deny God's Will. In so far as the mind tied into ego has greatly reduced its power, it thinks of what is actually its own reduced power or 'weakness' as strength. Further, because it involves itself in this greatly reduced experience of the full 'energy' or 'vitality' of Love and thinks of this as 'life,' what it calls 'life' is more correctly called 'death,' or a condition of greatly impoverished living. Of course, since accepting the ego enmeshes that mind in the highly reduced awareness of limited perceptions, such a mind comes to think of what it encounters in those perceptions as the sole criterion of truth or reality. And, in the sense that those perceptions further lead the mind to reject the full awareness of God's/Love's presence, it thinks of 'truth' as what is opposed to God.

2. Guilt as due to acceptance of the ego. Although I have emphasized how the mind, in entering separation, generates the idea of ego, this should not be thought of only as involving a purely 'mental' or cognitive form. Since the mind in its foundation is a creature originating from and existing as an expression of Love, it also has an affective or feeling aspect. This is the basis of its attraction toward the aspects of Reality that it focuses on and attaches itself to when it slips into the separated state. Just as the cognitive form that is generated so as to define its limits and uphold separation is the ego, there accompanies that formation a corresponding feeling that serves to bolster separation. As is stated:

> "1 The acceptance of guilt into the mind of God's Son was the beginning of the separation, as the acceptance of the Atonement is its end."(13,ln.,2,1)

That is, the first emotion that arises in separation is guilt, which is the feeling that arises along with the formation of the ego-idea.

This guilt is not the same as the feeling one usually has following engagement in a particular thought or action that one thinks is 'wrong.' Rather, it would better be called '**primary guilt**.' The essential nature of guilt is indicated in the following:

> "5 If you identify with the ego, you must perceive yourself as

---

[34] This referencing refers to those sections of the Workbook that are found in Part II that focus on special questions. 'pII' is 'Part II' and '12' is question 12.

> guilty. 6 Whenever you respond to your ego you will experience guilt, and you will fear punishment. 7 The ego is quite literally a fearful thought. 8 However ridiculous the idea of attacking God may be to the sane mind, never forget that the ego is not sane. 9 It represents a delusional system, and speaks for it. 10 Listening to the ego's voice means that you believe it is possible to attack God, and that a part of Him has been torn away by you. 11 Fear of retaliation from without follows, because the severity of the guilt is so acute that it must be projected."(5,V,3,5-11)

Although the emotion of guilt generally arises in our experiences from specific actions, words, or thoughts we think are violations of what the mind accepts as 'right,' 'correct,' or 'legal,' what is made clear here is that those specific forms of guilt are actually expressions of this primary guilt. As explained here, it is based on the initial act/thought that brought about separation: the decision to choose to focus on and then attach to a part of Reality. Since God's Will of complete Love is to be fully in Love's presence, this amounts to choosing to reject that Will-to-the-Whole in favor of one's own will-to-the-part. This is the core of the 'authority problem.' Since the ego was constructed so as to maintain that partial awareness, there is present in that fragmented mind the sense that it is opposed to the divine Will. Although God has not the slightest intent of punishing it, He does continue to will that mind's wholeness, since that would bring it complete happiness. The ego-dominated mind, however, interprets the presence of God's Will as a 'pressure' or 'coercion' toward wholeness and thinks of it as a threat to its continuance, perceiving it as an intention on God's part to destroy or punish it. That is, the ego is essentially a 'fearful thought,' (statement 7) as it anticipates it will eventually be dissolved. A mind dominated by ego thinks of this as a type of retribution God wills to impose on it. The feeling that it has for what it thinks of as impending destruction is central to primary guilt. Since that is a type of fear, primary guilt has fear as a major component. Indeed, it is the most fundamental type of fear.

But primary guilt also involves a more cognitive or conceptual content, as described:

> "8 It attributes to God a punishing intent, and then takes this intent as its own prerogative. 9 It tries to usurp all the functions of God as it perceives them, because it recognizes that only total allegiance can be trusted."(5,V,5,8-9)

That is, although God does not have any intention to punish, which would be totally inconsistent with Love, the mind that has formed and become attached to the ego-idea believes that it has usurped or taken over God's function as its creator and believes that God is offended by that, and will try to punish it for this attempted usurpation. This is another aspect of the 'authority problem,' which is further described:

> "3 The problem everyone must decide is the fundamental

> question of authorship. 4 All fear comes ultimately, and sometimes by way of very devious routes, from the denial of Authorship. 5 The offense is never to God, but only to those who deny Him. 6 To deny His Authorship is to deny yourself the reason for your peace, so that you see yourself only in segments. 7 This strange perception *is* the authority problem."(3,VI,10,3-7)

That is, by choosing to focus on only a part of Reality and attaching awareness to that part through the device of the ego-idea, the mind pretends to be the primary foundation or author of its own reality. In this it thinks of itself as a 'self-caused cause,' which on one level it understands is self-contradictory, but suppresses into unawareness as it fastens onto the ego-idea and all that follows from that. However, on the deeper level it feels this primary guilt for having entered into the self-contradictory condition. And that cloud of guilt obscures its clear understanding of what it is, as well as the nature of Reality.

From this, the following should be quite clear:

> "4 Love and guilt cannot coexist, and to accept one is to deny the other. 5 Guilt hides Christ from your sight, for it is the denial of the blamelessness of God's Son."(13,I,1,4-5)

That is, just as the full presence of Love is incompatible with fear, since guilt is a type of fear, Love is incompatible with guilt. As statement 5 points out, the particular effect of guilt is that it encloses the ego-dominated mind in a kind of wall that prevents that mind from being aware of the full presence of Love. Since the Christ Mind is defined as the level of the Son's Mind that has that awareness, primary guilt is what hides Christ from that mind's awareness.

This has several important consequences, as described:

> "1 The attraction of guilt produces fear of love, for love would never look on guilt at all. 2 It is the nature of love to look upon only the truth, for there it sees itself, with which it would unite in holy union and completion. 3 As love must look past fear, so must fear see love not. 4 For love contains the end of guilt, as surely as fear depends on it. 5 Love is attracted only to love. 6 Overlooking guilt completely, it sees no fear. 7 Being wholly without attack, it could not be afraid. 8 Fear is attracted to what love sees not, and each believes that what the other looks upon does not exist. 9 Fear looks on guilt with just the same devotion that love looks on itself."(19,IV,A,10,1-9)

As we saw before, the nature of fear in its deepest significance is that it is fear of Love. Here we further see that, since guilt is the basic form of fear and that the ego-dominated mind clings to guilt so as to maintain itself, the attraction to guilt involves the fear of Love. Fortunately, because Love is much more powerful than ego, fear, or guilt, in that It looks past them all to Its own presence throughout all Reality, It is the foundation of the ending of guilt, fear, and ego. However, since Love (which is the Will of God) does not impose Itself against the will of any mind, but simply offers Itself until that mind is ready to make the choice to accept It, the ending of guilt, fear, and ego can come only when that choice is made. Until that occurs, the fearing ego-dominated mind clings to guilt as a means to preserve the ego. That is its 'devotion' to guilt.

3. The inconsistency of the ego-idea. If we think through this notion of 'self-authorship,' we may see the core of the self-contradictory nature of the ego. That is, by attributing to the ego-dominated mind the notion that it has originated itself, that mind is thought of as a 'self-caused cause.' However, such a notion can be seen as self-contradictory by way of the following reflection.

A first observation indicates the basic flaw in the ego-idea:

> "6 The ego does not regard itself as part of you. 7 Herein lies its primary error, the foundation of its whole thought system." (6,IV,1)

That is, the mind that has accepted the ego-idea thinks of that idea as more fundamental than what it actually is. Rather than understanding the ego as something that has been constructed, it reverses the order, believing that it is the ego that generates the mind. Indeed, in systems such as Kant's, where the ego (which he calls the 'transcendental ego') plays the primary role as the foundation of the cognitive structure of the mind (what he calls 'ideas of reason,' 'concepts of understanding,' and 'forms of sensibility'), it is the ultimate foundation of the complex structure of the mind and its experience. This is quite in accord, at least in its general outline, with the Course's view. However, while it is understandable that the mind thinks this, it is essentially an error, since the mind exists more fundamentally as something without ego, and only constructs that idea.

The ramifications of this are further indicated:

> "4 I said before that you are the Will of God. 5 His Will is not an idle wish, and your identification with His Will is not optional, since it is what you are. 6 Sharing His Will with me is not really open to choice, though it may seem to be. 7 The whole separation lies in this error. 8 The only way out of the error is to decide that you do not have to decide anything." (7,X,6)

That is, the primary Reality is the created mind's relation to its Creator, God, whose Will or creative extension of Love is its ultimate foundation. It is by the choice of holding on to only a fragment of what is in that created perfect mind's awareness that the ego is formed within that very mind, which gives rise to the whole complex illusion that is the content of the experience of separation.

The substance of this error is actually quite simple: the belief that what is produced or caused (the ego) is itself the producer or cause of what actually produced it (the mind). In that sense, the ego is thought of as a 'self-caused cause.'

When we consider this belief carefully, its self-contradictory nature becomes clear. To be a cause is to be a factor that contributes to the existence of something or some characteristic of its existence. But in order for something to be a cause, it must itself exist. But if a thing were to be self-caused in regard to its own existence, it would have to exist prior to (either temporally or logically) its contributing to its own existence. But to exist prior to its own existence would require that it both exists (in order to be a cause of its existence) and doesn't exist (since it has been given existence). This is clearly inconsistent: ego both is and is not. But, because the mind is focused on an aspect of Reality, it loses clarity regarding this.

In an effort to maintain that focused awareness, it grasps at the symbol 'ego' (or whatever other form that involves that contradiction) and by clinging to it generates other contradictions. Some of these are:

1) The ego-dominated mind is separate from other such minds; vs.
    it is united with those minds in the 'whole' of the universe.
2) The ego-dominated mind wills to exist without limit, particularly in time; vs.
    it wills to be limited, i.e., the termination of its temporal existence.
3) The ego-dominated mind wills to feel unlimited pleasure/joy; vs.
    it wills to feel limits on that, which gives rise to the forms of pain/sorrow.
4) The ego-dominated mind is thought to be the same over time; vs.
    it is thought to be undergoing change and thus is different over time.
5) What is 'real' is limited (e.g., both spatially and temporally); vs.
    what is 'real' is unlimited; i.e., there must be something beyond any limits one might determine to account for what is within those limits.

Those who have some familiarity with Western thought will recognize in these the core of the 'antinomies' pondered by Kant, who showed that the truth of the one or the other is logically undecidable. The Course seems to indicate that this undecidability is due to the error of accepting the self-contradictory ego-idea.

In one sense, it is correct to say that the ego-idea is self-generated or is its own 'maker.' That is, it originates from the mind that chooses separation. However, once its inconsistency is clearly seen, it no longer has any viability and the mind that chose to 'invent' it can drop it completely. Indeed, this seems to be the whole point of the Course's learning process.

4. The 'world' as the result of the ego-error. Although the acceptance of the ego entrenches the mind in its own delusory separation, it also leads to the formation of what we may think of as the 'objective' region outside the particular mind. That is the realm we think of as the 'world.' This is the very complex system 'powered,' so to speak, by ego-driven guilt:

> "2 The world you see is the delusional system of those made mad by guilt."(13,In.,2,2)

The delusional system is the whole structure of the perceived world, which has the rest of the characteristics that are part of its madness, which will be described shortly. This is also the important insight focused on in the Workbook lesson:

> "I have invented the world I see."(W,32)

In light of this, the Course gives a simple verdict on the ego as a seriously flawed idea:

> "1 The ego is insane."(W,pII,12,2,1)

This fully agrees with the popular saying, "It's a mad, mad world." That is, the self-contradictory ego-idea lies at the core of all its thoughts regarding the world, which are simply projections of the mental forms that are present in the separated mind (somewhat like Kant's 'a priori forms'). Thus, as long as it thinks, perceives, and acts from the insane ego-idea, whatever it thinks, perceives, and does must be insane. That is, the ego-idea lies at the root of the separated mind's fundamental unwholeness or fragmentation, which is the root meaning of the word 'insane' (literally, in Latin, 'in' = 'not,' + 'sanus' = 'healthy, whole'). And from the Course's perspective, considering the havoc that it makes for separated minds, it generates major insanity even for those we might like to think of as more sane. From this, we can perhaps see the Course's emphasis on 'healing,' or making fully healthy or whole.

However, in a sense it is correct to say that the ego-dominated mind generates or is the author of 'reality,' if by 'reality' is meant a kind of relative reality such as the world of perception is considered to be. As is pointed out:

> "4 You dream of a separated ego and believe in a world that rests upon it. 5 This is very real to you."(4,I,4,4-5)

However, in the Course's view this is only an illusion. J.P. Sartre seems to hold that this is the only sort of reality attainable by the mind. He insists that the highest function of the mind is to accept complete responsibility for the world that it thus 'creates.' In a way, the Course would quite agree, in that each separated mind is the source of all that it experiences in the world that is formed out of its choice of separation. It also would agree with Sartre that such a world involves the formation of what is for it a hell of conflict with other ego-dominated minds. However, it holds that this relative 'reality' is not the only sort that the mind can experience. Fig. 14 is a representation of what arises from or in the separated mind. Although

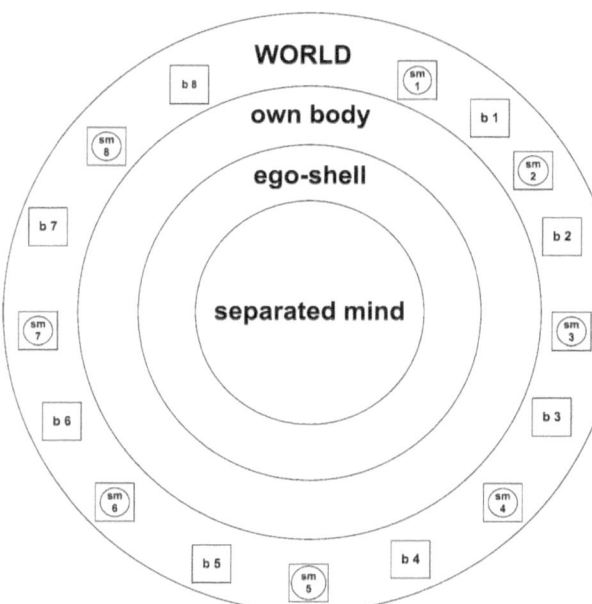

Fig. 14

much deeper, but often inaccessible to its awareness, is the Holy Spirit. What is most salient to it is its primary activity as a mind which has a limited power of extending, including both a limited awareness (perception) and limited producing (making). Its first production is the ego-idea and its structure of beliefs and feeling patterns, here called the 'ego-shell.' This is followed by its body, and finally the 'world' located in space and time. Some portions of the world are thought of as only bodies (labeled 'b'), and onto or into some of those bodies are projected similar ego-ideas (labeled 'sm'). Of course, this same sort of structure is occurring in all other separated minds connected with their ego-body complexes. In so far as they concur about what is contained in their projections, they exist in the same 'world.' In each of them there are some perceptions that belong only to their particular mind. But the contents that they agree on constitute what they consider to be the world that is 'real' for them. However, from the perspective of a perfect mind, that world is simply a shared hallucination or dream.

B. The core of the idea of 'illusory love.' Thus, ego is the form whereby the separated mind regards itself as different and separate from other separated minds, and also from any perfect minds that it might think of, such as God, the Son, the Holy Spirit, and other created perfect minds. It is out of this idea that illusory love arises, as indicated here:

> "1 Think of the love of animals for their offspring, and the need they feel to protect them. 2 That is because they regard them as part of themselves. 3 No one dismisses something he considers part of himself. 4 You react to your ego much as God does to His creations – with love, protection and charity."(4,II,4,1-4)

The analogy to the response of animals to their offspring points to the rather instinctive character of the reaction in the ego-dominated mind. The ego, a construction of the separated mind, is generated as a means for holding the content of that mind related to its interactions with what it thinks of as 'outside.' It is a moderately stable nucleus of perceptions (mostly associated with its body, its feelings, and its thoughts and memories), which constitute what it thinks of as its 'identity.' (This view is close to what thinkers like Hume and the Buddha observed). Because the mind constructed it as a kind of survival mechanism, that mind treats the ego with feelings that are superficially similar to God's response to what He creates. However, although the primary response to it is one of protecting it from dissolution, the feelings the mind thinks of as 'love' and 'charity' toward the ego are very different from what those terms refer to in relation to God or any perfect mind.

This is expressed quite strongly in:

> "2 You do not love what you made, and what you made does not love you. 3 Being made out of the denial of the Father, the ego has no allegiance to its maker. 4 You cannot conceive of the real relationship that exists between God and His creations because of your hatred for the self you made. 5 You

project onto the ego the decision to separate, and this conflicts with the love you feel for the ego because you made it. 6 No love in this world is without this ambivalence, and since no ego has experienced love without ambivalence the concept is beyond its understanding."(4,III,4,2-7)

In this passage, the word 'love' is used in two different ways. In statement 2, as in the last clause of statement 6, it refers to perfect love, or Love as present in perfect minds. Although one may have a feeling he calls 'love' for the ego, it is not really love, but only an imitation. Indeed, illusory love involves an element of hate, both for the ego and for the mind that made it. In statement 3, an even more startling point is made: the ego does not even have a commitment ('allegiance') to the mind that makes it. Of course, since the ego is only a constructed image, as such it cannot do anything. But the important point is that the separated mind, while tied into the ego-idea, although it may dimly recognize that it itself is the foundation of the ego, is unable to see that the originating mind that it actually is has any value in itself. It only identifies itself as the ego-dominated mind and regards the deeper mind that gave rise to its state as only having value to the extent that it upholds the ego-mind. It is profoundly split off from even itself. In statement 5, the term 'love' is used in the sense of 'illusory love.' Thus, the separated mind (you) regards the ego in two opposite ways. One is that the ego is given support for the simple reason that it was made by the separated mind, and also for the reason that the ego helps maintain that mind's condition of separation, which that mind regards as valuable. But the other is that the separated mind recognizes that its entanglement with ego generates the condition of suffering, and rather than accepting its own responsibility for that, it looks upon the ego as the 'thing' that gives rise to its suffering. Thus, the separated mind has a profound ambivalence toward ego: on the one hand, it 'loves' or wants the ego to continue so as to maintain its separated condition; on the other, it 'hates' the ego for being responsible for the unhappy condition it perceives itself to be in. This love-hate stance toward the ego is the most basic conflict present within the separated mind. The irony of this situation is that the separated mind is so focused on ego (one might even say, obsessed by it), that it is unable to understand the real nature of Love.

We can now easily resolve the seeming contradiction mentioned in Ch. I:

"The ego is totally unable to understand this, because it does not understand what it makes, does not appreciate it and does not love it."(7,V,9,6), i.e., the ego does not love what it makes; vs.

"This sickly picture of yourself is carefully preserved by the ego, whose image it is and which it loves, and placed outside you in the world."(20,III,5,6), i.e., the ego does love what it makes, that is, the image it makes of you.

In the first passage, the word 'love' should be understood in the sense of 'give Love in the absolute sense.' Thus, it simply states that the ego, or more precisely, the mind dominated by ego, does not give Love in the absolute sense to what it makes. This obviously follows from the insight that any mind dominated by the ego cannot give Love to anything at all. In the second passage, the word 'loves' should be understood in the sense of 'gives illusory love.' Thus, it states that the ego, i.e., the ego-dominated mind, gives illusory love to the image it has made of itself. Thus, because the word 'love' is used in two very different senses in the passages, there is no contradiction.

Although illusory love has some aspects that are somewhat similar to those of Love, in the Course's view it cannot be taken as a type of what might be called 'genuine love.' Although the term 'genuine love' is not used, we may think of there being only three meanings of the term 'love' that are sufficiently close to what it considers to be love so as to think of them as genuine types of love. Of course, Love is the most genuine sort of love. But there are two other types, perfect love and imperfect love, both of which are authentic types of love, although somewhat less complete in their expression. Illusory love, because it is so distorted and leads to such problematic consequences for a mind that accepts the idea, is simply an illusion of love, and should not be thought of as a genuine sort of love. Although ultimately based on Love, it is a severely distorted expression of It.

The incapacity of the ego-dominated mind to truly love is pointed out in the following:

> "3 You made the ego without love, and so it does not love you."(6,IV,2,3)

That the ego was made without love seems to hold in two ways. The first is that the ego-idea originates as the result of the separated mind's disconnecting itself from the wholeness of Love, which involves the awareness of the whole of Reality. That is, the process of forming the notion of ego involves a curtailing of or limitation on the awareness of Love in the mind that forms it. The second is that the result of that formation, the ego-idea itself, is within its very content empty of the full awareness of Love. Being 'Love-less,' the mind dominated by ego is not able to love even its own maker (although it may involve an impulse to use its maker for its own very narrow purposes.) That is, there is in the ego-dominated mind a strong element of self-hate. This self-hate coupled with the strong self-love as attachment to ego is the core of its fundamental conflict.

An important point regarding what upholds the ego's presence in the separated mind is in the following:

> "9 Without your own allegiance, protection and love, the ego cannot exist. 10 Let it be judged truly and you must withdraw allegiance, protection and love from it."(4,IV,8,9-10)

In a way reminiscent of the foundation of the Son's existence in God's extending Love to it, the ego originates and is maintained only by way of the separated mind's forming and upholding it. Of course, there is a profound difference between the Love that proceeds from God and the 'love' for the ego that proceeds from the separated mind. The latter is illusory love. This means that the ego-construct continues only if its engendering mind sees some value in doing so and does not withdraw its allegiance or commitment to it. The whole process of Atonement, the cessation of separation, rests on the separated mind's judging it truly or seeing clearly what it is and then abandoning all support for it. However, although this is simple in principle, carrying it out can be quite complex and difficult, since the ego-attached mind is hindered from clearly seeing and giving up its attachment by the very presence of the ego-idea operating within such a mind.

The incompatibility of ego with genuine love involves more than merely blocking the awareness of Love's presence in a mind immersed in the ego-idea, as is indicated in:

> "2 Being unable to love, the ego would be totally inadequate in love's presence, for it could not respond at all. 3 Then, you would have to abandon the ego's guidance, for it would be quite apparent that it had not taught you the response you need. 4 The ego will therefore distort love, and teach you that love really calls forth the responses the ego *can* teach. 5 Follow its teaching, then, and you will search for love, but will not recognize it."(12,IV,3,2-5)

This describes what amounts to a kind of 'double-bind' that ego puts a mind into regarding love. Not only does attachment to the ego *block* full and clear awareness of Love; it also *distorts* the separated mind's awareness of Love. This is due primarily to the fact that, by accepting the ego, the mind imposes and solidifies limits on its awareness. To accept the full presence of Love into such a mind would entail the abolishing of ego. Thus, the ego-bounded mind experiences a kind of being overwhelmed, a complete inadequacy, as it recognizes that the full awareness of Love would abolish the ego. In turn, this generates in the mind attached to ego two serious consequences. The first is a deep misunderstanding of Love, in which Love is perceived as a threat that would destroy the ego. This also involves the false belief that if the ego were destroyed, the mind attached to it would also be destroyed. This generates a second response within that separated mind: a feeling of profound fear. It seems to be a completely 'natural' emotion, since such a mind feels in Love's presence the impending collapse of its existence, a sense of its own death. (The nature of fear will be discussed more fully under the affective aspects of illusory love.) The combined result of this misunderstanding and fear is that the separated mind, primarily within its ego framework, sets up a substitute idea of 'love' that is acceptable to the ego. This substitute notion of 'love' is essentially illusory love. It is somewhat like real Love in certain respects, but is a major distortion of what Love really involves.

The acceptance of the ego-idea not only leads the mind to a very distorted view of love, but it also generates a very different sort of thinking in it. This is indicated in:

> "3 The thoughts the mind of God's Son projects or extends

have all the power that he gives to them. 4 The thoughts he shares with God are beyond his belief, but those he made *are* his beliefs. 5 And it is these, and not the truth, that he has chosen to defend and love. 6 They will not be taken from him."(14,I,3,3-6)

That is, the ego-attached mind is moved as a consequence of the presence of the ego-idea to form concepts and judgments through which the separated mind regards the perceived world. This is a kind of 'diluted' or impoverished version of the perfect mind's impulse to contain or comprehend within it a structure or idea that reflects what it is aware of. In the perfect mind, that idea is a complete or perfect reflection of the whole of Reality. But in the separated mind, since it is focused on only aspects of Reality, its thoughts/ideas are necessarily fragmented and focused on various aspects. This is the basis of the primary concepts such a mind generates, as well as the fundamental judgments it makes regarding the relationship of those concepts among one another. For example, some of its primary concepts are 'cause', 'effect,' 'whole,' 'part,' 'thing,' 'quality;' fundamental judgments include 'All causes have effects,' 'The whole is greater than the part,' 'All things have qualities.' These general judgments are applied to more concrete experiences, which have perceptual content (e.g., 'The flying rock broke the window,' 'This dollar is a small fragment of my wealth,' 'The Sun is bright,' etc.) We need not go into the various basic concepts and judgments of the separated mind or how it applies those to concrete experience. Philosophers have long been interested in such an inquiry. One of the most ambitious attempts at that was the focus of Immanuel Kant's *Critique of Pure Reason*, which is only one possible formulation of these fundamental structures and judgments. In Kant's view, as was noted earlier, all concepts and fundamental judgments rest upon what he calls the 'transcendental ego;' the Course also seems to place a priority on the ego-idea as the basis of all other ideas, including concepts and judgments. What is important here is how the separated mind forms concepts and judgments, that is, beliefs, in its thinking about love.

In all of those judgments, the Course is quite firm about their involving distortions. As it says:

"2 Knowledge is total, and the ego does not believe in totality. 3 This unbelief is its origin, and while the ego does not love you it *is* faithful to its own antecedents, begetting as it was begotten. 4 Mind always reproduces as it was produced. 5 Produced by fear, the ego reproduces fear. 6 This is its allegiance, and this allegiance makes it treacherous to love because you *are* love. 7 Love is your power, which the ego must deny. 8 It must also deny everything this power gives you *because* it gives you everything."(7,VI,4,2-8)

The problem is that the only fully adequate mode of awareness that is possible for a mind is its complete comprehension of the totality of Reality. If there is any fragmentation or focusing on one aspect or another, or even several, that awareness generally excludes awareness of those aspects not focused on. That is, in knowledge there can be no conceptual division between 'this' and 'that,' no judgment. However, because the separated mind has accepted the ego-idea as fundamental, whatever it thinks involves a further fragmenting mode of awareness. Of course, there is a fundamental dissonance or conflict in such a mind, at least in the Course's way of seeing this. On the one hand, such a mind is at its root an expression of Love: its very existence, all impulses to be aware, all emotions, and all impulses to do anything arise from the foundational 'energy' of Love. Since the ego-idea originates as a means for the focused mind to maintain its focused awareness, it supports a resistance in that mind to letting go of the awareness of the part and returning to awareness of the whole. Yet awareness of the whole is fundamental to the nature of Love. In this sense, as the focused mind recognizes the possibility of ending its focusing, it clings to that focusing and responds with an impulse to hold off letting go of the focusing mode. That impulse to hold off or keep away the mode of wholeness, as was pointed out above, is the basis of what is referred to as 'fear.' This seems to be the most fundamental, or primary, fear that is present in the separated mind. Thus, as statement 5 says simply, the ego is produced by fear, which arose as part of the guilt arising from the choice to be attached to awareness of only part of Reality. Further, once the ego-concept is embraced by the focused mind, since its fundamental feeling is fear, it responds to everything that this mind further experiences through the 'lens' of fear. All that it perceives is perceived, so to speak, through 'fear-colored glasses,' so that everything takes on a 'color of fear.' (This seems to be quite close to what Heidegger referred to as the pervasiveness of 'Angst' in all of our experience. More about fear in illusory love will follow.)

C. The characteristics of illusory love. Here, we consider the specific cognitive, affective, and behavioral aspects that are central to illusory love.

1. Cognitive characteristics of illusory love: beliefs it involves. We discuss here five of the most important beliefs that the ego-dominated mind forms and accepts.

a. Belief that love is limited, focused on body, and exclusive. Because illusory love is based on perception's limiting of awareness to a part of Reality and the confusion of perceptions that gives rise to false perception, it necessarily involves an idea that love is limited, as indicated in:

> "1 It is only the awareness of the body that makes love seem limited. 2 For the body *is* a limit on love. 3 The belief in limited love was its origin, and it was made to limit the unlimited. 4 Think not that this is merely allegorical, for it was made to limit *you*."(18,VIII,1,1-4)

Here we see three ways that illusory love involves limitation. The first is that it centers on the perceptual form we think of as the body. Because the ego-dominated mind is immersed in body-awareness, its main concern is focused on what relates to the body. Most of what it thinks of as love, for either oneself or for another, shares that body-focus. Non-body aspects of either oneself or others thus have a less significant place in one's thinking and acting. The second limitation, which is actually the foundation of the first, is that the full field of Love is contracted to a tiny portion of it: the ego and the body that the mind intimately associates with the ego, often even equating the ego-dominated mind simply with the body. This is particularly the case in modern scientific thought, much of which holds that mind and ego reduce to the physiology of the body. The third sort of limitation, though not explicit in this passage, is that in its relation to other ego-body forms, or other separated minds in the world, what it calls 'love' in any relationship must be selective, exclusively given to some with intensity, to a few with less intensity, and to most not at all. This is the point in the following:

"8 Here, where the illusion of love is accepted in love's place, love is perceived as separation and exclusion."(16,V,3,8)

In this sense, illusory love necessarily excludes many other separated minds. We will discuss this at greater length when we consider special relationships.

The question naturally arises: if the mind is essentially a non-spatial and non-temporal 'thing,' what is the origin of what is called the 'body' and the world of many bodies? While no detailed description is given in the Course about how the ego-dominated generates the body, it is clear that 'body' is primarily an idea that has as part of its meaning the notions of limitation, spatial location, and a kind of stability in its form while undergoing modifications over time. It can be thought of as a particular set of cohering perceptions that are the focus of what the separated mind thinks of as most important, but as perceivable by other minds similarly focused on their own bodies.[35]

We can only speculate how the body, with all its remarkable complexity, could originate following the adoption of the ego-idea. This can be outlined as involving a series of steps that parallels the formation of the physical cosmos itself. The most recent formulation of that begins with the formation of an 'energy-plasma' in space-time, then its consolidation in many places into elementary particles (tiny entities imaged as cohering perceptual forms that have special abstract characteristics), followed by the linking of those particles to form first atoms, then molecules, and finally cohering collections of molecules we call 'bodies' in a more general sense. This is followed by the development of the more complex molecular structures we call 'living,' which eventually evolved into the type of 'living bodies' that we identify with. Although there is clearly a strong dependence of what we perceive on the detailed conditions in 'our bodies,' it has not been explained how awareness arises from those conditions. Indeed, some have pointed out that the elaboration of the whole account of this explanation presupposes awareness as present in the original 'plasma energy,' and thus entails that any physiological 'explanation' of awareness is ultimately circular. In any case, the Course holds that awareness is primary or 'a priori' to the whole

---

[35] This view on the idea of 'body' is somewhat like that of David Hume.

cosmic-evolutionary sequence, which itself was initiated by the original fragmentation involved in the choice to focus on only an aspect of Reality. Since the Course offers no comment on how this happened, it remains an open-ended area of inquiry for us to speculate on. However, if the Course is correct that the whole process is founded on an idea that is itself self-contradictory, such speculation would be doomed to that same inconsistency. Perhaps this is why the Course makes the disclaimer:

> "1 This is not a course in philosophical speculation, nor is it concerned with precise terminology. 2 It is concerned only with Atonement, or the correction of perception."(C,In.,1,1)

Indeed, this is remarkably similar to the Buddha's response to metaphysical questions: "And why, Mlunkyaputta, have I not elucidated this? Because, Mlunkyaputta, this profits not, nor has to do with the fundamentals of religion, nor tends to aversion, absence of passion, cessation, quiescence, the supernatural faculties, supreme wisdom, and Nirvana; therefore have I not elucidated it."[36]

b. Belief in sin. One of the most problematic beliefs that the ego-centered mind fastens onto is the belief in sin. The term 'sin' has come to have a variety of meanings and connotations that the reader might infuse into the Course's comments. For that reason it will be important to understand the meaning that this teaching gives to it.

> "3 What is not love is sin, and either one perceives the other as insane and meaningless. 4 Love is the basis for a world perceived as wholly mad to sinners, who believe theirs is the way to sanity. 5 But sin is equally insane within the sight of love, whose gentle eyes would look beyond the madness and rest peacefully on truth."(25,VI,6,3-5)

Two things should be noted first. One is that, since in the Course's view only Love and its various manifestations or expressions constitute what is absolutely real, and sin is characterized as 'what is not Love,' it follows that sin cannot be truly real. This is a basic view that runs throughout the Course. The second is that, since the only sort of 'thing' that can be known or present within perfect awareness is the complete Reality of Love, for this same reason sin cannot be known. It is not within the realm or purview of truth. A further point is that, strictly speaking, neither Love nor sin is able to perceive. Rather, perception is what occurs only in minds. Thus, the second clause in statement 3 is more properly expressed: "A mind that is committed to either Love or the belief in sin perceives a mind that is committed to the other as insane." Accordingly, it follows that, as described here, the belief in sin so distorts the mind that it is unable to have any clear idea of what love really is. Indeed, such a mind regards real love as an utterly insane idea, and thus constructs an alternative idea that it calls 'love,' i.e., illusory love, such as will become clearer below.

---

[36] *Majjhima-Nikaya*, Sutta 63.

From this we may see that what the Course means by 'sin' is at its root a cognitive, rather than a behavioral or affective, idea. Indeed, the whole separation is primarily a matter of a cognitive shift, based on the mind's choice to focus on aspects of Reality instead of its Wholeness. This cognitive aspect of 'sin' is also emphasized in the following:

> "1 Darkness is lack of light as sin is lack of love."(1,IV,3,1)

That is, 'sin' refers to the state of awareness that the separated mind fastens onto by its very entry into the state of separation. It is important to note that although that state is experienced quite intensely by such a mind, it is only an illusion. Of course, that illusion is thought to be the way things really are. Although there is a perception of a lack of love, in fact, there is no lack of Love in any real being, since it is Love that gives any being its existence.

Nevertheless, within that state the mind forms a belief in sin that includes several other aspects. What seems to be the central aspect of that belief is described:

> "6 Sin is an idea of evil that cannot be corrected, and yet will be forever desirable."(19,III,1,6)

This notion of an 'uncorrectable evil' needs further clarification. From the perspective of any perfect mind, the only possible sort of 'evil' that could be considered is one in which a mode of awareness occurs involving a limitation on anything in Reality. This is precisely what occurs in the arising of the separated state. However, the Course is careful not to attribute to it anything other than a *deprivation* of full awareness, or knowledge, that is the condition found within every perfect mind. Rather than calling it 'evil,' which is fraught with fearful connotations, a more accurate way of describing it is as an 'error' or 'mistake.' This is the point in the following:

> "5 Sin is but error in a special form the ego venerates. 6 It would preserve all errors and make them sins. 7 For here is its own stability, its heavy anchor in the shifting world it made; the rock on which its church is built, and where its worshippers are bound to bodies, believing the body's freedom is their own."(22,III,4,5-7)

and:

> "And all sin is understood as merely a mistake."(W,359)

That is, a perfect mind capable of perceiving would understand sin for what it is. Such would be the mind of the Holy Spirit and possibly any separated mind that has come to see clearly the nature of the belief in sin. Thus, what the ego-dominated mind thinks of as sin or error that cannot be corrected, is only a matter of misunderstanding on the part of such a mind, i.e., it is simply a mistake. And, being a mistake, it is completely correctable. Of course, as long as such a mind remains attached to its belief in sin, it is in a 'bind' that prevents correction. But the 'uncorrectability' is due only to that mind's choice to make it so.

Here we should note that in so defining 'sin,' the Course goes beyond any particular religious belief. That is, while the term 'sin' is found in all Western religions, it has only analogues in non-Western religions (such as the Hindu and Buddhist term 'klesha,' which translates as 'defilement,' in the sense of an action which produces negative effects in one's karma). But, as defined here, it also has an analogue for atheistic views. That is, it is almost universally recognized by both theists and atheists, in so far as they accept the reality of time, that there are 'errors' or 'mistakes' that can be committed, which once done cannot be undone. This seems to be the basis of social systems that demand punishment for crimes. It is also central to the Eastern idea of karma that calls for some sort of compensation for evil deeds. Thus, although the term 'sin' may not be accepted by many thought-systems, most of them, even atheists, do accept the reality of what the Course understands by that word.

Related to this view of sin is how the mind believing in it considers punishment:

> "5 For sin and condemnation are the same, and the belief in one is faith in the other, calling for punishment instead of love."(13,IX,5,5)

That is, intimately associated with the acceptance that there is a mode of thinking, feeling, or acting that is an uncorrectable mistake or fault are two things: condemnation of the mind/person that engages in such thinking, feeling, or acting; and the demand for punishment as the only appropriate way of responding to that mind. Indeed, this seems to be the core of what most would regard as an 'evil action,' since it involves the rejection of the one 'committing the sin' and the visitation on that one of some sort of suffering experience beyond the suffering of being rejected. In the traditional Christian view, this has been depicted in the most dramatic images and ideas of 'hell' or even 'purgatory,' and is probably the basis of the various sorts of punishment that humans have devised even in this life for those they consider to have sinned. Thus, the widespread belief that Jesus had to suffer the horrors of crucifixion in order to compensate for the sins of humanity is fully consistent with the ego-based belief in sin.

While what we call 'guilt' has a very strong affective side, as we saw earlier, it also has a cognitive side. In a sense, the belief in sin seems to be the core of the cognitive response to the feeling of guilt, especially primary guilt. The Course speaks of this in the following:

> "3 For the idea of guilt brings a belief in condemnation of one by another, projecting separation in place of unity."(13,I,6,3)

That is, the act of condemning serves as a judgment of wrong-doing on the one who is condemned because the primary guilt has already set up the separated mind for accepting the belief it needs to be punished for its 'original sin' of choosing separation. When one observes either oneself or another, he inevitably regards that person from this perspective and projects upon him this judgment. Thus, we say such a person is 'guilty' of an immoral or illegal action.

While we are familiar with the effects the belief in guilt has on how we view others and ourselves, the foundation of that belief is explained as follows:

"3 For guilt establishes that you will be punished for what you have done, and thus depends on one-dimensional time, proceeding from past to future. 4 No one who believes this can understand what 'always' means, and therefore guilt must deprive you of the appreciation of eternity. 5 You are immortal because you are eternal, and 'always' must be now. 6 Guilt, then, is a way of holding past and future in your mind to ensure the ego's continuity. 7 For if what has been will be punished, the ego's continuity is guaranteed."(13,I,8,3-7)

The point that guilt calls for punishment is quite familiar in both theological and social theories and practice. This leads separated minds to set up various moral 'codes' in which certain types of actions, or even thoughts and feelings, are thought of as 'wrong' or 'sinful.' That is, although as such none of these are evil in themselves, they are considered 'evil' because the separated mind needs to have some sort of occasion on which to externalize its primary guilt. In a sense, morality is an invention of the separated mind that helps it deal with its own suppressed and forgotten 'original sin.' This might be expressed: since sin, punishment, and hell do not exist, the separated mind has to invent them so as to cope with its chosen error. The central idea in a judgment of guilt is that the one so judged is deemed deserving of punishment. What is overlooked, however, is this point that guilt serves as a mechanism for placing or holding the mind in time. Since punishment looks upon the past as real and projects the guilty mind into the future where punishment may be carried out, the acceptance of the belief in guilt is essentially a ploy to maintain the ego within the frame of time. And because beliefs the mind accepts have an effect of engaging it within the structure of what is believed, the belief in guilt acts as a means of holding the separated, ego-dominated mind outside the single unlimited Now of eternity and within the series of limited moments of time.

Thus, the belief in guilt, which is a part of the belief in sin, acts so as to place a barrier between the mind that accepts it and the presence of Love:

"4 Love and guilt cannot coexist, and to accept one is to deny the other. 5 Guilt hides Christ from your sight, for it is the denial of the blamelessness of God's Son."(13,I,1,4-5)

Simply put, belief in guilt as part of the belief in sin is essentially a denial of Love's presence. If a mind accepts belief in it, it must come up with something quite different from genuine love. In the Course's view, the substitute is the notion of 'illusory love' that is being described.

In applying the belief in sin/guilt to specific situations, the mind must make a judgment that a specific action is blameworthy and that the individual doing it is guilty. But in the Course's view, to make such a judgment is totally incompatible with real love. This has ramifications regarding what we think of as 'justice.' As the Course observes:

"3 Love is not understandable to sinners because they think that justice is split off from love, and stands for something

> else. 4 And thus is love perceived as weak, and vengeance strong. 5 For love has lost when judgment left its side, and is too weak to save from punishment. 6 But vengeance without love has gained in strength by being separate and apart from love. 7 And what but vengeance now can help and save, while love stands feebly by with helpless hands, bereft of justice and vitality, and powerless to save?"(25,VIII,8,3-7)

In this it becomes clear that such a notion of 'justice' is simply false, or more accurately, self-contradictory and thus meaningless. This also has serious consequences regarding the traditional idea of God's 'justice,' in which He is thought to mete out the punishment, particularly the infinite punishment of an 'everlasting hell' for finite transgressions, what by human standards would be regarded as unjust. In the Course's view, it is utterly absurd to attribute such to a God of Love. Yet such a view follows from an ego-dominated mentality.

A more accurate idea of justice is expressed in the following:

> "7 Without love is justice prejudiced and weak. 8 And love without justice is impossible. 9 For love is fair, and cannot chasten without cause. 10 What cause can be to warrant an attack upon the innocent? 11 In justice, then, does love correct mistakes, but not in vengeance. 12 For that would be unjust to innocence."(25,VIII,11,7-12)

That is, the only just response that real love can give to any error ('sin') is to correct it. This has the sole concern of helping the one in error move beyond his mistake to truth. Vengeance, which is the core of ego-based 'justice,' has no place whatsoever in true justice.

A third aspect of the belief in sin, closely connected with its intimate association with the importance of punishment, is indicated in:

> "1 Sin is not an error, for sin entails an arrogance which the idea of error lacks. 2 To sin would be to violate reality, and to succeed. 3 Sin is the proclamation that attack is real and guilt is justified. 4 It assumes the Son of God is guilty, and has thus succeeded in losing his innocence and making himself what God created not. 5 Thus is creation seen as not eternal, and the Will of God open to opposition and defeat. 6 Sin is the grand illusion underlying all the ego's grandiosity. 7 For by it God Himself is changed, and rendered incomplete."(19,II,2,1-7)

A first point is a clarification of statement 1. That is, 'sin is not an error' should be understood as an elliptical way of saying: 'For the mind that believes in sin, sin is not an error that can be corrected, but is uncorrectable.'

A further point is seen in statement 3: the belief in sin entails two very important ideas. One is that *attack, both by others and by oneself, is justified*. That is, punishment is nothing other than a kind of attack upon the 'sinner' that is fully justified. This goes to the root of why the belief in sin is accepted in the first place. That is, because the ego-centered separated mind chooses to maintain its separation, it needs to regard the presence of other minds that it perceives as threats to its continuance; thus, it feels compelled to attack them either grossly or subtly. By believing in sin, it sets itself up in a relationship to all others that assures that it will attack and that they will return attack.

A third idea that belief in sin entails is the belief that *guilt is justified*. This speaks more to the presence of the idea of guilt within one's own mind regarding what one may have done. Although there is a strong emotional component, here the focus is on the more conceptual judgment, mentioned earlier, involving condemnation of the one thought of as 'having committed a sin.' This generally involves the belief that one who has sinned deserves suffering as punishment.

The fourth and even more profound point is seen in statements 4-7. By accepting belief in sin as real, the mind must think of God as having failed to give Love in completeness to His creature. That is, He is thought of as having created an imperfect creature, and thus does not fully love that creature, something that is entirely inconsistent with the nature of God as perfect Love. That is, the belief in sin's reality involves a radical distortion of the mind's notion of God. This is the point in statement 7, that 'God is changed.' Of course, this means only that such a mind's idea of God is changed, not that God Himself is changed.

The overall place of the belief in sin in the ego-dominated mind is quite significant:

> "2 The idea of sin is wholly sacrosanct to its thought system, and quite unapproachable except with reverence and awe. 3 It is the most 'holy' concept in the ego's system; lovely and powerful, wholly true, and necessarily protected with every defense at its disposal. 4 For here lies its 'best' defense, which all the others serve. 5 Here is its armor, its protection, and the fundamental purpose of the special relationship in its interpretation."(19,II,5,1-5)

That the belief in *sin is considered to be the 'most holy' belief* in the ego's thought construction should make clear how important the Course regards understanding its nature. This was pointed out earlier in our discussion of guilt, where a passage refers to the fear-filled separated mind's 'looking on guilt with just the same devotion that love looks on itself' (19,IV,A,10,9). To think of sin as 'most holy' means that it can in no way be questioned. But since it involves affirming the reality of ego, that it is thought of as 'most holy' entails that the reality of ego cannot be questioned. As long as the mind accepts that 'most holy' belief, it is stuck in separation. The function of the Course (and the Holy Spirit) is to help the mind undo this belief. Of course, that requires a tremendous energy to make that belief, and with it the belief in and attachment to ego, dissolve.

Indeed, the undoing of that belief is considered to be the key to dissolving separation and returning to the wholeness of the perfect mind. But, as long as the mind holds onto its attachment to ego so intensely, it founders in the state of separation. This is a constant 'state of war.' While this may at first appear to be an exaggeration and not to correspond to our experiences, a little reflection makes clear that the compromises we make with others to form the 'social contract' only somewhat diminish the intensity and lethality of attack, but of its very nature does not bring about anything like real peace. Thus, it is only a more acceptable sort of 'war.'

c. Belief that love involves sacrifice. Another belief that is central to illusory love is that there can be no love without sacrifice. As is stated:

> "1 You who believe that sacrifice is love must learn that sacrifice is separation from love. 2 For sacrifice brings guilt as surely as love brings peace."(15,XI,4,1-2)

Although the word 'sacrifice' in its root meaning is literally 'to make holy' (from Latin 'sacer' = 'holy' + 'facere' = 'to make'), the dominant meaning is 'giving up of a desirable thing in behalf of a higher object.' This seems to be derived from the ancient practice of killing or burning (i.e., a kind of attack) something one deemed valuable by offering it to a deity, with the belief that this would please or gain favor from that deity. More closely related to the ego-dominated mind's idea of love, the thought is that if you truly love a person, a group, or an ideal, you will be willing to give up things like time, wealth or even your life to benefit that person, group or ideal. This is the usual interpretation of the statement attributed to Jesus: "Greater love has no man than this, that a man lay down his life for his friends" (John 15:13). In lesser forms we think of the importance of being willing to give up things we have for those we really love, and even think of such willingness as a test of 'true love.' Although the Course recognizes that people believe in such an idea, it rejects it as utterly incompatible with genuine love; indeed, it separates one from Love. The reason for this: sacrifice produces guilt.[37]

However, at first reflection such a claim does not appear to be correct. Since this is a very serious claim, it merits closer scrutiny. The following passage offers further light:

> "6 A tiny sacrifice is just the same in its effects as is the whole idea of sacrifice. 7 If loss in any form is possible, then is God's Son made incomplete and not himself." (26,VII,14,6-7)

The first point here is that the very idea of sacrifice involves a serious error. Whether one sacrifices something regarded as minor, such as some of one's time, or large, such as one's own life, its central meaning is that giving up what

---

[37] John's report of Jesus' statement can be interpreted in a very different way so that it is in accord with the Course's teaching. That is, if 'lay down one's life' is understood as 'set aside one's ego-dominated, limited mode of living and replace it with the unlimited mode of living in the Christ Mind's awareness,' the statement no longer can be understood as a call for sacrifice, but as a call for wholeness or true holiness. Indeed, that John's statement does not necessarily involve an idea of sacrifice is made even clearer when one finds that the word in the original Greek, 'θη,' usually translated as 'lay down,' can also be translated as 'set, fix, or establish,' which has no sense of 'sacrifice' at all.

one thinks of as being sacrificed involves some sort of loss. The problem is that engaging in any action or thought that involves the perception of loss involves affirming that one *can* be in a state of lack or incompletion. Of course, that is the whole idea of separation: it is a matter of taking on a type of awareness in which one sets aside most of Reality and fastens onto a tiny aspect or part of it. That is, when one engages in an act or even thought of choosing to sacrifice, he reinforces the mode of separation. This is the same as reinforcing the mode of ego-identification. But as we have seen, the whole idea of guilt is that it is a means of supporting that limited state. Accordingly, when one does anything that reinforces ego-identification, he reaffirms the belief in guilt. Thus, sacrifice by its very nature reaffirms the mind's acceptance of guilt, the point in statement 2 of the previous passage. This affirmation of and insertion into more guilt is somewhat different from what happens when one does something that one considers to be 'bad' or 'evil.' In fact, when one offers something in sacrifice, due to his belief that sacrifice is a noble or good thing, he thinks he is doing something 'very good.' The problem is that the socially accepted belief in sacrifice (recall that other minds are also embedded in the ego-dominated state) is actually an error of the whole collection of minds believing in it. It seems useful to other egos to have someone willing to 'sacrifice' things for them. However, when one thinks it through, it is simply a further reinforcement of their egos.

When one looks clearly at the idea of sacrifice, particularly in its original form of killing or burning possessions as an offering to a deity, such actions assume that the deity is somehow in need of those offerings. Such a deity is thought to be an entity with great power and a very great ego who demands that those believing in it submit their egos to its own. The dynamics of sacrifice may be seen to be more as a way imposing an obligation on the deity to use its power to aid the one sacrificing. That is, it is ironically a way of trying to impose guilt upon the deity so that it can be manipulated to take care of the sacrificer, protect him, etc. A little further extrapolation shows that, although we may not make sacrifices to any deity, we take much the same approach in our relationships with those we say we love. (Atheists and agnostics generally do not avoid this situation, in that their de facto 'god' can be money, power, fame, country, ideal, knowledge, etc., or whatever one holds to be of highest value, for which they also make sacrifices.) In the Course's view, although we may not recognize the full impact of what we are doing, any act of sacrifice further engages us in the state of ego-dominated separation. Even more insidious is the way in which it enters into our idea of love, as described:

> "7 Sacrifice is so essential to your thought system that salvation apart from sacrifice means nothing to you. 8 Your confusion of sacrifice and love is so profound that you cannot conceive of love without sacrifice. 9 And it is this that you must look upon; sacrifice is attack, not love. 10 If you would accept but this one idea, your fear of love would vanish. 11 Guilt cannot last when the idea of sacrifice has been removed. 12 For if

> there is sacrifice, someone must pay and someone must get. 13 And the only question that remains is how much is the price, and for getting what."(15,X,5,7-13)

Clearly, this is what the Course calls 'illusory love,' involving sacrifice and guilt, entailing the notion that it is something that can be traded, bought and sold. Such a belief must first be undone and dropped if one is to begin to understand what love really is.

Further, this notion of 'sacrificing love' is utterly meaningless in relationship to God. As is stated:

> "5 I am as incapable of receiving sacrifice as God is, and every sacrifice you ask of yourself you ask of me. 6 Learn now that sacrifice of any kind is nothing but a limitation imposed on giving. 7 And by this limitation you have limited acceptance of the gift I offer you."(15,X,2,5-7)

The separated mind, in much of its so-called 'religious' beliefs, projects onto God the idea of 'love' that it has itself constructed. While understandable that it does so, it completely misses what God's Love actually involves and the love He calls for from His creatures. Such ideas can only generate a view of God that is completely opposite to what He is: a being to be feared as the great 'Ego' who knows nothing of Love. As the Course observes:

> "1 How fearful, then, has God become to you, and how great a sacrifice do you believe His Love demands! 2 For total love would demand total sacrifice. 3 And so the ego seems to demand less of you than God, and of the two is judged as the lesser of two evils, one to be feared a little, perhaps, but the other to be destroyed. 4 For you see love as destructive, and your only question is who is to be destroyed, you or another?"(15,X,7,1-4)

Such a view could be better called a 'God of sin, guilt and fear, devoid of Love, and self-contradictory.' In the Course's view, this idea is completely insane. As is stated:

> "7 For it is guilt that has obscured the Father to you, and it is guilt that has driven you insane."(13,In.,1,7)

In a sense, since the idea of sacrifice is rooted in the guilt that is central to the belief in sin, acceptance of the belief in sacrifice as central to love is the 'nail in the coffin' that consigns the separated mind to a condition that might be called 'living death.' Fortunately, it is only an error that can be corrected, although as long as one insists on holding onto it the mind remains fragmented in its insanity.

d. Belief in specialness. The belief in ego and sin issues in perhaps its most important 'everyday' belief about how the separated mind is to relate with others in the world:

> "1 Specialness is the idea of sin made real. 2 Sin is impossible even to imagine without this base. 3 For sin arose from it, out of nothingness; an evil flower with no roots at all."(24,II,3,1-3)

When one first reads this, it may come with a great shock to think that 'specialness' might be so closely related to the belief in sin. This passage, however, is stated so strongly that it will be well to try to understand just what the Course is saying here and what is the basis of this insight. Indeed, all of Ch. 24 of the Text, "The Goal of Specialness,"[38] focuses on it. The term is not directly defined, but it seems to be used in the ordinary meaning it has in English, as the quality or state of being special. It would be good to review the most common meanings for the term 'special:'
    1: distinguished by some unusual quality, esp. distinguished by superiority
    2: regarded with particular favor and affection
These meanings connote the idea that anything that is thought of as special is regarded in comparison to other things, and in some way singled out as meriting greater consideration, having greater value than those other things. That is, when specialness is attributed to something it involves that thing's being separated from all other things and having more importance than them. In the Course's terms, this can be seen as an immediate consequence of separation. In the ego-enmeshed mind, this generates a belief that is foundational to all it thinks of and experiences. As the Course observes:
> "3 And thus does specialness become a means and end at once. 4 For specialness not only sets apart, but serves as grounds from which attack on those who seem 'beneath' the special one is 'natural' and 'just.' 5 The special ones feel weak and frail because of differences, for what would make them special *is* their enemy. 6 Yet they protect its enmity and call it 'friend.' 7 On its behalf they fight against the universe, for nothing in the world they value more."(24,I,4,3-7)

The origin of the 'setting apart' is in the primary shifting of awareness within the perfect mind toward that small portion of Reality that it focuses on and then attaches itself to. As we saw, the ego-idea is an act of such a mind that demarcates it from other minds. It also stabilizes that mind with regard to a further shifting of focus of awareness onto other aspects of Reality. By attaching itself to that idea, the focused mind thinks of itself as having boundaries and an identity equated to the idea itself. Thus, when that mind considers other aspects outside the ego, it thinks of itself as 'special' and 'more important' than anything else beyond it, including what it thinks of as other minds and other things. This is popularly expressed in the adage, 'Take care of number one.' Because it is constantly impinged upon by new perceptions (simply other aspects of Reality that it happens to focus on) and other separated minds (basically, projections analogous to what it thinks of as other ego's that it posits as present in at least some of those other things perceived), the separated mind thinks of the much larger realm outside its own ego-space to be much more powerful than it. Those other egos can impose

---

[38] In UM, the title is "Specialness and Separation."

their 'wills' upon oneself. Since one's own ego-mind occupies the position of 'most special,' within the belief in its own greatest importance it looks upon all other things and minds in terms related to its specialness. This includes their potential for negating one's specialness, even destroying it by terminating the body-mind entity the ego identifies with. Thus, everything beyond one's ego is 'beneath' oneself in importance or value. This generates, on some level at least, a regard for all other egos in terms of possible threat to oneself. That is, one thinks of them as possible enemies. (They also, by their own ego-attachment, regard themselves as the most important and me as a possible enemy). Indeed, whenever any other mind interferes with one's own specialness, the immediate response is to think of that mind as an 'enemy,' at least to some degree. This is articulated, perhaps exaggeratedly but insightfully, by J.P. Sartre in the play *No Exit*: "Hell is other people." It might also be noted that there is strong evidence that early humans attributed 'other mind' ideas to every entity they perceived, what is sometimes called 'animism,' and that modern young children seem also to do this much more than adults. However, even in the most 'rational' of adults there may be vestiges of animism present as when they become angry at a machine or object that they think is exerting a will against their own.

But there is a great irony in the very nature of ego-specialness. That is, specialness and ego arise only in a mind that regards itself in relation to other things, especially other minds. The notion of ego, 'I,' would not be present if the mind had no other 'ego' or 'egos' with which it compared itself as most important and separated itself from. This seems to be the point in statement 5, that 'what would make them special is their enemy.' Put otherwise, we would have no idea of specialness were it not for the presence in our perception of other minds who also regard themselves as special and compete with us for supreme importance. And, to the extent they are thought to negate our own supreme importance, they are considered our 'enemies.' Indeed, this seems to be the thought at the basis of Hobbes' notion of the 'state of nature' prior to the formation of society by the entering of individuals into the 'social contract' so as to be relieved from the awful 'condition of war' that egoistic minds 'naturally' are inclined to.[39]

As is indicated in statement 6, somewhat like Hobbes' idea of the social contract, the ego-enmeshed mind finds it necessary in order to meet the demands of its own specialness to make a kind of compromise with the specialness present in others: at least some among those others, who are on one level perceived and thought of as enemies, are allowed to indulge their own specialness if they allow us to indulge our own. These we call 'friends.' Whether intimates or only acquaintances or even simply co-citizens, they are seen as co-fighters within the greater battle against those more ruthless enemies that populate the world, which the separated mind thinks of as composed of countless other ego-centered minds committed primarily to each one's own specialness. Indeed, God

---

[39] *Leviathan*, XIII.

is thought of as the 'Supremely Special Mind/Spirit.'

The consequences of the belief in specialness intrinsic to accepting the ego are enormous. I have already mentioned one, which is expressed here:

> "1 Comparison must be an ego device, for love makes none. 2 Specialness always makes comparisons."(24,II,1,1)

Not only is comparison central to the formation of the belief in specialness itself, it continues to operate in all interactions with the world. Each object perceived, each person encountered, is weighed and judged in terms of how well it supports or detracts from one's own specialness. This can be seen as central to the idea of 'survival of the fittest.' But, whereas biological science defines 'fittest' as what is most successful in adapting to environmental conditions, for the separated mind what is fittest for it is what most successfully preserves its own specialness. Of course, in many social and political adaptations of that biological idea it has been given the egocentric meaning, whether it focuses primarily on the single individual ego of the most powerful person in a society, or on the collection of egos that constitute a whole society. Comparison plays a major role in most individual actions in relation to others. In modern societies it has been institutionalized as central to what is called 'education,' 'business,' 'politics' and even 'religion,' lying at the heart of what most think of as 'success.'

The core of what specialness engenders in any separated mind in its perception of others is described:

> "1 Specialness is a lack of trust in anyone except yourself. 2 Faith is invested in yourself alone. 3 Everything else becomes your enemy; feared and attacked, deadly and dangerous, hated and worthy only of destruction. 4 Whatever gentleness it offers is but deception, but its hate is real. 5 In danger of destruction it must kill, and you are drawn to it to kill it first."
> (24,IV,1,1-5)

This is very close to what is usually thought of as 'paranoia.' While few separated minds operate only from that extreme attitude, since it would be quite intolerable for most of us to live in constantly, we should not simply think of this description as not applicable to our own mind. That is, while most have others they trust to some extent and think of as friends and do not deal with harshly, the Course seems to be reminding even the kindest, gentlest soul that as long as there is any trace of specialness within it, there is a very deep and dark shadow lurking there. This is particularly clear, if one honestly examines one's own experience, in moments when one finds this attitude emerging even in the most intimate and 'loving' relationships, as when an argument occurs or where one thinks the other has betrayed him or her, or even on occasion when self-doubt fills the mind with great despair. Such moments have been reported by even the most saintly persons. Indeed, Siddhartha, who became the Buddha, and Jesus seem to have had such moments of encountering this inner darkness, which the Course holds is the consequence of the mind's accepting any sort of specialness.

The belief in specialness has other effects that we need not go into here (see Ch. 24 of the 'Text' for a fuller elaboration). Our concern is to understand the nature of love, particularly what is called 'love' as found within the ego-centered separated mind. An important passage in this regard is:

> "3 The demand for specialness, and the perception of the giving of specialness as an act of love, would make love hateful."(16,V,9,3)

Here it is pointed out that what the ego-dominated mind, committed to its belief in specialness, thinks of as love is itself saturated with specialness. We should recall that the fundamental awareness that is an essential characteristic of Love continues to operate in any separated mind, although greatly restricted due to the focusing in such a mind on only a limited portion of Reality. Similarly, the extending impulse of Love is likewise present in such a mind, but greatly restricted. We saw that this extending impulse involves a giving of what is within the extending mind. The passage here simply states that what the ego-dominated mind gives is its dominant quality: specialness. Exactly what it means to 'give specialness' is not further explained, but I may offer a suggestion. Obviously, such a giving mind would not be able to put specialness into another separated mind, since that other mind, by its being separated, is already engrossed in ego and specialness. However, what it can give is a kind of affirmation of that specialness so as to reinforce its presence in that other mind. Indeed, this seems to be what many think that love consists in: one person or mind supports and affirms the specialness of another person/mind. (This may call for re-evaluating Mr. Rogers' famous line.) Of course, the reason why this is done is so that the other mind reciprocates by giving specialness to oneself. This is a kind of 'mutual admiration' relationship, which forms the foundation of many of what the Course calls 'special relationships.' However, statement 3 makes a rather shocking assertion: this sort of giving makes love hateful! To understand what this might mean, we need to recall that specialness has the effect of engendering for the mind enmeshed in it a way of seeing the world in terms of enemies, competitors, and some sort of 'state of war.' When we think this through, it means that sharing, supporting or affirming another mind's specialness involves offering to it all those consequences. And what is hate but a matter of feeling toward another mind and offering it what would contribute to its misery and even possible destruction? Seen from the broader perspective of what 'giving specialness' involves, and thinking of such giving as a kind of 'love,' it becomes clearer that in this case we have an Orwellian situation in which 'love' means 'hate.'

e. Belief that Love is dangerous. Another belief that the ego fastens onto is a kind of corollary to the above. It is described:

> "1 The ego is certain that love is dangerous, and this is always its central teaching. 2 It never puts it this way; on the contrary, everyone who believes that the ego is salvation seems to be intensely engaged in the search for love. 3 Yet the ego, though encouraging the search for love very actively, makes one proviso; do not find it."(12,IV,1,1-3)

The passage does not capitalize the word 'love,' but clearly means by that word what love truly is. And since that is most clearly present in the highest type of love, which was called 'Love,' what it says about the ego's attitude toward love will be most intense regarding Love. Although the ego can have no clear idea of what Love actually is, it is surrounded by Love, which pervades all aspects of Reality, including those focused on by the separated mind. Thus, the mind attached to ego has some sort of subtle, perhaps even subliminal, awareness of Love's presence. The passage here says basically that whatever Love may involve or be, the ego considers it dangerous. This seems to be a kind of dim recognition that Love's full presence in the separated mind would dissolve the ego-idea. This may be the actual root of what Heidegger calls 'Angst' or 'fundamental fear.' However, there is within that mind also an obscured awareness of Love that it is drawn to. That attraction expresses as a kind of 'search for Love.' This operates even in its most dismal failures to complete that search, such as in the giving/affirming of specialness in what is only illusory love. However, because that mind is torn between its attachment to the ego and its attraction to Love, it sets up for itself the self-contradictory mandate: Seek for Love, but do not find it. And as long as it fails to see the absurdity of its condition, it is condemned to live like the mythical Sisyphus, perpetually trying to roll a stone to the top of a mountain only to find that when he nears the top it rolls back to the bottom, or like Don Quixote seeking to realize the impossible dream.

f. Beliefs concerning God. Although a number of modern intellectuals have given up the belief in a personal deity, the Course makes clear that for the separated mind that maintains that belief there is generally a notion of God that is essentially a projection of the ego. The Course agrees that humans generally project upon Him the most fundamental characteristic of the separated mind, that of the ego-idea. This may be explained as follows. The separated mind has a deep, even unconscious, awareness of 'something' beyond the limits of what it perceives, which it thinks of as 'the Unknown.' This is its awareness of the perfect mind of the Son that it is part of and of God, the creator of the Son. However, as in Fig. 15A, it projects (shown by the outward-pointing arrows) on both the Son and God the idea of an ego, which forms a very distorted notion of both. Thus,

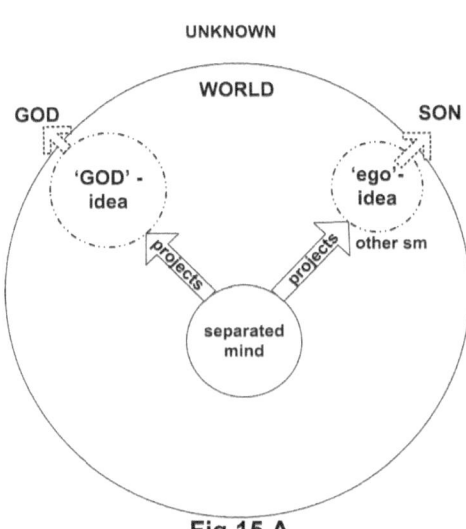

Fig.15 A

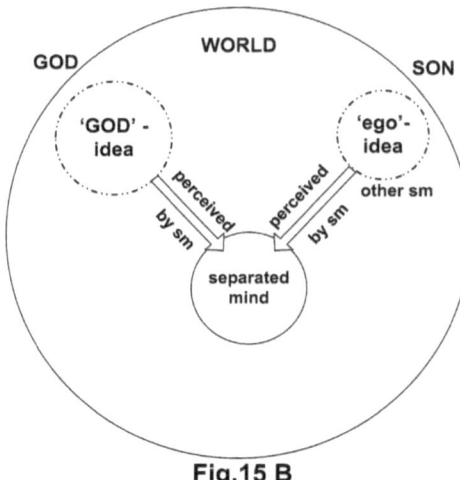

Fig.15 B

as in Fig. 15B, it thinks of and perceives in imagination the aspects of this projected idea as belonging to 'God' and possibly other 'higher minds.' It can have two responses to this perception, which is more precisely an image in its imagination. In the first, it believes that the 'larger' mind is responding to it in a manner that it would respond to another mind that rejected full awareness of it. That is, it thinks that God would feel hurt by its own rejection and want to hurt it back, or punish it. This is the basis of the fear central to primary guilt. This is typical of the response of many theists. In the second, the projected image is recognized for what it is, merely a projection, so that the idea imposed on the 'Unknown' is thought of as having nothing to do with what the unknown actually is. This is the view adopted by most agnostics and atheists. The Course fully agrees with the second, that the projected ego-characteristics thought to belong to God are illusory. However, it does not take the further step of concluding that all that the mind can possibly be aware of is restricted to perceptions and these projected ideas in imagination. Rather, there is also another mode of awareness possible beyond perception that a mind can come to. This is the main contention of most philosophies based on a deep mystical experience, such as are prevalent in Hinduism, many systems in Buddhism and Taoism in the East and of the mystical philosophies of the West, such as those found in Judaism, Christianity, Islam, and non-religious thinkers such as Plato, Plotinus, and possibly Hegel.

It will be helpful if we consider what the Course indicates are illusory attributes of God that the ego-dominated mind forms as central to its belief about God, particularly in that this false belief dominates much of what we find in current religions, both Western and Eastern. The following passage makes quite clear the Course's overall assessment of ideas of God as projections of the ego:

> "1 The projection of the ego makes it appear as if God's Will is outside yourself, and therefore not yours. 2 In this interpretation it seems possible for God's Will and yours to conflict. 3 God, then, may seem to demand of you what you do not want to give, and thus deprive you of what you want."(11,I,9,1-3)

When one looks closely at the ego-characteristics that the separated mind projects into its idea of 'God,' he finds very much what is ascribed to God in much religious thought, particularly in Westerns religions. In Appendix 1, "The Separated Mind's Idea of God," the Course's views on this are discussed with some thoroughness. Here are summarized some of the most important points: he is the creator of the physical universe, including our bodies; he divides the universe into various regions; he is quite arrogant, demanding exclusive worship and obedience to his commands; he institutes our guilt for the sins we commit as violations; he punishes us with a whole range of consequences, including pain, death, and even condemnation to everlasting hell; he demands that we offer him sacrifices and gives special care to those who offer them to him; he shows great anger and even rage; and in light of all of this, he inspires fear or even terror among his creatures. In the Course's view, such an idea of God is utterly absurd, just as is the ego-idea itself. The worship of such a deity amounts simply to idolatry.

Some thinkers have come to a very similar conclusion. Feuerbach, for example, although with a very different view on its final significance, pointed this out: "God did not, as the Bible says, make man in His image; on the contrary man, as I have shown in *The Essence of Christianity*, made God in his image."[40]

2. Affective characteristics of illusory love. Earlier we briefly considered how acceptance of the ego-idea involves the major concomitant emotion of fundamental guilt, whose quality is one of fear of being punished for its 'sin' of usurping God's Authorship, or claiming to be one's own 'author' or 'creator.' Although the acceptance of the ego-concept involves the cognitive commitments just described, it will be helpful to consider in more detail the affective or emotional consequences for the separated mind.

a. Fear. Here will be further clarified, first, what the Course says about its primary form; then, its particular applications.

Right from the beginning, there is pointed out a fundamental opposition between love and fear:

> "8 The opposite of love is fear, but what is all-encompassing can have no opposite."(In.,1,8)

The somewhat enigmatic second clause seems to deny any existence of fear, since Love is all-encompassing. However, the Course quite clearly acknowledges that fear is experienced by the separated mind. But this apparent inconsistency is readily resolved by interpreting the clause to say only that fear does and cannot exist in an absolute sense within the field of Reality. It nevertheless exists and plays a very significant role in the relative, and illusory, 'reality' of separation. Here we will try to reach a more precise understanding of what it means by 'fear.'

The Course's basic idea of fear is indicated in:

> "4 Everyone draws nigh unto what he loves, and recoils from what he fears. 5 And you react with fear to love, and draw away from it. 6 Yet fear attracts you, and believing it is love, you call it to yourself."(13,V,5,4-6)

---

[40]Lecture XX, *Lectures on the Essence of Religion*, p. 187.

The emotional response central to fear arouses the impulse to move away from what one fears. In this passage we see two levels or perspectives from which fear is considered. The first is one in which fear is related to some object that the feeling focuses on: a snake, an enemy, or in general an object that one perceives as endangering one's well-being. The second level is more subtle, being directed toward the presence of Love, either in Itself or in a particular manifestation or expression. On this level one may not have a clear understanding of what the 'danger' is, but because Love naturally draws one away from ego-embeddedness and the separated mind is attached to ego, it experiences fear of Love. On this same level, because the choice of ego-attachment is primary and fear supports remaining in that state, although fear may involve some unpleasant feelings, the mind is attracted to it, or feels a 'love,' in the sense of an attraction, for fear. This 'love' is obviously a form of illusory love, being only a very limited attraction. However, as pointed out in statement 6, because that mind thinks of it as intrinsically part of what it calls 'love,' it accommodates itself to the presence of fear, even welcoming it. This could explain the fascination many people have for things that intensify the feeling of fear, such as dangerous sports, horror movies, etc., particularly when that emotion does not involve an actual endangerment to the body. Of course, in that this intensifies the feeling of fear, from the Course's perspective, they may entail an even greater danger than bodily harm, since this can reinforce the separated state of mind by strengthening the presence of the fear of Love within that mind.

Another statement, which echoes the one found in the Course's Introduction, is the following:

"5 What is not love is always fear, and nothing else."(15,X,4,5)

Here the term 'love' seems best understood as 'Love,' the foundational 'energy' in God and all perfect minds. While that energy is what enables the separated mind to exist, because that mind focuses away from Love, it takes on a mode that excludes Love from the mind's clear awareness. This passage indicates that the turning away from that full awareness is itself a form of fear. That would follow because this turning away involves some sort of fundamental repulsion, arising from the choice of initiating separation, from the totality of aspects of Reality. While we can think of the initial impulse as an 'attachment' *to* the partial aspect or aspects (out of which the ego is formed), this also involves a counter-impulse *away from* the Whole. Although we might not think of that counter-impulse as fear, the passage here seems to say that it is the initial fear or what might be called '**primary fear**' that generates all the various particular fear responses within minds that have taken on this limiting mode of awareness. As was pointed out earlier (p. 91), fear is the central feeling in primary guilt.

This is further developed in the following:

"5 Fear and love are the only emotions of which you are capable. 6 One is false, for it was made out of denial; and denial depends on the belief in what is denied for its own existence. 7

By interpreting fear correctly as a positive affirmation of the underlying belief it masks, you are undermining its perceived usefulness by rendering it useless. 8 Defenses that do not work at all are automatically discarded. 9 If you raise what fear conceals to clear-cut unequivocal predominance, fear becomes meaningless. 10 You have denied its power to conceal love, which was its only purpose. 11 The veil that you have drawn across the face of love has disappeared."(12,I,9,5–11)

At first reading, statement 5 might seem to be a gross over-simplification, or even false. Humans recognize a great number of emotions, both positive and negative: love, contentment, desire, longing, hope, gladness, joy, delight, peace, fear, guilt, hatred, anger, despair, sadness, sorrow, depression, conflict, etc. Indeed, W. Parott lists 140 different emotions.[41] However, in the Course's view, all these various emotional states are seen as variations on the two most fundamental emotions or feelings, which it denominates as 'love' and 'fear.' That is, although the separated mind does experience various emotions, they all emanate from these two fundamental emotions/feelings. We have already seen that the term 'Love' refers to what is more than what we think of as an 'emotion.' While it includes feeling aspects, it also includes cognitive (knowing) as well as behavioral (creating) aspects. The affective aspect of Love is what the Course holds is the fundamental positive feeling; this includes peace, joy, and gratitude, which also have strong emotional content. Primary fear is quite different from Love, not only in its quality of being a repulsive impulse but also in its origination and foundation in the fragmentary awareness that is the basis of separation. That is, it arises only when an aspect of a perfect mind both focuses on aspects of Reality and attaches to that mode of awareness. Although it is difficult for our separated minds to see this clearly (indeed, the passage says that fear conceals something very important, which I suggest is precisely this), it seems that the key moment when fundamental fear arises is not simply in the act of focusing on an aspect, but when it attaches to that focused awareness. As we saw, it is central to the guilt associated with choosing that attachment and is the core of its belief in the sinfulness of 'usurping' the creative role of God. This attachment can be thought of as a kind of attraction, or a sort of 'love,' but it is unlike Love, which is an attraction to the Whole, in that it is only an attraction to the part. And since this excluding attraction is similar to Love in so far as it is an attraction, it seems to be the very root of 'illusory love.'

The last point can be understood as the substance of statement 6: primary fear (and illusory love) is based on denial, which is the denial that is part of the mind's attaching to focused awareness. In statements 7-11, we see a summary of the key to undoing fear and the separated state: simply observe what is going on in one's separated mind so as to see clearly how primary fear obscures or

---

[41] *Emotions in Social Psychology.*

conceals both the awareness of what that mind is doing to itself, which prevents its release from primary fear and restoration of awareness of the whole. Such penetrating mindfulness is the core of the release from the state of suffering within the teachings and practices of Buddhism, as well as in the teaching of J. Krishnamurti. (It may also be the core of the 'final liberation' in many other spiritual traditions, such as Hinduism, Yoga, Sufism, and even traditional Christian mysticism.)

A further important effect of fear is that it generates false perceptions:

> "4 Fear must make blind, for this its weapon is: That which you fear to see you cannot see. 5 Love and perception thus go hand in hand, but fear obscures in darkness what is there." (W,130,2,4-5)

If we recall that the origin of separation lies in the focusing upon an aspect or several aspects of Reality, while in one sense this awareness involves an illusion (the loss of knowledge), this focused awareness constitutes a true perception. That is, it is the accurate awareness of the aspect(s) of Reality that it is focused on. But once attachment to the ego-idea arises, since this involves primary fear, there is a serious distortion of even that focused awareness. That is, all that the ego-attached mind is aware of is filtered through that fear, which generates an awareness of these aspects that imposes on them the fearful 'darkness' that prevents that mind from perceiving them as they actually are. As long as that mind remains attached to ego, it will continue to distort what it is aware of, making its perceptions false. This has immense consequences for the mind's shifting from false to true perception. It seems to be the core of the Holy Spirit's function of helping such a mind move from the complex perception of this world, which is a radically false world, to the awareness of the Real World, which the Course claims to involve nothing but true perceptions.

Related to this distortion of perception is the distortion that fear generates in what the separated mind thinks of as 'love' in other minds. The following passage describes that as a particularly serious distortion of what it thinks about God:

> "1 Fear is associated then with love, and its results become the heritage of minds that think what they have made is real. 2 These images, with no reality in truth, bear witness to the fear of God, forgetting being Love, He must be joy."(W,103,2,1-4)

That is, as has already been pointed out, the separated mind, committed by its primary fear to the idea of illusory love, projects onto what it thinks of as God the thought that His love is also based on a similar primary fear. Instead of thinking of Him as completely at peace with everything, it sees 'God' as a super-ego wielding great power, imposing 'His Will' on all other minds, in a state of perpetual conflict with any that oppose Him, threatening them with punishment even to the extent of 'everlasting hell-fire.' Of course, such a deity could not be at peace either with those other minds or with itself, and if it had the least empathy with those opposing minds it could hardly be joyous. This would be particularly the case were it fully aware of the sorrow and suffering that is in its creature's mind that would choose to oppose 'its Will' and thereby fill itself with intense conflict. This would be especially intense for a 'god' who observed a mind so opposed to it that it would be sent into an everlasting hell. Indeed, this is a view widely accepted in traditional Christianity, which the Course considers a major distortion that is in need of correction. In its view, any doctrine that accepts the notion that God is to be feared is a major obstacle both to understanding God and to entering into His Presence. Such a belief is a necessary consequence of accepting the ego and its idea that fear is part of love. Further, as we will see below in our discussion of special relationships, this distorted idea of love plays a major role in the separated mind's idea of what love is in other separated minds.

b. Specific fears and guilts. Although primary guilt has at its core the feeling of primary fear that arises in the ego-dominated mind in relation to its choice to separate by attaching to the ego-idea, both fear and guilt operate not only on the fundamental or primary level. They also arise in relation to more concrete perceptual forms of ordinary separated experience, giving further support to the separated mind's entanglement in separation. The Course observes:

> "7 Anything that engenders fear is divisive because it obeys the law of division. 8 If the ego is the symbol of the separation, it is also the symbol of guilt."(5,V,2,7)

Here we should recall that the ego is itself an image or symbol that the separated mind constructs so as to enclose and uphold itself within the focused state of being separated or divided from the whole of Reality. It should be obvious that the feeling of fear, being a repulsive or distancing emotion, contributes to this. Thus, the feelings of guilt also contribute further to that divided state.

It also follows that, although primary guilt operates as long as the mind is involved in ego, it is generally not clearly aware of how primary guilt operates. This especially holds for various particular guilty feelings that arise from engaging in specific actions, words, or thoughts we think are violations of what the mind accepts as 'right,' 'correct,' or 'legal.' This is due to the fact that such a mind is preoccupied with the details shown by perception. Its experience of guilt is generally in relation to specific acts that it feels guilty about. However, those feelings of guilt are simply forms or concrete embodiments of primary guilt. That is, the separated mind perceives everything through, so to speak, 'fear-colored' or 'guilt-colored' lenses. Thus, those specific guilt feelings are projections of its primary guilt, just as its specific feelings of fear are projections of its primary fear. This situation will continue as long as the mind fails to observe what it is doing to its perceptions. The Course's function is to help it make that observation and undo the self-torture that separated minds bring to themselves.

The Course also speaks of several other sorts of emotions/feelings that arise out of the fundamental fear-guilt feeling that is rooted in the ego-dominated mind. If we look carefully at these, we can discern two basic sorts of such emotions, that can be thought of in terms of the well-known 'fight or flight' response found in most animals. The one sort is more active or confrontational, the other more passive or avoiding. Specifically discussed are two types of active feeling: hatred and anger; and two types of passive feeling: depression and what will be called 'false peace.' (It also mentions several others, but does not go into them at any length.)

c. Hatred. In many theories of the emotions, it is thought that the two fundamentally opposite feelings are love and hate (or hatred). While the Course agrees they are incompatible, as we have seen, it holds that hatred is not the primary negative emotion, but rather fear; and that hatred, like guilt, is one expression of fear. Concerning the opposition between love and hate, it states:

> "7 And hate must be the opposite of love, regardless of the form it takes."(M,7,4,7)

Since it does not offer a definition indicating otherwise, the Course can be presumed to use the terms 'hate' and 'hatred' in one of their generally understood English meanings, which are:

1) intense hostility toward an object that has frustrated the release of an inner tension
2) a habitual emotional attitude in which distaste is coupled with sustained ill will
3) a strong dislike or antipathy

In these definitions we can see three levels or degrees of hate. The first (def. 3) is simply a strong aversion to or dislike of something or someone. The second (def. 1) is a stronger feeling of dislike that involves a stance of hostility or feeling that the hated object is a kind of enemy or obstacle to one's own well-being; this can be either a momentary feeling or something more enduring. The third (def. 2) is a more permanent and intense feeling or disposition not only to dislike ('distaste') but also to will something negative (hurt or destroy) what is hated. In the passage cited, the Course seems to accommodate these various forms of hatred.

We have already noted the ironic situation that separated minds have in regard to their feelings toward Love, as involving both a fear of it and an attraction to it. This is further illuminated:

> "2 For love *is* treacherous to those who fear, since fear and hate can never be apart. 3 No one who hates but is afraid of love, and therefore must he be afraid of God. 4 Certain it is he knows not what love means. 5 He fears to love and loves to hate, and so he thinks that love is fearful; hate is love. 6 This is the consequence the little gap must bring to those who cherish it, and think that it is their salvation and their hope." (29,I,2,1-6)

This passage makes best sense if we keep in mind that the term 'love' in statements 2, 3, and 4 refers to Love. In statement 5, the first 'love' means 'love perfectly,' the second 'loves' means 'is attracted to,' the third means 'Love,' and the fourth is 'love as he thinks of it' or 'illusory love.' Or stated more clearly: "He fears to love perfectly and is attracted to hate, and so he thinks that Love is fearful, and hate is love as he thinks of it or illusory love." That is, because the separated mind is enmeshed in primary fear, it sees Love as a threat ('treacherous'): if Love were fully present, the ego would be dissolved. Further, that primary fear expresses in the form of what is here called 'hate.' The latter term seems to be understood as in def. 1) above. Since the full acceptance of Love would involve the dissolution of the ego, a mind enmeshed in ego cannot help but regard Love in any of its manifestations as its greatest enemy. Even further, since God is that Love, such a mind is afraid of God, fundamentally hating Him. But this hatred is not only on this fundamental level. Statement 3 points out that any state that involves hatred, even though it may seem to be directed toward some particular finite object, is an expression of primary fear. And because he has this profound fear of Love, he thinks of his attraction to fear as part of what he calls 'love.' This extends even further: since that primary fear also expresses as a hatred of Love, he thinks of what he calls 'love' as necessarily involving hatred. That is, what he calls 'love' necessarily involves hate. This contradictory idea can be seen as another consequence of the self-contradictory nature of the ego-idea. As we will see later in discussing how illusory love plays out in the interactions of the separated mind with other separated minds, this entwinement of 'love' (illusory love), fear, and hate has extremely serious consequences for one who remains fully immersed in the ego.

This indicates that the foundation of hate is fear as a fundamental repulsion from Love. Although there may be various objects of hate, as with fear, there is a fundamental or **primary hate** that is the strong dislike of or antipathy toward Love. This sets the separated mind at odds with Love, in a feeling that Love is the enemy which it thinks would destroy it. Of course, this perception is a complete distortion of Love, and is the result of its unclear, blocked awareness of what Love actually is. Hence, overpowered by this antipathy toward Love, the mind is simultaneously afraid of Love and attracted to the feeling of hate for It ('loves to hate'). Within this framework, it comes to the completely upside-down view that Love is something to be feared. In a rather Orwellian fashion, it is thought that what will best take care of it is hate; that is, 'hate is love.' Thus, this primary hatred toward Love surrounds such a mind; it also leads it to think that this hate is something that will protect or save it.

The 'little gap' mentioned in statement 6 is elsewhere elucidated:
> "1 You have conceived a little gap between illusions and the truth to be the place where all your safety lies, and where your Self is safely hidden by what you have made. 2 Here is a world established that is sick, and this the world the body's eyes perceive."(28,V,4,1-2)

That is, the distance that the separated mind sets up between what it *thinks* is real (which is actually an 'illusion') and the actual Truth or full awareness of Reality is what in essence constitutes the core of the separation. Of course, although it may seem to generate a huge gulf between illusions and Truth, there is actually only a very tiny distance between them, constituted by the choice to hold onto the focused aspects it has decided to become attached to. Yet, while this distance is a very small gap that can be easily remedied, as long as such a mind continues in that choice, primary hatred (as well as primary guilt and fear) continue to dominate it.

The Course speaks of three major types of object that hate is directed toward, what we might think of as three sorts of manifestation of that primary hatred. The first is toward the body, which it describes:

> "1 The thing you hate and fear and loathe and want, the body does not know. 2 You send it forth to seek for separation and be separate. 3 And then you hate it, not for what it is, but for the uses you have made of it. 4 You shrink from what it sees and what it hears, and hate its frailty and littleness. 5 And you despise its acts, but not your own. 6 It sees and acts for you."(28,VI,3,1-5)

From the context, it is clear that 'it' in statements 2-6 refers to the separated mind's body. Although the mind can direct its hate toward the body, particularly for its insufficiency, weakness, and many of the negative perceptions that come through it (perhaps this hatred lies at the base of the efforts often made to bolster, beautify, strengthen, and isolate it from unpleasant perceptions), the passage makes clear that this is only a matter of incorrectly imposing responsibility on it for what is actually the mind's own erroneous mischief. The body in itself is entirely neutral. This is made explicit in:

> "My body is a wholly neutral thing."(W,294)

All negative assessments of it are entirely a matter of how the mind chooses to use it: 'it acts for you,' and you simply make it a kind of scapegoat. And, because this whole process is overlooked, it becomes the object of hatred.

The second sort of object of hatred is other separated minds. As is stated:

> "5 You never hate your brother for his sins, but only for your own. 6 Whatever form his sins appear to take, it but obscures the fact that you believe them to be yours, and therefore meriting a 'just' attack."(31,III,1,5-6)

The point here is much like the one made by Hermann Hesse: "If you hate a person, you hate something in him that is part of yourself" (*Demian*). The Course again is quite clear that such hatred originates within oneself. From its view that this feeling has its basis in the act of choosing separation, it follows that, like hatred for the body, hatred for another is essentially a projection of the deeper-lying primary hatred. Of course, the unreflecting will fail to recognize how any loathing of another is actually a form of self-loathing. However, by observing this occurring in any act of hating another, one can find a sure remedy:

> "1 Look once again upon your enemy, the one you chose to hate instead of love. 2 For thus was hatred born into the world, and thus the rule of fear established there. 3 Now hear

God speak to you, through Him Who is His Voice and yours as well, reminding you that it is not your will to hate and be a prisoner to fear, a slave to death, a little creature with a little life."(30,II,3,1-3)

The key, from the Course's perspective, is to come to listen to the Voice for God or Holy Spirit, whose whole function is to correct the cause of the mind's self-inflicted suffering. His primary function is to help the mind see exactly what it is doing in each moment that it chooses separation. As it comes to full clarity, it recognizes the complete absurdity of this choice, from which spontaneously arises the cessation of that choice and its replacement with the choice to love truly.

The third type of object of hatred is toward God Himself, as described:

"1 The fear of God results as surely from the lesson that His Son is guilty as God's Love must be remembered when he learns his innocence. 2 For hate must father fear, and look upon its father as itself. 3 How wrong are you who fail to hear the call that echoes past each seeming call to death, that sings behind each murderous attack and pleads that love restore the dying world. 4 You do not understand Who calls to you beyond each form of hate; each call to war."(31,I,10,1-4)

Primary hatred, like primary fear and primary guilt, is the separated mind's response to the presence of Love. Since God is Love, these feelings are directed toward God, or more accurately toward the separated mind's idea of God. From the Course's perspective, since it is God/Love that gives existence to the mind that chooses to enter into the mode of separation, God's/Love's presence at the root of the mind acts as a constant reminder that the mind is short-changing itself by its choice of separation. While it is not God's intent to cause it fear, guilt, or hatred, its choice to remain in separation generates those feelings. Interestingly, if the Course is correct, it follows that however much a separated mind may say it loves God, as long as it persists in choosing the state of separation it fails to do so, and what it calls 'love' is only illusory.

A final point we may want to consider related to hate is the following:

"1 There are no triumphs of love. 2 Only hate is at all concerned with the 'triumph of love.' 3 The illusion of love can triumph over the illusion of hate, but always at the price of making both illusions. 4 As long as the illusion of hatred lasts, so long will love be an illusion to you."(16,IV,5,1-4)

Contrary to the popular idea that 'love conquers all,' as was pointed out in the discussion of Love, the whole notion of triumph is completely foreign to It. If we think it through, triumph or conquest is essentially an idea of overwhelming by force, so that it is the culmination of conflict. However, such a notion would admit the value and necessity of conflict, which is always a matter of one will imposing itself on another. The ego-dominated mind exists primarily by way of an attempt to impose the choice of separation on Reality. Thus, it sees all of existence as a conflict of wills. This it integrates into its idea of 'love,' which then engages in some sort of battle that it thinks of as aiming at the conquest/triumph of one will over another. (One is reminded of the Nazi propaganda film, *Triumph of the Will*, which in its historical context is an instructive lesson regarding how destructive such a notion can be.) Indeed, it thinks of love, whether love of another person or love of God, in precisely such terms. However, such a notion of love is a highly distorted illusion of love.

d. Anger. This is one the most aggressive emotions. It is the primary motivating force that leads to acting in terms of attack (discussed below). However, the Course brings anger back to the primary feeling of fear:

> "1 The relationship of anger to attack is obvious, but the relationship of anger to fear is not always so apparent. 2 Anger always involves projection of separation, which must ultimately be accepted as one's own responsibility, rather than being blamed on others. 3 Anger cannot occur unless you believe that you have been attacked, that your attack is justified in return, and that you are in no way responsible for it. 4 Given these three wholly irrational premises, the equally irrational conclusion that a brother is worthy of attack rather than of love must follow."(6,In.,1,1-4)

Like hatred, which in some form surrounds anger, it is rooted in fear. Although anger is almost always directed toward some specific object, it is a matter of projection of the deeper feelings related to separation. We have seen how the choice of separation leads the mind in that state to regard Love as a threat that it feels is trying to undo that state. In that sense, it perceives Love as constantly attacking it. On occasions when it regards something or someone outside itself as attacking it, the pent-up anger lashes out toward what it regards as the attacker. Of course, that mind considers this defensive response as right and the attacker as the one who is threatening it, so that the attacker is seen as responsible for the anger that is aroused. However, such a mind fails to observe the deeper-lying source within its own ego-walls and that it is only projecting onto the other what is actually in itself. Thus, the mechanism of anger is based on a failure of such a mind to be fully aware of what is going on within it.

While a mind dominated by ego may think that anger is appropriate in some or even most circumstances, we are told that this thought is based on three irrational premises, as indicated in statement 3. It will be instructive to consider how these premises are indeed irrational.

The first is a judgment that 'you have been attacked.' From the ego-perspective that judgment may seem to be true when the mind perceives another engaging in some sort of action, either verbal or physical, that appears to be intending harm to it. But such a perception is inconsistent with what is really true. Here we should recall that in Reality there is only the one mind of the Son that only seems to be divided between the two or more minds, one thought to be one's own and the other thought to be the other attacking mind or minds. Although in truth they are one single mind, perception insists there are separated minds. Thus, the one mind of the Son is not actually divided, so that it is false to say there are two or many separated minds. To hold they are multiple is inconsistent with their unity. Thus, to think they are multiple is irrational. This is simply another contradiction that originates from the idea of ego.

The second premise, that 'your attack is justified,' although it again seems reasonable if one accepts the content of perception, is inconsistent with the fundamental unity of what seems to be the multiple minds. In truth, it is the same mind that is generating the perception of both 'attacker' and 'attacked.' That is, in truth the mind called 'attacker' is the very same entity that is called the 'attacked.' Since one's own mind, on a deeper and truer level, is both giver and receiver of attack, for it to think that the inflicting of harm on another is right is to think that inflicting harm on oneself is right. But, the very notion of feeling attacked involves the idea that it is wrong to be harmed. Thus, to think that attacking another is justified is to think that it is both wrong to harm oneself and right to harm oneself, which is inconsistent or irrational.

The third premise, 'you are in no way responsible for it [i.e., the attack you perceive on you]' from the perspective of Truth involves believing that your mind did not generate the attack. However, it did generate it. Clearly, this is a contradiction and irrational.

Finally, the conclusion 'a brother is worthy of attack' seems justifiable from the perspective of the ego-dominated mind that accepts the three premises. But from the perspective of Truth/Reality, it involves the belief that the mind that appears to be other than my mind is really not my own mind, while in fact they are both the same larger mind. And although I think that I as a mind ought not be attacked or am unworthy of being attacked, nevertheless I, who really am the same larger mind, ought to be attacked, or am worthy of it.

That is, each of these four beliefs, when viewed from the perspective of Truth involves a contradiction and is irrational. However, the Course points out that whatever is perceived as an attack, when perceived truly, is simply a call for, or an expression of a need for, love.

> "10 That is the ultimate value in learning to perceive attack as a call for love."(12,I,8,10)

Although the ego-dominated mind is usually unable to perceive this, it is the perception of the Holy Spirit. Of course, as long as it chooses to listen to the ego, it will persist in the round of perceiving attack upon itself and responding with attack against the attacker. This is part of the cycle of violence that both Buddha and Jesus, and particularly the Course, point out can only end when one sees its absurdity and chooses to stop the cycle by recognizing that any 'other' separated mind is really the same as one's own true Mind. We will look at further aspects of attack later when we consider the behavioral aspects of illusory love.

Although the Course focuses on anger toward other persons, the irrationality and projected nature of anger toward things not having mentality should be obvious, particularly when the person believes that the machine or natural event has any sort of will. But such a response is only an expression of a much deeper level of the separated mind, which feels that Love (or the Will of God) is opposed to the will to hold onto the ego. Such experiences should serve as a reminder to any serious student of the Course that he or she still has things to work out in spiritual maturation. This can also be an indicator of the lack of maturity of any other person, particularly a person whom one might consider to be a 'master' or 'guru.'

There are several consequences of anger. The first, indicated in statement 4 of 6,in.,1,1-4 above, is that it interferes with giving real love to the one toward whom anger is directed. A second effect is described:

> "3 Projection means anger, anger fosters assault, and assault promotes fear."(6,I,3,3)

That is, there is generated a kind of circular or spiraling increase of fear. Thus, primary fear generates primary hate, primary hate generates specific fear/hate, the latter generates anger, anger generates attack, and because attack sets one up for counterattack from the one attacked, it intensifies the experience of fear. This also articulates the principle, taught by both the Buddha and Jesus, that it is important not to return attack with attack, but with love. The only way to break this truly vicious circle is to bring an end first to attacking behavior, then to the feeling of anger that inspires it, then to the hatred at its basis, then to the fear that generates the hatred. In the Course's view, this can occur fully only when the ego is no longer held on to.

Anger is observed also to have a close relationship with guilt:

> "3 All anger is nothing more than an attempt to make someone feel guilty, and this attempt is the only basis the ego accepts for special relationships. 4 Guilt is the only need the ego has, and as long as you identify with it, guilt will remain attractive to you."(15,VII,10,3-4)

We saw how primary guilt arises from primary fear as an anticipation of punishment for having made the choice of separation. The separated mind is quite aware of how guilt has the power to affect what it does, in that it leads it to try to avoid at least some of the unpleasant experiences that it thinks might come as punishment. Thus, guilt becomes a powerful means for manipulating others. Although one's own guilt is itself painful, by generating it in others it is perceived to give one power over them. By expressing anger toward them, one plays upon their feelings of guilt, and when done skillfully submits them to an extent to one's own power. This seems to be a major factor in moral and legal systems. Later we will see how this plays out in what are called 'special relationships.'

Although the separated mind tends to get absorbed in the details of perceptual experience, the Course insists that those details have little to do with anger:

> "1 Perhaps it will be helpful to remember that no one can be angry at a fact. 2 It is always an interpretation that gives rise to negative emotions, regardless of their seeming justification

by what *appears* as facts. 3 Regardless, too, of the intensity of the anger that is aroused."(M,17,4,1-3)

Like the body, facts as occurrences in the realm of perception have no capacity to generate anger (or indeed any other negative emotion). That emotion arises only from the meaning-structure in the separated mind, what is here called 'interpretation.' No matter how intense one's anger may be, it is entirely a function of that inner state which is projected onto the outer world of facts.

An important effect of anger is that it renders real peace impossible.

"3 God's peace can never come where anger is, for anger must deny that peace exists. 4 Who sees anger as justified in any way or any circumstance proclaims that peace is meaningless, and must believe that it cannot exist."(M,20,3,3-4)

It should be clear that anger's aggressive nature sets the mind at odds with what it is angry about. Of course, the momentary intensity of such an emotion is only a particularly strong perception that involves conflict, or absence of peace. At its deeper root, the presence of primary fear generates a perhaps milder but more pervasive type of conflict. As we have seen, such conflict must persist as long as the mind remains in its choice of ego-attachment and separation.

e. Depression. While hatred and anger are for the most part active, even aggressive, in their overall quality, there are also more passive emotional states that play an important part in the ego-dominated mind, as indicated:

"1 To identify with the ego is to attack yourself and make yourself poor. 2 That is why everyone who identifies with the ego feels deprived. 3 What he experiences then is depression or anger, because what he did was to exchange Self-love for self-hate, making him afraid of himself."(12,III,6,1-3)

Here, anger, the most aggressive negative feeling, is contrasted with the most passive, depression. When we reflect on the feelings already discussed, they can be seen as different responses to the separated mind's severely limited awareness of what it actually is. Which of these arises can be thought of as one of the alternatives in the fight-flight response. Anger moves toward fighting, depression toward fleeing. Rather than becoming aware of its unlimited Self, which can only occur in the full presence of Love, there arises the fear-filled perception of itself as unworthy of It. In this it tends to reject itself, which is a type of self-hate.

Depression is further described:

"2 Depression comes from a sense of being deprived of something you want and do not have. 3 Remember that you are deprived of nothing except by your own decisions, and then decide otherwise."(4,IV,3,2-3)

The mind that has made the choice of separation on some level is aware of the fact that it has shifted from a state of the complete abundance of unbounded Love, Joy, and Knowledge to one of greatly restricted feelings and awareness. However, because it loses clarity of how that occurred as the result of its own choice, it feels bereft or lacking. The feeling that arises is the essence of what might be called '**fundamental depression**.' Due to its forgetting that it and only it brought about this condition, it feels helpless, lost, and without the power to remedy the situation. This feeling is constantly with or in it. Of course, it makes efforts to fix the problem, such as entering into the world that it perceives in its restricted state and responding to it with the repertoire of beliefs and feelings that it has constructed as coping mechanisms, all basically modes of escape from its situation. However, there always lurks the profound depression that is its fundamental feeling, a sense of emptiness, futility, meaninglessness, and vanity. This is expressed in the following:

> "1 Do you realize that the ego must set you on a journey which cannot but lead to a sense of futility and depression? 2 To seek and not to find is hardly joyous."(12,IV,4,1-2)

That is, because there remains in every separated mind, at least dimly, the impulse toward satisfaction, pleasure, or happiness, and because within the framework of separation it experiences only very short-termed and very limited fulfillment of that impulse, it is constantly on the brink of recognizing or actually recognizing the basic futility of what it sees is the 'impossible dream.' At moments, it can run with Quixotic enthusiasm in search of joy, but always at least dimly it has the feeling, 'Vanity, vanity, all is vanity.' And, as seen from the perspective of a clear mind, that is the accurate assessment of most of its efforts in the world. What other response can this elicit but profound depression? Of course, all of this is only the result of choosing separation and solidifying it in the construction of and attachment to the ego, as is the point in:

> "3 Listen to what the ego says, and see what it directs you see, and it is sure that you will see yourself as tiny, vulnerable and afraid. 4 You will experience depression, a sense of worthlessness, and feelings of impermanence and unreality. 5 You will believe that you are helpless prey to forces far beyond your own control, and far more powerful than you. 6 And you will think the world you made directs your destiny. 7 For this will be your faith."(21,V,2,3-7)

No doubt, this is very much the substance of what the Buddha saw in discovering the first two Noble Truths: All within the world of perception involves a fundamental dissatisfactoriness ('dukkha'), and the cause of that dissatisfactoriness is the craving of the ego. However, if one stops there, one can easily be led to the further belief that the tiny embodied ego is only the effect of the conglomeration of impinging forces from the whole world, and that there is very little one can do about it. Depressing indeed!

Both the Buddha and the Course propose, however, that the situation has a remedy. For the Buddha, it was that dissatisfactoriness can be undone by removing its cause and that there is a path for doing so, which consists in becoming completely aware of the full range of activity that operates within the mind. For the Course, the remedy is very much like that of the Buddha, but with the added point that help is readily available if one chooses to accept it. That is, of course, the help of the Holy Spirit whose sole function is to guide every separated mind out of its self-imposed condition.

f. False peace. The other emotion, discussed by the Course, that is integral to illusory love and has a more passive quality is what can be called 'false peace' or 'the illusion of peace.' It is described:

> "1 Next, are the attributes of love bestowed upon its 'enemy.' 2 For fear becomes your safety and protector of your peace, to which you turn for solace and escape from doubts about your strength, and hope of rest in dreamless quiet. 3 And as love is shorn of what belongs to it and it alone, love is endowed with attributes of fear. 4 For love would ask you lay down all defense as merely foolish."(W,170,5,1-4)

and:

> "6 For fantasy solutions bring but the illusion of experience, and the illusion of peace is not the condition in which truth can enter."(17,VI,7,6)

Here is pointed out how there is a move on the part of the ego-immersed mind to counter its feelings of fear by generating something that is only an imitation of real peace. It consists of a feeling of security that comes when one is carefully insulated from fully interacting or relating with other minds. This can be a complete isolation from awareness of one's own feelings, particularly one's inner fear (what is sometimes called a 'schizoid' state), or of the emotions in others, particularly of their feelings of fear and pain. In the most extreme type it is what is called a 'psychotic state,' which allows such a mind to inflict pain on others without any feeling of the emotions of those they attack. While there are extreme situations in which a separated mind cuts off all awareness of those feelings, in most there is simply a withdrawal into something that one calls 'peaceful' by comparison to the intense awareness of those disturbing emotions. But there remains some degree of awareness of them, somewhat like a state of quiet that those within a fortress under siege by attackers might be in between periods of assault. But that is an uneasy quiet, since in it there is present the fear of the next assault. It may be called a kind of 'peace,' perhaps because it has an element of calm and diminution of disturbance, but it is not a state completely free of all conflict, the essential nature of true peace as viewed by the Course.

g. Other emotions. To round out our discussion of the emotional side of illusory love, it should be pointed out that the Course does recognize other emotions associated with it than the ones we've discussed here:

> "3 The upset may seem to be fear, worry, depression, anxiety, anger, hatred, jealousy or any number of forms, all of which will be perceived as different. 4 This is not true."(W,5,1,3-4)

In general, the Course sees that these 'upsetting' feelings, including worry, anxiety, jealousy, and others, as arising from the primary fear that stems from the mind's choice to cut itself off from the awareness of Love. Although they are

3. Behavioral characteristics of illusory love. There are also important consequences that follow from ego-attachment in regard to the behavior engaged in by the separated mind.

    a. Making. The first to consider is what the Course calls 'making:'

> "5 Fear and love make or create, depending on whether the ego or the Holy Spirit begets or inspires them, but they *will* return to the mind of the thinker and they will affect his total perception. 6 That includes his concept of God, of His creations and of his own."(7,VI,1,5-6)

The contrast here is between the perfect mind's unlimited mode of awareness, Love, which extends by producing in the unlimited way of creating, and the separated mind's limited mode which is dominated by fear and whose restricted productive extension is what is called 'making.' To understand this better, it will be useful to consider how 'making' is related to perception. We saw that perception is the limited mode of cognition that arises due to separation. Accordingly, separation imposes limits upon what we may think of as the more active aspect of Love, what the Course calls 'creation.' Here, the focus is on the major forms of that limited creative expression, due primarily to the mind's attachment to ego.

While the Course's most general term for limited expressions of the creative impulse is 'making,' a closer examination discloses that it has two broad categories. The first is the more primary sort that occurs at the very onset of separation. We have already seen that the first form made is the idea of 'ego' itself. This can be thought of as the primary 'cognitive' construction, since it is present prior to the making of the more 'material' constructions: the space-time structure of the world, and one's own and other bodies within that world. Indeed, the Course speaks of all of these, including the world itself, as being *made* by the ego-dominated mind. As it states:

> "1 The ego made the world as it perceives it..."(5,III,11,1)

This at first strikes the ego-dominated mind as quite puzzling, if not absurd, since it has come to accept the belief that the world is something that existed prior to its beginning as an embodied mind, which in one sense is correct. However, the Course insists that such a belief fails to recognize the deepest level of the ego-operation that it has forgotten, which is the very basis of the whole structure of the world. Although it is likely to dismiss such a claim as 'nonsense,' this dismissive thought fails to take into account the more primordial origin of separation, out of which the first result was the formation of countless ego-dominated minds. These, taken together as a kind of 'collective ego,' constitute the foundation of the whole complex order that exists in space and time.[42]

---

[42] I hope to discuss the question of how the world is made by the ego more fully in a future inquiry. Wapnick gives some indications of this in his *A Vast Illusion*.

This more fundamental making, which could be called 'mental making,' is also responsible for the beliefs and fundamental emotions generated by the ego-dominated mind, such as we have already discussed. This point is indicated in statement 6 of the earlier passage, which asserts that the separated mind made its concepts of God, of God's creations, and of its own creations. That is, all of its cognitive categories and beliefs are its own constructions.

The second general category of making focuses on very specific limited forms, particularly those made by human beings (although there is no excluding of minds or even other living and non-living things, such as the birds that make nests, the plants that make seeds, even rivers that make canyons and planets that make continents and oceans). With humans, their making includes many types of things made, from useful ones like tools, buildings, farms, cities, and vehicles; to beautiful ones like jewelry, works of art, music, dance, and stories; to more intellectual ones, like mathematics, the sciences, philosophies, and religions. They also make more problematic, even 'evil,' sorts of things, particularly the various things that bring pain and suffering, such as wars and various institutions of oppression of some persons by others.

While most of this making behavior, both 'good' and 'bad,' is the primary concern of human beings, the Course insists that all of it falls into one of two main classes. That is, it serves as a means either for further imprisonment in separation or for helping the mind find release from that. That is, it either tends to perpetuate the mode of limited making or to lead toward true creating, which is only fully possible within the state of Heaven. Which one it does depends on whether its primary guiding influence is the ego or the Holy Spirit.

Thus, in the Course's view, making is only in response to the perceptual mode, which involves some form of lack or limitation, as is described:

> "1 Since the separation, the words 'create' and 'make' have become confused. 2 When you make something, you do so out of a specific sense of lack or need. 3 Anything made for a specific purpose has no true generalizability. 4 When you make something to fill a perceived lack, you are tacitly implying that you believe in separation."(3,V,2,1-4)

Since all things made are based on the ego-idea that the mind has accepted, they take on the ego's characteristics. This ego-influence tends to make it think of all other minds as being like one's own ego-centered mind. However, the earlier passage very importantly points out that the separated mind is not completely stuck in acting under the direction of ('begotten by') ego. It is also capable of being directed or inspired by the Holy Spirit. In so far as the latter acts, it participates in the truly creating mode. In a sense, the whole purpose of the Holy Spirit is one of helping it shift from the making-mode to the creating-mode.

b. Attack. There are two specific types of problematic behavior that the Course gives great attention to: attack and what is involved in special relationships. First, let us consider attack. It was already clarified how anger leads to this other mode of acting. It is further observed:

> "10 That is the ultimate value in learning to perceive attack as a call for love. 11 We have already learned that fear and attack are inevitably associated. 12 If only attack produces fear, and if you see attack as the call for help that it is, the unreality of fear must dawn on you. 13 For fear *is* a call for love, in unconscious recognition of what has been denied."(12,I,8,10-13)

Since primary fear is present in such a mind, whenever its actions proceed out of that fear they involve some sort of attack. This can be either a blatant sort of aggression toward another mind or even an object, or a more subtle type of attack, which can be masqueraded with the appearance of gentleness, as a kind of tender coercion or 'friendly persuasion.' This can be so subtle or hidden to the acting mind that it fails to see how it is attempting to force what it intends upon an object or another person. This happens as long as that mind operates only from ego. However, on a deeper level (as perceived by the Holy Spirit and one who is guided by Him), that mind's attack-mode is actually an attempt to get outside its limits. It is what the passage refers to as 'a call for love.' Statement 12 is especially important where it says that 'only attack produces fear.' At first, this would seem to involve a circular situation (we discussed this earlier): attack issues out of fear, but fear issues out of attack. However, if we remember that the origin of primary fear is in the decision of the focused mind to form and hold on to the ego-concept, that very decision is itself the origin of the whole separation. That is, it is the initial aggression or attack on the Wholeness with which the perfect mind was endowed. If one revisits the story of Adam's 'fall,' which tradition has sometimes referred to as the 'original sin,' since the word 'sin' has so many confusing connotations, it could be called the 'Original Attack.'

Connected with the attacking nature of ego-mindedness, we find what seems at first to be a great exaggeration:

> "10 What is not love is murder. 11 What is not loving must be an attack. 12 Every illusion is an assault on truth, and every one does violence to the idea of love because it seems to be of equal truth."(23,IV,1,10-12)

Taken as stated, this says that any action that is done by an ego-centered mind is murder, what we think of as the most intense sort of attack on another so as to destroy him/her. While 'murder' has this basic meaning, it can also be used metaphorically to mean 'to put an end to, destroy' in a more general sense, such as 'to murder truth.' Taken in that more extended sense, we may see that any action that is not an expression of love involves, at least within the context of that action and the awareness within which it occurs, the ending of awareness of Truth or the whole of Reality. And when we recall that the awareness of Truth involves the awareness of God, the supreme Mind, whatever tries to negate that awareness is an attempt to 'murder' God. Yet, in the Course's view, although attack or acting from fear does negate or try to 'murder' God in the sense of making the attacker's mind unaware of God, this only occurs within that mind, not in Reality.

Here one may recollect Nietzsche's famous pronouncement, "God is dead."[43] It may have been for him that he successfully eliminated awareness of God from his own mind. However, the Course would go even further, by saying that not only that philosopher, but any mind that blocks Love's presence from it has, at least for the time it remains in that mode, killed Him for himself. Fortunately, however, it points out that this awareness can be restored, so that God is 'resurrected' within the murderer's mind once it learns to truly love.

The basis of attack is closely connected with the belief in specialness:

> "1 Specialness is a lack of trust in anyone except yourself. 2 Faith is invested in yourself alone. 3 Everything else becomes your enemy; feared and attacked, deadly and dangerous, hated and worthy only of destruction. 4 Whatever gentleness it offers is but deception, but its hate is real. 5 In danger of destruction it must kill, and you are drawn to it to kill it first." (24,IV,1,1-5)

Because the choice to separate remains upheld by attachment to the ego, which the ego-dominated mind thinks of as its specialness, that mind is committed to a kind of self-reliance that is limited to the false self enclosed by the ego, undoing true Self-reliance. Thus, it trusts only that impoverished 'self' and regards everything outside as a potential threat. Accordingly, it feels fully justified to destroy another whenever it thinks that other is an actual threat. Hence, there is justification for much of what are called the 'laws of war,' which are human applications of the 'law of the tooth and fang.' This may also be seen as justification of much of human destruction of the environment, which interestingly reflects back on it in terms of the serious possibility that collectively we are moving in the direction of our own demise by doing so. Perhaps the more 'primitive' peoples, by remaining close to Nature, see that the notion of specialness of human beings involves a severe danger, particularly when exaggerated.

c. Special relationships. A major type of behavior that is central to illusory love is the seeking and forming of what the Course calls 'special relationships.' Because this notion is integral to what many think of as 'love,' it will be examined with some thoroughness. We will first consider its overall view on how the separated mind thinks of other separated minds.

As we saw in the discussion of the formation of its idea of 'God,' in its relation to other beings in the world the ego-dominated mind engages in a twofold process of actively projecting onto at least some of those other beings and passively receiving perceptions of them in terms of its own self-imposed internal mental structure. That structure includes the more cognitive forms, such as the ego-idea itself and the various beliefs we've discussed, including the belief in space and time and other fundamental concepts, particularly the belief in sin and illusory love that revolve around sacrifice and specialness. But it is also domi-

---

[43] *The Gay Science*, Section 125.

nated by affective forms, such as the feelings of guilt, fear, hatred (along with desire), anger, and depression.

The relation that one separated mind (sm_1) has to another (sm_2) can perhaps be better illuminated by referring to Figures 16 and 17. In Fig. 16, is em-

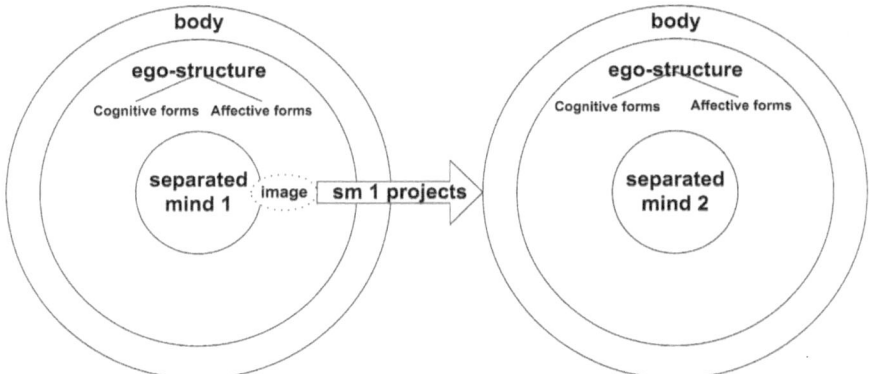

Fig. 16: Active side of perception of other

phasized the active mode in which sm_1 forms an image of its own inner structure, by which it projects onto sm_2 the various cognitive and affective forms that are within itself. In Fig. 17, since sm_1 accesses awareness of sm_2 primarily by way of

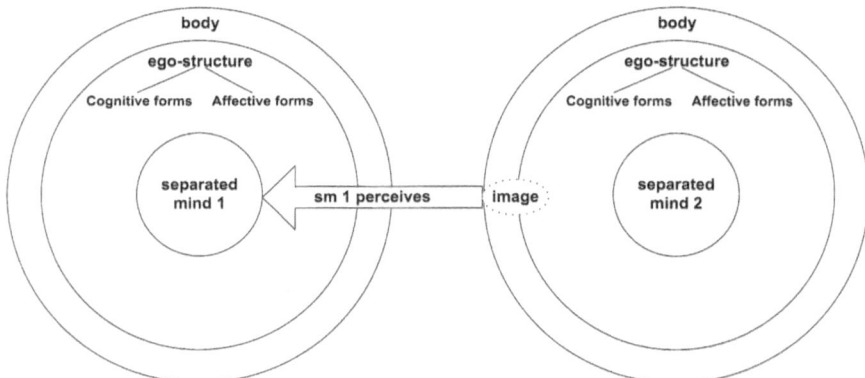

Fig. 17: Receptive side of perception of other

its own sensory organs (especially sight, hearing, and touch), it forms within it images that center on sm_2's body, but then further processes those images by way of its own ego-structure's forms. In effect, sm_1 does not perceive sm_2 'as he/she *is*' but only in terms of this constructed image of sm_2. The same is true for sm_2's perception of sm_1. As J. Krishnamurti points out, there is no actual conscious relationship between sm_1 and sm_2, but only a relationship between images. That is, both are largely constructions of each one's mind, having very little to do with who/what they actually are.

The projection of these images, which the Course calls 'shadow figures,' is discussed primarily in Ch. 13 of the Text. The following proposes how they are formed:
> "1 Each one peoples his world with figures from his individual past, and it is because of this that private worlds do differ. 2 Yet the figures that he sees were never real, for they are made up only of his reactions to his brothers, and do not include their reactions to him. 3 Therefore, he does not see he made them, and that they are not whole. 4 For these figures have no witnesses, being perceived in one separate mind only."
> (13,V,2,1-4)

That is, just as all perceptions in the separated mind are based on the choice to focus on some aspects of Reality, when the human mind encounters others it repeats that choice by focusing on only certain aspects of them and building up an image that it thinks accurately represents them. However, there is a twofold sort of illusion in that process. The one lies in the very nature of perception as an exclusion of many aspects in favor of a few. The other, even more problematic, sort of illusion is that the perceiving mind imposes upon what it perceives aspects that suit its primary impulse to form and maintain its own ego. This is the source of its false perceptions of others. Thus, a repertoire of images from past experiences dominates the separated mind's further perceptions, as it seeks to find what conforms to those old shadow figures.

The net result is that the separated mind, whose special relationships are dominated by the background of these shadow figures, lives in a condition that is mostly out of contact with what is actually the case. This is described:
> "1 It is through these strange and shadowy figures that the insane relate to their insane world. 2 For they see only those who remind them of these images, and it is to them that they relate. 3 Thus do they communicate with those who are not there, and it is they who answer them. 4 And no one hears their answer save him who called upon them, and he alone believes they answered him. 5 Projection makes perception, and you cannot see beyond it. 6 Again and again have you attacked your brother, because you saw in him a shadow figure in your private world. 7 And thus it is you must attack yourself first, for what you attack is not in others. 8 Its only reality is in your own mind, and by attacking others you are literally attacking what is not there."(13,V,3,1-8)

The important point here is that all special relationships, to the extent they are based on shadow figures, are actually insane. By this, we should recall, is meant the fundamental unwhole or fragmented mode of living and relating that is intrinsic to the ego-dominated mind. Although we may pretend that there is a type of 'sanity' in such a mind, this is only somewhat less insane than the more radically ego-dominated states of those we think of as 'extremely neurotic' or 'psychotic.'

In that sense, all separated minds live in a 'mad, mad world.' Hence, such special relationships are referred to as 'unholy relationships' as expressed in:

> "1 In the unholy relationship, it is not the body of the other with which union is attempted, but the bodies of those who are not there. 2 For even the body of the other, already a severely limited perception of him, is not the central focus as it is, or in entirety. 3 What can be used for fantasies of vengeance, and what can be most readily associated with those on whom vengeance is really sought, is centered on and separated off as being the only parts of value. 4 Every step taken in the making, the maintaining and the breaking off of the unholy relationship is a move toward further fragmentation and unreality. 5 The shadow figures enter more and more, and the one in whom they seem to be decreases in importance."
> (17,III,3,1-5)

That is, it is of the very nature of special relationships, unless corrected (as will be discussed in Ch. V as 'the holy relationship'), to deepen the separated mind's entrenchment in its fragmentation, which is the core of insanity or 'unwholeness.'[44]

Special relationships arise as an application of the separated mind's belief in specialness:

> "1 Specialness is the great dictator of the wrong decisions. 2 Here is the grand illusion of what you are and what your brother is. 3 And here is what must make the body dear and worth preserving. 4 Specialness must be defended. 5 Illusions can attack it, and they do. 6 For what your brother must become to keep your specialness *is* an illusion. 7 He who is 'worse' than you must be attacked, so that your specialness can live on his defeat. 8 For specialness is triumph, and its victory is his defeat and shame."(24,I,5,1-8)

That is, specialness permeates almost all thinking in the separated mind. Although we might hope that this thinking would be the basis for making good decisions, the problem is that if the content of that thinking is based on false ideas, it is very likely to engage in foolish decisions and actions. We saw earlier how the belief in specialness moves one to apply that notion both to oneself and to certain other separated minds. The basic problem here, according to the Course, is that to think of anyone as 'special' involves a radical misunderstanding or illusion regarding oneself and the other. Thus, that illusion leads the mind to make decisions that are wrong or erroneous. Underlying every decision is taking care of 'number one' or protecting one's specialness. Of course, since every separated

---

[44] Robert Perry gives further insightful observations on 'shadow figures' and special relationships, as well as the overall nature of 'illusory love,' in *Special Relationships: Illusions of Love*.

mind thinks it is special, there is inevitably a state of conflict that must arise from any such decision. Either one's own specialness is supported, in which case another's is to some extent suppressed, or another's is supported which entails the suppression of one's own. Indeed, Hobbes' observation about the 'state of war' is the necessary situation for any mind accepting specialness. From the Course's perspective, only the more overtly violent kind of war can be diminished by a 'social contract.' It is nevertheless still a state of war in which violence is only curbed by rules that make it more acceptable to those within it. This can involve the more intense sorts of battle involving victory and defeat such as are seen in the forms that humans still find acceptable, like the killing and destruction of the material underpinnings of people in other lands according to the so-called 'rules of war,' the various 'games people play,' ranging from sports to business and politics, or even the institutionalized forms of battle we call 'education' and 'cultural competition.'

The nature of the special relationship is clarified further:

"1 The special relationship has the most imposing and deceptive frame of all the defenses the ego uses. 2 Its thought system is offered here, surrounded by a frame so heavy and so elaborate that the picture is almost obliterated by its imposing structure. 3 Into the frame are woven all sorts of fanciful and fragmented illusions of love, set with dreams of sacrifice and self-aggrandizement, and interlaced with gilded threads of self-destruction."(17,IV,8,1-2)

The first point here is that out of belief in the ego's importance there is generated a remarkably complex structure and system of thought. Three of its primary principles are the importance of what it thinks of as 'love,' which is actually only an illusion of love; the importance of self-aggrandizement; and its counter-value of sacrifice. The notion of sacrifice can focus on either oneself or others, but it entails the willingness to have something in either of them be destroyed or limited for the 'good' of the special relationship.

These three principles can be seen as a kind of interpretation of the three Newtonian laws. The importance of maintaining/aggrandizing the limited ego-self parallels the law of inertia ('All masses tend to continue in a state of motion'). The principle of sacrifice, which involves a mechanism of imposing limits on ego-aggrandizing, is analogous to the law of force ('The change in the state of motion is proportional to the external force applied to it'). The principle of 'illusory love' can be seen as somewhat like the law of action and reaction ('Every action has an equal and opposite reaction'). This last point is made much clearer when we consider how what is thought of as 'love' involves the interaction of two or more minds and demands that each mind give to the other in the same way that other gives to it. That is, to take the simplest case, if mind A aggrandizes or supports the existence of mind B, mind B is expected to aggrandize or support the existence of mind A. Also, if mind A sacrifices (diminishes itself in some way or even lets itself be destroyed) for mind B, mind B is expected to be willing to do the same for mind A. Some writers, such as Erich Fromm (*The Art of Loving*), have compared this notion of love to a commodity exchange – it might be called the 'mercantile or trade idea of love.'

It is not difficult to see how these principles of the special relationship have been worked out as the 'elaborate and imposing frame' both in theories of interpersonal relationships and in the more complex theories of society. They seem to be accepted by much of psychology, sociology, economics, political science, and even the theologies of institutionalized religion.

While these psycho-social applications of the idea of 'illusory love,' particularly the role of the special relationship, may be interesting, the Course does not say much about them. Of much greater concern to it is its interpersonal significance, which is given further comment regarding its primary purpose:

> "4 The real purpose of the special relationship, in strict accordance with the ego's goals, is to destroy reality and substitute illusion."(16,V,9,3-4)

Although most separated minds have quite forgotten the original moment of separation and the formation of the ego-idea, this passage brings back that highly consequential beginning of the special relationship. Its main intent is to enable the separated mind to remain focused on only fragments of Reality and thus destroy its full awareness of it. In the Course's view, Reality by its very nature cannot be destroyed. However, by eliminating awareness of it, in effect it is destroyed or non-existent for the mind that becomes absorbed in what becomes the most important illusions for it: special relationships.

How this operates on a more fundamental level is further explained:

> "1 In the special relationship it does not seem to be an acting out of vengeance that you seek. 2 And even when the hatred and the savagery break briefly through, the illusion of love is not profoundly shaken. 3 Yet the one thing the ego never allows to reach awareness is that the special relationship is the acting out of vengeance on yourself."(16,VII,5,1-3)

We have already seen that there are two opposing values that are central to the special relationship: the one that supports/aggrandizes the mind's ego-dominated condition, the other that leads to sacrifice, some sort of diminishment of the entity, even its destruction. Of course, such a mind sees self-aggrandizement as more important, but it recognizes that sacrifice can be useful for achieving that, particularly if it is done by another. These two opposing values are the basis of the two main forms of special relationships: the *special hate relationship* and the *special love relationship*. The second is consciously seen as more important, but the first has its usefulness. In a moment, we will consider these types of special relationship, but first it would be good to consider the point of statement 3: the full nature of the special relationship is suppressed from awareness, since if it were clearly exposed the mind would begin to question its validity and value. However, because that dark side is covered over by its idea of illusory love, the mind fails to recognize the actual nature of what is called 'vengeance.' That is, vengeance is the infliction of pain or harm on someone one believes has caused him pain or harm. What is not recognized within the special relationship is that this 'someone' is actually oneself. Although tied into its ego-limits, that little ego-dominated separated mind is actually the same mind as what it perceives as the 'other mind.' In the Course's terms, in Reality they are both the one mind of the Son. However, because it decided to accept and be caught in the belief in specialness and immersed in its commitment to special relationships, it can see its 'neighbor as itself' only very dimly or even not at all. This it maintains even when the intensity of hatred is extremely great, since it is deeply attached to the idea of the special relationship.

The Course makes only one specific allusion to the special hate relationship:
> "1 Be not afraid to look upon the special hate relationship, for freedom lies in looking at it. 2 It would be impossible not to know the meaning of love, except for this. 3 For the special love relationship, in which the meaning of love is hidden, is undertaken solely to offset the hate, but not to let it go. 4 Your salvation will rise clearly before your open eyes as you look on this. 5 You cannot limit hate. 6 The special love relationship will not offset it, but will merely drive it underground and out of sight. 7 It is essential to bring it into sight, and to make no attempt to hide it. 8 For it is the attempt to balance hate with love that makes love meaningless to you."(16,IV,2,1-8)

In our earlier discussion of hate, it was pointed out that there is the primary hate closely associated with primary guilt and primary fear. It is from these fundamental feelings that particular instances of hate, guilt and fear arise as their projections upon particular forms in the realm of perception unfolding in time. It was also pointed out that primary hate is essentially a mode of fear in response to the 'pressure' of Love's presence that tends to dissolve attachment to ego, a response due to thinking that Love is its enemy. This generates in it a deep loathing and an engagement in activity that will help it either destroy or keep away its perceived 'enemy.' Primary hatred is then directed to particular forms, which it regards with specific feelings of hatred. This seems to be at the center of what the Course calls the 'special hate relationship.' In the passage just cited, three important observations are made. The first is that it is vitally important for the mind to observe such relationships closely, which means to observe them all the way to their roots in primary hate. What often happens, however, is that attention is given only to the details of the intense emotion one has toward the particular form. In that way, the understanding of what it is doing and the real nature of Love is further hidden from it. The second point is that primary hate is what actually leads such a mind to make for itself special love relationships. This seems to be based on the need to alleviate itself of the conflictive and isolating perceptions that are intrinsic to the hate relationship. That is, what it thinks of as 'special love,' which is at the center of illusory love, is primarily a reaction to primary hate. Finally, as long as the mind remains unaware of these deeper-lying processes, it must generate for itself and be entangled in a constant inner conflict between its effort to maintain its hate and its effort to compensate for that with illusory love. On a deep level this involves a fundamental contradiction, but whose inconsistency is not clearly understood. What holds its attention is these conflicting feelings so that Love is quite meaningless to such a mind.

The Course's overall estimation of this state of trying to live so as to fulfill this contradiction is given:

> "1 Do not underestimate the intensity of the ego's drive for vengeance on the past. 2 It is completely savage and completely insane. 3 For the ego remembers everything you have done that has offended it, and seeks retribution of you. 4 The fantasies it brings to its chosen relationships in which to act out its hate are fantasies of your destruction. 5 For the ego holds the past against you, and in your escape from the past it sees itself deprived of the vengeance it believes you so justly merit. 6 Yet without your alliance in your own destruction, the ego could not hold you to the past. 7 In the special relationship you are allowing your destruction to be. 8 That this is insane is obvious. 9 But what is less obvious is that the present is useless to you while you pursue the ego's goal as its ally."(16,VII,3,1-9)

The 'past' referred to does not seem to be only what may have happened in an earlier period of the separated mind's particular lifetime (or even of previous lifetimes if one expands that past by way of accepting that the separated mind may have reincarnated many times in previous bodies, about which the Course explicitly takes no position), but rather to the original 'beginning' of time, which was when the separation started, including the formation of the ego-idea. This generated for that separated mind the very unhappy feelings of fear, guilt, and hate, which it later thinks are being produced by something from 'outside.' That 'outside' is simply the rest of Reality which it feels is pressing in on it, although what is actually generating these unhappy feelings is its own ego-dominated mind reacting to that 'pressure.' This is its resentment for Love. In response, it concludes that it must somehow attack Love, which is what it thinks of as 'vengeance.' Of course, it is completely out of touch with Reality and thus can only be deemed insane. In fact, since it was the mind that generated the ego (the 'you' in statement 3 that is actually responsible for all this misery), the ego-enclosed region of that mind thinks of that 'you' as responsible for the whole unhappy condition and all the experiences it has undergone while in that condition. Thus, it also directs its vengeance toward that 'you.' In that sense, the ego-enclosed mind can be said to 'hate you,' and at the same time tries to uphold you, since without you it could no longer exist. (This 'you' is the Son's mind that is only dimly in awareness, even quite fragmented, but ultimately responsible for all that occurs in the mind.) Thus, the contradiction further unfolds: on the one hand, the ego-mind wants to destroy you, and on the other hand, it wants to preserve you. The first is expressed outwardly in terms of special hate relationships, whose logical end is 'kill and be killed.' The second manifests in terms of special love relationships. Thus, the idea of illusory love contains a view of love that both seeks to destroy you (and, therewith, also the ego) and to maintain you (and thereby the ego). Accordingly, this idea of love intrinsically involves its very opposite, hate. To attempt to live out such an idea is clearly insane.

The net effect of this insane mode of thinking/living is that the special love relationship is intrinsically bound up with the special hate relationship, as is observed:

> "1 The special love relationship is an attempt to limit the destructive effects of hate by finding a haven in the storm of guilt. 2 It makes no attempt to rise above the storm, into the sunlight. 3 On the contrary, it emphasizes the guilt outside the haven by attempting to build barricades against it, and keep within them 4 The special love relationship is not perceived as a value in itself, but as a place of safety from which hatred is split off and kept apart. 5 The special love partner is acceptable only as long as he serves this purpose. 6 Hatred can enter, and indeed is welcome in some aspects of the relationship, but it is still held together by the illusion of love. 7 If the illusion goes, the relationship is broken or becomes unsatisfying on the grounds of disillusionment."(16,IV,3,1-7)

Here is pointed out how the idea of the special love relationship is generated. On the one hand, the primary hatred, as we have seen, involves an impulse to destroy not only what is unpleasant but also the very mind that brings about that unpleasantness. In that sense, it has a will to die. On the other hand, the ego itself can continue only as long as that mind continues to think it, and the primary impulse of the separated mind is to maintain itself in separation. In this there is a will to live.[45] Faced with these two opposing impulses, it balances them off primarily by constructing for itself the idea of the special love relationship. Of course, it could relieve itself of the whole insane absurdity by 'rising above the storm,' which would involve seeing clearly what is occurring beneath the surface, which is the movement of primary guilt. Although this is what it will eventually see, as long as it holds fast to the upheaval of this insanity, it will be tossed about within the sea of its own self-made fear, guilt, hate, and special hate and

---

[45] The 'will to live' seems to be very close to Freud's idea of 'eros' or 'libido,' as the 'will to die' is like his 'thanatos.' Indeed, there are 40 different passages in UM (deleted in FIP) that make explicit reference to Freud. One passage is:
> "The concept of changing the channel for libidinal expression is Freud's greatest contribution, except that he did not understand what 'channel' really means, as a thinker who had come to important insights close to those of the Course."(UM, T 1 B 40i)

love relationships. In terms of the more concrete perceptual manifestation of this, what become most important are the love relationships. These offer some relief at times from the great disturbance of the storm. But these are only temporary 'breathers.' The nature of the special love relationship, being based on the idea of 'special love' which involves both attraction, sacrifice, and hate, must sooner or later move into a period when that relationship turns into one of hate. When this happens, the relationship has a tendency to dissolve unless it can be pulled back more to the 'loving' mode.

But let us look further into the nature and effects of the special love relationship. A brief passage points out some of its most important features:

> "1 The special love relationship is the ego's most boasted "gift, and one which has the most appeal to those unwilling to relinquish guilt. 2 The 'dynamics' of the ego are clearest here, for counting on the attraction of this offering, the fantasies that center around it are often quite overt. 3 Here they are usually judged to be acceptable and even natural. 4 No one considers it bizarre to love and hate together, and even those who believe that hate is sin merely feel guilty, but do not correct it." (16,V,3,1-4)

On the surface, as indicated here, the special love relationship involves its being estimated by the ego-dominated mind as its most important way of relating, its 'most boasted gift.' That is, the mind involved in such relationships considers the choice of entering them as the highest or best contribution it can make to the world. If we reflect on how in fact the variety of such relationships, ranging from parent-child, marriage, friendship and even commitment to one's work, social causes or political movements (in most cases, these are special relationships) occupy a position of primary importance in most human lives, it should be clear that these are the most significant aspects of life for them. However, although we tend to think of these as 'noble' or 'virtuous,' a closer examination discloses what is actually their darker side. This is that, if they are what the Course calls 'special relationships,' they are founded on guilt, which is rooted in the ego-idea. This guilt-foundation seems to involve two aspects.

One aspect is that it leads to an impulse to compensate for the choice of separating one's awareness from the fullness and completeness of Love. What occurs, however, is that there is only a very limited movement toward that compensation, and this is primarily based on an imagined fantasy of some sort of 'union with the other.' One is reminded here of the story related by Plato in *The Symposium*, where the poet Aristophanes tells of how human beings were originally formed as hermaphrodites, but because they were so happy and arrogant the gods decided to split them apart, so that one part seeks for the other so as to come back to the originally happy state. That impulse is what the poet holds is the nature of love. Although the allegory is hardly to be taken in its literal meaning, the Course would agree that what is thought of as 'love' by the separated mind is moved by this impulse to join in special relationships.

However, the passage cited above also points out a second, even darker aspect of special relationships: primary guilt is intimately connected with primary hate, which is the ego-mind's repulsion from true completion in Love. That is, there is a basic ambivalence in the 'love' of the special love relationship, which most separated minds experience as the oscillation between moments of deep attraction and feelings of great harmony with the other and moments of great revulsion, hate, and anger, often expressing as attack, which occurs in almost all special relationships. This holds for those between parents and children, spouses, friends, organizational involvements, work, and politics. At times, the dearest friend can seem to be one's greatest enemy. Of course, if the fantasy of union remains, those 'problems' can be 'overcome.' However, they are never really solved as long as they remain only 'special' relationships. They generally lead to either another round in the love-hate cycle or the dissolution of that particular relationship and its replacement by another.

Here, it should be pointed out that this sobering estimate of special relationships is not the final word for the Course. Others, like Schopenhauer who, in his pessimism, dismissed all human relationships as necessarily caught in the round of fleeting joy and sorrow, or like Sartre, in his estimation that other people are hell, have stopped at this point. The Course quite clearly teaches that the problem can indeed be solved through the process of transforming the special relationship into a holy relationship. But, more about that later (in Ch. V).

The 'love'-hate nature of the special relationship is succinctly summarized in:

> "3 The demand for specialness, and the perception of the giving of specialness as an act of love, would make love hateful." (16,VI,9,3)

The problem here is simply that the trading of specialness ("I give specialness to you so you will give it to me"), being based on mutual supporting of ego-based separateness, cannot escape the hate that is intrinsic, though perhaps at times submerged, to such relationships. One is reminded of the line of a song once popular, "I give to you as you give to me: true love, true love." In the Course's view, as demonstrated in the film it was featured in, 'true love' would be more accurately called 'illusory love.'[46] Indeed, much of what is celebrated in poetry, novels, and drama seems to be only the latter.

Another important characteristic of the special love relationship is its exclusivity:

> "1 You cannot love parts of reality and understand what love means. 2 If you would love unlike to God, Who knows no special love, how can you understand it? 3 To believe that *special* relationships, with *special* love, can offer you salvation is the

---

[46] The film is 'High Society,' which gives an interesting portrayal of the nature of illusory love, although it is there called 'true love.'

belief that separation is salvation."(15,V,3,1-3)

The first point here is that the special love relationship, by its very nature, focuses on only a limited portion of even the perceived world. It is the projection of belief in specialness, which sets apart one thing as being more important or valuable than another. Indeed, when one recalls that the initial act that starts the separation involves a selection of an aspect or part of Reality on which to maintain awareness, it is clear that such relationships are simply a replay of that act within the already very limited realm of what is perceived – a selection within that selection. The second point is that by directing one's attention and energy to special relationships, the mind becomes absorbed in a mode that makes it impossible to be fully aware of Love's presence. And, with that lack of awareness it is impossible to understand It. A third point is that the mind that dedicates itself to the pursuit of special relationships thinks that it will find in them some modicum of the completeness that it gave up when it chose separation. It believes that its suffering will be at least somewhat alleviated. Furthermore, because it holds that only a partial alleviation is possible, it identifies such relationships as its 'salvation.' This situation seems to hold for both those who seek some type of 'spiritual' salvation, such as what they think of as heaven, and those who reject such an idea but embrace the importance of involvement in the material order, whether it be the crasser commitment to money and power or the 'nobler' and more humanistic efforts of artist, writer, scientist, philosopher, or social reformer or revolutionary, who seek to move toward what they think of as a 'heaven on earth.'

The centrality of the belief in specialness is further supported by the thought that this is the truly 'natural' way to exist:

> "3 To the ego, unless a relationship has special value it has no meaning, for it perceives all love as special. 4 Yet this cannot be natural, for it is unlike the relationship of God and His Son, and all relationships that are unlike this one *must* be unnatural."(16,VI,1,3-4)

While it is in one sense true that all separated minds within the world pursue their own ego agenda more or less consciously, that this is *natural* is challenged here. What we usually think of as 'natural' is what is exhibited in the order of what we call 'Nature,' or the order disclosed by perception. Since that order is filled with separated minds, when looked at by a separated mind that is strongly inclined to perceive them in terms of its own ego-mindedness, it concludes that every such mind is in one way or another pursuing special relationships. Such is the view in almost all the sciences. In psychology, self-interest is considered to be the 'obvious' principle of all behavior. This extends to all the human sciences, like sociology, economics and political science. But it is also much the same for biology and can even be extended to physics ("All physical entities tend toward states and relationships that are most favorable to their continuance.") While we need not press this last point, it is quite clear that where we think of any form of mentality as being present, we think that it is natural to seek special relationships. However, the Course firmly rejects this idea of 'natural.' What is really natural is what is founded in what truly or absolutely exists. Of course, that is God and all arising from His creative extension. Since the foundation of that existence is Love, and Love knows no specialness or special relationships, what we usually call 'natural' is actually unnatural.

One of the consequences of pursuing special relationships is its effect on oneself, the relationship, and the other entity that one relates to:

> "3 If you single out part of the Sonship for your love, you are imposing guilt on all your relationships and making them unreal."(13,X,11,3)

That is, because special love excludes certain minds from it and is an expression of primary guilt, when one enters into a special relationship this tends to reinforce the intensity of that guilt. There is in this a kind of feedback on one's own mind, a reaffirmation of its own feeling of guilt. But it also projects guilt out into the surrounding world of other minds. This might be thought of as a kind of '*guilt-field*,' somewhat analogous to a gravitational, electric, or magnetic field, which tends to activate its own quality wherever it penetrates. In this way, such relationships can also reinforce the guilt in other minds, particularly if they have embraced the value of special relationships.

Earlier we saw how the belief in specialness is closely related to the belief in sacrifice and briefly pointed to how that applies in the special love relationship. This is further explained:

> "1 In such insane relationships, the attraction of what you do not want seems to be much stronger than the attraction of what you do want. 2 For each one thinks that he has sacrificed something to the other, and hates him for it. 3 Yet this is what he thinks he wants. 4 He is not in love with the other at all. 5 He merely believes he is in love with sacrifice."(15,VII,7,1-5)

Recall that the belief that love involves sacrifice is a reflection of the separation itself, which involves giving up or denying oneself awareness of the whole of Reality so as to maintain focus on a part of it. Because the separated mind generally is only very subliminally aware of that 'Original Sacrifice,' it repeats the process within the special love relationship. Although the mind is most deeply drawn to the full awareness of the Whole, it is attracted to perception of the part, if only briefly within the one Moment of Eternity. This pattern is replayed in the special relationship, where that mind is ready to sacrifice or give up fully connecting with all it perceives so that it can have the fleeting gratification of what the special relationship offers. It mistakenly thinks that 'giving up' or sacrificing is the 'price' it must pay for having the temporary satisfaction that seems to come in relating with another who is also willing to do the same. Of course, that mind resents that the other expects this of him and hates the other for that. However, the core of the matter is that such a mind does not actually look for the well-being of the other as an end in itself, but only for its own gratification. The other is simply a means for that, not something that is valued in itself. In that way, what it thinks of as 'love' is primarily a matter of only what supports its own ego-embedded state, which has nothing to do with real love at all. In this sense, it values sacrifice more than the other, who is a means to obtain it. As statement 5 bluntly observes, it thinks that it is 'in love' with or intensely holding on to sacrifice.

In this way, the separated mind thinks that love and being in a loving relationship necessarily involves sacrifice. As is pointed out:

> "9 Your confusion of sacrifice and love is so profound that you cannot conceive of love without sacrifice. 9 And it is this that you must look upon; sacrifice is attack, not love. 10 If you would accept but this one idea, your fear of love would vanish."(15,X,5,8-10)

One of the most serious problems in this, made clear by closer observation, is that sacrifice is a form of attack. That is, as pointed out earlier, to act in terms of sacrifice is to act without real love. But to do that is to block the awareness of Love's presence, which is most deeply a matter of trying to destroy Truth, which can only be present in the awareness of Love. This attempt to destroy Truth is *the most fundamental sort of attack*. Indeed, when one considers the original separation from this perspective, it involves the 'Original Attack' on Truth/Love. As long as one does not realize this, he is caught within the framework of illusory love. However, as statement 10 points out, if one is able to observe it operating in one's relationships, the full absurdity of doing so becomes clear and the block to Love's presence falls away.

Yet another consequence of trying to live in terms of special relationships, related to this last point that such living can only further fixate the mind in its belief that all love involves sacrifice, is the idea that the mind forms about God's love. This is the point in:

> "1 How fearful, then, has God become to you, and how great a sacrifice do you believe His Love demands! 2 For total love would demand total sacrifice. 3 And so the ego seems to demand less of you than God, and of the two is judged as the lesser of two evils, one to be feared a little, perhaps, but the other to be destroyed. 4 For you see love as destructive, and your only question is who is to be destroyed, you or another?" (15,X,7,1-4)

Such a view is particularly prevalent in the Western religions, especially traditional Christianity, where it is believed that God expects those who truly love Him to sacrifice to and for Him. There it is thought that Jesus made the 'supreme sacrifice' by dying so as to compensate for the sins of all mankind, and even that God both required and made the sacrifice of offering His Son Jesus, based on the belief that sin could be undone only by way of such a sacrifice. This is consistent with the view that 'total love' involves 'total sacrifice.' In the Course's view, however, all of this is simply a projection by the ego-dominated mind. When one considers closely such an idea of God, it entails the same contradiction that is essential to the idea of the ego itself. That would make God the epitome of what is to be feared, hardly a being any sane person would want to spend a second with, much less an unending time. Nevertheless, when the matter is so nakedly exposed, the ego-dominated mind generally gives one of three responses. For the 'religiously' committed, the response is, "One must have faith in the old view." To the theologian who remains committed but a little more thorough in his thinking, the response is, "It's a mystery that we cannot understand, so hold to the dogma as defined by the authorities." Those not tied to either religious perspective are likely to say, "It's utter nonsense." The Course would respond: "Such an idea is simply a mistake, a projection of the ego-dominated mind, and replaceable by a much sounder idea of God as infinite extending Love, in which there is no idea of sacrifice whatsoever."

A final point is the Course's view on sexuality, which is often especially important in special relationships. As was pointed out in Ch. I, the "Shorthand Notes" not only contains a good amount of material in which sexuality is discussed, but also states that this is a topic that the miracle worker must understand. While we think that what the Course says about the body found in FIP gives the essentials of what the miracle worker must understand, it will be important to give a fuller explanation of the matter. However, since its view is in relationship to giving miracles, which will be discussed in the next chapter, we postpone that explanation until the end of that chapter.

Chapter IV. 'imperfect love'

The third idea of love that the Course speaks of is what we might think of as the beginning of Love's clear presence within separated minds. Because those minds are dominated by the notion of illusory love, the awareness of what love truly is comes greatly colored by that false idea. As is pointed out:

> "5 You project onto the ego the decision to separate, and this conflicts with the love you feel for the ego because you made it. 6 No love in this world is without this ambivalence, and since no ego has experienced love without ambivalence the concept is beyond its understanding. 7 Love will enter immediately into any mind that truly wants it, but it must want it truly."(4,III,4,2-7)

It should be clear that the Course considers the ego to be the primary obstacle to both being aware of and living according to real love. This is particularly strengthened by what is here called that mind's 'love for the ego.' Thus, since the condition for there being a 'world' of finite things and minds is the presence of ego, whatever a separated mind is aware of is seen through that mind's lenses. Hence, both any idea of genuine love that it may have and any feeling or behavior that a separated mind is involved in has this 'ambivalence.' That is, although it may have some awareness of Love's presence, that awareness is overlaid or 'darkened' by the meanings related to illusory love, a kind of mixture of that and genuine love. Yet, as statement 7 reminds us, the only thing that keeps Love from being fully present is the choice of the separated mind.

The term 'imperfect love' is used only once in the Course, in an interesting comment about the closest early followers of Jesus:

> "2 The Apostles often misunderstood it, and for the same reason that anyone misunderstands it. 3 Their own imperfect love made them vulnerable to projection, and out of their own fear they spoke of the 'wrath of God' as His retaliatory weapon. 4 Nor could they speak of the crucifixion entirely without anger, because their sense of guilt had made them angry."(6,I,14,2-4)

The 'it' refers to Jesus' crucifixion. The point here seems to be that, although the close disciples of Jesus had come to an initial awakening of Love's presence, their minds were still strongly dominated by ego. The residue of primary guilt continued to operate within their own minds, which was in turn projected onto God. Their conditioning in the Biblical belief of a 'wrathful God' would probably have played a great part in this. In the Course's view, a clearer understanding of Jesus' teaching and a fuller realization of Love's presence would have undone that deeply rooted idea. But, until that was more fully learned, their minds could only realize this very imperfect love.

A. Charity as imperfect love. The more frequently used term for imperfect love is 'charity.' This is described:

> "6 Charity is really a weaker reflection of a much more powerful love-encompassment that is far beyond any form of charity you can conceive of as yet."(2,V,9,6)

This 'weaker' form of love that is realizable by separated minds is only the first stage of what the Course thinks of as genuine love. However, it is important to grasp what is meant by the term, since it is the condition that leads to perfect love. Because 'charity' has several English meanings, before we consider what the Course says about it, it will be helpful to consider them. 'Charity' is defined as follows:

1 Christian love:
   a: the virtue or act of loving God with a love which transcends that for creatures and of loving others for the sake of God
   b: divine love for man: love in its perfection
   c: the act of loving or the disposition to love all men
2 a: the kindly and sympathetic disposition to aid the needy or suffering: liberality to the poor, to benevolent institutions or worthy causes
   b: an act or series of acts of aid to the needy
   c: whatever is given to the needy or suffering for their relief
   d: an organization or institution engaged in the free assistance of the poor, the suffering or the distressed
   e: public provision for the care or relief of the needy
   f: the recipient of charitable assistance
3 a: (1) love or affection for others; a disposition to good will, kindliness, and sympathy
      (2) an act or instance of good will or affection
   b: an eleemosynary gift: a gift of real or personal property to the use of the public or any portion of it as distinct from specific individuals for any beneficial or salutary purpose
   c: an institution founded by a gift and intended for the use of the public
4: a disposition to liberal lenient tolerant judgment and toward minimizing shortcomings and putting the best possible construction on the characteristics or actions of others
5: a refreshment dispensed between meals in a monastery

Among these definitions can be seen a wide range of meanings. Indeed, def. 1a-c seem very close to what the Course means by 'Love' and 'perfect love.' However, def. 2-4 are the meanings found more commonly in usual parlance, which can be merely a 'nice' version of what the Course thinks of as illusory love. When the Course uses the term 'charity,' it seems to be taken with a meaning closer to the more commonly understood one. As we will see, it makes an important distinction between true charity, which involves at least some element of genuine love, and 'false charity,' which lacks it.

To get a better idea of what the term means in the Course, we will look at several passages. The first (which includes the previously cited passage):

> "3 However, as long as time persists, healing is needed as a means of protection. 4 This is because healing rests on charity, and charity is a way of perceiving the perfection of another even if you cannot perceive it in yourself. 5 Most of the loftier concepts of which you are capable now are time-dependent. 6 Charity is really a weaker reflection of a much more powerful love-encompassment that is far beyond any form of charity you can conceive of as yet. 7 Charity is essential to right-mindedness in the limited sense in which it can now be attained."(2,V,9,3-7)

The first point (statements 6-7) is that charity is a kind of manifestation of Love most easily accessible to minds, such as ours, tied into the separated mode. (One might call it a sort of 'love for dummies!') That seems to be the point of calling it a 'weaker reflection' (statement 6) of what is far beyond what those minds can conceive in their current state. A second aspect of it is that it is the key to healing (statements 3-4). 'Healing' refers not simply to the correction of physical abnormalcies, but rather to the fundamental 'making whole' or returning to the complete Wholeness/Holiness of the perfect condition that separation is a deviation from. A third aspect of charity is that, in its healing function, it primarily involves perceiving the one in need of healing in a manner much closer to his/her perfect state. A fourth aspect is that in charity there is a shifting of the mind toward the mode of awareness called 'right-mindedness' (statement 7), which is primarily a matter of perceiving all things as the Holy Spirit perceives them. These last two points are actually an essential aspect of what the Course refers to as a 'miracle.' In that sense, charity can be thought of as the primary operating basis of doing miracles.

Statement 4 also acknowledges that for many separated minds it is more difficult to perceive perfection in oneself than in others. This appears to be due to the fact that one is much closer and more attached to one's own ego-illusion than the ego-illusions of others. Nevertheless, because there is such an urgency to find healing for oneself, there is a kind of 'charity-network' that actually arises within the field of separated minds. This seems to be the point in:

> "3 To love yourself is to heal yourself, and you cannot perceive part of you as sick and achieve your goal. 4 Brother, we heal together as we live together and love together. 5 Be not deceived in God's Son, for he is one with himself and one with his Father. 6 Love him who is beloved of his Father, and you will learn of the Father's Love for you."(11,VIII,11,3-6)

That is, although one may more easily offer healing to another, that very healing generates a return of healing to the one offering it. While this at first only operates on the weaker love-level of charity, it has the effect of spreading throughout the realm of separated minds within that level. What is also indicated here is that, in referring to the student as 'brother,' the Author (Jesus) is indicating that his own success and continuing sending of Love through the 'charity-network' is a very helpful means for coming to one's own healing. In this, not only does one open to receive the healing/miracle offered by Jesus, but this is facilitated by its being offered by others within that network. The process eventually leads to a shifting from the level of illusory love to the level of charity/imperfect love, then to the level of perfect love, and finally to its completion in the level of Love or the 'Kingdom of Heaven.' We will discuss this process later in Ch V.

That charity is a kind of diluted manifestation of Love arises from the fact that it is its most accessible mode in the world of space and time. However, it is an important vehicle for healing that mode:

> "1 Charity is a way of looking at another as if he had already gone far beyond his actual accomplishments in time. 2 Since his own thinking is faulty he cannot see the Atonement for himself, or he would have no need of charity. 3 The charity that is accorded him is both an acknowledgment that he needs help, and a recognition that he will accept it. 4 Both of these perceptions clearly imply their dependence on time, making it apparent that charity still lies within the limitations of this world. 5 I said before that only revelation transcends time. 6 The miracle, as an expression of charity, can only shorten it."
> (2,V,10,1-6)

If we recall that the overarching concern of the Course is the achievement of the Atonement or complete healing of all separated minds, we can see that charity, as the 'driver' of miracles, has an extremely important role in that, for several practical reasons. One is that it accommodates the faulty ideas that preoccupy the separated mind of both the giver and the receiver of charity that is operating in the miracle. Another is that it helps the receiver recognize more clearly that he is in need of healing and help, along with his acceptance of it. The last is that, although charity operates in time, its effect is to lead to the lesser or greater 'leap' in time toward its ending, as is the effect of the miracle it produces. This, of course, is toward the completion of the Atonement.

B. The nature of miracles. Here I will try to characterize what the Course means by 'miracle' through a fairly detailed discussion, since it is such a central concept to the teachings. First, we consider its two basic meanings in the Course; then, what is excluded in its more frequently used meaning; and, finally and most importantly, the positive content of that meaning.

1. Two different basic meanings of the term 'miracle.' Within the 50 'Principles of Miracles' listed in the first section of the Text, although an explicit distinction is not expressed, a careful reflection shows that 'miracle' has two dif-

ferent, but related, senses or meanings:
- a. **'miracle' in the strict or primary sense**, which refers to something that occurs within the world of perception and applies to a limited range of objects. This is the sense in which the term is used most often in the Course.
- b. **'miracle' in a more generalized or secondary sense**, which applies to the more fundamental and universal level of reality. Since it is used much less often, we may call it the 'secondary sense.'

Within the principles, the secondary sense is found in only two statements. The first of these is in Principle 3:

> "2 The real miracle is the love that inspires them [i.e., miracles in the primary sense]. 3 In this sense everything that comes from love is a miracle."(1,I,3, 2-3)

That is, although 'miracle' is used in most cases to refer to a change taking place within minds imbedded in the world of perception, because that change originates in Love, which is the primary expression of God, who is completely beyond the world of perception, it also refers to Love as a miracle in so far as it is the primary cause of all more limited miracles. However, since the Course also makes it clear (in 13,VIII,3,6, discussed below) that the primary function of miracles is to help one return to the original, perfect state called 'Heaven,' and that miracles do not occur in Heaven because there is no need for them, while miracles are said to be creations of Love, not all creations, which are expressions of Love, are miracles in the primary sense.

The second principle using the term in the secondary or generalized sense is Prin. 24:

> "2 You are a miracle, capable of creating in the likeness of your Creator."(1,I,24,2)

This focuses on the idea that you and every other mind are, as creatures, expressions of Love. But again, as in Prin. 3, since created minds do not really exist in the world of perception (but only seem to be there), they are not miracles in the strict sense. There are also several other places later in the Text where the term 'miracle' is used in this broader sense:

> "7 You have lost the knowledge that you yourself are a miracle of God."(3,V,6,7)

> "1 This is the miracle of creation, that it is one forever."
> (13,VII,5,1)

> "7 The miracle of creation has never ceased..."(14,XI,11,7)

Since the Course's major concern is teaching the student what miracles are in the primary or strict sense, as well as how to engage in them, the remainder of our discussion will be focused on clarifying that meaning.

2. What miracles are not. The first thing that the Course negates of miracles is expressed early in the initial list of Principles:

> "1 The use of miracles as spectacles to induce belief is a mis-

understanding of their purpose."(1,I,10,1)

This serves as a correction of a widespread belief in popular Christianity. The stories of Jesus' performing miracles as spectacular demonstrations of super-power over Nature are often understood as simply his means of impressing his belief system on others. In the Course's view, this would be another ego-tactic: 'his teachings are true because he can overcome opposing forces.' The error here is that it completely misses the point of what his miracles were about: healing errors in the mind, which has nothing to do with 'conquest' or 'submitting' to the more powerful 'Great Ego' that God is thought to be.

A second idea of 'miracle' that is rejected is that they are equivalent to 'magic.' The Course makes clear that magic is in certain ways the very opposite of miracles:

> "1 All material means that you accept as remedies for bodily ills are restatements of magic principles. 2 This is the first step in believing that the body makes its own illness. 3 It is a second misstep to attempt to heal it through non-creative agents. 4 It does not follow, however, that the use of such agents for corrective purposes is evil. 5 Sometimes the illness has a sufficiently strong hold over the mind to render a person temporarily inaccessible to the Atonement. 6 In this case it may be wise to utilize a compromise approach to mind and body, in which something from the outside is temporarily given healing belief. 7 This is because the last thing that can help the non-right-minded, or the sick, is an increase in fear. 8 They are already in a fear-weakened state. 9 If they are prematurely exposed to a miracle, they may be precipitated into panic. 10 This is likely to occur when upside-down perception has induced the belief that miracles are frightening."
> (2,IV,4,1-10)

The core idea of magic is based on the belief that a limited form (material object, the body, words, images, or even concepts) has in itself the capacity to produce changes in other limited forms and particularly in the mind. In the passage cited, the focus is the attribution of power to a material thing that enables it to change another material thing, e.g., the use of medications to change the body from illness to health. In the Course's view, the mind that has gone into separation generates for itself a structure in which one limited thing seems to change other limited things, whether those limited things are what it thinks of as bodies or minds. This is not to say that magic is not accompanied by such changes. Physical forms are clearly related in ways such that the presence of certain forms is followed by changes in other forms. This is the basis of what are called 'scientific laws.' The Course does not dispute that, within the world that we perceive, laws operate and that effects follow when they are applied. It only points out that the miracle operates on entirely different, or higher, principles. Thus, what it calls 'magic' includes a whole range of causal relationships, from the more generally accepted ones disclosed by science and applied in medicine and other technologies, to those that science has not yet fully understood such as in 'traditional' healing. The latter includes the use of rituals or other types of symbolic suggestion, or 'psychokinetic' phenomena (materialization, dematerialization, teleportation, levitation, etc.)

Accordingly, the belief in magic has many forms, from the more naive form of 'shamanism' or 'witchcraft' to the more refined form of 'advanced medicine' and 'engineering.' But, in the Course's view, they all rest on the belief in this core idea. Of course, if the mind actually does accept that belief, what it experiences can be very much in line with it. And, if the mind is very attached to that belief, the Course does not counsel that it be simply dismissed (statements 5-8), since that could precipitate that mind into even deeper attachment to the ego-error.

Thus, to think of a miracle as a kind of magical process is to reduce it to something within the field of that radically false belief. That is, although there may be changes within limited forms that occur in genuine miracles, and those changes may elicit wonder in minds witnessing them (the word 'miracle' is actually derived from the Latin 'miraculum,' whose meaning derives from the verb 'miror' = 'to wonder, be astonished'), there is a much deeper meaning for the Course than simply a remarkable feat that evokes an outer puzzlement and wonder. Much more significant is the challenge to the mind on a deeper level: a shift in the way of being aware of or thinking about things perceived. This shift in awareness is central to what the Course means by 'miracle.'

Nevertheless, the ego-dominated mind generally responds to 'wonder' experiences, including the witnessing of genuine miracles, by thinking of them in terms of magic.

> "1 One of the ways in which you can correct the magic-miracle confusion is to remember that you did not create yourself. 2 You are apt to forget this when you become egocentric, and this puts you in a position where a belief in magic is virtually inevitable."(2,VIII,1,1-2)

That is, since the mind is committed to ego-separation, it can respond to wonder in such a way as to suspend its ego-system only temporarily, but then immediately runs back to it, perhaps slightly modifying the system to accommodate the 'anomalous' or 'odd' experience (in science, that is usually the grounds for searching for a new 'law'). Although the ego-system may have been challenged, usually it is simply adjusted so as to continue in ego-domination, and absorbs the experience under the category of 'acceptable magic.' However, as this passage points out, it is quite possible that a more radical correction takes place, which involves abandoning the belief in self-creation (the same as belief in ego). When that occurs, the experience is seen as a genuine miracle. But more about that below.

The Course also makes clear that miracles do not occur on the highest level of existence:

"6 The miracle, without a function in Heaven, is needful here." (13,VIII,3,6)

That is, they do not occur within the Universe of Love as it really is. The reason that they cannot occur in Heaven (although they can be thought of as emanating from it) is that their function is to correct errors or illusions, and since there are no illusions in that state of perfect awareness, they have no purpose there. Only in the secondary, more general sense of 'miracle,' as any expression of Love, can they be said to exist in Heaven. Indeed this is described as the 'miracle of creation,' as expressed in:

"7 The miracle of creation has never ceased, having the holy stamp of immortality upon it."(14,XI,11,7)

Thus, miracles in the primary sense only occur within the world of perception. Since that world is itself fundamentally an illusion, they are thus also illusions, but useful ones, like the Course itself.

Also negated of miracles by the Course is what is stated in Prin. 2:

"1 Miracles as such do not matter. 2 The only thing that matters is their Source, which is far beyond evaluation."(1,I,1)

The important phrase here is 'as such.' That is, in the Course's view, miracles are not something of value in themselves. What gives them any significance is what they are *for*. This implies that miracles must be understood as a *means* to something else. We may well anticipate, in light of what has been said about Love as being the ultimate foundation of Reality that is the basis of any true meaning, that this Source is Love.

3. What miracles are. There can be many ways to address this, particularly since the Course uses the term very frequently (570 times in FIP and 671 in UM). Here we focus on what it says about their purpose and core characteristic. Although this and the other discussiond may seem overly detailed, it may help to make this idea much clearer and understandable.

a. The purpose of miracles. In the broadest terms, the purpose of miracles is to facilitate the primary concern of Love with respect to separated minds: the Atonement. Indeed, Prin. 25 states:

"1 Miracles are part of an interlocking chain of forgiveness which, when completed, is the Atonement. 2 Atonement works all the time and in all the dimensions of time."
(1,I,25,1-2)

We saw earlier that 'Atonement' is the Course's name for the process by which separated minds are completely restored to the perfect state. That overall process is described here as an 'interlocking chain of forgiveness.' Thus, the whole Atonement can be thought of as a network in which there is a comprehensive extension of forgiveness to every separated mind that transforms them so that the illusion of separateness is dissolved. This is somewhat analogous to a 'chain reaction' in nuclear fission, but much more complete in that in a fission 'bomb' only a very small percentage of the energy bound up in the particles of the atoms is released. Although that process produces tremendous energy by comparison to simpler chemical processes (as in TNT), if all the bound up energy of the fission materials were released, for example in the nuclear explosion detonated at Hiroshima in 1945, that explosion would have been about 80,000 times more powerful than it actually was (16 kilotons of TNT) or about 128,000 kilotons of TNT. This physical analogue may give us some sense of how much more intensely active is the state of complete Atonement, when every limited material particle in the physical universe is 'decompressed' so as to release all its bound up energy! Although to our minds this is likely to be thought of as intensely destructive (in a sense, it does involve the ending of the limited mode that is intrinsic to separation), it may also serve to give a glimpse of the almost unimaginable increase of activity that is central to the state of complete release.

This principle also indicates that miracles play a very important role in this process of release. How that is so will be made clearer below. At the same time, the principle points out in statement 2 that the process occurs at every moment and on every level of the realm of separation, even when miracles appear not to be operating. Since miracles are not always occurring in our perceptual awareness, they are only one component of the Atonement. Later, we will see that they take on an increasingly important role in minds that have progressed in their own development. Suffice it to say here, both the purpose and the nature of miracles should be understood in terms of what is here called 'forgiveness.'

b. Their core characteristic: forgiveness. Forgiveness can be thought of as the miracle's core characteristic. Like the word 'miracle,' this has a significantly different meaning from the one usually associated with it. This new meaning is actually indicated in Prin. 26:

> "1 Miracles represent freedom from fear. 2 'Atoning' means 'undoing.' 3 The undoing of fear is an essential part of the Atonement value of miracles."(1,I,26,1-3)

That is, the overall nature of Atonement is not so much a matter of 'doing' something as of 'undoing' or letting go the erroneous ideas and perceptions that the separated mind has constructed for itself. Indeed, the forgiveness central to miracles is best thought of as a particularly effective way of undoing. As we saw in our discussion of illusory love, the most serious error that ties the mind into separation is the acceptance of the ego-idea and the concomitant fear that is central to the primary guilt that is generated thereby. Hence, a major purpose of miracles is to forgive or undo that primary guilt/fear and the mind's attachment to ego, along with undoing the ego-idea itself.

How the forgiveness in miracles operates is further described:

> "2 The miracle forgives because it stands for what is past forgiveness and is true. 3 How foolish and insane it is to think a miracle is bound by laws that it came solely to undo! 4 The laws of sin have different witnesses with different strengths. 5 And they attest to different sufferings. 6 Yet to the One Who sends forth miracles to bless the world, a tiny stab of pain, a

little worldly pleasure, and the throes of death itself are but a single sound; a call for healing, and a plaintive cry for help within a world of misery. 7 It is their sameness that the miracle attests. 8 It is their sameness that it proves. 9 The laws that call them different are dissolved, and shown as powerless. 10 The purpose of a miracle is to accomplish this." (27,VI,6,1-10)

Thus, miracles should be thought of as having their origin outside the 'field' of the world of separation. In that sense, they are 'meta-physical' or 'beyond the physical.' We might think of them as incursions into the space-time framework from outside that framework. Within the physical realm, things seem to operate according to various laws, such as those described by modern science. In so far as the separated mind accepts the thought that it is embedded within that realm, its experience is very much in terms of those laws. However, the Course points out here that there is a higher level or realm that is in no way bound by those particular laws. A mind operating from that level would look upon the lower one as a strange aberration of what it sees is real, a realm ruled by what is here called the 'laws of sin.' To call them that does not evaluate them as 'bad' or as even having any reality other than as the rather nightmarish invention that is deemed real by minds that have chosen to delimit themselves to the mode of awareness that generates such an experience. They could also be called the 'laws of insanity.' From the perspective of the higher realm, all forms of suffering are simply an indication of the same thing: a call for help to get out of the 'mess' that the mind has made for itself. And what the miracle does is to inject into that mind (or group of minds) the undoing of the distortion in it that is producing its misery. From the perspective of the separated mind, at least to some degree, the 'laws of nature' are suspended or abolished. Of course, to minds intensely clinging to that mode of awareness, this constitutes a major challenge that is felt as a threat to its mode of existing. Thus, the rejection of the possibility of miracles by those deeply committed to the ego-mode is widespread and understandable. This is particularly to be expected from those thinkers, such as philosophers and scientists, whose whole personal and professional commitment is one of insisting on the assumption that the 'laws of nature,' based on what perception discloses, are what is most fundamentally true and to which they must submit their lives.

As to the meta-physical level from which miracles originate, we are told:

"1 Forgiveness is the home of miracles. 2 The eyes of Christ deliver them to all they look upon in mercy and in love. 3 Perception stands corrected in His sight, and what was meant to curse has come to bless. 4 Each lily of forgiveness offers all the world the silent miracle of love."(W,pII,13,3,1-4)

That is, the 'home' of miracles rests in the state of complete forgiveness in the Christ Mind, the perceiving level of which is the Holy Spirit. Here we should recall that this Mind has not entered into the separated stated, although it has awareness that there are levels within 'regions' of the Son's mind that have. This perception of the realm of separation cuts right through it, completely letting it go and seeing it for what it is. Because it has no danger of slipping into the dream of separation, it can act as the origin of the undoing of the illusory awareness that may be present in any particular separated mind. Later, we will discuss how this operates from the perspective of a mind within the world of perception (the process of giving miracles).

One final passage related to the forgiving characteristic of miracles is described in Prin. 21:

> "1 Miracles are natural signs of forgiveness. 2 Through miracles you accept God's forgiveness by extending it to others."
> (1,I,21,1-2)

Two comments seem needed. The first relates to statement 1. What are called 'miracles' are perceivable from two perspectives. One is the higher level of the fully aware state of the Christ Mind/Holy Spirit, the other is the lower level of the separated mind. From the higher level, it does not seem fully accurate to call them 'signs of forgiveness,' since they are by their very nature acts of forgiveness or undoing of illusions. However, from the perspective of minds witnessing miracles, that is, minds in the separated state, they are indeed indications or signs that forgiveness has occurred. The second point relates to the idea in Prin. 25 concerning the 'chain of forgiveness.' That is, the overall atoning process is greatly facilitated when a miracle is received or accepted by any separated mind, since that serves to undo a significant portion of its illusions. However, what is even more important is that such a mind is thus enabled to offer miracles to others. This furthers the 'chain reaction.' Thus, the speed of the Atonement is greatly accelerated by this extension of miracles to others. This seems to be a part of what is referred to as the 'celestial speedup,' mentioned in the Original Texts and discussed later.

Related to the naturalness of miracles is the following passage:

> "4 The miracle is always there. 5 Its presence is not caused by your vision; its absence is not the result of your failure to see. 6 It is only your awareness of miracles that is affected."
> (W,91,1,4-6)

That is, although the perception of miracles may occur for separated minds only at particular times and circumstances, there is no time or place where they are not present. This is due to the fact that Love is always present, and its manifestation within the world of perception is what the Course means by 'miracle.' Here one may think of a kind of 'universal miracle' that underlies all of space and time, awaiting the opening of particular separated minds to bring them into their awareness. Hence, the miracle pervades all of nature on a deep level, and thus they are natural in the most fundamental sense.

This overall purpose of Atonement in general, and particularly of miracles, is further described:

> "1 A major step in the Atonement plan is to undo error at all levels. 2 Sickness or 'not-right-mindedness' is the result of

level confusion, because it always entails the belief that what is amiss on one level can adversely affect another. 3 We have referred to miracles as the means of correcting level confusion, for all mistakes must be corrected at the level on which they occur."(2,IV,2,1-3)

Here is emphasized the release of the separated mind from every sort of error. This can be on the level of external perception, such as perception of illness in either oneself or another, or on the deeper level here called 'not-right-mindedness.' In the latter, the mind's primary error lies in its ego-belief, which we saw further generates the perceptual structure it thinks of as its 'body,' and which is given further limitations such as the perceptual form called 'illness' (or in the extreme, 'death.') With that, it accepts the idea that the physical level can influence the mental, which is actually a matter of level-confusion. Indeed, the 'body' and the whole physical level are structures originally constructed by the mind itself, then thought to have arisen independently, even as what has generated the mind itself. The role of the miracle is to penetrate to the inner core of this very serious error and bring about a correct understanding of what has actually happened. It should also be pointed out that a particular miracle may not immediately undo *all* errors. As we shall see, the extent of its undoing errors is in proportion to the degree that it is accepted.

Prin. 33 further illuminates this point:

"1 Miracles honor you because you are lovable. 2 They dispel illusions about yourself and perceive the light in you. 3 They thus atone for your errors by freeing you from your nightmares. 4 By releasing your mind from the imprisonment of your illusions, they restore your sanity."(1,I,33)

Although the separated mind has implicated itself in its own self-constructed errors, from the perspective of the higher level it is really no less perfect and worthy of Love. What is positively present in that mind is the reality of the 'light' of Love's presence, although it is covered over or placed beyond its awareness by the awareness of those errors. The miracle allows those errors and their nightmarish consequences to be set aside or undone, at least to some extent. In so far as this occurs, the mind is restored to its original, perfect state.

This last point is the substance of Prin. 34, which states:

"1 Miracles restore the mind to its fullness. 2 By atoning for lack they establish perfect protection. 3 The spirit's strength leaves no room for intrusions."(1,I,34,1-3)

This restoration to 'fullness' is what the previous principle called 'sanity.' Here, we should recall that the primary meaning of 'sanity' is 'healthy,' which is the same as 'wholeness.' In the Course's view, true wholeness consists in the state of full awareness of Love, whose central characteristic we saw is complete 'oneness.' However, we should keep in mind that the complete return to fullness/sanity/health/wholeness does not necessarily happen as the immediate result of any particular miracle. Although this is possible, what usually happens is that illusions or blocks are only partially removed. As was pointed out, this is due not to some deficiency in the miracle, but to the resistance to its acceptance. Thus, the completion of the Atonement usually involves a series of many occasions of being offered the restorative help of the miracle.

The undoing/forgiving move of miracles generally takes place within the context of what we may think of as more concrete experiences. Those experiences are dominated by the separated mind's most salient mode of awareness, perception. Four other principles of miracles offer further insights into this. The first we consider is Prin. 49:

> "1 The miracle makes no distinction among degrees of misperception. 2 It is a device for perception correction, effective quite apart from either the degree or the direction of the error. 3 This is its true indiscriminateness."(1,I,49,1-3)

As we saw earlier, what makes perceptions erroneous or illusory is not so much the fact they are perceptions, but that they can be false. The point here is that what the separated mind perceives is a mix of true and false perceptions. That is, there is something in them that accurately reflects some aspect or aspects of Reality, but added to this is a form or content that does not pertain to that aspect or aspects. The latter is superimposed upon the true content, and the experience is one of false perception. The passage here makes clear a very important point: any addition of false content renders the perception erroneous. We may think of some perceptions as more erroneous than others. For example, we consider an hallucination as a much more serious illusion than an optical illusion, like a mirage; and an optical illusion as more serious than a misinterpretation of what we think of as an accurate perception, such as thinking that someone who only looks like an acquaintance is actually that acquaintance, or that such a 'misinterpretation' is more serious than a false perception of danger, such as the experience when one encounters a rattlesnake along the path while on a hike. However, such a 'hierarchy' of reliableness of perceptions, which estimates some perceptions as 'better' or 'more true' than others, in the Course's view in itself involves a serious error. That is, it dismisses the fact that all of these perceptions involve the projection of material onto the true content of perception. Indeed, what is overlooked is that almost all of the perceptions made by separated minds have this problem, and thus are misperceptions. What the miracle does, when it is fully accepted, is to dismiss every type of false perception as involving some sort of serious and misery-causing consequence. Indeed, such misperceptions fill our experiences of what is called 'illusory love' and run throughout our awareness of what we think of as 'our world.' The miracle moves toward undoing that whole gamut of falsehood so that the mind begins to perceive things 'as they really are.'

Thus, the field in which miracles occur is the realm of perception. Based on the fundamental principle that most perception involves some type of error based on the projection of false content, it begins a process of correction. Prin. 23 describes this as one of 'rearranging perception:'

> "1 Miracles rearrange perception and place all levels in true perspective. 2 This is healing because sickness comes from confusing the levels."(1,I,23,1-2)

A major problem in the separated mind's perception is that it is unaware of how it is confusing false content with true content. Its primary error is one of mixing content that comes from perception of one aspect or multiple aspects of Reality with content from another aspect or aspects, and not discriminating one from the other. Thus, in order to remedy that confusion, the miracle serves to separate the one from the other. For example, one may have the perception of a snake along the path one happens to be walking. But what is actually happening is that one's mind is projecting onto the form that is simply a piece of vine in the shadows the memory image of a snake that is present in imagination. However, once one becomes aware of this projecting process, that fear is dispelled. In a more 'miraculous' situation, one has a perception of his body as having the condition of some illness, such as tuberculosis. This includes aches in the lungs, perhaps fever and lethargy, and even lesions in the lung tissue. When one is offered a miracle, the miracle-giver shifts to a perception of seeing that person as completely whole in body and mind. This sets up a movement toward a shift in that person's status, first in mind and then in body, provided that the person accepts the miracle. This can be followed by a restoration to health, at least to some extent.

What occurs in this rearranging process is further described in Prin. 50:

> "1 The miracle compares what you have made with creation, accepting what is in accord with it as true, and rejecting what is out of accord as false."(1,I,50,1)

Here we see the core of the process of the miracle. That is, what happens is that the one giving the miracle does two things. First, he/she perceives the two components in the mind of the one needing the miracle: the conflictive structure that his/her mind has produced. Second, he/she distinguishes between the false or distorting aspects that this mind has imposed upon itself and the true perception of what he/she actually is as a being completely harmonious and filled with 'light.' Third, the miracle-giver sets aside the false aspects and lets the true aspects come forth into prominence and replace those false aspects. This is what brings about the healing of the one receiving the miracle.

What results is described in Prin. 37:

> "1 A miracle is a correction introduced into false thinking by me. 2 It acts as a catalyst, breaking up erroneous perception and reorganizing it properly. 3 This places you under the Atonement principle, where perception is healed. 4 Until this has occurred, knowledge of the Divine Order is impossible." (1,I,37,1-4)

This is perhaps the most succinct description of the miracle: a major, even culminating step occurring within a separated mind's process of Atonement, involving the correction of its false thinking by undoing its misperception and replacing it with true perception, so as to enable it to be restored to knowledge. From this, we may see that the 'wondrous' aspects are simply a matter of the way separated minds observing the miracle from the outside respond to it. Its central characteristic is this profound change in perception that leads to the full awareness of one's own perfection, in which one was created and in reality always is.

This same idea is expressed in a somewhat different manner in Prin. 41:

> "1 Wholeness is the perceptual content of miracles. 2 They thus correct, or atone for, the faulty perception of lack."
> (1,I,41,1-2)

What is emphasized here is that, through the miracle, the mind is returned to its original wholeness. Any unwholeness/unhealthiness/illness/insanity that may have been perceived by the separated mind is understood as due only to distorted perception. Once that is recognized, the faulty condition is completely set aside for it.

4. The process of giving a miracle. Now we may try to understand what, as experienced by a separated mind, is involved in the process of 'doing' a miracle. This is described in both general terms and in terms of what we can think of as involving several steps.

a. General nature of the process. There are two major overall characteristics of this described by the Course.

i. The miracle as an exchange. More generally, doing or working a miracle is described in Prin. 9 as an *exchange*:

> "1 Miracles are a kind of exchange. 2 Like all expressions of love, which are always miraculous in the true sense, the exchange reverses the physical laws. 3 They bring more love both to the giver *and* the receiver."(1,I,9,1-3)

Here is made clear that miracles occur primarily between two (or more) minds within the realm of separation, the world of perception. These I will refer to as the miracle-giver (abbreviated as MG) and the miracle-receiver (MR). The notion of 'exchange' involves the idea of something being transferred from one to another. The passage makes clear what it is that is transferred: love. Or perhaps it would be better to speak of this as Love, since Love is at the foundation of all forms of genuine love. Consistent with what was pointed out above, that exchange undoes or 'reverses' physical laws, the 'laws' to which the separated mind has submitted itself by its choice to enter into the ego-dominated mode. This should not be simplistically thought of as a changing of the arithmetic signs of those laws to their opposites, such as making Newton's law of force read something like $F = -ma$ (a 'reverse' of the Law of Force, which is $F = ma$). The 'reversal' referred to in Prin. 9 is much more radical. It involves completely moving outside the space-time structure that is characteristic of limited bodies or minds. This 'reversed' law is simply what was earlier called the 'Law of Love.' That is, of course, the law of creative extension, which is summed up in statement 3, that by its being given and received it increases what is given and received in both giver and receiver.

ii. The miracle as a service. Related to this idea of exchange is what is described in Prin. 18:

> "1 A miracle is a service. 2 It is the maximal service you can render to another. 3 It is a way of loving your neighbor as yourself. 4 You recognize your own and your neighbor's worth simultaneously."(1,I,18,1-4)

It should be obvious that giving a miracle is a service to the MR in that it moves to help. Since it serves to help the MR move toward the *complete* undoing of the separated state and returning it to the complete happiness or joy with which it was created, it is correctly described as 'maximal' or the greatest possible service one could do for another. But on a deeper level, since the MR is really the same as the MG, this service is done not only for the MR but also for the MG itself. As statement 4 indicates, in giving a miracle the MG recognizes not only the MR's worth or value, but also his/her own. That is, for the MG it serves as an occasion for dropping away his/her own illusions of perception. This will be made clearer when we discuss the effects of miracles.

b. The steps involved in the miracle. Although the Course does not analyze the process of giving miracles into numbered steps, its descriptions of what is involved can be seen to have eight distinct 'moves' or 'steps,' at least from the perspective of the separated mind.

Step i. MG perceives a deficiency or lack in another. It is a common experience of any separated mind to perceive deficiencies or problems as present in others, as well as in oneself. This can take the form of a simple physical lack, such as an illness (lack of health), a lack of sufficient material goods thought necessary for one's body, or as a more 'mental' lack, such as the presence of an emotional upset from loneliness or rejection or frustration or even the more intellectual sort of lack in the form of ignorance or an active desire to seek to understand something about the world. That is, there is a whole range of 'lacks' that we can become aware of in another. It is particularly those lacks that are thought of as causing another person to suffer that are the primary initial focus for the onset of giving a miracle. This is the point in Prin. 8:

> "1 Miracles are healing because they supply a lack; they are performed by those who temporarily have more for those who temporarily have less."(1,I,8,1)

Thus, at this first step of giving a miracle the MG perceives that there is a perception of lack in the mind of the MR. That perception of lack can also be in the MG's mind if he has only developed to imperfect love; that is, he may perceive in the MR something that he also thinks of as a lack, problem, or deficiency that he thinks of at first as 'really there.' For the MG who has come to perfect love, as we will see later, there is no perception of actual lack in the MR, although he perceives that the MR perceives some lack in himself.

This may be represented as in Fig. 18. That is, the MG perceives in the MR that the MR thinks that something is lacking (indicated by the shaded segment). Where the MG has only come to imperfect love, the MG may also think that something is lacking in the MR. The lack is what the MR thinks of as some sort of physical, emotional, or mental problem.

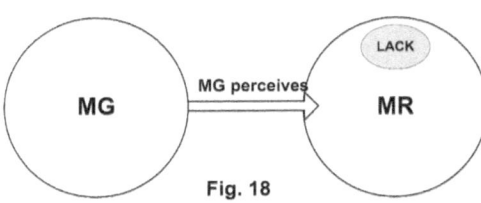

Step ii. Initial response of MG to MR. The response of a separated mind to the perception of a problem in another is described:

> "7 Every response you make is determined by what you think you are, and what you want to be *is* what you think you are."(7,II,2,7)

That is, how one responds is in terms of the image that one has of oneself. This includes a variety of possible responses, according to the development of the particular separated mind. Thus, we recognize even in ourselves that our responses to the perception of lack/suffering in another can be in several principal ways: with a feeling of indifference, revulsion, pity or compassion, or even a mixture of these. The parable of the 'Good Samaritan' points to such different responses. In a separated mind that has matured to imperfect love, which would generally be the situation of most serious students of the Course, there can be such a mixed response. But, when it has developed sufficiently to the point that leads to the giving of a miracle, it is the feeling of compassion and the impulse to help, as indicated in Fig. 19.

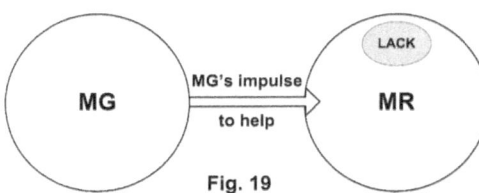

Step iii. MG's consideration of kind of help for MR. This initial response within any mind moved by compassion is followed by that mind's considering two major ways of offering help. The one is an earnest effort to offer some *limited* sort of relief: food, medical assistance, money, or a kind word; or perhaps to start a social campaign to alleviate the underlying conditions; etc. These are more 'ordinary' ways of acting from compassion. But, in the Course's view, the most effective and appropriate response is to move toward offering the MR a miracle.

This decision can only occur in a mind already sufficiently open to the influence of the Holy Spirit, as is pointed out in:

> "4 The Holy Spirit is the motivation for miracle-mindedness; the decision to heal the separation by letting it go."(5,II,1,4)

That is, on some level of the MG's awareness, there is a disposition to follow the deeper or higher impulse that is generally inaccessible to those strongly dominated by the ego. Although the Holy Spirit, by virtue of the function assigned to

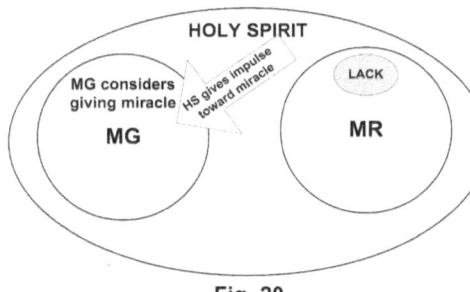

Fig. 20

Him, offers this impulse to every separated mind, those not yet developed so as to be able to receive those impulses will not be able to respond to them. How they have come to that stage of development seems to be by their either being given a miracle by someone else, or by serious dedication and hard work. In either case, this step is represented by Fig. 20, which depicts the MG's coming to the insight that giving a miracle is the preferable way of responding to the MR.

Step iv. MG's decision to listen to the Holy Spirit. In this fourth step, the MG recognizes that the higher mode of resolving the MR's problem must be done in conjunction with that higher awareness, which is that of the Holy Spirit. For the MG in imperfect love, he needs to choose to connect with the Holy Spirit so as to step beyond his ego-limits. Because he is also open to the higher possibility, he can choose to move toward that. Of course, in the MG that has realized perfect love, there is no such alternative; he immediately moves toward, or more accurately, is connected with that higher possibility. This step is represented in Fig. 21, where the MG opens to connecting with the Voice or Holy Spirit and asking for help.

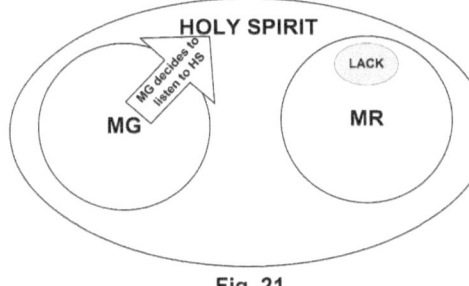

Fig. 21

Also, for the MG not yet matured to perfect love, there are two sub-steps within his connecting with the Holy Spirit. The first is one of simply choosing to connect with the Holy Spirit; the second is to open one's mind to listen to His Voice. In fact, this is a matter of the MG's recognizing that there are two levels within his own mind. This is indicated:

> "1 There is another vision and another Voice in which your freedom lies, awaiting but your choice. 2 And if you place your faith in Them, you will perceive another self in you. 3 This other self sees miracles as natural. 4 They are as simple and as natural to it as breathing to the body. 5 They are the obvious response to calls for help, the only one it makes."(21,V,3)

This may be thought of as shifting one's attention toward another dimension or realm beyond the perceptual. Since that higher or deeper level is always present, although one may not be consciously aware of it due to a more or less strong ego-awareness, all that is necessary is for the MG to choose to open and connect with it. In the Course's view, this higher level is the realm of Reality/God/Love; or thought of as a deeper level it is the same as what it calls the Self/Christ Mind/Holy Spirit. The term 'Voice' is used here for good reason. By that is meant a source of communication that originates within that higher level. How it communicates can involve a particular perceptual form, such as words, but also any other perceptual form (nonverbal auditory, visual, tactual, even smell or taste, a type of body sensation that we associate with an emotion, or simply an intuitive insight). Indeed, it may be useful for the MG to hold within his mind the idea, or even an image, of Jesus as a symbolic form that enables him more easily to connect with the Voice.[47] Of course, since Jesus was a human being whose mind became fully congruent with the Holy Spirit's Mind (and the Christ Mind), when one listens to the voice one thinks of as that of Jesus, he is listening to the Voice of the Holy Spirit. However, there does not have to be such a perceptual image in order for the MG to open to the Voice/Holy Spirit. Rather, there only needs to be a receptiveness to an 'energy' or meaning that originates beyond all perceptual forms, that is radically different from what is contained in ordinary associated meanings. We need not go into the details of what that difference is, since the Course does not elaborate on it. However, what is important here is that the MG makes the choice to open to connect with and listen to the 'Voice.'

The Voice of the Holy Spirit is further described:

> "1 The Voice of the Holy Spirit does not command, because It is incapable of arrogance. 2 It does not demand, because It does not seek control. 3 It does not overcome, because It does not attack. 4 It merely reminds. 5 It is compelling only because of what It reminds you *of*. 6 It brings to your mind the other way, remaining quiet even in the midst of the turmoil you may make. 7 The Voice for God is always quiet, because It speaks of peace."(5,II,7,1-7)

One of the important lessons that the MG needs to learn is how to discriminate between this 'Voice' and the many other voices that speak to him. All those other voices originate in the ego, either within oneself or in others. The passage here offers some indication of the way to make that discrimination: its being accompanied by a profound feeling of peace. But the central move of step iv is that one *makes the choice* to open to and listen to that Voice.

This will be recognized as what is sometimes thought of as prayer. Indeed, this is made clear in Prin. 11:

> "1 Prayer is the medium of miracles. 2 It is a means of communication of the created with the Creator. 3 Through prayer love is received, and through miracles love is expressed." (1,I,11,1-3)

---

[47] The role of Jesus in miracles is further describe in Step v. It will be discussed more fully in *The Holy Spirit and Jesus in A Course in Miracles*.

Here we see that the choice to listen to the Voice can be said to initiate the miracle within the MG's mind. However, one should be clear that the true initiation rests in the original communication of Love to that mind prior to the separation and which never ceases in Its concern to communicate with all separated minds. What the MG's choice does is to make his mind open to return to receiving that communication, at least to some extent.

Step v. MG listens to the Voice and receives guidance. In order to move toward the giving of a miracle, there must come into the MG's mind a recognition about the very perception of lack itself. This is indicated in Prin. 41, cited earlier, and repeated here:

> "1 Wholeness is the perceptual content of miracles. 2 They thus correct, or atone for, the faulty perception of lack."
> (1,I,41,1-2)

This points to a very important aspect of step i. That is, when one perceives a lack or deficiency in anyone, or even that another is perceiving such a lack in himself, there is present in that a false perception, based on two fundamental mistakes. The first is that one may identify the content of a perception as the reality of what the particular person actually is. While that content by its very nature as a perception involves limits, the further thought that this is the way someone actually is, is not warranted. From the higher perspective it is false. This is clearly stated in the following:

> "4 There is no emptiness in you. 5 Because of your likeness to your Creator you are creative. 6 No child of God can lose this ability because it is inherent in what he is, but he can use it inappropriately by projecting. 7 The inappropriate use of extension, or projection, occurs when you believe that some emptiness or lack exists in you, and that you can fill it with your own ideas instead of truth."(2,I,1,4-7)

and:

> "1 God asks for nothing, and His Son, like Him, need ask for nothing. 2 For there is no lack in him."(28,VII,1,1-2)

Thus, from the Course's perspective, any perception of lack or deficiency involves an error. Since we are here considering primarily the giving of a miracle by someone only matured to imperfect love, we should note that such an MG is also involved in some error and thus in need of having it corrected or healed. In that case, a perception of lack is in both the potential MG and the MR. For an MG that has come to perfect love, there is needed only the correction of the perception in the MR's mind. However, in both cases, this perception of some sort of awareness of lack in the MR is the first step in the process of giving a miracle.

Accordingly, if the MG has only developed to imperfect love, his mind needs to undergo a transformation. This is what the Holy Spirit brings about. The basis of that transformation lies in the fact that the Holy Spirit perceives the situation in the MR in a very different way, that is, as completely whole or without any lack. By opening to receive the communication from the Holy Spirit, the MG may be thought of as extending his attention and awareness into another dimension or realm beyond the ordinary perceptual. What enters into his mind is the way the Holy Spirit regards the MR.

This is roughly represented by Fig. 22. Although this may involve perceptual forms like those of ordinary communication, such as the hearing of words, the communication seems better thought of as an 'energy' or 'light', which is a meaning quite beyond such symbols. We need not go into the details of what that difference is, since the Course does not elaborate on it. However, what is important here is that the MG makes the choice to open to connect with and to listen to the 'Voice.'

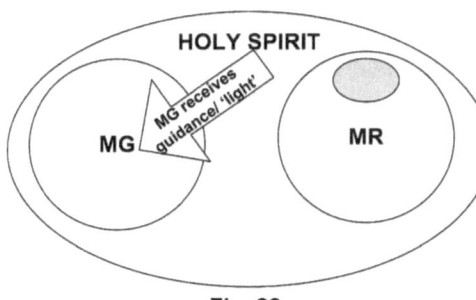

Fig. 22

However, an important point is made in Prin. 5 regarding the decision whether and to whom one will give the miracle:

> "1 Miracles are habits, and should be involuntary. 2 They should not be under conscious control. 3 Consciously selected miracles can be misguided."(1,I,5,1-3)

At first, one is confronted by what seems to be an inconsistency. That is, on the one hand there must be a *decision* to give a miracle. Deciding is of its nature voluntary and occurs within the field of consciousness. On the other, this principle tells us that the giving of a miracle should be involuntary and not under conscious control. This can be resolved by looking more closely at the process involved in the decision that is basic to giving a miracle.

First, the perception of the lack or deficiency within another person, as in the case of the MG who has only come to imperfect love, must be within the MG's field of consciousness. That is also accompanied by the response of compassion, which is the basis of the inclination to offer a miracle. But there remains the question: *is it appropriate to give a miracle to this person at this time?* The MG could make the choice solely out of his/her feeling of compassion. However, for the MG who has not yet come to full maturity, that feeling and the overall perception occur within a context that is still dominated by the ego or at least influenced by it. Indeed, this is characteristic of what such a mind thinks of as 'voluntary.' That is, if such a prospective MG consciously controlled that decision, there would be some element of ego-limitation entering into the process. The problem with this is that it would interfere with the very giving of the miracle as a process for healing the ego-block that is the basis of the perceived lack. Hence, the caution: consciously selected miracles can be misguided.

The reason for this is stated quite simply in the following:

> "4 The miracle worker must have genuine respect for true

cause and effect as a necessary condition for the miracle to occur."(2,VII,2,4)

That is, by his own choice the MR has gotten into the state in which he perceives a lack. This is the actual 'cause' of his problem. But the MG, just as God, must respect that choice. He cannot impose a miracle on a mind that still clings to its erroneous choice. However, where the MR's mind has already come to some degree of recognition of the folly of that choice, the MG can offer further help to enable it to open more fully to the undoing of its erroneous choice. Such is the condition that must be respected by the would-be MG. Thus, the MG must first ask whether it is appropriate to give a miracle to this person *now*.

What, then, is the way that the decision to give a miracle to whom can be 'involuntary?' This is explained in the following:

"1 I am the only one who can perform miracles indiscriminately, because I am the Atonement. 2 You have a role in the Atonement which I will dictate to you. 3 Ask me which miracles you should perform. 4 This spares you needless effort, because you will be acting under direct communication. 5 The impersonal nature of the miracle is an essential ingredient, because it enables me to direct its application, and under my guidance miracles lead to the highly personal experience of revelation."(1,III,4,1-5)

The 'I' is the Author, presumably the fully awakened mind that was known as Jesus and has realized the Christ Mind, or simply the Christ Mind/Holy Spirit. In considering this important passage, one must be careful not to interpret it as claiming that Jesus is or was the only person to have come to that realization. Indeed, one can read this passage as being an arrogant claim, instead of its deeply compassionate concern of helping the student be relieved of what could easily be perceived as an awesome, even fearful responsibility. That is, the 'only one who can perform miracles indiscriminately' or without concern for when or to whom to give them is the Christ Mind, in so far as He is able to perceive, i.e., the Holy Spirit. Nor should this be understood as claiming that only this particular name should be associated with that Mind. It could also be called the 'Buddha Mind' or any other name that refers to the foundational Mind, Entity, or Spirit that is fully aware of Love without any impediment. Only such a fully perceiving mind can be completely aware of the readiness of the MR to be open to being given a miracle and thus fully respectful of it. That Mind is precisely the same as what the Course calls the 'Holy Spirit' or one that is fully congruent with the His Mind.

The practical guideline offered in this passage is that any decision to offer a miracle should be based, not on one's 'personal' inclination, but on the decision of that perfect Mind. How that is ascertained is by the simple intention to ask and to listen to what it is told by the Holy Spirit. This moves that decision to what is called an 'impersonal' basis; that is, not rooted in one's own personal perception (although working *through* that). Indeed, by moving to this impersonal, or perhaps better, 'super-personal' or 'transpersonal' level, there is made possible one of the fullest interpersonal exchanges that can occur between separated minds. This guidance by the Voice for God is thus essential in the giving of a miracle.

We might also observe that the procedure of asking and listening to the 'Voice' regarding the decision of giving miracles seems to be very close to the approach taken by Socrates in making decisions. Plato tells us that his most admired teacher described how, whenever he considered a decision, he consulted what he called his 'daimon' or 'guiding spirit,' which manifested as a 'voice' within his mind. Although Socrates said that this daimon did not tell him what he should do, but only whether he should *not* do something he was considering, it is quite probable that this was primarily the particular mode that he received guidance from what the Course thinks of as the Holy Spirit. That it only communicated by way of a negative response may be an indication that Socrates had not yet fully learned the way of miracles. Although he had progressed along the path to awakening, from the Course's perspective, he seems to have had need of yet more undoing of the hold of ego before he would be able to hear the full communication of the Voice (or what in Plato's terms would be called 'nous,' which may be translated as 'intelligence' or 'mind.')

Step vi. MG opens to let perception be transformed by the Holy Spirit. This next step occurs immediately following the previous one. That is, once it is clear that the giving a miracle is appropriate, the MG decides to open fully to the higher level. This is the first phase of the process of actually giving the miracle. It is described in the first clause of the following:

> "8 The miracle worker begins by perceiving light, and translates his perception into sureness by continually extending it and accepting its acknowledgment."(9,V,7,8)

We can think of this as a matter of fully opening to and connecting with the higher level (Love, God, the Holy Spirit, Christ, or however it may be thought of) so that the MG receives and perceives what is here called 'light.' It is by virtue of the presence of that light that there is a transformation within the MG's mind.

However, it is important to be clear on the nature of the transformation that the MG undergoes. This 'light' brings to him an illumination of his own mind so as to perceive the MR in a very different way. This is described in Prin. 34:

> "1 The miracle dissolves error because the Holy Spirit identifies error as false or unreal. 2 This is the same as saying that by perceiving light, darkness automatically disappears." (1,I,39,1-2)

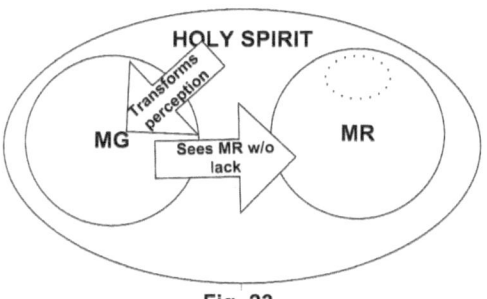

Fig. 23

This is represented in Fig. 23, where the arrow from the Holy Spirit brings His 'light' into the MG which completely undoes or lets go his perception of lack that was initially perceived as present in the MR. Here, I represent what the MG perceives regarding the MR as a dotted empty ellipse within the MR circle. Note that there is no longer any darkness in it for the MG, although it may remain for the MR. Thus, the MG's previous perception of deficiency is replaced by a perception of perfection or completeness in the MR. This elimination of the perception of lack is, of course, what the Course calls 'forgiveness.' As we saw earlier, it is simply a matter of letting it go and perceiving the MR as the Holy Spirit perceives him.

Prin. 4 indicates further what happens in making that connection:

> "1 All miracles mean life, and God is the Giver of life. 2 His Voice will direct you very specifically. 3 You will be told all you need to know."(1,I,4,1-2)

From this, we may describe the connecting to the Source as a matter of shifting from being in a mode in which one is consciously in a highly restricted form of living. This can be thought of as partaking only of a very small portion of the boundless Energy of Love that constitutes the greater, unlimited Life that is in each perfect mind. Of course, that limited little life is due only to the type of awareness that the separated mind has chosen to take on. But what happens in this step of the miracle-process is that the MG, to some degree at least, drops the limiting obstacles to Love's presence and shifts to a mode of consciously participating in or being one with Life.

Thus, the insights expressed in Prin. 38 may be seen as central to what might be called the 'core' of the miracle. As it points out:

> "1 The Holy Spirit is the mechanism of miracles. 2 He recognizes both God's creations and your illusions. 3 He separates the true from the false by His ability to perceive totally rather than selectively."(1,I,38,1-3)

We should first note that the original wording in Schucman's "Notes" uses the expression 'spiritual eye' instead of 'Holy Spirit' in statement 1. If one takes it as referring to the Holy Spirit, the emphasis is on the activity of a Mind that one thinks of as other than one's own. In a sense, this is correct if one considers his/her own mind as simply the separated mind. However, the Course is quite clear that the Holy Spirit is actually the same as the deepest level of one's own mind. To refer to this as the 'spiritual eye' would seem to be only a matter of emphasizing its connection with the mind that thinks of itself as separated.[48] Further, the use of the word 'mechanism' should not be taken as a thoughtless 'mechanical process,' but rather in the sense of a mental process for obtaining a result, which is one of its definitions.

What is central to the transforming process of the miracle is contained in

---

[48] This will be discussed more fully in *The Holy Spirit and Jesus in A Course in Miracles*.

statements 2 and 3. That is, because the Holy Spirit has the awareness of knowledge, which makes Him fully present to Love without any limitations and aware of all perfect minds, His Mind is in complete wholeness or unity. Yet, because His Mind also has perceptual awareness, it is cognizant of the true perceptions in any separated mind. Since those true perceptions are the actual foundation of any illusions or errors in the MR's mind, He is aware of the basis of those illusions, and in that sense 'recognizes' them. That He does not see those errors as such is made clear in:

> "3 I said before that the Holy Spirit cannot see error, and is capable only of looking beyond it to the defense of Atonement. 4 There is no doubt that this may produce discomfort, yet the discomfort is not the final outcome of the perception. 5 When the Holy Spirit is permitted to look upon the defilement of the altar, He also looks immediately toward the Atonement."
> (2,V,7,3-5)

This passage was also changed in the editing process so as to substitute 'Holy Spirit' for 'spiritual eye' in both statement 1 and 5. It has been pointed out that there is a debate regarding whether this change from the original involves a significant misinterpretation regarding the Holy Spirit, particularly whether He can or cannot perceive errors or mistakes. But the Course, after ceasing to use the term 'spiritual eye,' does state the following:

> "1 You undertook, together, to invite the Holy Spirit into your relationship. 2 He could not have entered otherwise. 3 Although you may have made many mistakes since then, you have also made enormous efforts to help Him do His work. 4 And He has not been lacking in appreciation for all you have done for Him. 5 Nor does He see the mistakes at all."
> (17,V,11,1-5)

and:

> "1 The Holy Spirit undoes illusions without attacking them, because He cannot perceive them at all. 2 They therefore do not exist for Him. 3 He resolves the apparent conflict they engender by perceiving conflict as meaningless."(7,VI,6,1-3)

Thus, since what is here called 'mistakes' or 'illusions' is equivalent to what is also called 'errors,' it is made clear that the statement that He cannot perceive error at all seems fully correct, at least as a matter of the Course's teaching.[49]

We may now return to the point in passage 2,V,7,3-5 that indicates how the Holy Spirit corrects the error or false perception. This is accomplished simply by His looking past the error ('defilement') to what is actually true about the situation. That is, He does not see what the separated mind might think of as a 'defilement,' but only what is true in that perception. This is essentially the point made

---

[49] Also discussed at greater length in the previously noted writing.

regarding His 'looking immediately toward the Atonement.' That seems to be essentially the same point made in statement 3 of the last passage cited, concerning how He resolves what for the separated mind is perceived as conflict. That is, what is understood as 'conflict,' 'error,' 'lack,' or 'deficiency' by either the MR or the MG is completely absent from His perception. Indeed, the core of the shift in awareness that is central to the transformation of the miracle is the replacement of that limited, erroneous perception by the Holy Spirit's 'whole' perception.

This is substantially the same point made in Prin. 39:

> "1 The miracle dissolves error because the Holy Spirit identifies error as false or unreal. 2 This is the same as saying that by perceiving light, darkness automatically disappears."
> (1,I,39,1-3)

That is, the correction induced by the miracle is not brought about by opposing the error or deficiency, which would require affirming that it is to some extent real. Such an approach could be called 'accentuating the negative.' The approach of the miracle is very much like the line in a popular song of the 1940's: 'accentuate the positive, eliminate the negative.' Indeed, this approach is entirely in line with one of the Course's primary images, that the condition of separation is like a dream, and Atonement is awakening from that dream. That is, one does not stop the misery encountered in a dream by 'fighting' the monsters, but simply by letting them dissolve in awaking. In that sense, a miracle might be thought of as a partial or 'mini' awakening.

Step vii. MG directs new perception to MR as healing light. Once this transformation of correction or healing has occurred in the MG, the MG is then able to look upon the MR in this new way. This is described in the second part of 9,V,7,8 (cited above, p. 172), which says that after perceiving the light, the MG is to translate 'his perception by extending.' That is, after having received healing of his own perception, he then directs his attention to the MR in this transformed mode, which can be thought of as 'offering healing light' to the MR. This is represented in Fig. 24 as the sending of light to him. In one sense, this is implicit in step vi, since the shift in perception that takes place there includes the MG's perception of the MR in this new way. However, in another sense, it can be thought of as the 'active' willing by the MG to direct his transformed way of seeing onto or into the MR. That is, this 'giving' step takes place immediately in the completion of step vi.

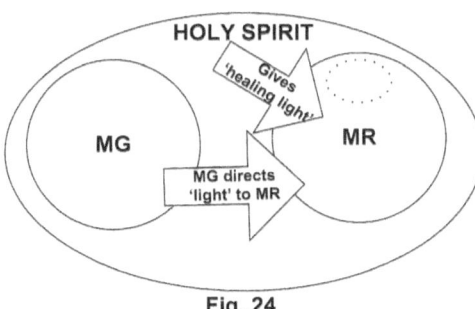

Fig. 24

Step viii. The MR chooses to accept the miracle immediately or later.

The final step in the miracle-process centers on the one to whom the miracle is given, the MR. This is represented in Fig. 25, in which the 'lack' has been removed; the dotted area used to indicate what once was perceived as a deficiency, but now completely undone. Also, since the Holy Spirit is always offering the 'light' of healing to every separated mind, the figure shows that 'light' moving directly from the Holy Spirit. What the MG has done is simply to act as a catalyst that opens the MR to receiving the 'light' that is always offered to him. Thus, although within the MG there has already occurred a change in perception, since the acceptance of Love is always a matter of free choice, an actual transformation of the MR in regard to the perceived lack or deficiency must wait until he or she accepts it.

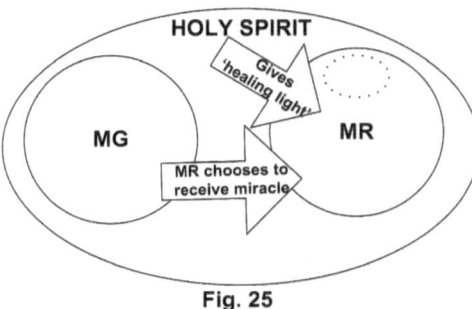

Fig. 25

This is the point in Prin. 35:

> "1 Miracles are expressions of love, but they may not always have observable effects."(1,I,35,1)

Thus, there may not be an overt change in the MR that occurs immediately. If the MR is resistant to the correction, blocked by fear or any clinging to the perceived deficiency, the transformation will not occur for him or her, at least in his or her completion.

However, this does not mean that the miracle has been completely blocked. It is only blocked until the MR chooses to accept it. This point is made in the following:

> "7 No teacher of God should feel disappointed if he has offered healing and it does not appear to have been received. 8 It is not up to him to judge when his gift should be accepted. 9 Let him be certain it has been received, and trust that it will be accepted when it is recognized as a blessing and not a curse."(M,6,2)

Here we are told that a miracle, once given, sooner or later will be accepted by the MR. It is just a matter of time. Thus, it is not possible to 'impose' miracles on anyone. As was stated in Prin. 9, they are an exchange that involves the conscious participation of both the MG and MR. This temporal deferral of a miracle's completion will be discussed below when we consider its effect on time.

c. The non-repeatability of giving a miracle. From what we've seen thus far, one might think that a particular MG may want to give several or even many miracles to the same MR. For example, if an MG perceives sometime later that the MR to whom he gave a miracle has not accepted it, he might be inclined to give another miracle to that MR. Or, possibly that MG may perceive that the same MR perceives some other lack in himself, and thus the MG may feel he should give another miracle to correct that other lack. But the Course counsels otherwise. In the Manual for Teachers, in response to the question, "Should healing be repeated?," it states:

> "2 Healing cannot be repeated. 3 If the patient is healed, what remains to heal him from? 4 And if the healing is certain, as we have already said it is, what is there to repeat? 5 For a teacher of God to remain concerned about the result of healing is to limit the healing. 6 It is now the teacher of God himself whose mind needs to be healed."(M,7,1,1-6)

Although this is concerned explicitly with 'healing,' and one could possibly conclude that it does not mean that another miracle should not be given by an MG to the same MR, further reflection seems to indicate otherwise. This has to do with the relation between the miracle and healing.

The following offers a basic distinction in this regard:

> "2 The miracle is the means, the Atonement is the principle, and healing is the result."(2,IV,1,2)

In this is made clear that what the Course means by 'healing' is the primary effect or result of a miracle. While it might be thought that 'healing' can be partial, such as we think of a particular disease as being healed when all of its symptoms have been corrected or removed but another physical or psychological 'lack' may remain, in the Course's view, such 'partial healing' is not what it means by that term. Rather, healing only occurs when there is the complete return to wholeness. Indeed, the etymological root of 'heal' is 'to make whole.' But, any partial healing would involve some aspect or aspects still not being integrated into complete wholeness. That is, healing, in the proper sense, can involve no remainder whatsoever of anything still not integrated into the completely united or whole state. This means that for the Course healing, in the strict sense, happens totally or not at all. In other words, it involves the full realization of the Atonement in the individual separated mind. However, it does recognize a kind of 'partial healing' that is a step or stage of greater wholeness in the temporal process of realizing Atonement. This is implicit in the separated mind's being able to live in terms of illusory love (the most unhealed state), imperfect love (coming to wholeness), and perfect love (fully healed). We will discuss these stages later.

It is also important to be aware that the word 'healing' has, even for the Course, two somewhat different meanings. The first is an overall resulting state, that results from the realization of the Atonement, the point in 2,IV,1,2,. The second is the process by which that realization occurs, which is the idea in M,7,1,1-6 above.

The relation between the miracle and healing as a process is also indicated in several other passages. One states:

> "4 In every miracle all healing lies, for God gave answer to them all as one."(26,VII,15,4)

This indicates that the miracle is the fundamental way by which true or complete healing is accomplished. That is, the process of healing occurs by way of giving and receiving a miracle. It is also important to note that the act of giving a miracle has a healing effect on both the MG and the MR:

> "5 If you perceive truly you are cancelling out misperceptions in yourself and in others simultaneously. 6 Because you see them as they are, you offer them your acceptance of their truth so they can accept it for themselves. 7 This is the healing that the miracle induces."(3,II,6,5-7)

In the case of the MG that has come only to imperfect love, his giving of a miracle brings healing, or the undoing of separation, both to himself and to the MR (provided the MR accepts it). Again, the fully healed state can occur in the MG only to the extent that he fully accepts it. For the MG that has come to perfect love, since he has already been completely healed in his own mind, there is no further healing in him as a separate mind, but rather an extension of his healed state to the MR when the MR decides to accept it.

The relation between healing, Atonement, and the miracle is also further clarified in:

> "1 Healing and Atonement are not related; they are identical. 2 There is no order of difficulty in miracles because there are no degrees of Atonement. 3 It is the one complete concept possible in this world, because it is the source of a wholly unified perception. 4 Partial Atonement is a meaningless idea, just as special areas of hell in Heaven are inconceivable."
> (M,22,1,1-4)

That is, healing as a resulting state is the same as the realization of the Atonement. Thus, healing in an individual separated mind is the same as that mind's realization of the Atonement. Further, statement 2 repeats the point that healing cannot be partial; it is something that occurs totally or not at all. In that sense, 'partial healing' is a self-contradictory idea. The important implication of all this is that the giving of any particular miracle involves much more than remedying a particular lack. Although the perception of such a lack may be the occasion for the MG's offering it, its primary intent is to move away from any trace of fragmentation or separation. In that sense, all particular miracles are essentially the same; and one is no more difficult than another.

In this light, it becomes clear that there can be no repetition of a particular MG's giving a miracle to the same MR. Giving it to that person once is all that can be done, simply because the healing-capacity of the miracle itself is total. In that sense, healing cannot be repeated by that MG for that MR. Of course, this does not mean that this particular MG cannot give a miracle to any other MR. Indeed, it is incumbent on him to do so, and as he matures to perfect love this becomes his habit or constant disposition in relating with any new MR.

This also does not mean that the particular MR cannot be given another miracle by another MG. Indeed, it is important for all other MG's to do so, not as a matter of offering the opportunity for healing to that MR, but for increasing the conditions that may help him/her to become acceptant of the Atonement. This seems to be another way of describing what was earlier discussed as the 'interlocking chain of forgiveness.'

Further, this does not mean that a particular MG should not stop offering love or help to the MR. Although the MR may not have come to full acceptance of what was given, the MG may remain solicitous to aid in that. But, in that solicitude he need not, nor cannot, offer 'another' miracle, since what was already offered was total healing that is simply taking time to find acceptance. Later, when we consider the nature of the 'holy relationship,' which is central to perfect love, we will further discuss the role of giving miracles and other modes of giving love to those to whom one may have already given a miracle. However, in the following section we will see a way that the Course proposes that one may help another by either giving a miracle or a lesser type of help.

d. A concrete 'visualization' for offering a miracle or help. These steps can be seen as operating in one of the lessons found in the Workbook Lesson 121. It will be helpful to look at the practice that this lesson describes:

"10. Begin the longer practice periods by thinking of someone you do not like, who seems to irritate you, or to cause regret in you if you should meet him; one you actively despise, or merely try to overlook. 2 It does not matter what the form your anger takes. 3 You probably have chosen him already. 4 He will do.

"11. Now close your eyes and see him in your mind, and look at him a while. 2 Try to perceive some light in him somewhere; a little gleam which you had never noticed. 3 Try to find some little spark of brightness shining through the ugly picture that you hold of him. 4 Look at this picture till you see a light somewhere within it, and then try to let this light extend until it covers him, and makes the picture beautiful and good.

"12. Look at this changed perception for a while, and turn your mind to one you call a friend. 2 Try to transfer the light you learned to see around your former 'enemy' to him. 3 Perceive him now as more than friend to you, for in that light his holiness shows you your savior, saved and saving, healed and whole.

"13. Then let him offer you the light you see in him, and let your 'enemy' and friend unite in blessing you with what you gave. 2 Now are you one with them, and they with you. 3 Now have you been forgiven by yourself. 4 Do not forget, throughout the day, the role forgiveness plays in bringing happiness to every unforgiving mind, with yours among them."
(W,121,10-13)

This procedure is clearly one to be used by a mind not yet matured to perfect love, since a mind so matured would not be able to think of anyone as in anyway annoying. It is also much more widely applicable for such a mind than is the process of giving a miracle, in that it can be used repeatedly in relationships that, as viewed by the one doing the procedure, are not totally healed. (Recall that giving a miracle to one person cannot be repeated.) Thus, this might be thought of as a process that helps prepare one to give miracles. Nevertheless, it involves several things found also in the steps of giving a miracle.

In par. 10, one mind, which I will call G, perceives another, R, as having some sort of deficiency or lack, as in step i. In this case, G is clearly one who has only imperfect love, since he/she perceives the other person as lacking in some way. In par.11, G's move to see R as having light may at first be taken as something entirely done by G. But steps ii through iv can be seen as completed by this section of the Workbook, which is a kind of general communication from the Holy Spirit to the student who has chosen to study and practice this section. However, in the act of choosing to have this perception, there is implicit the move of step iv, which is to choose to offer R a kind of healing. In the attempt to find the spark of brightness in R, what G is actually doing is engaging in something close to step vi, of connecting to the Source of Light or calling upon the help of the higher level, the Christ Mind/Holy Spirit. In G's continued act of holding R in that light and seeing it extend to encompass him/her, we can see something like step vii, the directing of the light of Love to R. This is strengthened in the process of par. 12, in which G further adds the quality that is predominant in his perception of someone he calls a 'friend,' which is essentially the quality of love that he has learned to realize within that relationship, but now further extended to R. This further transforms G's perception of R into an even more intense 'light' experience. Finally, par. 13 describes the even further perception (in imagination, of course) of R as returning light to G. This brings G to the letting go or forgiving of the deficiency formerly perceived in R. Of course, since R must himself make the choice to let go of the deficiency that he perceives, this does not necessarily immediately bring the transformation in R, as R perceives himself and the relationship. That can come only when R makes that decision. However, G has moved to be transformed to the degree that he has let go his own misperception of the deficiency in R.

We may also observe that this particular practice can be used for two different sorts of interaction with others. The one is in giving a miracle, which must be guided by the Voice as to whether it is appropriate, and also can be given only once to a particular person. The other is in the more general situation of relating to others where giving a miracle is not appropriate. That is, it can be used at any time and in any situation where one recognizes the need to offer Love. In this, we can see how using the perception of 'light' along with the intention to let it bring Love into a situation can be a particularly powerful and effective way of moving a relationship from one of conflict and discord to one of peace and harmony.

5. Effects of the miracle. As might be expected from what has been said, a miracle produces changes in the MR, as well as in the MG if he/she is in need of further healing, as indicated in Prin. 16:

> "1 Miracles are teaching devices for demonstrating it is as blessed to give as to receive. 2 They simultaneously increase the strength of the giver and supply strength to the receiver." (1,I,16,1-2)

The notion that any act of true giving, as understood by the Course, brings an increase to both giver and receiver is expressed in many places, such as the primary affirmation in Lesson 108 of the Workbook: "To give and to receive are one in truth." In the case of giving a miracle, since its essential process is one of letting go of a false perception and replacing it with a true perception, it should be clear that for the MG to give it he/she must first receive it by opening to the influx of the communication from the Holy Spirit. This is the 'increase of strength' that comes to the MG. Thus, the MG having only imperfect love is the first recipient of the miracle's transformative effect. Of course, to the extent that the MR is open to accepting it, there is a similar transformation in his/her mind.

a. Specific effects. Since the original perceptual error can relate to various sorts of perception, there are various changes that the miracle can introduce. It may help our understanding if we consider the specific types of change mentioned in the Course.

i. Healing of physical deficiencies. This is indicated in Prin. 24:

> "1 Miracles enable you to heal the sick and raise the dead because you made sickness and death yourself, and can therefore abolish both."(1,I,24,1)

Although it may at first seem more possible that the change in perception involved in the miracle might undo the basis of what we think of as sickness, it most likely strains believability to claim it can also undo what seems to be the much more final condition of death. Even in modern medicine there has been significant evidence amassed concerning what is called the 'psychosomatic' element in many illnesses and their cures, so it may not stretch too much our willingness to accept that there may be a way to produce healing by way of a more mental shift. Further, there are numerous well-attested reports of people alleged to have had 'miraculous' healings that medical science cannot explain. However, the undoing of death is much more problematic, due to the fact that it does not seem possible to reverse that process and, even more, the great rarity of claims where that seems to have happened. Instances of restoration of life after a significant period of 'being dead' are reported in the New Testament, such as Jesus' miraculous revivifying of Lazarus, of the daughter of Jairus, and of a young man being carried in his funeral procession. Of course, the reliability of these reports are greatly open to question, given that they were recorded long after their occurrence by ostensibly very biased writers, none of whom witnessed the events. Similar 'physical resurrection' miracles are reported in the Old Testament and in other religious traditions.[50] More reliable are the claims regarding two types of experience that can be thought of as a kind of restoration from death: near-death experiences (NDE) and cases of the reincarnation type (CRT), both of which have been extensively studied by scientists.[51]

However, when we consider the reason offered in Prin. 24, 'that you made both sickness and death,' we should give the initial skeptical judgment a second thought. That is, if it is true, as the Course asserts, that the mind generated the form we think of as the 'body,' then it also follows that the various conditions of the body must also be similarly generated. This would include not only what we think of as health and illness, but also the condition we call 'death' or 'dying.' From this perspective, it follows that an appropriate change in the mind's awareness would produce any sort of change, from the correcting of illness to the undoing of death. At least this is the claim made by the Course.

Indeed, the very first principle of miracles states:

"1 There is no order of difficulty in miracles. 2 One is not 'harder' or 'bigger' than another. 3 They are all the same. 4 All expressions of love are maximal."(1,I,1,1-3)

Although one may have difficulty accepting the reason for this (that all states that the separated mind enters into are generated by its own choice), it should be clear that if it is accepted it logically follows that the changing of any particular perception (from 'being dead' to 'being alive again') is in principle no more difficult than the changing of any other perception (from 'my hand is on the keyboard' to 'my hand is scratching my head'). The greater difficulty of the former change, from the Course's perspective, is that the mind does not believe it is possible, while it does believe the latter is.

ii. Release from the sense of isolation, deprivation, and lack. Prin. 42 puts the matter of restoration in a somewhat different way, describing three important aspects of it:

---

[50] See the Wikipedia article 'Resurrection' for an overview and bibliography.

[51] For CRT's, see J. Tucker and I. Stevenson's *Life Before Life: Children's Memories of Previous Lives*. For NDE's, see K. Ring's *Life At Death*. Recently, neurosurgeon E. Alexander makes a case for afterlife based on his intense NDE while 'brain-dead' in his *Proof of Heaven*. The Course has a very different view of 'resurrection,' clarified more fully in my book on Jesus and the Holy Spirit. It holds that it does not involve any sort of body. While it does hold that Jesus did indeed resurrect after going through the process of physically dying, his resurrection, although it may have incidentally generated a form similar to the body that was his prior to dying, that form was only symbolic for relating to his disciples. That is, since a body is essentially a limited object in space-time, to hold that it is intrinsic to the Reality of Jesus would be to think that such limits were part of his nature. The central idea of 'resurrection' is that of complete restoration to the original state of unlimited Being/Life that is totally beyond any limited bodily form.

> "1 A major contribution of miracles is their strength in releasing you from your false sense of isolation, deprivation and lack."(1,I,42,1)

That is, any perception of deprivation or lack, whether it be what we think of as a more emotional 'isolation' from others and the accompanying pain of loneliness, or a more external material deprivation, is in the mind only by its choice. Once it makes that choice it may find that it is 'caught' in its own self-enclosing perception because that is all that it is clearly aware of. However, it is possible for it, particularly after experiencing the misery that inevitably arises within that limited state, to come to the thought that there must be a better way and to choose to find it. This seems to be the first opening that the Holy Spirit responds to and begins to guide that mind to the point where it can move rapidly toward undoing its involvement in false perceptions. That movement commences when it learns to give miracles.

iii. Restoration of one's Identity and oneness with others.
The third specific result that comes in the miracle is described as follows:

> "1 Earlier I said this course will teach you how to remember what you are, restoring to you your Identity. 5 We have already learned that this Identity is shared. 6 The miracle becomes the means of sharing It. 7 By supplying your Identity wherever It is not recognized, you will recognize It. 8 And God Himself, Who wills to be with His Son forever, will bless each recognition of His Son with all the Love He holds for him. 9 Nor will the power of all His Love be absent from any miracle you offer to His Son. 10 How, then, can there be any order of difficulty among them?"(14,X,12,1-10)

Two points are important here. The first is that what is called 'your Identity' refers to the awareness of who or what the separated mind actually is, not in its limited condition but in its fullness. It can also be called 'awareness of the Self,' i.e., of the Christ Mind. As stated here, the miracle makes clearer that each separate mind's own Identity is the same as every other's. Thus, the MG and the MR, as a result of giving and receiving the miracle, come to a fuller realization that they are actually the same. This realization is, of course, a matter of degree. But, as the miracle is more fully accepted in either mind, to that degree they see that they are one, or share the same Identity. The second point is in statement 10. That is, since what occurs at the core of the miracle is the dropping away of false perceptions, and those false perceptions act as obstacles to awareness of Love's presence, the primary effect of the miracle is that it makes both the MG and the MR more fully aware of Love's presence. And as they realize that what is occurring is the dissolution of all false perceptions, they also see that dissolving one false perception is no more difficult than dissolving any other. Thus, there can be no order of difficulty in that dissolution process, which is given the name 'miracle.'

Closely related to the greater clarity regarding one's own Identity is the increased clarity regarding one's relation to other separated minds:

> "1 Miracles make minds one in God. 2 They depend on cooperation because the Sonship is the sum of all that God created. 3 Miracles therefore reflect the laws of eternity, not of time." (1,I,19,1-3)

Not only does one reach out to connect with the Source (Love/God) in the second step, but, by giving and receiving the miracle, the awareness of one's unity with other minds, particularly of the MG and the MR, becomes much clearer. This occurs first in the MG as a kind of response of witnessing the flow of energy or 'light' to the MR, particularly if the MG remains focused on the presence of that flow within him/her.

iv. Gratitude. As either mind observes the influx of the light or energy that brings correction, particularly the letting go of the false perception that blocks the awareness of Love's presence, it has a secondary response as it experiences that healing release. This is described in Prin. 31:

> "1 Miracles should inspire gratitude, not awe. 2 You should thank God for what you really are. 3 The children of God are holy and the miracle honors their holiness, which can be hidden but never lost."(1,I,31,1-3)

Although at first there may be some reaction of fear, which is an aspect of the emotion of awe, there is the sense of having been relieved of some heavy burden, which was part of the error's overall effect. As it becomes aware of this release, its deeper response is one of gratitude for having been brought to a 'lighter' condition. Even if the mind is consciously committed to an atheistic belief, and may only express a 'sigh of relief,' there is a sense of 'Thank God!' or 'Thank the Universe!' Of course, it may be more clearly conscious in the mind and issue in a more dramatic expression.

v. Genuine praise of the Creator. Whether only a sigh or a fully conscious canticle, this gratitude is described in Prin. 29 as follows:

> "1 Miracles praise God through you. 2 They praise Him by honoring His creations, affirming their perfection. 3 They heal because they deny body-identification and affirm spirit-identification."(1,I,29,1-3)

That is, the mind that is healed through the miracle, to the degree that it accepts the miracle, is restored to awareness of the relationship that it was originally given. This is a matter of recognizing, at least to some extent, the unlimited nature of the gift of Love. One way that this might be articulated, and indeed has been in almost all religious traditions, is in the expression 'How great Thou art!' In this there is not the slightest intention to 'flatter or 'manipulate' a higher being (often central to the ego-dominated mind in its 'religious' practices), but rather simply a choice to acknowledge the greatness of someone, in this case God. This seems to be the primary characteristic of praise in the deepest sense.

b. Most general effects on MG and MR. These more specific effects of the miracle may be better understood from a broader or more general perspective.

The first seven of these can be understood as aspects of inner healing.

i. Restoration of the mind to wholeness. Earlier it was pointed out that the purpose of the miracle is to restore the separated mind to complete wholeness. Indeed, that is the ultimate effect of any miracle if it is completely accepted. This is a point made in Prin. 34, where it is called 'fullness.'

> "1 Miracles restore the mind to fullness. 2 By atoning for lack they establish perfect protection. 3 The spirit's strength leaves no room for intrusions."(1,I,34,1-3)

Here we should recall that the fundamental reason for the formation of the notion and process of giving miracles lies in its serving as a means of realizing the Atonement. However, that realization involves the mind's restoration to awareness of its original wholeness, which is central to the unity of Love. Thus, if a particular mind receives or accepts a miracle, either as an MG or an MR, it moves toward that restoration to the degree that it accepts it.

ii. A sense of complete protection. As indicated in statement 2 of the last passage, this realization makes such a mind immune to slipping back into separation, giving it 'perfect protection.' It has been so 'energized' in the sense that its latent energy of Love has been activated that it cannot be collapsed into its former state. However, as was have pointed out, this condition only arises when that mind has come to a sufficient level or degree of acceptance of the miracle. Although any miracle given it will eventually have that effect, it may take time for it to actually occur. This amounts to the eventual maturation of the mind to perfect love.

Of course, this full realization generally does not occur immediately to either the MG or the MR in every instance of a miracle, particularly if its focus is on only one type of erroneous perception/lack. Rather, most miracles are only steps toward that. However, since any miracle makes the connection with the perfect Mind of the Holy Spirit, it opens the minds involved to move toward complete restoration. The only things preventing that are the obstacles still present in those minds.

iii. Undoing the cause of fear. It was pointed out how the miracle undoes particular feelings of fear. Related to that and the previous point is that not only is fear as a symptom undone, but also its very basis or root cause. This profound general effect of the miracle is also described in terms somewhat more abstract and philosophical, in relation to a radical undoing of the cause of limited awareness. Several passages discuss this undoing of cause as occurring on a succession of deeper levels, until it reaches the most fundamental level. The first is in relation to the cause of particular problems or deficiencies related to the body:

> "1 The miracle returns the cause of fear to you who made it. 2 But it also shows that, having no effects, it is not cause, because the function of causation is to have effects. 3 And where effects are gone, there is no cause. 4 Thus is the body healed by miracles because they show the mind made sickness, and employed the body to be victim, or effect, of what it made. 5

> Yet half the lesson will not teach the whole. 6 The miracle is useless if you learn but that the body can be healed, for this is not the lesson it was sent to teach. 7 The lesson is the *mind* was sick that thought the body could be sick; projecting out its guilt caused nothing, and had no effects."(28,II,11,1-7)

Here we see that the miracle operates so as to remove the immediate cause of dysfunction or illness in the body, by enabling the mind to see that both the fear that is the immediate cause of such dysfunction, and the cause of fear itself, lie in the very mind itself. But, as statement 2 points out, this causal relation is actually not real in an absolute sense. To be sure, the cause of fear, which is the mind that makes the choice of separation, is itself real, and the effect that is first fear and secondarily the dysfunction such as physical illness, have a kind of reality. But the latter is only relatively real. It appears to be real to the perceiving mind, but in fact it is only an illusion. That is, the cause of any illness is the mind's very thought that the body can be sick, which stems from the thought of guilt that projects the belief in the possibility of sickness onto the body. The miracle makes clear that this, not anything outside the body (germs, toxins, etc.), is the central cause of any illness. That is, it asserts that one's own mind is the cause of the dysfunction and that by correcting the mind the effect can be undone.

However, as statement 6 points out, it would be a major error itself to think that the primary concern of the miracle is the body's health. This is further indicated in Prin.17:

> "1 Miracles transcend the body. 2 They are sudden shifts into invisibility, away from the bodily level. 3 That is why they heal."(1,I,17,1-3)

Although the body's health is not to be dismissed as having no importance at all, since the presence of illness generally elicits further fear within the mind and intensifies one's involvement in the world of separation, there is something far more important than the body, something beyond it. This is the 'invisible' level that makes all visibility and all perception possible: the mind itself, or more exactly the 'light' of awareness flowing through the mind. The previous passage already indicated that the problem is not the body's condition, which is only a symptom of the actual problem: the mind's misthought. Hence, the miracle shifts its correcting process to this deeper causal level.

But the Course also teaches that this undoing of the root cause of error does not, as has been pointed out, necessarily occur immediately in the giving or accepting of a miracle:

> "3 The miracle is the first step in giving back to cause the function of causation, not effect. 4 For this confusion has produced the dream, and while it lasts will wakening be feared. 5 Nor will the call to wakening be heard, because it seems to be the call to fear."(28,II,9,3-5)

That the miracle is the first step in undoing the cause of error, which in itself is at its basis the act of denying the real Cause of the mind's own existence, is important to keep in mind. The undoing process occurs only to the extent that the miracle is accepted, and in most cases that acceptance is with reservations. Accordingly, it can only undo/forgive/correct to a limited extent. Some fears may be released, but others remain until one is willing to let go the fundamental commitment to the ego-idea. Put more positively, this is the same as answering what the Course calls the 'basic' or 'final' question:

> "14 And do I want to see what I denied because it is the truth?"(21,VII,5,14)

also formulated as:

> "4 Is this what I would see? Do I want this?"(21,VII,8,4)

Only then can there be complete awakening. Ironically, although the miracle is a call to that, it is at first perceived through the 'lens of fear.' However, eventually that will be dissolved. Of course, it is quite possible that a single miracle can fully complete the undoing process if the mind to whom it is given accepts it completely.

iv. Witness to truth. The general effect of the miracle is also described in terms of awareness, particularly of truth, as found in Prin. 14:

> "1 Miracles bear witness to truth. 2 They are convincing because they arise from conviction. 3 Without conviction they deteriorate into magic, which is mindless and therefore destructive; or rather, the uncreative use of mind."(1,I,14,1-3)

Given that the awareness of Reality, or Truth, is central to the removal of blocks to Love's presence, and that the miracle involves such removal, it follows that to the degree it is accepted by a mind, to that degree there follows the 'witnessing' of Truth. It is primarily that restored awareness that constitutes the certitude or conviction that comes with this. In so far as that does not occur, the miracle is looked upon as merely some sort of superficial change in the appearance of things, perhaps startling, but only thought of as a sort of magical manipulation of the physical world of perception.

v. Joy. We also saw that the awareness of Love, or Truth, involves profound Joy. This is the point of the following:

> "4 The miracle is therefore a lesson in what joy is. 5 Being a lesson in sharing it is a lesson in love, which *is* joy. 6 Every miracle is thus a lesson in truth, and by offering truth you are learning the difference between pain and joy."(7,X,8,4-6)

Here we should recall that the awareness of Love, Truth, and Joy are mutually entailed, since in a sense Love is Truth and Joy. Of course, this does not mean that the immediate experience following the giving or receiving of a miracle necessarily involves the full awareness of either Truth and Joy. That experience is limited or hindered to the degree one has not fully accepted the transformation that is essential to the miracle; but it is intensified to the degree it has been accepted.

vi. Denial of denial or awakening from the dream. Much the same insight is put in a grammatically and logically negative way in two other passages. The one reads:

> "1 Miracles are merely the translation of denial into truth. 2 If to love oneself is to heal oneself, those who are sick do not love themselves. 3 Therefore, they are asking for the love that would heal them, but which they are denying to themselves. 4 If they knew the truth about themselves they could not be sick. 5 The task of the miracle worker thus becomes *to deny the denial of truth*. 6 The sick must heal themselves, for the truth is in them. 7 Yet having obscured it, the light in another mind must shine into theirs because that light *is* theirs."
> (12,II,1,1-7)

Here is made quite clear the 'letting go' or 'undoing' and 'forgiving' character of the miracle. It is not so much an *adding* to of something into the mind, but a *removal* of what itself constitutes a taking away. The mind, by its choice of clinging to a tiny fragment of Reality, that is, the limited perceptions it focuses on, and supporting that by the further construction of the ego-idea and all the rest of the false perceptions that in turn support that idea, is in a state of denial or negation of what is actually true. Hence, the miracle amounts to a denial or negation of that denial. In statement 7 is noted the importance of being given a miracle by another who has already moved into that necessary denial of denial. Indeed, this is quite reminiscent of the approach found in Hindu Vedanta, called 'Neti! Neti!' ('Not this! Not this!'). It is also expressed in the tradition of Christian mysticism called the 'Way of Negation.'

This negative approach is further described in terms of the Course's often used reference to the dream state:

> "1 The dreams you think you like would hold you back as much as those in which the fear is seen. 2 For every dream is but a dream of fear, no matter what the form it seems to take. 3 The fear is seen within, without, or both. 4 Or it can be disguised in pleasant form. 5 But never is it absent from the dream, for fear is the material of dreams, from which they all are made. 6 Their form can change, but they cannot be made of something else. 7 The miracle were treacherous indeed if it allowed you still to be afraid because you did not recognize the fear. 8 You would not then be willing to awake, for which the miracle prepares the way."(29,IV,2,1-7)

What are here called 'dreams' are simply all the false perceptions, indeed almost all perceptions, experienced by the separated mind. In that sense, the whole of such a mind's experience is fundamentally no more than a complex dream, having the appearance of being 'real' primarily due to the agreement indicated by other minds (sometimes called 'intersubjective agreement') which we judge confirms some of those perceptions because others indicate they have similar perceptions. Although that 'real dream' is more stable and uniform than what we usually think of as dreams, in the Course's view, which claims to be the evaluation of a Mind that has awakened, it is nonetheless fundamentally a dream. Hence, the miracle is understood as an important means by which awakening from the dream is brought about. Indeed, this is much the same insight as found in the teachings of Buddhism, where the word 'buddha' means literally 'awakened,' and the one called 'the Buddha' is so-called because he is thought to have fully awakened. Also in Buddhism there is the notion of 'transmission' that is very similar to the Course's idea of giving a miracle. The Buddhist idea is that the learning of an important insight leading to awakening can be directly transmitted from a teacher who already has that insight to a student who is ready to receive it. Once transmitted, that insight may take time to unfold in clarity. That parallel to the miracle is quite obvious.

vii. Awareness of spirit. That fundamental level of awareness is the focus of Prin. 20:

> "1 Miracles reawaken the awareness that the spirit, not the body, is the altar of truth. 2 This is the recognition that leads to the healing power of the miracle."(1,I,20,1-2)

We earlier saw that what is called 'spirit,' as viewed by the Course, is the primary center of awareness and creative extension. In so far as it engages in either awareness or extension, it is said to have or be a 'mind.' Although created perfect, it can choose separation (and in us has done so on some level), so that the correction of any and all deficiencies that it experiences in that state can only be undone by addressing the cause at this most fundamental level. Of course, it can choose to remain on a secondary level, such as healing illnesses, etc. But, in that choice it condemns itself to slipping eventually into some other sort of deficient condition. However, when the miracle is taken all the way to the most fundamental level, it completely undoes the whole complex system of errors. Although articulated somewhat differently, this is quite close to the Buddhist teaching concerning the undoing of the cause of suffering, particularly in the Third and Fourth Noble Truth.[52]

The miracle's undoing of error on the most fundamental level is the point made in Prin. 30:

---

[52] The Third Noble Truth can be expressed: "The end of suffering is by way of ending its cause, selfish craving." The Fourth Noble Truth: "The ending of the cause of suffering is by the Eightfold Middle Path." What seems to be the most important aspect of this Path is the 7th, right mindfulness, which is a matter of seeing into the nature of the mind's ego-operations. I might also point out that a major difference between Buddhism and the Course is that the 8 aspects of the Buddhist Path place the responsibility very much upon the individual mind, while the Course recognizes that there is great help from the Holy Spirit. The Course might add a 9th aspect, which could be expressed: "Listen to the guidance of the Holy Spirit." In fact, since all the other aspects are contained within that 9th aspect, the Course could be said to have a 'Onefold Path.'

"1 By recognizing spirit, miracles adjust the levels of perception and show them in proper alignment. 2 This places spirit at the center, where it can communicate directly."(1,I,30,1-2)

That is, when the miracle is fully accepted, one's awareness is fully centered in or awakened to spirit and the foundation of all errors or false perceptions is brought to an end. Fully restored to the unlimited original state in which it was created (and from a higher perspective never slipped out of), it returns to the level of the original and eternal activity, or what is here called 'communication,' but which is its perfect mind's extending of unlimited awareness and creative Love to all within the Universe of Love.

Thus, when fully 'blossomed' or matured, the miracle is the key to the individual's full realization of the Atonement. This is described:

"3 The miracle sets reality where it belongs. 4 Reality belongs only to spirit, and the miracle acknowledges only truth. 5 It thus dispels illusions about yourself, and puts you in communion with yourself and God. 6 The miracle joins in the Atonement by placing the mind in the service of the Holy Spirit."
(1,IV,2,3-6)

Again, this refers to the 'fully ripened' miracle. The term 'reality' here clearly is not the pale imitation that the separated mind is aware of as the 'world of perception.' Rather, it is the primary Reality of the Universe of Love.

viii. Opening to giving further miracles. An important general effect of the miracle on the MG and MR is its initiation of the 'chain reaction' or what the Course calls the 'interlocking chain of forgiveness.' Since forgiveness/letting go of illusions or false perceptions is the core of every miracle, it could also be called the 'interlocking chain of miracles.' This point is expressed in:

"1 I give the miracles I have received."(W,159)

That is, the acceptance of a miracle has what we might think of as a 'positive infectious' effect, prompting any MR, once the miracle given it has been accepted to a sufficient degree, to become an MG. This is further described:

"1 To all who share the Love of God the grace is given to be the givers of what they have received. 2 And so they learn that it is theirs forever. 3 All barriers disappear before their coming, as every obstacle was finally surmounted that seemed to rise and block their way before. 4 This veil you and your brother lift together opens the way to truth to more than you. 5 Those who would let illusions be lifted from their minds are this world's saviors, walking the world with their Redeemer, and carrying His message of hope and freedom and release from suffering to everyone who needs a miracle to save him."
(22,IV,6,1-5)

A first point is that the reference to miracles in the plural (in W,159) should be understood as those given to oneself by various other minds. Although only one miracle can be given by each of them, there are potentially a countless number that can be given by the many other minds within the world of perception. These might be thought of as aspects of a single 'Great Miracle,' which is the manifestation of Love within the world of perception. A second point is that reception of a miracle, since it opens one to complete healing and the restoration of one's connection with the Holy Spirit and enables one to access the unlimited 'energy' within one's own mind, serves as the basis for giving miracles to others. Those others include both the original MG that first gave one a miracle, as well as all other minds. Thus, any MG is both a giver and a receiver of miracles. This relates also to the principle indicated earlier, that to give and to receive are one in truth.

c. Extended effects on others. It has been made clear that the number of separated minds is vastly greater than the two separated minds involved in a particular miracle. If this were the end of the story, involving the 'salvation' of only a few, the Atonement, as proposed by the Course, would be far from complete. Indeed, statement 6 in the last passage points to the role of the once-separated mind in the Atonement's completion, as one of entering into the service of the Holy Spirit. We next consider the miracle's effect on those beyond the MG and the MR. They are a major concern in Prin. 27:

> "1 A miracle is a universal blessing from God through me to all my brothers. 2 It is the privilege of the forgiven to forgive."
> (1,I,27,1-2)

This makes clear that not only are the few individuals (the MG and the MR) benefitted by a miracle, but in fact the whole collection of separated minds. While the Course does not discuss all the ways that every other mind is affected positively, it does indicate some important ones. One is described in Prin. 40:

> "1 The miracle acknowledges everyone as your brother and mine. 2 It is a way of perceiving the universal mark of God."
> (1,I,40,1-2)

The first point here is that the miracle, by shifting awareness from the erroneous perception of deficiency to the awareness of the wholeness, both of one's own mind and of all Reality, brings about an awareness of the unity of all minds that seem to be in separation. What this involves will be made much clearer when we consider the nature of what is called the 'holy instant,' which is central to this fuller awareness (see Ch. V). Suffice it here to say, in that awareness one enters into unlimited communication or connection with all other aspects of the one Mind (the Christ Mind) that is the foundation of all separated minds.

The second point concerns what is here called the 'universal mark of God.' Prin. 40 does indicate that this mark is something perceivable. Thus, it is not simply in some higher unperceivable mode. When we search further, we find that this expression is used nowhere else in FIP. However, something close to it is found in:

> "4 God *would* be mocked if any of His creations lacked holiness. 5 The creation is whole, and the mark of wholeness is

holiness."(1,V,4,4-5)

If the 'universal mark of God' is the same as the 'mark of wholeness,' which seems quite plausible, then we must ask if there is something perceivable related to Wholeness or Holiness. Indeed, this is the central point of Prin. 41:

> "1 Wholeness is the perceptual content of miracles."(1,I,41,1)

That is, wholeness is not only perceivable, but is the very content of what is disclosed by the miracle. This should not be thought of as the outer physical changes accompanying the healing of an illness, but rather the fuller or more interior perception. There may be other aspects that are apparent to the ordinary observer, such as the 'luminosity' that is sometimes reported present around people who have entered deeply into that transformed state. This is perhaps what is the basis of 'halos' or 'auras' that are perceived around such individuals, which would make the representation of 'saints' ('holy persons') more than simply a matter of artistic symbolism. Later, we will discuss in much more detail how this is what is disclosed in the experience of the 'holy instant,' which in the Course's view occurs at a somewhat more matured stage of the acceptance of the miracle. Briefly, it consists in the direct perception of how all within what is for the most part the highly fragmented perception of 'ordinary' experience is a completely unified whole. That perceivable wholeness is observed to be an attribute of every part of what is present in that perception. Since the miracle eventually brings the minds of the MG and MR to such a perception, and that mark is perceived in every seeming separate thing within the context of its perceptual content, the point of Prin. 40 is that this is both a perceivable 'mark' or characteristic of what is perceived and that it is universal, or pertains to all things within that perception. Of course, this remains generally beyond the limits of ordinary perception.

Other aspects of this perception include intense beauty, which is also described as characteristic of the 'holy instant' experience. One other passage that uses the 'mark' expression and seems close to 'mark of God,' and emphasizes 'beauty' is:

> "5 The Kingdom of Heaven is the spirit's right, whose beauty and dignity are far beyond doubt, beyond perception, and stand forever as the mark of the Love of God for His creations, who are wholly worthy of Him and only of Him." (4,I,12,5)

We will go into this further in Ch. V, when we consider the 'holy instant' more at length.

That the miracle has effects that extend beyond the MG and MR is also the point of Prin. 45:

> "1 A miracle is never lost. 2 It may touch many people you have not even met, and produce undreamed of changes in situations of which you are not even aware."(1,I,45,1-2)

Thus, although the MG and the MR are the focus or center of any miracle, and the primary shift in perception is in them, those effects reach far beyond them.

This may be thought of as similar to what is called a 'field-effect' in physics. For example, in the region close to a magnet there is produced a relatively strong magnetic field. However, those lines of magnetic force actually extend out into *all* of physical space, so that a movement of the magnet causes those lines to move everywhere else. The same is true of electrical and gravitational fields. Although the more distant effects may be very small, there is nevertheless some amount of effect everywhere in the whole physical universe. Of course, this analogy has its limits, but it serves to make plausible how the change in one mind can have an effect on other minds. Further, since the transformation of minds produced by the miracle is so profound and intense for the MG and MR, it has all the more capacity to affect other minds, even those quite far away or completely beyond the direct perception of either the MG or MR. Indeed, it is quite plausible to think of the transformation that masters like Jesus experienced as something like the beginning of a 'chain reaction' of transformations that continue to be catalyzed. This occurs both by way of 'energizing' the overall 'field of consciousness' primarily on Earth and by the process of offering miracles from person to person within that local field. It may well be that this process is accelerating, so that there may come an exponential increase of transformed minds upon the planet, which would of course produce a radical shift in the social and material activity of humans. The Urtext Manuscript does make mention of a 'celestial speedup,' which will be discussed further in Ch. V.

d. Effects on time. An intriguing effect of the miracle is in relation to time. This is referred to in four different principles, the first of which is Prin. 13:

> "1 Miracles are both beginnings and endings, and so they alter the temporal order. 2 They are always affirmations of rebirth, which seem to go back but really go forward. 3 They undo the past in the present, and thus release the future."(1,I,13,1-3)

Here is asserted not only that the miracle alters the temporal order, but it also gives an indication of what that alteration consists of. In statement 1, the point that it is a beginning and an ending merits reflection. It should be clear that, within the Course's larger view, a miracle is the beginning of a radical transformation within a separated mind. The culmination of that transformation involves a shift from an awareness that is saturated with content from past experiences, anticipated future images, and perceptions of what is actually present. The new awareness still has perceptual content, but that content is only in terms of the actual present, or true perceptions. Since the prior mode of perception, dominated by aspects that are past and future, ceases to operate in that transformed awareness, this can be understood as an ending of that older mode.

Statement 2 is more enigmatic. In what sense is a miracle an affirmation of rebirth, and what is its apparent 'going back' but actual 'going forward?' The answer is indicated in statement 3. The miracle undoes the past in the sense that it shifts the mind's awareness away from the hold of its habit of clinging to former perceptions whose images are held in memory. It is those past images that 'crowd out,' so to speak, the content of what is in the present. Indeed, much of what the separated mind thinks of as the 'present' is this mix of past, present, and future (memories, awareness of what is actually in the present, and images of what it anticipates as the possible or likely future). Thus, it only *thinks* it is aware of the present, but is aware of this mix. The miracle suspends that mode, so that what rises to prominence, and what is the only content in the transformed state, is what is actually in the present. This consists of a remarkably enlarged and more intensely clear content. We have already mentioned that this new mode of awareness is the perception of the holy instant. The Course refers to the content of that perception as the 'Real World.' We will defer discussion of this till later. However, if this new perception is indeed greatly enlarged both in content and intensity of awareness, it follows that it can be thought of as something like what must be the experience of passing from the womb out into the perceptual world, a new birth or a 'rebirth.'

From this perspective, statement 2 can be understood in the following fashion. The shift in awareness that the miracle brings would at first be felt as reviving something that had been lost. That is the state that existed prior to the separation. So viewed, it would be thought of as a 'going back' or 'recollection' or 'remembrance' of what had once been. Indeed, Plato seems to have made this a central idea in his teaching that the process of coming to know is one of recollection. Others, such as Wordsworth, have expressed a similar view.[53] However, while there is some value in thinking of this transformation as a 'going back,' it is better thought of as a 'going forward.' That lies in the connotation of the latter as continuing without end, rather than retrieving what has gone. Of course, either concept falls short, since they both are fundamentally temporal, while the transformed state is completely beyond time.

Yet, the Course recognizes that it is speaking to minds deeply immersed in temporality. Thus, it advises in Prin. 15:

> "1 Each day should be devoted to miracles. 2 The purpose of time is to enable you to learn how to use time constructively. 3 It is thus a teaching device and a means to an end. 4 Time will cease when it is no longer useful in facilitating learning."
> (1,I,15,1-4)

That is, as long as the mind is within the temporal order, it should make the most of the situation. Accordingly, it ought to engage in the most effective activity that will bring about its own transformation to the only state in which it can be truly happy. Here the Course is basically saying, 'become a student of the Course, since it is the quickest way to accomplish awakening.' Yet in this very principle it makes clear that once the separated mind has learned that most important lesson, all learning is completed, time is over, and it can remain in a far more satis-

---

[53] See Wordsworth's "Ode on Intimations of Immortality from Recollections of Early Childhood."

fying mode.

But, while the learning proceeds, the miracle has a very important impact on time itself, as described in Prin. 47:

> "1 The miracle is a learning device that lessens the need for time. 2 It establishes an out-of-pattern time interval not under the usual laws of time. 3 In this sense it is timeless."

(1,I,47,1-3)

The insight here, although quite simple in itself, is very puzzling for most separated minds. It is perhaps most easily grasped if we first consider the idea that the whole purpose of time, as seen by the Course, is for the separated mind to learn to undergo the transformation to a mode of awareness completely outside of time. This can be thought of as shifting to another dimension. That is, one can think of the temporal order as a series of points along a line. As long as one is within the line, its experience is one of moving from point to point or moment to moment. Its awareness is greatly limited to what happens to be associated with any particular point/moment. However, if the mind steps outside the line, its awareness becomes much more extensive: it cannot only see the whole line but the whole expanse of the plane that it is present in. Of course, this mathematical analogy is only to illustrate the possibility of another mode of awareness that is far more extensive than the temporally embedded mode.[54]

The 'out of pattern time interval' may be understood in the following way. This needs to be considered from two different perspectives. The first is that of the mind that has fully accepted the miracle and undergone the corresponding transformation. Although the awareness that comes with full acceptance of the miracle completely removes such a mind from the temporal mode in one respect, that mind still has a relationship with other minds remaining in that mode. That is, it can return to the temporal mode, which involves reinserting itself in some sort of body-awareness, so that it can interact with those untransformed minds. Its primary intent is simply one of giving more miracles to others as well as helping those to whom it has already given miracles to complete their realization of the transformed state. This must be the status of individuals like Jesus and very likely the Buddha. Thus, if we can assume they both realized full awakening prior to their physical deaths, their experience of others in the temporal order would have been of simultaneously perceiving the current problems of others as unfolding within time, but also perceiving them as having arrived at the end of that temporal unfolding. At the same time, they would not have been bound by any constraints that we think of as imposed by what are called the 'laws of nature,' although they could choose to operate within those constraints so as to be more effective in helping others. Of course, they could also choose to direct their bod-

---

[54] This idea is illustrated in a quite entertaining and imaginative way in the book *Flatland: A Romance of Many Dimensions* by E. Abbott. Several film versions are available.

ies or other modes of communicating in a variety of ways, such as Jesus' sudden 'materialization' into the gathering of disciples or his 'dematerialization' described as his 'Ascension.' This would also make possible his 'apparitions' at later times, either more intimately to only one individual, such as is reported in the lives of many 'saints' or even very pious individuals, or to groups of them. From a temporal perspective, this would enable such a mind to manifest at any time. That is, such a mind would have the capacity to do what science fiction has for many years called 'time-travel.' This is not all that far-fetched, considering that even theoretical physicists have come up with mathematical models for how that might be possible (worm-holes, time-warps, etc.). Indeed, this capacity to manifest, either in full physical form, with visual, tactual, auditory, and even olfactory perceptual features, or in a more limited form, such as the auditory impressions allegedly given to Schucman, would apply to the Holy Spirit, who we are told most usually makes use of a subtle auditory perception referred to as the 'Voice.' We should also note that similar sorts of manifestations are reported in other traditions, such as Mahayana Buddhism, which has developed a theoretical model of the three levels or 'bodies' of the Buddha, the Nirmanakaya (physical body), the Sambhogakaya (subtle or energy body), and the Dharmakaya (fully perfect mode) of the Buddha and numerous other highly advanced minds called 'Bodhisattvas.' Thus, for the mind completely transformed by the miracle, we may see that there is this 'out of pattern time interval,' which allows that mind to move freely around within what we think of as the temporal order.

The other perspective is that of the mind that has only partially accepted the miracle and thus only experienced a limited transformation. Because such a mind has not completely transcended the limitations that are intrinsic to the physical world, it does not have the freedom that will eventually come to it. However, it does have some degree of greater freedom in its activity of helping others. This may involve an increased ability to offer healing of illness in them, to understand their inner problems, or to work more effectively in solving social problems. If the biographies of the great saints of Christianity, Islam, Buddhism, Hinduism, Taoism, and many of the indigenous traditions are reliable, these record numerous instances of their unusual 'gifts' or 'powers' in service of others. Minds in this incomplete stage of transformation seem to affect the temporal order more by way of what we may think of as a 'speeding up' of natural processes (such as the healing of the body), which in another sense is a kind of 'collapse' of time. This is further discussed in the following passage:

> "1 The miracle minimizes the need for time. 2 In the longitudinal or horizontal plane the recognition of the equality of the members of the Sonship appears to involve almost endless time. 3 However, the miracle entails a sudden shift from horizontal to vertical perception. 4 This introduces an interval from which the giver and receiver both emerge farther along in time than they would otherwise have been. 5 The miracle thus has the unique property of abolishing time to the extent

that it renders the interval of time it spans unnecessary. 6 There is no relationship between the time a miracle takes and the time it covers. 7 The miracle substitutes for learning that might have taken thousands of years. 8 It does so by the underlying recognition of perfect equality of giver and receiver on which the miracle rests. 9 The miracle shortens time by collapsing it, thus eliminating certain intervals within it. 10 It does this, however, within the larger temporal sequence."
(1,II,6,1-10)

That is, as the miracle is even modestly accepted by a mind, that mind begins to step beyond the normal temporal process. This holds both for how it operates in the world affecting others and within its own further development. Thus, the time needed for a 'natural' process, such as physical healing or for its own learning, is reduced to the degree it accepts the transformation of the miracle. That is, as statement 2 indicates, from the perspective of a mind steeped in the separative mode, it appears that it would take forever, an infinity of time, for every mind to come to the Atonement, which the Course proposes is possible for each. (If one thinks of this clearly, such a mind would think of it as a kind of 'everlasting hellfire,' perhaps the meaning of what Jesus is reported to have alluded to.) That seems to be what is meant by the 'horizontal perspective.' However, the acceptance of the miracle undoes its encasement in the 'it would take forever' perspective and enables it to move closer to the mode of being completely beyond time. That is the 'vertical plane.' To the degree or height it rises in that plane, it approaches full transformation. Correspondingly, it sees into the nature of time, that it is merely a construction of its own mind and the minds of others like it. At the highest level of complete transformation, it moves to a totally different perspective in which it sees that the whole of time is contained in a single instant. That is, as statement 5 indicates, to the degree one accepts the miracle, it reduces or collapses the temporal order, so that when one fully accepts it, time is completely abolished. Of course, that generally occurs only for a particular mind, since it is its choice to accept or not to accept the miracle. Thus, the miracle, which is an occurrence within the temporal order, takes a certain amount of time to occur. It can be thought as beginning at the moment the MG offers it to the MR (step vii as I have called it). This might be imagined as an 'injection' of 'energy' into the relationship between the MG and the MR. That energy, once given, continues to be present for the MR to accept. We might think of this as a 'cloud of light' that remains around the MR, which that mind can access at any time it chooses to accept it. This is represented in Fig. 26. However,

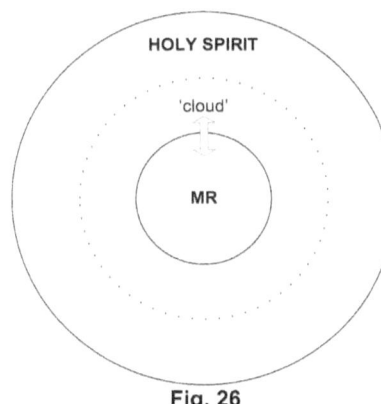

Fig. 26

this is subject to degrees of acceptance, so that at one later moment there can be a qualified influx of the 'energy' that has a corresponding correcting effect. Thus, the process of a particular miracle can, over a long period, have intermittent moments of acceptance in which there are 'jumps' of correction or healing that bring corresponding changes in that mind. This 'time-collapse' is represented in Fig. 27. What occurs here is that the segment of time that would otherwise have been required for the separated mind to move through is abolished to the degree that it accepts the miracle. This does not mean that it leaps ahead into the future in a manner that is sometimes imaged in modern movies, where

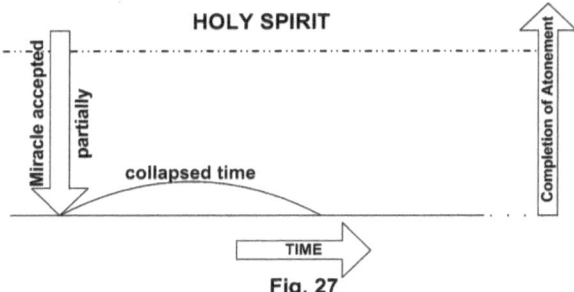
Fig. 27

others would have noticed that the person was absent in their world for a period; rather, it seems better understood as a matter of the deletion of a series of experiences that would have arisen if it had not accepted the miracle. Thus, when miracles occur, they place that mind 'ahead' in time in the sense of rendering unnecessary periods of experience that would have followed if the miracle had not produced the correction. As statement 7 points out, the period that is no longer needed to be passed through could be 'thousands of years.' Thus, statement 6 points out that the time it takes *for* a miracle to operate can be very small in comparison to the eliminated time interval that it affects or covers. Indeed, if the miracle is fully accepted, it brings about the complete collapse of time, as represented in Fig. 28. That is, the separated mind is brought to the completion of the Atonement, which is the same as the 'ending of time' or the ending of separation. Of course, that is not a matter of simple annihilation, but rather the restoration of the mind to its state of complete awareness of Love's presence, which

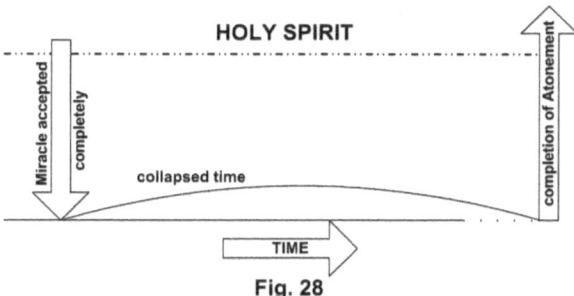
Fig. 28

the Course calls the 'Kingdom' or 'Heaven.' Statement 8 gives the basis for the miracle's power to bring about this collapse of time: 'by the underlying recognition of perfect equality' of the MG and the MR. In this, we may see the central factor that makes the miracle so powerful. That is, although the MG and MR appear to be *different* separated, limited, imperfect minds, they are in fact the *same* united, unlimited, perfect mind, the Christ Mind. When the MG chooses to draw in the 'light' fully, that mind moves to a recognition of the Christ Mind. It thereby becomes aware of the perfect equality between it and the MR. Here we should note that if the MG has not fully matured to perfect love, its recognition is obscured to some extent. However, if the MG is in perfect love, it has very clear awareness of its equality with the MR. In the latter situation, the MG operates out of the perception of the holy instant, in which this equality is clearly perceived. In the former, the perception of the Holy Spirit/Christ Mind, which can be thought of as 'looking' at the MR through the MG's eyes,' is fully aware of that equality. Thus, the act of choosing to accept the light/energy of the miracle, by either the MR or the MG, is what enables correction to occur. Furthermore, that correction occurs to the degree that the miracle is accepted.

Further, as statement 10 indicates, to the extent that any other minds have not made that choice, there remains the 'larger temporal sequence' of the world of separation. However, since each transformed mind recognizes its solidarity with all remaining separated minds, as the number of transformed minds increases, so is the sharing of miracles, which in turn accelerates the rate of transforming the remaining separated minds. From the perspective of those still in time, every one of them will eventually make the transformation which is the completion of the Atonement. But, from the perspective of the transformed mind, it is already completed; indeed, time never existed, since it sees that there is no time.

Understood in this way, the point made in Prin. 48 follows quite logically:

> "1 The miracle is the only device at your immediate disposal for controlling time. 2 Only revelation transcends it, having nothing to do with time at all."(1,I,48,1-2)

For the mind steeped in separation, it feels quite helpless in the inexorable grip of the laws of nature, whose primary variable is time, and seemingly totally beyond controlling it. However, since the substance of the miracle is to shift that mind beyond the temporal flow, by accepting it the mind comes to a condition in which it can control time, both for itself and for others. Of course, the concern for such control is only provisional. When it fully accepts the miracle, although it may choose to remain connected with the temporal world, it is also in a condition in which all time ceases, or the holy instant. Our little minds might regard that as a final death. However, its perception is of the Real World (discussed further in Ch. V). In one sense or on one level, because there remain other separated minds that have not realized this transformation, it is able to continue to operate within the world of perception so as to help them. But in another sense or on another level, it is already at the end of time or the completion of the Atonement. Thus, it is both within time and beyond it, somewhat as is the Holy Spirit.

One final observation may be made about the miracle and time as expressed in the following:

> "1 The basic decision of the miracle-minded is not to wait on time any longer than is necessary. 2 Time can waste as well as

> be wasted. 3 The miracle worker, therefore, accepts the time-control factor gladly. 4 He recognizes that every collapse of time brings everyone closer to the ultimate release from time, in which the Son and the Father are One."(1,V,2,1-4)

That is, the decision to accept the miracle is itself the decision to be miracle-minded. Once that has occurred, one begins to recognize the pointlessness of postponing any longer the acceptance of the responsibility to give miracles. Such a mind enters into the process of extending miracles to others, which is the same as accepting responsibility for the appropriate control and use of time as the means for releasing everyone from it.

6. The source of miracles. Earlier it was pointed out that the ultimate source of miracles is in the 'Energy' that is the foundation of everything. This 'Energy,' of course, is Love. This is made explicit in Prin. 3:

> "1 Miracles occur naturally as expressions of love. 2 The real miracle is the love that inspires them. 3 In this sense everything that comes from love is a miracle."(1,I,3,1-3)

This refers to both miracles in the primary sense (statement 1) and in the more general or secondary sense (statements 2 and 3). Thus, the giving of a particular miracle should be thought of as an intense manifestation of Love within the world of perception. That manifestation can be likened to an intense beam of luminous energy that stimulates the transformation of the MR, and, if needed, also of the MG, and then spreads from them to other separated minds.

Having this source, miracles are particularly powerful instances of something that is subject to the laws of this 'Energy.' This is described:

> "1 So would I liberate all things I see, and give to them the freedom that I seek. 2 For thus do I obey the law of love, and give what I would find and make my own. 3 It will be given me, because I have chosen it as the gift I want to give. 4 Father, Your gifts are mine. 5 Each one that I accept gives me a miracle to give. 6 And giving as I would receive, I learn Your healing miracles belong to me."(W,349,1,1-5)

We saw earlier that the Law of Love is quite simple: It gives totally of Itself. As applied to any created mind, since Love is given to it, its primary mandate is to give Love. For that mind, since the nature of true giving is that it involves receiving, by giving Love to another, it receives or intensifies It in itself. Since the effect of the miracle is healing or making whole, by giving it the giver is also either given healing or deepened in its awareness of wholeness.

Thus, this fundamental Law of Love entails that the giving of a miracle, by its healing effect, enables the MG to move to a very different way of viewing life, as described in the following affirmation that is one of the final practices central the Workbook:

> "3 I do not seek the things of time, and so I will not look upon them. 4 What I seek today transcends all laws of time and things perceived in time. 5 I would forget all things except

> Your Love. 6 I would abide in You, and know no laws except Your law of love."(W,346,1,3-6)

That is, as the student matures, he/she comes to recognize that there is only one law that needs to be followed: the Law of Love, which is expressed primarily by giving miracles. This is quite reminiscent of St. Augustine's observation about the primary principle or law of morality: "Love, and do what you will."[55]

7. Conditions hindering and helping miracles. The Course offers several further clarifications related to the conditions that both hinder and support the giving of miracles.

a. Conditions that block them. Three specific things that block miracles are weakness, doubt, and fear.

i. Weakness. What this involves is indicated in:

> "1 The meaning of love is lost in any relationship that looks to weakness, and hopes to find love there. 2 The power of love, which *is* its meaning, lies in the strength of God that hovers over it and blesses it silently by enveloping it in healing wings. 3 Let this be, and do not try to substitute your 'miracle' for this."(16,I,6,1-3)

What seems to be meant here is the presence of a perception of a lack of power in the mind of one wishing to give a miracle. Of course, such a perception will arise if the MG focuses on his/her own ability to produce a miracle. Since that self-perception is dominated by ego, which is the very cause of the perception of lack in the first place, it imposes on the process of giving release a contradictory idea that prevents release from occurring. By choosing to rely on one's own limited power, one is actually substituting an 'imitation miracle.' That is, such a mind would not be offering a miracle at all. The only correction for this is that the MG comes to recognize that the miracle rests on a power outside ego-limits, what is referred to as the unlimited 'power of Love' or the 'strength of God.' Thus, in order for the miracle to operate, the MG must set aside any sense that it rests on something that is part of his/her own limited mind, which by its very limitation involves what amounts to 'weakness,' but upon something far beyond those limits, that is, an unlimited power.

ii. Doubt. This seems to be closely related to the previous blocking condition, the point in:

> "1 One of the most difficult temptations to recognize is that to doubt a healing because of the appearance of continuing symptoms is a mistake in the form of lack of trust. 2 As such it is an attack. 3 Usually it seems to be just the opposite. 4 It does appear unreasonable at first to be told that continued concern is attack. 5 It has all the appearances of love. 6 Yet love without trust is impossible, and doubt and trust cannot

---

[55] In his "Homily 7 on the First Epistle of John."

> coexist. 7 And hate must be the opposite of love, regardless of the form it takes. 8 Doubt not the gift and it is impossible to doubt its result. 9 This is the certainty that gives God's teachers the power to be miracle workers, for they have put their trust in Him."(M,7,4,1-9)

This is more related to the MG's perception *after* the miracle is given. As was pointed out earlier, the transformation that comes in a miracle occurs to the degree that a mind accepts it. Also, acceptance can occur well after the time of offering it. This means that the MG, not observing any change in the MR, may think that the miracle 'has not worked.' However, that is only due to his/her still remaining in the time-bound mode and thinking that what has occurred is only what he/she perceives. If that happens, the response is one of doubt, which in turn raises in the MG's mind a block to its own transformation or healing. In such a state, the MG may be inclined to think the miracle has not been given, when it actually has. In turn, this may well produce a 'dampening' or 'slowing' of the transformation in both the MG and the MR.

From the Course's perspective, such doubting is more likely to arise in those who are just beginning to learn to give miracles. What we see here is that central to being an MG is the recognition that something exists quite beyond the field of separated awareness and that it can have effects on what is perceived within that field. This also calls for a willingness to accept or let that unperceived dimension come into operation through one's mind. This seems to be the essential feature of what may be called a type of 'faith' that is key to the occurrence of miracles.

In this we may further see why a miracle or healing cannot be repeated, which was discussed earlier in reference to M,7,1,2-6. While it can unfold or deepen in realization, both in the MR and the MG, once 'released' into the relationship between the MR and the MG, it will inevitably produce the healing transformation.

iii. Fear. This is the most obstructive block to the miracle, both in the MR and the MG. First, let us consider what it does in the MR, as indicated in:

> "5 Sometimes the illness has a sufficiently strong hold over the mind to render a person temporarily inaccessible to the Atonement. 6 In this case it may be wise to utilize a compromise approach to mind and body, in which something from the outside is temporarily given healing belief. 7 This is because the last thing that can help the non-right-minded, or the sick, is an increase in fear. 8 They are already in a fear-weakened state. 9 If they are prematurely exposed to a miracle, they may be precipitated into panic." (2,IV,4,5-9)

As we saw in the previous chapter, fear is a particularly powerful emotion that is generated by the mind that has chosen separation, which tends to hold it in that separated state. Thus, when one perceives that another actually believes that a lack or deficiency is present, it is important to be aware that that person's fear is closely related to that deficient condition. When a person who has matured to charity or imperfect love perceives such a person, he/she will naturally respond with the wish to help. However, it must first be assessed whether the dramatic change that might be brought through a miracle would only elicit an even more intense fear response ('panic') and thus produce an opposite effect of further blocking the transformation/healing. If that seems to be the case – and this is made clear if the MG consults with the Holy Spirit – this premature giving of a miracle would be unproductive. In such a situation, the Course advises that a more 'magical' approach (the use of something that is given healing belief), such as medication, ritual, etc., be used instead. Thus, the person is prepared to be more receptive to the miracle when it becomes appropriate to give it.

The importance of the MG's sensitivity to fear that may be present in the MR is further described:

> "3 This means that a miracle, to attain its full efficacy, must be expressed in a language that the recipient can understand without fear. 4 This does not necessarily mean that this is the highest level of communication of which he is capable. 5 It does mean, however, that it is the highest level of communication of which he is capable *now*. 6 The whole aim of the miracle is to raise the level of communication, not to lower it by increasing fear."(2,IV,5,3-6)

That is, the giving of miracles should not be thought of as a 'wholesale' sort of thing, or even perhaps as a gigantic 'give away.' A person who may have come to the state in which he recognizes the efficacy of miracles might be tempted to try to offer them to every person encountered. But that could itself be simply another 'ego-project' based on the thought that 'now *I* can do miracles.' In fact, no separated mind is the 'doer' of any miracle, but rather the vehicle or lens through which the real 'Doer' (Christ, the Holy Spirit, God, Love) produces healing. This does not mean to dismiss the importance of the MG in choosing to serve others, but only to make clear that the giving of miracles entails responsibility and sensitivity. Indeed, this underlies the point made earlier, that the would-be MG should always consult the 'Voice' concerning whether and to whom a miracle should be given.

The consequences of acting without this sensitivity and responsibility are described in the following:

> "1 Before miracle workers are ready to undertake their function in this world, it is essential that they fully understand the fear of release. 2 Otherwise they may unwittingly foster the belief that release is imprisonment, a belief that is already very prevalent. 3 This misperception arises in turn from the belief that harm can be limited to the body. 4 That is because of the underlying fear that the mind can hurt itself."(2,V,1,1-4)

That is, failure to recognize the state of the person to whom one would give a miracle can produce the opposite of what a miracle is intended to do: to further imprison, instead of liberate the MR from illusion and its misery. Statements 3 and 4 offer the reason for this: the receiving of a miracle involves the letting go or undoing of the belief that the body is essential to having existence, so that harming the body is equated with threatening that existence. The deeper basis of this, however, is that the mind, which on some level understands that it is responsible for all that occurs to it within its limited condition, believes that its choice to accept the transformation central to the miracle would bring some sort of harm or loss to itself. In the Course's view, this is based on the mind's attachment to the focused awareness that is intrinsic to separation. Thus, many separated minds may resist miracles simply because they have not yet matured enough to recognize that their attachment to belief in separation is precisely what is the basis of their misery. Accordingly, miracles should be offered only to those who are ready to take the next step in their awakening. Of course, only a Mind with far greater intelligence than any separated mind has adequate awareness of which ones are ready.

The MG, particularly in the stage of development in which imperfect love prevails, also has fears that can hinder the miracle. Indeed, this seems to be the basis for both the perception of weakness and doubt already discussed. But fear within the MG can interfere with the miracle more directly. The general nature of this interference is discussed in the following:

> "1 Both miracles and fear come from thoughts. 2 If you are not free to choose one, you would also not be free to choose the other. 3 By choosing the miracle you *have* rejected fear, if only temporarily. 4 You have been fearful of everyone and everything. 5 You are afraid of God, of me and of yourself. 6 You have misperceived or miscreated Us, and believe in what you have made. 7 You would not have done this if you were not afraid of your own thoughts. 8 The fearful *must* miscreate, because they misperceive creation. 9 When you miscreate you are in pain. 10 The cause and effect principle now becomes a real expediter, though only temporarily. 11 Actually, 'Cause' is a term properly belonging to God, and His 'Effect' is His Son. 12 This entails a set of Cause and Effect relationships totally different from those you introduce into miscreation. 13 The fundamental conflict in this world, then, is between creation and miscreation. 14 All fear is implicit in the second, and all love in the first. 15 The conflict is therefore one between love and fear."(2,VII,3,1-15)

This passage has been presented in full because it is particularly illuminating and very important for anyone who would give a miracle to understand. The primary insight of the Course is that everything that arises in awareness is based on the activity of the mind, or 'thought.' Thought can be either whole, as in any perfect mind, or fragmented, as in any separated mind. Within the latter, two sorts of further thought can arise. The one gives additional further support to fragmentation. The primary characteristic of this is that such thought is dominated by the separative feeling of fear. The other reverses this tendency and moves the mind toward wholeness. This is the essential feature of the miracle, and any other truly loving thoughts.

Any separated mind ('you') has a history of choosing fragmentation, and thus of thinking out of fear. Hence, it is stated that 'you have been fearful of everyone and everything,' including yourself. The basis of this comprehensive fear lies in the very simple fact that every idea or image that such a mind has is a construction it has itself made up, a projection of the fear-filled ego-idea upon everything it perceives. This is nothing more than a 'miscreation;' indeed, an expression of the truly creative power of the mind, but directed into the constrained limits that have arisen because of its choice to maintain awareness on a tiny part of Reality. That is, it is the cause of the distortions that run through everything it perceives. Of course, the real foundation of what is contained in those perceptions is the aspects of Reality that have actually been created by the one Cause, God, but which are so deformed by this projection of fear that they have the grotesque appearance of a 'world' that has almost no resemblance to the original. By its insistence on holding onto that appearance it opposes what is truly real, and thus enters into conflict. The truly real in no way opposes it, but simply remains what it is. However, such a mind interprets what thus arises as some sort of 'attack' by a greater 'power.' Ironically, all that true Power intends is that the separated mind be restored to the status of boundless peace and joy. Since that Power is Love, and fear is completely incompatible with Love, the situation is judged to involve a conflict between Love and fear.

Such a situation holds in every separated mind, including that of the would-be giver of miracles at the stage of imperfect love. Thus, when it comes to the point where it may choose to give miracles, it must confront that fear within itself. How that needs to be done is described:

> "1 You may still complain about fear, but you nevertheless persist in making yourself fearful. 2 I have already indicated that you cannot ask me to release you from fear. 3 I know it does not exist, but you do not. 4 If I intervened between your thoughts and their results, I would be tampering with a basic law of cause and effect; the most fundamental law there is. 5 I would hardly help you if I depreciated the power of your own thinking. 6 This would be in direct opposition to the purpose of this course. 7 It is much more helpful to remind you that you do not guard your thoughts carefully enough."(2,VII,1,1-7)

That is, since the separated mind itself chose or chooses to be fearful itself, no one else, not Christ, the Holy Spirit, or even God, can simply remove fear from it. That would be a violation of its own choice, which would actually be a violation of the very principle of Love, which gives not only awareness and creative capacity to whatever it creates, but in giving it creative capacity also endows it with the complete freedom to choose how it will use it. If another mind attempted to remove the fear that it chose for itself, it would cease to love that mind, that is, to affirm that mind's capacity to determine how it will use its thinking power. However, another mind, particularly one that is not caught in separation, can point out to it just what it has done to itself and continues to do. It then can move to clarity about what it has done and is doing. In the light of that clarity, it sees that it can either choose to continue in the fearful state or choose to let that fearful state drop away. In making the latter choice, which only it can determine, it takes the first step toward freedom. This is the choice that the Course refers to as one toward finding 'another way.'

Thus, the would-be MG, at least in the early stage of imperfect love, to some extent is choosing fear, even at the time he may want to choose to give a miracle. But, if he is to actually give a miracle, he must face that fear and choose to let it go. In doing so, he opens up to receive the light or 'grace' from the Holy Spirit/Christ Mind/God, which he then may pass on to the MR. The situation for the MG at this stage is described:

> "1 It has already been said that you believe you cannot control fear because you yourself made it, and your belief in it seems to render it out of your control. 2 Yet any attempt to resolve the error through attempting the mastery of fear is useless. 3 In fact, it asserts the power of fear by the very assumption that it need be mastered. 4 The true resolution rests entirely on mastery through love. 5 In the interim, however, the sense of conflict is inevitable, since you have placed yourself in a position where you believe in the power of what does not exist."(2,VII,1-4)

That is, the separated mind, tied into the choice of fear, as long as it maintains that choice, is unable to bring an end to fear. Indeed, it perceives fear as something that dominates it and in need of controlling or mastering. However, the very thought of 'mastery' is itself an idea of putting the ego in control. Thus, the ego, which continues to operate only through the support of the fear that it constructed, is confusedly thought able to bring some limit or mastery to that fear, while at the very same time it continues to generate that feeling. That is, the ego is completely unable to bring an end to fear. All it can do is *pretend* to control it (one thinks of the popular declaration, 'No Fear!' that one sometimes sees posted on vehicles), but all that such a mind has done is to suppress it into deeper levels of itself, where it continues to operate, often quite destructively.

However, although the ego is totally unable to bring an end to fear, the mind that has chosen the ego can make the choice that *begins* to undo it. In the case of the person offering a miracle, that choice must be made if the miracle is to be given. But this does not mean that all fear is completely eliminated by that choice. What usually happens is a temporary releasing of the domination by fear (and ego), as described in Prin. 28:

> "1 Miracles are a way of earning release from fear. 2 Revelation induces a state in which fear has already been abolished.

3 Miracles are thus a means and revelation is an end."
(1,I,28,1-3)

That is, in the initial choice to let fear go, that very choice invites the influx of Love into that mind. This may be especially instigated by the wish to bring healing to another, or to offer it a miracle. What then happens is that the 'energy' that moves into the MG can bring it further clarity about both the fear and the clinging to ego that still remains in it, so that it can choose an even more complete undoing of those two very limiting ideas. Thus, by giving a miracle to the MR, the MG finds further healing or movement toward transformation.

The undoing of fear by the miracle is also expressed in Prin. 26:

"1 Miracles represent freedom from fear. 2 'Atoning' means 'undoing.' 3 The undoing of fear is an essential part of the Atonement value of miracles."(1,I,26,1-3)

Although we discussed this principle earlier in regard to the general nature of the 'forgiving' or 'undoing' character of miracles as major events in the Atonement process, here we may understand how one of the most important 'undoings' is that of fear, particularly within the MG's mind. But we should also keep in mind that complete and permanent ending of fear generally does not happen immediately in the MR or even in the MG's giving of a single miracle. Rather, there is only an undoing of fear for the brief time and to the degree that makes it possible for the MG to receive and transmit the healing 'energy' to the MR. This is the point made in the passage cited earlier:

"3 By choosing the miracle, you *have* rejected fear, if only temporarily."(2,VII,3,3)

It may take many acts of such giving or receiving of miracles before either mind moves from imperfect to perfect love. Hence, the Course's emphasis on the importance of learning to *give* miracles as central to the transformation process of full awakening.

b. Conditions supporting miracles. The Course describes several conditions that are necessary in order for miracles to be given.

i. Pre-conditions for giving miracles. Several of these conditions may be thought of as 'pre-conditions,' in the sense that the MG must have come to a certain level of maturity before he/she is able to act in that capacity. The Course proposes three:

1) Purification. The first pre-condition is indicated in Prin. 7:

"1 Miracles are everyone's right, but purification is necessary first."(1,I,7,1)

What is meant by 'purification' is described in the following:

"5 Ideas of the spirit do not leave the mind that thinks them, nor can they conflict with each other. 6 However, ideas of the ego can conflict because they occur at different levels and also include opposite thoughts at the same level. 7 *It is impossible to share opposing thoughts.* 8 You can share only the thoughts that are of God and that He keeps for you. 9 And of

> such is the Kingdom of Heaven. 10 The rest remains with you until the Holy Spirit has reinterpreted them in the light of the Kingdom, making them, too, worthy of being shared. 11 When they have been sufficiently purified He lets you give them away. 12 The decision to share them *is* their purification."
> (5,IV,3,5-12)

Here is made clear that what is meant by purification is concerned with the removal or diminishing of the influence of thoughts based on ego. From what has been said, the separated mind's attachment to the ego is clearly the primary source of everything that interferes with the flow of Love in it. If ego-based thoughts are strong, the mind is unable to act as a transmitter of the miracle. One might think of them as like a 'monkey-wrench' thrown into the process. What the MG does is to receive the thoughts coming from God/Love/Christ/the Holy Spirit and then let them pass to the MR. But, even to begin this, the MG has to have come to some degree of diminishing the ego-block. Of course, the separated mind cannot help but raise such thoughts, since it is separated because it has chosen to hold on to ego. The problem with these 'impure' thoughts is that they are conflictive, which is ultimately rooted in the self-contradictory ego-idea, and their conflicting character makes it impossible for such a mind to give Love to another person. This does not mean that one cannot express them to another. Rather, that only generates conflict and opposition both within the other and between the one expressing them and the one to whom they are expressed. This is not at all what the Course means by 'sharing.' However, when the mind has developed to the point where it is able to hold a thought without raising its opposing thought, it is then able to give or share that thought. Indeed, it is the decision to share it that sets aside anything opposing it. We may think of this as something like a 'winnowing' process, in which the chaff (opposing thoughts) is separated from the grain. By sending the mix of positive and negative thoughts to the 'winnower' of sharing, what is communicated is only the positive. But this can happen only when the mind has sufficiently matured.

Here we should remember that this maturing is not something that the ego-dominated mind can *do*. It can only *choose to let it happen*. When that occurs, the higher level moves in to take the steps that move it along in its development. This development itself involves a kind of purification of the mind. This also makes it more receptive to the 'energy' behind the purifying process of separating positive from negative thoughts. The source of that is made quite clear:

> "7 Purification is of God alone, and therefore for you. 8 Rather than seek to prepare yourself for Him, try to think thus: 9 I who am host to God am worthy of Him. 10 He Who established His dwelling place in me created it as He would have it be. 11 It is not needful that I make it ready for Him, but only that I do not interfere with His plan to restore to me my own awareness of my readiness, which is eternal. 12 I need add nothing to His plan. 13 But to receive it, I must be willing not

to substitute my own in place of it."(18,IV,5,7-13)

That is, all the separated mind need, or even can, do is to make the choice to open to receive it and then let the 'Energy' of Love, primarily under the guidance of the Holy Spirit, take it through whatever steps are necessary to bring it to maturity. When it is sufficiently purified, as in the stage of imperfect love, it can begin to give miracles. When it is fully matured into perfect love, it gives them all the time. But more on this last point in Ch. V.

2) Ability to set aside fear. The second precondition for being able to give miracles is that fear be sufficiently set aside. This follows from what was said about the hindering effect of fear. Of course, any separated mind, by the very choice it makes to be separated, chooses to have fear. However, as was explained above, it can at times make a choice to reject fear, the point made in 2,VII,3,3, cited earlier on p. 204. But, like the problem of having a mix of positive and negative thoughts, this is possible only when the mind has come to a sufficient level of maturity. When it has so developed, only then is it able to be an MG.

3) Capacity for seeing equality. A third pre-condition, also related to how far the mind has developed, is that its perspective is one that can be described as 'seeing equality.' This is in regard to one's brothers, which includes both Christ and the MR, and to the perceived lack or deficiency. In relation to the first, the Course states:

> "4 The miracle is therefore a sign of love among equals. 5 Equals should not be in awe of one another because awe implies inequality. 6 It is therefore an inappropriate reaction to me. 7 An elder brother is entitled to respect for his greater experience, and obedience for his greater wisdom. 8 He is also entitled to love because he is a brother, and to devotion if he is devoted."(1,II,3,4-8)

The condition here is the attitude of the MG toward others involved in the giving of miracles. Not only does the MG need to see him/herself as equal with the MR, but with the Mind that it is its immediate source, the Christ Mind or the Holy Spirit. Clearly this equality is not a matter of what any of those minds are consciously aware of, but rather of recognizing each of them shares a complete sameness of value. Related to this is that the MG must not have any feeling of 'awe' toward that source-mind. The reason for this is further described:

> "1 Miracles should inspire gratitude, not awe. 2 You should thank God for what you really are. 3 The children of God are holy and the miracle honors their holiness, which can be hidden but never lost."(1,I,31,1-3)

Why miracles should not inspire awe becomes clear when we examine the nature of that feeling. There are several meanings of 'awe' in its modern usage:

1: fear mixed with dread, veneration, reverence, or wonder, as
  a. profound and reverent *fear* inspired by deity
  b. abashed reverence and *fear* inspired by authority or power

c: veneration and latent *fear* inspired by something sacred, mysterious, or morally impressive

d: reverent wonder with a touch of *fear* inspired by the grand or sublime, esp. in nature or art

In all of these definitions can be seen that awe includes some element of fear. Since fear, as we have seen, acts as a block to the miracle, it is clear that in so far as it involves fear, awe must generate some blockage to the miracle.

However, we should also note the following observations concerning awe:

"1 Awe should be reserved for revelation, to which it is perfectly and correctly applicable. 2 It is not appropriate for miracles because a state of awe is worshipful, implying that one of a lesser order stands before his Creator. 3 You are a perfect creation, and should experience awe only in the Presence of the Creator of perfection. 4 The miracle is therefore a sign of love among equals. 5 Equals should not be in awe of one another because awe implies inequality. 6 It is therefore an inappropriate reaction to me."(1,II,3,1-6)

and:

"2 I have said that awe is inappropriate in connection with the Sons of God, because you should not experience awe in the presence of your equals. 3 However, it was also emphasized that awe is proper in the Presence of your Creator."(1,VII,5,2-3)

While this reaffirms that awe is inappropriate toward any Son of God, including another separated mind, Jesus, the Christ Mind, or the Holy Spirit, primarily because it blocks the flow of Love between oneself and another, it nevertheless states that awe is an appropriate feeling for the separated mind to have toward God and what is directly from him (revelation). But, if awe involves some element of fear, how can it be an appropriate response toward the Creator, if fear has the effect of blocking the flow of Love? This apparent inconsistency may be resolved by two considerations. The first is that the separated mind, by its very own commitment to the ego, must feel some sort of fear when it begins to become aware of that Presence, since that Presence and its deepened awareness entail the dissolution of the ego. That is, on such an occasion that mind must have an emotional reaction that is a raising to prominence of its primary fear. However, this is only the initial response, which in so far as it continues to dominate that mind will block the full awareness of that Presence. The fearing aspect of awe is only one side of it. The other is what is called reverence, veneration, or wonder. What is central to the feeling of *reverence* is respect or honor; to the feeling of *veneration* it is respect inspired by sacredness or, in the Course's terms, Wholeness; to the feeling of *wonder*, it is a perception of the extraordinariness and amazed admiration. That is, awe involves both the feeling of fear and the feeling of immense worth of that toward which awe is felt. While the fear-aspect of awe does hinder a mind from union with the object of that feeling, the feeling of immense worth can override that fear. Of course, when the miracle is fully accepted, all fear is completely dissolved and the formerly separated mind returns to the state of feeling the unlimited worth of both God, itself, and every other perfect mind, in a condition of complete equality of worth.

The other sort of equality relates to the non-difference of difficulty among miracles, as stated in Prin. 1:

> "1 There is no order of difficulty in miracles. 2 One is not 'harder' or 'bigger' than another. 3 They are all the same. 4 All expressions of love are maximal."(1,I,1,1-3)

As we already saw, the only thing that could make one think that one miracle is more difficult than another is the thought that one perceived 'lack' or 'deficiency' is greater than another. If one believes this, that itself acts as a hindrance to giving a miracle. Thus, if one is to function as an MG, he/she must come to see this equality of all 'lacks'/'deficiencies.' What this means is that the MG needs to cease to be concerned about the content in the perception of the 'lack' and place attention on the Source that will correct that perception

ii. Conditions for giving miracles. The above are pre-conditions for giving miracles, which eventually arise in any mind that has made the choice to 'find the better way' of undoing the separation. Although they may take some time to be developed in a particular separated mind, once it has matured enough, it may then begin to act as an MG. But even here, at any occasion that such a mind chooses to give a miracle, there are two things or conditions that must be fulfilled for it to do so.

1) Miracle-mindedness and right-mindedness. The first is what the Course calls 'a miraculous state of mind,' which is in other places simply called 'miracle-mindedness,' as stated in Prin. 43:

> "1 Miracles arise from a miraculous state of mind, or a state of miracle-readiness."(1,I,43,1)

It will be helpful if we better understand what is meant, not only by the expressions 'miracle-mindedness' and 'miracle-readiness,' which are equivalent, but three other 'mindedness' terms used in the Course: 'wrong-mindedness,' or its equivalent 'not-right-mindedness,' and 'one-mindedness.' In general these all can be thought of as basic dispositions or orientations in a mind.

A first passage further clarifies 'miracle-mindedness:'

> "1 I have already said that miracles are expressions of miracle-mindedness, and miracle-mindedness means right-mindedness. 2 The right-minded neither exalt nor depreciate the mind of the miracle worker or the miracle receiver. 3 However, as a correction, the miracle need not await the right-mindedness of the receiver. 4 In fact, its purpose is to restore him *to* his right mind. 5 It is essential, however, that the miracle worker be in his right mind, however briefly, or he will be unable to re-establish right-mindedness in someone else."(2,V,3,1-5)

Here is made explicit that miracle-mindedness implies right-mindedness. What is characteristic of the latter is that it is a disposition in a mind that is still in the world of perception and that it is necessary in order for it to be able to give a miracle. Also involved in it is the previously discussed sense of 'equality' of both the MG and the MR. However, this does not mean that the MR has to have the miracle- or right-minded disposition. That disposition arises in a mind primarily by its being the receiver of a miracle, either directly from the Source or through the mediation of another mind within the world of perception.

The nature of right-mindedness is further clarified:

"1 The mind can be right or wrong, depending on the voice to which it listens. 2 *Right-mindedness* listens to the Holy Spirit, forgives the world, and through Christ's vision sees the real world in its place. 3 This is the final vision, the last perception, the condition in which God takes the final step Himself. 4 Here time and illusions end together."
(C,1,5,1-4)

"1 *Wrong-mindedness* listens to the ego and makes illusions; perceiving sin and justifying anger, and seeing guilt, disease and death as real. 2 Both this world and the real world are illusions because right-mindedness merely overlooks, or forgives, what never happened. 3 Therefore it is not the *One-mindedness* of the Christ Mind, Whose Will is One with God's."(C,1,6,1-3)

From this, we may see three broad sorts of states or dispositions possible for any mind. The most complete is 'One-mindedness.' It is the completely holistic awareness that is central to any perfect mind, such as the Christ Mind or the Mind of the Holy Spirit. Even in so far as that awareness may involve perception, it is oriented toward the Oneness of knowing and creating.

By 'right-mindedness' is meant the disposition in a mind within the realm of perception to move away from separation. From statement 2 in par. 5, we may see that right-mindedness involves more than the disposition to give miracles. In addition, it includes the disposition or inclination to listen to the Holy Spirit (which can occur even when no miracle is being offered) and also to let its perception blossom into perceiving the Real World. The last comes with the more mature development of a separated mind, and will be discussed further in Ch. V. The inclination to forgive, in the sense of letting go of false perceptions, seems best understood as the disposition to give miracles, or miracle-mindedness.

'Wrong-mindedness' refers to the disposition to choose to follow the dictates of the ego-idea that a separated mind has become immersed in. That includes the whole complex structure of beliefs, feelings, and behavior that was discussed in Ch. II.

Thus, there are only two basic sorts of mental disposition available for the separated mind, as described:

"2 You can be right-minded or wrong-minded, and even this is subject to degrees, clearly demonstrating that knowledge is not involved. 3 The term 'right-mindedness' is properly used as the correction for 'wrong-mindedness,' and applies to the state of mind that induces accurate perception. 4 It is miracle-minded because it heals misperception, and this is indeed a miracle in view of how you perceive yourself."(3,IV,4,2-4)

Besides their being the two basic possible dispositions, three other important points are made here. The first is that either of them can be matters of 'more or less.' One can be totally steeped in wrong-mindedness, or totally immersed in right-mindedness, or in a disposition that mixes aspects of both. This is completely consistent with the Course's overall view of the developmental nature of the mind's maturing from illusory love to imperfect love or charity (and that in many degrees), and from imperfect love to perfect love, which also may be thought of as either having degrees or simply being the highest state of maturity. The second point concerns the corrective nature of right-mindedness. That correction, as was pointed out earlier, is one of eliminating false perceptions by replacing them with true perceptions. The third point is that right-mindedness is an essential condition for the miracle, and thus that right-mindedness is included in miracle-mindedness.

The most essential feature of 'wrong-mindedness' or 'not-right-mindedness' is summarized in the following:

"4 All forms of not-right-mindedness are the result of refusal to accept the Atonement for yourself. 5 If you do accept it, you are in a position to recognize that those who need healing are simply those who have not realized that right-mindedness *is* healing."(2,V,4,4-5)

That is, the mind's condition comes down to a very simple choice: to reject or to accept the Atonement. This might be thought of as a variation of Hamlet's famous line: "To be or not to be: that is the question." Indeed, in the Course's view, 'to be' consists in being without any limitation, while 'not to be,' in being with limitations. Of course, the state of 'not to be' is generally not undone all at once after one makes the 'to be' choice, but involves the developmental process of letting go of all factors of limitation that the mind may have accumulated in its wrong-minded thinking.

How this relates to charity or imperfect love is indicated in a passage cited more fully earlier on p. 152:

"6 Charity is really a weaker reflection of a much more powerful love-encompassment that is far beyond any form of charity you can conceive of as yet. 7 Charity is essential to right-mindedness in the limited sense in which it can now be attained."(2,V,9,6-7)

That is, charity becomes active in a separated mind that has made the choice to come to right-mindedness. It is the first shift in the separated mind's transformation toward the Atonement. But it still involves the choice of holding on to the limitations that are endemic to wrong-mindedness. However, it is a necessary limited first stage in the separated mind's maturation.

Once the mind has come to this beginning stage of embracing right-mindedness, it begins to see the primary feature of the reason for its existence in the world of perception and time:

> "1 The basic decision of the miracle-minded is not to wait on time any longer than is necessary."(1,V,2,1)

Here is emphasized how a mind's shift from wrong-mindedness to right-mindedness also entails the commitment to the larger project of bringing miracles into the world it perceives. This is a part of the condition that disposes it to actually engage in giving miracles. Of course, as was made clear, it needs to guard against a kind of 'ego-enthusiasm' that might incline it to give a miracle without regard to the state of the potential MR, which can only be balanced by listening to the Voice regarding the appropriateness of giving it to a particular person at a particular time.

The progressive or developmental nature of the embracing of right-mindedness is also clarified in the following:

> "1 Salvation is nothing more than 'right-mindedness,' which is not the One-mindedness of the Holy Spirit, but which must be achieved before One-mindedness is restored. 2 Right-mindedness leads to the next step automatically, because right perception is uniformly without attack, and therefore wrong-mindedness is obliterated. 3 The ego cannot survive without judgment, and is laid aside accordingly. 4 The mind then has only one direction in which it can move. 5 Its direction is always automatic, because it cannot but be dictated by the thought system to which it adheres."(4,II,10,1-5)

In this we may see the role of right-mindedness in the overall process of Atonement. That salvation is right-mindedness should not be understood as saying that the mind's having made the choice is the same as its full realization of the Atonement, which is One-mindedness. Rather, that choice is the key for that realization to occur. Once chosen, the next step unfolds 'automatically' due to the acceptance of the correction of the fundamental error (that ego is to be upheld). This begins the process of dismantling the scaffold of all the subsequent errors, including the belief that one needs to make judgments. In a sense, prior to the choice of right-mindedness, the mind was 'automatically' in a self-sustained 'loop' of error. But, the new choice amounts to a breaking of that loop, so that Love can flow into the mind and 'automatically' reverse or undo the error-forming process. This is all part of the condition of dominance of right-mindedness in the MG's mind in order for it to be able to give a miracle.

A final passage related to this requirement of right-mindedness makes an important point:

> "8 You may feel that at this point it would take a miracle to enable you to do this, which is perfectly true. 9 You are not used to miracle-minded thinking, but you can be trained to

think that way. 10 All miracle workers need that kind of training."(2,VII,1,8-10)

In a sense, this may be thought of as a *pre*-condition that must happen before right-mindedness can come into a separated mind. That is, a mind not yet come to the point where it can make the choice necessary for it to be right-minded is very likely to think that it can't get out of its 'vicious cycle' (the 'loop') of wrong-mindedness without the help of a miracle. Indeed, that is precisely what it needs. However, once it is offered a miracle as an MR by an MG, it may then make the choice. In a sense, one might view Jesus as the initial MG among human beings, or at least as a very significant one within the 'interlocking chain of forgiveness.' However, the Course does make clear that there have been others, both among humans and elsewhere in the world of perception, who have made the choice:

> "1 This course has come from him because his words have reached you in a language you can love and understand. 2 Are other teachers possible, to lead the way to those who speak in different tongues and appeal to different symbols? 3 Certainly there are. 4 Would God leave anyone without a very present help in time of trouble; a savior who can symbolize Himself? 5 Yet do we need a many-faceted curriculum, not because of content differences, but because symbols must shift and change to suit the need. 6 Jesus has come to answer yours. 7 In him you find God's Answer."(M,23,7,1-7)

Thus, while the Course clearly recognizes that other teachers or initial realizers of Atonement have occurred within the human scene, it also points out to the student of the Course that his or her learning has been drawn to the particular teacher, Jesus. That is, while there is no claim of exclusivity or special superiority of his teaching, it will work for anyone who chooses to accept it. Of course, there remains the further question, as to whether Jesus was indeed the very first human to come to full realization of the Atonement. Although some interpreters of the Course do make that claim, it is not found anywhere in its teachings.[56] Indeed, we may speculate whether Jesus himself, like Siddhartha Gautama who

---

[56] One statement does indicate that Jesus has a kind of primacy:
> "2 He has established Jesus as the leader in carrying out His plan since he was the first to complete his own part perfectly."(C,6,2,2)

However, this does not say that others have not completed 'their part' after him, nor does it say that others have not completed 'their part' before him. For the latter, it only states that no one before Jesus completed 'their part' perfectly, which can be understood as allowing that they did so in an imperfect way. We should also be mindful that the Course is addressing human beings, so that it would not necessarily be claiming that Jesus was the first to complete his part perfectly within the whole universe. But this will be discussed more fully in my other book on the Holy Spirit and Jesus in the Course. In the Buddhist view, there were many others who became Buddhas prior to Siddhartha Shakyamuni, now called 'the Buddha.'

realized Buddhahood, had been preceded by someone who was the 'first' within the long scheme of time.

Here we might reflect that the most reliable opinion of scientists is that the space-time order has existed for at least 13 billion years, and that the star we call 'the Sun,' as well as the planet we call 'Earth,' most probably were preceded by other stars that generated the heavier atoms that are basic to our bodies. Thus, it is possible (even likely) that there have been many other 'masters' on thousands or even billions of other planets, who have preceded even Jesus and Siddhartha in coming to full awakening from the dream. This is made particularly poignant by the image that if one represented the whole of time by the length of one's arm, all of the 10,000 years of human history would be wiped away by the mere brushing of an emery board across one's fingertip (about 10 microns). Accordingly, given the Holy Spirit's assignment to bring separated minds to Atonement as quickly as possible, it seems quite unlikely that He waited all this time to begin to do so. Indeed, it may only be that we are just *very* slow learners, and that, as is expressed in Hindu and Buddhist stories, there have been many, many other places and persons who have preceded us in coming to full individual Atonement. It is quite possible that some of them acted as the teachers of Jesus and other great Teachers of Atonement, both within our solar system and elsewhere.

2) Setting aside attack. A second condition that must be present in the MG in order to give a miracle is described:

> "1 There is no sadness where a miracle has come to heal. 2 And nothing more than just one instant of your love without attack is necessary that all this occur."(27,V,4,1-2)

What is here called 'love without attack' may be understood as the complete setting aside of any impulse to aggression or act that seeks to bring harm to another, any word, or even any thought that tends toward that. Perhaps the most extreme example of this is Jesus' response to those who sought and carried out his execution by crucifixion. This is possible only for a mind that has the full presence of unconditional love. It seems also to have been the approach taken by Mohandas Gandhi and Martin Luther King in their efforts to bring about the letting go of the ego-centered repressive and sometimes destructive actions and policies of the British colonial rule and the racist legal and social system of the United States. Although one might focus on the violence and sometimes murderous actions of their oppressors, from the Course's perspective what is often overlooked is that they related to their oppressors without any action, word, or even wish to harm them. This is sometimes called the 'method of nonviolence,' but to think of that as a merely political 'method' for imposing change on others completely misses the core of their approach. That is, what they were offering to others was unconditional love without attack, or in the Course's terms miracles, both to the individuals with whom they interacted and to the whole society they were parts of.

However, the Course does not make the giving of a miracle subject to the MG's having such heroic and constant non-attacking state. All that is needed is that the MG be able to make the choice to relate in that way if only for a brief moment. That is sufficient for the transforming energy of Love to enter into his/her mind and to flow to the MR. Even if afterwards, as often is the case of those who have only imperfect love, there returns some impulse to attack, either mentally or verbally or in action, the MG has acted as a vehicle for the miracle, and the miracle's effects are quite independent of those lapses into the wrong-mindedness of the ego-dominated mind.

Thus, these two conditions of right-mindedness and non-attack are the only special ones that the Course indicates as necessary to be present in the MG's mind, beyond taking the steps of deciding to help another perceived as having a lack, calling on the Voice to ask that help flow into the relationship, and offering it to the MR.

8. General contexts in which miracles occur. It has been pointed out that the giving of miracles occurs when a particular separated mind has developed to a certain degree of maturity. Thus, they are given within the context of two sorts of overall circumstance of a particular mind. These are what is called 'charity'/'imperfect love' and 'perfect love.' Although the giving of a miracle is fundamentally the same process in both, there are some differences.

a. Miracles within imperfect love, or charity. Our focus here has been primarily on this weaker form of genuine love. The passage cited earlier (p. 153) is worth repeating in its fuller form:

> "1 Charity is a way of looking at another as if he had already gone far beyond his actual accomplishments in time. 2 Since his own thinking is faulty he cannot see the Atonement for himself, or he would have no need of charity. 3 The charity that is accorded him is both an acknowledgment that he needs help, and a recognition that he will accept it. 4 Both of these perceptions clearly imply their dependence on time, making it apparent that charity still lies within the limitations of this world. 5 I said before that only revelation transcends time. 6 The miracle, as an expression of charity, can only shorten it. 7 It must be understood, however, that whenever you offer a miracle to another, you are shortening the suffering of both of you. 8 This corrects retroactively as well as progressively."
> (2,V,10,1-8)

Thus, the MG who has come to the stage of charity, by his/her decision to move in the direction of Atonement, is able to access the Source of the miracle and offer it to the MR, who may at that point be quite unable even to consider Atonement due to his choice to cling to ego. However, this 'burst of energy' transmitted from the Source by the MG serves at least to open the MR's mind to the possibility of the 'other way.' At the same time, the MG, by having received that 'energy' to pass on to the MR, has also been given a boost in illumination appropriate to his capacity to integrate it into awareness. Thus, the MG is moved forward in his/her own healing process. For both, the acceptance of the Love 'energy' shortens time to the extent that this 'energy' (one meaning of the word 'grace' used by the Course) is accepted.

As to the point of statement 8, that the miracle corrects 'progressively,' this seems best understood as a matter of undoing, to some extent at least, a separated mind's immersion in wrong-mindedness, so that later experiences are not dominated by those earlier errors that have been corrected by the miracle. How it corrects 'retroactively' is less obvious. It could mean two things. One is that the correction occurring now somehow actually goes back to undo the errors occupying that mind at a previous time. However, if that were the case, then it would mean that the error that is undone at the moment of receiving the miracle, by this retroactive undoing had been undone prior to the acceptance of the miracle. That would require that the error could not be present in that mind at the time of the acceptance of the miracle, and yet it would be present in that mind at that time. This is clearly a contradiction. (This is much the same sort of logical problem that the idea of the science fiction image of time-travel into the past, where one actually goes back in time to cause the death of his own grandfather before he is able to initiate conception of any child, entails an obvious contradiction and is therefore impossible.) Thus, this cannot be the meaning of 'correcting retroactively.'

The other meaning is that the miracle only undoes the consequences that still remain to be worked out as a result of previous actions base on that error. This is related to what in the East is sometimes called the 'law of karma.' In the West, there is a similar idea which could be called the 'law of sin.' Both versions hold essentially that any action, particularly negative ones, involve the necessity of encountering at a later time some sort of experience to compensate for that earlier action. However, this retroactive correction can be understood as simply the undoing of the necessity of having that 'karmic' retribution. In the East, it is thought that certain rituals, such as bathing in the Ganges on certain holy days, can undo all of one's negative karma. In the traditional Christian tradition, one finds the belief that the ritual of baptism or confession (or, among Catholics, the performance of prayers that give 'indulgences') undoes those negative effects. The Course bypasses all these secondary ritualistic (and, to it, *magical*) procedures. What is called 'past karma' or the 'debt of sin' is completely dissolved to the extent that one accepts the miracle. Quite simple, indeed!

Still, there remains the problem that as long as the mind has not completely accepted the Atonement, it is also unable to completely accept the miracle. Thus, while in that state, such an MG or MR remains in the condition of imperfect love. Of course, it is possible to learn to get beyond that. Indeed, much of the Workbook gives daily lessons to aid that learning. For example, lesson 175 involves the affirmation:

"1 I give the miracles I have received.

2 God is but Love, and therefore so am I."(W,175,1-2)

This can be sincerely practiced even by a mind only at the stage of imperfect love. The mind acknowledges that it has received miracles and that it can and does give them. However, this is only in a manner that is appropriate for one at that stage.

b. Miracles within perfect love. Once the mind matures to the state of perfect love, it operates in a much different way. We will discuss this at length in the next chapter, but I note that its giving of miracles proceeds out of two very important further conditions that are characteristic of that state, what are called the 'holy instant' and the 'holy relationship.'

We briefly consider the first:

> "1 In the holy instant, you and your brother stand before the altar God has raised unto Himself and both of you. 2 Lay faithlessness aside, and come to it together. 3 There will you see the miracle of your relationship as it was made again through faith. 4 And there it is that you will realize that there is nothing faith cannot forgive. 5 No error interferes with its calm sight, which brings the miracle of healing with equal ease to all of them. 6 For what the messengers of love are sent to do they do, returning the glad tidings that it was done to you and your brother who stand together before the altar from which they were sent forth."(19,I,14,1-6)

That is, the experience of the holy instant involves a radically new sort of perception of others, of the world, and of oneself. At least while in it, there is no presence of error of any sort. Indeed, it is almost the same as the Holy Spirit's perception. However, because that mind still has a perception of other minds, it can offer them miracles according to their need of them.

The holy relationship also involves a radically new sort of mode of relating with other minds.

> "2 For in the miracle of your holy relationship, without this barrier, is every miracle contained. 3 There is no order of difficulty in miracles, for they are all the same. 4 Each is a gentle winning over from the appeal of guilt to the appeal of love."
> (19,IV,A,5,2-4)

In the fully matured holy relationship, which is central to every mind in perfect love, there is no limit to such a mind in regard to giving miracles. It fully sees that none are more difficult than others, and always recognizes when it is appropriate to give them. In this state, it recognizes the full truth of Prin. 6:

> "1 Miracles are natural. 2 When they do not occur something has gone wrong."(1,I,6,1-2)

That is, it recognizes that the sole point of remaining in the world of perception and minds that still think they are separated is to be a channel for miracles. In that sense, it also directly sees the full meaning of Prin. 5:

> "1 Miracles are habits, and should be involuntary. 2 They

should not be under conscious control. 3 Consciously selected miracles can be misguided."(1,I,5,1-3)

That is, being an MG is its constant disposition. The basis of this is its full congruency with the Mind of the Holy Spirit, rather than the limited sort of awareness that is intrinsic to what the Course calls 'consciousness.' Thus, it can make no mistake regarding the appropriateness of when or to whom to give miracles. But more will be said in Ch. V on both the holy instant, the holy relationship, and the giving of miracles by a mind matured to perfect love.

9. Summary and definition of 'miracle.' I may now offer a succinct summar description or definition of what the Course understands by the term 'miracle.' This may start with the central insight expressed in Prin. 12:

> "1 Miracles are thoughts. 2 Thoughts can represent the lower or bodily level of experience, or the higher or spiritual level of experience. 3 One makes the physical, and the other creates the spiritual."(1,I,12,1-3)

Thus, miracles are a kind of thought. Some thoughts are highly limited due to the choice of separation, and constitute what is called the physical or material level. Others move beyond those limitations and constitute the higher or spiritual level. Miracles are thus thoughts that serve to mediate between the higher and the lower levels so as to enable the mind bound within the lower level to move stepwise and eventually fully to the higher level.

Thus, a miracle may be defined as *a thought in which one mind, upon perceiving that another mind perceives a lack, chooses to accept another perception of wholeness, as perceived by the Holy Spirit/Christ Mind, and to allow the Light/Power of Love to flow through it to that other mind, thereby facilitating the letting go of that perception of lack and replaced by the perception of wholeness.*

C. The two primary concerns of imperfect love or charity: self-development and helping others. Although the giving of miracles is a very important expression of the mind that has developed to the stage of imperfect love, since such a mind is not as yet able to give miracles all the time and in all situations, it is clear that charity must be expressible in another way. That is, we may think of the giving of a miracle as an intense injection or burst of Love-energy within the world of perception, whose primary function is to speed up the process of transformation of both the MG and the MR. But, once a miracle has been given, it cannot be repeated to that person. How, then does imperfect love/charity manifest or operate at times when one is not giving a miracle?

There seem to be two main concerns beyond giving miracles that become central to imperfect love: furthering one's own development and helping others in their development. Indeed, both of these are aspects of the same primary concern of Atonement. From the Course's perspective, self-development involves primarily becoming dedicated to studying the Course. This can involve two major activities. One is the study and the practice of the Course's teachings. That seems to focus on further inquiry so as to come to a better understanding of the nature of the fundamental insights concerning the nature of each individual mind, both as caught in the separated 'dream' state and liberated in its deeper reality as an expression of the perfect Christ Mind, and the process by which it may pass from separation to the full awakening from that dream. By developing an understanding of these insights, it has a basis for engaging in the practical steps it needs to take as it moves toward Atonement. The other is learning to listen to the Voice for God. This seems to be the core of the 'universal Course,' of which *A Course in Miracles* is one expression. Indeed, these writings are only symbolic expressions of something more fundamental, and thus one must be careful about treating this particular expression as what is called an 'idol' by the Course itself. Like miracles, it is a means for a much more important end, and should be valued only in so far as it helps one attain that end.

The other concern of helping others is intimately connected with the concern for one's own development. That is, since others are in fact the very same as one's own Self, not in their separated appearance but in their fundamental reality as other 'fragments' of the Christ Mind, by helping them, one is literally helping oneself. Furthermore, it should be clear that the criterion of whether one is actually helping another is not primarily a matter of relieving their particular sufferings, or improving their physical, emotional, or intellectual states, or their economic, social, or political conditions, but of helping them undo the illusions that are the cause of any suffering and limitation that they may experience. Of course, this may involve any or all of those secondary improvements, since negative conditions can act as a major block to the undoing or forgiving of their illusions. It might express as helping by way of physical or limited psychological healing, or even economic, social, or political reform. However, those are only secondary concerns, having relevance in so far as they may be helpful toward the primary concern of undoing the fundamental illusions arising from ego. Indeed, as one engages in this process in relation to others, there is a lessening of the hold of ego on the minds of both the giver and receiver of that help. As this occurs, there also comes the lessening of the ego's effects: fear, guilt, anger, attack, and the grip of the beliefs it generates about sin, sacrifice, and illusory love. Along with the undoing of those illusions comes a radically different vision of oneself and of the world:

> "4 If I would remember who I am, it is essential that I let this image of myself go. 5 As it is replaced by truth, vision will surely be given me. 6 And with this vision, I will look upon the world and on myself with charity and love."(W,56,3,4-6)

That is, as a separated mind allows charity to operate within it, the ego-mode becomes increasingly weakened and finally is altogether dropped. This is a kind of rising from a more limited sort of charity to an increasingly purified and fuller version, till it culminates in the fullest mode of love available to separated minds, or more accurately, to minds still in the realm of separation: perfect love. We will come to that in Ch. V.

Thus, charity does not only have a transformative effect on the individual separated mind receiving it. As is stated:

> "3 Each one you see in light brings your light closer to your awareness. 4 Love always leads to love. 5 The sick, who ask for love, are grateful for it, and in their joy they shine with holy thanks."(13,VI,10,3-5)

That is, although this form of love may be imperfect, there is in it a kind of feedback effect. By giving it as forgiveness to others, it is also given directly to oneself, and others are further awakened to return it to the one who gave it. This, in turn, generates an even clearer and purer type of charity in the giver, enabling him to give an even less diluted form to others. This eventually leads to the even higher mode of perfect love.

D. 'False charity.' The Course also points out that there is a kind of counterfeit of charity, what could be called 'false charity,' that the student needs to be aware of and guard against falling into.

1. False charity in general. One aspect of it is described in the following:

> "1 When you 'forgive' a sin, there is no gain to you directly. 2 You give charity to one unworthy, merely to point out that you are better, on a higher plane than he whom you forgive. 3 He has not earned your charitable tolerance, which you bestow on one unworthy of the gift, because his sins have lowered him beneath a true equality with you. 4 He has no claim on your forgiveness. 5 It holds out a gift to him, but hardly to yourself."(W,126,3,1-5)

This false charity is closely connected with, in the Course's view, a very distorted notion of forgiveness. The latter is the idea that forgiveness is primarily a response to something one judges to be a 'sin.' In this, one considers the 'sin' to have really happened. This appraisal holds that what is regarded as sinful is real and imposes on the sinner both guilt and the requirement of punishment. While dismissing actual punishment, the person forgiving places himself on a higher level than the sinner, regarding him still as guilty for having really committed a sin. The sinner thus *deserves* no forgiveness, but out of a 'noblesse oblige' the 'forgiver' dismisses or lessens the punishment. Thus, the 'charitable' one deems himself superior to the other, and of course considers the other to remain obligated to him – a kind of subtle insistence that the guilty one owes something in return for that act of 'charity.'

It is readily clear that such a type of 'charity' is frequently what operates in what goes by that name. This is particularly present in those who give 'charity' so that their names are engraved on monuments and especially in the public's mind, as can be the case with so-called 'charitable institutions' and 'philanthropists.' If that is the motivation, what the givers get in return is little more than an enlargement of their egos, and often the increase in power within the community. In such cases, it is doubtful there is any trace of what the Course means by 'charity.'

The nature of false charity is further illuminated by the following:

> "1 The ego literally lives by comparisons. 2 Equality is beyond its grasp, and charity becomes impossible. 3 The ego never gives out of abundance, because it was made as a substitute for it. 4 That is why the concept of 'getting' arose in the ego's thought system."(4,II,7,1-4)

Here we see how false charity, in its ego-aggrandizing effort, completely fails to support the fundamental equality of all separated minds. It gives *in order to get*. In other words, its 'charity' is essentially a matter of buying recognition, power, or even possibly the relief one's own guilt. The latter was famously exploited by the system of 'sale of indulgences' in European Christianity, and may often be the actual operating principle in 'charitable' donations and works even today, which the givers think will obtain for them some sort reduction of their guilt and punishment, under the belief that God will forgive them their own sins which may have been 'committed' in the accumulation of their wealth. But we must be careful here. It is not that the Course considers some actions one may have done to be 'sins,' or even that false charity to try to compensate for such to be a 'sin,' since sin has no reality at all. Rather, the folly of false charity is that it is an illusory act based on ego and that its primary effect is to further embed the giver in ego- or wrong-mindedness.

2. False charity as 'forgiveness-to-destroy' (FTD). The most penetrating discussion of the central problem of false charity is found in the "Song of Prayer," one of latest parts of the Course claimed to have been dictated by its Author, in the section on 'forgiveness-to-destroy,' which will be referred to more briefly as FTD. Here, we need to recall that in the Course's view, both specific miracles and what might be called the 'Great Miracle' (the completion of the 'Atonement') have as their central process the removal of the blocks to the awareness of Love's presence. The term used to name the core activity of that removal is 'forgiveness.' This is simply a matter of letting go of beliefs, thoughts, feelings and actions that interfere with Love's awareness. In most specific miracles, forgiveness is restricted; in the 'Great Miracle,' it is complete. Thus, forgiveness is the central activity in the process of healing (which is primarily a restoration of wholeness). It was pointed out that the key to true healing is a matter of seeing the one being healed as perfect. In order to do that, one must let go the perception of the imperfection(s) that constitute the deficiency.

a. FTD in general. But forgiveness-to-destroy (FTD) is an idea of forgiveness that, although it may seem to 'let go' certain things, actually more deeply embeds the mind that thinks it is forgiving into the ego-mode. To understand better this serious distortion or 'illusion of forgiveness' (also integral to false charity), consider several passages in the "Song of Prayer." The first:

> "1 Forgiveness-to-destroy will therefore suit the purpose of the world far better than its true objective, and the honest means by which this goal is reached. 2 Forgiveness-to-destroy will overlook no sin, no crime, no guilt that it can seek and

> find and 'love.' 3 Dear to its heart is error, and mistakes loom large and grow and swell within its sight. 4 It carefully picks out all evil things, and overlooks the loving as a plague; a hateful thing of danger and of death. 5 Forgiveness-to-destroy *is* death, and this it sees in all it looks upon and hates. 6 God's mercy has become a twisted knife that would destroy the holy Son He loves."(S,2,I,2,1-6)

The first point is that FTD is closely connected to the whole reason that the world of separation was formed in the first place: to fortify the mind's belief and involvement in separation. The world's 'true objective' alluded to is to serve as a means for undoing the separation; for the Course, this is how the Holy Spirit perceives it. The second point is that FTD makes the notion of sin its primary focus. We have already seen that the belief in sin is generated by the ego as part of its 'thought-system' as a means of maintaining itself. This includes the beliefs in sin, sacrifice, and specialness; feelings of fear, guilt, hate, anger, and depression; and behavior that is primarily based on attack and focusing on special relationships. Thus, FTD is a particular kind of response that reinforces the ego network by making the notion of 'sin' and its variations (errors, mistakes, crimes), or what the separated mind thinks of as primarily 'evil,' its major focus.

However, the third point (in statement 5), that FTD is death, may not be immediately clear. Indeed, at first it seems to be quite an overstatement, possibly even nonsensical. But when we look more closely at what the Course means by 'death' we find that this statement points to a very profound insight. Although most of the definitions of 'death' relate to the termination of life in a body, there are several that have a wider sense. Two of these (4b and 4c in the dictionary) are:

1. a joyless dull tasteless existence: the state of being without full possession or enjoyment of the intellectual faculties
2. cessation or absence of spiritual life variously conceived as alienation from God, deadness to the appeals of spiritual ideals, annihilation of the spirit as a result of sin or unredeemable damnation

From these we can draw perhaps a meaning that is what the Course is indicating in 1: the state of not being fully alive (a kind of relative death) with respect to one or more of one's possible vital processes, such as emotional death, intellectual death, or spiritual death.

Thus, it should be clear that statement 5 in the last cited passage makes complete sense. This is because FTD is a counterfeit kind of 'forgiveness' that only further embeds one in the state of separation, which is actually a kind of 'living death.' How this is so will become even clearer if we consider the major forms that FTD expresses in. A first passage is:

> "1 Forgiveness-to-destroy has many forms, being a weapon of the world of form. 2 Not all of them are obvious, and some are carefully concealed beneath what seems like charity. 3 Yet all the forms that it may seem to take have but this single goal;

their purpose is to separate and make what God created equal, different. 4 The difference is clear in several forms where the designed comparison cannot be missed, nor is it really meant to be."(S,2,II,1,1-4)

Here it is noted that some forms of FTD are not quite as clearly recognized as what was called 'false charity.' But what is common to them all is their single goal: to maintain separation, the state of 'living death.' Connected with that goal is the further establishment in the mind that one portion of the perceptual world is unequal with another. This inequality is primarily a matter of thinking that one portion, aspect, or group of aspects is more important or of greater value than another. Of course, this is a further extension of the original assignment of greater value to one aspect of Reality in contrast to all other aspects that is the basis of the mind's decision to focus and hold on to those aspects which brought about the separation. It may be thought of as an application of that move to a particular group of perceptions within its field of contracted awareness. That is, what one perceives as 'another mind' is judged to be of lesser value than some 'other mind.' This more important mind can be either the one thought of as one's own or some other ('God,' 'Christ,' 'Holy Spirit,' or one with whom one has a special relationship.) These are illustrated in the three main forms of FTD.

b. The main types of FTD. The course discusses three sorts of FTD.

i. Arrogant FTD. The first of these is described:

"1 In this group, first, there are the forms in which a 'better' person deigns to stoop to save a 'baser' one from what he truly is. 2 Forgiveness here rests on an attitude of gracious lordliness so far from love that arrogance could never be dislodged. 3 Who can forgive and yet despise? 4 And who can tell another he is steeped in sin, and yet perceive him as the Son of God? 5 Who makes a slave to teach what freedom is? 6 There is no union here, but only grief. 7 This is not really mercy. 8 This is death."(S,2,II,2,1-6)

We might call this '**arrogant FTD**' since its central intent is to affirm the superiority of the 'forgiver' over the 'forgiven.' Clearly, in this case the mind thought of as having greater value is the 'forgiver's.' This can only reinforce the belief in separation, which true forgiveness focuses on ending. In arrogant FTD the 'forgiver' holds that the other has really committed a 'sin' that his 'superiority' condescends to 'forgive.' There is also an intent to make the 'forgiven' beholden to the 'forgiver,' a subtle intent to obligate him or make him enslaved to his 'nobility.'

ii. False humility FTD. The second form of FTD is indicated in:

"1 Another form, still very like the first if it is understood, does not appear in quite such blatant arrogance. 2 The one who would forgive the other does not claim to be the better. 3 Now he says instead that here is one whose sinfulness he shares, since both have been unworthy and deserve the retribution of the wrath of God. 4 This can appear to be a humble

> thought, and may indeed induce a rivalry in sinfulness and guilt. 5 It is not love for God's creation and the holiness that is His gift forever. 6 Can His Son condemn himself and still remember Him?"(S,2,II,3,1-6)

This could be called '**false-humility FTD**.' The problem is not that it emphasizes inequality between 'forgiver' and 'forgiven,' but that it focuses on another facet of separation, the belief in sin. Here, the 'superior' mind is the one that is thought of as 'God.' This does not insist so much on separation between one's brother and oneself, but on separation between God and both oneself and one's brother, who are also judged to be really sinful and thus unholy and separate from God.

This is further described, with an additional variation:

> "1 Here the goal is to separate from God the Son He loves, and keep him from his Source. 2 This goal is also sought by those who seek the role of martyr at another's hand. 3 Here must the aim be clearly seen, for this may pass as meekness and as charity instead of cruelty. 4 Is it not kind to be accepting of another's spite, and not respond except with silence and a gentle smile? 5 Behold, how good are you who bear with patience and with saintliness the anger and the hurt another gives, and do not show the bitter pain you feel."(S,2,II,4,1-5)

Since 'false humility FTD' emphasizes the belief in one's unworthiness, its intention is to intensify the sense of separation between separated minds and their Source because of their inferior value. And in the special variation, which could be called '*martyr FTD*,' the intention is to deepen the sense of sinfulness in both the 'forgiving' martyr who sees the inflicting of pain by the one he 'forgives' as something quite real, and thus a sin. But because the 'forgiver' regards himself as also a sinner, he considers the inflicted pain as something he deserves. On a subtler level, by becoming a 'martyr,' one thinks he raises his value in the 'view of God,' which lowers the value of the one he perceives as the cause of his martyrdom. Thus, the belief in the sinfulness and guilt of both the 'forgiver' and the 'forgiven' is made even stronger by the act of 'forgiving acceptance,' even though it may not have the arrogance of the first type of FTD.

The main problem in this is that it completely misses the primary concern of true forgiveness, as is explained:

> "1 Forgiveness-to-destroy will often hide behind a cloak like this. 2 It shows the face of suffering and pain, in silent proof of guilt and of the ravages of sin. 3 Such is the witness that it offers one who could be savior, not an enemy. 4 But having been made enemy, he must accept the guilt and heavy-laid reproach that thus is put upon him. 5 Is this love? 6 Or is it rather treachery to one who needs salvation from the pain of guilt? 7 What could the purpose be, except to keep the witnesses of guilt away from love?"(S,2,II,5,1-7)

That is, the whole intention of true forgiveness is the removal of obstacles to the awareness of Love's presence, and some of the greatest obstacles to that are pain, suffering, guilt and sinfulness. Because such 'forgiveness' tends to suppress that true awareness, it reinforces the state of living death, and hence is a type of FTD.

iii. 'Bargaining' FTD. The third main type of FTD the Course discusses is described in the following:

> "1 Forgiveness-to-destroy can also take the form of bargaining and compromise. 2 'I will forgive you if you meet my needs, for in your slavery is my release.' 3 Say this to anyone and you are slave. 4 And you will seek to rid yourself of guilt in further bargains which can give no hope, but only greater pain and misery. 5 How fearful has forgiveness now become, and how distorted is the end it seeks. 6 Have mercy on yourself who bargains thus. 7 God gives and does not ask for recompense. 8 There is no giving but to give like Him. 9 All else is mockery. 10 For who would try to strike a bargain with the Son of God, and thank his Father for his holiness?"(S,2,II,6,1-9)

This can be called '***bargaining FTD.***' Perhaps it is the most common form that we experience, thinking that it is the normal and appropriate way to live with others. Here the intent is to be willing to overlook perceptions that are considered to be offenses so that they are thought of as the 'price' to pay for what one perceives as benefits from the offender. The offenses are generally what the 'forgiver' considers to be relatively minor and tolerable, provided that the 'forgiven' recognizes his/her obligation to compensate for the offense by offering the benefit that the 'forgiver' perceives he is in need of. Generally, this is central to special relationships, the 'true love' or 'trade idea of love' that is actually only illusory love. Because each person in such a relationship is in it for the sake of satisfying some need, it is maintained as long as the 'bargain' is fulfilled. When that fails to happen, the relationship enters a crisis and can even move to one of the previously discussed forms of FTD, where one takes on the mentality of the 'martyr' or the 'sinner who deserves to suffer' or the 'arrogant superior.' In all cases, however, there is some level of perceived need that is the concern of the exchange. In this particular form, there is an agreement to accept one's obligation to fulfill the other's need, and to 'forgive' the 'sins' one has perceived to have been really committed against oneself. However, as indicated in the passage, it is actually a kind of agreement to be enslaved and to enslave.

In this form of FTD, there is a kind of 'alternating superiority.' That is, first one sees the other as of greater value with respect to some particular need or needs, then moves to the affirmation of one's own value regarding those needs with the expectation that the other acknowledge this. Of course, underlying this oscillation is each one's fundamental belief that he/she is most important. In this, we may recognize the core of what could be called a kind of 'personal social contract' that is central to the special relationship of illusory love. However, it can be clearly seen to be based on the ego's commitment to guilt, and accordingly is only a variation of the strategy to maintain separation. It has nothing to do with true forgiveness, but only further entangles one in attachment to ego and involvement in the cycle of suffering.

This passage also makes clear that this sort of FTD is completely unnecessary. It is not called for by God, whose only concern is that the separated mind return to the fullness of Love's awareness. Love, which even the separated mind has present within it although It is hidden from awareness, simply gives without asking for anything in return. It has no use for bargaining. Indeed, for a mind operating from Love such an idea is meaningless. In that very act of true giving, there is the receiving of a deeper awareness of Love's presence.

Commenting further on the futility and meaninglessness of FTD, the Course observes:

> "1 What would you show your brother? 2 Would you try to reinforce his guilt and thus your own? 3 Forgiveness is the means for your escape. 4 How pitiful it is to make of it the means for further slavery and pain. 5 Within the world of opposites there is a way to use forgiveness for the goal of God, and find the peace He offers you. 6 Take nothing else, or you have sought your death, and prayed for separation from your Self. 7 Christ is for all because He is in all. 8 It is His face forgiveness lets you see. 9 It is His face in which you see your own."(S,2,II,7,1-9)

That is, once one understands how FTD only binds one in the field of guilt and ego-limitation, one may discover what true forgiveness is. By learning to give that instead of FTD, one may move out of the enslavement that is intrinsic to the cycle of suffering. Thereby, one passes beyond the realm of 'living death' and returns to the fullness of Life, seeing the presence of the Christ Mind in everyone. This is what is called perceiving the 'Face of Christ.'

In a final passage, the nature of FTD is summarized:

> "1 All forms forgiveness takes that do not lead away from anger, condemnation and comparisons of every kind are death. 2 For that is what their purposes have set. 3 Be not deceived by them, but lay them by as worthless in their tragic offerings. 4 You do not want to stay in slavery. 5 You do not want to be afraid of God. 6 You want to see the sunlight and the glow of Heaven shining on the face of earth, redeemed from sin and in the Love of God. 7 From here is prayer released, along with you. 8 Your wings are free, and prayer will lift you up and bring you home where God would have you be."(S,2,II,8,1-8)

The main point is that anytime the separated mind associates 'forgiveness' with what reinforces the ego, it is not at all what the Course means by that term. If one sees this clearly, he is free to set it aside and move beyond the ego-mode and its condition of enslavement to its tyranny of limitation, fear, and sorrow. Thus, he comes into the realm of freedom; or more accurately, returns to what has been always his.

Thus, false charity, manifesting as FTD in all its variations, is abandoned as a mere diversion that greatly distracts the mind from living in terms of love. The failure to see this is one of the greatest factors operating in the separated mind that obscures whatever presence of Love it experiences. However, as those confusions are recognized for what they are and do to one's experience in the world, this form of illusory love can be purified first to imperfect love and then to perfect love, which is considered in the next chapter.

E. Sexuality as viewed by the Course. As was pointed out in Ch. I, the "Shorthand Notes" contains considerable material related to sexuality deleted in FIP. It also asserts:

> "I want to finish the instructions about sex, because this is an area the miracle worker MUST understand."(UM, T 1 B 40b)

Why that material was removed in FIP is not clear. However, while a careful study of that material may be useful for the student of the Course, it's central insights seem to be implicit in what FIP says about the role of the body.

The Course insists that the body is not in itself an 'evil' thing. As it states:

> "My body is a wholly neutral thing."(W,294)

It also states that the Holy Spirit makes use of all that has been formed by the mind in separation, which would include the body and special relationships, in the process of bringing it to Atonement:

> "1 God did not make the body, because it is destructible, and therefore not of the Kingdom. 2 The body is the symbol of what you think you are. 3 It is clearly a separation device, and therefore does not exist. 4 The Holy Spirit, as always, takes what you have made and translates it into a learning device."
> (6,V,A,2,1-4)

Thus, the body and the special relationship can be used for either intensifying separation or as a means for undoing it, that is, for making Love more fully present. The latter is the Holy Spirit's use.

As we have seen regarding miracles, the MG's perceptions give it the basis for deciding to offer a miracle or healing. When it so chooses, its decision can express in various ways, such as a silent thought, a word, or a gesture. It can even be in the act of giving a caress, a kiss, or sexual union. In either case, the essential move is the intention to draw the 'light' from a higher plane and to transmit it to the other. Thus, even sexual intercourse can be a mode of giving healing when it is an expression of Love. Thus, it can function like a miracle.

Of course, the body directed by the ego's impulses can also be an instrument of many sorts of ego-enhancing expressions. This can range from mutual pleasuring so as to strengthen the relationship's specialness, to only one's own gratification, or as a form of domination or even attack, as in the case of rape. That is, its neutralness can be informed by a variety of intentions.

Regarding the question of sexuality with various partners, the Course does teach that there is a most proper or 'natural' use:

and:
> "The only VALID use of sex is procreation."(UM, T 1 B 40 f)

> "The sex impulse IS a miracle impulse when it is in proper focus. One individual sees in another the right part for 'procreating the stock,'... and also for their joint establishment of a creative home."(UM, T 1 B 41)

Regarding the first passage, it is not clear what is the intended meaning of 'valid,' which has 10 definitions in English. The one that seems most appropriate is 'able to accomplish what it is designed or intended for.' Since sexuality as a biological mechanism obviously has procreation as its primary or 'most natural' function, this would appear to be correct, a point also made in the second passage. However, that passage also observes that it has a 'natural' use in the enhancing of the home relationship of those who have charge of raising children.

This does not mean that sexual expression for any other purpose is 'wrong' or 'sinful.' Indeed, as we have seen, the very notion of 'sin' is completely rejected by the Course. This is not to say that it advises indiscriminate promiscuity or even rape, generally considered 'sinful' by religions. But, in the Course's view actions can be mistakes if they generate fear and intensify attachment to the ego, either in oneself or in another.

Thus, if sexual union makes Love more fully present in the persons involved in it, it is both appropriate and healing. This would hold for heterosexual relationships of those either married or not married, as well as for homosexual relationships. The 'naturalness' of its use only for procreation does not mean that it cannot have a higher 'natural' use (as pointed out on p. 146), which is one that conforms with what brings about the greater awareness of Love's presence. Indeed, sex even within marriage can at times be far more contrary to that than a truly loving extramarital or homosexual expression.

However, homosexual union is viewed as more problematic than heterosexual union:

> "... homosexuality is inherently more risky (or error prone) than heterosexuality, but both can be undertaken on an equally false basis. The falseness of the basis is clear in the accompanying fantasies. Homosexuality ALWAYS involves misperception of the self OR the partner, and generally both." (UM, T 1 B 41ay)

That is, in homosexual relationships there is unavoidable misperception and thus a greater likelihood of the superimposition of fantasy. Of course, this very same sort of fantasy interference can happen in heterosexual unions as well. Nevertheless, this does not seem to entail that it is impossible for homosexual unions to be a genuine expression of Love; only that it involves greater challenges.

While this topic warrants a more thorough discussion of all statements regarding sexuality made in the "Notes," particularly those regarding 'sexual impulses' and 'miracle-impulses,' I think that what has been said here gives the substance of what they say. I hope to make a more thorough inquiry later.

Chapter V. 'perfect love'

Now we turn to what the Course holds to be the most complete type of love realizable within the world of separation, which it sometimes calls 'perfect love.'

A. Two meanings of 'perfect love' in the Course. The expression 'perfect love' is not used often (20 times) in the Course, and even then it appears to have two somewhat different meanings.

1. Perfect love as Love. The first major use of the term refers to Love as found in God and all other minds. Here we need to distinguish between perfect love as *actively* present in full awareness and *inactively* present or not in awareness.

The *active presence of perfect love* is found in God and all other perfect minds as indicated in the following:

> "1 To think like God is to share His certainty of what you are, and to create like Him is to share the perfect Love He shares with you."(7,I,6,1)

and:

> "5 For the real world has slipped quietly into Heaven, where everything eternal in it has always been. 6 There the Redeemer and the redeemed join in perfect love of God and of each other."(12,VI,7,5-6)

Other passages that use the term in this sense are (14,IV,4,9), (15,VI,2,1), (26,II,8,6), (26,V,10,7), (W,157,9,1).

However, one passage that uses the term in which it is *inactively* present to awareness is especially illuminating:

> "1 You have so little faith in yourself because you are unwilling to accept the fact that perfect love is in you."(15,VI,2,1)

That is, Love is present in even every separated mind, although such a mind may not be aware of it. One might think of it as present on a subconscious or unconscious level. We saw earlier that this must be the case under the Course's view that a thing can have real existence only if it is given that existence by God through His sharing with it His Being, which is Love.

2. Perfect love within the world of perception. A second idea of perfect love is in reference to minds that are still involved in the state of separation, but either briefly or continuously are more or less fully aware of Love's presence while still associated with a body and interacting with other separated minds and bodies in the world. That is, although their mode of awareness involves perception, they are not hampered by that. For example, the following seems to have this sense:

> "4 Perfect love casts out fear."(1,VI,5,4)

We will discuss this citation and others that refer to the active realization of perfect love in minds in the perceptual world or world of separation. Further, when using the term 'perfect love' in the rest of this inquiry, unless otherwise specifically noted, it will refer to perfect love within the world of separation.

Of course, this is the Holy Spirit's mode of loving in so far as He interfaces with minds still in separation. While His Mind is aware of knowledge, which includes the full awareness of Love, it also has perception of the world. In His perception, the world and all entities in it are perceived as 'saturated,' so to speak, with Love. That perception is central to what is called the 'Real World' (discussed later in more detail.) Thus, perfect love might be considered the last and highest stage or form of love that is attainable by a mind that is in a perceiving mode. From that perspective, perfect love would have been the type of love present in Jesus following his realization of the Christ Mind as he related to minds within the world and in the authoring of the Course and guiding minds after his physical departure from the world. Since the Holy Spirit is the Christ Mind in its function of relating with separated minds, it is also the type of love present within the Holy Spirit.

We should also note that, while the full expression '*perfect* love' is sometimes used to refer to perfect love operating or present in minds still perceiving in the world, there are several passages that use the word 'love' without the qualifier 'perfect' that appear to have that meaning. By examining those passages, as well as passages explicitly using the term 'perfect love' as present in a mind still in the world, we can come to a better understanding of the nature of this highest mode attainable by minds not fully returned to their originally perfect state.

Since the separated mind experiences life in the order it thinks of as time, most of it being in the state of rather complete immersion in separation, it begins its move beyond that condition in only brief shifts into the awareness of Love's presence. For a human being, according to the Course, much of her/his life attains only the very confused idea and experience of what is called 'love.' That, however, we have seen is for the most part the 'illusion of love.' But such a mind can begin to move beyond that mode when it learns to realize 'imperfect love' or 'charity,' and to express that in its relationships. The basis of this is referred to as an 'ambivalence' within even somewhat developed separated minds:

> "6 No love in this world is without this ambivalence, and since no ego has experienced love without ambivalence the concept is beyond its understanding. 7 Love will enter immediately into any mind that truly wants it, but it must want it truly. 8 This means that it wants it without ambivalence, and this kind of wanting is wholly without the ego's 'drive to get.'"(4,III,4,6-8)

That is, this ambivalence is due to the ego-dominated mind's being quite resistant to learning this. This ambivalence also prompts it to invent the distortions of 'special relationships,' and 'forgiveness-to-destroy,' which it can think are genuine expressions of love.

B. The separated mind's access to the realization of perfect love. As explained by the Course, the mind still tied into the perceptual order can access perfect love either briefly or more or less enduringly in what it calls the 'holy instant,' about which it speaks at some length. Here we will try to come to an understanding of that expression.

1. The general problem for the separated mind. We first consider a problem that exists for the separated mind when it tries to understand perfect love. This is described:

> "1 The Holy Spirit's Love is your strength, for yours is divided and therefore not real. 2 You cannot trust your own love when you attack it. 3 You cannot learn of perfect love with a split mind, because a split mind has made itself a poor learner." (12,V,4,1-3)

The difficulty here is that every separated mind is split to some degree. What is meant by 'split' is described:

> "1 In this world, because the mind is split, the Sons of God appear to be separate. 2 Nor do their minds seem to be joined. 3 In this illusory state, the concept of an 'individual mind' seems to be meaningful. 4 It is therefore described in the course *as if* it has two parts; spirit and ego."(C,1,2,1-4)

That is, the separated mind is divided into two 'parts,' 'levels,' or 'modes.' The most fundamental of these is what is called 'spirit,' which is the fundamental entity or being of such a mind; in several places this is called the 'Self.' In the Course's view, spirit is the primary reality of any entity, including both God and created entities. As we saw, in the spirit that is the Son, his mind has, by its choice, taken on the identification with some aspects of what it is aware of, which results in the awareness of multiple separate minds, each one thinking it is different from the others, although they are all the same identical mind. That is, they are in fact one and the same spirit. We also saw that the central idea that generates this awareness of separation is the ego. Thus, multiple egos appear to arise in the mind of the one spirit, and each one thinks of itself as different from the others, each with its 'individual mind.'[57] It has some awareness of its fundamental being or spirit, but primarily focuses on the distinctness and separateness of itself, even thinking that its one spirit is many. The 'split' that arises is in several

---

[57] The root meaning of 'individual' is 'undivided,' based on the Latin 'in' = 'not' + 'dividuus' = 'divided.' That is, it can mean 'completely undivided or indivisible.' That meaning has shifted to apply to something thought of as only undivided within itself, but divided or separate from other things. In full accuracy, only the perfect mind is truly an individual in the original sense, a point made repeatedly by J. Krishnamurti. See his *You are the World*.

respects. One is outward, between itself and what it thinks of as other separated minds. Another is more inward, between its own mind and the spirit of which it is actually a part. A third is between God and what it regards as itself. The latter two splits are generally not clearly perceived within the separated mind, although they profoundly affect its experiences. The most serious result of this split is that the separated mind has a great difficulty in understanding and realizing perfect love. Indeed, the point in the previous passage, that it cannot learn of perfect love, would seem to make it impossible for the separated mind to come to live in terms of such love. However, since the Course does propose that any mind in separation can come to such a state, this should be understood as saying that only in so far as the separated mind *chooses* to be divided is it unable to come to perfect love. If we recall that the split is due only to the mind's choice (or more accurately, the choice of an aspect of the Son's mind) of holding to the ego and the partial awareness that is perception, it follows that by making another choice it can move out of that condition. Since on its deepest level any separated mind remains in full connection with Love, learning of Love can be accomplished by turning its attention to that level. This is aided by the presence of the Holy Spirit, who acts as the mediator between the more superficial state of separateness and that deepest level. It is His function to undo the split and thereby enable the mind to understand and realize perfect love within it. That undoing is the Atonement, which may also be thought of as 'At-one-ment' or realization of unity.[58]

As noted earlier, one of the things that most entangles the separated mind in its unawareness of Love is the special relationship. This is further described:

> "1 Do not underestimate the intensity of the ego's drive for vengeance on the past. 2 It is completely savage and completely insane. 3 For the ego remembers everything you have done that has offended it, and seeks retribution of you. 4 The fantasies it brings to its chosen relationships in which to act out its hate are fantasies of your destruction. 5 For the ego holds the past against you, and in your escape from the past it sees itself deprived of the vengeance it believes you so justly merit. 6 Yet without your alliance in your own destruction, the ego could not hold you to the past. 7 In the special relationship you are allowing your destruction to be. 8 That this is insane is obvious. 9 But what is less obvious is that the present is useless to you while you pursue the ego's goal as its ally."
> (16,VII,3,1-9)

Here it is emphasized that special relationships place great focus on the past, that is, on images in the separated mind that are vestiges of previous experiences. It is those past images that give it something to focus on for generating its feelings of need, attraction, and caring, which it sees as the 'nice' side of special

---

[58] The expression 'at one' is used in this sense 23 times in FIP.

love, but also the feelings of hate, vengeance, and guilt, which give support to maintaining the operation of the ego. The cycle of conflict and suffering are the result, something that is here called 'insane,' in that it seeks both to destroy and to maintain the very mechanism of the ego. It was pointed out earlier that this is central to the self-contradictory nature of the ego-idea. Accordingly, if the special relationship acts as a major block to the awareness of Love and the realization of perfect love, it is necessary for that block to be undone.

The key to realizing perfect love lies in fully understanding the very simple truth of what is present within oneself. That is described:

> "3 Within yourself you love your brother with a perfect love. 4 Here is holy ground, in which no substitution can enter, and where only the truth in your brother can abide. 5 Here you are joined in God, as much together as you are with Him. 6 The original error has not entered here, nor ever will. 7 Here is the radiant truth, to which the Holy Spirit has committed your relationship."(18,I,9,3-6)

That is, perfect love, as primary Love, is already present in each separate mind, although for the most part not within that mind's awareness. Each is already connected with every other separated mind, as well as with God and all other perfect minds. However, that connection would best be described as 'unconscious.' The process, then, of realizing perfect love is simply one of shifting from this unconscious presence to a fully conscious awareness of what is already and always there.

2. The holy instant as key. Central to that process is the experiencing of the 'holy instant.'

a. The general nature of the holy instant. Its essential nature is described:

> "1 In the world of scarcity, love has no meaning and peace is impossible. 2 For gain and loss are both accepted, and so no one is aware that perfect love is in him. 3 In the holy instant you recognize the idea of love in you, and unite this idea with the Mind that thought it, and could not relinquish it. 4 By holding it within itself, there *is* no loss. 5 The holy instant thus becomes a lesson in how to hold all of your brothers in your mind, experiencing not loss but completion. 6 From this it follows you can only give. 7 And this *is* love, for this alone is natural under the laws of God."(15,VI,5,1-7)

Although the modifier 'perfect' is not used in statement 7, it is clear that the love present in the holy instant is perfect love while the mind remains in the world of perception. What is essential to the holy instant is that it involves three important experiences or realizations:

1) of the presence of Love within one's own mind
2) of the union of one's own mind with the Mind of its Creator from whom Love is given
3) of the union of one's own mind with one's brothers, i.e., all other

created minds, including all those one may perceive as separate from oneself

In those realizations, what is central is the primary recognition that the fundamental characteristic of Love is its giving nature and the awareness of how that giving process is present and operates within one's own mind. This does not mean that there is no aspect of receiving, since the mind in that state is quite aware that Love is being given to it. Thus, it recognizes that in giving to another mind there is also a returning of that same intention to give by the mind given to. (This we saw earlier is central to the Joy present in Love.) Hence, within the giving characteristic of perfect love there is also a receiving. As we noted earlier in our discussion of miracles:

"To give and to receive are one in truth."(W,108)

In that sense, giving *is* receiving. However, the primary move is one of giving. This points to a deeper meaning to the statement, "'It is more blessed to give than to receive" (Acts 20: 35).

We should also understand that these three realizations central to the holy instant can vary in degrees of clarity or intensity. What determines this is the extent to which the separated mind has or does not have obstacles in it that hinder it from entering into the complete experience. This also plays a role as to how long, from the temporal perspective, a mind remains in the holy instant.

Although the most important aspect of the holy instant is its being a kind of window or door through which the separated mind comes to the realization of perfect love, the very notion of a 'holy instant' has profound implications regarding its relation to time itself. Our usual idea of an 'instant' is that it is a fragment of time, which is experienced as a tiny duration having particular contents. From that perspective, an instant is sometimes thought of as an infinitesimally small portion of time, or even better, as the collection of all things occurring 'at once' or simultaneously within that tiny portion. However, when thought through thoroughly, one finds that the notion of an instant as an aspect of time involves contradictions. Some of the earliest reflections about this in Western thought were the intriguing discussions known as 'Zeno's Paradoxes.' Zeno, a student of Parmenides, proposed these paradoxes with the intention of showing that any view that involves any multiplicity of limited things is inconsistent. Zeno's particular focus was on the idea of time, which involves not only two but countless parts, which are intrinsic to what is called 'past,' 'present,' and 'future.' Although he gives many concrete illustrations (such as the argument that it is logically impossible for an arrow ever to reach a target, or more generally that the belief in the possibility of motion in space involves a contradiction), his central point is that if a thing is thought to exist as having a particular set of characteristics at any given moment, this logically entails that it does not exist in exactly that same particular way in a preceding or following moment. More simply, since only what is 'now' actually exists, what 'was' or 'will be' does not also actually exist. Thus, if we say a thing 'is now,' it entails it is not in a past or future moment. More generally, to say a thing is in time is to say that it both exists and does not exist, which is a contradiction. That is, the idea that there is time, or that things exist in time, involves the acceptance of the belief that the same thing both is and is not, both exists and does not exist. This was actually the view of Parmenides, so that Zeno's paradoxes can be understood as more concrete and visualizable applications of his teacher's more abstract principle. While Zeno's reflections have stimulated many attempts to show how they contain errors, the earliest being that of Aristotle and more recently that of W. Salmon,[59] we need not enter into that debate, but only point to it as indicative of how the notion of 'time' is fraught with serious logical problems and controversy. One is reminded of St. Augustine's comment: "What then is time? If no one asks me, I know; if I wish to explain it to one that asketh, I know not."[60]

To understand the Course's view, it is important to keep in mind that, for it, time does not exist in Reality, but is something that arises due to the separation. In Reality, what God and every perfect mind know is the complete existence of all that absolutely exists in a single Moment or unchanging Now or Instant of what is called 'eternity.' To think of this as an 'infinitely long time' would be a serious distortion based on trying to apply a category of thought formed by the separated mind to something that does not fit into that category. Of course, doing so involves a major illusion for that mind. Our usual notion of an 'instant' involves the idea that it does not contain what preceded it or will follow it (what would be regarded as the 'past' and 'future'). Such an idea of an instant as only a 'slice' of time leaves out of it most of what arises within the field of time. It is thus a greatly impoverished, tiny, even infinitesimal 'segment' of time that must be thought of as vanishing as soon as it arises. If time is thought of as the 'container' or 'realm' of all that can in some way be attributed existence, compared to the whole of time, an instant is so tiny that it is relatively non-existent. This is sometimes represented as a point in a line; the point being of zero length and the line of either finite or infinite length. Of course, when one thinks of the whole of time, or even a limited segment of it, as a collection of such infinitesimal points, it involves major conceptual confusions, such as some have argued are the gist of Zeno's paradoxes. In this way, one might propose that because there are an infinite number of instants in a temporal duration (or length) of a second, and that there are also an infinite number of instants in an hour (or a year or even 13.8 billion years, the currently believed age of the physical universe), a second must be as long as an hour (or year or 13.8 billion years).

The Course, however, has a very different view of what the 'instant' of the

---

[59] Salmon, W. C., 2001, *Zeno's Paradoxes*. For a briefer discussion, see http://plato.stanford.edu/entries/ paradox-zeno/

[60] *Confessions*, Book XI.

holy instant is. Simply put, although it can occur for a mind within the field of time, it is a shift in the separated mind's awareness into the single Eternal Instant of the Eternal Now. It is not merely a tiny 'slice' or infinitesimal duration within the flow of events from past to future, the boundary between those two that seems so brief that one could argue that it is non-existent. Rather, although to a mind embedded in temporality it may seem to last either very briefly or possibly even for a length of time, its actual nature cannot be assimilated to the category of time or any of its components. That is, the holy instant involves a shift in which awareness is fundamentally *beyond time*, or in 'timelessness,' although it may contain perceptual elements or aspects that can be thought of as within time.

It will be helpful to consider what the Course says about this:

> "4 Holiness lies not in time, but in eternity. 5 There never was an instant in which God's Son could lose his purity. 6 His changeless state is beyond time, for his purity remains forever beyond attack and without variability. 7 Time stands still in his holiness, and changes not. 8 And so it is no longer time at all. 9 For caught in the single instant of the eternal sanctity of God's creation, it is transformed into forever. 10 Give the eternal instant, that eternity may be remembered for you, in that shining instant of perfect release. 11 Offer the miracle of the holy instant through the Holy Spirit, and leave His giving it to you to Him."(15,I,15,4-11)

Here, it is clear that the holy instant should not be thought of in temporal terms. Although it can be experienced by a mind embedded in time, this is an occurrence that permits that mind to step outside of time into a radically different mode of being. This passage calls that mode 'holiness.' While that word has many connotations, its most fundamental meaning for the Course, as has been noted, is that of 'wholeness.' This is the primary unity or union of all that absolutely exists. It is a unity that does not exclude a *kind* of multiplicity, since there are many spirits with perfect minds. The foundation of that multiplicity is the primary dyad of God and His primary Creature (the Father and the Son). However, there is also the extension of that into the infinity of further creatures proceeding from His primary Creature, that is, into the rest of the 'Universe of Love.' It is also clear that, in the Course's view, this wholeness is not *fully* accessible to awareness except by way of the mode of awareness of knowing. That is, ordinary perceptual awareness cannot come to it. Accordingly, the 'instant' of the holy instant is the same as the single Eternal Instant or Now of Reality. In it the mind that has identified with separation shifts away from the separated state into an awareness of that wholeness. The point in statement 9, that 'it [holiness] is transformed into forever,' might be interpreted as saying holiness becomes something in a very long or endless time ('forever'). However, this is better understood as saying only that this holiness has no termination, but rather remains existing as it is. From the perspective of a mind in time, it would appear to go on for a very long or endless time. But, from the perspective of a mind immersed in that holiness, it would be only the single moment of its own infinite unfolding in unlimited Beauty and Joy. However, the mind can experience this timeless mode to some extent and then return again to the time-mode if it has not fully dropped all perception. Because this can occur while still maintaining some degree of perceptual awareness, but then opens eventually to a complete dropping of perceptual awareness, it can be thought of as a kind of 'bridging' awareness, which has both perceiving and knowing aspects. The Course indicates that this is facilitated by the Holy Spirit, when the mind is willing to attune to that awareness:

"2 I have already said that the Holy Spirit is the Bridge for the transfer of perception to knowledge, so we can use the terms as if they were related, because in His Mind they are. 3 This relationship must be in His Mind because, unless it were, the separation between the two ways of thinking would not be open to healing."(5,III,1,2-3)

Thus, the experience of the holy instant may be thought of as an entry into or participation in the Holy Spirit's mode of awareness, although it can be 'more or less' according to the degree of entering into that mode. As statement 7 observes, when this happens for such a mind, time 'stands still' or is completely transcended.[61]

b. Four types of experience in relation to the holy instant. Although the experience of the holy instant has profound effects on a separated mind, it does not necessarily entail that such a mind is completely severed from the temporal mode. This is made clear in the following:

"2 It is this shift to vision that is accomplished in the holy instant. 3 Yet it is needful for you to learn just what this shift entails, so you will become willing to make it permanent. 4 Given this willingness it will not leave you, for it *is* permanent."(15,IX,1,2-4)

A first point is that the experience of the holy instant involves what is called 'a shift in vision.' In this is indicated that the primary meaning of 'vision' is a mode of perception quite different from ordinary vision. This seems best understood as the holistic perception present in the Holy Spirit's Mind, the highest type of perception possible. A second point here is that the 'shift' to the experience of the holy instant requires the 'willingness' or choice of a particular separated mind. Although the holy instant is itself unchanging, it is possible for a mind to fail to experience it, if it chooses to remain outside that experience. Thus, for a mind there are four possibilities in relation to the holy instant:

    a) It may choose to remain completely beyond the experience of the holy instant. This is the situation for a mind completely caught in separation.

---

[61] The 'bridging' nature of the Holy Spirit's perceptual awareness will be discussed in more detail in *The Holy Spirit and Jesus in A Course in Miracles*.

b) Or, it may choose to experience the holy instant, but, because its choice is incomplete, it shifts back more or less completely to the temporal mode and loses awareness of the holy instant. In this, it is preoccupied with or focused on the contents of ordinary perception. However, there remains within it something of the quality of the holy instant, so that those perceptions take on a modified or even a very different meaning.

c) Or, it may choose to enter very deeply into the holy instant and not lose that awareness even while it returns to the temporal mode. Thus, it remains in the holy instant while experiencing the ordinary perceptual order. In this, there are both modes of wholeness (and non-temporality) and separation (and temporality), in a kind of superimposition of one upon the other.

d) Or, it may choose to completely leave the world of perception; this comes at the individual's completion of the Atonement.

The first three of these are what occur for a mind that is within the world of perception. The fourth is possible only for a mind no longer in that world. Here we briefly consider b) - d). Later, we will discuss b) and c) more fully.

i. The temporary holy instant. The second, or b), of these four possibilities we may call a '**temporary holy instant**' (or more precisely, 'temporary experience of the holy instant;' but I will use the shorter expression for brevity). Depending how far the holy instant has been entered into, the mind can return to temporality and the state of perception and separation. This can be in many degrees of intensity. For example, it may regard its 'breakthrough' as merely an illusion, perhaps thinking of it as 'almost dying' and in its returned state become quite fearful of the whole experience as it chooses again to give full sway to the ego. Or, it may think of it as a revelation from God[62] that gives it the obligation to be a messenger or 'prophet' to others, while at the same time failing to recognize how the ego begins to operate again and lead it to all sorts of insane thinking and behavior, such as exploiting its 'disciples'/followers in various ways, much dominated by the ego. However, in the more wholesome variations, the memory of the experience of the holy instant serves as a reminder of the further need for inner growth and genuine service in helping others also come to a realization of the holy instant.

It might be further pointed out that, although in the shallowest temporary holy instants there is a beginning realization of perfect love, the mind usually

---

[62] As the Course uses the term 'revelation,' the holy instant is clearly such, as can be seen in its description:

"1 Revelation is intensely personal and cannot be meaningfully translated. 2 That is why any attempt to describe it in words is impossible. 3 Revelation induces only experience."(1,II,2,1-3)

However, there seem to be other sorts of revelation than those involving the holy instant, such as Schucman's alleged hearing of the words of the Course.

slips back into imperfect or illusory love. Even following the somewhat deeper occurrences, as seem to have happened with the close disciples of Jesus, there seems to have been a return to imperfect love. That is, it is possible to have a temporary experience of perfect love, but then return to some level of obscuring Love's presence.

ii. The enduring holy instant. In the third possibility, described in c), which will be called an '**enduring holy instant**' (again, short for 'enduring experience of the holy instant'), the separated mind has come to the apex of what the Course considers to be its possible development while remaining in the world of perception. That it is possible for separated minds to come to this is pointed out in:

> "2 It is this shift to vision that is accomplished in the holy instant. 3 Yet it is needful for you to learn just what this shift entails, so you will become willing to make it permanent. 4 Given this willingness it will not leave you, for it *is* permanent."(15,IX,1,2-4)

The latter seems to be the state that Jesus is thought to have come to in his complete realization of the Christ Mind while still within the field of time. It is perhaps what was meant by being 'within the world, but not of it.' This is the same as the full realization of perfect love within the world. This may have also been the state reached by some of the great spiritual giants in all traditions, such as St. Francis of Assisi, Meister Eckhardt, John of the Cross, and Teresa of Avila in the Christian tradition; Siddhartha Gautama Buddha, Bodhidharma, Padmasambhava, and Yeshe Tsogyal in the Buddhist tradition; Krishna, Meera, Ramakrishna, and Ramana Maharshi in the Hindu tradition; Muhammad, Rumi, Rabia, Arabi, and Al-Hallaj in the Muslim tradition; Kabir and Guru Nanak in the Sikh tradition; and more recently J. Krishnamurti who shed all traditions. Of course, it is difficult to say who may have come to that state except by looking closely at their biographies, although such external facts can give us only probable evidence regarding their inner states. And, from the Course's perspective, it does not really matter, since its primary concern is to help the student come to the realization of the holy instant in all moments of living in the world as the major stage in the return to knowledge.

iii. The holy instant in the individual completion of the Atonement. In the fourth possible way of relating to the holy instant, described as d) above, the separated mind's completion of the whole purpose of the Course is fully attained. That involves the return to full awareness in the knowledge of the Wholeness of Reality, the abandonment of all illusions intrinsic to perception and time, and the complete restoration of the mind to Love's union with all other minds, including all perfect creatures and the original Creator. This is the state the Course calls 'Heaven.'

c. Only one holy instant. Although there are different choices that the mind can make regarding the holy instant, the Course makes clear that there is only one such instant. As it states:

> "1 You look upon each holy instant as a different point in time. 2 It never changes. 3 All that it ever held or will ever hold is here right now. 4 The past takes nothing from it, and the future will add no more. 5 Here, then, is everything."(20,V,6,1-5)

While separated minds may think there are many such instants, they are all encounters with the same Eternal Instant. One might think of this as like observing a mountain from different locations. Historically it has been reported that what is today called Mt. Everest was thought to be two different mountains: one given one name by the people to the south, and another name given by the people to the north. Later, the 'two mountains' were found to be only one.

This point is repeated, with an additional insight, in the following:

> "3 The holy instant is this instant and every instant. 4 The one you want it to be it is. 5 The one you would not have it be is lost to you. 6 You must decide when it is."(15,IV,1,3-6)

Here, we find an important idea about the relation between the eternal holy instant and the things we think of as instants within the field of time. That is, in our temporal mode we experience and think of multiple 'nows' or instants that are very brief or even infinitesimally short. The scientific study of the time-experience has made clear that what we think of as our perception of 'now' is actually a finite temporal segment as measured by a physical chronometer or clock. This is sometimes referred to as the 'specious present.'[63] Of course, that minimal length of time required for the mind/brain to register an experience of time is relative to what is accepted as 'physical time,' which has also been the object of research and speculation. It is currently debated whether the physical 'now' is of zero duration or whether there is a fundamental minimal time-quantum, a 'chronon,' that is the shortest period of time that holds within the physical universe.[64] However, while scientifically and philosophically interesting, these ideas are independent of the more fundamental concern here about the relation between the holy instant and the temporal instant. Two insights are important in this last passage. The first is that every 'now' in time is grounded on the more fundamental Eternal Now. One becomes aware of that Now in the experience of the holy instant. The second is that whether one remains in time or moves out of it is entirely dependent on the choice or decision of the separated mind. Thus, the holy instant can be clearly and fully present in awareness at any instant in time. But, for that to

---

[63] Studies of the specious present in relation to external sense-experience have yielded an approximate value of 25 to 240 milliseconds of 'objective' clock-time duration. This varies with the type of sensory mode and specific conditions like intensity of the stimulus. It may also vary in relation to other conditions, such as the subject's state of consciousness (e.g., extraordinary waking states, drug-induced states, meditative states, etc.)

[64] Some physicists have proposed that the 'chronon' may have a length of 10^{-23} seconds. But this is still a very speculative concept.

happen, such a mind must make the choice to enter it, as well as fulfill certain conditions that bring the removal of the blocks interfering with that experience.

d. The 'bridging instant.' Another point related to the 'instantness' of the holy instant is seen in:

> "1 How long is an instant? 2 As long as it takes to re-establish perfect sanity, perfect peace and perfect love for everyone, for God and for yourself. 3 As long as it takes to remember immortality, and your immortal creations who share it with you. 4 As long as it takes to exchange hell for Heaven. 5 Long enough to transcend all of the ego's making, and ascend unto your Father."(15,I,14,1-5)

The 'instant' this passage is referring to seems to be what might be called the **'bridging instant'** that occurs within the field of time. This is also referred to in:

> "3 What better way to close the little gap between illusions and reality than to allow the memory of God to flow across it, making it a bridge an instant will suffice to reach beyond?" (28,I,15,3)

But, unlike most instants in separative awareness, it involves moving out of time into the trans-temporal realm of the holy instant. The first passage may be understood as a further commentary on the 'decision' or 'choice' that is the primary requirement for coming to the holy instant. The separated mind, when considering such a choice, is undoubtedly confronted with an ambivalence between the two modes. On the one hand, there is the attraction of the ego-mode which is the basis of the experience of time. On the other, there is the attraction to the mode of wholeness/holiness that involves the dissolution of time. Both of these attractions are present within the separated mind. The ego-attraction is usually most salient, since it is what upholds the ego and saturates the separated mind's consciousness. Still, the attraction to wholeness remains present, although more or less dimly in the background or even entirely unconsciously, since that is the very foundation of the mind's existence. Thus, this bridging instant lasts as long as it takes for the separated mind to become ready to fully embrace the holy instant. This is the time it finds necessary to resolve that ambivalence, which may take hours, days, years or even lifetimes of learning to accept the guidance of the Voice that is always offering its reminder to each separated mind, but respectful of its decision to listen or not to listen.

Here, we should recall that, in the Course's view, the whole of time is contained within a tiny 'fragment' or 'level' of the one Eternal Instant. Thus, this passage, in asking how long an instant is, is simply pointing out that any time-measurement applied to it leads to many values. Since time, strictly, is not applicable to the Eternal Now, the question is a bit like asking, 'How long is a mind?' or 'How many meters length does an idea have?' (In philosophy, this involves what is called a 'category mistake,' i.e., applying a concept to something to which it is meaningless to apply that concept.) However, for the mind immersed in temporality, it has some sense to ask it. Thus, when asking "how long is an instant?," the answer is: "the amount of time that it takes a mind to move from the beginning of separation, i.e., the beginning of time, to the completion of the Atonement." For the separated mind, that may involve billions of years of temporal experience. For the mind in the perfect state of the eternal instant, it takes no time at all.

e. The holy instant and temporality. A final passage regarding the relation of the holy instant to temporality is the following:

> "2 For the past is gone, and what is present, freed from its bequest of grief and misery, of pain and loss, becomes the instant in which time escapes the bondage of illusions where it runs its pitiless, inevitable course. 3 Then is each instant which was slave to time transformed into a holy instant, when the light that was kept hidden in God's Son is freed to bless the world."(W,194,5,1-3)

This makes clear that a major effect of the holy instant is that it brings complete, although paradoxically temporary, ending of the past. We have already seen that the impetus of the ego-idea in the separated mind is to continue in its domination of that mind. This is assured by the remnants of the past, particularly in the guise of guilt which acts as the mind's 'springboard,' so to speak, that catapults it from the present moment into the following one with remnants of the past continuing to hold it in separation. However, if the past completely ceases to operate as the persistence of memory, there is no further impulse to move into a next moment or what is thought of as the future. That is, by the mind's shifting into the holy instant, however briefly or weakly, there is a complete collapse of time, and with that the ending of the limited perceptions or illusions that constitute the sequence it thinks of as time. In that sense, the mind is liberated from the chains of the limted causal sequence that is the fundamental generator of its time experience. Once the past ceases to operate as a force within the mind, any perceptual experiences that occur are no longer colored by the remnants of previous moments it may have experienced. Thus, it is fully in the present unfolding instant that would usually be experienced within the frame of memories that are thought of as the past and imagined anticipations that are thought of as the future. Thus freed of both 'sides' of time, it can fully experience what is present in the now. This may include perceptual content if the mind remains within the field of perceptions. This is the situation for a mind that has come to the enduring holy instant. That is, it is aware of only true perceptions. This constitutes perception of the Real World, which we will discuss shortly. But, if it has come to the point of dropping all perceptual awareness, it moves entirely out of the mode of perceptual content and returns to the original state it was created in, the mode of unlimited awareness, or knowing. Thus, the cited passage focuses on the new mode of awareness that includes perceptions. In that mode, recalling William Blake's observation, the doors of perception are fully cleansed and each object is perceived in a radically different way, involving no guilt, pain, grief, or sorrow. In terms closer to the views of Hinduism and Buddhism, this is a state in which there is complete release from the demands of karma, a state which in those traditions is realizable and is believed to have actually been realized by a significant number of individuals. That the mind can slip out of this timeless state is only due to its incomplete entering into the holy instant, which occurs if the mind still clings to any attraction to the ego-mode.

But now let us consider more closely first the *content*, then the *effects* of the holy instant.

3. Content of the holy instant. We first look at how the holy instant eliminates, at least temporarily, the limiting effects of the ego. Then we will focus on the new cognitive, affective, and behavioral aspects that it brings.

a. Limiting effects of ego that are eliminated or transformed in the holy instant. In Ch. III, we saw how the ego is the primary means by which the separation is maintained and how through it are constructed many different beliefs, feelings, and modes of behavior to support that. We also saw how that rather complex network or system makes it extremely difficult for the separated mind to understand itself as it really is, particularly with its way of preventing the mind from living with or in perfect love. The holy instant is the primary way by which that system is opened to be dismantled, not by its being attacked or the mind's being forced away from it, but by disclosing its fundamentally false basis and making clear that there is a totally different way of living/being. Here we look at how the principal ego-effects are impacted.

i. Cognitive aspects eliminated/transformed. Its attachment to the ego-idea leads the separated mind to several beliefs and ways of being aware that are adopted to uphold its involvement in that idea. Here, we consider passages that focus on changes that occur in the holy instant regarding some of these.

1) The ending of specialness. One of the most powerful ploys of the ego-mind to maintain itself is its belief in specialness. However, in the holy instant that illusory belief is dispelled:

> "2 In the holy instant no one is special, for your personal needs intrude on no one to make your brothers seem different. 3 Without the values from the past, you would see them all the same and like yourself. 4 Nor would you see any separation between yourself and them. 5 In the holy instant, you see in each relationship what it will be when you perceive only the present."(15,V,8,2-5)

The undoing of specialness, as indicated here, is due to the recognition that one need have no concern for what would usually be regarded as 'personal' needs. This seems to rest on the awareness of perfect love within oneself. That is, since such love consists in unlimited giving, and giving is itself intrinsically accompanied by receiving, the lack of limits on giving is recognized as lack of limits on what comes to that mind. Such a mind has only *one need*, not as something it lacks, but as its inner requirement for existing: to give completely. Further, this is reciprocated by its being given to completely. That is, Love flows into it, through it, out to all others, and back to it from all others. From that perspective, it sees all other beings as radically the same as it. This is due to the fact that there no longer functions in it an idea of the past, which was based on limited perceptions of the differences between oneself and those others. Within this awareness, which can include perceptions, the boundaries that formerly were thought to hold between oneself and others completely drop away, and all others are seen as non-different from oneself. In statement 5 of this passage, the point seems to be that in any case of entering the holy instant, however brief it may be and followed by a slipping out of it, the mind understands not only the relationships it may be focusing on at that particular instant, but *all* relationships, in the same mode of non-difference, free of the past, and only within the light of perfect love. This is called by some thinkers the 'non-dual state.'[65] The full realization of that may require the mind's further returning to and deepening of the intensity of the holy instant, followed by returning to the mode of time-bound awareness. But sooner or later it will come to a stable mode of an enduring holy instant from which it no longer slips away.

The reason for the undoing of specialness is quite simple:

> "7 For in the holy instant, free of the past, you see that love is in you, and you have no need to look without and snatch love guiltily from where you thought it was."(15,V,9,1-7)

That is, the primary reason for focusing on specialness is to fill the perceived void or emptiness within oneself due to the limits taken on by attaching to ego. In other words, it is sought after to make up for the perceived absence of Love, which moves one to engage in the game of special relationships. But, once the mind enters the holy instant, it becomes aware of the presence of Love within oneself. Thus, the need to seek the diminished imitation of Love that is called 'special love' is gone, since one is fully satisfied within the awareness of perfect love.

2) The shift away from and transformation of awareness of the body. In the Course's view, after adopting the ego-idea the separated mind forms a close association with the cohering set of perceptions it thinks of as the body so as to maintain the ego-dominated state. But with the understanding of the ego's illusoriness in the holy instant, the body no longer has the same relevance. Indeed, when the holy instant is entered into deeply, the primary perception is of something quite different, as indicated in:

> "1 In the holy instant, where the Great Rays replace the body in awareness, the recognition of relationships without limits is given you. 2 But in order to see this, it is necessary to give up every use the ego has for the body, and to accept the fact that the ego has no purpose you would share with it. 3 For the ego would limit everyone to a body for its own purposes, and

---

[65] Ken Wilber has discussed non-duality at length. See his *The Spectrum of Consciousness* or his more recent *The Integral Vision* for a fuller discussion of his view.

while you think it has a purpose, you will choose to utilize the means by which it tries to turn its purpose into accomplishment. 4 This will never be accomplished. 5 Yet you have surely recognized that the ego, whose goals are altogether unattainable, will strive for them with all its might, and will do so with the strength that you have given it."(15,IX,3,1-5)

The first point here is that the limiting mode of awareness central to specialness and special relationships is replaced by a very different sort of perception, since the need for limits central to the ego is no longer present. One perceives with the doors of perception 'fully cleansed' and sees each thing as having no boundaries. The second point concerns the new perception that rises into awareness, referred to as the 'Great Rays.' We will discuss this further when we consider the *new* content of the holy instant. The point in statement 5, that the ego's goals are altogether unattainable, is rooted in the fact that its goals are self-contradictory. That is, it seeks both to maintain itself and to bring about its own ending or death (entailed as a temporal limit by its very act of imposing limits on itself).

Going even further, the Course makes clear that as one enters more deeply into the holy instant, the significance of one's physical body diminishes:

> "3 In the holy instant there are no bodies, and you experience only the attraction of God."(15,IX,7,3)

What this seems to say is not so much that all perceptions of what we think of as a 'body' simply vanish. Rather, the notion of a limited body that the separated mind ordinarily thinks of is no longer operative. Briefly, what this involves is that there is a perception not involving any limits, in which the usual idea of 'body' is recognized as simply without correspondence to what is found in that experience. Again, we will discuss this later in more detail.

3) The ending of belief in sin. One of the significant beliefs in the ego-bound mind is in the reality of sin or uncorrectable error. This belief is accepted by both theists and atheists. For the religious, it is thought of as 'sin' or 'karmic debt.' For the atheist/agnostic, it is an error that can never be corrected or let go of (this is closely bound up in the belief in the reality of time, where an event, once having occurred, remains forever a part of the content of space-time). As might be expected, this belief is dissolved in the holy instant:

> "2 The holy instant will replace all sin if you but carry its effects with you. 3 And no one will elect to suffer more."
> (27,VI,8,2-3)

The perception or judgment of any action, either one's own or that of another, as sinful or uncorrectable error is only due to the domination of the ego over the mind having that perception or judgment. But, in the holy instant there is a complete suspension of that domination, so that in it the notion of 'sin' is replaced with what the Course holds is its more appropriate idea, 'correctable error or mistake.' This passage indicates that it is possible for the mind that has gone into the holy instant to 'carry its effect' of the non-existence of sin back into the more limited awareness of time-boundedness. If it does so, it is no longer able to perceive anything as 'sinful,' with all of the consequences of that. However, it seems clear that simply having the experience of the holy instant does not necessarily entail the abandonment of 'sin-consciousness' for those who slip out of the awareness of the holy instant. This seems to be the case in many Christian 'saints' who may have indeed (and quite probably did) come to the holy instant, but did not enter it very deeply, at least enough to permanently dissolve the belief in sin.

4) The elimination of exclusion. One of the first effects of the act in which separation originates is the exclusion of aspects or parts of, indeed most of, Reality, from the mind's awareness. This is reversed in the holy instant:

> "1 In the holy instant God is remembered, and the language of communication with all your brothers is remembered with Him. 2 For communication is remembered together, as is truth. 3 There is no exclusion in the holy instant because the past is gone, and with it goes the whole basis for exclusion. 4 Without its source exclusion vanishes."(15,VI,8,1-4)

One of the primary divisions that separation generates in relation to the world is the series of perceptions that are the basis of time. What is thought of as 'the past' is separated from what is thought of as 'the present.' However, when the mind enters the holy instant, it dissolves this division. While precisely what occurs in this mode of awareness is difficult for our time-bound minds to imagine or conceive, the Course makes clear that the direct awareness of the holy instant completely dissolves that division. Thus, although awareness of the past as past is gone, its real content (the true perceptions that were thought of as 'past') is not excluded from the present, since the holy instant is a different sort of 'present' that includes all moments of time. In that sense, the holy instant may be said to bring the 'dissolution of exclusion.'

5) The ending of judgment. Closely connected with the ending of exclusion, which includes the ending of the past, is the holy instant's effect on the judging process. As is stated:

> "1 The holy instant is the Holy Spirit's most useful learning device for teaching you love's meaning. 2 For its purpose is to suspend judgment entirely. 3 Judgment always rests on the past, for past experience is the basis on which you judge. 4 Judgment becomes impossible without the past, for without it you do not understand anything."(15,V,1,1-4)

The act of judging involves holding that what is judged either belongs to or does not belong to a limited class of objects that have a particular characteristic or set of characteristics, such as 'good' or 'bad,' 'big' or 'little,' 'true' or 'false,' etc. These classes are mental formations are called 'concepts.' They function so as to divide our experience into what fits within them and what does not so fit. Thus, judgments involve a mode of awareness that conceptually divides what is experienced. When one asks how this occurs, this passage indicates that it is always based on the past. This becomes clear when we reflect on how we form our concepts. For example, the concept 'dog' is derived from the memories of past experiences of things that have the general characteristics shared by dogs. While some thinkers, such as Kant, have argued that there are a number of very general concepts that are intrinsic to the mind's structure (what he called 'a priori forms'), the Course holds that all concepts, even those that Kant identified as a priori mental structures, are based on earlier experiences, and thus on the past.[66] Thus, from the Course's perspective, if the past is completely eliminated as occurs in the holy instant, there is no longer any basis for judging. Instead, there is only the 'pure present,' whose content is simply Love, which manifests in what the mind relates to as God and other perfect minds. Of course, this mode of awareness can be moved away from, so that the mind can return to the judging mode if it so chooses. Judgment is only suspended within the holy instant, not finally and completely, unless it chooses to enter totally and without reserve into that instant. This, of course, is the individual's full maturation to perfect love and ultimately the completion of the Atonement.

6) Cessation of illusions. Another consequence of the holy instant is the elimination of the distortions or illusions that arise from false perceptions:

> "5 Release your brothers from the slavery of their illusions by forgiving them for the illusions you perceive in them. 6 Thus will you learn that you have been forgiven, for it is you who offered them illusions. 7 In the holy instant this is done for you in time, to bring you the true condition of Heaven."
> (16,VII,9,5-7)

We should recall that there are two major sorts of illusion in the Course's view. The most serious are those that arise from the superimposition of perceptions from either memory or imagination upon true perceptions in the present so as to distort those true perceptions into false ones. A simple example is where one has the perception of a snake, but what is actually present is a vine or rope or stick. The Course holds that most of the perceptions by the separated mind are variations of this type of error, particularly influenced by the major distorting idea of the ego and its elaborate constructs of fear, guilt, false beliefs, etc. The other major sort of illusion is any awareness that involves perception, including true perceptions. They are illusory in the sense that they involve the focusing of awareness on only some aspects or aspects of Reality. Although they do not of

---

[66] Although the Course does not discuss it, it is quite possible that immediately after the initial formation of the ego-idea, prior to the formation of the body and the structure of the material world, the separated mind constructs or forms a set of basic ideas, such as Kant describes. These he calls the '3 ideas of reason,' '12 concepts of understanding,' and '2 forms of sensibility' (space and time). He considers these as 'a priori' or present in the mind as its internal structures which make all experience possible. However, these would have to be elaborations of the ego-idea, and in that sense be based on a kind of memory of that initial limited form.

themselves lead to the serious problems that false perceptions lead to, they obstruct the full awareness of Reality that can only come in the higher cognitive mode of knowledge. The point here is that in the holy instant all false beliefs (illusions of the first sort) are dropped, at least for the period the mind is in the holy instant. As was pointed out in our discussion of the nature of the miracle, this dropping or letting go of false perceptions is the core of what the Course means by 'forgiveness.' As statement 7 above points out, this usually occurs as a sudden moving outside of time but is then followed by a return to temporal experience, so that it is 'done for you in time.' However, since it acts as a clear experience of the non-temporal order, which at some eventual holy instant experience will bring the mind to a non-return to the temporal order and entry into the state called 'Heaven,' it comes to such a mind as a 'foretaste' of Heaven, in which *all* illusions, including true perceptions, are completely dropped.

7) The removal of 'darkness' by 'light.' Related to the ending of illusions is the cessation of what gives rise to them, or what is metaphorically called 'darkness' in the Course:

> "2 The darkness in you has been brought to light. 3 Carry it back to darkness, from the holy instant to which you brought it."(18,III,7,1-3)

The terms 'light' and 'darkness' are used in the Course in both a literal and a metaphorical sense. Already mentioned was how the holy instant brings a new perception of light in terms of the 'Great Rays.' In the present passage there is a more general notion of 'light,' in that 'light' refers to awareness and 'darkness' refers to any kind of obscuring of awareness. It will be helpful if we consider the Course's several different meanings of the term 'light.'

When one closely examines passages with the term 'light,' there emerges what we may think of as two major sorts of light: light within the level of perception and light within the absolute level of Reality. Within these levels there are varieties or sub-levels of light. Here I give a brief summary of the different sense of 'light' within those levels. For a more extensive discussion, see Appendix 2, "'Light' in *A Course in Miracles*."

Within the perceptual level (which has also been called the level of 'relative reality'), there are progressively 'brighter' or more comprehensive types of light. The lowest type refers to ordinary **outer physical light**, such as is emitted by the Sun. More significant are the various sorts of **inner light**, which refers to the types of awareness within the separated mind. The most basic of these is **visual light**, or the quality that is perceived through the eyes. This is somewhat generalized to what I will call **sensory light**, which makes possible any type of sensory awareness. Above that is an even more comprehensive level of **light of the imagination**, which includes not only the principle of awareness reflective of the ordinary sensory forms, such as experienced in sense-memory, but also the wider ranging experience called fantasy or constructive imagination. On a yet higher and more comprehensive level is the **light of understanding**, which en-

ables the mind to form concepts and judgments. At one place that meaning is made quite clear:
> "5 Understanding is light, and light leads to knowledge."
> (5,III,7,5)

Above this, although the Course does not give details about it, is what it calls the **light of reason**; this seems to be the type of awareness that makes possible two sorts of activities of the mind: the lower form is that of logical reasoning, and the higher form is that of the capacity to be aware in the most comprehensive sort of perception possible. The latter is clearly the 'Great Light' that is perceived in the experience of the Real World in the holy instant. This can be called the **light of the Real World.** In the Course's view, this is the highest level or sort of light within the mode of perceiving. Thus, within the realm or field of perception the mind can experience various degrees or levels of both light and darkness, in the sense that the higher in this series of 'lights' expands its awareness beyond the limits or 'darkness' of the lower levels.

'Light' in the absolute sense also has various types, although all of these, by virtue of the complete sharing within that level, are equal in intensity and comprehensiveness. Most fundamental is what can be called the **Light of Love**, which is the 'Energy' that is the basis of all that exists, both within the realm of absolute Reality and even in the realm of perception. Its presence in any perfect mind is what enables that mind to be aware or have knowledge. In that sense, it is also referred to as the **light of knowledge** or the **light of truth.** As viewed by the Course, that Light is present in the various perfect minds that make up Reality. The first is in God, which the Course refers to as the **Light of God**. But, as we've seen, the extending nature of that Light/Love produces what it calls **created light**. This is the foundation of awareness in all creatures. The primary creature is the Son, as **'being light.'** But the same is true for all other created perfect minds. Thus, the Course also speaks of the Holy Spirit and the Christ Mind as 'being light.' Thus, we have what can be called the **light of the Son**, the **light of the Holy Spirit**, and the **light of the Christ Mind.** Indeed, the whole of what the Course calls variously 'the Universe of Love,' 'the Kingdom,' or 'Heaven' is embraced by or filled with the **Light of Heaven**.

Accordingly, we may see these gradations or levels of light as increasingly intense or comprehensive sorts of light, or degrees of awareness, ranging from the lowest or 'darkest' level of minimal presence or even complete absence of even visual or sensory awareness to the highest perception possible (of the Real World), culminating in the most comprehensive of all light in the Light of Heaven, which is the full expression of the Light of Love. Similarly there are levels of darkness. This would include the darkness that the mind would be caught up in if it misunderstood anything due to its involvement in beliefs or limited feelings. In the Course's view, this is exactly what is done by attachment to the ego and the beliefs and feelings it generates. In the holy instant, however, there is a lifting of its involvement in that obscuring network. That darkness has been brought to the light of understanding and is illuminated in or by that instant. In this there is also the basis for that mind's bringing that understanding back into the mode of ordinary awareness, even if it retreats from the clearer awareness of the holy instant.

8) The ending of belief in vengeance. One of the serious distortions that come from the ego's dominance is the belief that vengeance, which is one of the major consequences of its belief in guilt and its highly distorted idea of justice, is a way of bringing order or 'salvation' to the world. However, as with the other ego-distortions, the holy instant lets the mind see through it and abandon it:

> "3 The holy instant is the opposite of the ego's fixed belief in salvation through vengeance for the past. 4 In the holy instant it is understood that the past is gone, and with its passing the drive for vengeance has been uprooted and has disappeared. 5 The stillness and the peace of *now* enfold you in perfect gentleness. 6 Everything is gone except the truth."(16,VII,6,3-6)

Thus, the absurdity of vengeance is seen quite clearly in the sufficiently deep holy instant, and the mind that returns to the temporal mode of perception can no longer entertain acting on its false premises.

ii. Affective aspects of ego eliminated in the holy instant. Just as the holy instant transforms the cognitive aspects of the ego-idea, it also brings important changes in the emotions and emotional dispositions.

1) The ending of fear. Earlier it was pointed out that the most fundamental emotion that dominates the separated mind is fear. The effect of the holy instant on this feeling is described:

> "4 Perfect love casts out fear."(1,VI,5,4)

and:

> "All fear is past and only love is here."(W,293)

Although these passages do not mention the holy instant, because the holy instant involves the awareness of the presence of perfect love, it follows that while the mind is in the holy instant all fear is dispelled.

The following passage makes clear the reason for this:

> "6 Fear arises from lack of love. 7 The only remedy for lack of love is perfect love."(2,VI,7,6-7)

Here we may recall that the arising of primary fear is the direct result of the mind's attaching itself to the focused awareness of only limited aspects of Reality and that the essential nature of Reality is Love. Thus, this act of focused attachment involves dismissing or setting aside some aspects of Love, or producing a state of lack of Love within its awareness.

An important consequence of the holy instant is that even if the mind slips out of that awareness and returns to more ordinary consciousness, that experience exercises a powerful influence in regard to fear:

> "5 Take this very instant, now, and think of it as all there is of time. 6 Nothing can reach you here out of the past, and it is here that you are completely absolved, completely free and wholly without condemnation. 7 From this holy instant

wherein holiness was born again you will go forth in time without fear, and with no sense of change with time."
(15,I,9,5-7)

Although this passage does not indicate how far the mind must be immersed in the holy instant for this to occur, the after-effect of fearlessness can pervade it even in its later experiences in time. This tallies with the reports of some regarded as 'saints' in all traditions who came to a point in spiritual development where fear no longer played any role in their lives. Indeed, if the Course's view is correct, it would follow that this absence of fear in the face of threats by others would be a clear indicator of an advanced stage of spiritual development.

2) The abandoning of guilt. The holy instant involves the transcending of the ego-mode of awareness. But guilt, the most basic and original type of fear, is one of the primary mechanisms that the ego engenders to maintain itself. Accordingly, it should be quite clear that guilt would be radically undone in the holy instant. Thus it is stated:

"2 In the holy instant guilt holds no attraction, since communication has been restored. 3 And guilt, whose only purpose is to disrupt communication, has no function here. 4 Here there is no concealment, and no private thoughts."(15,VII,14,2-4)

That the purpose of guilt is to disrupt communication may not at first be obvious. However, a little reflection makes this clear. That is, the ego exists primarily as a mode that excludes the full awareness of all aspects of Reality. Since other minds are constituted by their awareness of either all (for perfect minds) or a part (for separated minds) of Reality, the function of the ego is to set up a barrier between its own content and the content of other minds. Communication is a matter of awareness of the content of another mind, and full communication is the awareness of the content of all minds. Thus, ego-awareness is maintained by obstructing full communication, particularly with God whose authorship the ego-dominated mind thinks it has usurped (the 'original sin'). Guilt, as we have seen, in its primary form is the feeling that it has for what it thinks of as impending destruction due to one's choice to maintain focus on only a part of Reality. But, in the holy instant, the mind gets beyond that separative mode, so that the basis of guilt is removed.

However, if during the holy instant the mind drops guilt as completely meaningless, when it returns to awareness where the holy instant slips away, there is likely to arise an attraction to move back into the guilty condition. But this can be avoided:

"2 The holy instant is His most helpful aid in protecting you from the attraction of guilt, the real lure in the special relationship."(16,VI,3,2)

That is, because the holy instant has made clear that guilt is actually without a meaningful basis, this attraction is seen as quite pointless and productive of much suffering. Hence, the former experience of the holy instant generates a kind of 'protective shield' for that mind. Of course, it may choose to ignore the warning and get engrossed in the guilt-cycle, particularly if it has not come to full clarity about the folly of special relationships that are connected with ego-maintenance. If the intensity and depth of the holy instant are insufficient, such a mind may well slip into the mode of ego and guilt again, although it has as its ally both the guidance of the Holy Spirit and the recollection of the far more satisfactory state disclosed in the holy instant.

3) Other affective changes. Although no specific mention is made of other feelings that are changed in the holy instant, it is clear that those discussed as arising from the attachment to the ego-idea are no longer compatible with that mode of awareness: hate, anger, depression and the other negative emotions. However, a shallow temporary experience of the holy instant does not seem to bring their complete elimination, particularly when one returns to the ordinary state.

iii. Behavioral shifts related to the holy instant. Since behavior is largely determined by one's beliefs and emotional dispositions, it is significantly impacted within and following the experience of the holy instant.

1) The ending of the inclination to attack. In the holy instant, the basis for the separated mind to engage in attacking behavior is ended. This is described:

> "1 Only the different can attack. 2 So you conclude *because* you can attack, you and your brother must be different. 3 Yet does the Holy Spirit explain this differently. 4 *Because* you and your brother are not different, you cannot attack. 5 Either position is a logical conclusion. 6 Either could be maintained, but never both. 7 The only question to be answered in order to decide which must be true is whether you and your brother are different. 8 From the position of what you understand you seem to be, and therefore can attack. 9 Of the alternatives, this seems more natural and more in line with your experience. 10 And therefore it is necessary that you have other experiences, more in line with truth, to teach you what *is* natural and true."(22,VI,13,1-10)

That is, the awareness that comes in the holy instant, that one is not fundamentally different from his brother, undoes any basis for attacking behavior. The degree to which that awareness is realized greatly influences the elimination of attacking behavior, particularly in the awareness of such a mind after it returns from the holy instant into the mode of being in the world. If it is shallow, the attack-impulse in that mind will likely still have a residue; if profound, it will be greatly reduced or even altogether removed. Thus, it may be necessary for that mind to 'revisit' the holy instant before it has come to a sufficient depth of that awareness to completely undo the 'attack-habit' endemic to the ego-minded.

Thus, it is made clear that any sort of attack or inclination to it is incompatible with perfect love. As is stated:

> "2 Attack will always yield to love if it is brought to love, not hidden from it."(14,VI,2,2)

This seems to be the foundation of the principle expressed in Jesus' New Testament teaching, "But I say to you that listen, Love your enemies, do good to those who hate you" (Luke,6,27), and also expressed even earlier by Buddha, "For never does hatred cease by hatred here below: hatred ceases by love; this is an eternal law" (Dhammapada,I,5). Thus, the Course's teaching on this is fully in agreement with those other teachings.

2) The transformation of special relationships. Earlier we saw how one of the most serious ways in which the separated mind embeds itself in ego-mindedness is through its belief in the importance of and the pursuit of special relationships. These are radically challenged and set aside through the experience of the holy instant, as seen in:

> "1 Everyone on earth has formed special relationships, and although this is not so in Heaven, the Holy Spirit knows how to bring a touch of Heaven to them here. 2 In the holy instant no one is special, for your personal needs intrude on no one to make your brothers seem different. 3 Without the values from the past, you would see them all the same and like yourself. 4 Nor would you see any separation between yourself and them. 5 In the holy instant, you see in each relationship what it will be when you perceive only the present."(15,V,8,1-5)

That is, because the experience of the holy instant radically changes the awareness of others and removes the ego-basis for special relationships, those with whom one may have had such relationships are seen in an entirely different way. The key to this is the realization that one actually has no special needs that were thought satisfiable only through special relationships. In light of that, there comes the awareness that all those who had been perceived as 'different brothers' are actually recognized as not being different, so that none of them are seen as 'special.' Indeed, they are all seen as united with oneself rather than as separated. This does not mean that what is truly in them is dismissed, or even that one's relationship is dissolved. Rather, all of that is transformed into a very different sort of relationship, the 'holy relationship.' We will discuss that at length when we consider the 'new' content that comes by way of the holy instant. Also, this dissolution of special relationships does not seem to occur, at least fully, in the shallower experiences of the holy instant, even if within it their illusoriness is intimated. The complete dissolution seems to come only in the deeper experiences of it and finally is altogether realized only in the enduring holy instant.

3) Other behavior terminated or transformed. No other passages talk about how the holy instant dissolves or transforms other specific behavioral effects of the ego, such as 'making,' at least in the limited way that comes through the 'creative' impulse that operates in minds within the realm of separation. However, I may suggest that there does occur a new sort of making, which may be called *'illuminated making.'* That is, to the degree that the Light of Love operates actively within a mind, it can 'inspire' that mind to produce works that go beyond ego-making. For example, in the instances of the Buddha and Jesus, they spoke, taught, and did things having limited forms (sermons, instructions to followers, and miracles) that embodied meaning of extraordinary depth. These have continued to endure in the scriptures and practices that influence the lives of their followers. We may even think of the miracles they gave as leading to further miracles from those who received them down to this present day, as a kind of continuation of their transforming gifts to many millions. This inspired and illuminated making can also be seen in the lives of many of the great saints from all traditions – those of Judaism, such as Baal Shem Tov; of Christianity, such as Benedict, Francis of Assisi, Teresa of Avila, and Mother Teresa; of Islam, such as Arabi, al-Hallaj, Rumi, and Rab'ia; the 'mahatmas' of Hinduism, such as Ramakrishna, Aurobindo, and Gandhi; the great Buddhist 'masters' such as Padmasambhava, Dogen, and the Dalai Lama; as well as the holy men and women of Taoism and most indigenous religions. They have also given to their people works of Love that continue to awaken others to the presence of Love. A close study of the history of all these traditions would make clearer how in all of them there have been persons who not only came to the holy instant, but were led to inspired 'making' and 'doing.' In a more limited way, one can make the case that many of the greatest minds of mankind were those who experienced the holy instant to some degree and afterwards expressed that 'Light' in the form of the great literatures, such as that of Shakespeare and Goethe; or music, such as that of Bach, Mozart, and Mahler; or art, such as that of Da Vinci, Michelangelo, or even Van Gogh; or social builders, such as Ashoka, Jefferson, or M. L. King. This is not to say that all those inspired 'makers' were saints, since they often had the ambivalence of ego and Love operating in them. But that their great works can be understood as founded on the presence of the creative Light of Love is not an unreasonable explanation of their achievements.[67]

However, there are other specific positive aspects that the holy instant involves, to which we now turn.

b. New content in awareness arising in/from the holy instant. Before we consider this very important matter, it should be pointed out again that there are two levels of experience that need to be kept in mind. The first is the level on which the experience of the holy instant occurs. As was already indicated, there are many degrees of depth of that experience, ranging from a shallow encounter to a total immersion. This may be understood as related to the extent of the particular separated mind's attachment to or freedom from the obstacles that arise in the choice of separation. The second level is the mode of awareness that is present after the mind moves back into ordinary awareness. There can be a variety of responses in it, from 'fear and trembling' or even a return of intense egoism as it chooses once again to hold onto the ego-mode, to a major transformation into a profoundly reduced or even completely eliminated ego-influence

---

[67] Gopi Krishna makes a similar point in *The Biological Basis of Religion and Genius*.

and great love. There have been individuals in all cultures who have apparently gone into the temporary holy instant and upon returning to the ordinary state found a whole spectrum of changes, ranging from insanity to profoundly wise and loving attitudes toward life. One might read, for example, the biography of St. Francis of Assisi in which his numerous such experiences are followed by this whole range of after-effects. The need for multiple holy instant experiences seems to be dependent on what is necessary for undoing the hold of ego whose remaining obstacles can be clung to quite stubbornly. But there is also the effect even a shallow temporary holy instant can have on undoing those obstacles. This is its healing effect on the experiencer. We will discuss this last point when we consider the relation of the miracle to the holy instant, and the way it 'feeds back' into the separated mind so as to enable the mind to move into even deeper levels of experiencing it subsequent to a particular experience of the holy instant. Thus, while considering the content of the experience of the holy instant, we should keep in mind two things:

1) These contents can be *more or less* clear or complete.
2) What is carried over into ordinary time-bound experience afterwards can be quite limited or, in the shallower instances, hardly at all, or even in some cases provocative of an intensification of ego-domination as it confronts what it can perceive as great fear of the ego's dissolution.

i. A miniature of Heaven. One passage describes this in interesting terms:
"1 The holy instant is a miniature of Heaven, sent you *from* Heaven. 2 It is a picture, too, set in a frame. 3 Yet if you accept this gift you will not see the frame at all, because the gift can only be accepted through your willingness to focus all your attention on the picture. 4 The holy instant is a miniature of eternity. 5 It is a picture of timelessness, set in a frame of time. 6 If you focus on the picture, you will realize that it was only the frame that made you think it *was* a picture. 7 Without the frame, the picture is seen as what it represents."
(17,IV,11,1-7)

The three expressions 'miniature of Heaven,' 'miniature of eternity,' and 'picture of timelessness' merit reflection. The Course's ultimate aim is to bring separated minds back to their original condition called 'Heaven.' This is not some celestial paradise of super-embodied 'purified' egos as sometimes imagined and depicted by theologians of almost all traditions or described in visionary experiences such as sometimes occur in NDE's, but rather a state of complete oneness involving no material or limited mental modes that are characteristic of separated minds. There are two important features of awareness in the Heaven-state. One is that all 'fragments' of the perfect Christ Mind that had been perceived as separated minds, including what was thought of as 'one's own mind,' are recognized as simply the single and fully integrated Christ Mind, which is one's own Self. The other is the awareness of what was earlier called 'the Universe of Love.' This is the totality of perfect minds, including the primary Creator, who is the Source of the Christ Mind or Son; the Son's own creature (Son_2); that creature's creature (Son_3); and the whole infinite sequence of further created perfect minds. The expression 'miniature of Heaven' seems to have two senses. One is the awareness of the complete unity of all separated minds in the Christ Mind. Since this is only one 'portion' of the state of Heaven; it is aptly called a 'miniature.' The other is that it is only a perceptual, and therefore limited, reflection of the awareness of the whole 'Universe of Love.' This is usually interrupted by a return to a more limited temporal awareness, so that it is only a 'brief' encounter with that unlimited Wholeness. (The Course also refers to this as the 'perception of the Real World,' which will be more fully discussed later.) In that sense, it can also be called a 'miniature of eternity,' as in statement 4. That is, within that instant, which we should recall is the same in every occurrence of the holy instant, there is the cessation of time and the shifting into eternity or timelessness. However, because the mind can slip out of that mode of awareness back into time, from the perspective of the mind returned to the temporal mode it appears to *have* occurred with a past preceding it and a future following it, or to be surrounded or enframed by time. Hence, it is called a 'picture of timelessness' (statement 5). But, within the awareness of the holy instant there is no time at all. Since the Course does indicate that the separated mind can move into the holy instant and out of it repeatedly, from the temporal perspective there are many such occasions. One might think of them as consecutive steps into the holy instant, each subsequent one having greater depth and intensity, till the mind finally reaches a point where there is no more slipping back into the ordinary limited temporal mode, and either remains within time under the mode of the enduring eternal instant or fully returns to Heaven.

Here I might make some comments about descriptions of what are claimed to be experiences of Heaven by many who have had deep 'near-death experiences.' These generally contain a variety of details ranging from moving through a 'tunnel' toward a light, perceiving perceptual forms one thinks as relatives, then encountering a 'Being of Light' which sometimes is thought to be some holy person such as Jesus, Krishna, or the Buddha, or even a complete immersion in the Light, which the experiencer recounts as involving profound peace and bliss as well as an intense sense of certitude and knowing far beyond what may have been previously felt. A very interesting description of this is found in the neurosurgeon Eben Alexander's *Proof of Heaven,* mentioned earlier. This is particularly significant in that Alexander's commitment to the materialist explanation of consciousness prior to his own experience makes him especially qualified to evaluate the experience, at least as to the reliability of its contents. One of Alexander's conclusions is that it was, as the title indicates, an actual experience of Heaven. However, although it is quite plausible that what he experienced was something extraordinary, and very possibly something much 'more real' than what is found in ordinary experience, it does not follow that it was what the

Course refers to as 'Heaven.' Indeed, it is much closer to the experience of the Real World, or what is here called a 'miniature of heaven.'[68] Similar experiences are also reported among practitioners of meditative disciplines.

ii. Specific new cognitive contents. This 'miniature of Heaven' includes experiential aspects related to the entities that constitute Reality, particularly God, the Son, and aspects of the Son that have been experienced as other separated minds or 'brothers,' and communication with them.

1) The remembrance of God. This is clearly indicated:

> "7 In the holy instant, in which you see yourself as bright with freedom, you will remember God."(15,I,10,7)

This remembrance of God cannot be the cognitive process that we usually think of as 'remembering.' The latter is primarily a process of holding in awareness an image that is felt to be the same as or similar to some perceptual experience, either sensory, emotional, or conceptual (or even a combination of all three) that happened in the past. That is, remembrance in this sense is a matter of going back within the field of time. (How that might be possible is the subject of interesting philosophical and scientific inquiry, but we need not go into that here.) The remembering in the holy instant, however, cannot be a matter of going back in time, since it involves moving beyond the field of time. Thus, the remembrance of God cannot involve *recalling* some image, feeling, or concept that one has associated with the word 'God,' which entails referring to some past perceptual

---

[68] *Proof of Heaven*, Simon and Schuster, 2012. While Alexander's descriptions are very interesting, his interpretation of his experience may need closer scrutiny. For example, when he claims that he saw God, it is not clear whether he is claiming that his particular perceptions were of God, which in the Course's view is not possible, or whether there was something in those experiences that was beyond the perceptual aspects. The clarity of his experiences on the 'other side' and the certainty of their reality agrees with what others have reported in similar experiences. However, it would be misleading to think that they are the final mode of awareness of Reality. In the Course's terms, Alexander's experiences might be best thought of as beginning perceptions of the Real World, but still colored by the ego-habits that incline one to think of other minds in terms of limited bodies, such as the female entity that he tells of guiding him across the 'beautiful landscape.' Similar objections can be made in regards to the variety of 'vision experiences' that are described by some visionaries and mediums as being 'what Heaven actually is.' In the Course's terms, any sort of 'heaven' that involves limited bodies or events occurring sequentially in a 'higher' sort of time and space is at best simply an 'improved ego-plane.'

A similar hyper-physical structure has been described in Christian theology as the various 'mansions of heaven' and 'circles of hell,' in Hindu reflections as the 21 different planes called the 'lokas' (positive levels or heavens), 'patalas' (middle levels or worlds), and 'narakas' (negative levels or hells). Mahayana Buddhism also describes multiple planes of 'Pure Lands' (heavens) and 'demon realms' (hells). But particularly in the Hindu and the Buddhist views, those various planes are still less than the full Reality of Awakening, in that they all involve some type of spatio-temporal limits. The full realization of Awakening seems to be much closer to what the Course calls 'Heaven.'

content in the mind. Rather, the remembrance here is a matter of becoming aware of the presence of God that is at the foundation of one's very being, even though that awareness is generally obscured for the separated mind at most moments in time, due to the blockage of its awareness by the presence of the ego-idea. Since central to the nature of God is His connectedness to the Whole (the core of His Holiness), the term 'remembering' can be better understood by referring to its etymological roots, 're' = 'again' + 'member' = 'part.' The insight here is one of 'reconstituting in awareness all the members of the Whole, or all its parts into the actual Whole that it is.' It also follows that this remembrance can be more or less clear or intense. It can range from what we might call a bare intimation that remains somewhat obscured by perceptual details that are also prominent, to a fully clear and complete awareness of God and Reality without any admixture of perceptual content.

Exactly how God is experienced in the holy instant is not fully clarified. However, as was discussed earlier, it seems to be closely related to the higher perception of the 'Great Rays,' which we will discuss later in more detail. But we should keep in mind that in the holy instant awareness has characteristics of both cognitive modes, perception and knowledge. Perception seems to be the most salient aspect of the experience, but it is a very different sort of perception than is found in simple separation. Obviously, God cannot be perceived, at least as 'perceiving' is understood in the Course, since perception by its very nature involves some sort of limitation in awareness to particular aspects of what is perceived, and God is completely without any limitations. What must occur in this experience is that there is a partial awakening of the knowing mode, although not to its fullness. This 'dim knowing' is superimposed on the perceptual content, 'illuminating' it so to speak with the unitive quality that is central to knowing. In a sense, even the ordinary separated mind at any time has present to it the awareness of knowing, although its focus is directed to very limited perceptual details that render it actually unaware of God. That is, God is at every moment in time immediately present, but 'covered over,' as it were, by a perceptual 'cloud of unknowing' that complete focusing on perception involves. The experience of the holy instant can be thought of as a lifting of that cloud or a suspension of total focusing on perceptual detail. Of course, since this can occur in varying degrees depending on the willingness of the particular mind, the remembrance of God and all Reality is also a matter of degree.

2) Union with one's brothers. Not only does the holy instant involve what the Course sometimes calls this 'vertical' shift to the awareness of God/Love within oneself, but there is also a 'horizontal' inclusion in one's awareness of what is usually thought of as outside one's ego-bounded 'self,' particularly other minds.[69] This was briefly discussed in our consideration of the expression 'miniature of heaven.' It is further described:

> "8 Yet in the holy instant you unite directly with God, and all your brothers join in Christ. 9 Those who are joined in Christ are in no way separate. 10 For Christ is the Self the Sonship shares, as God shares His Self with Christ."(15,V,10,8-10)

In the Course, the term 'brothers' is used in two somewhat different ways. The first refers to all those within the realm of separation that are thought of as 'other' minds similarly tied into the belief in separation. That is, they are minds we think of as separate from ourselves and considered to have an ego similar to our own. From the Course's perspective, these can be thought of as 'fragments' of the single mind of the Son in so far as that mind has taken on the awareness of separation. This is also equivalent to one meaning of the term 'sons of God.' But there is a second meaning of the term 'brothers' as well as 'sons of God.' This refers to the whole collection of created perfect minds, which constitute the greater numerical portion of the 'Universe of Love.' In this particular context, the meaning that seems most appropriate is the first: all those minds that a mind not in the holy instant regards as like itself, limited and within the confines of an ego. To such a mind, even God, the Christ Mind, and the Holy Spirit are usually thought of as separate and within the confines of some sort of ego, though that ego is thought of as much bigger and more powerful. However, this is simply a projection of the ego-dominated separated mind. But, when such a mind enters into the holy instant, as the passage points out, that sense of separateness is either greatly diminished or even quite completely erased, at least for the period that it remains aware of the holy instant. Within that awareness, the mind sees not only that it is intimately united with God but that it is also one with all other 'fragments' of the Son's mind that are thought to have taken on the illusion of separation. Thus, it sees that what it regarded as its own separated mind and those of its brothers are all profoundly connected or united, or even better, that they are one and the same perfect Christ Mind. This awareness, as was pointed

---

[69] The term 'vertical' is used in the Course to refer to the mind's movement to fuller connection with the awareness of God's/Love's presence, as in:

> "'No man cometh unto the Father but by me' does not mean that I am in any way separate or different from you except in time, and time does not really exist. 2 The statement is more meaningful in terms of a vertical rather than a horizontal axis."(1,II,4,1-2).

'Horizontal' refers to the awareness of others within the level that its awareness is on, as in:

> "2 In the longitudinal or horizontal plane the recognition of the equality of the members of the Sonship appears to involve almost endless time. 3 However, the miracle entails a sudden shift from horizontal to vertical perception."(1,II,6,1-3)

That is, the horizontal plane for the separated mind includes all other minds that it thinks of as separated.

out regarding the general character of the holy instant as admitting of degrees of intensity or clarity of realization, is also subject to that variation in degree.

Thus, the lesser encounter with Heaven in the holy instant is not merely a private matter for the individual separated mind. While the holy instant can come to such a particular separated mind only by its decision to accept it, once it has come to it there are effects it has on other separated minds:

> "1 In the holy instant, you will see the smile of Heaven shining on both you and your brother. 2 And you will shine upon him, in glad acknowledgment of the grace that has been given you. 3 For sin will not prevail against a union Heaven has smiled upon. 4 Your perception was healed in the holy instant Heaven gave you."(19,III,10,1-4)

That is, within the holy instant the mind is aware of other separated minds, its brothers, in a very different way. It sees them as one with itself, and thus its perceptions of them no longer involve the illusions of judgment, fear, attack, and all the forms it formerly projected onto them, particularly the idea of 'sin.' This new mode of perceiving them, although it may not immediately or completely undo the state of separation in others, by seeing them in another 'light' they no longer have the reinforcement of their condition from the one offering that 'light' to them, so that they are now supported to move in the direction of their own liberation from separation. Thus, through the healed perception of the particular mind that enters into the holy instant, that mind now offers healing to all it perceives. This is the basis of the process of its giving miracles.

3) Perfect communication. Connected to the unitive 'Heavenly' state is the awareness of the sharing of the contents of one's own mind with all other minds, or what the Course calls 'perfect communication.' This is noted in:

> "5. ... the holy instant is a time in which you receive and give perfect communication."(15,IV,6,5)

This is further explained:

> "1 The necessary condition for the holy instant does not require that you have no thoughts that are not pure. 2 But it does require that you have none that you would keep. 3 Innocence is not of your making. 4 It is given you the instant you would have it. 5 Atonement would not be if there were no need for it. 6 You will not be able to accept perfect communication as long as you would hide it from yourself."(15,IV,9,1-6)

Here we may see a serious block to and a major condition for the occurrence of the holy instant, as well as what the Course means by 'perfect communication.' That is, it involves the complete sharing of the contents of one's mind and that of other minds. One might think of perfect communication as between only two minds, but if it is truly perfect it would also have to be with *all* minds. This does not mean that some of those minds are not aware of the contents of all other minds. The very nature of separated minds is that they choose to exclude from their awareness much of what is in perfect minds as well as what is in other separated minds. As is stated:

> "1 How can you do this when you would prefer to have private thoughts and keep them? 2 The only way you could do that would be to deny the perfect communication that makes the holy instant what it is. 3 You believe you can harbor thoughts you would not share, and that salvation lies in keeping thoughts to yourself alone. 4 For in private thoughts, known only to yourself, you think you find a way to keep what you would have alone, and share what *you* would share."
>
> (15,IV,7,1-4)

Thus, a major block to experiencing the holy instant is this choice to make some thoughts private or unshared. That is understandable as a means the ego-dominated mind uses to maintain its separateness, which it thinks makes it more secure, but in fact perpetuates its very limited and unhappy state. It can access the holy instant only when it is willing to let go of this concern for 'protecting' itself by being willing to share.

Yet, there does not have to be a conscious sharing, or even a willingness to share, in every mind in order for one separated mind to enter the holy instant. Its choice opens it to communicate with all other minds, both in having awareness of their contents and giving them its own; however, those other minds may be apprehensive about this 'violation' of their privacy. This might be compared to the experiences reported in encounters with highly advanced spiritual masters. Such masters are virtually impossible to hide any thought or feeling from, although the person encountering them does not choose to disclose many of his/her thoughts and feelings. Nevertheless, they report the sense of 'being completely seen through,' sometimes with a feeling of great discomfort. This can be thought of as type of unlimited telepathic 'mind-reading.' Related to this, as the above passage points out, one of the major blocks to entering the holy instant is the unwillingness to be fully transparent or willing to let another be aware of all the contents within one's mind. Conversely, an important condition for entering the holy instant is the willingness to let all those contents be given to all other minds, and of course the willingness to receive all the contents of all other minds.

4) A new perception of the body. It was pointed out that the holy instant brings with it an ending of the 'normal' way the body is perceived as a limited spatio-temporal form with which both one's own mind and other minds are closely identified. Now let us consider what replaces that. The first stage of that new perception is described:

> "2 For a time the body is still seen, but not exclusively, as it is seen here. 3 The little spark that holds the Great Rays within it is also visible, and this spark cannot be limited long to littleness. 4 Once you have crossed the bridge, the value of the body is so diminished in your sight that you will see no need at all to magnify it. 5 For you will realize that the only value

the body has is to enable you to bring your brothers to the bridge with you, and to be released together there."(16,VI,6,2-5)
Here, it is made quite clear that the holy instant does not completely terminate all awareness of the body, at least at first. In the earlier and less profound occurrences of the holy instant, perceptions of the body are commingled with a fuller awareness. The most salient feature of that perception is what is referred to here as the 'Great Rays.' As the above passage indicates, rather than the perception of a limited body there is the perception of unbounded rays of light associated with the awareness of oneself and every other being or mind that one is aware of. In another passage this is made even clearer:

> "1 In many only the spark remains, for the Great Rays are obscured. 2 Yet God has kept the spark alive so that the Rays can never be completely forgotten. 3 If you but see the little spark you will learn of the greater light, for the Rays are there unseen. 4 Perceiving the spark will heal, but knowing the light will create. 5 Yet in the returning the little light must be acknowledged first, for the separation was a descent from magnitude to littleness. 6 But the spark is still as pure as the Great Light, because it is the remaining call of creation."(10,IV,8,1-6)

If we look at this closely, we see three important terms: spark, Great Rays, and Great Light. In normal separated perception, all things including other minds are perceived only in terms of the more or less definite regions in space and time characteristic of limited perception of the body, such as visual perceptions that are dependent on the presence of physical light rays. In such visual perception, bodies are seen as bright or dark according to the intensity of those rays to which the eye responds. This corresponds to the lowest levels of meaning of the term 'light,' described earlier. But associated with the holy instant there is a new sort of perception that enters the perceptual field. What is called the '*spark*' seems best understood as referring to an initial perception that enhances the visual experience so as to include a limited center of light or even a limited surrounding field of light in and around other things. Thus, it is stated:

> "2 You will begin to understand it when you have seen little edges of light around the same familiar objects which you see now. 3 That is the beginning of real vision."(W,14,2,2)

This is not dependent on physical illumination, but is perhaps best thought of as superimposed on the visual image. Still, it is a perception, but no longer dependent on physical light, the physical eye, or even the other sorts of 'light' related to outer perception, imagination, understanding or conceptual reasoning. Rather, it is the first stage of the mind's perception of the higher light of the Real World. Indeed, there are many reports of ordinary people having such perceptions of luminosity around individuals thought to be 'saints' or persons of great spiritual development. This may be the basis of representing 'holy persons' as surrounded by halos or auras. The first stage of perception of higher luminosity, however, is expanded as the experience of the holy instant is deepened to the perception of the '*Great Rays.*' This seems best understood as referring to the mode of awareness that the mind has of both itself and other separated minds within the highest type of perceptual light. In this the mind perceives with increasing clarity both itself and all other minds as having no limits. In so far as that awareness is perceptual, it is a perception of seeing boundless light rays expanding outward; in so far as that awareness approaches knowing, it involves an intuitive 'seeing' of that same unlimitedness of each mind (including one's own) as extending to infinity. Ordinarily, the Great Rays are hidden and one is not even aware of the 'spark.' But, in the holy instant, echoing Blake, all things are 'perceived' as they really are, infinite.

The expression '*Great Light*' seems to be understandable in several ways. One is as the source of all that is present within any particular mind, including its infinite extension as these 'Rays.' Another is as the all-comprehensive luminosity or uninhibited perceptual presence of the realm of true perceptions, which is also called the 'Real World.' On a trans-perceptual level, the Great Light seems to be best understood as the ground of the total awareness and creativity of all perfect minds, which is Love or God. Of course, this would have to be the highest level of 'light.' Understood in this way, the usual awareness of the separated mind is one of only a tiny, even darkened, portion of the 'light' (the 'spark') that is present within the body that is the focus of perception. However, the holy instant opens that mind stepwise to these more complete perceptions, which of course far transcend ordinary visual perceptions, and finally moves beyond all perception into the awareness or light of knowledge.

Further details concerning the luminosity manifested in the deeper experiences of the holy instant are described somewhat later in Ch. 21:

> "1 Beyond the body, beyond the sun and stars, past everything you see and yet somehow familiar, is an arc of golden light that stretches as you look into a great and shining circle. 2 And all the circle fills with light before your eyes. 3 The edges of the circle disappear, and what is in it is no longer contained at all. 4 The light expands and covers everything, extending to infinity forever shining and with no break or limit anywhere. 5 Within it everything is joined in perfect continuity. 6 Nor is it possible to imagine that anything could be outside, for there is nowhere that this light is not."(21,I,8,1-6)

Here we find several important aspects of the 'expanded' perception, which seems to be a further elaboration of the highest type of light that can be perceived. One is the golden color of the light. This seems to involve something that may be both literal and analogous or figurative. That is, it indicates that there is a perceptual quality similar to our ordinary experience of the color of gold. Most people, indeed most cultures, have considered that particular color as especially beautiful or esthetically pleasing. While it may be difficult to determine whether that evaluation of this color is simply a matter of social conditioning or something more naturally or intrinsically related to our natural sensitivity (something innately more attractive), that this particular color is singled out as being characteristic of the luminosity of the deeper holy instant points to its being a feature of the perception in the holy instant. Of course, although gold has come to have a particularly great monetary value, which could contribute to our high valuation of that color, it may actually be that gold is felt so valuable because its color resonates with something more fundamental in the mind, such as is disclosed in its more mature experiences of the holy instant. If this is only meant figuratively in the sense that the quality of the light here is simply one of being of a higher esthetic value, and that the 'light' is actually not something perceptual but only a matter of deeper understanding beyond perception, the whole passage would have to be understood as primarily a metaphor. However, since the passage is quite detailed, it seems that the primary sense intended is that there is a color quality that is close to the ordinary perceptual quality 'golden,' but more intense.

This last idea meshes closely with the rest of the passage's description, which is also an extension of ordinary visual spatial characteristics. However, it far exceeds ordinary vision in several ways. One is the geometrical aspect, that it is *circular*. This circle, however, is not an ordinary objective circle, which visually occupies only a portion of the space within the visual field. That field is limited to the region in front of one's eyes, occupying only an arc of about 150 degrees horizontally and about 120 degrees vertically. That is, when we perceive a circle, it lies only within that region. But in the experience described, if one examines it closely, there is a complete circle of light, which would have to extend into the regions outside the ordinary visual field. That is, it involves a perception that is best thought of as a *circle completely encircling the perceiver who is at the center*. Further, that whole enveloping circle is completely *filled with this golden light*. Still further, that circle radiates outward in all directions *to infinity*. This is again quite different from ordinary visual perception, which is able to judge distances only to a finite radius. (Thus, the moon, sun and stars all appear to our eyes to be about the same distance away, which is a finite distance.) I might also add that this description, although stated in terms of a circular form, might more accurately use the word '*sphere*.' Indeed, since within the holy instant the content is not limited to what is only in a particular moment in time, but includes all of time, an even more accurate word would be '*hypersphere*' (a 4-dimensional sphere). Of course, because the Course is not attempting to give a completely precise description but makes use of terms that are readily graspable by most adults with a basic education, it keeps the terminology simple by calling it a 'circle.' However, if one were to try to refine the description most fully and accurately, the appropriate word could well be '*hypersphere of infinite dimensions*.' That is, the perceptual experience of the holy instant may well involve a direct intuitive perception of something that far exceeds our very limited habits of perceiving or even thinking. We will come back to this notion of 'golden light' when we discuss the holy relationship.

In this we may see that the holy instant acts a kind of 'bridging' mode of awareness that is to some extent perceptual yet also involving aspects of non-perceptual knowing. Thus, this experience of the '*Great Rays*' in the holy instant seems best to be understood as a radically new way of perceiving light. This term is used only seven times in the Course. Although it is an expression very close to something found in the visual experience of light, it seems to be best understood as referring to something present in Reality and an aspect of the highest mode of awareness, knowledge, which is entirely beyond perception. Thus, since the holy instant acts as a kind of 'bridging' mode of awareness that is to some extent perceptual yet also approaching non-perceptual knowing, this experience of the Great Rays in the holy instant seems best to be understood as a totally new way of perceiving.

One is reminded of the account of the so-called 'transfiguration' of Jesus in the *New Testament*, which is similar to a description of the 'transfiguration' of Krishna in the *Bhagavad Gita*, as well other descriptions of intense light surrounding other persons such as the Buddha and Muhammad. Even later individuals in those traditions are reported to have been experienced by some of their lesser-developed followers as enveloped in 'bright light.'[70]

Here, I might offer an observation that draws from modern physics. In one of its most recent formulations, each elementary particle is thought of as a probability-wave that extends infinitely into space and time prior to the moment it is actually observed. That act of observation is thought to 'collapse' this probability wave so as to give the particle a tiny location in space and time. However, before that perceptual observation is made, the particle can be thought of as being everywhere at all times. This is sometimes referred to as its virtual space-time property of 'non-locality.' From a somewhat different perspective, any particle (and any larger body composed of such particles) can be thought of as an energy field that is highly concentrated at a particular region of space-time, but also having some degree of presence at all other regions of space-time. As an energy structure, the Sun can be said to be 'located' at its particular place in the sky or Milky Way galaxy because its energy is more concentrated there. However, the Sun extends its luminous and gravitational influence throughout not only the whole solar system or even our local galaxy, but to the whole extent of space-time (as long as it is within that order). Thus, one can argue that it is fully compatible with the theory and observations of modern physics to hold that every body, including every star, planet, living body and tiniest elementary particle, as an energy field, in a sense can be said to be present everywhere. Of course, they are more intensely present at those places-times where they are observed to be (this accounts for the orderly structure of the physical universe), but in the strictest sense their energy-fields are present everywhere and everytime. From this perspective, physical reality needs to be viewed as an ordered collection of

---

[70] This luminous quality is a feature of what in the Tibetan tradition is called the 'rainbow body,' manifested by great masters. See the Wikipedia article on that topic.

interpenetrating energy-entities, each of which has only whatever space-time limits that the entire universe may have.

While this view from modern physics is only an intellectual construct, since the ordinary limits of sense-perception cannot access the details of it, the closest our ordinary minds seem to be able to approach an experience of that is by way of imagination. However, what the Course seems to be saying about the awareness that arises in the holy instant is that something very close to that construct is immediately experienced by the mind that enters into that awareness. Since the holy instant does not stop with perceptual awareness but moves into a mode that eventually sets all perception aside as unable to go there, it seems quite plausible that what we think of as the physical universe constitutes only a very tiny portion of the fuller Universe of Reality.

In cases where the mind generally slips out of the holy instant and returns to the ego-dominated mode for a period of time, it is fully restored to the perception of the body. However, even there the experience of the holy instant has a profound effect on such a mind regarding the separated mode and the body. There does not seem to be a complete returning to the old mode once the 'bridging' experience has occurred, at least if it is beyond a very shallow one. Now the body has a very different meaning. It is seen primarily as a vehicle for one's own coming back to the holy instant and for helping other separated minds come to it. We may again refer to the widely reported transformed attitudes that come to those having had deep near-death experiences. Such experiences seem to be very close in content to the holy instant and indeed may be special cases of experiencing it. Of course, there are other ways than nearly dying through which this can come to a person. Comparative studies of spiritual practices in all religious traditions make clear that numerous individuals have experienced something like, if not precisely the same as, the holy instant. Indeed, there are cases where this has happened to individuals quite spontaneously without any apparent conscious intent or disciplined practices on their part in what are called 'mystical experiences.' The reader may refer to Evelyn Underhill's *Mysticism*, W.T. Stace's *The Teachings of the Mystics*, or F.C. Happold's *Mysticism: A Study and an Anthology*, for accounts of such experiences.

For clarity regarding the holy instant experience, we consider briefly what the Course points out concerning the distinction between the holy instant and another type of 'expanded' awareness:

> "1 Everyone has experienced what he would call a sense of being transported beyond himself. 2 This feeling of liberation far exceeds the dream of freedom sometimes hoped for in special relationships. 3 It is a sense of actual escape from limitations. 4 If you will consider what this 'transportation' really entails, you will realize that it is a sudden unawareness of the body, and a joining of yourself and something else in which your mind enlarges to encompass it. 5 It becomes part of you, as you unite with it. 6 And both become whole, as neither is per-

ceived as separate. 7 What really happens is that you have given up the illusion of a limited awareness, and lost your fear of union."(18,VI,11,1-7)

This 'transportation experience' involves a release from some of the limits central to ego-mindedness. Those familiar with the findings of psychical research will recognize that this type of unusual experience is close to what falls under the general name 'extrasensory perception' (ESP). Specific types of ESP include a variety of experiences: clairvoyance, telepathy, out-of-body experiences, precognition and retrocognition. The first three involve primarily transcending the spatial limitations of ordinary perception and the last two have primarily a transcending of some temporal limitations. Indeed, right after the above passage a further comment is given:

"1 This can occur regardless of the physical distance that seems to be between you and what you join; of your respective positions in space; and of your differences in size and seeming quality. 2 Time is not relevant; it can occur with something past, present or anticipated. 3 The 'something' can be anything and anywhere; a sound, a sight, a thought, a memory, and even a general idea without specific reference. 4 Yet in every case, you join it without reservation because you love it, and would be with it."(18,VI,12,1-3)

That is, the 'transportation experience' can involve passing beyond either spatial or temporal limitations or even both.

One might conclude that the Course holds that such experiences are shifts into the holy instant. However, a little after the above passage, we find:

"6 In these instants of release from physical restrictions, you experience much of what happens in the holy instant; the lifting of the barriers of time and space, the sudden experience of peace and joy, and, above all, the lack of awareness of the body, and of the questioning whether or not all this is possible."(18,VI,13,6)

Here it is made clear that these 'transportation experiences' are not themselves experiences of the holy instant, although they have some similarities to them. While they can even include strong feelings of peace and love, they do not involve the primary awareness of union with God and with other perfect minds or all other fragments of the Christ Mind. One might think of them as indications that the mind may be approaching the holy instant awareness. Thus, it would be a mistake to think that because ESP occurs that the mind has come to the realization of the holy instant. Indeed, this error is not uncommon among those involved in the practice of inner disciplines, and it can even be quite misleading when a disciple concludes that his or her 'master' must be fully realized and liberated simply because he manifests such paranormal attainments. Although entering the holy instant generally entails having such 'transportation' experiences, having them does not necessarily entail having entered the holy instant.

Related to this is the variety of phenomena sometimes called 'psychokinetic' (PK). These involve the paranormal change of physical objects through mental activity. The only type of PK discussed by the Course is illness and healing of the body. In its view, these are primarily effects of the mind. However, from what it says about ESP, it follows that manifesting other PK 'powers' would not necessarily entail the holy instant, whose most important aspect is some degree of realization of the awareness of Love. Nevertheless, the realization of the holy instant may well be accompanied by the manifestation of PK. We may recall that the narratives of Jesus' life report numerous instances of his manifesting the power of levitation, materialization, dematerialization, teleportation, and of course physical healing. However, in a sense the whole process of the separation, which involves the formation of the body and the whole physical universe, can be thought of as a kind of super-materialization event, just as the final achievement of the Atonement is a kind of super-dematerialization. But the latter is intimately related to the realization of perfect love by way of experiencing the holy instant.

5) Perception of the Real World. The term 'Real World' has such a particular and important meaning in the Course's teachings that it will be very helpful if we try to come to a clearer understanding of it. But before we discuss that, we will consider again its view of what it calls 'the world.'

a) The illusory 'real,' or the realm of ordinary perception or 'the world.' The Course firmly challenges the ego-dominated mind's beliefs about what it thinks of as 'real.' That is founded on the belief that what is real is primarily based on what is disclosed by perception. While the Course provisionally indulges its students in that belief and wisely recognizes that this belief must remain in place as long as the mind clings to it, it also points out that a criterion of 'real' more reliable than perception is what is disclosed by the awareness of knowing, such as is present in all perfect minds. Even those that cling to the perceptual criterion recognize that they are sometimes misled by it into thinking that some things that are unreal are real (e.g., hallucinations, dreams, and perceptual illusions).

The characteristics of the world of ordinary perception make it utterly incompatible with the reality of God, whose existence is a primary fact of knowledge. The Course points out:

> "1 If this were the real world, God *would* be cruel. 2 For no Father could subject His children to this as the price of salvation and *be* loving. 3 *Love does not kill to save.*"(13,in,3,1-3)

That is, the presence of what we think of as 'evil' (death and any form of suffering or what can produce that) is utterly incompatible with the reality of a God of Love. Either God is not real or the world of perception is not.

It is further pointed out that the very nature of our mode of existing in the world contains the basis for the impossibility of our finding real happiness there:

> "3 You attack the real world every day and every hour and ev-

ery minute, and yet you are surprised that you cannot see it." (12,VIII,1,3)

While this may seem to be an exaggeration, the fundamental nature of ego-attachment, as we have seen, makes the separated mind perpetually engaged in a state of war, either on a conscious level or unconsciously engaged in the disposition to counter the other egos it thinks of as surrounding it. Since genuine happiness is not possible while one is engaged in a state of conflict, it follows that it cannot be found within this world. The only exception is that a mind can be at once operating (that is, engaged in perceiving and responding to perceptions) within the world, yet also in the higher unitive mode. This has been described in the expression 'being in the world but not of it.'[71] This would have to be the situation for persons like Jesus or the Buddha after they realized the Christ Mind/Enlight-enment. But, for most separated minds, there is only a brief and partial glimpse of true happiness, which is followed by a return to conflict. This occurs until the mind is fully released from ego-domination.

b) The central feature of the Real World. The primary teaching of the Course is that the insane mode of separation can and will be exchanged for an entirely different way of living and being. The key to that transformation is the realization of the holy instant. In it is a radically new mode of perceiving, which is that of what it calls the 'Real World.' As it counsels:

> "1 Sit quietly and look upon the world you see, and tell yourself: 'The real world is not like this. 2 It has no buildings and there are no streets where people walk alone and separate. 3 There are no stores where people buy an endless list of things they do not need. 4 It is not lit with artificial light, and night comes not upon it. 5 There is no day that brightens and grows dim. 6 There is no loss. 7 Nothing is there but shines, and shines forever."(13,VII,1,1-7)

In following this guided meditation, one comes to the condition that, as was already pointed out, is reached in the experience of the holy instant: the awareness of light. Let us try to get a better understanding of what is meant by this term 'Real World.'

A first point is that, although the separated mind is generally not aware of it, nevertheless it is *always present*.

> "8 Yet is the real world unaffected by the world he thinks is real."(29,IX,6,8)

This is not unlike what we are told by modern science. That is, although we think that reality is filled with solid objects having the colors and other perceptual quali-

---

[71] This expression is not actually found in the New Testament. However, it is clearly inferable from the statement attributed to Jesus: "... I do not pray that thou shouldst take them out of the world, but that thou shouldst keep them from the evil one. They are not of the world, even as I am not of the world."(John 17: 15-16).

ties we perceive, what is said to be actually there is something much vaster and different from what we are accustomed to thinking. Indeed, based upon the tiny portion of our sensitivity to what is present in physical reality, it has been said: "Reality is 99.999999% invisible." Although we conduct our lives based mostly on the very limited perceptions that lead us to think that what they deliver to us is reality, the unperceived world continues to 'do its thing' almost as if what we thought about it were less than a ripple from a stone thrown into a great ocean. And, while the instruments of science have greatly extended our capacity to gather information about physical reality, disclosing a universe of billions of galaxies of matter and an even greater proportion of matter that is called 'dark matter' (and more recently an even greater proportion of 'dark energy),' those most familiar with our understanding of physical reality have made it quite clear that, as Hamlet said, "There are more things in heaven and earth, Horatio, than are dreamt of in your philosophy." The Course proposes that what is actually there can be directly accessed by our minds, if only we let go of our attachment to the shackles that prevent our perceiving it.

That the Real World can be perceived is a major teaching of the Course. As it states:

> "6 The real world can actually be perceived. 7 All that is necessary is a willingness to perceive nothing else."(11,VI,2,6-7)

The scientific mind, which generally accepts to the belief that only through the perception of our five senses and their extensions through instruments can reality be accessed, is often not prepared to accept the possibility of the human mind's capacity to extend its awareness beyond any limits. That dogmatic blinder is here quite firmly dismissed by the Course. Moreover, this new mode of awareness is not only a return to what it calls 'knowing,' which we have seen has nothing to do with perception, but affirms that perception itself can be transformed so that the mind still in the world can actually perceive a fuller realm. And, as has been pointed out before, all that is necessary for that to happen is that the mind have true willingness to do so. However, that willingness entails the will to perceive nothing else. From this it follows that what prevents what may be called the 'Great Perception' is the mind's clinging to ordinary contracted perception.

Since the perception of the Real World is not what we think of as an ordinary sort of perception, it will be helpful if we understand just what sort of perception it is. This is indicated:

> "9 The real world is all that the Holy Spirit has saved for you out of what you have made, and to perceive only this is salvation, because it is the recognition that reality is only what is true."(11,VII,4,9)

Here we see two factors or aspects of the 'Great Perception.' The first is that it is closely connected with the Holy Spirit's involvement in the process of rectifying the separation. We will discuss His role in more detail shortly. The other aspect is that it involves coming to awareness, or recognition, of *only what is true*. Here we should recall that the separation originated by the focusing of a part or aspect of the perfect mind of the Son upon only a part or aspect of Reality. This awareness is of something that is actually real. Thus, it is a true perception. However, it is problematic in two ways. One is that by focusing on only a part, it loses awareness of all the rest of Reality. The other is that it goes further to attach its awareness to only that part, and further superimposes on that part aspects that it perceives in other parts of Reality, thus generating for itself false perceptions. What happens in the Great Perception, as described here, is that there is a clearing up of all those false perceptions. What remains is only true perceptions. This is further clarified in the following:

> "4 When you perceive yourself without deceit, you will accept the real world in place of the false one you have made."
> (11,VIII,15,4)

From this, it becomes clear that the Great Perception of the Real World involves perceiving the totality of all true perceptions. This passage might lead us to think that this involves only the totality of true perceptions that have accrued to the particular separated mind (and, perhaps, will eventually accrue to it in the future) within its excursion over time. However, this would seem to be too limited for two reasons. One is that the Great Perception is what arises in the holy instant, which is much more comprehensive than what pertains only to one particular separated mind. The other is that in the holy instant experience, as we have seen, there is a complete communication with all other 'brothers' or separated minds. The latter means that the particular separated mind would have access to not only its particular reservoir of true perceptions, but to the true perceptions of all other similar minds. Indeed, although the mind coming into the holy instant begins as a particular separated mind, while it is in the holy instant it does not make complete sense to speak of it as being 'particular,' since it is united with all other minds in the Sonship, at least while in it. The only thing that requires particularity, at least for the mind that is only in a temporary holy instant, is that it has something that draws it back into the temporal mode. Even in the case of the enduring holy instant, where there is association with a particular personality (such as Jesus), there must be some 'residue' of particularity, although on the deeper level it is still only the 'one mind' that is the Christ Mind/Holy Spirit. However this may be, it seems clear that the Great Perception contains all the true perceptions of all minds that have entered the mode of perceiving.

This new mode of perceiving is obviously radically different from the usual mode of the separated mind. But it is still a function of what the Course calls 'consciousness.' As it states:

> "3 *Consciousness* is the receptive mechanism, receiving messages from above or below, from the Holy Spirit or the ego. 4 Consciousness has levels and awareness can shift quite dramatically, but it cannot transcend the perceptual realm. 5 At its highest it becomes aware of the real world, and can be trained to do so increasingly. 6 Yet the very fact that it has lev-

els and can be trained demonstrates that it cannot reach knowledge."(C,1,7,3-6)

Here we see that the term 'consciousness' is used in a somewhat more restricted sense than is found in many English writings and translations of oriental texts on spirituality. For the Course, the wider term is 'awareness,' and 'consciousness' is only one sort of awareness and only occurs in relation to perception, as indicated here, which is the receptive aspect of a mind in so far as it holds perceptual awareness. Here is also acknowledged that consciousness has many levels, which seem to be related to the degree of openness to a more limited or more expanded range of perceptions. It has already been pointed out that human beings have many states or levels of consciousness, ranging from what we think of as ordinary 'waking consciousness,' but also more limited states, such as 'dreaming,' and more expanded states, such as the 'transportation experience' or ESP. What is significant in this passage is that the highest state or level of consciousness is the awareness or perception of the Real World. In saying this, it should be noted that beyond that level of perception there is an even fuller or totally complete state of awareness, which we have seen is called 'knowing.'

Further, the perception of the Real World, although the term 'seeing' is sometimes used, is not a matter of the process that we think of as mediated through the eyes. As is said:

> "1 The body's eyes are therefore not the means by which the real world can be seen, for the illusions that they look upon must lead to more illusions of reality."(C,4,2,1)

It has already been noted that in the early stages of this perception there is an influence on the physiological process of vision, which involves the perception of 'fields of light' around objects within the visual field. However, this is not a matter of 'sharpening' that visual process, but of the awakening of the perceptual ability that goes beyond physiological and physical processes. Here we should recall that much of what we think we 'see' in ordinary visual awareness involves the projection of aspects that are not actually in those objects. These constitute the superimposed content of false perceptions, and include material from past experiences (memories) and much of what we think of as the 'meaning' (both conceptual and emotional aspects) of what we perceive. That is, it generally is the case that much of the content of our perception is false perception: it is a mixture of content that is actually present and content that is superimposed from memory or imagination. Since the perception of the Real World includes only true perceptions, indeed a greatly amplified awareness of these, it also involves the dropping of the false elements of ordinary perception. Again, this produces a 'cleansing of the doors of perception.'

c) The Real World and the perception of the Holy Spirit and Christ. That the Great Perception arises within a separated mind by the action of a higher Mind has already been indicated. In Ch. II, we briefly considered some aspects of the Holy Spirit's perception, which enables Him to carry out the task of guiding and healing separated minds in the process of the Atonement. A much more detailed discussion of that will be given in *The Nature of the Holy Spirit and Jesus in A Course in Miracles.* Summarily, His perception is a single cognitive act involving the holistic perception of all true perceptions in all separated minds, as is seen in:

> "7 There is no conflict anywhere in this perception, because it means that all perception is guided by the Holy Spirit, Whose Mind is fixed on God. 8 Only the Holy Spirit can resolve conflict, because only the Holy Spirit is conflict-free. 9 He perceives only what is true in your mind, and extends outward only to what is true in other minds."(6,II,11,9)

This is the same as the perception of the Real World. Statements 7 and 8 make clear that His perception excludes any content that in any way involves conflict, even if separated minds perceive such, which is possible only due to their distorting true perceptions into false ones. Statement 9 emphasizes the absence of false perceptions in His awareness, as was noted in 11,VII,4,9 on p. 272. This exclusion of any erroneous content is also indicated in:

> "3 I said before that the Holy Spirit cannot see error, and is capable only of looking beyond it to the defense of Atonement."(2,V,7,3)

The positive content of His perception will be considered in the following section 1)), such as it is perceived in the full holy instant and the matured holy relationship. Indeed, in its fullness, the once-separated mind's perception is congruent with or the same as the perception of the Holy Spirit/Christ Mind.

Some passages also speak of the Christ Mind's perception or the 'vision of Christ,' such as:

> "7 Through the eyes of Christ, only the real world exists and only the real world can be seen."(12,VII,11,7)

and:

> "2 Beyond this darkness, and yet still within you, is the vision of Christ, Who looks on all in light."(13,V,9,2)

In the first, it is made clear that the Christ Mind, in so far as it is attributed perception, has the perception of the Real World. In the second is emphasized both that the Christ Mind's awareness is in each separated mind, although blocked from that mind's awareness, and that by being beyond this darkness it is one of 'light.' What is important here is that, since the Christ Mind and the Holy Spirit are the same entity, in so far as there is perception in the Christ Mind, it is actually the perception of the Holy Spirit. Here we should keep in mind that their difference is only one of emphasizing one or another aspect of that same Mind.

This is made even clearer when we consider the following:

> "5 The Holy Spirit is in the part of the mind that lies between the ego and the spirit, mediating between them always in favor of the spirit."(7,IX,1,5)

That is, the Holy Spirit may be thought of as located in a region just beyond the ego 'shell,' which is the boundary that the separated mind sets up for itself so as to separate it from all else, including other separated minds, the Holy Spirit, the Christ Mind, God, and the rest of the Universe of Love. This is represented in Fig. 29 as a small band, surrounded by a dotted circle, which is in turn surrounded by a larger circle. The ego-shell band is the ego-boundary. The surrounding band represents the Holy Spirit. That larger circle, which is not actually separated from the region within the dotted band, is the Christ Mind. We might further draw arrows that point both *into* the tiny circle and *outward* from the Holy Spirit region into the larger circle, to indicate what is called the 'mediating' between ego and spirit. In this passage, 'spirit' seems best understood as the spirit which is the fundamental reality of the Son. Of course, this diagram has its limitations, in that the outer circle, to be more accurate, would have to be of infinite radius. Even further, within that larger circle it would be necessary to draw an unlimited number of small circles, each representing another separated mind. Still further, the larger circle would represent the Son within a moment of time before the Atonement is completed. To be even more complete, that larger circle would have to have overlapping it countless other circles of infinite radius, each representing one of the perfect minds that compose the Universe of Love. However, such a geometrical figure obviously cannot be drawn. Nevertheless, this may have some usefulness for aiding our minds in getting a rough idea of the nature of the Course's view of Reality.

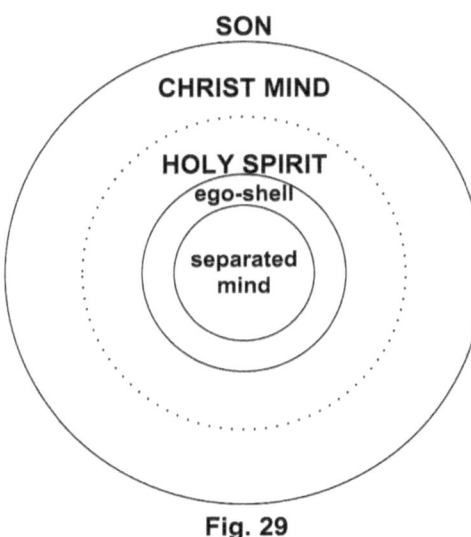

Fig. 29

I need to emphasize again that, if we are to avoid a serious inconsistency, the Holy Spirit and the Christ Mind need to be understood as the same entity. Strictly speaking, the Christ Mind *as* Christ Mind only knows. Thus, it does not directly perceive the Real World. That perception belongs to that aspect of the Son's Mind that is the Holy Spirit. Thus, since the Christ Mind and the Holy Spirit are the same entity, the Holy Spirit should be thought of as the aspect of the Christ Mind that perceives, while the Christ Mind is that aspect of the Holy Spirit that knows. Accordingly, the phrase 'vision of Christ' refers to the perceiving aspect of the Christ Mind that is the Holy Spirit. This will be important to keep in mind in the following. Again, this will be discussed more fully in my next book.

1)) The Holy Spirit's direct perception. While the Course does not directly assert that the Holy Spirit perceives the Real World, it does follow from several statements, such as those already cited. It is particularly important to note that His perception is radically different from that of the separated mind. This is made clear in the following:

> "3 He separates the true from the false by His ability to perceive totally rather than selectively."(14,IV,10,3)

That is, since the Holy Spirit perceives totally and only perceives truly, His perception must be of *the totality of all true perceptions*. This is the same as the complete perception of the Real World.

Thus, in His function of undoing the separation, He is described as having the basis for giving the perception of the Real World to those who think they lack it. The passage cited earlier (p. 272) bears repeating and further comment:

> "9 The real world is all that the Holy Spirit has saved for you out of what you have made, and to perceive only this is salvation, because it is the recognition that reality is only what is true."(11,VII,4,7-9)

While this reference to 'you' might be read as saying that what He has saved is restricted to what one particular mind has perceived truly, since it is addressed to every potential student of the Course, it should be understood as the whole set of true perceptions generated in the collection of all separated minds. If we consider that the whole world of perception is constituted by the fragmented perceptions of innumerable separated minds, this seems best understood as saying that the Holy Spirit's perception, that is, the Real World, is constituted of all their true perceptions, including those that are thought of by separated minds as 'past,' 'present,' and 'future.'

Further insight into how the Holy Spirit brings about the transformation at the heart of the separated mind's coming to this new perception is indicated by the following:

> "9 Yet to find the place, you must relinquish your investment in the world as you project it, allowing the Holy Spirit to extend the real world to you from the altar of God."(12,III,10,9)

Once the particular mind comes to the point where it is willing to let go of the world as it has perceived it, the Holy Spirit actively engages in what is here called 'extending' His perception to that mind. This may be thought of as active engagement in sharing His total perception with that mind. Here we should recall that the Holy Spirit is actually within every separated mind at the interface between the ego and the Christ Mind that it is a part of. Thus, the Holy Spirit acts as a mediating agent that supplies the fuller awareness in the Christ Mind to the particular separated mind. That fuller awareness has two levels or stages. The first is perceptual (the perception of the Real World), which involves the fullest possible mode of perceiving, and thus some type of limitation that is intrinsic to perceiving, but clearly without the aspect of temporality. In view of what was said about the 'Great Rays,' it seems best thought of as a boundless spatiality that is filled with something analogous to the perceptual quality of light. The second involves the complete abandonment of the remaining limitations of the perceptual mode and the restoration of knowing. That, of course, is the full awareness of Love and all Reality in the single timeless or eternal Instant that is Heaven.

That the perception of the Real World is also in some way present in the Christ Mind is indicated in the following:

> "5 The Holy Spirit keeps the vision of Christ for every Son of God who sleeps. 6 In His sight the Son of God is perfect, and He longs to share His vision with you. 7 He will show you the real world because God gave you Heaven. 8 Through Him your Father calls His Son to remember. 9 The awakening of His Son begins with his investment in the real world, and by this he will learn to reinvest in himself. 10 For reality is one with the Father and the Son, and the Holy Spirit blesses the real world in Their Name."(12,VI,4,5-10)

It may be helpful to think of this in the following manner. The separated mind can be thought of as usually focused on a very narrow range of perceptions that change as time passes. The totality of its perceptions over its temporal existence can be represented as in Fig. 30 as a small circle or sphere (sm 1) that contains all those perceptions. Since these involve both true and false perceptions, true perceptions are above and the false ones below. Immediately surrounding sm 1 is the Holy Spirit, which can be represented as a band or shell. His awareness is of all the true perceptions within the little ego-bound circle/sphere. But it is also directly around every other separated mind (represented by two other similar separated mind circles) and aware of their true perceptions. Since His awareness is directed to the true perceptions in the interior of all those limited minds, this awareness is represented by an arrow toward the interior of those circles. However, since the Holy Spirit is the same entity as the Christ Mind, His awareness is also directed outward (arrow pointing upward). The Christ Mind, of course, is the Son's Mind in so far as it has not slipped into the divided condition of separation. Thus, it has the awareness of knowledge, despite the experience of the separation in the tiny 'blip' or level of the Eternal Instant within those little regions of the Son's Mind. This is the basis for the Holy Spirit's knowing awareness. But, because the Christ Mind is also one with the

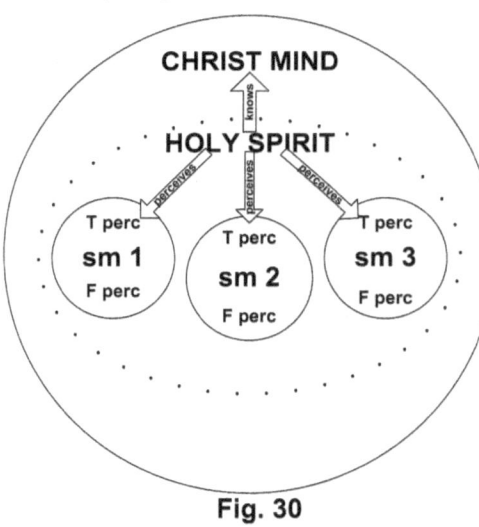

Fig. 30

Holy Spirit, the Christ Mind can also be said indirectly to have the awareness of perception. Of course, that perception is the same as the Holy Spirit's, that is, the perception of the Real World. In the above passage, the latter is referred to as the 'vision of Christ.' That is, the Christ Mind, as the Holy Spirit, has this perception so that all separated minds can find the fullness of perception that is the perception of the Real World, and pass through it on to the complete awareness of knowing, which is the state of Heaven. We will consider more about the Christ Mind's perception shortly.

We should also recall a point made earlier regarding the intention of the Holy Spirit to complete the function given him:

> "3 The eagerness of the Holy Spirit to give you this is so intense He would not wait, although He waits in patience. 4 Meet His patience with your impatience at delay in meeting Him. 5 Go out in gladness to meet with your Redeemer, and walk with Him in trust out of this world, and into the real world of beauty and forgiveness."(17,II,8,3-5)

What is called 'eagerness' seems to refer to the Holy Spirit's participation in the intense attraction of Love, which powerfully draws every mind toward realizing complete awareness. Since the Holy Spirit poses no obstacles to that attraction, He has an overwhelming 'desire' or eagerness to accomplish His task. But at the same time, He has complete respect for the freedom of each separated mind to choose either its bondage or its freedom, which is the basis of His patience or willingness to wait until any separated mind chooses freedom. Interestingly, because the Holy Spirit is completely outside time, He is already at the end of time when all separated minds have made that choice. He may be thought of as looking into a 'great hypersphere,' which is the Real World, through a kind of 'window in time,' a window that allows him to see all moments of time, but only their true aspects, all at once.

2)) The Christ Mind's 'perception.' Perception in relation to the Christ Mind, or more simply Christ, is clarified in the passage cited earlier (p. 275):

> "7 Through the eyes of Christ, only the real world exists and only the real world can be seen."(12,VII,11,7)

Of course, in the Course's view, the term 'Christ' does not only refer to the person Jesus, who realized the Christ Mind, but to the higher Mind that is present, albeit unconsciously, at the foundation of every separated mind and will ultimately be realized by all of them. What is made clear here is that the Christ's perception is solely of the Real World. That Christ is present and intimately close to every separated mind is also made clearer in another passage previously cited in part (on p. 275) :

> "2 Beyond this darkness, and yet still within you, is the vision of Christ, Who looks on all in light. 3 Your 'vision' comes from fear, as His from love. 4 And He sees for you, as your witness to the real world. 5 He is the Holy Spirit's manifestation, looking always on the real world, and calling forth its witnesses

and drawing them to you."(13,V,9,2-5)

This makes four important points. The first is that what is called 'the vision of Christ' is present within every separated mind ('you'), at least as a potential mode of awareness. The second concerns the meaning of 'the vision of Christ.' Earlier, it was pointed out that the term 'see' is understood in the Course as one of the types or levels of awareness corresponding to the various levels of 'light.' The highest level is the awareness of Love called 'knowing.' As statement 3 indicates, Christ's 'vision' or awareness comes from Love: indeed, it is the primary and most perfect awareness possible. It is this awareness that illuminates the Holy Spirit, thus giving rise to the Holy Spirit's perception of the Real World. The third point is that, although this capacity of awareness is present, it is blocked by fear, which seems best understood not as a particular fear but the primary fear that we discussed earlier. Of course, particular fears have the effect of reinforcing that primary fear. The fourth point is in statement 5, which seems to say that Christ is the Holy Spirit's manifestation, emphasizing the priority of the Holy Spirit, which would make the Christ derived from the Holy Spirit. However, one could also say that the Holy Spirit is the manifestation of the Christ. Given the higher state or level of the Christ's awareness, this would seem to be a more accurate statement. Yet, if the Christ and the Holy Spirit are understood as the same entity, one could also correctly describe it as in the first clause of statement 5. However, if we recall that the formation of the Holy Spirit was the first response of God to the Son's making the choice of separation, and that part of His response was the formation of the Christ Mind by preserving a level of the Son's Mind from slipping into separation, we can see that the Christ Mind would be correctly described as the Holy Spirit's manifestation. Of course, all of these formations happen instantly rather than in any temporal sequence. In another sense, since it is the Holy Spirit that facilitates the separated mind's coming to clear awareness of the Christ Mind, which could be described as 'making the Christ Mind manifest' to the separated mind, the Christ Mind would thus be correctly described as the 'manifestation of the Holy Spirit.'

We should keep in mind that the whole of time's billions of years occur within the tiny 'blip' that is an infinitesimal subset or level of the Eternal Instant. It is so inconsequential within the Eternal Instant that once the Atonement is completed, it is as if the separation never happened. What thus becomes clear and resolves any possible inconsistency is that the rest of statement 5 should be understood as saying that it is the Holy Spirit, rather than the Christ, who is *directly* 'looking on the Real world' and 'calling' and 'drawing' separated minds toward the perception of the Real World and thence to the full awakening of knowing that is the innermost awareness in the vision of Christ.

The place of the Christ Mind in the process of re-awakening is summarized:

"1 When you have seen this real world, as you will surely do, you will remember Us. 2 Yet you must learn the cost of sleeping, and refuse to pay it. 3 Only then will you decide to awaken. 4 And then the real world will spring to your sight, for Christ has never slept. 5 He is waiting to be seen, for He has never lost sight of you. 6 He looks quietly on the real world, which He would share with you because He knows of the Father's Love for Him."(12,VI,5,1-6)

The metaphor of sleeping is important in the Course. As we have seen, it refers to the condition of the mind in separation relative to its original condition. Christ is that level of every mind that never entered into separation. It never slept. Instead, it is the fully awake Mind that is aware directly of Reality and indirectly of the Real World through the Holy Spirit in so far as perception has any relevance for bringing separated minds into wakefulness. In so far as the Christ Mind, through the Holy Spirit, maintains the full awareness of the Real World, it is similar to what is referred to as the 'storehouse consciousness' of the Mind-Only School of Buddhism, although what it stores is only true perceptions. When the separated mind begins to awaken, it retrieves the fullness of the Christ Mind's/ Holy Spirit's perception of the Real World. When fully awakened, it lets the Real World drop and opens to the complete restoration of knowledge, which is central to the state of Heaven.

d) Content of the Real World. Although it is impossible for a mind not having experienced the holy instant to grasp clearly or fully the content of the perception of the Real World, we may get something of an idea by considering what the Course says about it. We first look at what it says is absent from it, then its positive content.

1)) Specific things absent from the Real World. Several things present in our familiar world of separation are not within the Real World. We already saw that in the holy instant there is no perception of limited bodies. Since the Real World is primarily perceived in the holy instant, bodies as limited forms cannot be present in it, as well as the conditions that we associate with them. Thus, it is asserted:

"1 In the real world there is no sickness, for there is no separation and no division."(11,VIII,10,1)

Sickness is generally thought of as primarily of the body, but it is also mental. Its characteristic is perhaps best described as some sort of malfunction in the body's or the mind's processes. That such malfunction is not possible in the Real World seems to stem from the absence of a body in the limited sense and the completely free flow of all mental activity, whose blockage is usually the basis for mental illness. This is closely connected with the absence of any type of division or separateness of all that is within the whole 'field' of the Real World.

Also connected to this absence of limited bodies is the absence of death, as is described:

"2 God does love the real world, and those who perceive its reality cannot see the world of death. 3 For death is not of the real world, in which everything reflects the eternal. 4 God gave you the real world in exchange for the one you made out

of your split mind, and which is the symbol of death."
(12,III,8,2-4)

A first point relates to how God loves the Real World. Since God does not perceive at all, He cannot have awareness of the Real World as such. Strictly speaking, only the Holy Spirit (and all minds that share His perception) have such an awareness. However, this does not mean that God's Love does not extend to the Real World. Indeed, His Love extends to every separated mind as aspects of the one mind of the Son. In the same way, His Love extends to or penetrates all perceptions (even false ones) as that which is the foundation of all those fragmented acts of awareness. Accordingly, He can be said to love the Real World. A second point is related to death. As we saw earlier, death is one of the primary characteristics of the ego-dominated condition that places the mind within the world of limited bodies. Obviously, where such bodies do not exist, death cannot occur. This seems also to be closely related to the absence of temporality in the Real World, since the holy instant takes the mind outside time. That is, in its primary meaning, what we think of as death is the conclusion of the embodied separated mind's temporal sequence. If there is no such sequence, death cannot occur.

Related to the absence of death is the absence of any fantasy. As is stated:

> "1 This loveliness is not a fantasy. 2 It is the real world, bright and clean and new, with everything sparkling under the open sun. 3 Nothing is hidden here, for everything has been forgiven and there are no fantasies to hide the truth."(17,II,2,1-3)

The absence of fantasies seems to be the direct consequence of the Real World's involving only true perceptions. This is because the nature of any fantasy is the formation of an image, that is, a type of perception, that does not reflect the presence of something real. Fantasies or memory images can be imposed on true perceptions of some aspect or aspects of reality to form false perceptions. As long as the mind is clear about what is only a fantasy or memory it can avoid this superimposition that generates a false perception. However, when the mind is totally immersed in the perception of only what is real, it has no place for either memories (the past) or fantasies (unconnected with realities). Further, if one thinks of the awareness of what is called 'death,' particularly of one's own death, it is invariably a matter of something in imagination or fantasy. Thus, the absence of fantasies in general includes the absence of the particular fantasy that is the meaning of 'death.'

b)) Specific things present in the Real World. Several passages point to a more positive content of the Real World. The first that we consider is:

> "2 Only loving thoughts are recognized, and because no one is without your help, the Help of God goes with you everywhere."(11,VIII,10,2)

This may be thought of as the underlying or pervading quality of the Great Perception. As was pointed out, in the holy instant perfect love is realized as the fullest possible awareness of Love's presence within the perceptual mode. Thus, the whole content of the Real World is saturated with the quality of love.

The luminous quality of the Real World is also further described:

> "1 This world of light, this circle of brightness is the real world, where guilt meets with forgiveness. 2 Here the world outside is seen anew, without the shadow of guilt upon it. 3 Here are you forgiven, for here you have forgiven everyone. 4 Here is the new perception, where everything is bright and shining with innocence, washed in the waters of forgiveness, and cleansed of every evil thought you laid upon it."
> (18,IX,9,1-4)

Here we see what seems to be the Course's most concrete details of the Real World's structure: a circle (or perhaps better, a sphere) of light shines with a great brightness (recall the passage cited on p. 265 that refers to the brightness of that light). It is important to note that this luminosity is not primarily a matter of intense visual brightness, which to our usual experience is quite painful beyond a certain limit. Rather, it is a brightness that is based on the absence of guilt, a quality of innocence. This might be better thought of as the quality that we sometimes perceive when looking at a newborn baby sleeping peacefully. One might call it a 'transcendental purity.' Thus, although there may be something analogous to what we perceive in a bright sunrise or sunset, the brightness here seems to be of a very different order than physical brightness, but closer to the quality of innocence, but with an intensity far greater than we can access in ordinary experience.

Another characteristic or quality of the Real World is described:

> "1 All this beauty will rise to bless your sight as you look upon the world with forgiving eyes. 2 For forgiveness literally transforms vision, and lets you see the real world reaching quietly and gently across chaos, removing all illusions that had twisted your perception and fixed it on the past. 3 The smallest leaf becomes a thing of wonder, and a blade of grass a sign of God's perfection."(17,II,6,1-3)

What is here called 'beauty' is somewhat like the 'transcendental purity,' but an extension of what is called 'beauty' in the more limited ordinary experience. Here, the beauty seems to arise as the result of the complete letting go (forgiveness) of all traces of negative perceptions so that everything within the Real World is experienced as having this intense aesthetic quality, perhaps to an unlimited degree. As statement 3 indicates, all particular things (e.g., leaves and blades of grass) are perceived to be penetrated with this quality. Since the awareness of such particular things seems to occur only within the context of ordinary perception, this would refer to the state that includes the perception of limited objects. That would either occur when the mind takes with it the awareness of the holy instant back into the temporal mode of awareness, either for a period following the deeper experience that involved the unlimited mode of awareness or permanently for the mind that has come to full and unwavering union with the Christ Mind (in the enduring holy instant). I may also note that this passage is reminiscent of the highest stage of realization of love as described by Plato in his recounting of Socrates' conversation with the wise-woman Diotima: "And, turning his eyes toward the open sea of beauty, he will find in such contemplation the seed of the most fruitful discourse and the loftiest thought, and reap a golden harvest of philosophy, until, confirmed and strengthened, he will come upon one single form of knowledge."[72]

There are two other, more cognitive, aspects of the Real World that the Course indicates. The first is in relation to choice:

> "1 There is no basis for a choice in this complex and over-complicated world. 2 For no one understands what is the same, and seems to choose where no choice really is. 3 The real world is the area of choice made real, not in the outcome, but in the perception of alternatives for choice. 4 That there is choice is an illusion. 5 Yet within this one lies the undoing of every illusion, not excepting this."(26,III,6,1-5)

This seems to be more of an insight or realization regarding all that the separated mind had regarded as the act of choosing prior to this experience. That is, there is seen that within in the ordinary perceptual mode there is really no choice at all. Indeed, there seemed to be many things to choose and many acts of choosing. However, all of them reduced to only one: between what holds the mind within the world of separation and what gives it freedom from that world. That is, all seeming particular choices are simply variations of the same commitment to ego. However, while in that ordinary state, they seemed to be real choices. But, within the context of the Real World, they are seen to have all been the same and thus not choices at all. The only real choice is between holding onto or undoing illusions.[73]

The second is an insight into the purpose of the world:

> "1 The real world is the state of mind in which the only purpose of the world is seen to be forgiveness."(30,V,1,1)

For the separated mind, the world seems to have many possible purposes, or even to have none at all. But within the awareness of the Real World its purpose is seen with complete clarity and certainty: forgiveness. Of course, this is the process of letting go of all that the separated mind had thought of as real and of value, which when fully realized entails the ending of all the illusions it has made for itself.

A final passage summarizes the key points of what is found in the Real World:

> "4 The spark of beauty or the veil of ugliness, the real world or

---

[72] *Symposium*, 210d.

[73] This closely parallels J. Krishnamurti's reference to the truly meditative state as one of 'choiceless awareness.' See his *The First and Last Freedom*.

> the world of guilt and fear, truth or illusion, freedom or slavery – it is all the same."(17,III,9,4)

That is, taking the first parts of these disjunctions as being intimately connected, the Real World involves the absence of any ugliness, any guilt or fear, any illusion, or any bondage, and the presence only of the spark of beauty, or as was pointed out, the perception of beauty in ever-growing intensity; truth, that is, only true perceptions; and freedom, which is perhaps best thought of as the state of being able to love perfectly. This is the insight in:

> "7 To feel the Love of God within you is to see the world anew, shining in innocence, alive with hope, and blessed with perfect charity and love."(W,189,1,7)

Of course, it is in the perception of the holy instant that this occurs as a prelude to the complete realization of Beauty, Truth, and Freedom that the perception of the Real World opens to, that is, Heaven.

iii. New affective content of the holy instant: new/transformed feelings. As we saw that old ego-based feelings were eliminated or transformed, we consider now the new affective aspects of the holy instant. The separated mind entangles itself in many confusing feelings that are dispelled when one enters the holy instant. The Course specifically mentions five sorts of emotion or feeling that replace them: what it calls the 'one desire,' invulnerability or safety, peace, joy, and love.

1) Only one need/desire. The first 'new' feeling is related to the emotion of desire, which expresses as various feelings of attraction related to the different needs that are perceived as arising in response to the ego and its body identification. In the holy instant this is radically revised:

> "4 In the holy instant there is no conflict of needs, for there is only one. 5 For the holy instant reaches to eternity, and to the Mind of God. 6 And it is only there love has meaning, and only there can it be understood."(15,V,11,4-6)

The single need that is recognized in this state is simply the need for love, that is, for the complete realization of perfect love, which is the union with Reality. Although this realization may not be complete, particularly in the early stages of experiencing the holy instant that are followed by a return to a lesser mode of awareness, it consists primarily in the impulse to give or share all that it is with other minds, including those in separation and those in their perfect state. This is the one 'desire' that is its single concern. This need is further described:

> "10 For in the holy instant you will recognize the only need the Sons of God share equally, and by this recognition you will join with me in offering what is needed."(15,VI,6,10)

That is, there is the feeling of solidarity with all other minds, particularly those not yet come to the fullness of their realization of that same need within themselves. This seems best equated with what might be called a 'universal compassion' in that it is sensitive to their suffering due to the incomplete presence of Love's awareness. This prompts the mind that is in the holy instant to aid those other minds in so far as they are in need of that realization, which is the sole adequate solution to their suffering. However, this experience of their suffering is not of the pain they undergo but of their not yet realizing perfect love. In that sense, all particular sufferings are perceived as different expressions of this one desire in so far as it is not yet experienced as satisfied, that is, as a call for love.

2) Invulnerability/safety. Related to the ego-based emotion of fear is its counter-emotion of 'invulnerability' or 'safety.' Since perfect love completely undoes fear, and perfect love is experienced in the holy instant, it follows that perfect love brings with it this feeling of invulnerability to the degree that the holy instant is entered. Although not specifically stated in relation to the holy instant, the following passages make this clear:

> "2 Love cannot suffer, because it cannot attack. 3 The remembrance of love therefore brings invulnerability with it."
> (10,III,3,2-3)

and:

> "2 Surrounding me is everlasting Love. 3 I have no cause for anything except the perfect peace and joy I share with You. 4 What need have I for anger or for fear? 5 Surrounding me is perfect safety."(W,348,1.2-5)

This could be thought of as a feeling of complete security and absence of any fear of suffering. It seems to involve the feeling of release from all perception of threat from the outside and of conflict within, which leads to the feelings of peace and joy. Here we may recognize the fundamental insight of the Course's Introduction:

> "2 Nothing real can be threatened. ... 4 Herein lies the peace of God."(In,2,2 & 4)

This necessarily comes to the mind upon the realization of perfect love, which occurs in the holy instant.

3) The feelings of perfect peace and joy. These emotions in the holy instant are what could be thought of as included within the feeling aspect of perfect love and the emotional aspects that we have seen are central to Love. They are indicated in:

> "1 In the holy instant the condition of love is met, for minds are joined without the body's interference, and where there is communication there is peace."(15,XI,7,1)

and:

> "6 In these instants of release from physical restrictions, you experience much of what happens in the holy instant; the lifting of the barriers of time and space, the sudden experience of peace and joy..."(18,VI,13,6)

The first passage points out how the feeling of peace is grounded in the perfect communication within the holy instant. Although what is often called 'peace' is only an absence of conflict and the emotional anxiety and tension that are usually associated with conflict, a deeper sort of peace, closer to what that term fully refers to, is the feeling of complete harmony and connectedness with all other minds. Some spiritual writers refer to this as the 'dilation of the heart.' Since perfect communication involves the expansion of awareness beyond all bounds, this feeling of 'unbounded dilation' is perhaps the best characterization of what complete Peace is as an emotion.

The second passage also affirms this 'dilation' feeling as one of being aware emotionally of the unboundedness that is central to the holy instant. It also indicates the fourth emotional aspect, joy, as a primary feeling that arises in it. Although it does not elaborate further on the nature of this joy, since the primary characteristic of the holy instant is its unboundedness, we may infer that this feeling of joy is also unbounded, or what is called 'Joy,' which is central to Love (discussed in Ch. II).

This does not mean that every experience of the holy instant involves a maximal intensity of these emotions, but only that it enters into an awareness of them that far exceeds 'ordinary' versions of them. As the mind enters more deeply into the holy instant by dropping away further obstacles to its awareness, it would seem to find correspondingly even more intense and complete awareness of those emotions. Accordingly, it follows that the peace and joy found there are in proportion to the intensity that it is entered into.

4) The feeling of love. The fifth type of emotion that is felt within the holy instant is related to the fundamental Reality and foundation of all existence. This is described:

> "7 To feel the Love of God within you is to see the world anew, shining in innocence, alive with hope, and blessed with perfect charity and love."(W,189,1,7)

Although in the Course's view love involves more than a feeling or emotional manifestation (it includes cognitive and behavioral aspects as well), it does recognize that is has a profound, perhaps the most profound, affective aspect, which is related to the clear presence of Love in one's awareness. Indeed, what is experienced in the holy instant is the fullest awareness of that feeling that is possible for a mind still in the separated state. To the degree that the mind enters the holy instant, to that degree it enters into that feeling. As this passage also indicates, it is in that affective state that the Real World is disclosed.

iv. New behavioral aspects arising in/from the holy instant. There are also what might be called new ways of behaving that arise from the experience of the holy instant. Here we need to keep in mind that the holy instant, although it is in one sense a participation in the Eternal Instant, is a 'bridging instant' between time and the Eternal Instant. A mind fully present in the Eternal Instant can have only one type of action or 'behavior,' which is that of creating. But in the holy instant, it can engage in action related to minds still deeply immersed in time, and thus its action is what is more like what we usually think of as 'behavior.' Thus, the notion of behavior needs to be enlarged beyond our usual idea. Indeed, the Holy Spirit is primarily a mind whose 'behavior' is that of carrying out the process of Atonement. While He is fundamentally in the Eternal Instant, He is also in the holy instant as the power that gives rise to all that happens within it. When a separated mind has the experience of the holy instant, it is enabled to participate in the Holy Spirit's action to the degree it has entered into that experience. However, this activity is outside time and thus cannot be what would be thought of as 'behavior' in the usual sense. In order for it to behave or act, it must have some sort of involvement in the world of perception, which is to have a relation to limited beings in space and time.

We have distinguished between the temporary holy instant and the enduring holy instant. In the former, there are two important factors that give it its temporariness. One is that the particular separated mind, owing to the obscuring presence of ego, is not yet able to enter fully into the holy instant. The other is that those same obscuring ego-aspects lead to its stepping out of the holy instant back into the temporal mode. This does not mean that all aspects of the holy instant are completely lost. Although that does seem to be possible if the mind chooses to relapse fully into ego-mindedness, there can also remain vestiges or traces of the holy instant's qualities. In that state, the mind comes back to the mode of imperfect love. Subsequent experiences of the holy instant can bring further elimination of ego-aspects, which makes for an even deep deeper experience of the holy instant. If the holy instant is only temporary, the further re-entries into the 'ordinary' temporal mode can be more fully freed of ego-aspects and lived in terms of a much closer approximation to perfect love. Eventually, that separated mind is completely purified of ego, so that it experiences no opposition between the holy instant and the temporal mode. That is, it remains in the holy instant while living in the world. This is the enduring holy instant.

Since such a mind has no personal reason to immerse itself in the temporal order, the question arises: why does it come back into the world? Indeed, since the final state is complete return to full perfection that is beyond all time or limits, the state called 'Heaven,' why does such a mind not simply abandon the illusion of the world? This seems to be because it has completely gone beyond all limited ego-awareness and has fully merged into the awareness of the Holy Spirit, which is the Christ Mind that continues to relate to minds that remain in separation. This includes the recognition that there remain those other separated minds, whom it sees as aspects of itself and still in need of the liberation of Atonement. Thus, it sees it still has a function of participating in the completion of the Atonement. In its identification with the Holy Spirit's Mind, it remains within the world in whatever form may be useful to help in that completion. This seems to be precisely the status of Jesus after his complete realization of perfect love.

This idea is not unique to the Course's teachings. It is very much like the principle expressed in the Mahayana Buddhist idea of the Bodhisattva. Briefly, this is that any fully enlightened being will remain in the world (samsara) until all other beings have attained enlightenment.

It might also be pointed out that the Holy Spirit is the most perfect instance of a mind that is at once in the timeless state of creative extension and related to the time-bound state by producing effects in the world, or behaving in the proper sense. His activity is fully related to all true aspects of the perceptual realm, that is, to all separated minds and all that they perceive truly. What the separated mind discovers in the holy instant is a mode of awareness and action or behavior that approximates the Holy Spirit's mode to the degree that it enters the holy instant. Just as the Holy Spirit's action produces effects upon the world, such an embodied mind also produces similar kinds of effects. Or more accurately, in so far as that mind enters the holy instant does its activity or behavior become congruent with that of the Holy Spirit. This is the foundation of what is referred to as the holy relationship.

With this in mind, we may better understand the four major new behavioral modes described by the Course: living in the holy relationship, giving miracles, bringing salvation to the world, and participating in the 'celestial speedup.' In fact, these are not so much differing sorts of activity, since any of them involve the others. Rather, they should be thought of as having differing emphases of intentions and contexts, ranging from more strongly personal connections, to a more extended set of connections with other particular separated minds, to the whole realm of separated minds that coexist with oneself, and finally extending to all separated minds within the space-time order. Although the Course does not refer to them as 'modes of behavior,' this term seems useful for obtaining greater clarity. Further, in our discussion of these behavioral aspects, we will see other details regarding the cognitive content of the holy instant experience, in so far as the Course speaks of that particular content as arising in the exercise of that behavior. We begin with what seems to be the central one.

1) The holy relationship. We already saw how the belief in specialness, the focus of ego-dominated behavior, is alleviated or even eliminated or transformed in the holy instant. Here we consider what it is replaced with.

a) The holy relationship in general. One of the most important aspects of the holy instant is that it brings into realization this very different type of relationship. Here we may recall that the special relationship is one of the most problematic confusions that arise from ego-attachment. We saw how it is central to illusory love. The holy relationship may be thought of as a transformed special relationship. The holy instant is the primary basis for bringing about that transformation. Its general nature is described:

> "1 The holy relationship is the expression of the holy instant in living in this world. 2 Like everything about salvation, the holy instant is a practical device, witnessed to by its results. 3 The holy instant never fails. 4 The experience of it is always felt. 5 Yet without expression it is not remembered. 6 The holy relationship is a constant reminder of the experience in which the relationship became what it is."(17,V,1,1-6)

As we have seen, when in the holy instant the mind recognizes its oneness with all other minds, including other separated minds. Since it generally steps out of the holy instant and back into the time-bound mode of being in the world, when it does so it can return to those relationships it regarded as special now perceived from a radically different perspective. Although it sees those other persons as separate to some degree, thinking and living with thoughts and feelings different from its own, engaged in actions based on their connection with their bodies which it perceives as different from its own, it carries with it something from the awareness that arose when in the experience of the holy instant. The degree of that new awareness appears to be dependent on the depth or intensity it entered into the holy instant. This seems to be the point of calling it an 'expression of the holy instant in living in this world.'

The holy relationship is not realized all at once, but continues to develop over time. The special relationship is usually not suddenly fully transformed, but gradually moves toward a more complete realization of the characteristics of the holy instant within the context of relating to still separated minds in the world. This serves to reverse the divisive or 'unholy' qualities of the special relationship, as is described:

> "1 The holy relationship, a major step toward the perception of the real world, is learned. 2 It is the old, unholy relationship, transformed and seen anew. 3 The holy relationship is a phenomenal teaching accomplishment. 4 In all its aspects, as it begins, develops and becomes accomplished, it represents the reversal of the unholy relationship."(17,V,2,1-3)

In this we can see the developmental nature of the holy relationship: it goes through a beginning stage, a growth stage, and a final maturation. Thus, the process of unfolding the holy relationship may be thought of as returning to the only legitimate use of time. That it goes through these various stages means that in the early stages there may be many disturbances and conflicts as the mind within the budding holy relationship struggles with the undoing of the old ego-mode and takes on the mode of wholeness or holiness. In the accounts of Western spiritual development, one finds descriptions of this three-staged process, such as the 'way of purgation,' the 'way of illumination,' the 'way of union.' There are also the often cited difficult sub-phases of the 'dark night of the senses' and 'dark night of the soul.' (A concise overview of these stages is given by Happold, and a more extensive one by Underhill.)[74] The Course itself also discusses six stages or 'periods' in the process of the teacher's development. These focus more upon the quality of the progressive shifts in awareness that the separated mind goes through, which seem closely correlated to the various sub-phases recognized in the Western view.[75] These stages should be understood to hold both for the deepening levels of change in the more externally oriented holy rela-

---

[74] F. Happold, *Mysticism: A Study and an Anthology*; E. Underhill, *Mysticism*.

[75] These phases are discussed in the Manual For Teachers (M,4,I,3-8). Wapnick holds that there are three major stages, discussed in *The Stages of Our Spiritual Journey*.

tionship as well as for the more interior transformation within a particular separated mind.

Holy relationships can be thought of as special relationships transformed or transforming into a very different mode of being in the world of perception. This is further described:

> "3 I have said repeatedly that the Holy Spirit would not deprive you of your special relationships, but would transform them."(17,IV,2,3)

and:

> "1 Your special relationship will be a means for undoing guilt in everyone blessed through your holy relationship. 2 It will be a happy dream, and one which you will share with all who come within your sight. 3 Through it, the blessing the Holy Spirit has laid upon it will be extended."(18,II,7,1-3)

The first passage makes clear that the process of Atonement does not involve the simple elimination of special relationships, but rather their being fundamentally transmuted in a way that retains the relationship, but removes the ego-centered specialness. The second passage further explains that the primary shift that occurs in this transformed special relationship is that guilt, the original basis for the special relationship, is undone. We saw earlier how guilt leads to the 'bargaining' quality of most strong relationships for the separated mind. This is the primary characteristic of what it thinks of as 'love' (actually, illusory love). In light of the absence or reduction of guilt, at least within one of the minds who has moved to this other mode, this undoing of guilt affects others, particularly those who are participants in the holy relationship. Another important aspect indicated here is the role of the Holy Spirit. That is, the primary operating principle of the holy relationship, as of the holy instant, is that the mind formerly resistant to the Holy Spirit's guidance has let go of that resistance. As we will see, it is this opening up to the Holy Spirit's 'Voice' that is central to entry into the holy instant. Although most step back from the more intense awareness of the holy instant into the more ordinary awareness of everyday perception, they carry with them something of that greater openness to the 'whole' or 'holy' quality of the holy instant, which has this transforming effect on special relationships. The description of the resulting relationship as a 'happy dream' refers to the fact that, although all perceptual awareness is primarily a construct of the separated mind, which is usually experienced with much suffering and unhappiness, the transformed perception of the world that comes with the holy relationship is relatively much happier, and thus is called a 'happy dream.' Of course, this is still a long way from the full and complete happiness of the final return to the Heaven state. But the Course is also careful to point out the following:

> "1 It is no dream to love your brother as yourself. 2 Nor is your holy relationship a dream. 3 All that remains of dreams within it is that it is still a special relationship. 4 Yet it is very useful to the Holy Spirit, Who *has* a special function here. 5 It

will become the happy dream through which He can spread joy to thousands on thousands who believe that love is fear, not happiness."(18,V,5,1-5)

That is, although the perceptual content of the holy relationship, like all perceptual content, is unreal in an absolute sense and thus most accurately like a dream, its core and true significance is not a dream. That core is the perfect love that is a manifestation of Love in a particular mind. This means that the holy relationship, although it expresses within the world of time and space, in its essence is beyond that world. The 'dream' quality is a matter of its being within the framework of the world, appearing to undergo changes in details as time passes. But its reality is beyond the world, grounded in the Eternal Instant.

b) Content of the holy relationship. While much of what is experienced in this relationship, especially in its more advanced or mature stage of development, has been described in our discussion of the Real World, we consider here further aspects that pertain primarily to the holy relationship. The first is described:

> "8 Did you see the holiness that shone in both you and your brother, to bless the other? 9 That is the purpose of your holy relationship."(20,III,8,8-9)

This 'seeing of holiness' seems to be related to the perception of light, perhaps as a perception of something like an 'aura' or a halo, discussed earlier. Indeed, those images are probably reflective of some sort of perceptual experience of luminosity around the bodies of saintly people, sometimes observed by those not yet having experienced the holy instant. Thus, we also saw that the Course makes use of the term 'light' not only in a metaphorical sense of deeper understanding, but in a perceptual sense of a strong visual impression. Although it is not given great elaboration, an interesting distinction is made between ordinary vision and what is called 'real vision' in a passage previously cited (p. 264):

> "2 You will begin to understand it when you have seen little edges of light around the same familiar objects which you see now. 3 That is the beginning of real vision."(W,15,2,2-3)

As was also pointed out earlier, real vision involves a higher type of perception, culminating in what is called the 'vision of Christ;' it is related to a greater sensitivity to the real basis of true perception as founded in the subtler details of all visual objects, which discloses that they are all more accurately perceived as 'energy fields' that have no sharp demarcation of the limits of what we usually perceive and think of as 'bodies.' Since this perception of the 'little edges of light' is said to come when the separated mind moves closer to the healed state, it could be called a 'holier' perception of light.

The seeing of holiness in oneself and one's brother that comes in the holy relationship should not be confused with merely heightened visual impressions. The proper meaning of 'holiness' is 'wholeness' or connectedness or union with all Reality. This is not something that can itself be experienced as a sensation, but is on a much higher level of awareness. That is not to say the awareness of wholeness/union/holiness does not have effects on sense-perception. Indeed, when it becomes strongly present, it is the basis of the most complete perception possible, that of the Real World. This is what the Holy Spirit actually perceives and what the mind once caught in separation eventually comes to perceive. This seems to be the point in the previous passage where it says that seeing holiness is the purpose of the holy relationship (statement 9). Perhaps this 'seeing of holiness' is best described as perception strongly influenced by the intuitive awareness of wholeness or unity that is the core of Love, a kind of superimposition of holiness upon perception. We will discuss this further shortly.

A second aspect of the awareness of the holy relationship is indicated here:

> "1 A holy relationship starts from a different premise. 2 Each one has looked within and seen no lack. 3 Accepting his completion, he would extend it by joining with another, whole as himself. 4 He sees no difference between these selves, for differences are only of the body. 5 Therefore, he looks on nothing he would take."(22,In.,3,1-5)

Although in the earlier stage of the holy relationship the mind is still greatly aware of the body, both of its own and of those it is related to, and that awareness necessarily involves a perception of limits and even limitations and deficiencies connected with the body, in the more developed stages it recognizes that there is no lack or incompleteness either within itself or in those it is related to. Indeed, seeing no lack in itself and seeing that its own Self is the Self of the other, this absence of lack in the other is directly understood. Any perception of lack is on a superficial level. The ramification of this is that the one so perceiving has no basis for wanting to take something from any other. Because he *is* the other, he already has what the other has. The only need, as discussed earlier, is for the full and complete realization of perfect love both within what one thinks of as one's own mind or as another mind.

Related to the perception of luminosity, a third thing that arises in awareness in the holy relationship is described as 'the golden light.' A passage using the expression is:

> "1 Beyond the body that you interposed between you and your brother, and shining in the golden light that reaches it from the bright, endless circle that extends forever, is your holy relationship, beloved of God Himself. 2 How still it rests, in time and yet beyond, immortal yet on earth."(22,II,12,1-2)

This adds further details related to the perception of 'golden light' that we discussed earlier (21,I,8,1-6, on p. 265) in relation to the luminosity experienced in the holy instant. Again, this seems to be meant both literally and metaphorically. The metaphorical sense would refer to the higher perception that comes when the holy relationship reaches its maturity. In that fuller perception, the true perception of both oneself and one's brother (the 'other' in the relationship) involves the absence of any spatial or even temporal limit as to how far either mind extends. Since it goes out infinitely in all directions or dimensions of space-time, it is best thought of as a circle, or more accurately a hypersphere (a four-dimensional sphere) of infinite radius that is 'boundless' spatially and 'forever' temporally. That it is described as 'golden light' is of course a visual metaphor, since the particular color 'golden' that we are familiar with is a particular type of visual experience. As we saw earlier, that metaphor suggests what we connote with the term 'golden:' both the intense aesthetic response of its beauty and perhaps the preciousness related to the metal from which it gets the name. It also seems to involve a non-metaphorical element in the assertion that an intensely golden color is a perceptual quality characteristic of the highest perceptual experience that a mind can have. Thus, the color experienced in this higher perception is said to be a close match to the ordinary visual color of gold.

Although the mind comes to the clear perception of the infinite golden light only in the more advanced stages of development of the holy relationship, the passage indicates that it is nevertheless actually present at all times, despite one's not having awareness of it. Also, although the Course does not make this fully explicit, it is very probable that the mind comes to that perception during the more intense experiences of the holy instant. This is entirely consistent with the reports of some intense mystical or near-death experiences, where the experiencer is in that state for a limited period but then returns to a more ordinary mode, although his or her relationships with others are powerfully transformed as a result of the experience. Those reports often describe the experience as including the awareness of an intense white or golden light.

c) The holy relationship as bringing access to the Real World. These three new aspects of awareness – the perception of holiness, the perception of no lack, and the golden luminosity – along with what was described before about the Real World, may be understood as part of the more general new cognition that comes through the development of the holy relationship as an opening to the perception of the Real World. This is indicated in:

> "1 The holy relationship, a major step toward the perception of the real world, is learned."(17,V,2,1)

While this passage only briefly speaks of it as a 'step' toward the perception of the Real World, it makes clear what the primary culminating point is in the holy relationship's development. As we saw, the term 'Real World' denotes the highest mode of cognition that can occur within perception. It is what the Holy Spirit, who is essentially the same as the Christ Mind as it interfaces with the world of perception, perceives. This is a single, unified and completely harmonious awareness of all aspects or parts of Reality in so far as those aspects are perceived.

Although the holy relationship is a step toward perceiving the Real World, that actual perception seems best understood as occurring within the more advanced experiences of the holy instant. Indeed, since the 'luminosity' is an aspect of even the more shallow encounters with the holy instant, we might think of that luminosity as the first opening to a restrained or partial perception of the

Real World. As the mind is further purified of ego, which acts as an obscuring obstacle to this perception, the Real World is correspondingly perceived with greater clarity. Since the holy relationship serves as an important step to this, the more mature that relationship becomes, the clearer is its perception of the Real World. As the separated mind comes to the full development of the holy relationship, although the Course does not give a precise description, what seems to happen is that its perception deepens and becomes more capable of uniting with the fullness of the holy instant. This grows in intensity so that its awareness merges with the Holy Spirit's perceptual awareness. That is, it comes to the full perception of the Real World. As it does so, the once separated mind drops all remaining traces of separateness, and in this it realizes its identity with the Christ Mind.

Related to the 'light' description is another passage that brings out two further aspects of the holy relationship:

> "1 This holy relationship, lovely in its innocence, mighty in strength, and blazing with a light far brighter than the sun that lights the sky you see, is chosen of your Father as a means for His Own plan. 2 Be thankful that it serves yours not at all. 3 Nothing entrusted to it can be misused, and nothing given it but will be used. 4 This holy relationship has the power to heal all pain, regardless of its form."(22,VI,4,1-4)

The first point is that the intensity of this higher luminosity is compared to the 'blazing' light of the sun. The analogy seems to indicate that something quite dramatic occurs in the transformation, reminiscent of the fusion of two atoms of hydrogen that expresses in the release of energy that is enormously different from the relatively unenergetic state prior to that fusion – something parallel to what happens at the detonation of a hydrogen bomb. One is reminded of the awe expressed by J. R. Oppenheimer when he witnessed the first nuclear explosion, quoting from the *Bhagavad Gita*: "Brighter than a thousand suns!" That reference is to the transformation Arjuna witnessed when he saw his friend Krishna transformed into his fuller mode of Vishnu. One might draw a parallel to the transfiguration of Jesus witnessed by his closest disciples. In this we may understand that the holy relationship, when fully developed, makes clear the immensity that dwells only potentially in all separated minds.

d) Synchronicity in the holy relationship. Related also to the spatio-temporal contexts of holy relationships, the following passage gives a further important insight:

> "2 Each teaching-learning situation involves a different relationship at the beginning, although the ultimate goal is always the same; to make of the relationship a holy relationship, in which both can look upon the Son of God as sinless. 3 There is no one from whom a teacher of God cannot learn, so there is no one whom he cannot teach. 4 However, from a practical point of view he cannot meet everyone, nor can everyone find

> him. 5 Therefore, the plan includes very specific contacts to be made for each teacher of God. 6 There are no accidents in salvation. 7 Those who are to meet will meet, because together they have the potential for a holy relationship."(M,3,1,2-6)

That is, the various relationships that arise in the temporal journey of separated minds are all purposeful and carry with them specific lessons related to the process of the Atonement. They are all parts of the 'plan' that is orchestrated by the super-intelligence of the Mind of the Holy Spirit. This is especially true for those special relationships that are transformed into holy ones. Although the separated mind is generally unable to see the order and reason in these meetings (and partings), very few, if any, at least on some level, can totally dismiss what C.J. Jung called 'synchronicity' or 'meaningful coincidence' of the beginnings of some of the most important special relationships and particularly of holy ones.[76] One might want to think of these as 'mere coincidences,' but even the most hard-minded rational skeptic feels 'a vestige of superstition' or a feeling of 'uncanniness' about them. The more open-minded will find the Course's insight offers a much more satisfying explanation, even on the intellectual level, than closed skepticism. However one might respond to its explanation, it stands as an important principle in the Course's view on relationships and how and why they arise.

This last point is particularly elucidated in the following:

> "1 You have been called, together with your brother, to the most holy function this world contains. 2 It is the only one that has no limits, and reaches out to every broken fragment of the Sonship with healing and uniting comfort. 3 This is offered you, in your holy relationship."(18,I,13,1-3)

When one thinks of the relationships that have had or currently have the greatest meaning in one's life, the insight here enframes them so as to give them both a sense of why they have arisen and a direction toward which they are unfolding: the complete healing of the world of separated minds.

e) The final stage of the holy relationship. This is the condition of being completely healed, which is also described:

> "1 The holy relationship reflects the true relationship the Son of God has with his Father in reality."(20,VI,10,1)

That is, to borrow a phrase used by Plato to describe time, the holy relationship is a 'moving image of eternity.'[77] However, that cryptic expression is given fuller meaning here: what is imaged is the relationship that exists eternally and without limits between the perfect mind of the Son and the perfect Mind of His Creator-Father. Of course, the core of that relationship is Love. This implies that if one would want to come to an understanding of Love while in the world, there can be

---

[76] The idea of 'synchronicity' or 'meaningful coincidence' is discussed by Jung in *Synchronicity: An Acausal Connecting Principle*.

[77] *Timaeus*, 37d.

no closer approximation of it than is found in the holy relationship, particularly in its full maturity. If one were to assume with the Course that Jesus fully realized this in his own life, then from one's narrow limits of realization there could be no better place to find it exhibited than in Jesus' life. To be sure, that can only give an 'outsider's' understanding. A fuller grasp, at least in the Course's view, would be found in the realization of that relationship within one's own relationships, possibly even in the relationship that is available with the person Jesus although he is perceptually absent. But, perhaps that is the meaning of what the Course also says:

> "4 It is His [God's] Love that joins you and your brother, and for His Love you would keep no one separate from yours. 5 Each one appears just as he is perceived in the holy instant, united in your purpose to be released from guilt. 6 You see the Christ in him, and he is healed because you look on what makes faith forever justified in everyone."(19,I,10,4-6)

That is, each and every person that one meets has within him or her the presence of the Christ, which can be seen within the framework of the holy relationship that is deeply infused with the awareness contained in the holy instant. Since Christ is really present there, that is the place where He may be seen. This is what is called 'seeing the Face of Christ.' Indeed, one of the practices in the Workbook focuses on coming to that perception:

> "1 Select one brother, symbol of the rest, and ask salvation of him. 2 See him first as clearly as you can, in that same form to which you are accustomed. 3 See his face, his hands and feet, his clothing. 4 Watch him smile, and see familiar gestures which he makes so frequently. 5 Then think of this: What you are seeing now conceals from you the sight of one who can forgive you all your sins; whose sacred hands can take away the nails which pierce your own, and lift the crown of thorns which you have placed upon your bleeding head. 6 Ask this of him, that he may set you free: 7 Give me your blessing, holy Son of God. 8 I would behold you with the eyes of Christ, and see my perfect sinlessness in you."(W,161,11,1-8)

This practice seems to be concerned with opening the mind to the most important encounter possible within the holy relationship, i.e., of perceiving the Face of Christ. The foundation is clearly in the context of a simple special relationship that one chooses to be the focus of its transformation into a holy relationship. The apex of that transformation is just this seeing of Christ in both the other person in that relationship and within one's own self. To be clear, this is not a matter of overlaying an image of what one might think of as the person Jesus; that would be both a block to seeing the Christ in him/her and a kind of dismissal of the truth that that person is an embodiment or manifestation of Christ. Rather, it seems to consist in an awareness that is the same as that which the Holy Spirit has of both. Of course, from that more restricted awareness it can and must expand to one's relationship with every other separated mind. This is the fullness of the Holy Spirit's/Christ's awareness.

2) Full engagement in miracle working. The last cited passage brings us to the second major behavioral aspect of the holy instant and perfect love. This light/energy is not merely a display for its own sake, but has within it the power of transforming other separated minds. That seems to be the gist in saying in the previous passage's assertion that it can 'heal all pain.' That is, although the holy relationship involves a profound cognitive and affective transformation, it also entails other important behavioral consequences, one of the most significant of which is engagement in miracles. As the Course states:

> "1 The holy instant is the miracle's abiding place. 2 From there, each one is born into this world as witness to a state of mind that has transcended conflict, and has reached to peace."(27,V,3,1-2)

The idea expressed here is that as the separated mind enters more fully into the holy instant, it discovers the key to release its energy that is the basis for giving miracles. Here we should recall that the only place where miracles are needed, or even possible, is in the world that exists as the result of the perceptions of the collection of all separated minds. As we have seen, the holy relationship is one that intensifies the depth of the holy instant experience, which it brings back into the world of separation. Besides benefitting the minds that play the central role in the holy relationship, the Love that is its foundation must extend into the world, and the giving of it is primarily through what the Course calls 'miracles.' Indeed, in our discussion of the process of giving a miracle, the most important step for the MG was the shifting of one's perception from seeing a lack in the MR to seeing the MR as without that lack (step vi as we have analyzed the process). Since what is central in the matured perception of a mind in the holy instant is that there is no lack in anyone, it follows that such a mind is actually carrying out this central step of miracle-giving at all times it may be operating within the world. That is, it is giving miracles all the time.

As is further explained:

> "1 To overcome the world is no more difficult than to surmount your little wall. 2 For in the miracle of your holy relationship, without this barrier, is every miracle contained. 3 There is no order of difficulty in miracles, for they are all the same. 4 Each is a gentle winning over from the appeal of guilt to the appeal of love."(19,IV,A,5,1-4)

The first point here is the reference to the holy relationship as itself a miracle. This brings out the further insight that, since a miracle is based on the attunement of the mind of the miracle-giver to the whole Mind of the Holy Spirit/Christ and allowing that Mind to transform or heal whatever is perceived as in any way deficient, the foundation of the holy relationship is just this attunement to the Holy Spirit. The more fully one attunes to that Mind, the more complete is the holy relationship. This means that in such a relationship between two people who have until that time been involved in a merely special relationship, the more completely either of their separated minds connects with the Holy Spirit, the more completely will their relationship be a holy one. However, the extending nature of Love that is active in the Holy Spirit's Mind (as also in the minds of those in the holy relationship by their participation in Love), calls for the further giving of miracles to other separated minds. As indicated in statement 4, the effect of that is the release from entanglement with guilt that blocks the awareness of Love's presence in those separated minds.

This undoing of guilt is the core of the miracle's healing. It is described:

> "1 A holy relationship, however newly born, must value holiness above all else. 2 Unholy values will produce confusion, and in awareness.[78] 3 In an unholy relationship, each one is valued because he seems to justify the other's sin. 4 Each sees within the other what impels him to sin against his will. 5 And thus he lays his sins upon the other, and is attracted to him to perpetuate his sins. 6 And so it must become impossible for each to see himself as causing sin by his desire to have sin real. 7 Yet reason sees a holy relationship as what it is; a common state of mind, where both give errors gladly to correction, that both may happily be healed as one."(22,III,9,1-7)

Here we see that the holy relationship, being firmly based on the recognition that the holiness or wholeness of Love is the most important value, impels the mind embracing it toward the undoing of all false beliefs. The specific belief mentioned here is the belief in sin. The dynamic of the holy relationship is such that each one in it, by their commitment to holiness, reinforces this undoing of the attachment to that destructive belief.

This healing of cognition is clearly central to the holy instant, the experience of which we have seen is the foundation of the holy relationship. This is indicated in:

> "1 As you begin to recognize and accept the gifts you have so freely given to your brother, you will also accept the effects of the holy instant and use them to correct all your mistakes and free you from their results. 2 And learning this, you will have also learned how to release all the Sonship, and offer it in gladness and thanksgiving to Him Who gave you your release, and Who would extend it through you."(17,V,15,1-2)

We see here again a kind of 'feedback' process of facilitating the undoing of one's own mistakes by giving that undoing, or forgiveness, to another. This is, of course, central to the process of giving a miracle. One can see here even more

---

[78] Reflection on statement 2 makes clear that the words 'and in awareness' do not make clear grammatical sense. It makes more sense if ', and' is deleted. This phrasing may have been due to Schucman's inaccurate 'hearing' or recording of the Voice's words, perhaps due to a distraction. It is puzzling that it was not corrected in the editing process.

why the holy relationship is so important: it is a kind of first focus for the giving and receiving of miracles. Given that special relationships are the ones that occupy much of our time and energy, it makes complete practical sense that one would begin to apply the healing process in their context. Miracle-giving thus naturally would start by healing those most intimate special relationships, transforming them into holy ones, and then extending to other relationships. If one recalls the Biblical principle, "Love thy neighbor as thyself," this can be understood as: "Begin the process of healing by truly loving or giving miracles to your 'neighbors', i.e., those with whom you have the closest relationships, which then brings healing to your own self."

3) The bringing of salvation to the world. The third sort of behavioral change due to the holy instant is in an even wider context than that of giving miracles. That is, the correction of fundamental errors or mistakes, which is a central effect of the holy instant on the holy relationship, is also central to a much larger function in the world with respect to other separated minds. This is described:

> "1 You who are now the bringer of salvation have the function of bringing light to darkness. 2 The darkness in you has been brought to light. 3 Carry it back to darkness, from the holy instant to which you brought it."(18,III,7,1-3)

The expressions 'bringer of salvation' and 'bringing light to darkness' expand the significance of both the holy instant and the holy relationship in connection with the function of giving miracles. Salvation in the Course's view is nothing less than the full completion of the Atonement or complete healing of every separated mind within the world of perception. As any of those minds comes more fully into the holy instant and reaches a greater maturity in the holy relationship, it has a correspondingly far-reaching role as a 'bringer of salvation,' or 'savior.' In the Course's view, Jesus, having come to the fullness of the holy instant and the highest maturity in the holy relationship, is thus appropriately called a 'savior of the world.' This is even the traditional understanding of his role as 'the Christ.' However, the further meaning added by the Course is that not only the person Jesus, but each and every other separated mind is moving toward that role. Indeed, it makes much more sense of how each separated mind, as it approaches that maturity, acts as the means through which increasing portions of the world have their darkness brought to light, that is, find salvation. Thus, each mind becomes an integral part of the whole process of bringing light or salvation to all other parts. Not only does each separated mind come to being *like* Christ, but to the realization that it *is* Christ, the only Son of God. This is very much like the Mahayana Buddhist teaching regarding the Bodhisattva, who also takes on the responsibility of bringing enlightenment to all other sentient beings.

Here we see the profound importance of giving miracles. They are not only the means by which one or a few in intimate, holy relationships move toward this highest realization, but they can be given to all other separated minds:

> "1 How easy is it to offer this miracle to everyone! 2 No one who has received it for himself could find it difficult. 3 For by receiving it, he learned it was not given him alone. 4 Such is the function of a holy relationship; to receive together and give as you received."(22,IV,7,1-4)

That is, the particular set of separated minds that an MG has come to have a holy relationship with is only the start of a much broader sharing of the healing 'light' of miracles. They can be offered to every other separated mind in the world: those in close relationship (one's family, friends, or neighbors), those in less intimate relationship (one's acquaintances), and even to everyone that one has even the slightest contact with. This seems to be what is implied in Prin. 6, which states:

> "1 Miracles are natural. 2 When they do not occur something has gone wrong."(1,I,6,1-2)

The effect of this extension of miracles, based on the holy relationship, to an ever widening range of others is indicated in two passages:

> "1 Through your holy relationship, reborn and blessed in every holy instant you do not arrange, thousands will rise to Heaven with you."(18,V,3,1)

and:

> "1 It is no dream to love your brother as yourself. 2 Nor is your holy relationship a dream. 3 All that remains of dreams within it is that it is still a special relationship. 4 Yet it is very useful to the Holy Spirit, Who *has* a special function here. 5 It will become the happy dream through which He can spread joy to thousands on thousands who believe that love is fear, not happiness."(18,V,5,1-5)

Several points should be noted. The first is that one should not underestimate the effects that the holy relationship has upon the whole collection of separated minds that constitute the world. First, it catalyzes the transformation of thousands; then it spreads to thousands of thousands. Although not made explicit, one can extrapolate this mathematically from a thousand, to a million, to a billion, to a trillion, etc. This effect does not necessarily occur instantaneously, since it depends on two factors: the offering of miracles by the minds for whom their relationship has matured to a holy one and the accepting of them by others not yet reciprocally in such a relationship. Within the temporal framework, this may take more or less time. It also depends on the degree to which those giving miracles have matured in the holy relationship.

In this insight we may see an explanation of the growth of what is called the 'Christian religion.' That is, Jesus and his closest disciples/friends would be instances of the original holy relationships based on Jesus' realization of the enduring holy instant. This small group then expanded, gradually growing until it now includes almost two billion. Of course, from the Course's perspective, many of that number seem to be in very early stages of development, some even in complete violation of the original principles. But some appear to be to be very advanced (e.g., Mother Teresa). The same insight could be applied to the Hindu, Buddhist, Muslim, and other religions, all of which have many millions of adherents.

4) The celestial speedup. Here we consider what can be thought of as the fourth behavioral effect of the holy instant, its extension in time. If we assume, even hypothetically, that this extension has continued in the 2,000 years since Jesus is said to have walked on the planet and afterwards continued to be in holy relationships with human beings, there seem to be relatively few who have themselves come to full maturity in that regard. However, that should not lead us to underestimate or even dismiss the effectiveness of his transforming influence, since a thousand years is no more than a very tiny 'sub-blip' within the 'blip' that, in the Course's view, is the billions of years of time since the original act of separation. On the contrary, one might argue that the presence of the Course as a clarification and correction of many misunderstandings about the nature of the process of Atonement is itself acting as a very significant accelerator of that process as it is occurring on Earth. Indeed, in one communication that is said to have come to Schucman but not included in the FIP version, the Course is itself described as having a role in the 'celestial speedup.' Although passages using this term were deleted in FIP, UM contains two references to it:

> "You and B [Bill] DO have special talents which are needed for the Celestial speedup at this time. But note that the term speed-up is not one which relates to the TRANSCENDING of time."(UM, T 1 B 41m)

and:

> "'Many are called but few are chosen' SHOULD read, 'ALL are called but few choose to listen. Therefore, they do not choose RIGHT.' The 'chosen ones' are merely those who choose right SOONER. This is the real meaning of the celestial speed-up. Strong wills can do this NOW. And you WILL find rest for your Souls. God knows you only in peace, and this IS your reality."(UM, T 3 F 23)

Related to the idea of a speedup, the Course describes the miracle and the holy relationship in something like those terms:

> "2 Otherwise a miracle will be necessary to set the mind itself straight, a circular process that would not foster the time collapse for which the miracle was intended."(2,VII,2,2)

and:

> "2 A holy relationship is a means of saving time. 3 One instant spent together with your brother restores the universe to both of you."(18,VII,5,2-3)

While we need not here go into the more involved details of the Course's view on time, these two passages make clear two important ideas.[79] The first, which was discussed in Ch. IV, is that whenever a miracle is given, one of its effects is a 'leap' forward in time toward the full Atonement, in which all time ends. This 'leap' is the 'time collapse,' which is generally only a partial elimination of the temporal sequence, a kind of jumping ahead that eliminates what would otherwise be a necessary interval. Since the holy relationship makes the giving of miracles a 'natural' process, it follows that, as the second passage indicates, such relationships involve a major saving of time. However, the time collapse in miracles and holy relationships might be understood as simply an interpersonal thing holding only for those immediately within the miracle or holy relationship. But, as we have seen, both the miracle and the holy relationship have effects beyond these few minds that extend throughout the whole collection of separated minds. Thus, if each miracle produces some sort of time-collapse for the MG as well as for the MR if she/he accepts it, as the number of people giving and accepting miracles increases, this would have a growing effect on the overall time-flow both locally on earth and throughout the whole space-time cosmos. That is, the Course itself may well be contributing to this celestial speedup by way of its being seriously studied and practiced by a growing number of people. This seems to be the point in the passages referring to a *'celestial* speedup.' The word 'celestial' is clearly something beyond the limits of the personal. From that perspective, it might further be pointed out that the increase in interest and study of the Course since its first appearance would lead to the increasing disposition to give, and probably the actual giving of, miracles, as well as the formation of holy relationships. Thus, its teachings would itself involve a saving or speeding up of time within the whole realm of separated existence (what is called 'the physical universe'), at least on this planet. When we further note the greatly increased interest in and dedication to spiritual maturation in the last fifty years found in many traditions (Christian, Muslim, Hindu, Buddhist, Taoist, etc.), this might well be understood as a widespread growth in spiritual consciousness within humankind, each following other versions in which the Course is articulated.

C. The occurrence of experience of the holy instant. Since experiencing the holy instant plays such a central role in the Course's curriculum of learning/realizing perfect love, it will be helpful if we discuss in somewhat more detail what brings that experience about. I first give further clarification of the two primary ways that it is experienced in relation to time, then discuss the conditions

---

[79] Wapnick offers valuable clarifications regarding the Course's views on time in *A Vast Illusion: Time According to A Course in Miracles*. It is interesting to note that there he makes no mention of the 'celestial speedup.' In *Absence From Felicity*, where he does discuss the term, he evaluates it as not to be taken seriously. I think he may be mistaken in that regard. My clarification of it proposes that it is integral to the teachings, although it is not essential to understanding and realizing the Course's primary aim of Atonement.

304   Ch. V. 'perfect love'

that are necessary for it to occur, and finally the stages of how that experience unfolds to its full realization.

1. The two main types of experience of the holy instant while in perception. As we have already briefly pointed out, the holy instant can be experienced by minds still in separation with varying degrees of intensity or depth and either temporarily, followed by a reduction or loss of the awareness of that experience, or permanently, which maintains that awareness even in the temporal mode. This is made clearer in several passages. First we discuss the temporary holy instant, then the permanent one.

a. Temporary holy instants. Since the experience of the holy instant is itself a mode of awareness that is completely outside of time, it may at first sound like an oxymoron to speak of it as temporary. However, when properly understood there is no inconsistency. This is addressed in the following:

> "1 For a time you may attempt to bring illusions into the holy instant, to hinder your full awareness of the complete difference, in all respects, between your experience of truth and illusion. 2 Yet you will not attempt this long. 3 In the holy instant the power of the Holy Spirit will prevail, because you joined Him. 4 The illusions you bring with you will weaken the experience of Him for a while, and will prevent you from keeping the experience in your mind. 5 Yet the holy instant is eternal, and your illusions of time will not prevent the timeless from being what it is, nor you from experiencing it as it is."(16,VII,7,1-5)

The usual experience of the separated mind is temporal, having the three sets of perceptions it calls the 'past,' 'the present,' and 'the future.' Each set usually has some content that is similar in each, so that the mind thinks of certain patterns as undergoing change, sometimes remaining partly the same and partly different, sometimes completely ending, sometimes completely arising anew. For example, one observes a tree in autumn whose leaves a month before were green but now are yellow, orange, brown, and gold. The pattern of the tree with its leaves is in certain ways the same, but in other ways quite different. Then a leaf detaches from a branch and twirls down to the ground. Still, the tree is much the same in shape, but with a tiny difference. And, as more days pass and all the leaves have fallen, we think it is still the same tree, though now quite bare of any foliage. There is also a complete ending of that shape for our awareness when we turn away from it and look upon a house instead. The form of the tree has completely disappeared and there has arisen in its stead the form of the house. That is our usual way of perceiving, quite deeply rooted in our habits of thought that we call 'time.' However, in the holy instant, the mind shifts to a very different mode. The only content is a present without a past or future. There is no change, no shift in content, no boundary or limit between observer and observed. And here our words begin to fail, since they are formed from the contents of the time-bound experience, and any use of them can only distort the content of this timeless experience. In normal separated awareness, there is also the space-bound nature of usual experience that is rooted in what we think of as the difference between oneself, the subject of the experience, and what one is aware of, the object. In the holy instant, this division between subject and object also drops, or at least is profoundly changed. Even calling it 'experience' can lead to a distortion, since what is meant by that word is drawn from the usual spatio-temporal mode. Indeed, as the passage indicates, the force of habit of the spatio-temporal mode pushes the mind to try fit the holy instant into the molds it has long been attached to, which can only distort this radically different mode. As long as those habits continue to press into the new mode, the mind will be prevented from completely entering it.

This force of habit can soon pull the mind away from the new mode to bring it back to the old one, as is described in the context of the perceptions that constitute a relationship that has been a special one:

> "7 Have you consistently appreciated the good efforts, and overlooked mistakes? 8 Or has your appreciation flickered and grown dim in what seemed to be the light of the mistakes? 9 Perhaps you are now entering upon a campaign to blame him for the discomfort of the situation in which you find yourself. 10 And by this lack of thanks and gratitude you make yourself unable to express the holy instant, and thus lose sight of it."(17,V,11,7-10)

That is, the memories that are central to special relationships, based on the perception of error or even 'sin' and founded on the ego's acceptance of guilt and fear as guiding emotions, prompt the mind to return to that old way. Although awareness in the holy instant was one of complete union between one's own and that other mind, and of the absence of any limits in each, the re-entry into the spatio-temporalizing mode brings back the sense of separation and limitation. Although the other was recognized as an expression of pure Love, the slipping back into the old mode of divided perception brings back the old uneasiness (discomfort). This is projected onto the other as its origin, extinguishing for the while the profound feeling of gratitude that was present in the holy instant.

While there are probably many specific things that can trigger this loss of the awareness of the holy instant, the Course discusses three. One is described:

> "3 Your difficulty with the holy instant arises from your fixed conviction that you are not worthy of it. 4 And what is this but the determination to be as you would make yourself?"
> (18,IV,3,3-4)

Here we see two levels of the operation of the old habits. One is *the belief that one is not worthy of the holy instant*. This feeling of unworthiness seems best understood as an expression of the feeling of primary guilt, which we may recall is based on the presence in the fragmented mind, usually sub- or even unconsciously, the recollection that it has chosen to believe that it is its own creator, what the Course calls 'usurping the role of God.' The second, deeper level, which gives rise to the first, is *the decision to form and hold onto the idea of 'ego.'* That idea is one of establishing barriers between oneself and all the rest of Reality, and through which one adopts the belief that the ego is the principle at the basis of both oneself and all the other contents in one's mind. In a sense, this is true regarding the separated mind's contents, particularly the whole system of subsequent ideas and feelings that constitute most of the ego-dominated mind's experience. What pulls the mind out of the holy instant, which is a shift away from ego-dominated awareness, is the fixation on or attachment to the ego-idea that has been the basis of the separated mind's long odyssey across the vast ocean of time.

Closely related to this is another habit that tends to pull one away from the holy instant:

> "1 You *have* received the holy instant, but you may have established a condition in which you cannot use it. 2 As a result, you do not realize that it is with you still. 3 And by cutting yourself off from its expression, you have denied yourself its benefit. 4 You reinforce this every time you attack your brother, for the attack must blind you to yourself."(17,V,13,1-4)

That is, even though the holy instant is actually present (but beyond awareness for most separated minds) at every moment of time, it is particularly blocked from awareness by accepting *any impulse to attack another*. Attack is most fully actualized when expressed in and through the body. As is explained:

> "1 Attack is always physical. 2 When attack in any form enters your mind you are equating yourself with a body, since this is the ego's interpretation of the body."(8,VII,1,1,2)

That attack is always physical does not mean it is always an outright assault on a body. Rather, it is always in relation to the perception of the limitations that are intrinsic to the body, either another's or one's own. Thus, attack occurs whenever the mind enters into a mode of perceiving another as something to defend oneself from. It can be an overt physical action, such as murder, assault or a response to counter that, a verbal expression that intends to push another away or preserve what one thinks of as one's 'self,' or even a thought that is prompted by a similar impulse. When we consider most of our thoughts carefully, it becomes surprisingly clear how in much of our lives we are engaged in attacking in this sense, either crassly or subtly. It is the great force of this inclination to attack, strengthened by years (or possibly lifetimes) of reinforcement, that rises up so easily after one returns to the mode of perceiving, even after having an experience of the holy instant in which that habit was at least briefly suspended. As long as this inclination remains as part of the ego-idea, the mind will be drawn out of the holy instant experience.

A further insight on the nature of the attack habit is seen in a passage cited earlier (p. 254), which will be worth considering further, particularly after our discussion of the holy relationship:

> "1 Only the different can attack. 2 So you conclude *because*

you can attack, you and your brother must be different. 3 Yet does the Holy Spirit explain this differently. 4 *Because* you and your brother are not different, you cannot attack. 5 Either position is a logical conclusion. 6 Either could be maintained, but never both. 7 The only question to be answered in order to decide which must be true is whether you and your brother are different. 8 From the position of what you understand, you seem to be, and therefore can attack. 9 Of the alternatives, this seems more natural and more in line with your experience. 10 And therefore it is necessary that you have other experiences, more in line with truth, to teach you what *is* natural and true.

"1 This is the function of your holy relationship."
(22,VI,13,1-10;14,1)

This contrasts the two levels of relative and absolute reality. Since on the absolute level there is no difference between separated minds, on that level it is impossible to attack. This is what one becomes aware of while experiencing the holy instant. However, since that awareness admits of differing degrees and intensity, if it is only shallow there is not sufficient strength in it to bring the mind experiencing it into full conviction and stable permanence in it. In the level of separation or relative reality, the mind has the experience of the attack mode that we think of as 'normal' and intrinsic to living ('the struggle to survive'). When the separated mind first encounters the holy instant, it goes into a mode of awareness in which the other level is deeply challenged but not undone. Because the separated mind is so steeped and entrenched in the ego-habit, it is in need of a 'jolt' that throws it beyond that habit. Although it is only brief and shallow at first, this makes clear that its former way is seriously questionable. But questioning is not the same as full certainty. Hence, it needs to have more experiences of the holy instant before it can completely shake itself loose of the ego and the impulse to attack. What is especially important here is the role of the holy relationship. It arises and deepens in a stepwise transformation of special (ego-dominated) relationships through deeper and more intense experiences of the holy instant. This makes it the primary context for the process of full awakening. Here we see the intimate connection between the holy relationship and the holy instant in the Course's program of learning.

This brings out the third cause for the mind's slipping out of the holy instant. That is its *need for further learning*. As is stated:

"1 The holy instant does not replace the need for learning, for the Holy Spirit must not leave you as your Teacher until the holy instant has extended far beyond time."(15,VIII,1,1)

In this it is made clear that a single experience of the holy instant does not automatically undo the long-entrenched and deeply rooted attachment to the ego. That the experience of the holy instant occurs at all is the result of two factors. The primary factor is that of the presence of Love, which is the very foundation of the separated mind's existence and is always exerting an influence or 'pressure' to release that mind from its self-imposed condition. The primary manifestation of that presence is through the Holy Spirit, who is ever ready to offer guidance within the mind in the form of the 'Voice for God' and the experiences mediated through others in the world outside who offer opportunities for opening to that presence. Within the latter there can be the many miracles given to such a mind. As the mind opens to the Holy Spirit it also learns to offer miracles to others, which in giving them also further opens that mind to its own healing. The other factor is the willingness of the separated mind to accept three things: the guidance of the Holy Spirit, the miracles given it, and opportunities to give them. Without that willingness, it must continue in its separation until it comes to the point where it decides to open to Love's presence. However, the decision to open is generally only partial and with reservations. As long as it is ambivalent in its decision, it can enter into Love's presence only partially. At some point in its itinerary through time, its decision to receive the Light of Love is sufficient to bring about a breaking away from the usual temporalizing mode and enter into the holy instant. However, that is only to the degree that it has decided to embrace it. Any reservation or holding back draws it to return into the temporalizing mode, where it continues to experience the problems of that mode until it comes to the point where it chooses once again for Love. Thus it oscillates between the holy instant and the temporalizing mode, gradually learning to make the full and unreserved decision to return to Love, at which point it enters into a mode of unswerving and constant experience of the holy instant.

b. The enduring or permanent holy instant. While temporary experiences of the holy instant are what is usually the case, the deepening of learning can bring one to the realization of that awareness without cessation. This seems to be the point in:

> "1 The holy instant is nothing more than a special case, or an extreme example, of what every situation is meant to be. 2 The meaning that the Holy Spirit's purpose has given it is also given to every situation. 3 It calls forth just the same suspension of faithlessness, withheld and left unused, that faith might answer to the call of truth. 4 The holy instant is the shining example, the clear and unequivocal demonstration of the meaning of every relationship and every situation, seen as a whole."(17,VIII,1,1-4)

It was already pointed out that the holy instant is accessible in every moment in time, provided the mind is willing to accept it. Although that more intense experience of perfect love and union with God and one's brothers is usually only temporary, when the mind returns to the temporal mode it brings with it remnants of that awareness. This is the foundation of the early and middle stages of development of the holy relationship. It might be thought of almost in a mathematical way: *the depth of the experience of the holy instant brings afterward a proportionate deepening of the awareness of perfect love in that relationship.* It follows that there comes a point in that deepening where the holy relationship is pervaded by that awareness, and eventually the point at which the holy instant is fully present in all moments for a mind still in the perceiving mode. That is, there is no 'slipping away' from the holy instant, a kind of superimposition of that non-temporal awareness on the temporal mode of perceiving within the world. Indeed, this is very close to the mode of perception of the Holy Spirit, who both perceives what is within time and knows the fullness of Love that is beyond it. However, it has two important differences. One is that there is an association of that mind with a particular body. The other is that such a mind has experiences in limited space and time. This association with a body that operates in space and time is important in the Atonement process, since it makes possible communication with other separated minds. The Course points out:

> "1 How can the Holy Spirit bring His interpretation of the body as a means of communication into relationships whose only purpose is separation from reality?"(17,III,5,1)

Thus, the mind that has come to this stage of development serves as a vehicle for being a teacher in the highest sense. This seems to be the whole point of Jesus' remaining in a body after his realization of the Christ Mind. It may also explain why Siddhartha remained in the body 43 years more after reaching Buddhahood. Many have considered J. Krishnamurti also to have been the most recent major teacher. He remained in the body for more than 60 years after realization of what he called 'Intelligence' and was referred to by some as 'the World Teacher.'

What the Course refers to as the experience of the holy instant appears to be another name for what scholars speak of as mystical experience, particularly the kind of mystical experience some call the 'mysticism of love.'[80] Those studies also make clear that in all spiritual traditions beginning mystical experiences are only relatively brief elevations to the mode of timelessness and union, followed by a return to ordinary experience, although that ordinary experience often has a decidedly transformed character of greater love for and greater sense of connection with others. In the more advanced stages of mystical development, there can come the permanent presence of the higher mystical state even while engaged in temporal awareness. Some refer to this as the 'unitive life' or the 'way

---

[80] The term 'mystical experience' in popular usage includes a whole variety of unusual experiences, ranging from ESP, aura perception, mediumship, even schizophrenic episodes. However, scholars generally do not include these, but reserve the term for experiences whose primary feature is a suspension of the dualistic mode of awareness and its replacement with the awareness of being one with reality. Also occurring is a state of 'timelessness' and profound feeling of certainty or intense reality of its contents. Although there is not complete agreement among all scholars as to what it includes, E. Underhill, W. T. Stace, and F. Happold list 6 to 8 characteristics and also distinguish several major types of mystical experience. The reader may want to consult their writings.

of unity.'[81] From what is known of their biographies, it is quite probable that the persons named the Buddha, Jesus, St. Francis of Assisi, Muhammad, Rumi, Ramakrishna, Ramana Maharshi, and J. Krishnamurti (and others) came to that stage of development. In the Zen tradition, this state is said to be attained by the real 'masters' and is referred to as 'mujodo no taigen' ('actualization of the supreme way in daily life').[82]

However, as was pointed out in our discussion of the Real World, in the Course's view even this highest state of realization of perfect love within the world is not the final conclusion of the separated mind's development. Beyond this is the further shift in awareness in which all perception is completely dropped and the intense beauty of the Real World is replaced by knowledge, which is the awareness of Reality as the unity of all perfect minds in their limitless act of giving and receiving infinite Love, which is the boundlessly increasing Joy of Heaven. This final state is the culmination of the whole Atonement process. It consists in the return of the separated mind (indeed all separated minds) to the full awareness of its (their) original and essential nature.

2. Conditions and practices promoting the experience of the holy instant. Several passages cited indicate conditions that must exist within the separated mind before the holy instant can be entered, as well as practices it can do that facilitate experiencing it.

a. Conditions necessary for the occurrence of the holy instant. The Course mentions two conditions that must be fulfilled.

i. Choosing not to hold onto 'ego-thoughts.' One important condition is described:

> "1 The necessary condition for the holy instant does not require that you have no thoughts that are not pure. 2 But it does require that you have none that you would keep."
> (15,IV,9,1-2)

By 'impure' thoughts is meant those that are derived from and supporting the ego, since these are the primary thoughts that act as obstacles to being aware of Love's presence. If such thoughts had to be gotten rid of before one could enter the holy instant, the mind would be in a serious bind, since it is only by entering the holy instant that those thoughts can be removed. We have seen how the mind's entanglement in separation is reinforced by those thoughts, but that what initiates it is the mind's choice to attach to the ego. Hence, it is necessary for the mind to go through a 'purification' that eliminates these thoughts. Thus, this condition amounts to ceasing to will to hold on to these obstacles, which, since the mind is always engaged in willing, involves choosing or willing *not* to hold on to them.

---

[81] Described by Happold, *Mysticism: A Study and an Anthology*, pp. 94-100, and more extensively by Underhill in *Mysticism*, pp. 413-443.

[82] See P. Kapleau, *Three Pillars of Zen*, pp. 55-56.

ii. Giving up desire to be in charge and letting the Holy Spirit be in charge. A second condition is that the mind must abandon the wish or desire to determine what happens in one's release from the state of separating, as described:

> "2 If you already understood the difference between truth and illusion, the Atonement would have no meaning. 3 The holy instant, the holy relationship, the Holy Spirit's teaching, and all the means by which salvation is accomplished, would have no purpose. 4 For they are all but aspects of the plan to change your dreams of fear to happy dreams, from which you waken easily to knowledge. 5 Put yourself not in charge of this, for you cannot distinguish between advance and retreat." (18,V,1,2-5)

The problem of wanting to be in charge is that the mind is greatly enclosed by the ego, and to be in charge is the same has having one's ego in charge. Of course, the ego's prime commitment is to maintaining itself. The holy instant is a state of awareness in which the ego is, at least within that instant, no longer dominating. Thus, choosing to be in charge necessarily prevents entering it. The Course's alternative is to choose to let the Holy Spirit, the Mind completely free of ego, be in charge.

To the ego-dominated mind, the prospect of letting another mind be in charge seems to be contrary to its current commitment. Thus, letting the Holy Spirit have complete charge at first is a formidable challenge, making it very difficult. This is central to the purification process and is often experienced as what is referred to as a 'dark night of the soul.' But in fact, if one can get past that perception, the following points out that it is actually quite easy:

> "1 It is this that makes the holy instant so easy and so natural. 2 You make it difficult, because you insist there must be more that you need do."(18,IV,7,1-2)

The key here seems to be that the primary step is to make the choice to move away from ego-control and let universal intelligence (the Holy Spirit) coordinate the process. By following that guidance, no mistakes and confusions will arise, as must necessarily come from the very limited 'intelligence' of the ego. The only problem here is the challenge of being fully willing to let that Mind be in charge.

iii. The 'little willingness.' The third condition, and what seems to be the most important, for coming to the experience of the holy instant is what is called the separated mind's 'little willingness,' discussed at some length in Ch. 18, Sec. III, which has that sub-title. The key passage seems to be:

> "1 The holy instant does not come from your little willingness alone. 2 It is always the result of your small willingness combined with the unlimited power of God's Will."(18,IV,4,1-2)

This indicates two aspects that are central to the occurrence of the experience of the holy instant. The first is that there must arise within the particular separated mind a definite formation of a shift in its volition toward living in 'another way,' that is, beyond ego-domination. That it only has to be 'little' seems to refer to the fact that the mind may still have some ambivalence (inclination to remain with the ego and yet to get beyond it) and thus is only weakly or partially committed to the alternative way. It may also be very unclear in its understanding of its own situation, which is quite likely due to its long-standing mental habits of choosing ego-domination.

The second aspect is that, although the separated mind needs to have this willingness, the actual occurrence of the experience of the holy instant is not something that it generates or produces. Rather, its actual source is in God or Love. All that the 'little willingness' does is to set aside to some extent the obstacle that impedes the holy instant from arising.

Indeed, if we recall that the separation was initiated by the volitional act or choice to remain focused on a tiny portion of Reality, and that God cannot cease to offer Love to that mind, but also remains respectful of that mind's choice, it is only when the separated mind makes a reversal of that choice that the separated mode can be undone. Then Love can move into it so as to clear away all the rest of the remaining obstacles to awareness of It, which of course may for that particular mind require considerable time. Indeed, although for the separated mind God/Love had waited patiently for aeons, He/It never ceased to act upon it so as to open it to make this all-important choice. It is the development of this 'little willingness' that is central to what I've called the Course's 'Onefold Path.'

b. The practices proposed in the Course. This process, simple in principle, does not mean that the separated mind need not engage in deliberate exercises that will facilitate entering into the holy instant. First we consider what the Course has to say about its practices in general, then we discuss what seem to be the primary realizations that come in doing those practices.

i. The nature of the practices. As the Course states:

> "4 You can practice the mechanics of the holy instant, and will learn much from doing so. 5 Yet its shining and glittering brilliance, which will literally blind you to this world by its own vision, you cannot supply. 6 And here it is, all in this instant, complete, accomplished and given wholly."(15,II,5,4-6)

It may at first be surprising to see the expression 'mechanics of the holy instant,' since that connotes a kind of rote, superficial ritual that operates with unawareness, like a machine. Here, one is reminded of the practices of repeating mantras or doing various repetitive exercises that, as J. Krishnamurti points out, can merely lull the mind into a kind of hypnotic state of dullness, at most producing a release of tensions and even physical, emotional, and mental relaxation and a kind of calmness, sometimes even in the deeper levels of the mind, but failing to open awareness to the deepest levels. Such would be quite useless also for the Course's learning purposes. They would lead only to a kind of expanded ego-consciousness, possibly even accessing so-called 'supernormal' powers (such as the siddhis or occult powers described in the *Yoga Sutras*), but actually only embedding the mind even more deeply in ego-based separateness.[83] However, 'rote mechanical practices' does not seem to be the intended meaning of 'mechanics' here. One definition of the term makes 'mechanics' synonymous with 'mechanism,' one of whose meanings is defined as 'the combination of mental processes by which a result is obtained.' As was pointed out earlier in relation to the statement that the Holy Spirit is the 'mechanism of miracles' (p. 174), this in no way implies a mindless mechanical procedure. Rather, it can be understood as referring to the practices that the Course recommends and actually proposes in the Workbook. These are 365 mental exercises, engaged in on a daily basis, often in several periods of focused practice and sometimes even every hour of the waking day. However, this passage makes it clear that all of those practices should not be confused with the primary shift in awareness that is the holy instant. Indeed, when one looks closely at those practices, their primary intention can be seen to be precisely that of preparing the separated mind to make that shift. In general, this is similar to the practices found in all spiritual traditions if correctly understood. Whether those of the Course, the Protestant 'Practicing the Presence,' the Jesuit 'Spiritual Exercises,' the Orthodox 'Prayer of the Heart,' the Sufi 'dhikr,' Buddhist 'zazen,' 'mahamudra' or 'mindfulness,' Hindu 'yoga,' or Taoist 'nei-yeh,' they should never be considered to be ends in themselves. It is also a serious misconstrual to see them as only means to some sort of inferior aim such as relaxation, increasing personal power, etc, although they can be so used (which may even be appropriate in their use for reducing fear). Rather, they are primarily practical tools for breaking the habit of ego-attachment and letting the 'Light' of a higher mode of awareness flow or even rush in, which in the Course's terms is the entry into the holy instant.

Related to this, those practices need to be understood correctly. As is described:

> "4 In preparing for the holy instant, do not attempt to make yourself holy to be ready to receive it. 5 That is but to confuse your role with God's."(18,IV,5,4-5)

Here it is made quite clear that the achievement of great skill in doing any practice has little to do with real holiness. The state of wholeness that comes in the holy instant *is given, not achieved*. All exercises that one may engage in are concerned with helping the mind make the simple choice of being guided to receive that gift. Indeed, any thought that one has become a 'master' of either the Course's or any other practice is simply another ego-block. The guru 'businesses,' both Eastern and Western, are often headed by men or women who may have great skills in certain mental practices, even being able to do all sorts of mental feats like mind-reading, materialization, communicating with spirits, etc. They sometimes have huge followings of disciples, who in some cases satisfy

---

[83] The 'siddhis' are discussed at length in Bk. III. See *Yoga Philosophy of Patanjali* by Swami Harihar-ananada Aranya.

their own ego-need for adulation and accumulate huge wealth. But, in the Course's view, none of this has anything to do with genuine holiness. Indeed, it can be the very opposite in that it only deepens the hold of ego on the so-called 'master,' making him or her the center of major separation between oneself, one's followers, and particularly all those who don't follow them. Of course, this occurs within more conventional religious organizations dominated by a sort of 'entrepreneurship' mentality that seems entirely inconsistent with the teachings of the religion's founder. But, we need not belabor this criticism of 'religions.' The primary point is that the student of the Course must recognize that none of his/her practices have the effect of making him or her holy. Rather, they can only prepare one's mind to receive the wholeness of the holy instant, which in the Course's view is the only authentic holiness.

Thus, the 'leap' into the holy instant does not require that one first clean up, so to speak, his mind/soul. As is stated:

> "1 Never approach the holy instant after you have tried to remove all fear and hatred from your mind. 2 That is *its* function. 3 Never attempt to overlook your guilt before you ask the Holy Spirit's help. 4 That is *His* function. 5 Your part is only to offer Him a little willingness to let Him remove all fear and hatred, and to be forgiven."(18,V,2,1-15)

This can be seen as a correction of a common misunderstanding found in many spiritual traditions. In the Course's view, they mistakenly hold that one has to engage in a rigorous 'purification' process of removing from oneself all accumulated negative habits or inclinations that stem from fear, hatred, and guilt, and cultivating positive habits by one's own efforts. When the process is understood correctly, purification comes from the holy instant itself. For that to happen, the primary condition necessary is to make the choice without reservation: "Let it be."

This point is made even clearer in the following:

> "1 It is impossible to accept the holy instant without reservation unless, just for an instant, you are willing to see no past or future. 2 You cannot prepare for it without placing it in the future. 3 Release is given you the instant you desire it. 4 Many have spent a lifetime in preparation, and have indeed achieved their instants of success. 5 This course does not attempt to teach more than they learned in time, but it does aim at saving time. 6 You may be attempting to follow a very long road to the goal you have accepted. 7 It is extremely difficult to reach Atonement by fighting against sin. 8 Enormous effort is expended in the attempt to make holy what is hated and despised. 9 Nor is a lifetime of contemplation and long periods of meditation aimed at detachment from the body necessary. 10 All such attempts will ultimately succeed because of their purpose. 11 Yet the means are tedious and very time consuming, for all of them look to the future for release from a

state of present unworthiness and inadequacy."(18,VII,4,1-11)

In this we find several important insights. The first is regarding the nature of 'preparation.' To prepare is always a matter of focusing on the future based on a memory of something from the past. This is to engage intentionally and intensely in a time-affirming process. Certainly one can prepare for many things: exams, careers, etc. However, all those things are only various modes of being in the world, and thus of being engaged in time. By and large, they are fundamentally ego-affirming. The second insight is that it is quite possible to engage in such preparation, even with a truly spiritual intent or aim. In fact, we are quite familiar with the stories of the Buddha and his many-year search for enlightenment, as well as similar spiritual searches in all other traditions that have culminated in genuine spiritual realization. The Course does not deny that such has actually happened. However, those searches were successful not because they were long and arduous. Success depended only on one thing: the decision to embrace holiness which is available at every instant, provided one so chooses. The third insight, and perhaps the most important in regard to the Course, is that no 'struggle with sin,' no 'great effort,' no 'long time' is really necessary. Indeed, all of that is only a matter of deferring the fulfillment of the single requirement for entering the holy instant, which brings the realization of perfect love and the completion of the Atonement: simply make the choice to accept it. In that choice, one saves him/herself a lot of time, effort, and trouble.

Thus, we see that in the Course's view, what is called 'spiritual realization,' 'salvation,' 'nirvana,' 'moksha,' 'mujodo no taigen,' etc., requires only one thing on our part, which is the third condition, 'the little willingness.' It is further described:

> "3 But trust implicitly your willingness, whatever else may enter. 4 Concentrate only on this, and be not disturbed that shadows surround it. 5 That is why you came. 6 If you could come without them you would not need the holy instant. 7 Come to it not in arrogance, assuming that you must achieve the state its coming brings with it. 8 The miracle of the holy instant lies in your willingness to let it be what it is."
> (18,IV,2,3-8)

That is, it occurs when 'your willingness' so chooses. Although its Source is God or infinite Love itself, that Source is blocked only by one's choice to hold on to the ego. Once the choice is made to release it, the holy instant comes of itself. When this is understood, then learning to make that choice becomes the only concern that one seriously committed to the spiritual path need focus on. The absence of that choice is actually the choice to separate and is the only thing that generates the numerous 'shadows' (all the illusions generated by the ego: fear, guilt, anger, hatred, special love, etc.) One need not dance or fight with those shadows in an effort to defeat them. The only requirement is to learn this willingness. However, this choice is not merely a matter of saying or even thinking words that sound as if they articulate the choice. It must come from the very core or heart of the mind, from the deepest level of the will. When that happens, the holy instant dissolves all the shadows.

ii. The major insights whose realization is central to entering the holy instant. The Course's whole curriculum comes down to this very simple matter: learning the willingness to choose the holy instant. It offers many insights that must not only be understood intellectually, but more importantly must be existentially 'seen' or realized. In one sense, the 365 exercises of the Workbook offer a sequential opportunity for that. However, there seem to be certain insights that are particularly important, which we consider here.

Insight 1: There is nothing I can do. The first realization that the separated mind needs to come to is that there is nothing *it* can *do*. This, as well as the second insight, seems to be the primary focus of lessons 1 through 26. The idea of this first insight is described briefly:

> "12 I need do nothing except not to interfere."(16,I,3,12)

It is also the culminating focus of Lesson 25:

> "I do not know what anything is for."(W,25)

The basis of this is expressed in:

> "4 And it is only fear that you will add, if you prepare yourself for love. 5 The preparation for the holy instant belongs to Him Who gives it. 6 Release yourself to Him Whose function is release. 7 Do not assume His function for Him."(18,IV,6,4-7)

That is, any attempt to do anything that one thinks would help develop the needed willingness not only will not work, but will actually generate another obstacle of fear. This is because what one may try to do proceeds from a particular thought in one's mind, and all such thoughts are tinged or even deeply colored by the ego, which is surrounded by fear. Thus, what one might try to do will be inclined to generate more fear within one's mind. When one sees this clearly, he understands that the only way he can get beyond this dilemma is by being guided out of it by a Mind that is not caught in ego. That, of course, is the Holy Spirit. Thus, the mind simply wills to let itself be guided by that Mind, even in the elementary step of learning true willingness. With that very 'little' initial willingness, the Holy Spirit can now come in to take the steps that are necessary to undo the whole set of inner obstacles interfering with the learning process.

It is also interesting to note that this insight is part of one of the final group of practices offered in the Workbook:

> "5 God has already done all things that need be done. 6 And I must learn I need do nothing of myself, for I need but accept my Self, my sinlessness, created for me, now already mine, to feel God's Love protecting me from harm, to understand my Father loves His Son; to know I am the Son my Father loves." (W,337,1,5-6)

That is, the insight is integral to the fundamental intention of the means that are offered to the student for realizing its teachings. The same is true for the rest of the primary insights, which are either implicit in every practice or at times repeated as part of the practice. Thus, all of these primary insights should be thought of as part of a larger holistic insight which constitutes the substance of the Course's teachings.

Insight 2: Attachment to the body is absurd. Since one of the most entrenching beliefs that holds the separated mind within its entanglement with the ego is its attachment to the body, it is necessary for it to realize just what that involves. The problem and its solution is described:

> "4 Here does the Son of God stop briefly by, to offer his devotion to death's idols and then pass on. 5 And here he is more dead than living. 6 Yet it is also here he makes his choice again between idolatry and love. 7 Here it is given him to choose to spend this instant paying tribute to the body, or let himself be given freedom from it. 8 Here he can accept the holy instant, offered him to replace the unholy one he chose before."(20,VI,11,4-8)

The main point is that the Holy Spirit first needs to make fully clear the folly of living by ego, particularly in its belief in the supreme importance of the body. This comes by recognizing that the way of the ego is actually a kind of 'religion' that worships death, and that the body, as a form with limits in space and time, necessarily involves its own mortality. But, in order to see this clearly, the separated mind is shown the full nature of this, which is that the ego is a fundamental contradiction: while it wills to exist, that very willing involves willing its own cessation of existence. What is described here in words is, of course, only an abstraction. This part of the lesson must be an existential encounter, in all of its emotional fullness and intensity, with the radical absurdity of the ego-minded mode, which is one that would be appropriately described as a 'living death.' However, under the guidance of the Holy Spirit, that encounter with one's own death is only brief, acting as a kind of catharsis that brings the mind to the realization that it has no need whatsoever to engage in this 'idolatry' of the deity 'Ego-Death-Body.'

Although the first 25 lessons of the Workbook involve a gradual disclosure of this insight, Lesson 26 seems to be most directly concerned with its full impact:

> "My attack thoughts are attacking my invulnerability." (W,26)

What stands out here is the fundamental contradictoriness of concern about the body. This can be stated more clearly: Commitment to the body's reality involves protecting it. Protecting it involves attacking anyone or anything that threatens it. However, that very attacking of anyone or anything generates for it the conditions of being attacked and destroyed. That is, dedication to the body's existence as a central concern involves dedication to its destruction. Having seen this clearly, it is now ready to direct the will to the only thing that has any value: finding entry into the condition having no limits, the holy instant.

This stage of learning seems equivalent to what in mystic literature is called 'the way of purgation.' However, it is different from how that way is conceptualized in many traditions as a long-enduring and frightening period. Of course, it can be long enduring and very frightening and full of suffering if the mind delays making the choice. But, if the mind gives itself fully to the direction of the Holy Spirit, that stage can occur within as little as a second, or even less, of time. This perhaps parallels Jesus' own confrontation with death in the form of the crucifixion. The notion of 'encountering one's own death' or the 'death of the ego' is found in most biographies of the mystics, from the Buddha's encounter with Mara, to the shaman's 'dying experience' prior to becoming a full-fledged healer.

Insight 3: The Holy Spirit is the only one capable of directing the separated mind to its freedom. The importance of being willing to be directed by the Holy Spirit is described in the following:

> "6 Be happy, and you gave the power of decision to Him Who must decide for God for you. 7 This is the little gift you offer to the Holy Spirit, and even this He gives to you to give yourself. 8 For by this gift is given you the power to release your savior, that he may give salvation unto you.
>
> "1 Begrudge not then this little offering. 2 Withhold it, and you keep the world as now you see it. 3 Give it away, and everything you see goes with it. 4 Never was so much given for so little. 5 In the holy instant is this exchange effected and maintained. 6 Here is the world you do not want brought to the one you do."(21,II,3,6-8;4,1-6)

In this we may see a kind of 'feedback' process that begins to operate with greater intensity. That is, the very simple decision to place all further decisions in the hands of the Holy Spirit frees the separated mind from the poor basis (the distorted ideas of his own ego-dominated mind) for making further specific decisions within the time-bound limitations of the perceptual world. This enables it to listen to the Holy Spirit's decisions, which He communicates to that mind so that it may move more steadily in the direction of its release from ego-domination.

Within the Workbook, this insight can be seen to be the primary concern of lessons 27 through 49. It is particularly the focus of the following:

> "God's Voice speaks to me all through the day."(W,49)

What follows in the other lessons is direct guidance toward the central process that undoes the blocks preventing entry into the holy instant. This is particularly facilitated in that mind's being guided to give miracles to those brothers it encounters ('release your savior' in the preceding passage), which enables those brothers, having found release, at least to some extent, to return the same miracle-minded intent to it. Through this process, although it is only a 'little offering' of that simple willingness, one takes the initial step toward transcending the world of ego-bound perception. This opens such a mind to entering into the holy instant, which further deepens that willingness, so that the formerly severely entangled mind comes to the transforming experience of the holy instant, or more accurately, to the series of such experiences that are central to the process of growing development of the holy relationship (or holy relationships).

Insight 4: It is necessary to make the choice of inviting Love to enter.

When the mind is sufficiently prepared and ready, it is able to come to the further realization that it can and must make the choice of inviting love, or better Love, to enter into it. This is first focused on in Lesson 46:

"God is the Love in which I forgive."(W,46)

Later, the focus on welcoming Love is repeated in various forms, either explicitly as Love, or as light, joy, or truth. In this way, the holy instant is described as 'your invitation to love':

"1 The holy instant is your invitation to love to enter into your bleak and joyless kingdom, and to transform it into a garden of peace and welcome. 2 Love's answer is inevitable. 3 It will come because you came without the body, and interposed no barriers to interfere with its glad coming. 4 In the holy instant, you ask of love only what it offers everyone, neither less nor more."(18,VIII,11,1-4)

One might think that, since the holy instant is primarily an experience given by God through the Holy Spirit, it is not correct to call it an invitation of the separated mind but rather an invitation of the Holy Spirit. However, this passage makes clear that in that 'little willingness' there is realized the opening step to the holy instant. Of course, the holy instant is *always* offered by the Holy Spirit, but it is blocked by the unwillingness of the separated mind to receive it. Thus, this decision to place one's status in the Holy Spirit's hands constitutes the separated mind's invitation for Love to enter. In a sense, it is the turning point in such a mind's itinerary through time to reciprocate God's invitation that is always open.

However, it is one thing to accept an invitation and another to actually follow through. Although the separated mind may have decided to give the 'little willingness,' there still remains the process of learning that brings its full realization. One might liken this to accepting an invitation to a wealthy man's banquet. The invited person sends notice that he will come, but first his clothes must be changed to something appropriate and he has to make the trip to the banquet hall. Such intermediate steps are necessary also in coming to the full realization of the holy instant are described:

"3 The holy instant in which you and your brother were united is but the messenger of love, sent from beyond forgiveness to remind you of all that lies beyond it. 4 Yet it is through forgiveness that it will be remembered."(18,IX,13,3-4)

That is, the 'readying' that is necessary before one can arrive at the full-fledged holy instant is the 'cleaning up' of the obstacles that still block it. This 'cleaning up' is here described as 'forgiveness.' We should recall that the primary move in that is one of letting go what acts as an obscuring factor to the awareness of what is always present. As one learns to do this, more and more such factors drop away. As they drop away, the holy instant shines ever more brightly and completely.

Insight 5: Forgiveness is the fundamental key to freedom. Although the 'undoing' that is forgiveness is implicit right from the beginning of the Workbook, it is given clear focus in most of lessons 61 through 170. The first of these is Lesson 62:

> "Forgiveness is my function as the light of the world."(W,62)

The realization of this insight is emphasized from many perspectives in many of these lessons, from understanding the nature of what needs to be forgiven (grievances) to the importance of the process in which forgiveness is the core process (giving miracles).

The nature of forgiveness as understood in the Course is perhaps most succinctly stated in the following:

> "1 What is the holy instant but God's appeal to you to recognize what He has given you? 2 Here is the great appeal to reason; the awareness of what is always there to see, the happiness that could be always yours. 3 Here is the constant peace you could experience forever. 4 Here is what denial has denied revealed to you."(21,VIII,5,1-4)

That is, the holy instant is blocked by the act of denying most of Reality in favor of only a tiny portion or aspect of it. That tiny portion is constituted only by an affirmation of that tiny portion, including the construction of and attachment to the idea of the ego. We have already seen that this idea is actually self-contradictory, although its inconsistency is covered over and hidden by the name 'ego' and all its consequent ideas projected upon further perceptions. Thus, the basis of separation lies in its denial of the full Truth of Reality in preference to a tiny fragment of it. Understood from this perspective, entry into the holy instant, which even in its initial stage of being experienced, is based on a denial of this denial. This negation of the negation that is fundamental to the separation logically is the same as the affirmation of what was negated: the Reality of Love, and the unity between God and all created minds

Insight 6: Entry into the holy instant opens the door to freedom. The rest of the Workbook (Lessons 171-365) can be seen as emphasizing that the holy instant is actually right at hand at any moment. The student is most directly invited to see this in Lesson 182:

> "I will be still an instant and go home."(W,182)

Prior to that lesson, there is a gradually building preparation for this lesson. After it, the lessons emphasize underpinning and deepening the mind's understanding of what the holy instant entails. Indeed, the final lessons, 361-365, are identical in the focus:

> "This holy instant would I give to You. Be you in charge. For I would follow You, certain that Your direction gives me peace." (W,361-365)

Thus, if the student has diligently practiced all the lessons, he/she concludes the practices with the affirmation of this most important realization. Even if the holy instant has not yet fully opened in awareness, the mind is disposed to letting it be guided through whatever further steps it must take for that to happen.

The Course gives a concise description of what occurs in the holy instant as follows:

> "1 I stand within the holy instant, as clear as you would have me. 2 And the extent to which you learn to accept me is the measure of the time in which the holy instant will be yours." (25,IV,5,1-2)

From this, since the 'I' referred to is best understood as Jesus as fully identified with the Christ Mind/Holy Spirit, we can conclude that what the separated mind encounters or realizes in the holy instant, at least to some extent, is the Christ Mind itself. This is not an acceptance of some other mind that is separate from it. Rather, it is a recognition that what had been experienced as one's own mind in separation is now experienced as one with or identical with the Christ Mind/Holy Spirit. Or, stated slightly differently, it experiences that it *is* Christ. Of course, initially that experience is somewhat qualified and blurred, but as the experience matures the mind realizes more and more that in its deepest reality it is Christ, the Son of God. This seems to be the fuller meaning of the following:

> "1 The holy instant is truly the time of Christ."(15,X,2,1)

This may at first seem to be perplexing if one reflects on it critically. That is, the holy instant, as we have seen, is strictly speaking completely outside time. However, this passage says it is a kind of time, 'the time of Christ.' This may be understood in the following way. Although the holy instant is a mode of awareness outside time, viewed from a mind still within time, such as one returning to the time-mode of awareness, it would be thought of as a period in which the separated mind is one with Christ. That period would have a duration, judged within the time-framework, as long as the separated mind was 'away' from usual time-awareness. From that perspective, it would be viewed as the 'time of Christ' or the period of time in which Christ is manifested in such a mind. For most separated minds, the process of full realization is a series of such 'times of Christ,' each of them not yet fully matured and lasting only a limited time, even though it induces profound changes in those minds after they return to the temporal mode (after stepping out of the holy instant). In the maturing mind, these times of Christ become deeper and longer, until at last they come to the fully enduring experience of the holy instant. In the Course's view, this fully enduring time of Christ is what happened in the individual mind of Jesus. In that sense, it is fully appropriate to refer to him as 'Jesus the Christ,' which is perhaps the correct meaning of the commonly used expression 'Jesus Christ.'

A final consideration that may help us better understand this process of entering into the holy instant, which opens the separated mind to perfect love, will focus on several passages in the Workbook. The first is:

> "1 Release the future. 2 For the past is gone, and what is present, freed from its bequest of grief and misery, of pain and loss, becomes the instant in which time escapes the bondage of illusions where it runs its pitiless, inevitable course. 3 Then is each instant which was slave to time transformed into a holy instant, when the light that was kept hidden in God's Son

is freed to bless the world."(W,194,5,1-3)

This particular exercise comes after many days of preparatory practices. In it, the student confronts a fundamental obstacle: his attachment to the time-mode. The practice here focuses on guiding her/him to come to two realizations: 1) of how that attachment is the source of its difficulties, and 2) of how letting go of that attachment allows a completely different meaning to emerge regarding each moment: that it is a holy instant. Of course, this is only preparatory, although a major preparatory step, which readies the mind to anticipate what will come when the holy instant is entered.

The second passage is the one cited on p. 320 (W,361-365), which is the focus of the last five lessons of the Workbook. These are the primary words of the practice and are the focus of a longer period of contemplation at the beginning and the end of each day. They are also to be used to help focus the mind on the Presence of God and open it to the guidance of the Holy Spirit at the beginning of each waking hour. This practice is not a matter of simply reading, but a meditative recitation that gives the mind a focus on thoughts and feelings so as to bring one's whole being into that Presence. In this particular practice, repeated for the five concluding days of the year of practices, we can see how it is geared to make use of words that, if taken seriously, can bring the mind to the realization of the holy instant. Of course, the words are not themselves all that important, nor are they even necessary. What is important is the mind's discovering that 'little willingness,' which when fully realized is all that is necessary for the Holy Spirit to enable Him to do His work. As was explained, the core of His work is to facilitate the full experiencing of the holy instant, which is nicely summarized:

> "5 The holy instant thus becomes a lesson in how to hold all of your brothers in your mind, experiencing not loss but completion. 6 From this it follows you can only give. 7 And this *is* love, for this alone is natural under the laws of God."
> (15,VI,5,5-7)

Once this is fully realized, the individual's full achievement of the Atonement occurs with no further difficulties.

I may also point out that these six insights can be seen as correlating to the central realizations that are central to what has been called 'the mystic way' by some scholars of mysticism. The insights 1-3 are the focus of the 'way of purification or purgation;' insights 4 and 5, of the 'way of illumination;' and insight 6, of what is called 'the way of union,' 'the unitive life,' or the 'spiritual marriage.'[84]

D. The process of returning to Love: Atonement. We may conclude our discussion by pointing out how the overall intention of the Course is toward what it calls the Atonement. The process of Atonement is described summarily:

> "6 Fear arises from lack of love.

---

[84] See E. Underhilll's *Mysticism*, esp. Part Two, Ch. III, Ch. IV, and Ch. X.

> 7 The only remedy for lack of love is perfect love.
> 8 Perfect love is the Atonement."(2,VI,7,6-8)

That is, the separated mind is caught in the web of fear, which is the state that arises when one does not have the awareness of Love's presence. This faulty awareness can be corrected only by realizing perfect love. When that is completely realized, the process of Atonement is completed, whose final stage is the realization of or return to the eternal state of Heaven.

That process involves four major stages or states of the separated mind:
  I. complete separation and the formation of illusory love
  II. the opening to imperfect love
  III. the realization of perfect love in the world of perception, the central feature of which is the perception of the Real World and maturing of the holy relationship
  IV. the full realization of Love, or Heaven

As we have seen, the third stage is best thought of as a continuous development, involving many 'jumps' or 'leaps' that are greatly aided by the experience of the holy instant, each one deeper than the previous one. We also saw how that third stage may be divided into three sub-stages:
  a. the initial stage, involving holy instants of limited duration
  b. the intermediate stage, involving a more or less stable move between the holy instant and the temporal mode, but focused on the maturation of the holy relationship
  c. the mature stage, which culminates in the stable and enduring experience of the holy instant even while in the temporal order

However, stage IV involves the final dropping of even the perception of the Real World, which still has some limitations intrinsic to perception, and the complete return to Heaven. The Course makes clear that the perception of the Real World, however beautiful and 'heavenly' it may be, is not the final state for the separated mind in the process of the Atonement. As it states:

> "2 Christ's Love for you is His Love for His Father, which He knows because He knows His Father's Love for Him. 3 When the Holy Spirit has at last led you to Christ at the altar to His Father, perception fuses into knowledge because perception has become so holy that its transfer to holiness is merely its natural extension. 4 Love transfers to love without any interference, for the two are one."(12,VI,6,2-4)

That is, the full experience of the Real World is the last stage prior to the mind's complete letting go of the inherently divisive mode of awareness that is perception. From that most complete perception possible it passes to the completely undivided mode of knowing. This is the recovery of the state of Heaven, in which Love is fully present and flowing through the mind and given to all other perfect minds. Not only is its awareness without any limitations, but it is also restored to the unlimited extending of Love in the act of creating. Since in that state there is no trace of division, all minds that were formerly thought of as separate from itself are completely one. That is, it and they are the one Mind of Christ and in full realization of their true Identity as the Son of God. All time is completely set aside in the timeless experience of the Eternal Instant, which includes the infinite increasing Joy that we spoke of in our discussion of Love.

As for the duration of the experience of the Real World, the Course points out:

> "2 Perception will be meaningless when it has been perfected, for everything that has been used for learning will have no function. 3 Nothing will ever change; no shifts nor shadings, no differences, no variations that made perception possible will still occur. 4 The perception of the real world will be so short that you will barely have time to thank God for it. 5 For God will take the last step swiftly, when you have reached the real world and have been made ready for Him."(17,II,4,2-5)

That is, although the full perception of the Real World is the apex of what one can be aware of within the mode of perception, it is still short of the most complete awareness of knowing. Once it has been realized, it has no further purpose other than as a stepping-stone to what is beyond it. No further lessons involving the removal of obstacles to Love's awareness are needed. Since it has no further purpose, the Real World is quickly dissolved or transformed into the higher mode of unobstructed knowing/creating. This is the state of non-perceptual knowledge of Reality as infinite Love expressing in the relationship between all perfect minds, including both unlimited giving involved in creating, boundless Peace, and infinitely increasing Joy.

From the perspective of a mind still in separation, the process seems to take a very long time. However, in the Course's view, from the perspective of any perfect mind, this whole 'process' is already completed even in this present moment, since such a mind does not really exist in time (or space) at all.

Epilogue

I offer a few comments retrospectively regarding what has been discussed in the preceding pages.

The first is that the primary intent of all that has been said is to propose a way of clarifying the ambiguities in the Course that often puzzle its students and almost certainly call for great effort on the part of scholars to try to disentangle. It has been my concern to offer clear definitions of the principal terms and to show the various meanings that they seem to have in various contexts. Hopefully, this will make the efforts of students and scholars less taxing and permit them to recognize and better understand the central insights of its teachings.

The second is that I have sought to show that some of the instances where the Course seems to assert conflicting, even contradictory, ideas, can be understood as quite consistent and coherent. Related to this, I should point out that it is very easy to find 'inconsistencies' in the wording of the Course material. This is probably true for every writing, including the Bible and all other scriptures, that has issued from the human mind (the only exception perhaps being those by logicians, who take it as their major concern to avoid contradicting themselves). However, there is a widely accepted principle in philosophical discourse, known as the 'principle of charity,' that obligates any serious discussant to give a writer or a speaker the 'best possible interpretation' of what is articulated in words, rather than to 'nitpick' on particular formulations, which is more a sign of immature sophistry than a serious commitment to discovering truth. However, this does not mean that unresolvable inconsistencies within a view are to be ignored. Indeed, as many have pointed out regarding the Bible, there seem to be very serious contradictions within it that cannot be escaped without some sort of logical 'violence.' However that may be, with the Course I think the view I've offered does resolve the serious apparent inconsistencies that I've discussed. (Whether the rest of its 'inconsistencies' can be resolved is still to be determined by serious inquiry.)

Also related to how what is offered here resolves some of those apparent inconsistencies, I should make it clear that some, if not all, of my clarifications involve interpretations and further developments of the Course's explicit teachings. This is particularly the case for the views proposed regarding the 'one Son - many Sons' problem, the infinite sequence of created perfect minds ($Sons_n$), the identity of the Christ Mind and the Holy Spirit, the view that miracles can be given only once by a particular MG to a particular MR, and what is referred to by the Course as the 'spark,' the 'Great Rays,' the 'golden light,' and the 'Great Light.' While my explanations have sought to show that the teachings are logically consistent and coherent, there may well be alternative interpretations that do so as well or even better. The Course itself recognizes the importance of such consistency, as is expressed in:

> "1 We are not inconsistent in the thoughts that we present in our curriculum. 2 Truth must be true throughout, if it be true. 3 It cannot contradict itself, nor be in parts uncertain and in others sure."(W,156,2,1-3)

That is, the Course insists that its own insights are fundamentally logically consistent, so that any interpretation is bound by the requirement of not containing any contradictions. While it is quite possible that interpretations differing from what is presented here may also fulfill that requirement, I am at this time not aware of any such alternatives.

Thus, what has been proposed here may serve as an example of how the teachings may be understood as having a great coherence. If alternative interpretations can be found by others, particularly ones that correct any misunderstandings that I may have slipped into unawares, they will be most welcome to the dialogue that focuses on understanding the truth that may be contained within its teachings, as well as to disclose any errors my interpretations may contain. Of course, they are obligated to conform to the Course's own requirement of logical consistency.

Indeed, I believe that further sincere and careful dialogue is quite likely to disclose even deeper insights into the Course's teachings. Even if one doubts the claims about its authorship from Jesus, the document stands as a remarkable intellectual and spiritual edifice that may give valuable suggestions regarding how what we encounter in ordinary and extraordinary experience may be understood. In this there may be a framework for a deeper understanding in many fields of inquiry, from cosmology and physics to psychology, sociology, and comparative religion. Especially for the latter, the Course, as I have indicated in several places, may provide important conceptualizations in relation to the phenomena that are the focus of psychical research, most particularly those of mystical experience.

Related to the last point, although I have taken many opportunities to point out the similarities between the Course's teachings and those of the other great spiritual and religious teachings of humanity, it is also important to be clear how its teachings differ from those others. Indeed, I have written a short essay, *The Five Principal World-views and A Course in Miracles*, to that effect, which will be published as a separate booklet. It is my hope that others will pursue this comparative approach so as to facilitate a better understanding of what is distinctive about the Course's teachings.

A fourth area of comment is that the recent controversy and conflicts over the various versions of the Course that have arisen among students of the Course do not at all seem to be necessary. They are reminiscent of the sectarian conflicts in the early periods of Christianity, Hinduism, Buddhism, and Islam, which unfortunately continue to this day. Differences of understanding can generate valuable dialogue that brings better understanding of the original teachings. However, it is quite incongruous that they lead to any sort of violence. That violence can take many forms, from subtler attitudes of disrespect or even contempt for those who differ from one's own view, to verbal expression of those feelings, to actions of attacking others by way of deception and violation of society's laws, followed by intense acrimony toward the brothers who thereby have become regarded as adversaries or enemies. It can even express in physical attack, such as occurred in early Christianity up to fairly recent times. The latter seems quite incongruous with the teachings of the New Testament. Fortunately, it has not occurred among brothers who are students of the Course, although some of the other sorts of violence have been observed.

I am personally of the opinion that there is no serious conflict among the various versions of the Course and that each of them offers important insights not emphasized in, perhaps even not included in, the others. That is, they seem best thought of as *complementing*, rather than opposing one another. Of course, it remains an important work for those of a scholarly bent of mind to examine carefully all the versions, note their differences and discern in what ways they might indeed be incompatible, or whether those apparent incompatibilities can be resolved. One such point of dispute focuses on the terms 'Holy Spirit' and 'spiritual eye' (the latter being absent from FIP), which will be considered closely in the next-planned book.

My fifth, and perhaps most important, comment is that what I have presented is by no means intended to be a substitute for the original teachings themselves. I stand in awe of the immensity and profundity of what seems to me to be one of the greatest pieces of spiritual literature ever to have been written. No intellectual, philosophical, or theological commentary can possibly match it as a symbolic matrix for promoting inner realization. Thus, my hope is that the present inquiry will help the earnest seeker to approach the profundity of the inner life that moves within its words. For that, one can only go to the original writings.

In closing, if this effort helps a few people come to a better understanding of the Course, it will have been worth the effort of publishing it. Even if it had not come to that stage, the study, meditation, and reflection that went into its writing have served me well in my own personal search for Truth. May it also so serve the reader.

Appendix 1: The Separated Mind's Idea of God

'God' as a projection of the ego-idea. The Course is quite clear that much of what we think of as 'God' is fundamentally a projection of the ego-dominated mind itself. That is, it echoes thinkers like Feuerbach, who proposed that God is made in the image and likeness of man, rather than the reverse that is found in Genesis I.[1] This was already recognized by some ancient thinkers such as Xenophanes, who observed: "Yes, and if oxen and horses or lions had hands, and could paint with their hands, and produce works of art as men do, horses would paint the forms of the gods like horses, and oxen like oxen, and make their bodies in the image of their several kinds."[2]

In the Course's view, separated minds, because they arise from the self-imposition of limits upon the unlimited perfect mind of the Son, place themselves in a situation where their creating impulse is also limited. The general term for that is referred to as 'making.' This is summarized:

> "5 Fear and love make or create, depending on whether the ego or the Holy Spirit begets or inspires them, but they *will* return to the mind of the thinker and they will affect his total perception. 6 That includes his concept of God, of His creations and of his own. 7 He will not appreciate any of Them if he regards Them fearfully."(7,VI,1,5-7)

Although there are many secondary types of 'making,' the primary type is the formation of the various limited mental forms, first that of its own 'ego,' but then the ideas and concepts foundational to the separated mind's operations. As this passage points out, the ego-idea is the basis for further ideas. Statement 6 makes explicit that these limiting ideas are also imposed on what it thinks of as God and what it calls 'reality.'

The effect of this is that our ideas of God are often projections of our own minds, as is the point in:

> "1 The projection of the ego makes it appear as if God's Will is outside yourself, and therefore not yours. 2 In this interpretation it seems possible for God's Will and yours to conflict. 3 God, then, may seem to demand of you what you do not want to give, and thus deprive you of what you want."(11,I,9,1-3)

That is, what is contained in the ego-idea is imposed upon what one thinks of as God. In this particular passage, since the ego contains within it a notion of will,

---

[1] *Lectures on the Essence of Religion*, Lecture XX.

[2] Xenophanes of Colophon, Fragment 15, in *Ancilla to the Presocratic Philosophers*.

which is one of limited productive impulse, God is also thought of as having a will. Further, God's Will is thought to be much more powerful than one's own, since it is deemed to be responsible for the production not only of oneself but of all other selves as well as the whole world the mind finds itself in. Being a great Will, the separated mind thinks of that Will as in some ways in opposition to one's own (of course, it also thinks of any wills present in any other separated minds as having this opposition of will). This is based on the ego-dominated mind's own formation of 'opposition' and perhaps the origin of the notion of 'negation' that arises from its choice to be aware of only a portion of Reality. However, if the notion of 'will' is more accurately applied to the Reality of God, the Course calls for an important correction to this more limited idea of 'will:' there neither is, nor can be, any opposition in God's Will itself.

The traditional Christian view, particularly its ideas based on the descriptions of what are thought to be certain human interactions with God that are clouded by ego, is strongly dominated by this notion of God as the most powerful 'Ego.' Indeed, that is one interpretation of the ancient Hebrew word said to be God's name, 'Jahweh,' which translates as 'I am Who am' or 'I am the One Who is' or 'I am what I will be.' If one accepts that the Bible accurately describes how God has interacted with people, He seems to have many of the characteristics that belong to the separated mind's ego. We will discuss these later.

However, the Course is very clear that to think of God in such terms involves a major distortion. Indeed, it holds that acceptance of such a deity is actually a type of idolatry. As it states:

> "1 The ego is idolatry; the sign of limited and separated self, born in a body, doomed to suffer and to end its life in death. 2 It is the 'will' that sees the Will of God as enemy, and takes a form in which it is denied. 3 The ego is the 'proof' that strength is weak and love is fearful, life is really death, and what opposes God alone is true."(W,pII,12,1,1-3)

That is, the separated mind takes a limited idea, which is its own production, and then imposes it upon what it thinks of as the ultimate Being. In so doing, it actually forms for itself an image in its own likeness. Because the ego-dominated mind considers the ego to be the most important form having its highest value, this places that form, along with the 'God' that it holds also has that form, in the forefront of what it thinks of as 'religion.' This projected idea of God thus makes its religion a matter of idol-worship or idolatry. Since the ego-idea involves several serious inconsistencies, the projecting of it onto God also makes 'God' a self-contradictory notion.

The Course also points out that this is a situation that the separated mind has set up for itself. Its choice of separation has led it to invent an idea of the 'supremely holy' which is actually unwhole, insane, or sick:

> "3 All forms of idolatry are caricatures of creation, taught by sick minds too divided to know that creation shares power and never usurps it. 4 Sickness is idolatry, because it is the

belief that power can be taken from you. 5 Yet this is impossible, because you are part of God, Who is all power. 6 A sick god must be an idol, made in the image of what its maker thinks he is. 7 And that is exactly what the ego does perceive in a Son of God; a sick god, self-created, self-sufficient, very vicious and very vulnerable. 8 Is this the idol you would worship? 9 Is this the image you would be vigilant to save?" (10,III,4,3-9)

In this we may recognize the important insight that the act that leads to separation involves dividing or partitioning Reality and taking that partitioned structure to be what is actually real. In doing so, it has generated for itself a condition of illness, fragmentation, unholiness, or insanity. Ironically, although coherent with that choice, it formulates for itself the notion of a 'God' who is itself divided from the rest of Reality, one who is also sick or insane.

Attributes projected onto God. Several passages make quite clear that the separated, ego-dominated mind has constructed for itself its own idea of 'God' and included in that idea several basic characteristics of itself. The first of these is described:

"3 To the ego, the *ego* is God ..."(13,II,6,3)

Thus, in line with what has already been pointed out, the most fundamental attribute of this idea of God is that *He is an ego*. Since the ego is an idea that involves at its root the imposition of limits which make it different and separate from other beings, God as 'Ego' must be different from other beings and also separate from them. This may be seen in traditional theological views where the 'place of God' in the 'Holy of Holies' of the temple supports the ego-concern of being separate. This seems to be the basis of the contrast of the 'holy' or 'sacred' from the 'profane.'[3] It is also the basis for attributing to certain people (priests and saints) a greater value, to certain places (temples and churches) a greater 'holiness,' and to certain actions (religious rituals, including sacrifice) as more important than others. Indeed, the 'religious' life so understood is one of separation and division, as opposed to union and wholeness, which are the true characteristics of both God and holiness.

The reason for the imposition of these 'unwhole' ideas on God is given:

---

[3] This is the core idea of the 'sacred' as presented by Mircea Eliade in *The Sacred and the Profane* and to some extent by Rudolf Otto in his *The Idea of the Holy*. These give what seems to be an accurate assessment of the traditional Biblical 'idea of the holy' as that which is 'completely Other' (in German, 'ganz Andere') or separate. The Course holds that this is only an illusory ego-generated idea, actually one that is as self-contradictory as the ego-idea itself. However, the Course does hold that there is indeed a much deeper sense of 'completely other' that is indeed the core of holiness; this holds that what is truly holy is completely other than what is found within the field of the separated mind's perception.

> "1 The ego is the part of the mind that believes in division."
> (5,V,3,1)

and:

> "2 The ego always seeks to divide and separate."(7,IV,5,2)

Thus, if God is the 'Great Ego,' He must necessarily divide and separate Himself from all other things. Indeed, the traditional Christian view often takes God as the 'great separator' or 'great divider,' both in the act of creating the world,[4] in imposing separating/dividing demands on people, and in the judgment that comes to them upon the completion of their lives on earth.

The deeper level of this projected illusion upon God is pointed out in the following:

> "1 While we have recognized that the ego's plan for salvation is the opposite of God's, we have not yet emphasized that it is an active attack on His plan, and a deliberate attempt to destroy it. 2 In the attack, God is assigned the attributes which are actually associated with the ego, while the ego appears to take on the attributes of God....
>
> "1 The ego's fundamental wish is to replace God. 2 In fact, the ego is the physical embodiment of that wish."
> (W,72,1,1-2;2,1-2)

That is, the mind attached to the ego, by its very commitment to separation, must form a means to uphold that commitment. Hence, it constructs a view of how it is to be 'saved' from its own self-contradictoriness by constructing this idea of God, who is viewed as at once being the primary Great Opposer of one's own will and the one who will mysteriously undo that opposition. Of course, the deeper basis for this invented idea of God is to replace the Reality that is God.

In line with the basic idea of the ego as the most important object within its awareness, it also projects onto God its own concern for recognizing *His own supreme importance*:

> "1 The Bible repeatedly states that you should praise God. 2 This hardly means that you should tell Him how wonderful He is. 3 He has no ego with which to accept such praise, and no perception with which to judge it."(4,VII,6,1-3)

Again, we may see this aberration as central to much of what is thought to be the major concern of traditional Christian (as well other religious traditions): the offering of 'praise' to God, understood as adulation and admiration of and submission to the 'Great Ego' who is voraciously hungry for and in need of the worship of lesser beings. Some scholars have compared this to the demands made by the most powerful people in ancient societies (i.e., the Hebrew Jahweh being like a

---

[4] "And God saw the light, that it was good; and God divided the light from the darkness."(Genesis, I:4) That is, one reading of this is that God is said to have intentionally produced separation/division as part of his very first creative act.

tribal sheikh or chief). However, the Course sees this as more deeply a symptom of the ego–dominated mind, which craves for its own worship and praise. Although the Course does not reject the importance of what it calls 'genuine praise' of God, that is a matter of something totally different from groveling admiration of a 'little' ego before a 'bigger' Ego.

The absurdity of this ego-projected idea of 'God' leads the Course to a view that would be quite sympathetic to atheists and agnostics. Thus, it states:

> "1 Bringing the ego to God is but to bring error to truth, where it stands corrected because it is the opposite of what it meets. 2 It is undone because the contradiction can no longer stand. 3 How long can contradiction stand when its impossible nature is clearly revealed?"(14,IX,2,1-3)

Long has it been pointed out that such a notion of God is fundamentally inconsistent, so that no person having clear rationality would believe in it. That is, as we saw earlier, the idea of ego itself involves numerous contradictions, although they are overlooked by the ego-committed minds even of the atheist or agnostic. Thus did Nietzsche proclaim, after examining the traditional idea of God: "God is dead."[5] This logically follows for any idea of God based on 'ego,' since death is intrinsically a part of the meaning of that idea. Of course, it does not follow that this is the only legitimate idea of God, and the Course is clear that there is an alternative, such as was described in Ch. II.

There is also an interesting observation regarding the reason that so many accept this contradictory idea of God:

> "3 Loudly the ego tells you not to look inward, for if you do your eyes will light on sin, and God will strike you blind. 4 This you believe, and so you do not look. 5 Yet this is not the ego's hidden fear, nor yours who serve it. 6 Loudly indeed the ego claims it is; too loudly and too often."(21,IV,2,3-6)

That is, as part of its scheme to keep itself within the ego-framework, the separated mind imposes on itself a requirement that it must not look too closely at its idea of God. It uses many ploys to do this: "If you question it, God will strike you blind or dead; so you must have unquestioning 'faith.'" Or, "The idea of God is beyond human grasp, and thus seems to involve inconsistencies; but these are not really inconsistencies, but only 'mysteries' that are beyond reason and its grasp." The Course has a very different response: "Yes, the idea is only a thought-construction based on the projection of one's own ego, and if one remains with reason and patiently examines it, there is another very different idea of God that is both consistent and far more satisfying."

One of the most widely accepted ideas of God, particularly in Western religions, is that *He is the Creator of the universe of material things in space and time*. The Bible begins with what is said to be a description of the six days, peri-

---

[5] F. Nietzsche, *The Gay Science*, Section 125.

ods, or phases of His creative action, and throughout much of the Old and New Testaments one finds descriptions of what are said to be His communications and interactions with human beings, particularly with the small group that identified themselves as members of the Hebrew or Jewish society. The Course is very clear that much of what is attributed to God is simply further aspects of the ego-idea that separated minds have generated for themselves. It also points out that if God is the unlimited Creator whose essential nature is Love, it is impossible for Him to create anything limited, since that would involve His both loving and not loving what He created, clearly a contradiction.

Among the features said to be of God's creative action is that *He intentionally created the human body*. The Course observes:

> "1 To this carefully prepared arena, where angry animals seek for prey and mercy cannot enter, the ego comes to save you. 2 God made you a body. 3 Very well. 4 Let us accept this and be glad. 5 As a body, do not let yourself be deprived of what the body offers. 6 Take the little you can get. 7 God gave you nothing. 8 The body is your only savior. 9 It is the death of God and your salvation."(W,72,6,1-9)

The body, in the Course's view, is the concrete form of limitation that the separated mind thinks itself to have. By placing responsibility for that in God, it is actually shifting the causal basis of the body onto something that it considers beyond its feeble power. However, in this move it elevates the actual basis, the ego, to the position of the highest power. The book of Genesis is usually interpreted as saying that the body was originally made immortal, since eventually God tells Adam that he will die if he eats of the tree of knowledge of good and evil. However, this can also be explained as saying that this projection of the separated mind is simply clarifying the full ramification of what it means to have a body, i.e., death is a necessary effect of being in the bodily state of having spatial and temporal limits. In any case, since the body is thought to be the primary vehicle that allows the separated mind to exist, that mind concludes that it must hold onto the body, and thus that it is necessary for its 'salvation.' In this passage, of course, all that is intended is to make clear what acceptance of the ego-idea involves. While the concern of Genesis is primarily to offer human beings an explanation for their situation, the principle that bodily existence entails eventual death holds for all things in the physical world.

The Course is quite clear on what is the actual origin of the world:

> "1 The ego made the world as it perceives it, but the Holy Spirit, the reinterpreter of what the ego made, sees the world as a teaching device for bringing you home."(5,III,11,1)

That is, rather than indulging the student with his long-held inclination to shift responsibility for the world he perceives onto some imaginary deity, who is only a blown-up version of his own ego, it simply dismisses that as an illusion. From that perspective, the mind can come to recognize that what it has itself made (jointly with all other ego-dominated minds) can be understood very differently.

Even the 'heaven' that is usually thought to be a part of that world is only another ego-illusion.[6] Thus understood, the meaning of that world takes on an entirely different meaning: it is the arena for teaching the separated mind how to undo all of its illusions, including the illusion that it thinks is God, the illusion that it thinks is the world, and the illusion that it thinks is itself.

Closely related to the necessity of death of anything bodily, the Genesis account is usually understood as saying that God is the one who inflicts death upon living things:

> "4 For as long as you feel guilty you are listening to the voice of the ego, which tells you that you have been treacherous to God and therefore deserve death. 5 You will think that death comes from God and not from the ego because, by confusing yourself with the ego, you believe that you want death."
> (12,VII,14,4-5)

Of course, if God is a 'Great Ego,' it follows from this that death comes from Him. The Genesis story seems to say that because Adam and Eve disobeyed God, upon learning this *He felt offended and judged them guilty, then sentenced them and all their descendants to die, along with all sorts of suffering.* However, the Course is very clear that God, being Love, is utterly incapable of anger, judgment of sinfulness, or willing pain or death for anyone. Again, the 'God' described in this interpretation of Genesis is only a projected ego-image, an illusory fantasy of the guilt-ridden ego-dominated mind. This would be inconsistent with God's being Love.

Genesis also lends itself to thinking of *God as an arrogant entity*, indeed, the most arrogant of all entities. Again, the Course makes clear that such a notion is simply the exaggeration of the projected ego-idea. As it points out:

> "9 Correction is of God, Who does not know of arrogance."
> (9,III,7,9)

Since arrogance is the symptom of a mind that holds its ego is vastly superior to others, the separated mind is inclined to think of God as the 'Supreme Ego.' Indeed, throughout the Old Testament, one finds many stories where God supposedly demanded that He be given the highest adulation, even that there were places where He was thought to be present as very special 'holy' ground, and that those who are His worshipers have access to the privileges of being very special or 'chosen' people. But, the Course again gently dismisses all of this as mere projection of the ego-dominated imagination. In this we may recognize the ego's belief in specialness as what is projected onto the idol it thinks is 'God.' In contrast, what is actually the case:

> "3 You are alike to God as God is to Himself. 4 He is not spe-

---

[6] In that view, 'heaven' is imagined as a realm in which the ego can continue with other egos, including the 'Great Ego' it thinks as God, and is simply a variation of bodily existence.

cial, for He would not keep one part of what He is unto Himself, not given to His Son but kept for Him alone."(24,II,10,3)

We saw in our discussion of 'specialness' how this quality is merely a further elaboration of the ego-notion itself, holding that there is something within it not present in anything else. Thus, if God is thought of as special, He is thought of as having within Himself a vast array of 'things' that He has not shared. This is usually construed as the basis of His great superiority and power. However, the Course makes clear that any failure to share all that He is would amount to His failing to love fully, which would actually be not to love at all.

Related to this belief in incomplete sharing, the Course points out that one of the important ideas generated by the ego is the belief in sacrifice. This idea is found almost universally among religions, whether the shamanistic practices of sacrificing fruits, animals, or even human beings, the Hindu rituals of the fire-ceremony and other symbolic sacrificial offerings, the popular Taoist and Confucian practices of offering sacrifices to ancestors, the Hebrew and modern Jewish ritual of sacrificing the Seder lamb, or the widely accepted interpretation of the Christian ritual of the Eucharist. It is even in the secular belief in sacrificing portions of one's wealth for the benefit of society or of one's life in defending it. This notion that *God demands sacrifice* is perhaps most thoroughly worked out in the Christian theological doctrine that God demanded the sacrifice of His own Son in order to compensate for the 'real' sins of human beings.

However, the Course is quite clear that this idea has nothing whatsoever to do with what God is really about:

"1 Sacrifice is a notion totally unknown to God."(3,I,4,1)

This stems from the fact that God has no awareness whatsoever of lack in anyone or anything that really exists, nor any idea of the deficiency the separated mind thinks of as 'sin' and its accompanying idea of guilt. Nevertheless, because the separated mind is caught within the confines of its own self-generated idea of ego, it thinks that sacrifice is important for it and projects onto God the notion that He demands it.

The mischief of this idea is described in the following:

"1 Do not underestimate the power of the devotion of God's Son, nor the power the god he worships has over him. 2 For he places himself at the altar of his god, whether it be the god he made or the God Who created him. 3 That is why his slavery is as complete as his freedom, for he will obey only the god he accepts. 4 The god of crucifixion demands that he crucify, and his worshipers obey. 5 In his name they crucify themselves, believing that the power of the Son of God is born of sacrifice and pain. 6 The God of resurrection demands nothing, for He does not will to take away." (11,VI,5,1-6)

That is, although within its depths the separated mind has the choice of affirming either the idea of the 'Ego-God' or the actual Truth of Who and What God really is, by choosing separation it enters into the framework of the former. This amounts to an enslavement to its own self-constructed idol, and exacts from it a mode of existing filled with suffering. Prototypical of that mode is the requirement to be crucified, because it thinks its idol demands that it undergo suffering. In fact, since God by His real nature has everything that really can be had, there is in Him no basis whatsoever for demanding anything. The only demand, whether of obedience, sacrifice, or any sort of punishment including death is what that mind's own construction, the ego, imposes upon itself and projects upon its idea of God.

One result of this distorted idea of God is that He is thought of as a Being who needs to be distanced from that mind. As is pointed out:

> "4 For if God would demand total sacrifice of you, it seems safer to project Him outward and away from you, and not be host to Him. 5 To Him you ascribed the ego's treachery, inviting it to take His place to protect you from Him. 6 And you do not recognize that it is what you invited in that would destroy you, and does demand total sacrifice of you. 7 No partial sacrifice will appease this savage guest, for it is an invader who but seems to offer kindness, but always to make the sacrifice complete."(15,X,1,4-7)

That is, if God calls for the pain and suffering that is essential to sacrifice, he is certainly not someone that the separated mind would like to be near. Ironically, the belief in such a mind sets it up for both needing to appease that deity, since it is thought to be the condition necessary for its own continuation, and also to avoid him since he imposes the limits of sacrifice and eventually death or cessation. That is, being a projection of the contradictory idea of 'ego,' this 'God' is the centerpiece of a completely self-contradictory 'religion.' In the Course's words, it is utterly insane.

On the contrary, it is made quite clear that such a notion must be completely abandoned:

> "6 The memory of God must be denied if any sacrifice is asked of anyone."(26,I,4,6)

The simple reason for this is that acceptance of such an idea of God, an image that is an idol, actually blocks the mind's awareness of Him as He really is. The situation for such a mind is that it is imprisoned in its own thought-construction:

> "2 It is not your will to be imprisoned because your will is free. 3 That is why the ego is the denial of free will. 4 It is never God Who coerces you, because He shares His Will with you."(8,II,32-4)

That is, although one's will is entirely free to choose either the complete awareness of knowing or the highly restricted awareness of perception, in making the latter choice it actually negates its own infinitely greater freedom in favor of an extremely limited illusion of freedom. But, far from imposing anything on that mind, God only offers it the possibility of choosing once again, without any coercion. Indeed, all coercion is only a construction of the mind that chooses to embed itself in ego.

Closely related to the idea that one must distance himself from God is the same primary feeling arising from acceptance of one's own ego: fear.

> "1 How fearful, then, has God become to you, and how great a sacrifice do you believe His Love demands! 2 For total love would demand total sacrifice. 3 And so the ego seems to demand less of you than God, and of the two is judged as the lesser of two evils, one to be feared a little, perhaps, but the other to be destroyed."(15,X,7,1-3)

This passage clearly points out how the belief that God demands sacrifice unavoidably entails that *He is to be feared*. Indeed, because such a deity demands total sacrifice, the separated mind in its own self-interest considers it far better to hold onto its own ego-dominated condition. The reason: such a deity is a 'god of death,' and the mind's deeper impulse to life insists that even the paltry sort of life it has is better than submission to what would actually be more accurately called a 'God of Darkness.'

The basic root of the fearfulness of God lies in the very nature of the ego's belief in specialness:

> "1 The fear of God and of your brother comes from each unrecognized belief in specialness. 2 For you demand your brother bow to it against his will. 3 And God Himself must honor it or suffer vengeance."(24,I,8,1-3)

When one reflects upon what the Course indicates is the nature of the ego, i.e., an idea that sets off one part of Reality from the rest and endows it with great importance or specialness, it becomes clear why this projected idea of God would entail fear. That is, although the mind has through its attachment to the ego-idea arbitrarily held onto a small portion of Reality, the far greater portion calls to it so as to allow its complete satisfaction. But, to come to that, it must let go of the ego-idea. Thus, it interprets that call as something that jeopardizes or threatens its current condition, and so feels fear of it.

The fearfulness projected onto God is closely connected with four other offshoots of the ego-idea. One of these is described:

> "8 If the ego is the symbol of the separation, it is also the symbol of guilt. 9 Guilt is more than merely not of God. 10 It is the symbol of attack on God. 11 This is a totally meaningless concept except to the ego, but do not underestimate the power of the ego's belief in it. 12 This is the belief from which all guilt really stems."(5,V,2,8-12)

Here it is made fully clear that guilt is only a consequence of the belief in ego, having nothing whatsoever to do with what God actually is. In holding that *God is the basis of guilt*, the mind has merely projected this aspect onto its idea of deity, something that is completely unconnected with what God actually is.

Similarly, the notion that *God punishes* is only another projected aspect of the ego-belief:

> "6 The ego believes that by punishing itself it will mitigate the punishment of God. 7 Yet even in this it is arrogant. 8 It attributes to God a punishing intent, and then takes this intent as its own prerogative."(5,V,5,6-8)

Thus, in believing that God has any intent or even any idea of punishing, the mind again projects onto God what is only an aspect of its own ego-idea.

Closely related to the view that God thinks of anyone as guilty or punishes anyone is the ego-based idea that *God condemns or judges* anyone:

> "1 You need not fear the Higher Court will condemn you. 2 It will merely dismiss the case against you."(5,VI,10,1-2)

The 'Higher Court' alludes to what is thought of as God's concern for judging anyone in terms of having disobeyed His 'commandments' or violated what is thought to be His 'Will.' This is possible only for a mind that perceives itself as somehow lacking or imperfect, which is totally beyond God's awareness. Thus, any belief that God condemns is merely a projection of one's ego-idea.

Similarly, the ego-based belief that *God intends suffering for any of His creatures* is firmly rejected by the Course:

> "5 God wills no one suffer. 6 He does not will anyone to suffer for a wrong decision, including you."(8,III,7,4-5)

As was pointed out earlier, since God is Love and Love extends only happiness and joy, it would be completely inconsistent for God to impart suffering, or unhappiness, to anyone. Rather, such an idea is rooted only in the same basic illusion that projects ego or any aspects of ego onto God.

A major idea of traditional Christian theology is that *God condemns those He judges unjust and sends them to an everlasting punishment in hell*. Here again the Course considers this to be a part of the ego-dominated mind's projection. Indeed, were He to do this to His creature it would be the same as doing that to Himself. As is pointed out:

> "3 Would God condemn Himself to hell and to damnation? 4 And do you will that this be done unto your savior? 5 God calls to you from him to join His Will to save you both from hell."(24,III,8,3-5)

Of course, such an idea is completely inconsistent with the notion that God is unlimited Love. Indeed, a point made repeatedly throughout the Course is that hell is the actual present state of the separated mind, and that the whole aim of the Course is help it move out of that hellish state and into the state that it was originally created in, called 'Heaven.' In a sense, this is a complete reversal of the dominant view of traditional Christian beliefs.

Related to the separated mind's projection of specialness onto God are three closely associated characteristics. The first is that *God is partial*. In many places in the Bible, for example, one can interpret it as saying that God prefers certain individuals or groups (such as the prophets or the Hebrews) over others. However, that is simply the way of the ego-dominated mind. On the contrary:

> "2 God is not partial. 3 All His children have His total Love,

and all His gifts are freely given to everyone alike."(1,V,3,2-3)

That is, any notion that God prefers anyone over another is completely contrary to His being Love, which is all-inclusive.

Similarly, the ego's fascination with and devotion to special relationships is also projected in the separated mind's idea in God. Here the Bible is especially open to the interpretation that earlier the Hebrews (the 'Chosen People') and later the Christians are loved by God more than others, i.e., that *He has special love*. But, in the Course's view, this is simply another illusion:

> "2 If you would love unlike to God, Who knows no special love, how can you understand it? 3 To believe that *special* relationships, with *special* love, can offer you salvation is the belief that separation is salvation."(15,V,3,2-3)

Here again, we may see an effect of the ego-idea as it is imposed on what the separated mind thinks of as God, which is of course only an idol having nothing to do with what God actually is.

Stated another way, both partiality and specialness are fundamentally different aspects of the same ego-characteristic, *exclusiveness*. As the Course points out:

> "2 The ego projects to exclude, and therefore to deceive."
> (6,II,12,2)

This may be seen in the primary act that originates separation. That is, the initiation of separation lies in the choice of the perfect Mind of the Son to focus on only an aspect of Reality, in which the rest of Reality is excluded. This is not 'wrong' or 'sinful' or 'evil,' and that choice can be made freely. However, in further choosing to hold on to that narrowed awareness (perception) by constructing the ego-idea within that level of the Son's Mind, it enters into the state of exclusive awareness, or separation, until it comes to realize the folly of that choice and lets it go.

One final characteristic of the separated mind's idea of God deeply rooted in the projection of the ego onto Him is the belief that *God can be angry or wrathful*. Indeed, there are many instances in the Biblical account, particularly in the Old Testament, where God is portrayed as becoming extremely angry, even viciously attacking people in His wrath. Most notable is the story of Noah, but also the wrath of God that destroyed Sodom and Gomorrah as well as the story of the destruction of the worshipers of the 'Golden Calf' when Moses descended from Mt. Sinai. Throughout Christian history, the tendency has been to think of the great catastrophes suffered by people as the result of God's anger. However, the Course is again quite clear in the following:

> "2 The Apostles often misunderstood it [the Crucifixion], and for the same reason that anyone misunderstands it. 3 Their own imperfect love made them vulnerable to projection, and out of their own fear they spoke of the 'wrath of God' as His retaliatory weapon."(6,I,14,2-3)

and:

> "1 It is extremely hard for those who still believe sin meaningful to understand the Holy Spirit's justice. 2 They must believe He shares their own confusion, and cannot avoid the vengeance that their own belief in justice must entail. 3 And so they fear the Holy Spirit, and perceive the 'wrath' of God in Him. 4 Nor can they trust Him not to strike them dead with lightning bolts torn from the 'fires' of Heaven by God's Own angry Hand. 5 They *do* believe that Heaven is hell, and *are* afraid of love."(25,VIII,6,1-5)

That is, the mind dominated by ego is compelled to project into its idea of God the way it responds to things it perceives as 'sin' or 'attack.' Even the Apostles, as close as they were to their master, often seemed to be unable to get beyond this compulsion.

This is more fully explained in the following:

> "1 The ego's use of projection must be fully understood before the inevitable association between projection and anger can be finally undone. 2 The ego always tries to preserve conflict." (7,VII,2,1-2)

That is, if the separated mind's idea of God is primarily a matter of projecting the ego-idea onto Him, one would expect anger to be one of His major characteristics, which is quite closely connected with the belief that He is to be feared. But, once again, the Course makes clear that the origin of the separated mind's view of God is based on a major distortion due to its constructing for itself an 'idol' or image that has its own principal characteristics. This should give welcome relief in the understanding that these features have nothing whatsoever to do with what God actually is. The Course's view is that God is simply infinite Love that gives only of Itself to what It creates, and that this involves the giving of only what is complete perfection, joy, and happiness. This is quite the opposite of the ego-dominated mind's projected distortion of itself. Indeed, the concluding lessons of the Workbook are prefaced by the following observation:

> "3 And we are saved from all the wrath we thought belonged to God, and found it was a dream. 4 We are restored to sanity, in which we understand that anger is insane, attack is mad, and vengeance merely foolish fantasy. 5 We have been saved from wrath because we learned we were mistaken. 6 Nothing more than that. 7 And is a father angry at his son because he failed to understand the truth?"(W,fl[7],In.,5,3-7)

That is, the whole point of the Course is to undo completely this ego-projected notion of God by making clear it is only that, and to lead to the correct understanding and realization that God is only Love.

---

[7] 'fl' means 'Final Lessons.

Appendix 2. 'Light' in the Course

The term 'light' has been used in most spiritual traditions as an important aspect or even direct descriptor of the highest reality. This is particularly true in the Western traditions, where light is said to be an essential property of God Himself.[1] The Course also makes frequent use of the word 'light' in the sense of luminosity – 784 times in various grammatical forms in FIP and 827 times in UM. In Ch. V, a summary of its principal meanings was given. Here is offered a more detailed discussion of those meanings.

When one closely examines the various passages using the term, it becomes clear that, although one of its meanings refers to what is experienced in visual sense-perception, there are also other metaphorical meanings that go beyond visual perception. What seems to run throughout all those various meanings is that 'light' primarily refers to the mind's cognitive capacities or activities. Indeed, we find that it refers to each of the various levels or degrees of the mind's awareness, or what the Course refers to as various sorts of 'vision' or 'seeing.' As it states:

"1 Vision depends on light. 2 You cannot see in darkness." (13,V,8,1-2)

Here are two important insights. The first is the dependence of vision, or more generally cognition, on light. That is, some sort of light is a condition necessary for awareness to occur. One might think of this as the objective or ontological condition that makes awareness possible. This would hold for the various sorts of awareness, including the highest called 'knowledge' and all the various sorts of limited awareness called 'perception.' The second is that light is contrasted with darkness, which similarly refers to deprivation of light or some sort of limitation on awareness. Thus, we would expect that there are as many sorts of darkness as there are of light.

However, the term 'light' is not simply a cognitive metaphor. It also entails something much more active, the point of the following:

"2 You cannot see in darkness, and you cannot make light. 3 You can make darkness and then think you see in it, but light reflects life, and is therefore an aspect of creation. 4 Creation and darkness cannot coexist, but light and life must go together, being but different aspects of creation."(W,44,1,2-4)

The important point here is that 'light' is closely related to 'life.' If we think of 'life'

---

[1] 1 John 1: 5: "This is the message we have heard from him and proclaim to you, that God is light and in him is no darkness."

as referring to the internal activity of those things we think of as living, or perhaps even as what makes possible that internal activity, we may see that in the presence of the various sorts or levels of light we may find similar sorts or levels of activity. That is, there is a dynamic aspect of light, which may be thought of as closely connected with the sorts of processes originating in beings that have awareness. This would range from very simple and limited responses to basic perceptions of an entity, such as moving about, to what the Course considers the highest activity it calls 'creating.' Although we will focus here on the cognitive features of light, we should also recognize that there are various sorts of life-activities that correspond to the various levels of awareness.

In what follows, it will be most useful to consider the Course's views on light in reference to these four major concerns:
1) how it contrasts with darkness
2) the various types or levels of light within two broad categories; these will be called 'relative' and 'absolute'
3) spirit as the source of light, particularly in reference to God, perfect minds, the Son, the Holy Spirit/Christ, and separated minds
4) the process of the separated mind's realizing the highest sort of light

I. The contrast of light with darkness. The Course, in various passages, harkens back to our ordinary experience of light as something that is in opposition to darkness. Indeed, the second sentence of Genesis observes: "The earth was without and void, and darkness was upon the face of the deep; and the spirit of God hovered over the face of the waters." Some have pointed out that this seems to imply that some sort of darkness provided the 'region' into which creation could be placed, perhaps even that darkness coexisted with God before creation. Of course, that would make darkness, or what might be called 'Darkness,' a primary reality along with God. However that may be, the Course is very clear that it does not accept such an idea. As it states:

"1 Darkness is lack of light as sin is lack of love."(1,IV,3,1)

That is, in its view, darkness should not be thought of as having any sort of positive existence. It is only the result of placing limits ('lack') upon light. Indeed, what is indicated indirectly here (and made explicit elsewhere), is that light is closely associated with love; or, more in line with what was said earlier, with absolute Love. Here, we should recall that the primary Reality is Love, and that any limitation imposed on Love is only a matter of imposing limits by a mind (center of awareness) upon its own awareness. That is, 'darkness' refers to something that is fundamentally or absolutely unreal or illusory, the effect of self-imposed limitations. Thus, the notion of a self-existing original 'Darkness' is rejected.[2]

---

[2] The Course is quite different from 'dualistic' Gnosticism, which postulates two fundamental Realities, Light and Darkness. The Course, although much more coherent, is closer to 'non-dualist' Gnosticism. See K. Wapnick's *Love Does Not Condemn*.

Indeed, since light, or perhaps what would better be called 'Light,' is characteristic of the only fundamental Reality, in an absolute sense, darkness does not exist at all, as follows from:

> "3 It is impossible to conceive of light and darkness or everything and nothing as joint possibilities. 4 They are all true or all false. 5 It is essential that you realize your thinking will be erratic until a firm commitment to one or the other is made. 6 A firm commitment to darkness or nothingness, however, is impossible. 7 No one has ever lived who has not experienced *some* light and *some* thing."(3,II,1,3-7)

Thus, 'darkness' for the Course is only a metaphor for the condition of limited awareness. That there is or might be anything completely deprived of light is quite impossible. Such would be total non-being. Of course, to speak of something that is 'total non-being' would be to posit a 'being' that is completely deprived of being, 'something that both is and is not,' which is clearly a contradiction and without meaning. Accordingly, 'darkness' is a term that has only relative application.[3]

That darkness has nothing whatsoever to do with absolute Reality is also made clear in the following

> "3 No darkness abides anywhere in the Kingdom, but your part is only to allow no darkness to abide in your own mind. 4 This alignment with light is unlimited, because it is in alignment with the light of the world. 5 Each of us is the light of the world, and by joining our minds in this light we proclaim the Kingdom of God together and as one."(6,II,13,3-5)

The 'Kingdom' is, of course, a synonym for 'absolute Reality.' That there is no trace whatsoever of darkness within it, refers to the complete absence there of any limitation upon awareness. It is a state of 'unlimited Light.' It also follows that the whole concern of any separated mind is one of undoing all limitations on the light within it so as to be fully in the presence of that Light. This is equivalent to its having removed all darkness from it.

In our earlier discussion (Ch. V), it was pointed out that the perception of the Real World involves the removal of the mind's focused limitations on its perceptual awareness. From the perspective of the separated mind, its own awareness

---

[3] Some interpretations of the Taoist symbol called the 'Tai Chi' or 'Great Ultimate' hold that light and darkness are fundamental properties of being. While this seems to be the case for the various forms within limited existence, it does not apply to the more fundamental level of the Tao Itself, which is the 'One' that gives rise to the fundamental 'two' of yang and yin, light and darkness. Most of that view is about conditions that dominate the dualistic realm (for the Course, the realm of separation), but with an intention of enabling the particular mind to return to the primordial unity, which is congruency with the Tao. Although expressed in different ways, Taoism seems to be in general agreement with the overall concern of the Course.

can be thought of as only a 'spark:'

> "1 In many only the spark remains, for the Great Rays are obscured. 2 Yet God has kept the spark alive so that the Rays can never be completely forgotten. 3 If you but see the little spark you will learn of the greater light, for the Rays are there unseen. 4 Perceiving the spark will heal, but knowing the light will create. 5 Yet in the returning the little light must be acknowledged first, for the separation was a descent from magnitude to littleness. 6 But the spark is still as pure as the Great Light, because it is the remaining call of creation."(10,IV,8,1-6)

That is, the highest sort of light that can be experienced through perception, here called the 'Great Rays' or 'Great Light,' is considered to be actually present at all times within the separated mind. It is only covered over due to the choices made by that mind, 'darkening' it to what to that mind's awareness is only this tiny spark. Thus, that darkness holds only due to the choice of both one's own mind and the minds of others who also perceive only this spark. Thus, darkness has only a qualified existence by virtue of the choice of separated minds. In that sense, separated minds might be called 'darkness-makers,' although what they make is only an illusion.

Another image, drawing on the Christian story of the birth of Jesus, is that of a 'star':

> "1 The sign of Christmas is a star, a light in darkness. 2 See it not outside yourself, but shining in the Heaven within, and accept it as the sign the time of Christ has come."(15,XI,2,102)

Here the Course makes use of the astronomical perception that is particularly instructive. Our understanding of the nature of stars is that they are in fact like our Sun, which when perceived close-up and directly, are so brilliant that their luminosity would blind our physical eyes. The darkness that the numerous stars seem to be imbedded in, of course, is only the effect of the eye's removal from proximity to them. Indeed, astronomical instruments make clear that the whole of space is filled with 'light' rays whose frequencies our eyes are not sensitive to. That is, if we could actually see the full spectrum of all such rays, we would experience a tremendous brilliance even in the 'darkest' night. Thus, from a purely physical perspective, what is called 'darkness' is only an effect of the selective sensitivity of our eyes, so that on that very limited physical level we are actually within a universe of unceasing light. Any darkness that we perceive is only the effect of the limitations of our organs of perception, and not something that exists within the physical world. This holds true even for the interior of the deepest, darkest cave, in which is present a great variety of electromagnetic or light waves. This includes the regions recently discovered to be so-called 'black holes.' Although they are 'dark' even to our instruments, their very existence requires that they be filled with light. That is, there is no place within the physical universe where there is complete darkness.

From the Course's perspective, darkness of any sort is simply the effect of the limited mode of awareness that the separated mind takes on by its choice. Every single object, whether what seems to be a piece of lifeless matter or a human being, or even an abstract idea, is to some extent covered over or contained within what it calls a 'frame of darkness:'

> "1 Accept God's frame instead of yours, and you will see the masterpiece. 2 Look at its loveliness, and understand the Mind that thought it, not in flesh and bones, but in a frame as lovely as itself. 3 Its holiness lights up the sinlessness the frame of darkness hides, and casts a veil of light across the picture's face which but reflects the light that shines from it to its Creator."(25,II,7,1-3)

In this is indicated the contrast between what each separated mind really is and what it is perceived to be. The 'frame of darkness' refers to the confining or limiting structure that reduces it to a distorted and extremely limited fragment of the totality confined within a tiny portion of space and time. Indeed, space and time are themselves formations that seem to reduce the unlimited Light to this 'spark' surrounded by great darkness.

Related to this is the expression 'dark companions,' which appears three times in the Course. The first of these is:

> "6 Walk in light and do not see the dark companions, for they are not fit companions for the Son of God, who was created *of* light and *in* light. 7 The Great Light always surrounds you and shines out from you. 8 How can you see the dark companions in a light such as this? 9 If you see them, it is only because you are denying the light. 10 But deny them instead, for the light is here and the way is clear."(11,III,4,6-10)

Here 'dark companions' refers to particular limited forms that the separated mind may perceive. The context does not make it clear what these forms may be: other human beings whose minds are greatly dominated by ego and thus have a highly limited awareness of light, 'disembodied' separated minds that are like that, such as what might be thought of as 'devils' or 'demons,' that are like that; or only forms in imagination that have a quality that evokes great fear.

Since the notions of 'devil' and 'demon' as 'beings of darkness' have played a major role in traditional Christian thought as well as in other religious views, it will be valuable to understand the Course's view on the matter. Although the term 'demon' is found nowhere in FIP, 'devil' occurs in nine places. We should also note that 'demon' or 'demons' occurs in three places in UM, 'devil' or 'devils' 13 times, as well as an associated expression 'possession' 39 times. While some students of the Course think that FIP's editing out of references to demons and most of the material that discusses possession constitutes a serious loss of important insights into the teachings, I am of the opinion that this is not the case. Indeed, it seems to have been a wise choice by Schucman, since that material is found only very early in the "Notes" and seems to have addressed Schucman's own special concerns as a psychologist and as a person long interested in Biblical teachings. Particularly in light of what is found in FIP regarding 'devil' and 'dark companions,' I think we can come to its central insight on these matters by considering only what is in that version. Of course, it would be good if someone were to do a more complete scholarly study that considers both. But what is said here offers what I think is the substance of the Course's view.

The following gives a succinct summary of what is generally understood by the word 'devil:'

> "4 The 'devil' is a frightening concept because he seems to be extremely powerful and extremely active. 5 He is perceived as a force in combat with God, battling Him for possession of His creations. 6 The devil deceives by lies, and builds kingdoms in which everything is in direct opposition to God. 7 Yet he attracts men rather than repels them, and they are willing to 'sell' him their souls in return for gifts of no real worth. 8 This makes absolutely no sense."(2,VII,2,4-8)

That is, what is meant by the term is an entity that is thought to be a spirit having a mind whose intention is to compete with God to control His creations, particularly human beings. He is considered to have great power, even rivaling that of God, which enables him to wage his war to gain control. He is also thought of as extremely clever, which is the basis of his use of deception as part of his strategy. Thereby he organizes vast regions ('kingdoms') within the world so as to better achieve his goal. Although all of this would make him extremely repulsive and frightening to any human being, he is nevertheless quite attractive, both in his overall manner and by way of what he promises to give those who submit to him. How it 'makes no sense' will be discussed below.

The point of 'selling' one's soul is reiterated in another passage:

> "5 'Psychic' abilities have been used to call upon the devil, which merely means to strengthen the ego."(M,25,6,5)

Those familiar with Goethe's *Faust* will recognize in the above description a very accurate portrayal of the drama's particular devil, 'Mephistopheles,' to whom Dr. Faust sold his soul in exchange for the gifts of restored youth, the power to seduce the innocent Margaret, and protection from any who might try to stop Faust in his pursuits. But it also makes clear the folly of Faust's bargain, which ends with the loss of his beloved and his own death, at least in Part I of the story. Thus, such a 'bargain' makes no sense in that it would be quite irrational to give so much to get so little. Of course, that story is taken from Goethe's Christian Biblical and theological background, which he quite magnificently incorporates into his masterwork. Both the Old and New Testaments contain portrayals of devils, such as Satan and Beelzebub, as well as accounts of demon-possession. Later in history we also find numerous reports of alleged encounters with devils/dem-ons, including stories of their apparitions to saints and their possessions of infants, children, adults, and even places or buildings, which are sometimes the substance of stories and movies that have a remarkable fascination, even for 'true believers.' Though inspiring fear, they are nevertheless attractive to many.

However fascinating such stories may be, the Course's overall evaluation of the 'devil/demon' idea is given in the last clause of the previous passage: any interest in them involves primarily a will to 'strengthen the ego.' That is, the sole basis for the appeal is that it resonates with one's own ego so as to increase its hold upon the mind. Here we should recall that the primary basis of perceiving egos in other beings in the world is the projection of one's own ego-idea upon what is perceived. This is not to say that there are not within other separated minds the presence of an ego, but rather that one's perception of an ego in them arises from that projection from one's own mind. The Course is quite clear that such projecting is not the only way to perceive others. The alternative is to see them as brothers who are one with oneself; that is, to see in them the Face of Christ. In so perceiving them, not only is their fearful quality dispelled and healing brought to them, but there is also the healing of the fear in one's own mind as one's own attachment to the ego-idea is reduced or even dissolved.

Thus, although such forms of darkness may seem to be quite 'real' to many, especially to those deeply imbued with traditional religious ideas, the Course offers a very different evaluation:

"5 The dark companions, the dark way, are all illusions."
(11,III,5,5)

Here we should recall that every perceptual form, whether thought of as 'bad' or 'good,' is on the deepest level an illusion. Particularly all those we regard as 'bad,' such as those we think of as 'diabolical' human beings, or for even forms experienced perceptually as 'devils' seeming to exist on a 'higher plane' or present in other human beings who are thought to be possessed, are illusory due to the superimposition of perceptions that are not actually present. That is, any form of darkness is fundamentally only a projection of one's own ego onto another region of the world of perception. That does not mean that our minds do not treat them as 'really there.' However, if one is more fully aware of their nature, their 'reality' simply dissolves in the light of the holistic vision of them as aspects of the Real World and by perceiving in them the Face of Christ.[4]

This is further clarified in:

---

[4] The story of Jesus' three temptations by Satan, described in Matthew 4: 1-11, can be understood as involving first his permitting to arise from his own ego the projected form of 'Satan,' which offered him the various temptations in a visual and auditory form; then his seeing through them as being merely projections of his own ego, whereupon they simply collapsed or dissolved. Of course, that does not mean that 'Satan' was dissolved for all other separated minds. Rather, it indicates what any separated mind must also do. A similar sort of experience is said to have happened when Siddhartha meditated for 40 days under the Bodhi Tree, in his encounter with Mara, the Buddhist equivalent of the archdemon Satan, and saw that form as only a projection of the deepest level of his own ego, following which Mara dissolved and he entered into Enlightenment as a Buddha.

> "1 The mind can make the belief in separation very real and very fearful, and this belief *is* the 'devil.' 2 It is powerful, active, destructive and clearly in opposition to God, because it literally denies His Fatherhood. 3 Look at your life and see what the devil has made. 4 But realize that this making will surely dissolve in the light of truth, because its foundation is a lie."(3,VIII,5,1-4)

That is, the Course very simply resolves many confusions and long debates as well as the experiences of terror that have arisen from the separated mind's acceptance of some sort of external 'devil' by equating that to the belief in separation, which is principally founded on the acceptance of the ego-idea. In that sense, the essence of the 'devil', as well as any other form of darkness, is the ego-idea itself.

Related to the point made above, there is another reason for the view that there can be no being that is thought of as a 'devil' who is forever opposed to God:

> "8 You cannot enter God's Presence with the dark companions beside you, but you also cannot enter alone. 9 All your brothers must enter with you, for until you have accepted them *you* cannot enter. 10 For you cannot understand wholeness unless you are whole, and no part of the Son can be excluded if he would know the Wholeness of his Father."
> (11,III,7,8-10)

Here we see that the idea of a being who is incurably and forever outside Heaven is completely inconsistent with God's being Love. That is, even if we assumed there is some super-separated mind like a devil within the world of perception, such a mind would simply be a variation of our own separated minds. It might be much smarter and more powerful than we, perhaps existing in a different sort of space with a 'subtle' body and able to maneuver 'supernaturally' within it. But it would still be only a fragment of the Son's perfect mind. Thus, since God's Love responds with his plan for complete Atonement, that mind would have to be included in the completion of that plan. That is, in more traditional terms, even Satan must be redeemed, since without him Love would not be complete. Thus, in the Course's view, Satan or any other devil or any other 'dark companion,' if it is perceived within the world as a separated mind, is a brother that Love embraces as Its own.

Although the choice of separation draws the mind into the condition of darkness, the Course is very clear that this illusion or darkness cannot blot out all light:

> "3 Each dream has led to other dreams, and every fantasy that seemed to bring a light into the darkness but made the darkness deeper. 4 Your goal was darkness, in which no ray of light could enter. 5 And you sought a blackness so complete that you could hide from truth forever, in complete insanity. 6 What you forgot was simply that God cannot destroy Himself.

7 The light is *in* you. 8 Darkness can cover it, but cannot put it out."(18,III,1,3-7)

Thus, all that can happen is that the light or awareness that is the essential and fundamental nature of each separated mind can only be placed temporarily into a condition of 'darkness' or limited awareness. Caught within its choice of imposing limits upon its awareness, the fragment of the perfect mind can so circumscribe and limit its awareness of light that it seems to be in 'utter darkness' or 'blackness.'[5] Here we can imagine the very energy that constitutes the structure of an atom as an instance of a mind that has so completely reduced its awareness that the only reaction it has to the world about it is the gravitational, electric, and magnetic forces acting on it. But, even those forces are in some sense a form of 'light.' Although we might think of it (and the fragmented mind at its core) as completely covered by darkness, it cannot be totally extinguished. Such a 'reduced mind' still has within it the presence of some sort of light. It is the presence of Light (unlimited Awareness, or what the Course calls 'knowledge') in every separated mind that is the basis of its very existence and of the possibility of its moving out of darkness (limited awareness) back into the full realization of what it actually is. We will discuss this after we consider the various meanings of 'light' and the sorts of light that the Course speaks of.

II. Two basic levels and the various sorts of light. Throughout the Course, one finds two fundamental levels or 'realms' of experience that the mind can enter into or operate on, which has been called 'relative' and 'absolute.' Although only the latter has a truly real existence, for the mind in separation and committed to perception, the relative is what seems to be most real. Since that is the level that is most familiar and accessible to separated minds, the Course constantly appeals to the contents of that lower level of experience in order to bring it some understanding of the higher level, and ultimately to help minds caught within that lower level to be released from it and return to what it holds is the only true Reality. Accordingly, the term 'light' has two very different, although related, meanings. Here, we first consider the various types of light on the more familiar lower, relative level, and then the true Light of the higher, absolute level.

A. Relative light or perceptual light. Since in the Course 'light' refers to that by which the mind has awareness, we find various sorts of light corresponding to how awareness ranges from the most concrete to the most abstract. There is a kind of 'natural' order that goes from light in a visual sensory sense; then, more generally, light related to any sort of sensory awareness; then, the light that func-

---

[5] This is reminiscent of the observation in the Isha Upanishad: "Into blind darkness enter they that worship ignorance; into darkness greater than that, as it were, they that delight in knowledge," tr. by R. Hume. Here 'knowledge' refers to rational or intellectual knowledge, which is the highest sort of perceptual awareness. For the Course, 'knowledge' is completely beyond that mode.

tions within imagination and memory; next, the light that operates within the context of conceptual understanding and the light that enables the human mind to carry out reasoning; then, the light that is the basis of the mind's awareness of itself; and, finally, the light that discloses the Real World. All but the last of these are present in most human experience, while the highest of these relative or perceptual lights is more rarely encountered. In addition, the Course also refers to an idea of 'outer' or physical light that the modern mind is generally familiar with, which it contrasts with the various sorts of 'inner' lights. We begin with this last distinction

1. Outer light. Our habits of thought generally recognize that there is a physical form called 'light' present in and moving through nature. Science currently describes this as undulating waves of electromagnetic energy, whose presence stimulates the optic nerves to send signals to the brain, which then are said to give rise to visual experience of colors and shapes. This seems to be the kind of light discussed in:

> "3 Light cannot penetrate through the walls you make to block it, and it is forever unwilling to destroy what you have made. 4 No one can see through a wall, but I can step around it."
> (4,III,7,3-4)

Here, we should note that the modern idea of physical light is itself a rather complex construct that has only emerged within the last several centuries of scientific study. Its primary experiential basis is in the content of ordinary visual perception, which directly discloses nothing about its having a wave structure. Of course, that construct has been greatly elaborated and extended to include a much broader notion of physical light, including many wave forms that are completely invisible to us – radio waves, infrared, ultraviolet, x-rays, and gamma rays. Even the very notion of its 'wave' structure has been found insufficient, so that it is thought to have both wave and particle (quantum) characteristics, and some theoretical models even propose that it is based on an even more fundamental structure of what are called 'strings' and 'membranes' that exist within a higher dimensional level. The passage here uses the term only to serve as a metaphor for the directly observed experience of how within the sphere of physical light there occur blockages to its movement which are associated with a curtailment of its action upon other physical objects, including one's own eyes. Indeed, if one pursued the characteristics of physical light as currently disclosed by science, there may be many further interesting parallels between it and the general nature of perceptual awareness. But that would have little instructive value to the average student, for which the Course is designed.

2. Inner light. Since the content of experience is the Course's focus of concern, the term 'light' most often is better thought of as an 'inner light,' or what could also be called 'psychological light,' which is directly encountered in immediate experience.

a. Inner light in general. An important aspect of the inner light is described in the following:

> "1 In order to see, you must recognize that light is within, not without. 2 You do not see outside yourself, nor is the equipment for seeing outside you. 3 An essential part of this equipment is the light that makes seeing possible. 4 It is with you always, making vision possible in every circumstance."
> (W,44,3,1-4)

This does not seem to deny that ordinary visual perception occurs only when a sufficient amount of physical light is present. However, as is quite well established even by science, there must also be present some internal activity within the mind. Modern neuroscience argues that this is the neural activity in particular parts of the brain. However, that same science has also established that even the responses in the brain's optic region can occur without the person's experiencing visual perception. In addition, those neural activities must interact with other areas of the brain before the person has the experience of seeing. That is, there must also be the 'inner light' that enables the particular visual sensory forms to have an active presence in the person's mind. Here, the Course is very clear that the brain is not the primary 'equipment' needed for any awareness. As it states, that equipment is not 'outside you.' In the Course's view, the body, including the brain, is only a small fragment of the mind. Contrary to what has become almost a dogma of modern neuroscience, awareness does not arise from brain/neural activity, although the content of awareness can be greatly determined by that activity.

This is made particularly clear and unambiguous in the following:

> "1 You also believe the body's brain can think. 2 If you but understood the nature of thought, you could but laugh at this insane idea. 3 It is as if you thought you held the match that lights the sun and gives it all its warmth; or that you held the world within your hand, securely bound until you let it go. 4 Yet this is no more foolish than to believe the body's eyes can see; the brain can think."(W,92,2,1-4)

Currently, the opinion dominates in neuroscience that all thought, consciousness, and awareness are effects of the brain. The Course flatly rejects that idea, even going so far as to ridicule it as utterly absurd. Unfortunately, it does not substantiate its position with a clear argument. The only indication of the basis for its view is by way of the two analogies (that the sun is lighted by a match and that the world is contained with one's hand) and perhaps the more insightful claim that it would be made fully clear by examining carefully the nature of thought.

Here I may offer a reflection in that direction. That is, thought is essentially the act of a mind that enables it to grasp the unity of many different things. Those things can be separate in space (such as the objects referred to by the concepts of 'mountain,' 'river,' or more generally 'spatial location') or separate in time (such as 'birth,' 'war,' or more generally 'day' or 'instant'). These rather simple thoughts and the judgments we accept about them are not spatially or temporally determinate, i.e., do not apply only to specific objects in space and time. However, the body and all its parts, including the eyes and the brain, are all spatially and temporally determinate. Thus, to claim that the eyes or the eyes together with the brain fully determine the content of such thoughts proposes that the properties of those bodily parts completely determine the content of those thoughts. The problem is that this would require that a particular, determinate brain state would fully characterize an indeterminate thought. Mathematically, this involves the assertion that a particular finite and limited set of conditions adequately correlates to an infinite or unlimited set. Stated otherwise, this amounts to saying that a finite set is infinite or not limited, clearly a contradiction. This holds for very ordinary sorts of thought (from simple visual forms to very abstract concepts). For the higher mode of perceptual awareness that comes with the experience of the holy instant, where awareness includes elements totally outside time or space as well as no limits whatsoever, the utter inability of the brain to serve as the explanatory basis is augmented by what may be a factor of infinity beyond that of ordinary conceptual thought. This perhaps is the point made in comparing the brain-reductionist view to believing that one could hold the whole world in one's hand or that a match illuminates the sun. But, I leave this discussion to another occasion.

The nature of the inner light is further elaborated in:

> "1 The Atonement can only be accepted within you by releasing the inner light."(2,III,1,1)

What is indicated here is that this inner light, although it is highly limited when the mind focuses on the modes of visual or other sensory awareness, has a potential for being enlarged or expanded to a much greater extent. That is, the light that makes possible very ordinary, sensory awareness, although limited greatly in that situation, is the very same light or principle of awareness that operates in the realization of the Atonement. This is fully consistent with the Course's idea that the infinite Light has been 'darkened' for any particular separated mind by its placing upon itself the limitations that are central to separation.

Later, we will see how this removal of all limits upon the inner light is what is said to occur as the culmination of the process of Atonement. However, although reduced to only a 'spark' in the separated mind, even the basic light of ordinary vision is in essence the very same light that operates in the highest mode. As it states:

> "1 True light that makes true vision possible is not the light the body's eyes behold. 2 It is a state of mind that has become so unified that darkness cannot be perceived at all. 3 And thus what is the same is seen as one, while what is not the same remains unnoticed, for it is not there."(W,108,2,1-3)

That is, even ordinary visual perception is an expression of the 'true light' that is the foundation of the awareness that arises in Love's extension as knowledge.

Indeed, what occurs in ordinary visual awareness is that the object seen in a certain way becomes united with the one that sees. This very basic unification between perceiver and perceived, although limited to the particular forms characteristic of visual perception, is a very limited form or mode of the unlimited unifying that is made possible by the undarkened 'true light,' or Light.

b. The levels of inner light. Next, we consider the various ways in which the inner light is found or expressed within the separated mind.

i. Visual light. The type of light that we think of as most directly experienced is the sort seen through the eyes in terms of shapes, colors, and various intensities of that sense-mode. Earlier was cited a passage that holds on all levels of light and seeing. However, its most obvious sense is on the very basic level of ordinary visual perception. I repeat it here:

> "1 Vision depends on light. 2 You cannot see in darkness."
> (13,V,8,1-2)

Related to visual perception through the eyes, this can be understood in two ways. The first is that such perception has some sort of dependence upon the presence of outer, physical light. The second and more important way is that this perception depends on the presence of the inner light of awareness, since without whatever makes that awareness possible the presence of the outer light does not bring about such perception. The corresponding 'darkness' that renders it inoperative is the failure of the basis of awareness to be present in relation to the particular body it is said to occur in. As was pointed out, the Course holds that the foundation of this visual awareness lies in the awareness or Light that is constitutive of the mind, although the particular separated mind may have lost clarity and understanding of what that Light consists of.

The reason for the limitation of awareness to only the relatively contracted visual forms lies in its having chosen to be thus limited. This is further explained:

> "1 Eyes become used to darkness, and the light of brilliant day seems painful to the eyes grown long accustomed to the dim effects perceived at twilight. 2 And they turn away from sunlight and the clarity it brings to what they look upon. 3 Dimness seems better; easier to see, and better recognized. 4 Somehow the vague and more obscure seems easier to look upon; less painful to the eyes than what is wholly clear and unambiguous. 5 Yet this is not what eyes are for, and who can say that he prefers the darkness and maintain he wants to see?"(25,VI,2,1-5)

That is, having chosen the severely limited focused awareness that depends on its relationship with the body (and most particularly the eyes), the separated mind sets itself into a habit of responding to this tiny portion of Reality. It becomes so dependent on that condition that when the intensity of the visual information exceeds a certain amount, it experiences pain from the overabundance of stimulus entering the eyes. Hence, it actually feels comfortable only within the presence of a very restricted amount of physical light, which also corresponds to a restricted intensity of the inner light's activity. This is apparently closely related to the way that the body has been constructed with a twofold aim. One is to give the separated mind *some* awareness of what is occurring around it so that it can satisfy some of its ego-needs. But, the other is to keep that awareness greatly *restricted* so as to keep the ego-state continuing. Thus, what it may like to think of as 'seeing' and 'light' is in fact a severely contracted state that is more accurately a kind of 'blindness' and 'darkness.'

Also related to this habituation to the conditions of awareness through the physical eyes is the mind's being caught in great unclarity regarding what it is actually perceiving. That is, because it has only a very limited awareness of what it sees, the nature of those objects is fraught with ambiguity. In a passage somewhat reminiscent of Plato's 'Divided Line' explanation of the various levels of cognition, the Course observes:

> "1 Reflections are seen in light. 2 In darkness they are obscure, and their meaning seems to lie only in shifting interpretations, rather than in themselves."(14,IX,6,1-2)

The 'reflections' alluded to here seem to be meant in several ways. One is that in the visual perception of a reflected image, say on the surface of a still pond or in a mirror, there must be the presence of both the outer physical light and the internal light of awareness so as to render it present to the mind. However, such images are always subject to multiple interpretations, affected by both the outer conditions operating and the internal flow of thoughts, such as memories and the play of fantasy. Yet, as they are more fully illuminated, by either a stronger physical light or a more focused inner awareness, the ambiguity is reduced and the meaning rendered clearer. The other meaning of 'reflections' can be understood as referring to direct visual seeing. In this we need to recall that, in one sense, all visual forms are reflections, both of physical light and inner light. That is, impinging physical light, whether from the Sun, the Moon, or any artificial source, whenever it makes an object perceivable, involves the reflection of that light from the object into the perceiver's eyes, carrying with it the information about the object's form and other visual properties. The same is true of the inner light. That is, the inner light is of itself undifferentiated and takes on particular characteristics by its being 'reflected,' so to speak, from the particular visual pattern one perceives. Thus, both the outer and the inner light, to the extent that they inform the mind about what is perceived, have absent the particular characteristics of the object, and they reflect from that object carrying with them the object's peculiar characteristics. 'Darkness' can obscure what is being perceived in two ways: one, by being insufficient to render the object's characteristics perceivable; the other, by the light's having its own properties overwhelm and hide the object's properties (e.g., if physical light is itself a strong yellow, it makes the object appear to be yellow; or if the inner light is dominated by a particular color or even an emotion, it colors the object accordingly.) However, although the Course shows that it is attuned to the way visual perception operates, it is not greatly concerned with offering a general explanation of that process; its main concern is to acknowledge the important factors of outer and inner light as necessary for visual perception to occur.

ii. Sensory light. On a somewhat more general level, the Course also speaks of 'light' in reference to the sensory awareness operative beyond only that of vision:

> "2 Look at this body in a different light and it looks different. 3 And without a light it seems that it is gone. 4 Yet you are reassured that it is there because you still can feel it with your hands and hear it move. 5 Here is an image that you want to be yourself. 6 It is the means to make your wish come true. 7 It gives the eyes with which you look on it, the hands that feel it, and the ears with which you listen to the sounds it makes." (24,VII,9,2-9)

Although visual sensory awareness is the most widely experienced type for most human beings, it would be a mistake to conclude that those who are blind are somehow not to be included. In this passage, the term 'light' refers to what makes one aware via the body, and it specifically mentions the modes of hearing and tactile feeling. Thus, the term is applicable to these other types of sensory awareness. Further, although the Course does not anywhere refer to smell or taste as sensory modes (as also any of the other sensory modes such as those sometimes called 'somatic' sensations), since these are obviously types of perception, their being experienced can be thought of as made possible by the presence of a 'light' that brings them into awareness.

iii. Light of imagination. Yet another sort of light is that which makes possible the awareness that occurs in the experience of concrete images closely resembling those of the visual and other sensory modes. This is alluded to in:

> "3 Each dream has led to other dreams, and every fantasy that seemed to bring a light into the darkness but made the darkness deeper. 4 Your goal was darkness, in which no ray of light could enter."(18,I,3,3-4)

This passage recognizes that in the operations of imagination we call 'dreams' and 'fantasies' there is a kind of light, which is of course the awareness that renders the contents of what is imagined present to the mind. It also points out that there is in this, as in almost all other perceptual awareness, an attempt to remove oneself from unlimited awareness, or Light.

A second passage also addresses the light of imagination as experienced in dreaming:

> "3 Yet in darkness, in the private world of sleep, you see in dreams although your eyes are closed. 4 And it is here that what you see you made. 5 But let the darkness go and all you made you will no longer see, for sight of it depends upon denying vision. 6 Yet from denying vision it does not follow you cannot see. 7 But this is what denial does, for by it you accept

> insanity, believing you can make a private world and rule your own perception. 8 Yet for this, light must be excluded. 9 Dreams disappear when light has come and you can see." (13,V,8,3-8)

Although this specifically refers only to the experiences of the ordinary dream-state, there is implicitly acknowledged the whole gamut of perceptual forms that arise without the input from sensory organs, including those we call 'remembered' and 'fantasized.' Thus, this more interior sort of experience is made possible by the presence of a correspondingly higher level of 'light' as the principle of such awareness. However, as statements 8 and 9 indicate, the light of imagination is itself an impoverished type of light relative to the fuller Light that is possible for the mind.

iv. Conceptual or rational light. At yet another level, the human mind is capable of even greater generality by way of its forming abstract concepts. One aspect of it as the **light of understanding.** This is indicated in the following:

> "5 Understanding is light, and light leads to knowledge." (5,III,7,5)

Although the term 'understanding' has numerous meanings, on the simplest level it refers to the mind's capacity to recognize a single pattern or set of properties that can belong to multiple individual things. For example, the concept 'triangle' has fundamentally the same meaning in the numberless particular occurrences of different sorts and particular instances of triangles. What stands out in such awareness is the basic unity that runs through the many sorts and concrete instances. This light of understanding is even more powerful in its capacity to recognize union or separation between concepts that occurs in the forming of various sorts of judgments. For example, 'All humans are created equal' unites two concepts ('humans' and 'created equal'), while 'No humans are dogs,' separates two concepts.

Related to this conceptual light is the even more comprehensive capacity of the mind to carry out processes of reasoning, what the Course calls the '**light of reason**:'

> "4 Sickness and sin are seen as consequence and cause, in a relationship kept hidden from awareness that it may be carefully preserved from reason's light."(26,VII,2,4)

One way that this light is applied may be illustrated: 'All men are mortal, Socrates is a man; therefore, Socrates is mortal.' Apparently lower animals lack this capacity or light, at least to any great degree. Thinkers have pointed out that it is the presence of this light that has enabled our species to accomplish many of its achievements, such as those of science, technology, law and government, literature, and philosophy.

v. The light of apperception. A still 'higher' sort of light within the realm of perception is that which is the basis of what is sometimes called 'apperception.' This is indicated in:

> "2 Let yourself be brought unto your Self. 3 Its strength will

be the light in which the gift of sight is given you. 4 Leave, then, the dark a little while today, and we will practice seeing in the light, closing the body's eyes and asking truth to show us how to find the meeting place of self and Self, where light and strength are one."(W,92,10,2-4)

The notion of apperception refers to the capacity of an individual mind to have awareness of itself. That is the point made in statement 2. This may be thought of as a self-reflective type of awareness, which is different in content from the awareness of what is different from oneself. In statement 4, there are acknowledged two different sorts of apperception: of self and of Self. The first is a much more limited awareness which is the perception of the separated mind's own ego-dominated activity. The second is awareness of the unlimited activity that is central to the perfect mind. This second apperception occurs both perceptually in the perception of the Real World and non-perceptually in the state of knowledge. In this context of the relative level, it is a matter of a limited awareness, and thus only perceptual. The light at its basis, which is limited and to some extent distorted, is quite different from the unlimited Light of Self-awareness that is present in any perfect mind.

vi. Light of the Real World. The previous five sorts or levels of 'light' are fairly easy for human beings to identify as present within themselves. They constitute the gamut of types of 'light' operative within our species' particular mode of ordinary perceptual awareness. However, there is still another type of perceptual light that can be experienced by us, although it seems to be much less common than the others. Here I refer to what from the Course's perspective may be called the '**light of the Real World**:'

"1 This world of light, this circle of brightness is the real world, where guilt meets with forgiveness. 2 Here the world outside is seen anew, without the shadow of guilt upon it. 3 Here are you forgiven, for here you have forgiven everyone." (18,IX,1,1-3)

This light is the basis for the profoundly transformed mode of awareness that is held to be available to every separated mind. We discussed some of its features in the section on the Real World, but will here note several important things about that light.

The first is that in activating this highest of perceptual lights the mind experiences not only a profound expansion of its overall awareness, but also an extremely powerful affective shift:

"2 This world you bring with you to all the weary eyes and tired hearts that look on sin and beat its sad refrain. 3 From you can come their rest. 4 From you can rise a world they will rejoice to look upon, and where their hearts are glad. 5 In you there is a vision that extends to all of them, and covers them in gentleness and light. 6 And in this widening world of light the darkness that they thought was there is pushed away, until it is but distant shadows, far away, not long to be remembered as the sun shines them to nothingness."(25,IV,3,2-6)

Here we are told that the expansion of awareness that comes with this intensification and extension of awareness beyond the mode available prior to its occurrence has something extremely remarkable about it: that all the aspects of darkness, or limitations of awareness, rapidly drop away. This melting away of limitations seems to play a powerful role in generating the feelings of intense joy, both in the release of what was formerly experienced as various sorts of pain and the access to a kind of 'fullness' that brings great satisfaction.

Related to this undoing of all traces of perceptual darkness, including the limits in the light itself, is the following indication of what might be called the 'hugeness' and the beauty of the light that constitutes the Real World:

> "1 Beyond the body, beyond the sun and stars, past everything you see and yet somehow familiar, is an arc of golden light that stretches as you look into a great and shining circle. 2 And all the circle fills with light before your eyes. 3 The edges of the circle disappear, and what is in it is no longer contained at all. 4 The light expands and covers everything, extending to infinity forever shining and with no break or limit anywhere. 5 Within it everything is joined in perfect continuity. 6 Nor is it possible to imagine that anything could be outside, for there is nowhere that this light is not."(21,I,8,1-6)

The radical difference of this light is expressed in its 'golden' quality, perhaps suggestive of the profound feeling of value that it is perceived to have. Also, its lack of both spatial and temporal limits that 'extend to infinity' indicates that there is in this perception an extensiveness that is totally beyond all other lower sorts of perception. Further, that the whole perception is 'filled with light,' indicates yet another radical difference from other sorts of light in that nothing present within it involves any sort of darkness, lack, or absence of that luminous quality. Finally (in statement 5), there is directly perceived, not just as a matter of intellectual or conceptual abstraction, the connectedness and mutual presence of all aspects within every other aspect. Thus, this highest perceptual light, although it has some resemblance with the limited light of ordinary perception, is vastly different from it.

Closely related to the light of the Real World are what seem to be two variations of that light, both of which seem best thought of as different ways of thinking of that light as applied within the context of particular perceptions. The first is the light that makes possible the awareness of what the Course refers to as the 'vision of Christ.' This is indicated in:

> "1 Christ's vision has one law. 2 It does not look upon a body, and mistake it for the Son whom God created. 3 It beholds a light beyond the body; an idea beyond what can be touched, a purity undimmed by errors, pitiful mistakes, and fearful thoughts of guilt from dreams of sin. 4 It sees no separation. 5

And it looks on everyone, on every circumstance, all happenings and all events, without the slightest fading of the light it sees."(W,158,7,1-5)

The perception that occurs within the vision of Christ is one that includes ordinary forms, such as those of particular individual persons, but transformed in such a way that what is seen within that person is how he or she is an aspect of the Real World. It can be more or less intensely clear, depending on the depth into which the mind so perceiving has entered into the awareness of the Real World through the experience of the holy instant. As the passage notes, the ordinary perception is so transmuted that another person is perceived as completely beyond any negativity and as connected with all other aspects within the field of perception. It involves no aspect of separateness, and the person is perceived as only a facet of the much more comprehensive entity that is the Christ Mind. This will be discussed at greater length in my other work, *The Holy Spirit and Jesus in A Course in Miracles*.

The second is expressed somewhat differently, where the Course also speaks of a light that is basic to the awareness of the holy relationship:

> "1 This holy relationship, lovely in its innocence, mighty in strength, and blazing with a light far brighter than the sun that lights the sky you see, is chosen of your Father as a means for His Own plan."(22,VI,4,1)

The perception that is primary in the holy relationship is fundamentally the same as what is called the 'vision of Christ.' It admits of degrees of intensity of awareness, depending on how far the particular mind has matured in that vision. For those in a mature holy relationship, their perception of each other involves, as indicated here, an intense light. This seems best understood as the same light that makes the Real World perceivable. As was discussed in Ch. V, since this perception is holistic, the perception of the other also includes his or her intimate unity with all other minds that prior to that maturity have been perceived as separated minds. If those other minds are not yet so matured, they may continue to perceive themselves as separated. However, the light of the vision of Christ or the holy relationship moves the mind to perceive all things as parts or aspects united in the Real World.

Nevertheless, the Course is quite clear that the light that is the basis of this highest or most complete of all possible perceptions, which can be variously called 'light of the Real World,' 'light of the vision of Christ,' or 'light of the holy relationship,' is not the most complete or perfect light. As it states:

> "7 Perception can reach everywhere under His guidance, for the vision of Christ beholds everything in light. 8 Yet no perception, however holy, will last forever."(13,VIII,2,7-8)

That is, although the light that illuminates the vision of Christ and the Real World is the maximal type of light within the realm of perception, beyond it is the still higher light that is the basis of cognition and life that are present in all perfect minds. That brings us to the following sort of light.

B. Absolute light. The ultimate foundation of awareness is, in the Course's view, Love. This may be thought of as an 'Energy' that operates within all minds, including that of the primary Mind of God, the perfect minds that arise from His creative extensions, and even the imperfect minds that arise due their choice to enter separation. This supreme Light is referred to in a number of ways.

1. The foundational Light of Love. Several passages indicate aspects of this most fundamental light. The first:

"4 Only the creations of light are real."(1,I,24,4)

Although the Course sometimes uses the word 'real' in a relative or limited sense, here it is meant in the sense of what is most truly real, or what was also called absolutely real, or Real. In saying that only the creations of light are real, it is not to be understood that Reality should be attributed only to what is created. Rather, both the uncreated Light that is the foundation or Source of creative extension and what that Light creates can be called Real. As was explained earlier, this includes Love Itself as well as the particular entities, which the Course calls perfect minds or spirits, in which It is present without limits: God, the Son, and the infinity of creatures ($Sons_n$), the whole collection of which constitute the Universe of Love.

Within that Light is the complete absence of any sort of 'darkness':

"1 Darkness is lack of light as sin is lack of love."(1,IV,3,1)

This makes fully clear that, since the ultimate Reality is only Light, anything that might be considered 'darkness' is fundamentally lacking in Reality. This holds for both Love itself, which can be called the most perfect Light, and any perfect mind/spirit, whether uncreated or created. It also follows that the darkness or curtailment placed on that Light by way of the separation is itself not Real. Thus, the passage's point that what a separated mind might think of as 'sin' is absolutely unreal.

Although this primary Light is present within a multiplicity of entities, the Course is clear that this multiplicity is constituted of the same '**One Light**:'

"6 How beautiful indeed are the Thoughts of God who live in His light! 7 Your worth is beyond perception because it is beyond doubt. 8 Do not perceive yourself in different lights. 9 Know yourself in the One Light where the miracle that is you is perfectly clear."(3,V,10,6-9)

While the passage speaks here of the 'One Light' in terms of a particular separated mind's ('yourself') relation to that Light in the context of a miracle, it is clear that this light is singular or one in relation to all miracles, all separated minds, and even all perfect minds. Here we may recall that the primary characteristic of Love is its essential unity; Light, being but another way of referring to Love, would also have that unity. We next consider various ways the One Light is spoken of.

a. Perfect Light. This fundamental Light is also described as 'perfect:'

"1 You are a mirror of truth, in which God Himself shines in perfect light."(4,V,9,1)

The idea of perfection refers to that which is fully complete (Latin, 'per' = through + 'factum' = made or produced) and admitting of no further addition or improvement upon it. Thus, God was described by St. Anselm as 'that beyond which nothing greater can be thought.' For the Course, this perfection belongs primarily to the Light of Love, which is the core or essential nature of God and out of which God is prompted to further extend or create. I should point out that if God is considered only by Himself, He in one sense is lacking, for there needs to be fulfilled the full extension of Love in Him. Thus, the basis of His impulse to creatively extend Himself is the Light/Love of which He is constituted and which necessarily extends to and is present in the whole of Reality. Accordingly, seen in its more complete context of the act of creation, the Perfect Light admits of no further addition or improvement.

b. Eternal Light. The Course also speaks of this primary Light as 'eternal:'

> "1 Be you not separate, for the One Who does surround it has brought union to you, returning your little offering of darkness to the eternal light."(18,IX,2,1)

In the second clause, 'it' refers to the tiny portion of Reality that the separated mind has enclosed within its ego-idea and thinks of as itself. What is important here is the expression '**eternal light**,' which makes clear that the foundational Light Itself does not exist in time, but in the single all-inclusive and unending Eternal Now or Instant. Because it supports even separated minds as the foundation of their existence, it expresses in the lower limited forms of light within the relative level of perception. Of course, that expression is unreal in an absolute sense; it only seems to exist to those minds in the aspects of the fundamental illusion that is the realm of perception.

c. Unlimited Light or Great Light. This Light is not only described as non-temporal, but also as unlimited:

> "1 There is a light that this world cannot give. 2 Yet you can give it, as it was given you. 3 And as you give it, it shines forth to call you from the world and follow it. 4 For this light will attract you as nothing in this world can do. 5 And you will lay aside the world and find another. 6 This other world is bright with love which you have given it. 7 And here will everything remind you of your Father and His holy Son. 8 Light is unlimited, and spreads across this world in quiet joy."(13,VI,11,1-8)

In saying that the primary Light is unlimited, although this may at first seem to claim that it occupies an infinite space, what is actually asserted is that its existence is not spatial. This necessarily follows in the denial that it is in time, since time and space are both frameworks upon which the mind constructs its notion of a world that involves separate things (places and events). In itself, the primary Light has no spatial characteristics whatsoever. However, because the separated mind enters into the space-time framework and the awareness in that mind is possible only by some presence, although greatly limited, of that Light, this primary Light does manifest to separated minds within the world in a restricted form. This is the point of the last clause of statement 8. Thus, although the primary Light has no temporal or spatial characteristics at all, because it operates within separated minds, it seems to have temporal and spatial qualities for those minds.

Similarly, It is also sometimes referred to as the '**Great Light**,' as in:

"6 But the spark is still as pure as the Great Light, because it is the remaining call of creation."(10,IV,8,6)

and:

"7 The Great Light always surrounds you and shines out from you." (11,III,4,7)

d. Light of Truth. Although the eternal and unlimited features of the primary Light are by way of negation of what dominates the separated mind's experience, the Course speaks of what we should think of as more interior properties, which we consider next. The first is referred to as the '**light of truth**:'

"4 But realize that this making will surely dissolve in the light of truth, because its foundation is a lie. 5 Your creation by God is the only Foundation that cannot be shaken, because the light is in it."(3,VII,5,4-5)

This passage contrasts the primary, unlimited, and absolute Light with the derived, limited, and relative light that dominates the separated mind's awareness. That the more fundamental Light is called the 'light of truth' is intimately connected with the idea that all that is Real has its existence by virtue of the presence of that Light within it. Here we should recall that this 'Energy' has both an ontological and a cognitive aspect. As Love is that which is primarily Real, and the fundamental property of Love is extending by way of giving existence to what is totally like itself, it is that which gives rise to all that is called 'Real' by the Course. But, because it also has what is connoted in its being called 'Light,' that is, its capacity to make what is Real fully present within awareness, it also has its cognitive aspect. It is the latter that is emphasized in using the expression 'light of truth.' What is present to any mind in which it is fully present is the awareness of all that is Real. This is precisely what the Course means by 'truth,' or what was also called 'Truth.' This expression is also used in reference to the function of the Holy Spirit:

"1 Like you, the Holy Spirit did not make truth. 2 Like God, He knows it to be true. 3 He brings the light of truth into the darkness, and lets it shine on you. 4 And as it shines your brothers see it, and realizing that this light is not what you have made, they see in you more than you see."(14,II,4,1-4)

Here it is made quite clear that the light of truth is not something produced by the Holy Spirit, but what He conveys or transmits to the separated mind in its learning the lessons of the Atonement. That is, the light of truth is simply the uncreated Light of Love.

e. Light of Knowledge. Closely related to this last notion is what the Course

calls the '**light of knowledge**.' As it states:
> "3 Across the bridge that He provides are dreams all carried to the truth, to be dispelled before the light of knowledge. 4 There are sights and sounds forever laid aside."(W,pII,7,1,3-4)

This passage describes the final stage of the Atonement process in which the Holy Spirit brings the formerly separated mind back to its original state. This is described as involving the full arising of the primary Light, here called the 'light of knowledge,' or better the 'Light of Knowledge,' in that mind. What is emphasized in the phrase is that this Light is the basis of the awareness that is central to the highest cognitive mode called 'knowledge.' Of course, that this would be the effect of that Light upon any mind in the perfect state is completely coherent with what the Course says about knowledge.

2. God as the primary center of Light. Although the primary Light of Love is best thought of as an intelligent, creative Energy, it is found in various centers that the Course refers to as 'spirits' in which it functions as the foundation of the activity that expresses through what is called 'mind.' The Spirit/Mind of God is the original and uncreated center in which that Light/Love is eternally present. From that Mind the Energy extends, both in terms of the awareness called 'knowledge' and of the productive impulse called 'creation.' Accordingly, God is described as 'light:'
> "3 God is the light in which you see."(W,44,6,3)

Although this refers to God as 'light' in the context in which the separated mind ('you') sees, and could be understood as 'light' on the lowest relative level of sensory vision, it may also be understood as saying that God operates as light or the principle of awareness on all levels. This includes the very highest level of the Son's perfect mind, which 'you' are. That is, God's being light could be thought of only in reference to the capacity for awareness in a creature, whether a perfect mind or in its separated state. However, the idea is made much more strongly in:
> "3 God is the only light."(W,58,4,3)

Here, we find the view that not only is God light by virtue of an effect that He produces upon other minds, but that He is light in His very essence, indeed, 'the only light.' This becomes much clearer when we consider that the most fundamental sort of light is the Light, or basis of awareness, that is essential to Love, and that God is the original 'locus' or center, which the Course calls 'spirit,' understood as any center in which there is a mind through which Love operates, in which Love is present. That is, God is the primary entity in which Light is present, and in that sense the 'Primary Light.' This gives a much deeper meaning to John's assertion: "God is light." (I John 1:5)

3. Created light. But the Course, as we have seen, also holds that it is the very nature of Love to extend creatively. Accordingly, the Light that is God extends to produce a second entity or spirit within which that perfect Light is present, called the Son, and from or through the Son produces further created centers of that Light.

a. The Son. The Son is referred to as light in the passage cited earlier:

> "6 Walk in light and do not see the dark companions, for they are not fit companions for the Son of God, who was created *of* light and *in* light. 7 The Great Light always surrounds you and shines out from you. 8 How can you see the dark companions in a light such as this? 9 If you see them, it is only because you are denying the light. 10 But deny them instead, for the light is here and the way is clear."(11,III,4,6-10)

What is important here is the assertion that the Son is 'created of light and in light.' This seems to assert that the substance of the Son, like that of the Father (God), is this primary Light. Hence, the Son has the same extending characteristic, which is the basis of both His knowing awareness and His creative production of yet another perfect mind.

This gives another, deeper meaning to the references to 'light' in both the Old and New Testaments. In Genesis I, where the second act of creation is described by way of God's saying "Let there be light," this may be understood as simply an assertion regarding the initial productive action on God's part. Rather than saying that God introduced light into existence from a condition that lacked it, it can be understood as saying simply that He extended the Light within Himself so as to produce another entity or mind (the Son's) that was exactly like Him. In my understanding of the Course, this single creative act by God is the only one by Him. It would follow, at least as the Course views it, that the rest of the 'six days' of creation are only constructions of minds within the condition of separation, with some 'echoes' of the original and primary creative act of God. One such 'echo' is the comment that 'He made man in His own image and likeness,' as a very distorted reference to what was actually produced in His creative act. That is, all the formations of days 2 through 6 are ego-projections of the separated mind. In the New Testament, there are several important references, the first being in John 1: "4 In him was life, and that life was the light of men. 5 The light shines in the darkness, and the darkness has not overcome it." Here, 'light' is intimately associated with the 'Word,' of whom Jesus is considered to be the incarnation, but in this case that light is in reference to the way it/he illuminates the minds of human beings. But in 1 John 1:5, previously alluded to, we find a statement very close to what the Course holds regarding God Himself as being, since He is not created, an uncreated light: "5 This is the message we have heard from him and declare to you: God is light; in him there is no darkness at all." That is, both the older tradition of the Bible and the teachings of the Course are in agreement that there is an uncreated Light, which is present in the Father. However, there is a difference, in that the Course holds that the Light in the Son, although perfect like that in the Father/God, is a created perfect Light, although it shares all the characteristics of the uncreated Light.

b. Other perfect minds. While the Course does not have much to say about the further creations subsequent to the Son, it does make the following

observation:
> "4 Only the creations of light are real."(1,I,24,4)

This seems to be best understood as saying that only what is constituted of Light is real. This would include both God, His creature (the Son), and all creatures that are produced by the creative extension of the Son. It was pointed out that this logically includes the infinite sequence of Sons$_n$ beyond the Son directly created by God. That is, all those creatures are themselves beings of Light, since they are perfect and complete entities produced and existing by virtue of the presence of the Light of Love.

c. Holy Spirit as light. It was clarified how the Course teaches that the Holy Spirit is produced or created by God in His response to the Son's choice to enter into the condition of separation. He is not a new entity different from the Son, but a part or level of the Son's Mind that has a special function. As we should expect, He is described as also being light:

> "1 The Holy Spirit is the light in which Christ stands revealed. 2 And all who would behold Him can see Him, for they have asked for light."(13,V,11,1-2)

That the Holy Spirit is constituted of Light is fully consistent with the teaching that all things in Reality have Love as their essence, and that Love is Light. That is, the Holy Spirit can be thought of as a particular expression of Light, distinguished by His special function of correcting the error of the separation. His being constituted of Light is further indicated in:

> "5 Understanding is light, and light leads to knowledge. 6 The Holy Spirit is in light because He is in you who are light, but you yourself do not know this."(5,III,7,5-6)

In this passage, the emphasis is on His being the basis of the illumination that the Course refers to as the 'light of understanding,' which was pointed out as focusing on the conceptual level with the separated mind. But, His Light is also central to the overall function that He has of returning such minds to the full awareness that remains potential within them, that is, His function as 'Communication Link:'

> "1 The Holy Spirit is described as the remaining Communication Link between God and His separated Sons. 2 In order to fulfill this special function the Holy Spirit has assumed a dual function. 3 He knows because He is part of God; He perceives because He was sent to save humanity. 4 He is the great correction principle; the bringer of true perception, the inherent power of the vision of Christ. 5 He is the light in which the forgiven world is perceived; in which the face of Christ alone is seen."(C,6,3,1-5)

Although the Light within the Holy Spirit actually operates in all instances where the separated mind is elevated from a lower to a higher level of awareness, it is particularly important in bringing it to the highest type of perceptual awareness, the holy or 'whole' perception of the Real World. That is indicated in statement 5 where in its broadest meaning it is called the 'forgiven world' and in application to any particular part of that world it is called the 'Face of Christ.'

d. Light of Heaven. The most comprehensive sort of absolute light is that which includes the totality of Reality. This can be thought of as the presence of Light that pervades and unites all perfect minds. It is variously referred to as 'the light of Heaven,' or as what illuminates 'the Kingdom' or 'the Universe of Love.' Here are cited passages that refer to each of these. The first:

> "12 How better could your own mistakes be brought to truth than by your willingness to bring the light of Heaven with you, as you walk beyond the world of darkness into light?" (25,IV,5,12)

This seems best thought of in terms of what operates within the level of absolute Reality so as to enable all particular minds within it to be aware of all that is present there. It is the basis of the knowing in which absolute Truth is present within each perfect mind's awareness.

It is also referred to as the illuminating principle of the Kingdom:

> "3 No darkness abides anywhere in the Kingdom, but your part is only to allow no darkness to abide in your own mind. 4 This alignment with light is unlimited, because it is in alignment with the light of the world. 5 Each of us is the light of the world, and by joining our minds in this light we proclaim the Kingdom of God together and as one."(6,II,13,3-5)

Here again the supreme Light is referred to in relation to its having an effect upon the world of perception. Because that Light is present at the foundation of every separated mind, it has the capacity to transform the world that it perceives into something radically different. What is characteristic of the lower world is the presence of limits on awareness. But, within that presence there operates the unlimited Light. When the mind realizes its actual nature, it immediately finds itself restored to its original state of unlimited awareness, or returned to the Kingdom of Light of which it has always been a part, although not aware of it.

The third expression for this most comprehensive aspect of Light is in reference to 'the universe of love.' As is stated:

> "1 The light that joins you and your brother shines throughout the universe, and because it joins you and him, so it makes you and him one with your Creator. 2 And in Him is all creation joined."(22,VI,15,1-2)

This passage can be understood on two levels, a lower and a higher one. On the lower level, what we think of as the 'universe' within the realm of perception, which includes the totality of space and time, is said to be connected ('joined') and united not simply by some physical energy, but by the light of awareness that is present in all separated minds within it. However, on the higher level, this refers to the more fundamental universe that is the totality of all perfect beings, or the universe of love, or better, the Universe of Love. What connects or unites all entities within it is the one Light of Love. Thus, when understood as what it actually is, the physical universe or the universe disclosed by perception is actually grounded on that higher Universe (indeed, but an extremely tiny portion of it), in which the founding principle is the Light of Love. But only the latter is truly Real.

III. Spirit as source of light. It has been pointed out that the locus of all the various types of light, as seen by the Course, is within the minds of the entities it calls 'spirits.' This includes the spirits of unclouded perfect minds and of imperfect or separated minds. Here we consider what it has to say about how spirits are that out of which light emanates.

A. More generally. Spirit is thought of as having as its essential nature this characteristic of being illuminative:

> "3 Spirit is beyond humility, because it recognizes its radiance and gladly sheds its light everywhere."(4,I,12,3)

Here, we should recall that Love is more accurately thought of as a more primordial 'Energy.' In that sense, it is perhaps better thought of as 'impersonal' in its fundamental nature. This is a view acknowledged in the Oriental traditions, which refer to the most fundamental principle as 'Brahman' in Hinduism, 'Tao' in Taoism and Confucianism, or 'Dharmakaya' in Buddhism. All of these views can be thought of as primordially 'atheistic,' if by 'atheism' is understood the view that the most foundational reality is not a 'theos' or 'god' in the sense of a personal entity. Such a view is also found in some of the deepest thinkers in the Western traditions. For example, Plato's 'world of ideas' does not have a personal deity; the same is true of Aristotle's 'Prime Mover' (which is not thought of as a personal being), as well as of Plotinus' 'One.' Interestingly, it can be seen among some Christian theologians, such as Meister Eckhardt, who referred to the 'Godhead' as being more fundamental than the persons of the Trinity. However, this is not to say that the 'Energy' does not have a particular 'center' or 'centers' in which it is present in an unlimited way. Thus, while one might want to think of these views as 'atheistic' from one perspective, they also accommodate a basic 'theism' from another perspective. In this particular passage, what is made clear is that any such center, which the Course calls 'spirit,' since it is constituted of Light, must also emanate light. This follows, as was pointed out, from the fact that this 'Energy' is Love, whose primary property is to extend its unity.

B. In particular. The various spirits, or centers in which Love is present, can correspondingly be thought of as centers from which Light emanates. We briefly consider these as having that property:

1. God as ultimate, uncreated spirit. The Course holds that there is one uncreated center, God, also called Father, whose nature is Love. As it states:

> "4 The light is so strong that it radiates throughout the Sonship and returns thanks to the Father for radiating His joy upon it."(5,In.,3,4)

In this we may see that God must have within Him the characteristics of that

Light without any limitation. That is, He must have unlimited awareness and creativity.

2. Created spirits. Thus, being constituted of Light, He must extend that Light. It is by virtue of the Father's radiation of the Light within Himself that the Son is produced. This is the first creature, who is described:

> "4 God's guiltless Son is only light."(13,VI,8,4)

That is, the Son, like the Father, is constituted of the very same unlimited Light of Love.

But, as was discussed in Ch. II, the Course makes clear that the Light in the Son must also have the unlimited awareness and unlimited creativity of the Father:

> "7 Each voice has a part in the song of redemption, the hymn of gladness and thanksgiving for the light to the Creator of light. 8 The holy light that shines forth from God's Son is the witness that his light is of his Father."(13,VI,8,7)

That is, the Son creates His own creature, which I have called Son_2, which, being like the Son, must also create. Thus, there is the infinite sequence of perfect creatures, all of whom are spirits or centers of unlimited Light.

3. In separated minds. Because the Son's mind has also the freedom to choose to focus and attach its awareness to limited aspects or parts of Reality, it can enter into the condition of separation, as the Course holds it has done so in us. Nevertheless, that Light does not cease to operate within separated minds, although those minds are greatly diminished in their awareness of it. As is stated:

> "1 God has lit your mind Himself, and keeps your mind lit by His light because His light is what your mind is."(7,III,5,1)

The primary function of the Course is to help separated minds become aware of the presence of this unlimited Light within them. One of its exercises focuses on the following:

> "3 I am the light of the world. 4 That is my only function. 5 That is why I am here."(W,61,5,3-5)

To call a separated mind 'the light of the world' even in its separated condition seems to refer to the idea that it continues to act as a center from which light, although limited, emanates from it. Indeed, as viewed by the Course, its limited light, conjoined with the limited light of all other separated minds, is what gives rise to the world of perceptions. Of course, the concern is to restore the separated mind to fully operating as it actually is. In the case of minds not yet so restored, they are described:

> "2 Those who seek the light are merely covering their eyes. 3 The light is in them now. 4 Enlightenment is but a recognition, not a change at all. 5 Light is not of the world, yet you who bear the light in you are alien here as well. 6 The light came with you from your native home, and stayed with you because it is your own."(W,188,1,2-6)

Although the Light is present in any separated mind, its choices block its awareness of it. The only thing that needs to occur is for it to make the choice to let go of that block. This is also the point in:

> "1 There is a light in you the world can not perceive. 2 And with its eyes you will not see this light, for you are blinded by the world. 3 Yet you have eyes to see it. 4 It is there for you to look upon. 5 It was not placed in you to be kept hidden from your sight. 6 This light is a reflection of the thought we practice now."(W,189,1,1-6)

Thus, the condition of separation is only a temporary effect of self-imposed limitations on the awareness of what is always and irrevocably within it, and its limited emanation of light.

IV. The release of the Light. From one perspective, the practical teaching of the Course can be described in terms of releasing the separated mind from the experience of limited light to unlimited Light, which we discuss here.

A. Aim of releasing the Light. The separated mind is said to be really only Light, but caught within the foolish choice of attachment to limited awareness or light. Thus, the primary, and actually the only, problem it faces is to undo that attachment. What this entails is that it choose or aim at what is described:

> "1 When a mind has only light, it knows only light. 2 Its own radiance shines all around it, and extends out into the darkness of other minds, transforming them into majesty."
> (7,XI,5,1-2)

That is, its single intention must be to have within its awareness the fullness of light. Of course, that is the clear awareness or knowledge of the fundamental or primary Light, which it and all other things in Reality actually are. This involves the complete elimination of any sort of 'darkness,' i.e., any limitations imposed upon the Light that it is aware of.

This has a physical analogue in how physics regards material objects. Such objects are thought of as composed of elementary particles, each particle itself a spatially confined 'standing wave' of light-energy. Einstein's equation $E = mc^2$ states that all such material objects, characterized by their m(mass)-value, can be transformed to the unbounded state E(energy), a mode that extends through space. That is, all material objects can be liberated so as to exist as what is more properly called light. In that sense, the liberated mode of matter would be in its having returned to its original condition of light, out of which the material form coagulated. This is quite similar to the return of the separated mind to its original condition of being only Light.

From this perspective, the separated mind needs to come to the realization that it has a single goal, which is described:

> "4 Fear seems to live in darkness, and when you are afraid you have stepped back. 5 Let us then join quickly in an instant of light, and it will be enough to remind you that your goal is

light."(18,III,2,4-5)

Elsewhere, the Course points out that the primary block, or darkness, that arises in its separated experience is fear. Fear is what impels the mind to distance itself from what it fears. In that sense, although it *is* Light, what it comes to fear in adopting the ego-idea is the very Light that it actually is. This is compared to the state of being in a dream:

> "6 If a light is suddenly turned on while someone is dreaming a fearful dream, he may initially interpret the light itself as part of his dream and be afraid of it. 7 However, when he awakens, the light is correctly perceived as the release from the dream, which is then no longer accorded reality."(2,I,4,6-7)

This analogy points to the way in which a sleeping person can respond to the presence of a strong sensory light that might stimulate his own awakening. Its presence is distorted and perceived as some sort of threat and danger to his well-being. In one sense, such a stimulus does indeed threaten the dream-state, since it tends to undo or destroy that state. However, the dreaming mind that is attached to the dream state greatly deprives itself of a much fuller experience. When correctly understood, the external stimulus is seen as a pathway to a much more wholesome condition. Similarly, the separated mind, although it may at first feel threatened by and be fearful of the presence of the greater Light that might be seeping into its awareness, is only depriving itself by identifying with that fear. When it comes to the point of seeing through the fear, it may open to the wholesome awakened state.

What operates in the process of awakening is the basic principle described here:

> "4 Whenever light enters darkness, the darkness is abolished."(2,VII,5,4)

This principle applies on all levels, from the physical, to the various sorts of perception. One may think of it as operating in the process called 'biological evolution,' where we find a slow emergence of more comprehensive sorts of light or awareness. The lowest or most limited is that of physical light, which is received and emitted by all material things. In living organisms there arises the rudimentary sort of 'light,' such as chemical responsiveness to the environment as well chemical imposition on the environment, as exhibited in the simplest living things, the prokaryotes and the eukaryotes. Their very primitive 'light' as a type of awareness seems to correspond to the sensation of smell and taste in humans. In more developed organisms, this 'light' diversifies into the various sorts of sensory perceptivity not fundamentally different from that of our five external senses. On a still more developed level, organisms come to a much more complex 'light' that emerges into whole perceptual units that allow identification of various sorts of 'things.' Even further development brings the complex neural networks that allow organisms to experience an even more complex sort of 'light' exhibited in imagination and memory. In human beings, there emerges the yet more complex sort of 'light' that enables them to form concepts and to reason. From this perspective, the apex of biological evolution is found in those human beings that activate the highest perceptual 'light,' that experienced in the perception of the Real World or what is called by others the 'mystical experience.' However, it would be erroneous to conclude that the Course has a narrowly anthropocentric view of the levels of light, holding that only humans can access this highest perceptual light. Although it does not discuss other biological forms, it clearly can accommodate the presence in the space-time realm of many other species that have awareness. It is even compatible with the view that not only what we think of as 'living organisms' can experience various sorts of light, but that there may be a great variety of minds within the universe very different from the particular array discovered by our sciences. Indeed, it is quite possible that physical bodies such as planets, stars, or even what are called 'galaxies' have their own peculiar sort of perceptual light and experience in ways far different from what we and other living forms experience here on Earth. It was not long ago when the opinion of the greatest human minds generally held that the stars and planets all had their own minds and were referred to as 'gods' or 'devas' (Sanskrit for 'shining ones'), and that there are 'spirits' of countless sorts that exist on other planes of space and time. It would be mere arrogance to assume that the only sorts of perceiving beings are the ones that we have been able to examine in our laboratories. In any case, the principle described above would hold for any such separated mind, which in the Course's view, whether a lowly bacterium, a human being, or a 'god,' is to some degree in the condition of darkness, and can be brought to a state in which that darkness is removed, either partially or totally.

Complementary to this general principle of the releasing power of Light is this description of what prevents that release:

"3 There is no darkness that the light of love will not dispel, unless it is concealed from love's beneficence."(14,VI,2,3)

That is, no obstacle or block is insuperable. All darkness seeming to be present in any separated mind can and eventually will be removed. What removes that darkness is the Light itself; what prevents the removal is simply the choice that such a mind makes to uphold the darkness

B. The major steps in the release. Accordingly, the Course is essentially a set of instructions in the process for enabling Light to operate fully. When one examines the following passages, one can see a series of 'steps,' described in terms of 'light,' that bring this about. These are outlined here:

Step I. Asking for light. Since the presence of darkness or the blocking of Light's presence is fundamentally only a matter of so choosing, the undoing of darkness must begin with a reversal of that choice:

"3 Ask for light and learn that you *are* light."(8,III,1,3)

Although the separated mind does not clearly understand what it may be asking for, it can come to the insight that there is a 'higher' light that it may think of as coming from a higher Source. This involves a kind of faith in that it recognizes that it can and must move beyond the limits into the 'unknown,' or rather 'unperceived,' which is beyond its current condition of awareness. Such a choice is very likely one that has been made for every student of the Course, long before he or she even heard of it or began to study it. It also seems very likely that this step occurs to people entirely outside the tradition of Christianity. Indeed, it operates in any mind that comes to the realization that something that may be called 'truth' may be accessible to its awareness, whether that mind be the most hardened atheist or the most accepting believer.

Step II. Calling for the Light in the Holy Spirit through some person in whom the Light is more fully present. Although the Light is present within every separated mind, most of them are greatly dominated by the ego-idea. But, the presence of another person in the world who has realized the Light can serve as a great help in enabling them to move more fully into that same realization. In the context of the Course, this is the primary role of Jesus:

> "8 My purpose, then, is still to overcome the world. 9 I do not attack it, but my light must dispel it because of what it is. 10 Light does not attack darkness, but it does shine it away. 11 If my light goes with you everywhere, you shine it away with me. 12 The light becomes ours, and you cannot abide in darkness any more than darkness can abide wherever you go."
> (8,IV,2,8-12)

Here the alleged Author of the Course, who may be thought of as Jesus, makes clear that his intention is to bring the Light into, or more accurately awaken the Light already in, all others. This seems to be quite close to the condition described in Jesus' healing of the blind man Bartimaeus in response to his cry as that teacher was passing by and Bartimaeus called out to Jesus: "'What do you want me to do for you?' Jesus asked him. The blind man said, 'Rabbi, I want to see.'"(Mark 10: 51) From the Course's perspective, Bartimaeus, in calling on Jesus for the Light, was perceiving that the teacher was one in whom the Light was present to a much greater degree than in himself. That is, the person or form of Jesus acted as a symbol that more vividly manifested the presence of the Light than what Bartimaeus was then aware of. By his calling on the Light in Jesus, he was actually opening to the Light within himself.

The Course does make clear that the name and form of Jesus is a very useful symbol in this step. However, it also makes clear that he is not the only such symbol. It seems fully consistent with the teachings that other symbols, such as those of the various 'saints' within the Christian tradition or the holy persons like the Buddha, Lao Tse, and the 'rishis' of Hinduism, can also function in this way. Indeed, the biography of the 19th century Hindu Sri Ramakrishna tells how that man realized the Light by using symbols taken from various Hindu traditions,

Christianity, and Islam.[6] In all these traditions, the Course holds that it is the same Mind of Light which it calls the Holy Spirit that is brought into more direct functioning within the separated mind. Indeed, the Light may be more fully manifested than in oneself in many people that one encounters, even varying in its manifestation, so that they may act as 'transmitters' of the Light, or better, as 'removers' of the blocks to It.

Step III. Seeing light in all brothers. Related to the last point, attachment to some external form or symbol is itself a block to further realization of the Light. A further step that this opening involves is one of recognizing that the Light one seeks is present in all other separated minds. This is described:

> "2 The mind we share is shared by all our brothers, and as we see them truly they will be healed. 3 Let your mind shine with mine upon their minds, and by our gratitude to them make them aware of the light in them. 4 This light will shine back upon you and on the whole Sonship, because this is your proper gift to God."(7,V,11,2-4)

Once a separated mind opens to choosing Light, it begins to understand that Light is actually present in every other mind. This is called 'seeing the Face of Christ.' If one considers Jesus as being born as a separated mind, but one that quickly came to the realization of who/what he actually was, it becomes clear that his ministry was based on his recognition that Light was present in all he encountered and that his concern was one of helping them to realize that they were not different from him, at least in their potential. Thus, it becomes extremely important for any separated mind's full realization to have this recognition in all others it encounters. This is, of course, the primary reason for giving miracles. As statement 4 points out, when one sees the Light present in others, the effect is that the Light in them shines back into oneself, thus deepening and intensifying one's own realization of the Light.

Step IV: Giving forgiveness to all others. This step in one way can be thought of as a part of step III. However, what it emphasizes is that not only must the developing mind perceive the Light in others, but it must also actively engage in a process of removing all the blocks to their awareness of Light's presence. That is the activity of giving miracles, the most essential feature of which is that of forgiving or letting go of false perceptions and letting the light from the Holy Spirit flow to the miracle-receiver. This is described:

> "4 The world I look upon has taken on the light of my forgiveness, and shines forgiveness back at me. 5 In this light I begin to see what my illusions about myself kept hidden."(W,57,5,4)

Here, we may see how being a miracle-giver is an essential role incumbent upon every separated mind that would fully 'see.' In our discussion of the giving of miracles for a mind only at the stage of imperfect love, the giving of miracles is

---

[6] See *The Gospel of Sri Ramakrishna*, Swami Nikhilananda.

limited and sporadic. But, for the mind that has more fully awakened to perfect love, the offering of miracles occurs almost, if not completely, in an incessant way to everyone encountered by that mind. The importance of this lies in the fact that what occurs in doing so is that all false perceptions are completely dissolved or eliminated from such a mind while it remains in the realm of perception.

There are several other passages that speak of the realization of Light within this step. One of them makes clear that this is not a matter of taking in some sort of Energy or Light from an outer source, but rather of releasing fully the Light already present within one's own mind:

> "2 Let yourself be brought unto your Self. 3 Its strength will be the light in which the gift of sight is given you. 4 Leave, then, the dark a little while today, and we will practice seeing in the light, closing the body's eyes and asking truth to show us how to find the meeting place of self and Self, where light and strength are one."(W,92,10,2-4)

Here it is made fully clear that the Light that one comes to realize is the Light that constitutes one's own Self. As viewed by the Course, that is simply the Son as God created Him. In this sense, the realization of the Light is not so much a matter of accumulating or adding on something, but a matter of removing the obstacles, the various forms of darkness (the ego-idea and its beliefs together with all the fears and limited false perceptions that obsess it, including the 'dark companions') that interfere with the awareness that is and has always been present.

This same insight is stated somewhat differently in a passage cited earlier (p. 368):

> "2 Those who seek the light are merely covering their eyes. 3 The light is in them now. 4 Enlightenment is but a recognition, not a change at all. 5 Light is not of the world, yet you who bear the light in you are alien here as well. 6 The light came with you from your native home, and stayed with you because it is your own."(W,188,1,2-6)

That is, that there seems to be a lack or limited presence of Light is only an illusion based on the choice that persists in time until it is reversed. The separated mind is not changed to something else, but simply comes to see what it has always been, or rather always is. Thus the Course uses a metaphor for this realization that is perhaps the most accurate: it is a matter of awakening from a kind of gigantic dream, in which the many other separated minds that seem to be within that dream are also dreaming along with it, but which sooner or later will awaken. Indeed, from one perspective, they are already awake.

The importance of miracles is also noted in:

> "3 Let us ... recognize that we are being introduced to sight, and led away from darkness to the light where only miracles can be perceived."(W,92,11,3)

In this we may see a kind of 'feedback' effect that operates in the mind of the miracle-giver. First, it is the opening to the Light that makes the giving of a miracle possible. But then, since this involves the dismissal or letting go of some sort of darkness (the illusion of lack), the result is a clearer awareness of the Light. This enables the miracle-giver to move ever more quickly toward the full awareness of the Light.

Step V: Opening to the world of Light, or the Real World. This step should be thought of as one that involves a growing intensity rather than a sudden shift or 'step.' It is the final phase of the process of transformation of the separated mind within the world of perception. It is summarily described:

> "5 You and your brother are coming home together, after a long and meaningless journey that you undertook apart, and that led nowhere. 6 You have found your brother, and you will light each other's way. 7 And from this light will the Great Rays extend back into darkness and forward unto God, to shine away the past and so make room for His eternal Presence, in which everything is radiant in the light."(18,III,8,5-7)

This describes the central shift in awareness that occurs in the experience of the holy instant, which involves the opening of awareness to the Real World. As was explained earlier, that experience is a matter of degree, although there is a major shift that occurs in the initial occurrence of that experience. It was also pointed out that this shift, at least in the beginning, is usually followed by a return to the habitual ego-dominated state, although even that state undergoes important transformations in which the ego-domination is diminished. As the experience deepens and becomes more intense, there is a gradual release of attachment to the ego-idea so that the particular mind eventually operates completely free of it. In terms of 'light,' this can be thought of as a shift toward being completely in the perceptual awareness of Light, or more accurately, in a state in which the Light of Love fills the whole of one's perception.

There are several important effects related to this growing luminosity. One is in relation to the perception of the body:

> "2 In His perception of the world, nothing is seen but justifies forgiveness and the sight of perfect sinlessness. 3 Nothing arises but is met with instant and complete forgiveness. 4 Nothing remains an instant, to obscure the sinlessness that shines unchanged, beyond the pitiful attempts of specialness to put it out of mind, where it must be, and light the body up instead of it."(25,III,5,2-4)

Because the mind is firmly connected to the Light and that Light fills its perception, it perceives the form it thinks of as its body as completely penetrated with that Light. Although the very notion of the body as something limited in space and time involves an aspect of 'darkness' (recall that the core meaning of 'darkness' is simply that of limitation on awareness), even it is perceived in terms of the true perceptions that constitute its form. From a perspective of current physics, one might describe this as involving the direct perception of the 'field characteristics' of the body that make it only a particular concentration of energy within the whole of space-time, yet having a presence throughout all of space-time. That is, the body is perceived as radiating its presence to all of the physical universe.

But, not only is one's own body so perceived. All other objects, including the bodies of others as well as other physical forms, are perceived as having a similar luminosity.

> "5 So perfectly can you forgive him his illusions he becomes your savior from your dreams. 6 And as you see him shining in the space of light where God abides within the darkness, you will see that God Himself is where his body is. 7 Before this light the body disappears, as heavy shadows must give way to light. 8 The darkness cannot choose that it remain. 9 The coming of the light means it is gone."(29,III,3,5-9)

That is, the experience of other separated minds shifts from awareness of the limits and limitations of their bodies to the presence of the Light that is in them. As statement 7 indicates, this involves a shifting of focus on the particular bodily forms of others to their being centers of Light that radiate throughout the whole world of perception. From that perspective, the universe is perceived as a unity of countless interpenetrating spheres (or perhaps better, four-dimensional hyperspheres) of Light, the centers of which are the various particular minds that have thought they were in separation.

More generally, this perception holds for all particular limited forms that the separated mind thinks of as located in various places within the field of its perception. This is described as perceiving all within a 'picture of light:'

> "1 The picture of light, in clear-cut and unmistakable contrast, is transformed into what lies beyond the picture. 2 As you look on this, you realize that it is not a picture, but a reality. 3 This is no figured representation of a thought system, but the Thought itself. 4 What it represents is there. 5 The frame fades gently and God rises to your remembrance, offering you the whole of creation in exchange for your little picture, wholly without value and entirely deprived of meaning."
> (17,IV,15,1-5)

This particular passage focuses on the shift away from the 'picture of light' to the complete awareness that comes when the mind is fully restored to its original state. However, what is first experienced at the most mature development of the experience of the holy instant is the fully complete perception of the Real World. It is that perception which is the content of this 'picture of light.' It is also called a 'miniature of eternity' and a 'picture of timelessness:'

> "4 The holy instant is a miniature of eternity. 5 It is a picture of timelessness, set in a frame of time."(17,IV,11,4-5)

Thus, the picture of light may be thought of as the content of the perception of the fully matured experience of the holy instant. In it, all that one perceives is Light as extending throughout all that it perceives. This includes all of what is present in space and time, viewed not through the visual organs or even one's conceptual awareness, but perceived in a single comprehensive perception of all that is present within space-time.

The overall effect of this perception is described:

> "3 What has been locked is opened; what was held apart from light is given up, that light may shine on it and leave no space nor distance lingering between the light of Heaven and the world."(26,IX,5,3)

That is, all things that the matured mind perceives, which extends to the whole of space and time, are perceived simply as filled with intense light. This light, because it is within the confines of perception, is not itself the full Light of Love, although it is the result of the presence of Love within all those things perceived. One might think of this as a 'stepped-down version' of Love, so that it would be correct to say it involves a perception of Light/Love, although not as Light/Love actually is in its fullness. The full awareness of Light/Love is accessible only through the mode called 'knowledge.'

The Course makes clear that a mind having such a perception can still operate within the world of minds that have not yet come to this perception. However, it does so in a radically different manner from that of minds still influenced by ego. This is described:

> "6 And the light of Christ in you is given charge of everything you do."(31,VIII,2,6)

That is, what such a mind has come to is a state of being identified with the Christ Mind. The ego-idea has been completely dissolved for it, so that the only basis for what it does is the non-ego awareness that is said here to be filled with the 'light of Christ.' This is also described as having only the 'vision of Christ.' Of course, since the awareness of Christ is, strictly speaking, only the perfect mode of knowing, and the Holy Spirit is His Mind's awareness in so far as it is able to perceive, this light of Christ is the same as what can be called the 'light of the Holy Spirit.' Such is claimed to have occurred in the person Jesus.

So filled with that light, such a mind has a single concern: the giving of its vision to all minds that still remain in separation. Hence, it engages in the fulfillment of that concern:

> "2 This world you bring with you to all the weary eyes and tired hearts that look on sin and beat its sad refrain. 3 From you can come their rest. 4 From you can rise a world they will rejoice to look upon, and where their hearts are glad. 5 In you there is a vision that extends to all of them, and covers them in gentleness and light. 6 And in this widening world of light the darkness that they thought was there is pushed away, until it is but distant shadows, far away, not long to be remembered as the sun shines them to nothingness."(25,IV,3,2-6)

Thus, the very presence of the Course may be understood as an expression of the fully awakened and realized mind of Jesus, working through the guidance of the Holy Spirit, so as to awaken all other minds still in separation to the Light that is within them. From this perspective, it is a particularly straightforward and effective expression of that Light that follows in the tradition that may be traced back to Jesus, and even prior to him in the more ancient stories found in the Old Testament that point to the very beginning of creation in the words said to have been spoken by God: "Let there be Light!"

Step VI. Return to the fullness of Light, or Heaven. This process of illumination is not, however, fully completed in the transformation of the separated mind's awareness to that of the Real World. Although that is an important and necessary step, it does not involve the total forgiveness or letting go of *all* illusion. The final step must even let the Real World go so that forgiveness may be fully like what is thought of as forgiveness in God, whose Light dissolves the whole illusion of separation:

> "1 Father, forgiveness is the light You chose to shine away all conflict and all doubt, and light the way for our return to You. 2 No light but this can end our evil dream. 3 No light but this can save the world."(W,333,2,1-3)

Here it is important to recall that God's response to the separation is such that He completely dismisses, and in that sense forgives, the whole illusory complex in a single act of His Mind. Although that complex seems for separated minds to last for billions of years, it is only a minor 'blip' within God's awareness. As the separated mind fully opens to the Light that it is, it also comes to this awareness.

The Real World, although it is a 'world of light,' it is still based on the selective awareness of perception. As long as that mode of awareness remains, the mind excludes something from what it sees. This can be remedied only by the elimination of even the last traces of 'darkness' or limitation that any perception involves:

> "12 How better could your own mistakes be brought to truth than by your willingness to bring the light of Heaven with you, as you walk beyond the world of darkness into light?" (25,IV,5,12)

What is here called the 'light of Heaven,' as we saw earlier, is nothing but the pure and unrestricted Light of Love. Although perception may only involve true perceptions, as is the perception of the Real World, those perceptions are nevertheless focused and limited aspects of the whole of Reality. That is, the Light of Heaven is far more inclusive than what can be found in any perceptual awareness, however great it may be.

Thus, the final step involves what is described as 'crossing the bridge:'

> "3 Across the bridge that He provides are dreams all carried to the truth, to be dispelled before the light of knowledge." (W,pII,7,1,3)

The 'bridge' is the shift in the mind's awareness that transfers it from the perception of the Real World, however magnificent and beautiful it may appear to be, to the infinitely greater and more beautiful cognition that is knowledge. In that alone is the fullness of the Light made completely present, as it illuminates with total clarity the infinity of perfect minds, including God and all those produced by way of His sharing of the Love that is His essence, which constitutes and fills the Universe of Love.

A Selected Bibliography

Abbott, E. *Flatland: A Romance of Many Dimensions*, Create Space Independent Publishing Platform, 2014

A Course in Miracles, Combined edition 3, Foundation for Inner Peace, 2008; includes the Preface, Text, Workbook, Teachers Manual, Clarification of Terms, Psychotherapy, and Song of Prayer.

A Course in Miracles Urtext Manuscripts, Miracles In Action Press, 1st edition, 2008. This includes nearly all material found in the "Shorthand Notes" but not included in FIP, as well as important Appendices that discuss the various versions.

Alexander, Eben. *Proof of Heaven: A Neurosurgeon's Journey into Afterlife*, Simon & Schuster, 2012

Aranya, Swami Harihar-ananada. *Yoga Philosophy of Patanjali*, SUNY Press, 1983

Aristotle. *Physics*, Oxford University Press, 2008

Augustine of Hippo. *Confessions*, Penguin Classics, 1961
  Homilies on the First Epistle of John, tr. by Boniface Ramsey, New City Press, 2008

The Bhagavad Gita, Penguin Classics; revised edition, 2003

Buber, Martin. *I and Thou*, Touchstone, 1971

Buddha. *The Dhammapada*, tr. by Irving Babbitt, New Directions Books, 1st printing edition, 1965
  Teachings of the Compassionate Buddha, ed. by E. A. Burtt, New American Library, 2000

Barrington, Amy. *Love Remembered: An Experiential Journey Through a Course in Miracles*, Miracles In Action Press, 2009

Carroll, Robert Todd. *The Skeptic's Dictionary: a Collection of Strange Beliefs, Amusing Deceptions, and Dangerous Delusions*, John Wiley and Sons, 2003.

Eliade, Mircea. *The Sacred and the Profane*: *The Nature of Religion*, Harcourt Brace Jovanovich, 1987

Feuerbach, Ludwig. *Lectures on the Essence of Religion*, tr. by Ralph Manheim, Harper & Row, 1967

Fromm, Erich. *The Art of Loving,* Harper Perenial Modern Classics, 2009

Gardner, Martin. *Weird Water and Fuzzy Logic, Weird Water and Fuzzy Logic,* Prometheus Books, 1996

Goethe, Johann W. *Faust, A Tragedy,* Norton Critical Reader, 2nd ed., W. W. Norton & Co., 2001

Groeschel, Benedict J. *A Still Small Voice,* Ignatius Press, 1993

Happold, F. *Mysticism: A Study and Anthology*, Penguin Books, 1991

Heidegger, Martin. *Being and Time*, Harper & Row; English Language Edition, 1962
Hesse, Hermann. *Demian*, Harper Perenial Modern Classics, 2009
Hobbes, Thomas. *Leviathan*, Penguin Classics, 1982
Howe, Carol M. *Never Forget to Laugh: Personal Recollections of Bill Thetford, Co-Scribe of A Course in Miracles*, self published, 2009
Hume, David. *Treatise of Human Nature*, Oxford University Press; 2nd edition, 1978
Hume, R. E. *The Thirteen Principal Upanishads*, Oxford University Press, revised edition, 1974
Jampolsky, Gerald. *Love is Letting Go of Fear*, Celestial Arts, 2004
Teach Only Love, New York: Bantam, 1985
Jung, C. G. *Synchronicity: An Acausal Connecting Principle*, Princeton University Press, 2010
Jesseph, Joe R. *A Primer of Psychology According to A Course in Miracles,* Outskirts Press, 2008
Kant, Immanuel. *Critique of Pure Reason*, Palgrave Macmillan, revised edition, 2003
Kapleau, P. *Three Pillars of Zen: Teaching, Practice, and Enlightenment*, Anchor, 1989
Krishna, Gopi. *The Biological Basis of Religion and Genius*, Institute for Consciousness Research, 2006
Krishnamurti, J. *The First and Last Freedom,* Harper & Row, 1975
You are the World, Harper & Row, 1972
Master Teacher (Charles Buell Anderson). *Love: The Sum and Substance of Our Eternal Reality*, Endeavor Academy, 2011
Miller, Douglas P. *The Complete Story of the Course*, Berkeley: Fearless Books, 1997
Understanding a Course in Miracles: The History, Message, and Legacy of a Spiritual Path for Today, Celestial Arts, 2011
Newport, John P. *The New Age Movement and the Biblical Worldview: Conflict and Dialogue*, Wm. B. Eerdmans Publishing Co., 1997
Nietzsche, Friedrich. *The Gay Science*, Vintage, 1974
Nikhilananda, Swami. *The Gospel of Sri Ramakrishna*, Ramakrishna-Vivedananda Center, 1969.
Otto, Rudolf. *The Idea of the Holy*, Oxford University Press, 2nd edition, 1958
Parmenides. "Fragments," in *Ancilla to the Presocratic Philosophers*, by Kathleen Freeman, Basil Blackwell, 1956
Parrott, W. *Emotions in Social Psychology*, Psychology Press, 2001
Perron, Mari. *A Course on Love: Combined Edition*, Take Heart Publications, 2014

Perry, Robert. "Are There Many Sons or Just One Son," www.circleofa.org/library/articles/are-there-many-sons-or-just-one-son
 Reality & Illusion: An Overview of Course Metaphysics, Circle Publishing, 2002
 Special Relationships: *Illusions of Love*, Robert Perry, 1992
Plato. *The Republic*, Dover Publications, 2000
 The Symposium, Penguin, 1974
 Timaeus and Critias, Oxford University Press, 2009
Rice, Kevin. *The Game of Love: Changing the Rules Changes Everything*, Litho Printers & Bindery, 2nd edition, 2009
Ring Kenneth. *Life at Death, A Scientific Investigation of the Near-Death Experience*, Coward, McCann, and Geoghegan, 1980
Salmon, W. C. *Zeno's Paradoxes*, 2nd edition, Hackett Publishing Co. Inc., 2001
Sartre, Jean-Paul. *No Exit*, Samuel French, Inc., 1958
Schucman, Helen. *Helen Schucman Autobiography*, downloadable at www.acim-archives.org
Skutch, Robert. *Journey Without Distance: The Story Behind A Course in Miracles*, Foundation for Inner Peace, 2001
Thetford, William. *William Thetford Life Story*, downloadable at www.acim-archives.org
Tucker, J. and I. Stevenson. *Life Before Life: Children's Memories of Previous Lives,* St. Martin's Griffin, 2008
Underhill, E. *Mysticism - A Study in the Nature and Development of Man's Spiritual Consciousness*, E. P. Dutton, 1961
Vahle, Neal. *A Course in Miracles: The Lives of Helen Schucman and William Thetford*, Open View Press, 2009
Wapnick, Ken. *Absence from Felicity: The Story of Helen Schucman and Her Scribing of A Course in Miracles*, Foundation for A Course in Miracles, 2nd edition, 1991
 Christian Psychology in A Course in Miracles, Foundation for A Course in Miracles; 2nd edition, 1992
 Ending Our Escape from Love: From Dissociation to Acceptance of A Course in Miracles, Foundation for A Course in Miracles, 2011
 Ending Our Resistance to Love: The Practice of A Course in Miracles, Foundation for a Course in Miracles, 2004
 Fifty Miracle Principles of A Course in Miracles, Foundation for a Course in Miracles, 4th edition, 1992
 Life, Death and Love: Shakespeare's Great Tragedies and A Course in Miracles, Foundation for A Course in Miracles, 2004
 Love Does Not Condemn: The World, the Flesh, and the Devil According to Platonism, Christianity, Gnosticism, and 'A Course in Miracles', Foundation for a Course in Miracles, 2nd

edition, 1989

The Stages of Our Spiritual Journey (The Practice of A Course in Miracles), Foundation for A Course in Miracles, 2009

A Vast Illusion: Time According to 'A Course in Miracles,' Foundation for a Course in Miracles, 2nd edition, 1991

Wapnick, Ken, and W. Norris Clark. *A Course in Miracles and Christianity: A Dialogue,* Foundation for a Course in Miracles, Reprint edition, 1995

Whitson, William W. Ph.D. *Myths and Misinformation: William Newton Thetford and the Central Intelligence Agency*, Foundation for Inner Peace, 2012

Wilber, Ken. *The Spectrum of Consciousness*, Theosophical Publishing House, 1977

The Integral Vision: A Very Short Introduction to the Revolutionary Integral Approach to Life, God, the Universe, and Everything, Shambhala, 2007

Williamson, Marianne. *A Return to Love: Reflections on the Principles of 'A Course in Miracles,'* HarperOne, Reissue edition, 1996

Xenophanes of Colophon. "Fragments," in *Ancilla to the Presocratic Philosophers*, by Kathleen Freeman, Basil Blackwell, 1956

Some useful Internet resources:

A Course in Miracles Archives: www.acim-archives.org/   Set up in 2009 as the ACIM Archival site of The Foundation for Inner Peace and the Foundation for A Course in Miracles, it offers original and authentic material from its historical collection

A Course in Miracles Resource Website for ACIM Students: www.miraclestudies.net/   Set up by Joseph Jesseph, this site contains insightful essays on the various versions of the Course, particularly regarding the publication of the 'unauthorized' versions.

A Course in Miracles Explained: www.acimexplained.com/

Circle of Atonement: www.circleofa.org/   Established in 1993 under the leadership of Robert Perry focusing on the Course's teachings.

The Community Miracles Center: www.miracles-course.org/joomla Worldwide community for anyone who is interested in the Course's teachings

Course in Miracles Society: www.cimsmiracles.wordpress.com

Foundation for A Course in Miracles: www.facim.org/ Founded in 1983, the Center was established as a school focusing on the Course. In 1993 it established an academy of learning as an aid and reinforcement to students' study of A Course in Miracles. In 1995, it founded the Institute for Teaching Inner Peace through A Course in Miracles (ITIP-ACIM), primarily to reflect the close relationship between the Foundation for Inner Peace External and the Foundation for A Course in Miracles

Foundation for Inner Peace: www.acim.org/ The earliest ACIM organization, founded in 1975, it was established as trustee and publisher of the Course. It published the first edition of ACIM

Institute for Personal Religion and Miracles Magazine: www.miraclesmagazine.org/ Led by Jon Mundy, one of the leading teachers on the Course

Miracles in Action Press: www.miraclesinactionpress.org/ Led by Doug Thompson, it offers the various versions of the Course as well as links to numerous videos of talks related to the Course. Most useful is The Scholar's Toolbox, which links to primary source documents in "facsimile" (photocopy of original manuscripts) form and in searchable "e-text" typed transcripts, as well as Concordances. Included are copies of all the versions of the Course prepared by the Scribes which have come to light. It includes the following:

1) Primary Source library: The Scholar's Toolbox I
2) Concordances: The Scholar's Toolbox II
3) High Resolution Notes facsimile manuscript images
4) HLC "synthesized" Audio (not currently on line)
5) The Annotated HLC (e-text)
6) The Urtext Manuscripts in Seven Volumes (e-text)
7) Bibles and Concordances
10) ACIM On-line copies: HTML files for Notes, Urtext, HLC, and FIP versions
12) All ACIM versions reviewed with on-line copies
13) The Original Dictation combining both Shorthand Notes and Urtext Manuscripts chapters one through eight

Miracle Distribution Center: www.miraclecenter.org Dedicated to helping make the teachings of A Course in Miracles more available and to aid course students in their practice of its transformational principles. Founded in 1978

van Harskamp, Anton. "A Modern Miracle; or: The Ruthless Logic of A Course in Miracles," at thegroundoffaith.net/issues/2011-10/CourseInMiracles

Websites primarily critical of the Course:

"A Course in Miracles, another devilish attempt that proves Satan is losing," www.bibleprobe.com/miracle course

"A Course in Miracles," www.apologeticsindex.org/c08

Branch, Rick. "A Course InMiracles," www.watchman.org/profiles/pdf/courseinmiraclesprofile.pdf

Contender Ministries: www.contenderministries.org/coursein miracles.php

Conway, Timothy. "A Brief Critical Analysis of A Course in Miracles, ACIM,"www.enlightened-spirituality.org/ ACIM_critique

Giganti, Sharon Lee. "A Warning About A Course in Miracles" www.newagedeception.com/new/free-resources/5-a-warning-about-a-course-in-miracles

Hryczyk, Edward R. "A COURSE IN MIRACLES" www.ewtn.com/library/newage/course.txt

In Plain Site: www.inplainsite.org/html/a_course_in_miracles

Lighthouse Trails Research Project: www.lighthousetrails.research.com/courseinmiracles.htm

Moran, Tracy. "A Course in Brainwashing," www.ewtn.com/library/NEWAGE/BRAINWAS.TXT

Sina, Ali "A Course in Miracles or in Brainwashing?" www.faithfreedofreedom.org/Articles/sina31214

Skeptics Dictionary: www.skepdic.com/cim.html

Szimhart, J. "A Course In Miracles: an Examination," www.jszimhart.com/essays/a_course_in_miracles

Wise, Russ. "A Course In Miracles A Biblical Evaluation," www.leaderu.com/orgs/probe/docs/thcourse

INDEX

absolute love or Love 9, 24-84
  as basis of awareness 71-2
  as basis of existence 67-8
  effects of 41-7
    freedom 45-7
    gratitude 44-5
    Joy 42-4
    Peace 41-2
  essential characteristics 25-41
    all-inclusive 38-9
    creating/extending 28-36
    eternal/timeless 37-8
    knowing 28
    limitless/infinite 36-7
    sustaining 39
    uniting 25-8
  excludes 47-53
    comparison 50-1
    fear 47-8
    illusion 48-9
    judgment 49-50
    symbol 52-3
    triumph 51-2
  in created perfect minds 66-74
    in Son 68-73
    in other created p.m. 73-4
  in creatures 'after' separation 81-2
    in Christ Mind 81
    in former separated minds 81
    in Holy Spirit 81-2
  in creatures 'during' separation 74-81
    in Christ Mind 74-5
    in Holy Spirit 75-79
    in separated minds 79-81
  in God 25-66
    'after' Atonement 65-6
    originally 25-53
    in response to separation 53-66
    forgiveness in 65-6
    as Light 360-2
  in Universe of Love 82-4
  Law of Love 39-1, 46, 201
A Course in Miracles 4-7
  author of 2, 4, 16-18
  main parts 4-5

  origin 4
  practices in 312-22
  referencing systems 6-7
  scribes 4
  versions, 4-6
    Foundation for Inner Peace (FIP) 5
    Hugh Lynn Cayce (HLC) 5
    Urtext Manuscripts 6
    Shorthand Notes 4
    Thetford Transcript 5
    Urtext 4
anger 126-9, 339-40
Angst 48, 100, 115
apperception 356-7
Atonement 11, 17, 60-6, 154, 161, 181, 164, 177-8, 234
  full completion 66(n), 81-4, 197, 224, 269, 299, 309
  individual completion 66(n), 190-1, 198-9, 216, 240-4,
  plan of Atonement 60-5, 349
  process of 66, 76, 97, 162, 191, 207, 215, 322-4
attack 106-7, 26-7, 133-5, 254-5, 306
  'Original Attack' 134, 148
  as self-contradictory 126-7
Augustine of Hippo 44, 201, 237
aura/halo 192, 264, 292
authority problem 86-7, 90-1
awareness 27, 273-4
  as based on Love 71
  knowing/knowledge 28, 58
  and light 250, 342-3
  as receptive mode of uniting 27
  perceiving/perception 11, 54, 58
  unexplainable physiologically 101-2, 352-3
awe 184, 209-10

beauty 192, 239, 283
Blake, William 244, 265
body 54, 60-1, 124, 162, 182(n), 186, 196, 246-7, 263, 306, 316-7
  basic idea of 54, 101
  in holy instant 246-7, 263-70, 281
  as neutral 124

body (cont.))
    not central to awareness 352-3
    not created by God 333
    origin of 54, 57, 95, 101, 249(n)
    'rainbow body' 267(n)
'bridging instant' 243-4
'bringer of salvation' 300-1
brothers 236, 261, 373
Buber, Martin 72
Bodhisattva 39, 40, 196, 288, 300
Buddha 95,102,113, 130, 171, 189, 196, 216(n), 255, 304, 314, 317, 347(n)

cases of the reincarnation type 182
cause 51, 92-3
celestial speedup 160, 193, 289, 301-3
charity 151-3, 214, 217-8
    English definitions of 151-2
    'false charity' 222-29
    as imperfect love 151-3
    and right-mindedness 214
choice
    of return 79, 92, 125, 168-9, 176, 207, 214-5,234,239,243,283-4,315,318-9
    of separation 54-5, 57, 61-3, 84, 86-7, 94, 128-9, 233, 256, 280,
    only one choice 214, 283-4
Christ Mind, or Christ 60-3, 74-5
    after Atonement 82
    CM''s perception 75(n), 275, 279-81
    different function from Holy Spirit 63-4
    Face of Christ 228, 297, 347, 365
    identity with Holy Spirit 60-5, 274-6
    level of Son not in separation 47, 58, 60-3, 67, 91
    Love in 74-5, 82
    manifestation of Holy Spirit 280
    present in separated minds 64
    Self of separated minds 75
    'time of Christ' 321
    vision of Christ 75,275-80,292,358-9,377
communication 262
    Holy Spirit as link 63, 365-6
    perfect communication 262-3
conparison 50-1, 113
consciousness 273-4
creation 28-36, 66-7
    as extension 28-30, 33, 67

    in Son and perfect minds 32-4
    as necessary 72
    as what is created, or creature 67
creator
    Creator (God) 28-33, 322-3
    perfect minds as creators 29-34
creature 66
    as perfect 34
    as thought 30-1, 35-7, 66
crucifixion 79, 104, 151, 217, 316, 336

daimon 23, 172
darkness: 250-2, 341-49
    absence of light 102, 250, 257, 342
    Biblical idea 33(n), 341-2
    'dark companions' 345-8
    'frame of darkness' 345
    'God of Darkness' 337
    as limited awareness 250,343,344-5,349
    removal of 175, 250-3, 294, 369-78
    unreality of 342-5, 349, 360
death 89,181, 224-5, 281-1, 291-2,333-4,336
    'being-toward-death' 45
    ending of 182, 281
    'god of death' 337
    living death 89, 110, 225, 317
    of God 333
depression 129-30
    fundamental depression 129
devil/demon 345-8
dream 55, 62, 95, 175, 188-9, 221, 291, 355, 370, 374

Eckhardt, Meister 367
ego 19, 55, 86-9
    basis of 'world' idea 55, 88-9, 93-5
    guilt in 89-92
    as idea of division/separation 54,86,330-1
    its idea of salvation 1114, 146, 333
    as idolatry 88-9, 329-30
    origin of 55, 87
    projected onto God 330-2
    self-contradictory 92-3, 95-7, 330(n)
    as symbol 88-9, 93
enduring holy instant 241, 308-10
eternal 37-8
Eternal Instant/Now 37, 56-7, 62, 79, 237-9
exclusion 28-9, 100, 247-8, 339

extending, extension 27-8, 35-6
extrasensory perception (ESP) 269, 274

Face of Christ 228, 297, 347, 365, 373
'Fall of Adam' 87
false charity 222-9
    forgiveness-to-destroy (FTD) 223-9
        arrogant FTD 225
        bargaining FTD 227-8
        false humility FTD 225-6
        martyr FTD 226-7
false peace 131
Father 28, 31-3, 51, 39(n)
fear 47-8, 99-100, 117-20, 203-8, 285-6
    in general 47, 91-2, 117-20
    of God 337-8
    particular fears 118, 121, 280
    primary fear 100, 118-9, 205, 280
    release from 119-20, 207, 252-3
Feuerbach, Ludwig 116-7, 328
forgiveness 65-6, 157-64, 319-20
    God's forgiveness 64-6
    interlocking chain of 157-8, 179, 90, 215
    as undoing 65-6, 158, 189
forgiveness-to-destroy (see 'false charity')
freedom 45-6, 196, 279
    absolute freedom 46
    complete freedom 53
    freedom from 46
    freedom to 46
    separated mind's one free choice 283
Freud, Sigmund 143(n)
Fromm, Erich 139

genuine love 97
Gnosticism 2, 342(n)
God 24-66, 258-60, 270-1, 328-40
    awareness of separation 58-61
    as primary Creator 28-33, 72, 322-3, 332
    forgiveness in God 65-6
    holiness of God 27, 259
    knowledge in God 28
    as Light 360-1, 363, 367
    Love in God 25-66
        after completion of Atonement 66
        as God's essential nature 24
        in response to separation 53-66
        originally 25-53
    no perception in 58
    human ideas of 107, 115-7, 327-39
    uncreated perfect Mind 24
Goethe, Johann 346
'golden light' 265-6, 293-4
'Great Light' 265, 362
'Great Perception' 272-3
'Great Rays' 246-7, 264-7, 344
guilt 89-96, 104-7, 337-8
    as demand for punishment 104
    as form of fear 91
    'guilt-field' 146-7
    primary guilt 89-92
    relation to time 105
    specific guilts 121
    undoing of guilt 253-4, 291

hatred 122-6
    definition of 122
    primary hate 123
healing 94, 153, 156, 163, 177-81
    physical healing 181-2
    non-repeatability of 177-9
Heaven 11, 17, 55, 66, 146, 257-9
    Light of Heaven 250, 366, 378
    miniature of Heaven 257-9
    as original state 154
    as Reality 55, 190
    as Universe of Love 34-5,70-1,73-4,82-4
Heidegger, Martin 49, 100
hell 104, 106, 111, 121, 259(n), 338-9
Hesse, Hermann 124
Hobbes, Thomas 112, 138
holistic 77, 213
holiness, holy 27, 152, 238, 291-2, 329-30
    God's holiness 259
    seeing of holiness 292-3
holy instant 235-322
    in Atonement 241
    as beyond time 238-9
    'bridging instant' 243-4
    conditions for holy instant 310-2
    content of holy instant 245-303
        affective aspects 252-4, 285-7
        behavioral aspects 254-6, 287-303
        cognitive aspects 245-52, 256-85
        light in holy instant 250-52, 263-7
        degrees of 236, 240, 256, 261, 287, 304

holy instant (cont.)
    enduring holy instant 241, 308-10
    general nature of holy instant 235-9
    in Atonement 241
    one holy instant 241-3
    practices leading to 312-22
    relation to time 244-5, 321-2
    temporary holy instant 240-1, 288, 304-8
holy relationship 220, 289-97
    as access to Real World 294-5
    content of 292-4
    in general 289-92
    miracles in 219-20, 297-300
    role in celestial speedup 302-3
    synchronicity in 295-6
Holy Spirit
    'after' Atonement 82
    as 'Bridge' 239
    as communication link 63, 365
    different function from Christ Mind 63-4
    gentleness 79
    judgment in 79-80
    knowledge in 64-5
    as 'light' 251, 365
    Love in 76-80, 82
    origin of 60-74
    patient teacher 78-9
    perception in Holy Spirit 76-8, 274-9
        holistic 77, 275
        of Real World 77-9, 271, 279-81
        only true perception 76-7, 275-6
        outside time 78
    present in separated minds 64, 276
    role in Atonement 63-5, 76, 79
    role in miracles 167-77
    same entity as Christ Mind 60-5, 274-6
    Voice for God 20,24,81,124,168,172,196
horizontal plane 197, 261(n)
Hume, David 87, 101(n), 95
hypersphere 266, 279, 293

idea (see 'thought')
idolatry 88-9, 116, 317, 329-30
illusion 48, 55-6
    cessation of 249-50, 283-4, 333-4
    two basic types 136, 249
illusion of love (see 'illusory love')
Illusion Capacity (IC) 47, 53-5

illusory love 9-10, 85-149
    based on ego 86-100
    core idea of 95-100
    characteristics 100-48
        affective aspects 117-31
        cognitive aspects 100-17
        behavioral aspects 131-48
            attack 133-5
            making 131-3
            special relationships 135-48
imperfect love 10, 150-230
    as charity 151-3, 214
    miracles in 153-221
    two primary concerns 221-2
        helping others 221
        self-development 221-2
imperfect minds 11
infinite (see 'limitless')
interlocking chain of forgiveness 157-8, 179, 190, 215
I-Thou relationship 72

Jesus
    author of Course 1-2, 4, 13, 17
    as Christ 19, 64, 75-6, 232, 241, 321
    congruent with Holy Spirit 64, 171
    crucifixion of 104, 148, 217, 318
    primacy in Atonement 216(n), 300
    resurrection of 182
    role in miracles 168
    as useful symbol 168, 182(n), 372
    transfiguration of 267, 295
Joy 42-4
    increase of 44, 58 66, 73, 83-4
judgment 49-50, 248-9, 331, 336
    as basis for 'world' 99, 249(n)
    ending of 248–9
    evaluative judgment 49
    factual judgment 49
    Holy Spirit's judgment 79-80
    last/final judgment 79-80
Jung, Carl 296
justice 105-6
    false justice 106
    true justice 106

Kant, Immanuel 37, 92-4, 99, 249
karma 104, 218, 245

Kingdom 198, 343, 366,
knowing/knowledge 28, 53, 76, 99
Krishna, Gopi 256(n)
Krishnamurti, J. 120, 136, 233(n), 241, 284(n), 309, 312, 321

last/final judgment 79-80, 331
Law of Love 40-1, 46, 201
life 89, 173, 341-2
light 250-2, 341-78
    absolute Light 251, 359-67
        created light 251, 363-6
        eternal Light 361
        God as Light 251, 363, 367
        'Great Light' 264, 362
        light of Heaven 251, 366
        light of knowledge 251, 362-3
        light of Truth 251, 362
        as Love 251, 360-2
        perfect light 360-1
        unlimited light 361-2
    as condition for awareness 249, 341-2
    contrast with darkness 242-49
    in holy instant 250-2, 263-7, 282-3, 292
    in miracles 161, 170, 172, 175, 177, 179-80, 206
    'picture of light' 376
    relative light 250-51, 349-59
        conceptual light 250, 356
        inner light 250, 350-3
        light of imagination 250, 355-6
        light of apperception 356-7
        light of Real World 251, 294-5, 357-9
            'circle of light' 243, 265-6, 282-3
            'golden light' 265-6, 293-4, 357
            'Great Rays' 263-7, 344
        light of reason 251, 356
        light of understanding 251, 356
        outer, physical light 250, 350
        sensory light 250, 355
        visual light 250, 353-5
    releasing of Light 369-78
    spirit as source of 367-9
limitless 36-7
'little gap' 123-4
'little willingness' 311-2, 315, 322
longitudinal plane (see 'horizontal plane')

love
    English meanings 7-8
    4 main ideas
        absolute love, Love 9, 24-84
        Illusory love 9-10, 85-149
        imperfect love 10, 150-230
        perfect love 10, 231-324
    genuine love 96
    Law of Love 40-1, 46, 201
    as Light 369-2
    only one love 67

magic 155-6, 219
making 132-3, 328
    'Illuminated making' 255-6
'mark of Wholeness' 192
mechanics, mechanism 173, 313
'miniature of Heaven' 257-9
mind 10-1, 69-70
    characteristic of 69
    imperfect (separated) minds 11
    perfect minds 10-1, 27-9
miracle 153-221
    conditions for 201-17
    contexts of 217-20
    defined 220
    effects 181-200
        inner healing 185-91
        on others 190-3
        on time 193-200
        physical healing 181-2
    as exchange 164-5
    forgiveness as core characteristic 157-64
    in general sense 154
    'Great Miracle' 191, 224
    in strict sense 154
    no order of difficulty 178, 182-4, 211
    not repeatable 176-9
    role of Holy Spirit in 167-76
    as service 165
    Source of 200-1
    steps in giving 165-77
miracle-mindedness 211-6
mystical experience 116, 269, 309, 370

natural, two ideas of 146
near-death experience 182, 258-9
Nietzsche, Friedrich 134, 332

onefold path 189(n), 312
One-mindedness 212-4
'Original Attack' 134, 148
'original sin' 87, 104-5, 134, 253
Otto, Rudolf 330(n)

Parmenides 31(n), 237
peace 41-2, 296-7
    false peace 131
perception 54, 76-8, 119-20
    as focused awareness 54
    false perception 76, 100, 119-20, 162, 251
    'Great Perception' 272-3
    holistic perception 78, 213, 240, 275
    not in God 58-9
    true perception 77, 120, 194
perfect love 10, 231-324
    holy instant in 235-322
    holy relationship in 288-303
    miracles in 219-20, 297-9
    two meanings of 231-3
perfect mind 11, 27-9
    as light 35-6, 367-8
Perry, Robert 13(n), 35(n), 138(n)
plan of Atonement 60-5, 348
Plato 18, 23, 172, 144, 194, 283, 296, 354, 367
praise 184, 331-2
process 37-8, 56-8
projection 28-9, 87(n), 94, 111, 115, 126,
    141, 205, 328
psychokinesis (PK) 156, 270
punishment 18, 23, 104-7, 119, 128, 172,
    223, 336, 337-8
purification 208-10, 310-1, 314, 322
Real World 77, 271-87, 310, 323, 357-9, 374-8
    central characteristics 271-4
    content of 281-7
    'Great Perception' 272-3
    'miniature of Heaven' 257-8
    as perception of Christ 279-81
    as perception of Holy Spirit 77, 274-9
    as step to Heaven 323-4
reality 11, 53, 55-6
    absolute reality, Reality 11, 39, 55
        as Thought 61, 70-1
    relative reality 55-6
resurrection 182
referencing systems 6-7

religious teachers, other 80-1
remembering 258-9
revelation 240(n)
right-mindedness 211-5

sacrifice 108-10, 14
    as absent from God 148, 335-7
    as attack 148
    as ego belief 107-10
    principle of 139
    in special relationships 139, 147
salvation (see Atonement) 17, 114, 146,
    215, 289, 300-2, 333
    ego's idea of 333, 339
    'bringer of salvation' 300-1
    as special relationship 146
Sartre, Jean-Paul 94, 112, 145
'Satan' 87(n), 346-8
Schopenhauer, Arthur 145
scribes 4
Self 63, 75
separation 11, 53-8
    as activation of Illusion Capacity 53-4
    body in 55
    ego as central 55
    God's awareness of 58-60
    impossible for God 47
    as never really happening 57-8
    origin of 53-8
separated mind 11, 80-1
    focused on ego 55
    light in 349-59, 368-9
    Love in 80-1
    origin of 54-5
sequence 56-7
sexuality 8-9, 229-30
shadow figures 136-8
sin 102-7, 247-8
    Course's definition of 103
    ego's most holy idea 107
    'original sin' 87, 104, 134, 253
    requires punishment 104
Son 31
    as creating 34
    as differing from God 53
    Illusion Capacity in 46, 53
    levels of Sons mind 47, 58
    as Light 251, 363-5, 368

Son (cont.)
    as like God 32-3, 51
    only one Son 32
    as Word or 'Logos' 61-2
Sons of God 34, 35(n), 60, 71, 261
space 37, 47, 55, 69, 132, 216, 266, 304
    as generated by ego 57-8, 132
    hypersphere 266, 279, 293
'spark' 264-5, 343-4
specialness 110-4, 339
    definition 110-1
    ending of 245-6
special relationship 135-48
    exclusivity in 145
    sacrifice in 139, 147-8
    special hate relationship 140-2
    special love relationship 142-4
    three principles of 139
    transformation of 255
spirit 30, 35, 69-70, 189-90
    definition of 69
    as source of light 367-9
    as thought 30, 37
    two main types:
        created 33
        uncreated (God) 31
spiritual eye 173-4
stages of development 290, 308-9, 323
symbol 52-3, 87, 215
    ego as symbol 89-93, 121, 335-8
    Jesus as symbol 168, 182(n), 372
synchronicity in holy relationship 295-6

Taoism 343 (n)
temporary holy instant 240-1, 304-8
thought (idea) 30, 37, 61-2, 69-70
    as aspect of created entity 61-2, 67
    as created entity or spirit 30, 61-2
    as uncreated Entity (God) 30
    in separated mind 205
time 37-8, 55, 47, 56-7, 105, 142, 236-8, 242-5, 304
    collapse of time 196-9, 244, 303
    as fragment of Eternal Instant 57-8, 62, 79, 243-4
    formation of 55, 135, 248-9
    instant in 236-8, 242-3
    'time of Christ' 321

    unreality of time 237
    Zeno's paradoxes 236-7
transfiguration 267, 294
transmission (Buddhist) 189
'transportation experience' 268-9
Trinity 73(n)
triumph 51-2, 125-6
truth 49, 89, 123, 187, 362

union, uniting 25-9, 44
    in extending 28-9
    in Joy 44
    in knowing 28
'universal Course' 39, 221
'universal mark of God' 191-2
Universe of Love 34-5,37,70-1,73-4,82-4, 366

vengeance 106, 140, 142, 252
vertical plane 197, 260 (n)
vision of Christ 275-80, 292, 358-9, 377
voice
    as author 4
    as guide 20, 24, 81, 124, 168, 172, 196
    in miracles 168-72

Wapnick, Kenneth 4(n), 61(n), 290(n), 302(n), 342(n)
wholeness 25-7 (also, see 'holiness')
will:
    ego/separated mind's 93, 111,125, 143
    of God 37, 48, 62, 89, 329
    in miracles 176
    in transformation 239, 263, 272
    'a little willingness' 208-9, 308, 311-2, 315, 322
    will-to-the-whole 90
    will-to-the-part 90
'the world,' world of perception 39, 270-71
    as illusory 55, 94-5, 270-1
    as relatively real 56, 94
    result of ego-error 55, 93-5, 132, 333-4
wrong-mindedness 212-5

Zeno's paradoxes 236-7

www.ingramcontent.com/pod-product-compliance
Lightning Source LLC
Chambersburg PA
CBHW030133170426
43199CB00008B/49